Early

*K*ENTUCKY

Settlers

The Records of Jefferson County, Kentucky

Early
KENTUCKY
Settlers

The Records of Jefferson County, Kentucky

From The Filson Club
History Quarterly

**With a Preface by James R. Bentley, Director
The Filson Club**

CLEARFIELD

Reprinted for
Clearfield Company by
Genealogical Publishing Co.
Baltimore, Maryland
2002, 2007

Excerpted and reprinted from
The Filson Club History Quarterly,
with added Preface, Table of Contents, and Index by
Genealogical Publishing Co., Inc., Baltimore, 1988.
Added matter copyright © 1988 by Genealogical Publishing Co., Inc.
Baltimore, Maryland. All Rights Reserved.

Library of Congress Catalogue Card Number 87-83670
ISBN-13: 978-0-8063-1213-2
ISBN-10: 0-8063-1213-0

Made in the United States of America

Published with permission of
The Filson Club

Preface

THE FILSON CLUB was established in Louisville, Kentucky on May 15, 1884 to collect, preserve, and publish historical materials, especially those pertaining to Kentucky. Over the past century the Club has flourished and is now well established as the oldest continuously operating historical society for Kentucky. The Filson Club is an independent research library deriving its support from gifts and bequests. Its collections include a library of some 50,000 volumes, the second largest newspaper collection in the state, maps, sheet music, microfilm, and ephemeral items such as theatre programs, broadsides, and invitations. The manuscript department houses the best collection of Kentucky manuscripts of the pioneer, antebellum, and Civil War periods. Among its more than one million items are personal and family papers, diaries, records of organizations and business firms, and some genealogical collections. The photographs and prints department holds approximately 50,000 photographs and several thousand historical prints. The Club's museum is particularly strong in portraits, textiles, silver, and weapons, but owns many other interesting items.

The Publications office is in charge of *The Filson Club History Quarterly* and book publishing. The Club began book publication in 1884. *The Filson Club History Quarterly* was started in 1926. While its focus has always been history, many articles of direct interest to genealogical research have been printed. Those pertaining to specific families were reprinted in *Genealogies of Kentucky Families from The Filson Club History Quarterly* (Genealogical Publishing Company, 1981). Source records have also been printed from time to time in the *Quarterly*. The most notable are those reprinted in this volume covering early Jefferson County, Kentucky.

Most of present-day Kentucky was included in Fincastle County, Virginia until the establishment of Kentucky County, Virginia in 1776. In 1780 Kentucky County was divided into three new Virginia counties—Fayette, Lincoln, and Jefferson. These three counties are the parents of Kentucky's present 120 counties. The early

v

records of these three counties are therefore extremely important for genealogical research in the state.

The Jefferson County records reprinted in this volume are Minute Books A and 1 (1781-1785); Will Books 1 and 2 (1784-1833); Bond and Power of Attorney Book 1 (1783-1798); and Division Book 1 (1797-1832). All are basic for genealogical research and we are glad to see them made widely available in one book. They are certain to provide answers for many researchers.

James R. Bentley, Director
The Filson Club

Contents

Early

*K*ENTUCKY

Settlers

———————— ⋙✵⋘ ————————

The Records of Jefferson County, Kentucky

MINUTE BOOK A, JEFFERSON COUNTY, KENTUCKY
MARCH, 1781—SEPTEMBER, 1783

Copied for publication
BY ALVIN L. PRICHARD

IN THREE PARTS

*

INTRODUCTION

In the May, 1780, session of the Virginia Assembly it was enacted that from and after the first of November, 1780, the County of Kentucky should be divided into three counties, and that a court be established by the justices of the new counties on certain days. The court day fixed for Jefferson County was, as set forth in Hening's *Statutes*, the first Tuesday in every month.

The earliest minute books of this first court of Jefferson County are probably less generally known than other early court records, yet they contain a great amount of historical data. Minute Book A is of particular interest. During the period which it covers, from 1781 to 1783, the records of the court were kept with engaging informality, and consequently it contains wills, deeds, inventories, records of polls, and many other records which would ordinarily be searched for elsewhere.

As an instance of this informality, it contains no prefatory statement of the personnel of the first court, but scattered through it in various places are entries showing that in June, 1783, William Pope, Gentleman, and William Oldham were magistrates, and that Richard Chenowith, Gentleman, was sheriff in August, 1781, while in September, 1783, he appears as

*The page references found in this transcription refer to pages in the original Minute Book A.

Justice of the Peace. John May was Clerk *pro tempore* as early as March 7, 1781, until August 7, 1781, when Meredith Price began his entries as "Clk Jeff Cur," which continue until the last, June 3, 1783. George May was Surveyor.

The first instrument recorded is the will of John Copage, written October 8, 1780, before the new counties were created, and consequently he styles himself "John Copage of the County of Kentucky," as also does the second testator, "Joseph Irwin of Kentucky county." The later documents are designated "Jefferson County, State of Virginia."

Probably the entries of most human interest to residents of Jefferson County are the will of Colonel John Floyd and the inventory of his estate. The will is not dated, but was probably written in the two days he lived after riding into the Indian ambush where he received a fatal wound. The will was probated June 3, 1783. So many years have elapsed since the institution of slavery existed in this country that it seems strange for a moment to see Colonel Floyd, one of the noblest and most gentle of men, providing for the sale of certain property or its exchange for slaves, as the executors "may think best for the benefit of my wife & children."

In comparison with the inventories of other estates Colonel Floyd seems to have had a comparatively large personal estate in addition to the lands he possessed, yet it seems pitifully small to the present-day reader. The brief appraisers' lists in this book, cataloguing in rude form and with sometimes barbarous spelling the meagre effects which sufficed the early pioneers, afford a far more graphic conception of the hardships and privations they endured than the pen pictures of the most eloquent historians.

Among the records in Minute Book A are the names of four men, Leighton White, Henry Preator, Edward Murray, and Abraham Taylor, who served with George Rogers Clark in the Illinois campaigns; and five more, Benjamin Briggs, John Pearman, John McCullam, William McCullam, and John Ash, who were in the Continental Army, and absent on duty in 1779 when the land commissioners held their hearings in Kentucky.

Dowdall's Station was known to exist before 1784 (*Collins* II:18,100), but an entry on page 8 fixes it prior to June 25, 1781, for in a lease of land and a ferry to George Grundy of that date he is bound to grant the same privileges to the inhabitants of Dowdall's Station as they had formerly enjoyed. The station was

2

in what is now Bullitt County, near Shepherdsville, and the ferry was operated across Salt River.

A number of fascinating minor touches appear in the record. In the articles of indenture of John Stewart, page 35, Michael Humble engages to instruct him "in the art & mystery of Blacksmith & Gunsmith," and "that he will, at no time, expose him the said John to the danger of the Enemy, more than is the Common custom, or usage of one in his Circumstances." On page 31, Benjamin Pope and James Patton sell to Marsham Brashears six hundred and sixty acres of land for 165 gallons "of good merchantable whisky," further stating that the land is "what is commonly known, or accepted, as Secondrate land." Page 19 recites that "Satisfactory proof made to the Court that the lower part of Daniel Sullivan's right ear was bitt off in a fight with John Carr."

Apparently the original Minute Book A was worn out by frequent consultation, for the little volume now in the Jefferson County Clerk's office is a copy in uniform handwriting and bears at the conclusion of the last entry the following attestation: "In Witness whereof and that the foregoing are truly Copied from the records of my office I the Clerk of said Court do hereto set my hand this 28th day of May, 1816. Worden Pope."

It is fortunate that some years ago Mr. R. C. Ballard Thruston attended to having the transcribed copy photostatted, for even that copy itself is in none too good condition. The paper is exceedingly brittle, and the edges are breaking back into the text and obliterating many words. The copy prepared for publication in THE HISTORY QUARTERLY was made from the photostat copy in the archives of The Filson Club. Words which were illegible were checked against the Worden Pope copy. In addition, difficult names were checked against the Jefferson County Marriage Records, and the land entries in Jillson's *Old Kentucky Entries and Deeds*, Filson Club Publications No. 34. In spite of these precautions there are a few words which could not be deciphered. In some instances it has been extremely difficult to distinguish an "i" from an "e," even under a strong glass. This, however, is of minor importance, since most of the pioneers, having little access to dictionaries, spelled phonetically, and many curious forms of spelling resulted.

The original page numbers are here indicated in brackets; and every effort has been made to follow the form of the original, except that instead of using superior letters in smaller type for the final letters of abbreviations they are here preceded by apostrophes.

PART 1

In the name of God amen: I John Copage of the County of
Kentucky, being of Sound, & disposing memory & judgment;
blessed be God for the Same.   Knowing that it is once appointed
for All men to die, tho the approaches of death be uncertain, I
do therefore design to Settle all my wordly estate, that God hath
bestowed one [sic] me, so that no difference may arise about it
after my dissease.   In manner & form following, vizt.   Item.
I give & bequeathe unto my beloved wife, the choice of my three
negroes, Bob, Jude, Luce, during of her natural life; the other
two, I desire to be left in the hands of my father in law, for the
use & support of raising of my children in the most usefull, and
suitable manner, that he shall, or may think fit, until they shall
become of Age, and that he may have the rule, and guidance of
the same.   Item.   I give & bequeath also all my moveable
estate, unto my beloved wife Susannah Copage.   I also appoint
Thomas Harrison Executor of this my last Will & Testament.
As witness my hand this eight day of October Seventeen hundred & eighty—

Sign'd Sealed & delivered In   )   his
presence of Benja Roberts,   )   John x Copage (seal)
                         his   )   mark
Henry Hall, William x Rice)
                        mark   )

At a Court held, & continued, for Jefferson County on the
7th March 1781.   The above will proved by William Rice, and
to be recorded, & a certificate granted to Thomas Harrison the
Executor for obtaining a probate.
                    Teste John May Clk. Jeff. Cur P. T.[1]

I Joseph Irwin of Kentucky county do make, & ordain this
my last Will & Testament—in manner & form following (ie)—I
bequeathe unto my Son Joseph Irwin, two tracts of land, lying
in the County of Westmoreland, in the state of Pennsylvania,
one containing by estimation four hundred acres, whereon I
formerly lived, on Turtle Creek, the other adjoining Henry
Small, or dirty camp, on the same Water course, & containing
by estimation three hundred, & thirty acres, to him, & his heirs
forever—also all my possessions in the aforesaid County of

4

Kentucky, both real & personal—I give & bequeathe unto my Brother John Irwin, one certain tract of land, in the aforesaid County of Westmoreland, containing by estimation three hundred acres on the waters of Pocket Creek about two miles off the Allegany river to him & his heirs forever. [Page 2] Lastly I nominate, & appoint James Bard, & Andrew McCullock, whole & sole Executors of this my last will & testament. In witness whereof I have herewith Set my hand & Seal this xiiith October M.DCCLXXX.

Sealed & acknowledged in   )
presence of Mer'th Price, Sam'l) Joseph Irwin (Seal)
Harod, Philemon Waters, W Pope)

At a Court held for Jefferson County, on the 7th March 1781—The above will proved & ordered to be recorded, and it appearing to the Court, that there is danger of the estate being wasted, the Executors not being present, to undertake the executorship thereof, administration is granted Benja Pope.

        Test John May clk Jeff Cur P. T.

KNOW ALL MEN by these presents that I Nicholass Meriwether, of Louisa County, have & do by these presents constitute & appoint my friend Meredith Price, attorney in fact, within the County of Kentucky, & every transaction by him made, in my behalf in said County, shall be binding on me, my heirs Exrs admrs & assigns forever—Witness my hand & Seal this xxxth May MD.CCLXXX.

Seal'd. & Delivered in presence of) Nicho Meriwether (Seal)
Jno. Floyd, Jno Dickey   )

At a Court held for Jefferson County, on the 7th March 1781. The within power of attorney proved by the oaths of the Subscribing Witnesses, and ordered to be recorded.

        Test John May Clk Jeff Cur. P. T.

Satisfactory proof made to the Court, that the following Warrants of survey, upon Treasury rights, had been issued by the Register of the Land Office, towit, one for Six thousand, five hundred, in the name of Isaac Momson, one other in the name of John Davidson, for 1000 acres, one other in the name of Sam'l Samris for five hundred acres, one other in the name of Peter Burner for one thousand acres, one other in the name of Chafield Tuttle, for three hundred, one other in the name of Christopher Hogland, for Six hundred, one other in the name of Fulker Fulkerson, for three hundred, one other in the name of Martin Wykoff, for one thousand, one other in the name of Andrew Dine, for five hundred, and one other [Page 3] in the name of Moses Tuttle, for one thousand, three hundred acres, and that there are good reasons to believe that the Said Warrt are lost—ordered, to be certified. 7th March 1781.

Test. John May Clk Jeff Cur

Jesse Pendergrass an infant Son & heir of Garrett Pendergrass² dec'd, made proof by the oath of Margaret Pendergrass Widow, of the said deceased, that the said Garrett acted under a warrant, or Brevet, as the Second in command of a company of guides to the armies, commanded by General Forbes, in the year 1758, and by General Stanwix, in the year 1759—That he was engaged in the said Service, by Colo Adam Steven & continued therein till he was regularly discharged; that he received Lieutenants pay, & that he was an Inhabitant of Virginia, at the time of entering into the Service, & also at the time of his death, and that he the said Garrett never in his lifetime, nor the said Jesse, since his death to the Knowledge of the said Margaret, ever before made proof of such Services, in order to obtain a Certificate thereof; or ever obtain'd. any warrant for such Services, under the King of Great Britain's proclamation of 1763—

At a Court held for Jefferson County on the 7th March 1781 then the above proof made.

Test John May, Clk Jeff Cur P. T.

Administration of the estate of Robert Travis granted Jane Travis, who entered into bond of three hundred thousand pounds with James Patton & Benja Pope Securities.

Admn of Adam Grant estate granted Jane Grant his Widow who entered into bond of Ten thousand pounds, with Benja Pope & Meredith Price Securities.

Admn of John Cline's estate granted Ann Cline, bond entered into of twenty thousand pounds, with Meredith Price, & Will Oldham Securities.

Adm of Joseph Irwin's estate granted Benjamin Pope, bond entered into with Meredith Price, Security in two thousand pounds.

Administration of John Montgomery estate granted William Galloway bond of Six thousand pounds, with George Pomeroy & James Galloway Securitys.

William Spangler appointed Guardian to Thos George an infant orphan of John George & bond entered into with Benja Pope security.

March 7th 1781.   Teste John May C. J. C. P. T.

[Page 4] THIS INDENTURE made this Seventh day of March in the year of our Lord, one thousand, Seven hundred & eighty-one between William Spangler blacksmith of the County of Jefferson of the one part, & Thomas George an Infant orphan of John George deceased, of the other part Witnesseth, that the said Thomas George, by & with the approbation & consent of the Court of the said county of Jefferson, and for and in consideration of the covenants & engagements hereinafter entered into by the said William Spangler, hath, & doth by these presents put, & bind himself to the said William Spangler, as an apprentice, to serve him the said William Spangler, in the said capacity of an apprentice until the eighth day of July, which shall happen, in the year of our Lord, one thousand, seven hundred, & eighty eight,—And the said Thomas George doth covenant, promise, & agree, to, & with the said William Spangler, that he will honestly, diligently, & faithfully serve him as an apprentice, for & during the term afforesaid—That he will not, at any time, during the said term absent himself, from the service of his said Master but will in all things faithfully discharge the duty of an apprentice, according to law.

In Consideration whereof the said William Spangler doth covenant, promise, and agree, to & with the said Thomas George, his Executors & admr that he the said William Spangler, shall, & will find for the said Thomas George clothing, washing lodging & food suitable to his Condition, and such, as is usual found apprentices—also teach him the art & mystery of a Blacksmith, that he will teach him, or cause him to be taught at his the said William Spangler's expence, to read, write, & Cypher as the law requires of Masters, in cases of Orphan apprentices bound under

7

order of Court & whenever he shall be freed from his apprenticeship, by Serving out his time as aforesaid, that he will pay him his freedom dues according to law, and that he will in the meantime at his own expense, pay all poll Taxes, which shall be imposed by law on the said Thomas George. IN Witness whereof the parties to these presents hereunto Severally Set their hands & Seals, the day & year first within written.

	)	Will Spangler (Seal)
Seal'd & deliver'd	)	his
In presence of	)	Thos x George (Seal)
		mark

At a Court held for Jefferson County on the 7th March 1781—This Indenture was acknowledged by the parties approved of by the Court & ordered to be recorded. Test John May clk J Cur P. T. Recorded by Mer'th Price Clk Jeff Cur.

[Page 5] At a Court held for Jefferson on the fourth of April 1781.

Administration of the estate of John Westevall, granted Samuel Westevall, who entered into bond of four thousand pounds, with John Kingston, & Peter Austergess Securities—

John Burbridges will proved by Thos McQuaddy—

William Linns Do [will] proved by Thomas McCarty

Test John May Clk Jeff Cur P. T.

At a Court held for said County on the 7th August 1781.

Administration of the estate of Daniel Hall granted Sarah Hall, & bond of twenty thousand pounds entered into with Dennis Pursel Security—Adm of William Brashear's estate granted Anne Brashear & Bond of three hundred thousand pounds entered into with Benjamin Pope & Reuben Cave, Securities—

Adm. of James McClorklan's estate granted May McClorklan, & bond of four thousand pounds, Jesse Clark Security—

Adm. of James Brown's estate granted Henry Floyd, bond of twenty thousand pounds Merideth Price & Benjn Pope Securities—

Teste Mer'th Price Clk. Jeff Cur

George May, asse & enters one thousand acres, part of a Treasury warrant No. 4866, on the waters of Harrod's Creek, to

8

join on his east, or back line, from the river, the whole length thereof, and to extend the same line, in the Same direction 150 poles, from each Corner, thence off at right Angles, to said line Eastwardly, for quantity, Also 400 acres on Otter creek, a branch of the Ohio, to begin on the east side of said creek, at the mouth of a Cave spring branch, and to run East, to a large hill, thence up with the foot of the same, to the head of the bottom, above said May's upper Mill Seat, then West, across the Creek, to the hills, on the West side of the Creek, then nearly North, till opposite nearly to said Mill, seat, then a north west course, to include a spring mark'd by Edward Bulger, then down the hill till opposite to the Beginning—thence a straight line to the same—The above entries made before John May, Gent former Clerk, & at the request of Geo. May Gentleman, ordered to be recorded.

Returned to Jefferson Court, the 6th day of March 1781—to be recorded.

Test. John May C. J. C.

[Page 6]   Surveys made & recorded in Jefferson County.

1781			
March	28	Peter Shepherd...................	404
	22	Same...........................	900
	23	Same...........................	600
April	5	Levin Powell....................	2000
March	29	William Barnaby Sears............	1000
	15	Jacob Myers.....................	400
	20	John Fitch......................	1000
	26	Same...........................	300
	28	Isaac Cox.......................	1000
	30	Same...........................	400
	28	David Cox.......................	1000
	8	Nicholass Meriwether.............	400
	26	David Mitchell & George Wilson....	653
Sep	15	Nicholas Meriwether.............	12
March	8	Same...........................	1000
April	2	John Burnett....................	100
	3	Evan Williams...................	600
	3	Moris Brady.....................	300
March	8	James Coburn....................	400
	12	William Brashears...............	400
	31	James Rogers....................	1000
	8	Squire Boone....................	400

9

	27	Adam Wickersham................	400
	18	Thomas McGehee..................	450
	8	Squire Boone....................	1000
	8	Morias Hansbrough..............	500
	8	Robert Tyler....................	500
	8	John Eastwood..................	900
	8	Squire Boone....................	122
March	8	Merideth Helms.................	352
	8	Squire Boone....................	200
	8	John Larne.....................	1000
	31	Sarah Boone....................	250
	8	John Cline.....................	300
	27	Adam Wickersham................	1000
		Robert Tyler....................	400
Mar	8	William Bryan...................	500
	8	Thomas Peirce..................	200
Ap	17	James Brind....................	977
	17	James Roney....................	970
June	25	Anguis Cannon [Camron?].........	600
	27	Mark Hardin....................	1000
	16	John King......................	1000
	12	John Hardin....................	1000
	14	Same..........................	500
	26	Edward Worthington.............	560
	29	Joseph Hughes..................	1000
	12	John Hardin....................	1500
	8	James F. Moore.................	300
	17	Richard Swan...................	1000
	29	Aaron Lewis....................	200
	28	Mark Hardin....................	500
	15	John Hart......................	125
	8	Benham Shaw...................	100
	21	Thomas Stansbury...............	800
	20	William Stewart.................	1000
	23	James Pinix....................	400
	20	Henry Lee.....................	1000
	19	William Stewart.................	500
	21	John Deumiah [?]...............	1000
	20	William Stewart.................	800
	20	Same..........................	600
	20	Joseph Cartwright..............	400
	20	Same..........................	500
	20	William Stewart.................	500
	20	Same..........................	500
		[Page 7]	
"	20	Joseph Cartwright..............	500
"	30	Abraham Fry...................	500

10

,,	20	Jacob Froman.....................	500
,,	20	James Overton....................	1000
,,	20	William Stewart..................	600
,,	12	Thomas Helm.....................	500
,,	23	Gerrard Briscoe..................	158
,,	20	Charles Stewart..................	1000
,,	26	Osborn Sprigg....................	500
,,	19	William Stewart..................	422
,,	11	John Severns....................	300
,,	4	John Vertrees....................	400
,,	17	Jacob Funk......................	50
,,	18	David Mitchell & Geo Wilson.......	400
,,	20	Edmund Egleston.................	1600
,,	30	Martin Hawkins..................	1000
,,	20	Martin Hardin...................	1000
,,	28	John Askins.....................	1000
,,	28	William May.....................	300
,,	20	Joseph Cox......................	1000
,,	20	Martin Hawkins..................	1000
,,	19	Isham Watkins...................	400
,,	20	Patrick McGee...................	400
June	15	John Hart.......................	200
,,	30	Basil Prather....................	500
Aug	3	John Vertrees....................	323
June	11	Andrew Hynes....................	100
	17	John Severns....................	300
Aug	11	Chas M. Thruston................	1400
June	9	Andrew Hines	400
1781			
Aug	18	Jacob Vanmetre..................	800
June	13	John Vertrees....................	255
July	11	Stephen Rawlins.................	50
Aug	11	Chas M Thruston.................	400
June	11	Jacob Funk......................	200
Ap	4	John Baker......................	400
Mar	28	Saml Withrow & Jno Corkey Owens .	1000
July	14	Andrew Hines....................	400
,,	21	William Stewart..................	800
		Same...........................	600
June	13	Thomas Helm....................	400
Aug	18	Peter Shepherd..................	500
,,	13	Chas M Thruston.................	2000
Mar	31	James Samuels...................	184
Aug	28 √	Isaac Finley....................	400
March	8	Meredeth Helms.................	375
		Abraham Vanmetre...............	800
		Peter Cline.....................	200

11

		John Pean.....................	500
		Jacob Meyers..................	100
	21	Peter Mansons................	1000
	21	Jno Lewis & Rich'd May.......	1000
	31	John Gratton.................	500
July	21	John May.....................	400
June	8	Robert Tyler.................	400
Sep	6	Robert Wickliffe senr........	400
	1	Mark Harden..................	400
	30	Katey Hardin.................	200
	30	Robert Travis................	500
	1	Lydia Hardin.................	200
	6	Martin Hardin Wickliffe......	400
	1	Benjamin Hardin.............	800
	5	Chas Wickliffe..............	400
	28	Robert Wickliffe............	400
	4	Thomas Prather.............	400
		Same.......................	1000

A true list of Surveys made in Jefferson County prior to this date Septr 8th 1781 Geo May S J O

Copy Test Mer'th Price Clk Jeff Cur

[Page 8] Adm of William Lynn' estate granted George Slaughter Gent bond entered into of Seventy thousand pounds with Rich'd May & Peter Austingess Securitys. April 4th 1781.

Teste John May Clk Cur

Administration of John Westovells estate granted Samuel Westovelle & bond entered into of forty thousand pounds, John Kingston, & Peter Austingess Securitys April 4 1781

Test John May Clk Jeff Cur

THIS INDENTURE made this 25th day of June 1781 between George May attorney in fact of Jacob Myers of the one part, & George Grundy Senr of the other part both of Jefferson County WITNESSETH, that for & in consideration of the sum of three hundred pounds, Current money of Virginia in hand by s'd Grundy to the said May the receipt whereof is hereby acknowledged, he the said George May, as attorney in fact for the said Jacob Myers, hath granted, leased, and to farm let, one certain tract of land, containing four hundred acres, and lying at the Station Known by the name of Dowdalls, and at the ferry, together with the said ferry, to the said George Grundy, for the whole space & term of one year, ensuing the date hereof,

12

giving the said George Grundy full power & authority respecting the premises & to make, and enjoy all profits, as well from the said ferry, as now Kept by said Grundy, as otherwise from said land, save only that the said Grundy is not to be allowed, to waist timber, Provided that nothing herein shall be Construed, to affect, or in any wise take away any former indulgence, that may have been given by the said Jacob Myers to the Settlers at present at the said Dowdalls station & on said land, but they to remain on the same footing, they were left upon by said Jacob Myers, Hereby excluding any other person from the priviledge of Keeping a ferry, on the said land. Witness my hand & Seal this day & year above mentioned.

Sign'd & Seal'd in the presence of   George May (Seal)

               her

Benjamin Price Margret   x   Bell   atto for Jacob Myers

              mark

At a Court held for Jefferson County on the 7th August 1781. The above lease acknowledged by George May Gentleman & orderd to be recorded.

             Test Mer'th Price Clk Jeff Cur

[Page 9] Aprile 18th 1781. We Peter Demaria George Pomre [Pomeroy] & Arthur Parks, being apointed by the Court of Jefferson County Virginia, being duly Sworn, do apraise the goods, chattels, & estate of John Westervell lately slain, in manner following Viz

	Dollars'
To a peach nursery................................	200
To a quantity of Corn.............................	
To dried puncans.................................	10
To a pair of hand mill stones......................	350
To a Kuler [cooler] 40 basket & old Clothes 30.......	70
To a pair of Shoes................................	40
To Shugar at 30 dollars per Lb. 40 Lb [and] ¾.......	1222
To a pair of Tongs 60 a tramel 60ᵗ.................	120
To a tramel 60, a mattock 80......................	140
To an Ax 80—an ax 100...........................	180
To a broad ax....................................	110
To 2 Iron Wedges & maul rings....................	80
To 1 mill peck & hand mill Irons..................	60
To 1 ho. 20, 1 Do 40. 1 Do. 10...................	110

To a howel 20	20
To a large Clivis link & small Clivis	60
To 2 small Clivises	20
To an augur 60. 1 Do 20	80
To Drawing Knife	15
To an Inshave [?]	20
To a Chest & 18 spoons	65
To woollen yarn, 2 L and a quarter at 37 Dollars	83
To 2 puter Dishes	160
To 7 Ditto plates	126
To Paper box & Salt Cellars	10
To a bason	40
To a handerchief & Buckskin	40
To a bucket & Looking glass	30
	Dollars
To a bucket & Looking glass[5]	30
To a bucket, Pail & Funnel	30
To Linnen yarn 10½ lb. at 40	420
To a Rug	300
To a feather bed & Pillows	150
To 3 Pillows & an old rug	15
To Cups & saucers	10
To 40 Boxes at 10 Dolls p pr[6]	40
To a roundbore gun & half bushel Salt	180
Amt Carried forward	4606
Amt brot forward	4606
To an old Saddle	100
To 2 pair of neting needles	8
To brimstone 8 a bell 60	68
To a mare	4000
To 16 quarts hempseed at 20 d p qt	320
To 1 bridal, gimblets & Rule	25
To 13 qts flaxseed, at 10 Doll'rs pr qt	130
To Potatoes	25
To a Cow	1600
To Chisils & gouge	40
To Branding Iron	20
To a syth nib & wedge	5
To a pair of Compasses & 2 files	20
To a foot Edge	20
To 3 Plains 40 a fleshfork	55
To Sundries of old Iron	15
To Hammer, gimblet & Chalkline	15
[Page 10]	**Dollars**
To Plough Share & Coulter	100
To a Cattle [Kettle] 100 a pot 300	400
To Smoothing Irons	100

14

To 2 Books 10. old Book 8	18
To an old shirt & Jacket	10
To old buttons 5 a Cloak 20	25
To 6 piecis of Childrens Cloathes	20
To an old goon [gown]	15
To a small bag with bullets	70
To Patches 12, 4 Knives & 6 forks 60	72
To a quilt Peticoat	200
To a Peticoat 80, 1 Do 70	150
To a Lincey Do[7]	70
To Childrens Cloaths	40
To Tobacco 50″ at 5 Dollars	250
To Childrens Cloathes	40
To Chimniy Valines[8]	15
To Childrens Cloaths	50
To a Ribband 30, 1 Do 30, 1 Do 20	80
To 2 bedgoons & aprone	80
To Shints [shirts?] & Patches	20
To a Table Cloth	100
To a small shint [shirt?]	20
Amt Carried over	3020[9]

Inventory of John Westewelts estate brought over

	Dollars
Amount brought forward	
To Caps & Tinders	100
To gloves & Sundries	15
To Silk Ribbon for a bonnet	120
To a goon 80, a Do 100	180
To 2 pillow Cases 80, 2 Do 80	160
To a Check apron	100
To 1 Pini,[10] Do 100. 1 Do 100	200
To Petticoats 50. 1 shawl 300	350
To a Sheet 300	300
To 2 shifts or bodies	300
To Small Bedgoon	80
To Soing thread 25 a Coat 500	525
To a great Coat 400 a blanket 50	450
To Powder Horn	100
To 6 pr Stockings	180
To a Churn & Beans	100
To 9½ yarn 25 Dollars p. lb	237
To Candlemoles & Canister	24
To a Bottle & oyl of Turpentine	20
To a Small Cattle & Tallow	60
Amount Carried forward	3601

Amount bro forward...............................	
To old Trowsers, & britches......................	5
To Big wheel spindle & Sundries.................	40
To Cask & Sundries..............................	15
To pocket book & Sundries......................	15
To a gun barrel.................................	10
To an old Cattle................................	5
To a hansaw....................................	50
To a syth 40, a wheel.	190
To 2 old bags..................................	20
To 1 Pair of Wool Cards........................	40
To Stockin yarn................................	100
To Cotton Do..................................	100
To an old hatt 10, a jug 20.....................	40
To a bag 30 a bell 30 [should read 60]	670
	670°

Peter Demaree, Arthur Parks, George Pomeroy

At a Court held for Jefferson County on the 7th August 1781. The above Inventory was returned to Court & ordered to be recorded.

Test Merth Price Clk Jeff Cur

[Page 11]

A Poll taken for Delegates for Jefferson County 3d April 1781

Isaac Cox	John May	Willis Green
Edward Tyler	George Grundy	Thomas McCarty
Thomas Applegate		Thomas Applegate
Thomas Spencer		Thomas Spencer
John Carr		John Carr
Samuel Brown		Samuel Brown
Henry Wade		Henry Wade
Earnest Miller		Earnest Miller
John McCausland		John McCausland
Henry Spilman		Henry Spilman
James Pursley		James Pursley
Moses Cherry		Moses Cherry
Joseph Greenwall		Joseph Greenwall
Leyton White		Leyton White
George Grundy x		Hugh Corkran
Hugh Corkran		John Sellars
John Sellars		Isaac Kellar
Isaac Kellar		Saml Harod
Samuel Harod		James Stevenson
Jas Stevenson		Danl Sullivan

16

Dan'l Sullivan		Peter Austergess
Peter Austergess		Benjamin Taylor
Benjamin Taylor		Samuel Jacks
Samuel Jack		John Hinkston
Jno Hinckston		John Caghey
Jno Caghey		George Grundy Junr
George Grundy Jr		Moses Timplin
Moses Timplin		James Crooks
Jas Crooks		William Aldridge
William Aldridge		Jonathan
Jonathan		Cunningham
Cunningham		George Dickins
George Dickins		Joseph Brown
Joseph Brown		William Smily
William Smiley		Samuel Westervill
Saml Westervelle		John Whitacre

[Page 12]

Isaac Cox	John May	Willis Green
John Whitacre		John Wray
John Wray		John James
John James		Thomas Purcell
Thomas Purcell		Michael Humble
Michael Humble		John Camp
Abraham Whitacre x		Aquilla Wallace x
John Whitledge x		John Young
John Camp		Jacob Vanmetre
Aquilla Whitacre x		Mathew Jeffries
John Young Young		Proctor Ballard
Jacob Vanmeter		Christo'r Windsor
Mathew Jeffries		John Hinch
Proctor Ballard		William Shannon
Christo'r Windsor		George Wilson
John Hinch		Samuel Herick
William Shannon		James Stewart
George Wilson		Benja Hansberry x
Samuel Hinch		John Doyle
James Stewart		John Handley
John Doyle		David Hawkins
John Handley		John Hawkins
David Hawkins		
John Hawkins		

At a Court held for Jefferson County on the 7th August 1781—The above Poll returned by Richard Chenoweth Gent Sheriff & ordered to be recorded.

Test Mer'th Price Clk Jeff Cur

17

[Page 13]
An Inventory of the goods of Daniel Hall dec'd

	£	
One pyde Cow £ 600 one Red Cow 600	1200	
One Brown Cow £ 600 one Red Cow 540	1140	
One Sorrel horse £ 2000, one Bay horse 1800	3800	
One sheep £ 84, 1 Pinch back Watch 480	564	
One Rifle gun 420, 1 saddle £ 120	540	
One Bed & furniture £ 600 one Ditto 550 £	1150	
3 Coverlid, £ 600, 1 Teakettle 84	684	
The Wearing Clothes of Daniel Hall £ 600	600	
3 Blankets, a piece of Worsted and 1 yd of silk	340	
One hackle, a pair of Stilyards [Steelyard]	120	
A Steel trap, a broad ax, & mattock	340	
Sundry Iron Tools, & Chains	564	
Some pewter, £ 210, one wheel £ 60, a buckskin £ 36	306	
Two pots & 2 kettles 240	240	
£	11398•	

Estimate & 'prais'd this 31st day of August in the year of our Lord, 1781, The above goods & chattels as mention'd, An in Witness whereof we have Set our hands hereunto.

	Morris Brady
N. B. There is a few things belonging)	Shadrack Carter
to the estate cannot be had as yet)	Evan Williams

At a Court held for Jefferson County on the 3d April 1782. The above Inventory returned & ordered to be recorded—

Test Mer'th Price Clk Jeff Cur

Administration of Thomas Talbot's Esta granted Drusilla Talbott & bond intered into of fifty thousand pound, with James Stewart Security.

Same Samuel Wells's estate granted his Son Samuel Wells & bond of ninety thousand pounds, John Floyd & William Pope Gentlemen Securities—

Same Dennis Downing granted Margarett Downing & bond for Ten thousand pounds, David Hawkins Security—

Same Peter Austergess granted James Austergess & bond of twenty thousand pounds, Samuel Hobbs & Paul Froman Securities—

18

Same Abraham Vanmeter granted Elizabeth Vanmeter &
bond of three hundred thousand pounds, with John Vertrees &
William Hill Securities—

The above administrations granted, at a Court held for
Jefferson County, on the 3rd December 1782 (1) [sic]

Test Mer'th Price Clk Jeff Cur

[Page 14]

At a Court held for Jefferson County the 3d December
1781—It appearing to the Court that the following Persons, are
intitled by virtue of an Act of Assembly passed May last, to
four hundred acres of land, each, Orders that the County
Surveyor lay off to them accordingly viz:

Thomas Banfield	Ann Cline
James Hamilton	Martha Hughes
James McKegg	Charity Thornton
John Thixton	Jemima Hougland
John James	Joanna Farrow
Peter Lovell	Sarah Morgan
Daniel Lovell	Ann Shores
John Cline	Mary McKenzie
Sam Ray	Sarah Payne
Reuben Case	Jane Grant
John Coy	Mary Holmes
William Hall	Jonathan Harnett
Moses Timplin	Anthony Junkus [?]
John Mundall	James Stewart
John Hughes	James Harriss
Zachariah Hold	Thomas Dillian
Joseph Case	Thomas Spencer
Lydia Case	Samuel Young
William Hold	Rachel Hargiss
Reuben Blackford	Thomas Brown
James Swan	Henry Watson
John Martin	Thos Applegate
Henry Grass	Jacob Hoffman
William Galasby	Mary Stevens
Jacob Case	Ruth Harriss
Cornelius Bryan	Jno Mayhue Harriss
Robert Gilmore	Susannah Harriss
Catharine Darling	Peter Newkirk
Rachel Ricker	Robert Holmes
Margaret Vanleeve	Boston Damewood
Barbara Lyburn	Daniel Lynder
Jemima Lemaster	Miles Hart

19

Benja Wright
William Lagston
Samuel Watkins
Jacob Gun
Abram Raymond
Corrod Custard [sic]
Dinah Kennedy
John Tewell
John Alsey
Francis Adams
Niel Doherty
Elizabeth Faith
Graves Wapshot

Mary Westoville
Sophia Voress
Jane Weach
Mary McGlaughlin
Mary Gakin
John Donne
Israel Dodge
Daniel Campbell
Allen Campbell
Lambert Darling
David Johnson
John Galloway
William Mitchell
Joseph Mitchell
Samuel Demara[11]
Arthur Park
Joseph Park
George Seaborne
Joseph Collard
Henry Davis
Martin Curts
George Yent
George Pomeroy
Spencer Collins
Susanna Dickens
Peter Cummins
John Helm
John Shaw
Peter Warren
John Barnett
William Cummins
John Demara
Charles Morgan

Griffin Tillis
John Williams
Elisha Freeman
Elisha Freeman junr
John Sinclair
John Hamilton
William Martin
James Dunbar
John Dunlap
John Shaw
George McManniss
John McManniss
Christian Wyman

[Page 15]

Saml Damarie junr
Elias Newkirk
Tobias Newkirk
William Lock
John McLean
James Hougland
James Mays
John Spencer
Henry Countryman
Richard James
John Kennedy
James Pursley
Ozias Welch
Soloman Kersinger
Isaac Froman
Matthew Bartley
John Greenywalt
Charles Morgan junr
James January
Jacob Williams
Daniel Lout
Robert Mosely
John Voress junr
Daniel Byers
Isaac Keller
Henry Keith
Elizabeth Duncan
Jos Fleming
David Hart
Saml Hobbs
Margaret Downing
James Scaggs
John Roberts

20

Thomas Harrison
Edward Combs
Christian Wyman junr
James Stevenson
John Thompson
John Burk
Turner Oliver
Elizabeth Higgins
Catharine Galasby
Moses Spears
John Gilmore
Haden Whorton
Joshua Archer
Christopher Schulz
Joseph Glenn
Luke Voress
William Lee
John Lee

Andrew Gregory
John Voress
George Cravetson
Mathew Mays
John McCasline
Christopher Jones
Thomas Beard
Mary Beard
Joseph Beard
William Burrass
Michael Teets
Samuel Morton
Jeremiah McNew
John Williams
James Colvin
James Doherty
Dennis Purcell
Thomas Collins

[Page 16]

Peter Bartness
John Hawkins
John Keith
Walter Wright
John Riker
William Arnett
Samuel Stuthard
Samuel McAddams
Henry Scaggs
Peter Countryman
Peter Countryman jr
Richd Gregory
George Jones
John Niel
John McCasline
Jos Greenywalt
Samuel Miller
Christopher Miller
Benja Johnson
Chas Kennedy
Frederick Honsault

John Honsault
Mary Gray
Jos Brooks
Thomas Morton
James Voress
David Hawkins
Jane Archer
Robert Foreman
Jane Arneson
John Cameron
Cornelius Bogart
John Sutherland
James Shannon
Jacob Hobbs
George Hinch
Charles Harebridge
John McCumsey
William Downs
Ceirsey Cisidon [sic]
Margaret Higgins

Test Mer'th Price Clk Jeff Cur

John McCullom gives Satisfactory proof to the Court, that
he was prevented from laying his claim before the Commissioners, on account of his being on the Continental Service, and
appearing to the Court that he is intitled to the Preemption of a

21

thous'd acres of land, lying on the Cainey Run of the South fork of Simpsons Creek, including the foundation of a cabbin, about Ten foot square, & an half-acre deadned, with a large ash tree marked, J McC.C made the 20th May 1776—

The above proof made at a Court held for Jefferson County 4th December 1781.

Test Mer'th Price Clk Jeff Cur

Louisville Oct'r 15th 1781.

IN obedience to an order of Jefferson Court to us directed we the Subscribed have invantaried & appraised the estate of James Brown deceasd, and [Page 17] is as followeth

To 3 yds blue broad cloth £ 400 4½ yds flannel £ 180....£	580
To 3 yd white linnen £ 270, 4 doz brass buttons £ 60.....	330
To pocket Compass £ 100, 1 Brass Kettle £ 200........	300
To Small Pocket Knife £ 15,1 Napsack 24..............	39
To pair old blue Overalls & flannel bag £ 30, 1 pocket book £ 6..	36
To pair Silver Sleeve buttons (old) £ 27, 2 blankets £ 180.	207
To Pair old long breeches.............................	30

Ben Pope, Phil Waters, Jas Patten) ....£1512'

At a Court held for Jefferson County on the 4 December 1781. The above Inventory returnd & orderd to be recorded

Test Mer'th Price Clk Jeff Cur.

A list of the appraisment of Abraham Vanmetre deceasd, the widow Elizabeth Vanmetre, Ex'rs Richard Chenoweth Gent. Thomas McCarty & Robert Tyler—

	Specie	.
The big old Cow & Calf 200/. broken hornd Do & Calf 200/	£ 20	
A white Cow & Calf 160/. Black heifer & young 160/...................................	16	
A mottled faced Cow 160/. a heifer, with her tail part off 50/........................	10	10
A young Bull 50/. a black horse 400/..........	22	10
A Negro Man namd General.................	100	
A large pot 13 or 14 gallons & Bail............	1	10
A 3 or 4 gallon pot & Bail 10/. a gallon pot & Do 6/...................................	"	16

A pair of Steellards, draws 120 wt 12/6, a frying pan with a hole 2/6......................	`"`	15
A Riffle gun, with mountaing 100/. 1 Riffle Do without box & some mountain £ 5.........	10	
A pitchfork 6 d., 2 pot racks 10 /. 1 large Chain 4/. 1 grid Iron 6/......................	1	6
1 pair fire tongs 6/. 1 Lamp 1/6, 1 old hackle 5/. 1 Teakettle 12/......................	1	4.6
A Driper of Pewter, 6 Dishes. 13 Plates, 4 basins & 1 Tankard......................	4	
2 Bed ticks & half Set of Curtains, Cover-lid &c.	3	
1 side Saddle 20/. 26 spools 2/. 1 half bushel 6/.	1	8
1 Steel trap 25/. 2 sythes 12/. 1 mattock 6/. 1 Pitchfork 2/6......................	2	5.6
1 ʃrow 4/. 14 harrow teeth 20/. 1 Drawing Knife 6/	1	10
Swingle tree Irons 3/. hand Mill Do 12/........		15
2 Iron wedges 14/. old Iron 4/. 7 axes & 1 Tomhook £ 3..............................	3	18
3 hoes & 1 dough knife 16/. 1 augre & Pruning Knife 6/..............................	1	2
1 pair hinges, hooks, & Door handle, hitch-.....		10
1 pr window hinges 6/. 2 Chisels & gouge 4/6....		10.6
[Page 18] £		
1 old Spit 6/. 1 large bell, & Iron Coller 20/. 3 pieces Steel 7/4........................	1	7.10
1½ augre 1/6, 1 hammer 2/6, 1 Sett Plow Irons Screw & belt 20/......................	1	14
1 spade 6/. 1 whip Saw 75/. New Iron 90/. 2 spinning wheels, 20/.....................	9	11
2 Clivises & pins 4/. 1 Saw 20/. 1 heifer with Calf pide Color 150/....................	8	14
1 Sorrel Mare with white on her face...........	7	10
1 Brown Mare, with a blaze in her face.........	16	10
1 Large 10 gallon Kettle 60/. 1 grine Stone 3/...	3	3
£	[blank]	

At a Court held for Jefferson County, on the 8th March 1782. Returnd to Court & orderd to be recorded—

Test Mer'th Price Clk Jeff Cur

IN obedience to an order of the County Court of Kentucky to us directed, we the Subscribers appraised the estate of Thomas Davis as follows viz

	Currency	Specie	
2 Cows £ 2400. 1 Roan mare £ 1500, 1 gray Do £2000....................£	5900 £	29	10

3 Beds & furniture 6000 £. a quantity of Pewter £ 400	6400	32	
1 Teakettle, & Teaware £ 300, 1 spice mortar & Pestle £ 200	500	2	10
1 Box Iron & heaters £ 150, 1 skillett Ladle fleshfork & candlestick £150	300		15
2 Pair Cards, 2 Padlocks & 1 heckle	100		10
A quantity of farming tools £ 800—1 Trunk £ 100	900	4	10
4 Sickles, 3 pains of glass £ 160, 3 spinning wheels £ 500	600	3	
Some feathers £ 130, 2 heifers £ 1200	1230	6	11.6
Isaac Cox, Isaac Davis, Arrington Wickleff	£16090⁹	80	7.6

At a Court held for Jefferson County on the 5th March 1782. The above Inventory returnd to Court & orderd to be recorded.

Test Merth Price Clk Jeff Cur

Louisville Oct 15th 1781.

In obedience to an order of Jefferson Court to us directed have inventoried & appraised the estate of Joseph Erwin deceasd & is as followeth—

To a Coat & waistcoat £ 250. an old blew Do 1 Do £ 50 . £	300
To Pocket book 6 £—Part of an old shirt £ 3	9
To old blanket 6/. 2 Bushels Salt £ 180⁹	480.6
	£ 789/6

Henry Floyd, Edward Holsman, James Patten

At a Court held for Jefferson County. on the 5th March 1782—The above Inventory returnd & orderd to be recorded.

Test Mer'th Price Clk Jeff Cur

[Page 19]

KNOW ALL MEN by these presents, that We Samuel W. Culbertson and Daniel Sullivan of Jefferson County, are held & firmly bound unto the administrator of William Linn deceasd in the full, and just sum of five hundred pounds, Specie, Currency of Virg'a value receivd of him, for which payment, well, & truly to be made, We bind ourselves, jointly & severally, our joint, & several heirs, Exrs administrators, & assigns, jointly by these presents, Seald with our Seals, & dated this xxvɪth day of February m.dcclxxxɪɪ—Now Know Ye, that whereas the aforesaid William Linn, did by his last will & testament devise, unto Ann Linn Daughter of Letticia, a negro winch namd Margarett, and unto the said Letticia, all the household furniture, which said legacies, the above namd Samuel W. Culbertson, as first friend to said Legatees, hath taken in possession therefore The condition of the above obligation is such, that if the above bound Saml W. Culbertson, his certain attorney, heirs, or assigns, shall deliver up unto the aforesaid adminstrator, the said legacies, or so much thereof, as is proportionable to discharge the debts of the said Deceasd.when thereunto lawfully requested, then the above obligation to be void, else to remain in full force & virtue—

Seald & deliverd In presence of) Saml. W. Culbertson (Seal)
Mer'th Price. Thos Spencer   )

  At a Court held for Jefferson County on the 5th March 1782. The above bond provd & ordered to be recorded.

Test Mer'th Price Clk Jeff Cur

  Satisfactory proof made to the Court that the lower part of Daniel Sullivan's right ear was bitt off in a fight with John Carr—orderd that the same be admitted to record.

Test Mer'th Price Clk Jeff Cur

  Administration of John Sisney [Cisnea] estate granted Mary Sisney Bond intered into of eight hundred pounds, Specie, Philip Phillips, & Joseph Kirk Patrick Securities—

  Same of David Hinton's Estate granted, William Chenoweth, & Bond of four hundred pounds specie, John Vertrees, and Joseph Bozur [Bozier?] Securities.

  [Page 20] Same Henry Hougland' estate granted James Hougland, and bond of one thousand pounds, Specie, Richard Chenoweth, and Thomas Curry Securities.

  At a Court held for Jefferson County on the 5th March 1782 The above administrations granted.

Test Mer'th Price

  William McCullam proves to the Court, that he improved land in the County of Kentucky, in the year 1776 April 10th. on the East fork of Simpsons Creek joining Joseph Coxs pre Emption, on the North side thereof, whereon some peach trees were planted & WM'C cut on a blew ash and that he was prevented from laying his claim, before the Commissioners on account of his being in the Regular Service, wherefore the Court were of opinion, that he is entitled to a Pre-emption of One thousand acres.

JOHN Ash proves to the Court that he improved land in the County of Kentucky, in the year 1776, lying on the Westerly fork of Ash Creek, with JA cut on a beech near the improvement, and adjoing John Ash, Senr & that he was prevented from laying in his claim before the Commissioners, on account of his being in the REGULAR Service, Whereupon the Court are of opinion that he is intitled to a pre-emption of One thousand acres.

The above proof made at the March Court 1782

Test Mer'th Price Clk Jeff Cur

Adm granted of Jonathan Wright's estate to Benja Wright with Thomas Hargiss, & John Carr Securities in a bond of Sixty pounds–specie—March 5th 1782.

Test Mer'th Price Clk Jeff Cur

KNOW ALL MEN by these presents, that I Mary Cisnea of Jefferson County State of Virginia, administratrix of the estate of Jonathan Cisnea, late of this said County, deceasd have made, ordained & constituted and by these presents do make, ordain & constitute & in my place & stead, put & depute my trusty & loving friend, John Friend of Bedford County State of Pennsylvania, my true & lawful [page 21] attorney, for me, and in my name, and for my use, to ask, demand, sue for, levy & recover all such sums, & Sums of money, debts goods, wares dues, accompts & other demands whatsoever, which are or shall be due, owing, payable, and belonging to me, or said estate, or detained for me, any manner of Ways, or means, whatsoever, by any person, or persons whatsoever, in said state of Pennsylvania, giving, & granting unto my said attorney, by these presents my full, & whole power, strength, & authority in, & about the premises, to have, use, and take all lawful ways & means in my name for the recovery thereof and upon receipt of any such debts, dues, or Sums of money, acquittances, or other discharges for me & in my name, to make Sale & deliver and generally, all and any other act, and acts, thing or things, device, & devices, in the law whatsoever, needful, and necessary to be done, in the premisses for the recovery of all, or any such debts or Sums of money, aforesaid, for me, and in my name, to execute & perform as fully, and amply, to all intents & purposes, as I myself, might or could do, if I was personally present or as if the matter required more special authority than is here given— And attorneys one or more, under him, for the purposes aforesaid, to make & constitute and again, at pleasure to make, ratifying, allowing & holding, for firm, & effectual, all, and whatsoever my said attorney shall lawfully do, in & about the premisses, by virtue hereof. IN WITNESS whereof I have hereunto set my hand & Seal this 5th day of March 1782.

Seald & deliverd In   )   her
)   Mary   x   Sisney (Seal)
presence of   )   mark

At a Court held for Jefferson County on the 5th March 1782. Mary Cisnear personally came into Court & acknowledged the above letter of attorney to be her act & deed Whereupon It was admitted to record
                                Test Mer'th Price Clk Jeff. Cur[1]

Received of Mr George Dickens a certificate from the Commissioners of Kentucky, for one thousand acres of Land, which is assign— I am to pay all expenses, and when a right can be got by the said Certificate to the land, then I am to make George Dickens, a good and lawful deed to one half the said land, and the part next to [Page 22] Simon Butler[12] is for Dickens. In case any fraud use by myself to words Dickens, I forfeit all my, the s'd land. Given under my hand this 26th April 1780
Test Mer'th Price, Jn'a Fleming)   Geo: Thompson (Seal)

At a Court held for Jefferson County, on the 5th March 1782 The above receipt Bond, provd & ordered to be recorded
                                Test Mer'th Price Clk Jeff Cur

At a Court held for Jefferson on the 5th March 1782   Ordered that the County Surveyor lay off, the following persons, four

27

hundred acres of land, each agreeable to act of Assembly passed, May last—

David Evans.
Ann Martin
James Shields
John Friggs Junr
Samuel Saunders
Rachel Searcy
Abigail Clark
William Goodwin
Martin Rowe
Thomas McCurrddy
   [McCunddy ?]
John Faver
Archibald Lockhart
Samuel Duncan
David Douglass
Mary Brown
George Owens
Lewis Ward
John Nelson
Elizabeth Faver
Hannah Moore
William Rice
Rachel Vancleave
James Beggus [?]
Samuel Martin
Osborn Bland
Thomas Hurley
James Abbott
Samuel Abbott
Edward Scidmore
Eneas Harnett
Joseph Black

William Tyler
Thompson Randolph
Mary Galloway
Abnar Hawkins
Edward Goodwin
Urania Meredeth
William Monroney
William Day
Jane Spear
Sarah Tren
Thomas Burk
Benja Roberts
James Holmes
Isaac Woollard
Adam Moddrel
Rebecca Moddrel
Lawrence Smith
Samuel Wilson
James Cook
Julian Phelps
Jesse Clark
Ann Hawkins
Amoss Goodwin
Ann Asher
Sylvester Munroney
James Lewis
Rebecca Faulker
Ruth Wade
Nimrod Duncan
Sarah Paddock
Richard Breeding

Test Mer'th Price Clk. Jeff. Cur.

[Page 23] Administration of the estate of Robert Eakin granted William Goodwin and bond entered into of One hundred pounds, Specie, with William Spangler, & Robert Eakin Securities.

Same Abraham Keller's estate granted Isaac Keller, with James Sullivan & Daniel Sullivan Securities in a bond of Six hundred pounds, specie—

Granted April Court 1782.   Test Mer'th Price Clk Jeff Cur

¹The original bears this notation on the margin: "Original taken out of the office."

²The name Garret Pendergrass was also spelled Pendergrest (*Illinois Historical Collections*, VIII:21), and Pendergrast. (*Collins*, II:615.) He was killed and scalped by Indians at Harrodsburg January 28, 1777. (Bodley's *George Rogers Clark*, 39.) Colonel William Fleming in a diary entry of January 19, 1783, mentions one Wilson, "who married Wid'w Pendergrass." (Bodley's *History of Kentucky*, 326.)

³It is possible that Spanish milled dollars are referred to, for early Kentucky prices were high, but such items as "To a mare...4000" seem to indicate that they were Continental paper dollars, issued originally with a par value of 4 shillings 6 pence. (Shuckers' *The Revolutionary Finances*, 22.) These depreciated so rapidly that by May, 1781, one Spanish dollar equalled between 500 and 1000 of the Continentals. (*Op. cit. 90*.) This money was used in Kentucky and Illinois, because friction arose in 1780 between the Illinois Regiment and the Vincennes French over the recall of certain issues. (Bodley's *Clark*, 153.) The disputed issues were of 1777 and 1778, and were recalled because of counterfeiting. (*Journal Continental Congress*, XIII:21-2.)

⁴This is properly trammel, the hook for suspending kettles over the fire.

⁵This item was evidently copied twice, because with it included, the sum is 4636, but, omitting it, the appraisers' total, 4606, is correct.

⁶This item is unintelligible, although the writing is legible.

⁷"Lincey," given more frequently as "linsey" or "linsey-woollsey," is a familiar word in pioneer writings, representing the homespun cloth of cotton and wool.

⁸"Valines" is evidently intended for valances, or draperies.

⁹This addition is incorrect, but is given as found in the original. Many similar instances will be encountered.

¹⁰This word is unintelligible unless it be a corruption of pina, a fine material for handkerchiefs and other articles of this character.

¹¹In other places Demara is spelled Demaria, Damarie, and Demaree.

¹²This Simon Butler is probably Simon Kenton, who assumed the name of Butler when he left Virginia in the belief he had killed William Veach, his rival in love. It was not until 1782, eleven years afterward, that he learned otherwise and resumed the name of Kenton. (*Collins*, II:442,449.)

¹³Opost was a common name among the Kentuckians for Vincennes. (*Illinois Historical Collections*, VIII:300.)

MINUTE BOOK A, JEFFERSON COUNTY, KENTUCKY
MARCH, 1781—SEPTEMBER, 1783

Copied for publication

By Alvin L. Prichard

In Three Parts

Part Two *

In the name of God, Amen: I Mary Christy of Jefferson County State of Virginia widow, being at this time Sick, and weak, in body but of sound, mind, memory, & understanding & calling to mind that it is appointed for all to die Do make my last will & Testament, in manner & form following to wit— I Commit my body to the Earth, to be enter'd in a decent and Christian like manner, at the discretion of my Executors, & for as much, as it hath pleasd Almighty God, to bless me with some wordly estate, I give & dispose of the same as follows.

Imprimis—I give & bequeath unto William Christy, my eldest Son, the house and lott, I at present occupy in Louisville to hold to him & his heirs forever—Item, I give and bequeathe to my son Thomas Christy, my right of & to a pre-Emption Warrant for four hundred acres, on Licking Creek, to hold to hold [sic], to him & his heirs forever—Item. I give & bequeathe, all & singular, my household furniture, the bedding & pewter, only excepted, to my Daughters, Sarah Christy & Jenny Christy, and I do direct that the same be sold, as soon as convenient after my decease and the same applied towards the education,—and clothing of the said Sarah Christy & Jenny Christy,—I also bequeath one black Cow & Calf and one horse at the Opost¹¹ if found, to be Sold, and applied as aforesaid,—Item. I give & bequeath all my cash in hand & all my debts & residue of my estate unto my Children, William, Thomas, Sara & Jenny to be equally divided amongst them, & lastly I the said Mary Christy hereby revoke all other & former wills [Page 24] wills, and

---

*The page references found in this transcription refer to pages in the original Minute Book A.

declaring this to be my last, true & proper will do make & constitute my friend Mr. George Wilson Sole executor thereof—
In Testimony Whereof I have hereunto Set my hand & Seal this
twenty fifth day of August anno Domine, one thousand, Seven
hundred, and eighty one—

Signd Sealed, deliverd pronounced, and)
declared by the said Testatrix as her last)
will, & testament, the words "of Pitts-)   her
burg" and the words "my eldest son")Mary x Christy (Seal)
being first erased, & interlined, in the)   mark
presence of us, Thomas Harrison, Hen-)
ry Floyd, John Sinkler—)

    Louisville August 26th 1781.   I the aforesaid Mary Christo-
pher[14] do hereby declare, this present instrument in writing to be
my lawful codicil to my foregoing will: and I do hereby declare
the same to be accepted and taken, as the same.   I appoint
Joseph Nicholson of Pittsburg as joint Executor, with my Executor George Wilson whom I appointed my sole Executor, & I do
hereby appoint the said Joseph Nicholson to be guardian over
my Children, and I recommend the charge, & care of my Son
Thomas Christy, to my dear friend Israel Rowland and my
Daughter, Saray & Jenny to the care & tuition of Martha
Nicholas, wife of Joseph Nicholas, [sic][15] my Executor as aforesaid   Dated August the twenty sixth, as the Codicil of the
foregoing will—Witness my hand & Seal

Sealed, & deliverd before us who at   her
her request have subriced [sub-   Mary x   Christy (Seal)
scribed] our names, Tho Harrison:)   mark
Henry Floyd, John Sinkler)

    At a Court held for Jefferson County on the 2d April 1782.
The above will proved, & admitted to record
                         Test Mer'th Price Clk Jeff Cur

    To ALL PEOPLE to whom, these presents shall come, I
Richard Brashears, of Jefferson County in the state of Virginia
Send greeting
KNOW Ye that I the said Richard Brashears, for & in considera-
tion of the sum of four hundred pounds specie, to me in hand

31

paid [Page 25] paid by Marsham Brashears of the said County—
The receipt whereof I do hereby acknowledge, have granted,
bargained, & sold, and by these presents for me & my Heirs, Do
grant, bargain & Sell unto the said Marsham Brashears, and to
his heirs & assigns a certain plantation & tract of land, situate in
the County of Jefferson aforesaid & about three miles, West of
the painted Stone on the Waters of Brashears's creek, and
adjoining my pre-emption right of one thousand acres, it being
the same land that was granted to me as my improvement right,
as by the location of my said Settlement, right may more fully
appear. Together with all & my right & title of in, & to the
same—
To HAVE, and To HOLD the hereby granted tract of land, &
premises to the said Marsham Brashear, his heirs & assigns, to
the only proper use and behoof of the said Marsham Brashears,
his heirs, and assigns forever: subject only to the claim of the
state: and I the said Richard Brashears do hereby Covenant,
Covenant, for me, & my heirs to, and with the said Marsham
Brashears, and his heirs & assigns, that I the said Richard
Brashears shall & will WARRANT and forever Defend the said
tract of land, & premisses to the said Marsham Brashears, his
heirs & assigns, by virtue of these presents.

In Testimony whereof I have hereunto Set my hand &
Seal the twenty fourth day of December One thousand, seven
hundred & eighty-One.

Sealed & delivered In presence)
of Mer'th Price William Pope) R'd. Brashear (Seal)
Josiah Phelps, Mark Thomas)

At a Court held for Jefferson County on the 5th of March
1782—The above deed poll proved, and Orderd to be recorded
Test Mer'th Price Clk Jeff Cur

At a Court held for Lincoln County, the 15th day of May,
1781. I do hereby certify that Abraham Taylor proved to this
Court, that he was intitled to a settlement & pre-emption in
Kentucky District on account of his having been in the Regular
Service, in Colo. George Rogers Clarke Regim't. where he continued till he was discharged and that he never before obtain
any certificate for the same.

[Page 26] Test William May C. J. C: At a Court held for Jefferson County on the 2nd April 1782. Ordered that the above Certificate be sufficient proof to the Court, and that a certificate issue accordingly.

Copy Test Mer'th. Price Clk Jeff Cur

Know all Men by these presents that I James Meriwether of Louisa County, in the state of Virginia, have and by these presents nominate & appoint my trusty friends, Benjamin Pope, William Pope, and Meredith Price attorneys for me on the Western Waters, and any transaction being made by them, or either of them shall be binding, on me, my heirs, & assigns forever: WITNESS my hand, and Seal this xiith April. MD.CCLXXXI

Seal'd & delivered In presence of   )
Philemon Waters. James Dundas)   Ja's Meriwether (Seal)
Hardy Hill   )

At a Court held for Jefferson County on the 7th May 1782 The above power of attorney proved & ordered to be recorded.

Test Mer'th Price. Clk. Jeff. Cur

IN the name of God Amen: I Charles Coulson, now being in full helth and strenth, both of body and mind—this is my last will & testamony—That all my lands, goods, & chatels, fall into the hands of my father Charles Coulson, and them totally to be at his disposel, only too Mairs, one of them to my Sister Jean's oldest Child: and the other to my Brother Willm's oldest Child: and fifteen hundred pound, to my Bruther Niblock's oldest Child, As for my accounts in the Curntrey. Cuntory [sic]—they air in the hands of Morton Brashear's at the falls of Ohio; and Col'n Norman Bruse haith in his hands sum land warants, which that I left with [blank] pollas, out for said land, and thair is sum money I let Mr. Springer, that he was to Send me, whiskey down,—if he shold not have sent it, his reciet, for the same, is now in the hands of Morton Brashear's, with a bill of Sail for a Cow & Calf, & many other accounts against William Shannon for Services, dun from the fourth of May of wan hundred, & seventy dollars per day [Page 27] accomt against the stait of Virginia, for Services dun at the saim per day—the rent whair of

Col'n George Slater was to give to Moton Brasheirs the Men that is now upon my Plais, thair time is up. next Spring. althow I left a pow'r of a turney, in the hands of Norman Bruse, to act for me, with regard to Seting [seeding(?)] of it again, and to receiving my part of the Crop; and I now appoint Jonothan Rogers and William Pope Executors of my Affairs, at falls of Ohioh and Col'n Andrew Bruse, Executor of my affairs, in the stait of Maryland, sow I resine my body to the graive, & my sole to God, June the twentyeth Wan thousand—

Test	)	1781
Jn'o Baily	)	Charles Coulson (Se—)
James Brown	)	my father lives in York County, in the state
Jonathan Rogers)	of Spennsylvania in Manahon Township
	)	within Nineteen miles of York Town—

At a Court held for Jefferson County, on the 7'th May 1782. The above will proved & admitted to record

Test Mer'th Price Clk Jeff Cur

Know all men by these presents that I Richard Brashear, Capt of the Illinois Department, have made, ordain'd Constituted and appointed. and by these presents for me my heirs & assigns do. make ordain nominate, & appoint my friend Marsham Brashear of Louisville in the County of Jefferson, & State of Virginia, my true and lawful attorney to ask, receive, demand of, & from, all persons, or persons, all such sums [sic], or sums of money, likewise discharge all debts, dues, & demands, that shall appear just and also to act, in a full & lawful manner, in the premises, as if I myself was present, and I do by these presents Covenant and grant that I will at all times ratify & confirm all such lawfull acts and things as the said Marsham Brashear shall & may do in the premises, by Virtue here off. IN WITNESS whereoff I have hereunto set my hand, and Seal this thirteenth day of April one thousand Seven hundred & eighty two

R'd. Brashear (Seal)

Delivir'd In presence of us   )
Ben Pope Ja's. Patten Mark Thomas)

[Page 28] At a Court. held for Jefferson County on the 7th May 1782. The above power of attorney proved & admitted to record

Test Mer'th Price Clk Jeff Cur

Leighton White came into Court, & proved by the oath of Sundry witnesses that he has Served in Colo Clarke's Regiment, as a Soldier, from July 1779 till July 1780—that he came down the river Ohio, with Colo Clarke in May 1778; and served as a Soldier till the reduction, of the Several posts, at the Illinois, after which he return'd to this County of Kentucky, and in February 1779. built a cabbin, then in Kentucky, now Jefferson County, on a north branch of Green river, heading Southwardly of Hardin's Creek, in the fork of two runs about four miles from Hardin's Settlement, near which a cabbin is white oak, tree marked L. W. and claiming a pre-emption of 400 acres, to include such Cabbin: which he desired to locate, as follows, To begin at the branch, at the first large fork, below the S'd Cabbin and to run West 253 poles, thence N 253 poles, then E 253 P. Thence to the Beginning: and it being the Courts Opinion that he is entitled to the preemption of the said land—a Certificate is granted him for the same accordingly April 3d 1781.

Test John May Clk J. Cur

Apraisment of Samuel Wells decest, affects, apraised by us first being sworn, James Quoturmous Peter Newkirk William Lock.

	£		
1. Mare £ 25 1 Do. £ 16 . . . . £	41		
1 Cow & heffer Caf	8		
1 Cow & Caf £ 7. 1 Ditto £ 5.10	12	10	
1 Do £ 8 1 Ditto £ 6.10	14	10	
1 Cow £ 6.1—Bul £ 6 10			
1 heffer 30/	14		
1 heffer 30/. 1 small Stear 27/8	2	17	8
1 Small Stear 27/6 1 two year do 30	2	17	6
4 Sows & eight pigs	7	10	
£			
1 Sow & 6 shots 5 12	5	12	
1. Sow & 8 Ditto	3		
1. Chest & Table 50/	2	10	
2 Dishes, 1 bason & other Sundrys	4	8	
1. Tekettle & Tepot		17	
three Steal traps	3	15	
2 axes, & 2 mattocks	2	6	
Chese 54/2 Bar share [?] plows 7.2.2	9	16	2
1 Shovell plow	1	6	

	£		
1 Whip Saw & Cross Cut Saw	4	7	6
1 Sett harrow teeth & other sundrys	2	11	
Two Ewes & 1 lamb	1	15	
Six Weathers	7		
4 Sickles & tu locks	1	9	6
Seven pair of hinges	1	1	
1 ho. & other sundries		10	
1 Lock Chin [16]	1	5	
2 pair of Chains	2	10	
1 pair of Stelyards	1	10	
1 gun barrel & Sundry		18	
1 box Iron & spice mortar		14	
two pair of Cards		6	
2 Hackls		14	
1 Grid Iron		6	
1 Cutting box & Knife £		15	
1 Negro fellow Jacob	75		
1 Wench Cate	80		
1 gal Sarah	30		
1 gal Cis	27	10	
1 gal Nan	20		
		[blank]	

Jas. Quertermous
Peter Newkirk
Wm. Lock

At a Court held for Jefferson County on the Second of April
1782. The Inventory above, return'd & ordered to be recorded
Test Mer'th Price Clk Jeff Cur

KNOW ALL Men by these presents that I David Douglass,
now of Jefferson County State of Virginia, being about going to
New Orleans, as also for other good causes & considerations,
moving me hereunto have made, ordained, authoriz'd, and
appointed, and by these presents do authorize & appoint my
trusty, & loving friend George Wilson, of the falls of Ohio, and
County & State aforesaid, my true & lawfull attorney, for me,
and in my name, and to my use, to ask, demand, sue for, recover,
& receive of the sundry persons, who now are, indebted to me,
agreeable to a schedule, with my said attorney now left, all such

sum, or sums of money, debts, & duties whatsoever, which now
are due, and owing, unto me, the said David Douglass, by &
from the said Sundry persons, as also, all other moneys, now due
or to become due and owing unto me, by any other ways, or
means, or any other person, or persons whatsoever, and to have
use & take all lawful ways, & means, in my name, or otherwise for
recovery thereof, [Page 30] by attachment, arrest, distress, or
otherwise, and to agree, & compound for the same and acquittances, or other sufficient discharges for the same for me, and
in my name to make, Seal, & deliver—And to do all other lawfull
act, and things whatsoever, concerning the premises, as fully and
in every respect, as I myself might, or could do if I were personally present—

AND attornies, one, or more under him, for the purposes
aforesaid to make, & at his pleasure, to revoke, ratify, and
Confirming, all, & whatsoever my said attorney shall, & will in
my name, lawfully do, or cause to be done, in, and about the
premisses by virtue of these presents, IN WITNESS whereof I
have hereunto set my hand, Seal this third day of May anno
Dom: one thousand, Seven hundred, and eighty-two

Seal'd & deliver'd In presence of)
Robt George. J. Donne   )   David Douglass (Seal)
Rich'd Chinoweth   )

At a Court held for Jefferson County on the 7th May 1782.
The above power of attorney proved & admitted to record.
                                    Test Mer'th Price Clk Jeff Cur-

IN obedience to an order of Jefferson Court, we the subscribers
being first sworn before William Pope Gent; one of the Magistrate, of said County, have valued, & appraised the estate of
Abraham Keller deceas'd an Inventry whereof is as follows viz:

1 Sword 80/. 1 Rifle gun & bullet mould, 80/. 1 Regimental coat & waistcoat 40/..............................	£ 10		
1 Regimental coat, & waistcoat 90/. 1 Calico Jack Coat & waistcoat 36/. 1 gingham Do & Do 40/..........	8	6	
1 silk waistcoat 30/. 1 Cloth Do 12/.6.. 1 man's hatt 45/. 1 blanket 12/....	4	19	6

	£		
1 half moon, 22 Coat buttons, 1 silver Knee buckle, 1 pr garters 2 Steels & old razor......................		7	
10" Lead 10/. 1 old trunk 5/. 1 brass Kettle 20/. 1 Ironpot & hooks 23/..	2	18	
3 pewter Basons, 1 plate, & 3 spoons 25/. 3 knives & 3 forks 6/. 2 Chain 5/. 1 [illegible] 5/..............	2	1	
£	28	11	6

Aquilla Whitaker   )
      his   )   Moses Kuykendall
Abraham x Whitaker)   Jo's Archer
      mark   )

At a Court held for Jefferson County, on the 7th May 1782. The above inventry return'd to Court & admitted to record

              Test Mer'th Price Clk Jeff Cur—

[Page 31] KNOW ALL MEN by these presents, that we Benjamin Pope & James Patton of the County of Jefferson, & State of Virginia for & in consideration of one hundred, & Sixty five gallons of good merchantable whisky to us this day delivered by Marsham Brashears, of the County aforesaid, We the said Benjamin Pope, & James Patton, for us, our heirs, Executors, & administrators, do Covenant, promise, grant, & agree, to & with the said Marsham Brashears, and his heirs & assigns in, manner & form following, that is to say—that we the said Benjamin Pope, and James Patton, shall, & will, on or before the first day of May next ensuing the date hereof, by a good, & sufficient deed, & assurance, in law, grant, & convey to the said Marsham Brashears, and to his heirs and assigns, in fee simple, six hundred, and sixty acres of land, of what is commonly known, or accepted, as Secondrate land, the same to be laid off on Floydsfork, of Salt River. four miles below the Buffaloe Crossing; and on the east side of said Floyd Fork. Provided Nevertheless, that if it shall so happen that we the said Benjamin Pope, & James Patton shall not be able to grant & convey the premises aforesaid, to the said Marsham Brashears, in manner aforesaid—then, and in such case, we & each of us, Do jointly covenant & grant that we will by a like sufficient deed, & assurance in law, convey, & assure to the said Marsham Brashears, and to his heirs, & assigns in fee Simple a like quantity of Six hundred, & Sixty acres of land, equal in quality to the aforementioned—the same to be laid off on the said Floyds Fork, and not to exceed five miles from the aforesaid premises—and lastly for the true performance, of all & Singular the Covenants herein contain'd we bind ourselves, our heirs Executors & administrators, in the penal sum of one thousand pounds, lawful money. of Virginia, in specie, firmly by these presents IN Testimony whereof we have hereunto sett our hands & Seals, this Sixth day of May one thousand, Seven hundred & eighty-two

Sealed & delivered in the present of us)   Ben Pope (S)
)   Jas Patten (Seal)

Notwithstanding the term of the first of May is mentioned in the foregoing instrument, it is the intention of the parties that [Page 32] the term shall be extended untill by the laws & ordinances of the state will permit

Josiah Phelps,   )
Rich'd Chinoweth Capt)
James Berwick   )

At a Court held for Jefferson County, on the 7th May 1782. The above instrument of writing fully proved & order'd to be recorded
        Test Mer'th Price Clk Jeff Cur[1]

IN pursuance to, and order of the Worshipful Court of Jefferson Cty. held the 18th of August 1781. Geo: Grundy, Jas Samuel, & David Hawkins, being first sworn, do estimate the movable part of Wm. Brashear decd estate: in paper Currency, as followeth—

	£	
To one Negroe Boy . . . .£	7000	
To two Cows & Calves £ 1000, and two heifers £ 900	1900	
To 7 Axes £ 130, To some cisels Augurs, & other Irons	1070	
To 1 foot adds, & 4 siccles, & other Irons £ 25	25	
To another parcel old Iron £ 14. To one handsaw box & flat iron	40	

	£		
To 6 oald hoes, 2. Mathooks & 2 Mall rings £ 100	100		
To one frying pan £ 14. To Clivises Traces & hames, £ 10	24		
To 3 oald Cests £ 20 & three old Chairs & Table £ 10	30		
To 3 Beds & furniture £ 120 To 2 Reeds & hatchel £ 60	180		
To 9 Pewter plates 2 Dishes, one bason & Some spoons	60		
To one washing Tub, 3 pales & 2 Buckets, & some other vessels	15		
To one oald flax, wheel £ 10 3 Pots & Duch oven	710		
To one oald gun £ 30. and one old horse £ 15	45		
To his Wairing Apparel £ 55	55		
To Virginia paper Currency £ 25 o. g. Continental Do £ 64.4	89	4	9
To feathers to the Amount of £ 30. & an old plow £ 12	42		
Paper Currency £	10499	4	9

	£		Specie		
1782 February 15'h then appraised in specie					
To one Cow, & Calf £ 5, & three Deer skins in the hare	3	15	[sic]		
To one gouge & some other oald Tools		3			
£	5	18	& 10499	4	9

[Page 33] At a Court held for Jefferson County on the 7th of May 1782. The above Inventory returned to Court, & order'd to be recorded

Test Mer'th Price Clk Jeff Cur[17]

At a Court held for Jefferson County on the 7th May 1782. Satisfactory proof being made to the Court, that the following land warrants, were lost viz't. one in the name of JOSHUA WRIGHT for 3000 acres, one other in the name of ISAAC COX for 2000: one other in the name of JOHN COX for 2000. One other in the name of David Cox for 2000—one other in the name of

William Taylor, for 1000: Orderd that Certificates of the Same
be granted.

Test Mer'th Price Clk. Jeff Cur

A poll taken April 2'd for Delegates of the Assembly of
Virginia—

John May	Squire Boone
James Sullivan	John Martin
Aquilla Whitacre	Samuel Westerfield
David Standiford	John Harriss
Samuel Wells,	William Goodwin
Robert Eakin	John Tuell
John Martin	William Stafford
John Thixton	William Lock
Jacob Case	William Spangler
George Wilson	John Voress
Peter Coleman, 10	John Vertrees,
John Pryor	James Dunbar
Philip Lutes	Samuel Watkins
Cornelius Bryan	Jacob Gum
William Goodwin	Francis Galloway
George Ownes	James Voress
James Catermous[18]	John McLean
James Austinguss	Morias Hambury

William Shannon	Isaac Marrison
James Sullivan	Robert Ackin
Aquilla Whitacre	John Thixton
David Standiford	John Prior
Samuel Wells	William Stafford
Jacob Case	John Voress
George Wilson	James Dunbar
Peter Coleman	James Galloway,
Sam'l Westerfield	James Voress
Philip Lutes	John McLean
John Harriss	John Sinclair
Cornelius Bryan	Abraham Chaplain
George Owens	Joseph Kirkpatrick
John Tuel	
James Catamus[18]	
James Austengus	
William Lock	
Moses Kuykendall	

John May Cont'd	John May Cont'd
William Spangler	David Douglass
John Vertrees	George McManus
Moses Kuykendall 20	Benja Pope
Joshua Archer	Meredeth Price
Samuel Watkins	William Pope
Jacob Gumm	Thos Banfield
James Steward	Henry Floyd
Morras Hansbury	Rich'd Chenoweth shff
Arthur Park	
Robert George	
Mark Thomas	
Isaac Kellar	
James F Moore	
Robert Gilmore	
Benj'a McLeland	
James Hogland	
John Mundall	
John Handly	
John Crawford	
John Helm	
John Crittindin	
Thomas Spencer	
Peter Warren.	
Daniel Sparks.	
Isham Floyd	
Sebastian Demar	
Johnson Campbell	
Daniel Sullivan	
Geo R Clarke	
George Pomeroy	
Thos Pursley	
Jacob Barrackman	

Squire Boone	William Shannon Cont'd
John Sinclair	Joshua Archer
Arthur Lock	James Steward
William Cummins	William Cummins
John Nelson	John Nelson
Robert Gilmore	Robert George
Benja Mcleland	Mark Thomas
James Hogland	Isaac Keller
John Mundall	James F Moore

John Handly	John Crittinden
John Crawford	Thos Spencer
John Nelson	Daniel Sparks
Peter Warren	Isham Floyd
Sebastian Demar	Abraham Chapman
Joseph Kirkpatrick	Johnson Campbell
George Pomeroy	Dan'l Sullivan
George McManus	Geo R. Clark
Benjamin Pope	Thomas Purley
Meredeth Price	Jacob Barrackman
William Pope	David Douglass
Henry Floyd	Thos Banfield—
Rich'd Chinoweth shff	

At a Court held for Jefferson County on the 7th May 1782.
The above poll return'd & order'd to be recorded—
Test Mer'th Price Clk Jeff Cur

[Page 35] THIS INDENTURE made the xviiith February Anno Domini MD.CCLXXXII. Between James Steward of the County of Jefferson of the one part and Michael Humble of the County of Lincoln of the other part WITNESSETH, the said James Steward, by and with the consent, and approbation of his Son John Steward doth by these presents bind him the said John apprentice to the aforesaid Michael Humble for, and during the space of four years, to commence from the date of these presents, to learn the art & mysterys of Blacksmith & Gunsmith, and also doth engage that the said John Steward shall not absent himself from his said Master's business with his the said James Stewards advice, or consent, but in all things faithfully & truly obey his said Master's lawful commands. IN consideration whereof he the said Michael Humble doth oblige himself to use his utmost endeavors, to learn, & instruct the above named John Steward in the aforesaid art, & mysterys of blacksmith & Gun Smith, & every other mechanical art, that he the said Michael Humble is acquainted with if thereunto required by the said James, or John Steward, & that he will, at no time, expose him the said John to the danger of the Enemy, more than is the Common custom, or usage of one in his Circumstances, and that he will find him in sufficient meat, drink & clothing, such as is usual in this Country during his apprenticeship, and that he will, **at**

43

the expiration of the said term, give unto the said apprentice, such clothing at least, as he shall receive with him the said John Steward, For the true performance of the above presents the said parties bind themselves each to the other in the penal Sum of One thousand pounds, Specie Currency of Virginia & have interchangeably Set their hands & Seals, the day & year above written.

Seal'd & deliver'd In presence of)   James Stewart (Se[al])
Ben Pope, Wm Pope Mer th Price)   John Stewart (Se[al])
)   Michael Humble (Se[al])

    I hereby engage to send the within nam'd John Stewart, to school Six months in case an opportunity, should offer during his apprenticeship
    Witness my hand & Seal, the day & year within written.

Test Ben Pope W Pope &)   Michael Humble (Seal)
    Mer'th Price   )

    At a Court held for Jefferson County on the 7th May 1782. The [Page 36] The above named proved & ordered to be recorded.

                   Test Mer'th Price Clk Jeff Cur

    KNOW ALL MEN by these presents that I John Girault Captain in the Illinois Regiment, in the Service of the State of Virginia, being about to embark for the Settlement of the Natchez with the permission of my Superior Officer, as also for divers other good causes and Considerations moving me hereunto, have made, ordain'd authorized, and appointed. And by these presents, do make, ordain authorize & appoint, my trusty and loving friend William Clark, Lieutenant, in the Regiment aforesaid, and in the service of the State aforesaid, my true, & lawful attorney, for me & in my name, and to my use, to ask, demand, sue for, recover & receive of the Commonwealth of Virginia, all such Sum & Sums of money debts and duties, whatsoever which now are, or here after Shall be due, and owing unto me the said John Girault, by & from the said Commonwealth of Virginia, as also all other monies now due or to become due & owing to me, by any other ways & means, or any other person or persons whatsoever, and to have use & take all lawful means in my name, or otherwise for recovery thereof, by attachment, arrest, distress or otherwise, & to agree & compound for the same, & acquittances, or other sufficient discharges, for the same, for me, and in my name to make Seal & deliver & to do all other lawful acts & things whatsoever, concirning the premisses as fully, in every respect, as I myself might, or could do if I were personally present, and attornies, one or more under him for the purposes aforesaid, to make, & at his pleasure to revoke—ratifying all & whatsoever my said attorney shall in my name—lawfully do, or cause to be done in & about the premisses by virtue of these presents. In Testimony whereof I have hereunto set my hand & Seal at Fort Nelson, at the falls of Ohio this thirteenth day of April one thousand Seven hundred and eighty two

Sealed & delivered In presence of)   Jno Girault (Seal)
Jos Calvit Jas Finn   )   Cap:

At a Court held for Jefferson County on the 4th. June 1782 [Page 37] The above power of attorney proved and order'd to be recorded.

Test Mer'th Price Clk Jeff Cur:

KNOW ALL MEN by these presents that I George Dickeans, of Louisville, in Jefferson County & State of Virginia, for & in consideration of thirty pounds in Specie to me in hand paid by Charles Lecount of the same place, the receipt whereof I do hereby acknowledge have granted, bargained & Sold, And by these presents do grant bargain & Sell to the said Charles Lecount & to his heirs & assigns, a certain lott & piece of ground, Situate in the town of Louisville aforesaid, known in the plan of the said Town No. Thirty Seven, adjoining John Crawford, on the West, John Vickroy on the East, and the river Ohio on the North: containing half an acre (it being the same lott, and piece of ground, which John Townshind, by his Certain bill of Sale, bearing date the Sixth day of September, one thousand Seven hundred, & eighty to me did convey) Together with all my right title, and interest, of, in to the Same—and all & Singular the buildings, improvements, and appurtenances, thereunto belonging: To HAVE, & To HOLD the said premisses, with the appurtenances, unto the said CHARLES LECOUNT, his heirs, & assigns, to the only proper use and behoof, of the said Charles Lecount, his heirs, and assigns forever; Subject only to the claim of the CHIEF LORD of the fee, thereof, and I do hereby covenant, and agree, to Warrant & Defend, the above granted premises against me, and my heirs, & against all persons claiming by, from, or under me, to the said Charles Lecount, his heirs & assigns, by these presents: In Witness Whereof I have hereunto set my hand & Seal this ninth day of October one thousand, Seven hundred and eighty one:

Sealed, & delivered In presence of)
And'w Scott John Sinkler   )   George Dickens (Seal)
James Berwick   )

At a Court held for Jefferson County on the 4th June 1782— The above bill of Sale proved & admitted to record
Test Mer'th Price Clk Jeff Cur

[Page 38] KNOW ALL MEN by these presents that I George Dickens of Louisville, Jefferson County, & State of Virginia, for & in consideration of the Sum of thirty pounds, in specie to me in hand paid, by CHARLES LECOUNT of the same place, The receipt whereof I do hereby acknowledge have given, granted, bargained & Sold, And by these presents do grant, bargain, & Sell, unto the Said Charles Lecount, and to his heirs & assigns, a certain lott & piece of ground, Situate in the Town of Louisville aforesaid, Known in the plan of the said Town No. thirty Six, adjoining Moir's Street, on the north, on the Main Street, on the West, and on the Ohio river on the East, containing half an acre—(It being the Same land, which a certain Jacob Myers, by his bill of Sale, dated, the eighth day of March, one thousand, Seven hundred, and eighty did convey to John Townshend, which Said John Townshend, by his bill of Sale dated the ninth day of May, in the Same year did convey to John Vickroy, and which the Said John Vickroy by his bill of Sale dated the Sixteenth day of October in the year aforesaid to me did convey) Together with all my right, title, and interest, of in & to the Same with all &. Singular the buildings, improvements, & appurtenances, thereunto belonging. To HAVE, & TO HOLD the said premises, with the appurtenances, to the said Charles Lecount, his heirs, & assigns forever subject only to claims of the Chief Lord of the fee thereof—and lastly I do hereby Covenant to Warrant, the aforesaid premises against me, & my heirs, & against all persons claiming, by, or under me: to the Said Charles Lecount his heirs & assigns by these presents. IN

46

Witness Whereof I have hereunto Set my hand, and Seal, the ninth day of October, one thousand Seven hundred & eighty-one

Seal'd & deliver'd In the presence of us.) George Dickens (Seal) And'w Scott, John Sinkler James Berwick)

At a Court held for Jefferson County. on the 4th June 1782. The above bill of Sale, proved, & admitted to record
Test Mer'th Price Clk Jeff Cur¹
[Page 39]

Know All Men by these presents that I George Dickens of Louisville Jefferson County, & state of Virginia for & in consideration of one hundred pounds in specie to me in hand paid by Charles Lecount, of the Same place, the receipt whereof I do hereby acknowledge, have granted, bargained, & Sold, And by these presents do grant, bargain, and Sell unto the said Charles Lecount, all & Singular One moiety, and half part of a Certificate for One thousand acres of land on the waters of Licking Creek adjoining Sampson Butler, which said land is now held jointly, by me, & George Thompson, as will more fully appear, by an instrument in writing under the hand, of the Said George Thompson, dated the 26th April 1780 will more fully appear, together with all improvements & appurtenances, of in and to the Same— To Have & To Hold the said premisses to the said Charles Lecount, his heirs & assigns, to the only proper use, & behoof of the said Charles Lecount, his heirs & assigns forever Subject only to the claim of the Lord Of The Fee thereof— and I the said George Dickens against me & my heirs, and against all manner of persons claiming by from, or under me, the above mentioned moiety of the Said tract of land, & premisses to the said Charles Lecount, his heirs & assigns, Shall and will Warrant & forever defend by these presents—In Witness Whereof I have hereunto Set my hand & Seal this Ninth day of October anno Domini, one thousand Seven hundred and eighty one.

Sealed & deliver'd In presence of us. The)
words "on the waters of Licking Creek")George Dickens (Seal)
being first interlined, also the words "in)
specie".   )
And'w Scott,John Sinkler James Berwick)

At a Court held for Jefferson County on the fourth of June 1782—The above bill of Sale proved, & ordered to be recorded.
Test Mer'th Price, Clk. Jeff. Cur¹

47

[Page 40] To ALL PEOPLE, to whom these presents shall come GREETING—KNOW YE, that I GEORGE DICKEANS of Jefferson County & State of Virginia, for, and in consideration of the trust & confidence, I repose, in my friend CHARLES LECOUNT, of the said County, have made, ordained, Constituted, and appointed, And by these presents do make, ordain, constitute, and appoint the said Charles Lecount my true & lawful attorney, in and over all & Singular my estate, & property, as well real, as personal, Westward of the Kanaway, and the Cumberland Mountains, hereby giving full power to my said attorney, as well to ask, sue for, receive, and demand, all and Singular my debts due me, as also to Sell, alienate, grant, & convey, or otherwise, to lease or to farm lett, all, and Singular my lands, and Tenements, in the said Country, as to my said attorney shall Seem most for my benefit and advantage, in as full and ample a manner, as if I myself was personally present—And lastly, I the said George Dickeans do hereby covenant, that I will at all times hereafter, when thereunto required, ratify, and Confirm all & Singular, all such lawful acts, & things, as my said attorney Shall do in the premises, by virtue of these presents—IN WITNESS Whereof I have hereunto Set my hand & Seal this Ninth day of—October one thousand, seven hundred, & eighty. One

Sealed & deliver'd In the presence)   George Dickens (Seal)
of us. And'w Scott   )
John Sinkler, James Berwick   )

At a Court held for Jefferson County on the 4th June 1782—The above power of attorney proved, & admitted to record.
Test Mer'th Price. Clk. Jeff. Cur

On the motion of Richard Chenoweth Gentleman, Ordered that his Mark be recorded. viz: A Crop off the left ear, and a Swallow-fork in the right—
Test Mer'th Price Clk. Jeff. Cur

[Page 41] IN OBEDIENCE to an order of Jefferson Court we the Subscribers, being first Sworn have apprais'd the estate of Mary Christy deceas'd—An Inventory whereof is as followeth Viz:

1 black Cow & Calve..................£	10	
1 feather bade & furniture.............	15	
1 Ditto & Ditto.....................	12	

48

Item	£	s	d
1 Hand Mill @	3		
1 Small Dutch Oven	1	10	
1 4 gallon Pot @	1		
2 frying pans		15	
13 small Puther plates)			
2 small Do Driper)	3		
3 puther basons)			
1 Small Tea pot)			
1 small puther bottle)			
1 brase Candlestick)		15	
1 Tea Canister Brick)			
2 pair Candle Snuffers)			
1 X Cut Saw 30/.1 pot rack 20/	2	10	
1 foot Edge & 2 drawing [illegible]		18	
1 pack Saddle & 1 old riding Saddle		12	
1 Sett of plow Irons	1	15	
1 Lock Chane		15	
1 old plow shear & 2 mattocks)			
1 Breyer Seyeth, 1 spad)	2	10	
2 axes, 2 Clevis's with pins)			
9 sickles		9	
2 spick gimelets 1 gouge)		10	
1 Chisle & 1 pitchfork)			
Carried on	56	19	
Brought up £	56	19	
2 locks without Keys		6	
2 mawl rings		6	
1 Small pot Rack		12	
Sundry pieces of old Iron	2	10	
2 Handsawes 2 howes)	11	14	
1 Iron Wedge 1 hammer)			
2 glass Tumblers 1 Bangly[19]		18	
3 Cups & 4 Sacers		6	
1 pr Iron Tongs		10	
1 Glass Bottle		3	
1 large Chist		15	
1 Butter Pott		10	
2 Small Chists		7	6
1 old brace kettle 21 spoons		13	6
1 Teakettle & 5 old Chairs		19	6
2 Tables (old)		10	
6 old knives & three forks		6	
1 pair Glass eyes		6	
1 Close basket		1	
1 Churn & Washing Toob)		10	
3 old piggens 1 old Jair)			

1 ager, 1 old how, 1 Currie Comb).......		10	
& 1 Luking Glass)			
4 Hens & 5 ducks, 4 Cocks)............		17	6
2 Canteens 2 horse Collows)			
	£	69	10

Ben Pope, Jas. Patton, Thomas Harrison

At a Court held for Jefferson County on the 4th June 1782. The —[Page 42] The above Inventory return'd and admitted to record

Test Mer'th Price Clk Jeff Cur

A RETURN of the property belonging to the estate of Robert Travis deceas'd

To Sundry old Clothes............................£	210
To pr Silver Shew buckles 1. Stock Buckle & pr Sleeve Buttons..	180
To parcel of glass & Earthen Ware £15 1 Side Saddle £150...	195
1 Man's Saddle £ 60 1 Dixinary grammar & Sundry other books £ 270..............................	330
1 Slate £ 18—a parcel of yarn, wool & Indigo £ 96.......	114
1. Bed, Bedsted & furniture £ 1000 1 Do with furniture £ 500..	1500
1 Ditto with some furniture £ 500 2 Rifle barrels from forge £ 120....................................	620
1 Smooth Bore gun & 2 naked Barrels................	30
2 Dutch plow plates, & part of Bar of Iron............	84
1 Handsaw, Drawing knife & adds...................	75
3. old gun locks £ 45. 2 Horse Bells £ 30..............	75
2 Brass Cocks £ 30, a parcel of old files £ 18...........	48
1. Box Iron & Brass articles, £165 1 Screw Augre £ 30..	195
A parcel of Bar led £ 30 9 Peuter Plates £ 135. 5 Do Basons £ 90.....................................	255
2. Pewter Dishes..................................	60
1 Wooden Bole. 1 Tin Funnel 3 old Pewter Plates, Some Pewter Spoons—Some old knives & forks, 1 Grater & c.....................................	60
1 p. Wool Cards £ 15. 1 Sett of flatt Irons £ 30........	45
1 Coppey Book 1 Razor, 1 p Sissers £ 24 1 Pottle Pot[20] £ 36..	60
1 Earthen pan & Pot £ 9. 1 Iron Pot & Bales £ 15 1 Dutch oven & Bales £ 18 £ 72.................	72

50

1. Broiling Iron £ 18 1. Frying Pan £ 30	48
1 Iron Pot Rack, shovel, & other Iron Articles	51
1. Tennant Saw, 1 old Narrow Ax £ 36	36
1. Piggin, 2 Sifters, 1. Bred Tray £ 9. 1. Bed, Bedsted & furniture £ 300	309
1. Squaer Table & Chair £ 48 1 Iron Kettle £ 150	198
1 Sett Iron Traces & Hames	45
1. Gray Horse £ 2500 1. Bay Mare £ 2500	5000
2 Cows & Calves £ 2300 1. Pot & Bales 2 hackles £ 75 . . .	2375

At a Court held for Jefferson County on the 4th June 1782. The above Inventory return'd & admitted to record—

Test Mer'th Price Clk. Jeff Cur

[Page 43] Administration of the estate of James Robinson deceas'd granted Philip Barbour, who entered into bond of one thousand pounds Specie with Abram Chaplain Security

Test Mer'th Price Clk. Jeff Cur

We the subscribers, being chosen: do proceed to appraise the estate of Adam Grant deceas'd as followeth

1 Red Cow & Earling £ 750 L Do £ 800. 1 Do £ 700 . . . . £	2200	
1 Rifle £ 150 1 Ditto £ 250 1 Smooth Gun £ 30 . . .	430	
1 Pot & Bales £ 60 1 Frying Pan £ 30 1 Flat Iron £ 75	105	
1 Tea Kettle £ 45 1 pr Steelyards 45: 1 Narrow ax 15	105	
2 old Broad hoes £ 15 1 pr Wool'd Cards £ 18 1 Do Too Do 90/	37	10
14 Pewter spoons £ 33. 3 Do Plates £ 30. 1 Lot Iron wedges £ 30	93	
Sundry Iron Articles £ 66 2 pr. Iron Traces £ 90 .	156	
1 Linnen Wheel & Spools, £ 45 Sundry wooden ware £ 30	75	
1 square Table £ 12. 1. Black Man £ 2000	2012	
1. Plow share & Coulter £ 75 1 Mattock £ 30	105	
Sundry Iron Articles £ 135 1 Grind stone £ 30 . . .	165	
2 Bells £ 36 1 small Broad Hoe £ 6. 1 Hand Mill £ 300	342	
£	5845	10

At a Court held for Jefferson County on the 4th of June 1782. The above Inventory return'd & admitted to record

Test Mer'th Price Clk. Jeff Cur

L Leonard Helm[21] of Jefferson County & state of Virginia, do make, and ordain this my last will & testament in manner & form following vizt—I devise unto my Children Sally, Achiles, & Molly Helm, an equal distribution of all my land, debts, & accounts on the Western Department of Virginia, and if either of my said Children should die before they come of age, or mary, it is then my desire that their proportion of said estate be equally devided between [Page 44] the Surviving children, or their heirs—Lastly I constitute my friends William Pope and Henry Floyd, whole & sole Executors of this my last Will & testament. In Witness whereof I have hereunto Set my hand & Seal this twenty Second day of May Anno Domine one thousand Seven hundred and eighty two—

Leon'd Helm (Seal)

Seal'd & acknowledg'd In presence of)
Wm McCraken Jos Archer   )
Wm Johnston Mer'th Price   )

At a Court held for Jefferson County on the 4th June 1782. The above will proved & admitted to record

Test Mer'th Price Clk Jeff. Cur

This is to certify that Henry Preator, served under me, at the Reduction of the Illinois—Given under my hand Falls of Ohio Novem'r 28th 1779—

G R Clark Com'd in C'f Dept do Ils

This is to certify that Edward Murray, Served as a Soldier in Illinois Detachment, until the reduction of the different posts in that Country Given under my hand Falls of Ohio Novem'r 23d 1779   G R Clark[1]:

At a Court held for Jefferson County on the fourth of June 1782 On the motion of Captain Abraham Chaplain the two certificates above was admitted to record

Test Mer'th Price Clk. Jeff Cur.

Agreeable to an order of Court held for Jefferson County 4th
June 1782 We the subscribers have appraised the estate of
Leonard Helm deceased according to law:

Two Coats, & one Waistcoat.................£   5
one Hatt 3/. one pair Shoes 3/. Blankett.........____14____

                                        £   5   14
    Given under our hands 17th June 1782 Louisville:
        Marsham Brashear Geo Owens, Edw'd Holeman:

At a Court held for Jefferson County on the 2d July 1782.
The above Inventory of Leonard Helm's Estate return'd &
order'd to be recorded—
        Test Mer'th Price Clk. Jeff. Cur

[Page 45] Agreeable to an order of Court held for Jefferson
County, the fourth of June 1782 we the subscribers according to
law have appraised one Negroe Man nam'd Caesar, said to be
the property of James Robertson's to one hundred, & Sixty
pounds Specie—Given under our hands this 6th June 1782.
Louisville
        Marsham Brashear
        Thos Harrison
        Henry Floyd

At a Court held for Jefferson County on the 2d July 1782.
The above Inventory was return'd & order'd to be recorded
        Test Mer'th Price Clk Jeff Cur

Inventory of the estate of James Robertson deceased—A Cer-
tificate for his pay as Lieutenant of Artillery for one year ten
months, & Seven days—
One negro man Slave named Casar
A Certificate for said Negroes pay as an Artificer for fourteen
    months & two days:
A Certificate for said Negroe's pay for two hundred & four days
    Services in like capacity
        Falls of Ohio July 1 1782
        Phil Barbour

The above Inventory return'd by Philip Barbour Gent,
July Court 1782. & admitted, at his request to record
        Mer'th. Price Clk Jeff. Cur

In the name of God, amen: I, Hezekiah Moss of Jefferson
County, being weak in body but of Sound memory, blessed be

God, do this eleventh day of May, in the year of our Lord one thousand Seven hundred, eighty & two, make this my LAST WILL, and Testament in manner following that is to say. First I give to my Daughter Elizabeth four hundred acres of land, which I have purchased from George Grundy, Known by Dan C. Meredy's place, Also I bequeath to my beloved wife, four hundred acres of land which I have lately purchased from William Hardin—Also I give [Page 46] to my son Hezekiah three hundred acres of land which I have bought of Thos Clark, together with two hundred & fifty acres of land which I have bought of John Camp—Also I give to my said Daughter Elizabeth one milch cow, which is to be in the care of my dear wife until time, time [sic] her widowhood only also I give to my Dear wife One black Cow which is now in my Custody—also I give to my Dear Wife one black horse during her widowhood only, and after said horse shall be delivered, to my Daughter Elizabeth—also I order that my Stock of hogs, after my debts may be paid: whatsoeven shall remain, may be divided between my dear wife, Daughter & Son, in three equal parts, & I ordain Reuben Case, & Jacob Vanmatre my sole Exr's of this my Last Will, to take care, & see the same, perform'd according to my true desire, Interest, & means—and for their pains I give each of them

IN witness whereof I the said Hezekiah Moss, have to these, to this my last Will & Testament Set my hand & Seal, the day and year above written—Sign'd Seal'd, & deliver'd In presence of us—

John Byrns, Edward holeman:)   his
Joseph Glenn   ) Hezekiah x Moss (Seal)
)   mark

At a Court held for Jefferson County on the 2d July 1782 This last Will & Testament of Hezekiah Moss was fully proved and admitted to record
       Test Mer'th Price Clk Jeff Cur

An Inventory of the goods & of Hezekiah Moss dec'd Aug 2'd 1782: we the subscribers chosen to preas Hezekiah Moss' estate deces'd Joseph Brooks.

value one brown Cow, & Calf to be worth eight pounds.....................£	8	
one Pided Cow & Calf £ 7. One yearling bull 30/.........................	8	10
One Sow & five pigs £ 3..............	3	

	£	s	
To a Sow with Shoat, or her her/Liveth [?]	1	15	
To a black Sow with a white list round her middle	2	10	
To a white Sow 45/. Black Two Barrows 55/. 9 Shoats £ 7 1. Barrow 40/.	14		
To white Sow 35/. Black & white sow 25/.	3		
To Black Horse with some white feet	25		
To a Horse £ 6 To one Well, & the third of 20/	7		
To 1. Bell 6/. An ax, & old iron 30/. 2 pair Chanes 50/	4	6	
[Page 47]			
To two Gun barles, & Gun lock 50/. a Smooth bore gun 20/	3	10	
To a Chest 20/. 4 Chear 12/. a walnut book 12/. a mattock 12/	3	16	
To a Shumaker hamer & pinchers		7	
To a Reasor, & Ten quart & some Small articles		5	
To a pese of old iron belonging to a wagon		5	
To a pot & Kettle 50/. & 1 Bedstead 6/	2	16	
To a beason & pleat & five spoons 20/	1		
To a Churn & some wooden veasels 12/		12	
To a pare of Brace Buckles 1-/.6		1	6
To a hunting Shirt & Jackeat Stockings & Stoak	1	10	
To Six dear skins, in the hear 20/. a bed, a case 60/	4		
To a Bag 5/ a p. wool Cards, 6/		6	
To a water Toob, Salt troff, & two brine barels	1		
To a little Spinning wheel		6	
To 1 wiskey Barrel 2/. An old pewter Teapot 2/		1	
To a Plow & Irons, £ 3 a dres'd doe skin 3/	3	3	

John McCasland, James Pursel Joseph Brooks Exhibited to the worshippel the court of Jefferson, County the 6th August 1782—

Reuben Cave) Executors
Jacob Vanmatre)
Test Mer'th Price Clk Cur

A List of goods, & chattels, being the whole of William Eakin deceased, approved by Philip Lute, John Thickstow & Robert Gilmore, for William Goodwin administrator this third day of July 1782.

To 1 Black Mare & Colt appraised at . . £	30		
To 1. Red Cow & Calf £ 7 1 Two year old horse colt £ 16	23		
To 1 Cow £ 6, a young Cow & Colt £ 6 1 Ditto 6 £	18		
To a white heifer & two year old bull	6		
To a Brass Kettle 40/. for a Small iron Kettle, & small skillet 12/	3		
For Two Smoothing Irons, 9/. 1 falling ax 8. 1 Pot rack 12/	1	9	
For a pot rack 12/. 3 Pewter dishes 30/. 6 Pewter Plates 18/	3		
[Page 48]			
One Pewter Tea pot & Tin Cannister 12/ . . . . £		12	
For 1 Bible, & three other books 15/. 1 old Rifle Gun 35/	2	10	
To a mattock, an Inch Augre 20/	1		
Three Chisels, a gouge, & small draw Knife		12	
A Hammer & a pair of Nippers & an old hoe		8	
For a pair of Plow Irons & hangings	2		
For a pair of Fetters 2/. and a Bell 5/		8	
For a Side Saddle £ 5 for a hone		6	
£	96	13—	

At a Court held for Jefferson County, on the 3d July 1782— The above Inventory returned & admitted to record
Test Mer'th Price Clk Jeff Cur

A list of goods & chattels, (the estate of William Spangler deceased) aprised by James Stergus, James Quertermas, & John Thixton for Margarett Spangler administrix, this 7th day of July 1782

To a yoake of oxen, aprised at £ 20. 1 yearling horse Colt £ 4 . . . . £	24		
To a young Mare & Colt £ 20 To a Mare £ 8	28		

56

Item	£	s.	d.
To Six sows, & 13 young Pigs	6		
To one old Sow & twelve Shoats £ 7 16/. .	7	16	
To thirty Bee hives at two dollars each . . .	21		
To a Sett of Smith Tools, To an Anvil	10		
To a Bellows £ 4—To a vice £ 4	8		
To Two old Sledges, & other smith Tools .	3		
To one Stake. 39/. 1 Pair of Stelleards 20/. 1 p fire Tongs 6/	3	5	
To one Iron Kettle 67 lb at 6/. pr lb	5		
To one Large Iron Pot £ 3 1 Do £ 3 1 Less Do 45/	8	5	
To a Small Iron Kettle 20/. 1 Dutch oven 55/	3	15	
To a Large Iron Kettle 6 £ 3 pairs of Iron Chains & two pair of Hems 36/	7	16	
To a Pair Duble tree hangings 6/. 1 skillet 2/6		8	6
To one Barrel & Keg 6/. 4 Chopping axes 30/	1	16	
[Page 49]			
To a Small broad ax, & frow & Drawknife . . . . £		12	
To a grind Stone 10/. 2 old hoes 3/. a pot rack & old Chains 12/	1	3	
To a pair of plow Irons & hangings 45/. 1 Cross Cut saw 40/	4	5	
To 4 Augurs & a handsaw 12/6		12	6
To a Mill Peck, 3 gimlets & Chisel & square		8	
To a Hempheckle 15/. a Frying Pan 10/.	1	5	
To a Rifle gun 25/. 1 smooth Bore Do 25/.	2	10	
To Big wheel 14/. 2 Spinning wheels 20/.	1	15	
To a Check Reel 3/ three sythes 20/. 3 Sickles 7/6	1	10	6
To a Bar & a peice of Steel 58/9 1 small ps steel 6/3	3	5	0
To 51 lb. Bar Iron a 1/3 pr 1	3	3	9
To old Iron 12/ old Copper 37/. 6 a Box with old Irons 3¾	4	2	10
To a Sett of Waggon Boxes	4	6	
To a Big Chest 20/. 1 Chest a 10/. 1 Do 5/. 2 Boxes 6/	1	17	
To a Parsel of Book, 35/. Pewter 40/. files 8/. 1 P. Plow Irons 20/	4	3	
To a pair of Wool Sheers 5/ Bed & Bed-Clothes 45/	2	10	

To a Set of Harrow teeth 37/6 1 ox Cart & Yoke £ 7 15	9	12	6
To wooden Vessels 17/6 1 Candle mole 3/	1	0	6
To young apple Trees £ 4 young Peech Do 124 31/	5	11	
To Mattock & other old Irons 10/ Powder & lead 9/		17	
To a Red Cow & Calf £ 6 a Cow & Calf £ 6 a year old heifer 40	8		
To a Cow & Calf £ 6 a Weaver Loom 40/	8		
To a Black Cow & Calf £ 6 a steer 35/	7	15	
To a White Heifer 25/ a Small steer 20/ an old Cow & Calf £ 6.15	9		
To 1. Black Cow £ 5/10 2 heifers £ 4 a small steer 20/	10	10	
£	241	3	

An Inventory of the estate of Jonathan Cisnea deceas'd

A Dark Bay Mare £ 20 a Red Cow £ 4 10 ....£	24	10	
A Spotted Cow £ 4. a spotted Haffer £ 3 1 Ewe 12/	7	12	
Three Pewter Dishes 14/. 8 pewter plates 14/. 4 Do Basons 23/	2	11	
Spoons & c 5/9. a Frying pan 4/. 2 Pots 12/6. 1 Spinning wheel 6/	2	8	3
A Broad ax & 4 old axes &c 21/ 1 Rifle gun 40/	3	1	
Utensils for husbandry 57/6 Pot hooks & Lumber 6/9	3.	4	3

[Page 50]

a hackle 15/. a Side Saddle 20/ Books 5/	2		
a Bead & Beding 70/ a Bead & c		3	6
The 3d August appraeced by us			
£	45	10	11

At a Court held for Jefferson County, on the 6th August 1782. The above Inventory return'd & admitted to record—

Test Mer'th Price Clk Jeff Cur

Artikel prass't of Petore Stirgess by James hoglin, James Anderson, Cristefer Shotts

	£	s	d
A Mere & Colt £ 18 1 Rifel Gun £ 5 1 Broad ax 8/...................£	23	8	
1 Narrow ax 6/. 1 Mattock 5/ 2 pair pot tramels 15/..................	1	6	
2 Chisels & Gouge 3/6 1 Augur 4/6 1 Sythe & nib 5/....................		13	
Plow shear & Coulter 37/6 1 Pot 31/3..	3	18	9
1 p Smoothing Irons 6/. 1 nal hammer 1/6		7	6
½ dosen pewter plats 12/ 2 puter Dishes 18/...............................	1	10	
1. puter Basen 4/ 4 Cups & Sasers 2/6 4 Trewns shoes [?] 1/..............		7	6
½ dozen spoons 3/. 3/ Iron Traces & 1 p hains & heaks....................		17	
½ doz Chears 18/. Iron Trumpery 10/. a stock Lock 3/...................	1	11	
1 Bed & furniture £ 7 Coat & Waistcoat £5...............................	12		
1 par Ne buckles & Slef buttons & broch 22/6...............................	1	2-	6
1 p Ovealls & Drawers 9/. 2 Shirts 15/9.	1	4	9
1. p thread, Stockins 8/ 2 Huting shirts 18/	1	6	
2 p Leather breaches 43/ 1 cot 35/ 4. p. Wooling Stockings 24/............	5	12	0
	55	4	0

At a Court held for Jefferson County on the 6th august 1782 The above Inventory of Peter Austingus, return'd & order'd to be recorded.

Test Mer'th Price Clk. Jeff. Cur

Know all men by these presents, that I Valentine Crawford, of the County of Bedford Gentleman: am held & firmly bound unto Dorsey Pentecost, of the County aforesaid Esquire, in the sum of One hundred pounds lawful money, of Pennsylvania, to be paid to the said Dorsey Pentecost, his certain attorney, Executors administrators [Page 51] or assigns To which payment well & truly to be made I do bind myself my heirs Executors & administrators, firmly by these presents Seal'd with my Seal'd & dated this fourth day of January in the year of our Lord, one thousand Seven hundred, & Seventy three, and in the thirteenth year of the Reign of our Sovereign Lord George the Third by

the grace of God King of Great Britain & c. The Condition of
the above obligation is such, that if the above bound Valentine
Crawford, his heirs Ex'rs adm'n or any of them shall & do well
& truly pay, or cause to be paid unto the above nam'd Dorsey
Pentecost his certain attorney Ex'r adm'rs or assigns the just &
full sum of Fifty pounds lawful money aforesaid, on the twenty
fifth day of December next without any fraud, or further delay,
Then the above obligation to be void, else to remain in full force
& virtue—
Sealed & Delivered In presence of)   Val. Crawford (Seal)
John Stevenson James Berwick)

At a Court held for Jefferson County, August 17th 1782
James Berwick came into the said Court & made oath that he
saw Valentine Crawford, deceased, sign Seal & deliver the above
bond dated the fourth day of January 1773. to Dorsey Penticost
therein mentioned, and to the best of his deponent's Knowledge,
the Same was given by the said Crawford, to the said Penticost
in part payment of certain lands situated on Buffaloe, on Char-
tees Creek ²², then sold to the said Crawford, by the said Penticost in the presence of this deponent, and further this Deponant
saith not
                      Copy Teste Mer'th Price Clk Cur

assignments on the back of the bond—
I assign over the within bond to Robert Thorn, it being for
value rec'd. As witness my hand, this 21st day of February, 1779
Christopher Beeler)   Do's Penticost

Assignments continued
I assign the within bond to Francis Dade attorney at law, as
abislute day [sic] for so much, for value rec'd. Witness my hand,
& Seal this 19th day of September 1773.

             her   )   his
Tes't Matthew Jefferes Isabel x Jefferes) Robt R.T. Thornton (Seal)
            mark   )   mark

[Page 52]
I assign the within bond to Mr Ezekiel Hickman, for value
rec'd of him. Witness my hand & Seal this 2d day of November
Anno Domini 1783.

Teste Ezekiel Hickman Jun'r)   Francis Dade (Seal)
Fra's Hickman   )

I assign the within bond to Mr Samuel Wells, for value rec'd of him Witness my hand, & Seal this 7th day of December 1773.

Teste Jun'r   Ezekiel Hickman (Seal)
Ezekiel   Iramel Hickman
                      Copy Teste Mer'th Price Clk Jeff Cur[1]

A List of the appraisment of the effects of John Williamson deceased—his widow Executor

	£	s	d
A crop of corn, appraised to............	13	7	6
A crop of flax £ 5, a crop of hemp 40/ Potatoes 20/.....................	8		
a young horse £ 7. 10 a white Cow £ 5 a white heifer Calf 35/............	14	5	
a black Cow & heifer Calf £ 6 a Brindled Cow £ 4 10......................	10	10	
A. Red yearling Heffer, 52/6/ A Black Do 35/ A white Bull 50/.........	5	01	6
A. Spotted heffer Calf 30/. a spotted, black & white Sow & Six shoats...	2	0	
A White Sow & six pigs 25/............	1	5	
5 Large hogs, 3 Barrows, & 3 Sows, £ 5, O–	5		
Plow Irons, Swingle & clevis...........	1	13	
2 p. Heams, & Iron Traces, 12/6 1 Bell & Iron Collar 5/.................		17	6
P. Maul Rings, & 3 augers.............		10	
2 Axes 11/ 1. Tramble 7/6. 1. Draw-knife 2/ old Iron 7/6..............	1	8	
old Man's Saddle 10/ 2 spinning wheels..	1	15	
Amount carried forward			
Amount brought over £			
A piece of Steel 2/. 1. Pott 4 gall's 10/..		12	
1. Small mettle Kittle, 6/– 2 Veeding hoes 17/.........................	1	3	
2 Churns & 1 Buckett.................		5	
1 Bed Tick & Blankett & Coverlett......	1		
A Box Iron & heater..................		1	6
A Smooth Bored Gun & Powder horn ...		15	
A Sifter & 25 spools..................		3	
[Page 53]			
3 Reeds, one 6 C one 5 C one Coverled ..£		17	
1 Loomb 45/ 4 Weavers shuttles 8/.....	2	13	
1 old quilt..........................		2	6
£	79	3	6

Appraised by Rich'd Chenoweth
Thomas Curry John McMannis

61

AN Inventory of the estate of Richard James deceased.

	£	s	d
A Rifle gun 24/-3 lb Buffaloe yarn 5/....	1	9	
2 p'a flax & tow yarn		3	9
1 ax 10/. 1 weeding hoe 3/- 1 Carpenter's compass & rasp 4/		7	
1 Ladle 5/ 1 p Cards 2/- 1 spelling Book 3/		3	
£	2	19	9

We the subscribers agreeable to order of Jefferson Court. have appraised the above mentioned articles on oath—Given under our hands, this 29th day of July 1782
Tho's Helm Jacob Funch, John Handley [23]

I have Sold to William Pope of Louisville four hundred acres. of land on the South fork of Beargrass Creek being Faith's Preemption joining Allen's line Eastward which I do Warrant, and Will defend to said William Pope his heirs & assigns against all persons Whatsoever, binding hereby myself & my heirs Given under my hand & Seal this Ninth day of Feb'y 1781
Test Mer'th Price)   Jno Todd (Seal)

Proved & admitted to record 7th Jan'y 1783
                                        Test Mer'th Price Clk Cur

[Page 54] Jonathan Rodgers effects August 15th 1782

	£	s	d
1 Pockett book 6/ 1 Mare & Colt £ 18 .. £	18	6	
1 Spur pair shoes, & Buckles 14/6		14	6
1 Pair Nee buckles, & stock buckel 12/ 1 P Stockins 3/		15	
1 Pot 15/ 1 sackel & p breeches Cloth 50/	3	5	
1 Jacket silk 20/ 2 Jackes [sic] 15/ 1 p logins 3/	1	3	
1 Bibel 6/ 1 Set old plow Irons & Screws 15/	1	1	
1 old Mattock & 2 old axes 16/ 2 Clivis' & Link 8/	1	4	
1 ho. swingle Tree Irons, & Shov'l		10	
1 Bell. & foot adzes 9/ 1 Rasor, awl & file 5/		14	
2 Chisels 5/ 1 Chist lock 6/ 1 p lether Briches 15/	1	6	

fore drest deer Skins, 35/- 1 Lock Chain 20/	2	15	
1 Coat & Jackett 90/ 1 shirt & 2 Stocks 20/	5	10	
1 Coat & Jackett	1	10	
1 Negroe girl	40		
Fifteen hundred Virginia Dollars	75	0	0
Three hundred & Seven, Dollars—			

The above Inventory return'd the 7th January 1783 & ordered to be recorded

Test Mer'th Price, Clk. Jeff. Cur

---

[1]The original bears this notation on the margin: "Original taken out of the office."

[9]This addition is incorrect, but is given as found in the original. Many similar instances will be encountered.

[13]Opost was a common name among the Kentuckians for Vincennes. (*Illinois Historical Collections*, VIII:300.)

[14]The name is as given, although it is Christy in the signature and other parts of the document.

[15]The names are as given, Nicholas and Nicholson, although they evidently refer to the same person.

[16]By "chin" is probably meant "chien," meaning the cock or hammer of a gun. (French-English glossary, Sawyer's *Firearms in American History*, p. 109.) If this surmise is correct, the Kentuckians evidently borrowed the term from the Illinois French.

[17]The appraisers in this inventory and in that of Thomas Davis (p. 77), where the scale of depreciation is 200 to 1, do not seem to have followed the General Assembly's act of November, 1781, where the scale was fixed for December of that year at 1000 paper dollars for one dollar specie. (Hening's *Statutes* X:473.)

[18]This name well illustrates the phonetic basis of pioneer spelling. In this book it appears as James Quoturmous, Quertermous, Quertermas, Qutermous, Catermous, and Catamus. Jillson's *Old Kentucky Entries and Deeds*, p. 275, gives three other forms, Quattarmus, Quarkermus, and Quatremus, while the *Early Jefferson County Marriage Records* (Filson Club Archives) has it Quertermus and Quertermousy.

[19]Perhaps a glass ornament.

[20]A four-pint pot.

[21]Leonard Helm was one of Clark's four captains on the Kaskaskia Expedition, and was in command of Vincennes when Hamilton captured it. His intrepid refusal to surrender without terms, although almost all the militia had deserted and he stood nearly alone in the fort, is one of the finest examples of courage in our history.

[22]This is probably Chartier's Creek, now in Allegheny County, Pennsylvania. (Crumrine's *The Boundary Controversy between Pennsylvania and Virginia*, map, p. 518.) Cf. Shurtee's Creek, Bodley's *George Rogers Clark*.

[23]The assumption is justifiable that this was the John Handley who was a trustee of and most active in founding Vienna, now Calhoun, McLean County. See article * on the beginning of old Vienna in the April issue of THE HISTORY QUARTERLY.

*Refers to the April 1929 issue of THE FILSON CLUB HISTORY QUARTERLY.

MINUTE BOOK A, JEFFERSON COUNTY, KENTUCKY
MARCH, 1781—SEPTEMBER, 1783

Copied for publication

By Alvin L. Prichard

In Three Parts

Part Three

To all to whom it may Concern—Elizabeth Carter of Jefferson, County & Commonwealth of Virginia: Relict, & widow of William Fowler, deceased, Sendeth greeting. Know Ye that the said Dame Elizabeth Carter for & in Consideration of the sum of Ten pounds specie, to her in hand paid by John Fowler son & heir at law of the said William Fowler The receipt whereof she doth hereby acknowledge hath remised releas'd, and forever quit-claim'd And by these presents doth remise, release & forever quit-claim unto the said John Fowler all, & all manner of dower, and right & title of—dower whatsoever, which the said Dame, Dame Elizabeth Carter now hath, may, might, or should or of right ought to have or claim of in or out of all and every the lands, tenements & hereditaments whatsoever which were the said William Fowler's her late [Page 55] husband, at any time during the coverture between him the said Elizabeth situate in Loudon County & Commonwealth aforesaid—or elsewhere, and also all manner of actions, and writs of dower whatsoever, so as neither she the said Dame Elizabeth Carter, nor any other Person for her, or in her name any manner of dower, or writ of Action of Dower, or any right, or title of Dower, of or in the said lands, Tenements, or hereditaments, or for or in the said lands or part or parcel thereof, at any time hereafter shall or may have claim or prosecute against the said John Fowler, his heirs, or assigns. In Witness whereof she hath hereunto affixed her hand, & Seal this seventh day of January in the year of our Lord seventeen hundred & eighty three.

sign'd Seal'd & Delivered	)	Elizabeth Carter X (Seal)
In the presence of us	)	her mark
Richard Lee, William Harrison	)	
Shedrach Carter	)	

At a Court held for Jefferson County, on the 7th January, 1783. Elizabeth acknowledged this Conveyance Whereupon it was admitted to record

Test Mer'th Price Clk. Jeff. Cur

I John Williams do make this my Last will & is as followeth viz: It is my desire that my friend Morias Hansbrough take my too small sons William & Rawleigh & one bed—2'd That my Daughter Sarah have the bed I now ly on, my Cow & Calf, and to have the care of my little Daughter, Barshelea. 3'd that Robert Akin have my son John, & my Daughter Santha. 4th I leave my son George Sullivan Williams the residue of my estate after my just debts are paid—Lastly: I leave my friend Morias Hansbrough, Executor to this my last will & Testament:

Seal'd & deliver'd In presence of)	his
Henry Floy & Benja Pope)	Jno x Williams (Seal)
)	mark

At a Court held for Jefferson County on the 8th January, 1783 The above will proved & admitted to record

Test Mer'th Price Clk. Jeff Cur

[Page 56] October the 29 1782. The last will & Testament of John Ash.

In the name of God who gave me, my being, I resine my Soul to him that gave it: and then my Will is, that all my lawfull debts to be paid out of my estate. & then whatsoever remains, I give & bequeathe to my Wife Elizabeth and to the Child she is now going with forever: both the estate I now have and my part of my fathers likewise—and my desire is that my Brother who is hear shall have his equal part with me, and if any of my Brothers that are now in Captivity should return my desire is that they should have an equal part of my father's estate
Given under my hand as above—

Test Hugh M Clughan)	his
Morias Hansbrough)	John x Ash (Seal)
his)	mark
David Allen x)	
mark)	

This will proved by the Oath of David Allen in the 4th February 1783: & admitted to record—

(cop'd. 66th. [Sic]) In the name of God amen I, John Floyd of Jefferson County being of sound mind & memory do make,

Constitute & ordain this my last WILL & Testament: that is to say I give, I give to my wife Janny Floyd all the land Contained within the lines, of the tract I now live on, that lie on the north side of Beargrass and to be laid off from the other part of the tract by the meanders of Beargrass, to her & her heirs forever— I give to my Son William Preston Floyd the residue of the two thousand acres I live on lying on the South side of Beargrass, including the stations of Hoglins & New Holland, and divided from the tract mentioned, by the meanders of Beargrass Creek, to him & his heirs forever: I give to my Daughter Mourning Floyd, & to my Son not baptized, now called George Floyd, all that tract of land lying in Fayette, called Woodstock containing Four thousand acres, more or less, to be equally divided between them according to quantity & quality, so as for both to have the advantage of Springs, & water courses, to them & their heirs forever—I give to the Infant with which my wife is now pregnant fourteen [Page 57] hundred acres of land, on the waters of Harrods Creek, being the tract I purchased of Colo Trigg to it & its heirs forever. The four hundred acre tract of land, which I purchas'd of Colo Todd adjoining the land I live on, at the north West end, I leave to be Sold by my Exrs when they shall adjudge it necessary or exchang'd for Slaves, as they may think best for the benefit of my wife & Children—All my other lands including my Entries, on the branches of Floyds Fork & Harrods Creek, and all entries made for me in the Surveyors Books (except 500 acres on Floyds fork, or Bull skin, sold to John Veech, & of which two he has his choice, and also except 600 acres, on the Ohio disposed of to Colo Todd, and to be transfr'd to his heirs, as well, as the 500 acres to Veech) are to go & descend to my wife & all my Children, to be equally divided amongst them according to quantity & quality, except so much thereof as may be thought by my Ex'rs should be sold for the purpose of purchasing Slaves for the benefit of my family for paying for building or finishing a house already begun, & furnishing the same, for my wife and Children to dwell in. all or either of which they are hereby authorized, to do Should they think it best for the advantage of my family—all my Stock & other estate except what is hereafter disposed of, are to be kept together for the support & mainte-nance of my wife & Children—all slaves which are owing to me or that may be purchased for my estate, are to be equally divided among my wife & all Children, as they come of age or marry. and in case my wife or any of my Children should die before they have an heir, that part of my estate shall go & descend to all the Survivors, and to be equally divided amongst them—My Ex'rs to Convey. to the heirs of Colo Stephen Trigg, one thousand acres of land in Fayette, called the Royal Spring Tract and also convey to the heirs, of John McClelland, fourteen hundred acres, or so much thereof, as a legal title, is obtain'd for, and no more in my name. as ass'n of John McClealland, lying on the north side the Royal Spring Tract, and to take up an assignment of mine of the Royal Spring now in the hand of Sarah Wilson—I give to the youngest Son of Robert Davis dec'd Twenty five acres of land in Amherst, where I formerly lived—It being the land I had of his Father, to him & his heirs forever: I give all my lands in Amherst to my Father to be disposed of as he shall think fit. all my lands in [Page 58] Bottetourt are to be disposed of by Colo William Preston and after Settling his acct's against me the balance of the money & other effects which he may get for it to be put in the possession of my wife for the support of my family And for the assistance of my Brother Isham in removing me to this Country I give him a two thousand acre entry on Floyd's fork call'd the Horse shoe Bottom,—My other Brothers Robert & Charles are desired to finish the surveying thereof which I have undertaken for others and to receive half the money due me for my Locations: I have made for absent people & also to survey and pattent all my lands entered for me, except those disposed of, for which they are, each of them, to receive four hundred acres in any part they may chuse, of my locations, in this County. not already disposed of, and to be laid off in such a manner as not to spoil the figure of the remaining part—I do hereby nominate & appoint William Pope, Gent, & my wife, Jenny Floyd, Ex'rs of this my Last will: who are to be allow'd for their trouble whatever the County—Court may adjudge reasonable for their trouble &c

Sign'd Seal'd & pronounced in presence of)   Jno Floyd (Seal)
Charles Floyd, Robert Floyd,   )
Robert Eakin   )

At a Court held for Jefferson County, on the 3d June 1783. This Last will & Testament of John Floyd Esq. deceased, was proved, & admitted to record.

Test Mer'th Price Clk. Jeff. Cur

We the undernam'd Subscribers, being appointed by the Court of Jefferson County, to appraise the estate of the late deceased. Colo John Floyd being duly Sworn according to law, have appraised as followeth towit

	£	S	D
8 Cows & Calves.......at £3.10 each ...	28		
3 Cows and Calf or Strapper.........at £3 10 each ...	10	10	
4 one old Heffers, and 2 yearlin Stears....at £1.5 each ...	7	10	
5 3 old Stears.........at £2 each.....	10		
1 3 old Stear..........at £2..........	2		
1 4 year old Ditto....................	2	10	

[Page 59]

	£	S	D
1 Two year old Heffer.................	1	5	
14 large hogs consisting of Sows & pigg & Barrows.........a 17/..	11	8	
14 young Sows & Shoats.......a 7/3..	4	18	
15 pigs or half grown shoats.....3/.....	2	5	
1 Black horse 12 years old.............	12		
1 Dark Bay horse 10 years old.........	15		
1. Bright Bay Do 4 years old..........	18		
1 Bright Bay Mare 2 years old & Colt....	15		
1 Iron pot weighing 44 lb...a 11 d plb..	1	16	8
1 Do Kettle........27½...at 10 d.....	1	2	11
1 Dutch oven......12½...at 10 d	0	10	5
1 Iron Kettle......20.....at 10 d.....	0	16	8
1 Do Pott.........44.....at 10 d.....	1	16	8
1 Do.............38.....at 10.......	1	11	8
1 Cross Cut Saw 35/ 1 whipsaw 40/...	3	15	
2 pair Hames & Chains, old Collar & 2 old Clevises....................	1		
Iron Lumber 5/ 2 old hoes & 2 old axes 13/...............................		18	
Candle mould, 1/6 4 old pails & 1 Cooler 5/...............................		6	6
16 Harrow Teeth 10/ 1 Shovel Plow 4/ 1 Common Do 20/................	1	14	
1. Churn & wooden Lumber 6/.........		6	
Waggon Tire & other irons, belonging to a waggon........................	6		
Compass Chain & other Instruments....	7		
1. Rifle gun £4 2 Smooth Do 20/......	5		

Item	£	s	d
1 Bead & Beadstead & furniture £ 7 1 Do £ 8	15		
1. Ditto £ 6 1 Table 6/ 1 Chest 18/. 3 old Trunks 5/	7	9	
1 spinning wheel & Reel 12/. 6 Chairs 7/		19	
19 worn pewter plates 15/ 4. Pewter Dishes 20/	1	15	
1 Small worn pewter Basin 1/ 9 Do spoons 2/.		3	
7 Delf plates 7/ 10 knives & forks 6/		13	
4 Tea Cups & Saucers 4/ 1 Tea pot 12/.		6	
1 Copper Teakettle 6/ 4 TinCanisters 2/		8	
2 Brass Candlesticks 4/ 1 Large Bottle 3/		7	
1 Pr old dividers 1/ 1 Bible 20/ 7 books) Pocket volumes 6/)	1	7	
2 Table Cloths 6/ 2 Weathers 12/		18	
6 acres of wheat & Rye	6		

[Page 60]

Item	£	s	d
9 hives of Bees 90/ 2 old hoes 6/	3	16	
1 Man's Saddle 45/.	2	5	
1 fire shovel 1 Smoothing iron & 1 Tomhawk		10	
Total amount £	218	15	2

Given under our hands, this 7th day of June 1783

Jno Leach
Samuel Burk
Daniel Sullivan
Aquilla Whitaker

I William Morton do make this my Last Will & Testament revoking all others and is as follows Viz:

1st It is my will that John Dunlop have my black horse, and dun Cow & her heifer: My blew sow & four shoats, also his own bed & furniture: 2nd I leave the residue of my stock in the care of my friend John Hamilton who is to Keep on for the use of John Raboom [sic]: 3d I leave my whole estate real & personal to my Stepson John Raborn after the legacy above written is

69

paid—& Lastly I leave my friends Benjamin Pope & Henry Floyd Executors to this my Last Will.

sign'd & Seal'd In presents of
     his
Wm   x   Morton (Seall)
    mark

John Williams   )
George Sullivint Williams)
         her   )
Mary Rice   x   )
       mark   )

At a Court held for Jefferson County, on the 3d June 1783: This Last will & Testament of William Morton, was proved & admitted to record.

Test Mer'th Price. Clk. Jeff Cur

[Page 61] IN obedience to an order of Jefferson Court here-unto annext we the subscribers being first sworn before William Pope Gentleman one of the Magistrates for said County have valued & appraised the estate of William Linn deceased. an Inventory whereof is as followeth Viz:

1 Negroe Man Tom.....................£	4000
1. Ditto Boy Moses £ 7000 1 Wench Marg't £ 8000.....................	15000
1 Ditto Wench Phillis, £ 6000 1 Do Boy Bateest £ 4000...............	10000
1 Do Boy Jack.......................	2000
15 Harrow Teeth £ 135 1 X Cut saw £ 300...........................	435
2 Pots hooks & Bales £ 330 1 Small Tub £ 15.........................	245
1 Buckett 90/ 1 Tub £ 30 2 Brass Kettles £ 200.....................	320
4 Collars £ 80 2 pail, & 1 half buckett £ 5	134
1 Churn £ 30. 1 Dutch oven, Bale & Cover £ 150.....................	180
1 Dutch oven & Gridle...............	150
1 Rifled gun pouch Horn & Bullet moulds	750
1 Ditto horn & pouch £ 500. 1 Large pot & hooks 270 £...............	770
1 Pitching ax £ 120. 1 Broad Ditto £ 75.	195

Item	£	s
2 Broad hoes £ 24 1 spindle frog of a hand-Mill & Grinding Iron........	64	
3 Chisils 2 Augers, 1 gouge 1. bell, & parcel old Iron.................	135	
1 Graining Knife & Collar Needle £ 15 2 Cart boxs £ 12................	217	
3 Clivises link & swingle Trees £ 55 1. melting Ladle £ 3.............	58	
1 Handsaw £ 75 a parcel leather £ 200 p pot hooks £ 6.................	281	
1 Cow & Calf £ 100 1 Do 1000 1 heif'r £ 700 L Do £ 775...............	3475	
1 Do £ 850 1 Do 750 1 Do 700 2 Heifers £ 300....................	2600	
1 yearling £ 150 2 Sows & Pigs £ 2200..	2350	
1 Sow, barrow, & 3 pigs, £ 900. 122 Barr Iron £ 549.................	1449	
2 Leather Collars Hames, & Iron Chains .	300	00
1 Bed quilt, sheet, Curtains & p. pillows..	1000	
1 Bed Cover & 1 pillow £ 250. 1 Trunk £ 200..........................	450	
1 Black Walnut Table £ 150 4 Chairs 60 £ 210..........................	210	

[Page 62]

Item	£	s
1 Small Box £ 9, 1 spinning wheel £ 100 .£	109	
3 Large Pewter Dishes £ 150 6 Small basons £ 90.....................	240	
17 Delph £ 68 1 Salt Cellar & 4 Tumblers £ 15.........................	83	
2 Cups & Saucers £ 3 3 Razors, hone strop & oyl Botl 100..............	103	
6 Silver Tea spoons £ 150..............	150	
1 Pocket Compass £ 6 2 smoothing Irons £ 45.......................	51	
1 Copper Tea Kettle £ 40 1 Small Looking Glass £ 3.................	43	
1 Fiddle & Bow £ 24 1 womans Saddle & Bridle £ 1000....................	1024	
1 Tin Funnel £ 6, 1 qt Bottle £ 4/10.....	10	10
1 Green Coat £ 120 1 Red Do £ 150......	270	
1 p Leather overalls £ 60 1 p plush breeches £ 100...................	160	
1 p Cotton Drawers £ 4 10 3 Linnen Stocks £ 3.......................	7	10
1 Silk Jackett £ 6 1 Bedstead £ 24.....	30	

71

1 Linnin Table Cloth..................	21	
1 p Shoe & Knee buckles, & 1 stock Do..	240	
4 lb Cotton thread, £ 72 5¾ Linnin Do £ 50..............................	122	
8 lb hemp £ 40 11¾ lb yarn 85 £......	125	
½ Buffalo wool 6/ 100 Bushels corn 1200£	1200	6
5 Bushels potatoes £ 52 10 1½ bushel) hempseed £ 67 10 ½ Do Salt £225) 1 Do Beans £ 24................)	369	
30 lb Bacon £ 144 40 lb Pork £ 96......	240	
1 Foot adze £ 18 Wheat & Barley growing £ 700........................	718	
1 Bush'l Flax Seed £ 15 1 p hand mill stones 40........................	55	
2 Hives Bees £ 200 1.................	215	
Rich'd Chenoweth	18180	6
Thomas McCarty	34130	
Edw'd Tyler £	2310	6

A just & true Inventory & appraisement of the goods, and chattels to us produced by the administrator of the estate of Evan Hinton deceased, taken at Clark's Station in Lincoln County, by us the underwritten subscribers, being appointed appraisers [Page 63] by order of the Court of Jefferson County, and duly sworn May 24th 1783

1 Dutch oven 30/ 1 Pot 24/ 1 frying pan 6/..............................£	3	
2 Puter Basins 15/ 3 Do plates & 4 spoons 15/.......................	1	10
1 puter Tankard 3/ wheel Irons & Buckett 4/.......................		7
1 old bed quilt & Blankett.............		10
1 Bed Bolster & pillow................	2	10
1 Pepper Box & fork 2/ 1 Hand saw 12/.		14
1 Certificate from the Commissioners....	4	5
1 Cow & Calf 50/ 1 Testament 6/.......	2	16
A Large Smith's Vice..................	2	10
£	18	2

Samuel Kirkham Wm Feild William Crow

Inventory of the Estate of William Russell deceased.

	£	s
2 Cows & Calves 20£ 1 Sheep 20/ 1 pot 25/	22	5
5 pewter plates, & a pewter pint cup	1	5
Some wooden Ware 10/ 2 Coats 70/	4	
£	27	10

Jefferson County Aug't 22 1782 appraised the above articles of the estate of William Russell deceased to Twenty Seven pounds Ten Shillings. Benja Linn. Philemon Waters, William Cleaver.

We the undernamed subscribers, being apointed & duly sworn, to appraise the personal estate of Arthur Park late deceased, do appraise the following articles this 29th of March one thousand, Seven hundred & eighty three:

	£	s
The old Pyded Cow & Calf . . . .£	3	15
A Brindled Cow & Calf 65/ Pink Do & Calf 95/	8	
Cut horn'd pyded Cow & calf	3	15
A young white Cow 70/ Crooked horned Cow 70/	7	
A Red Cow 80/ a yearling Bull 20/. a barren Heffer 30/	7	10
[Page 64]		
A spotted Cow 80/ a brown 2 year old heffer 40/ . . . .£	6	
2 Drawn Steers 80/ 1 Red year old Heffer 40/	6	
1 Sorrel Mare £ 14 1 Horse £ 12 1 Sow 20/	27	
1 English Dictionary 10/ Burges Sermons 15/	1	5
Sundry Books 27/ 4 Puter Basons 20/	2	7
2 Small Besons, 3 porringers		6
1 Dozen spoons 1 pint, 1 Tea pot al puter		12
Tea Cups & Sundries		12
1 Teakettle 5/ 1 Large Iron Kettle 70/	3	15
1 Pot & hooks 20/ 1 Small Do & Do 10/	1	10
1 Iron Griddle 12/ 2 pot Trambels & Chaine 15/	1	7

Item	£	s
2 Smoothing Iron 12/ 1 Grid Iron shovel & Tongs 20/...............	1	12
1 Bed & Beding £ 8 1 Do 35/..........	9	15
1 Trunk & Chest 17/. 1 Looking glass 30/...............................	1	17
1 hare Sive 3/ 1 small Box & Sundries 23/.............................	1	6
1 Foot Edge 6/ 1 Jointer & Jack & Smoothing plane 10/..............		16
1 plow plane & two other planes 12/......		12
Ten chisels & three gouges 23/ 8 augers 30/...........................	2	13
Three drawing Knives, & one turning Crank, & gouging................		18
1 howel inshave [?] spoke & shave........		6
2 gun locks 6/ Cutting Knife & steel 10/.		16
Sundry old Iron 10/- Steel & old Iron 14/	1	4
3 axes 18/. 1 Mill peck frow & spoke shave 8/............................	1	6
3 Saws & Square 30.....................	1	10
2 Candlesticks & flesh fork.............		3
1 Set of Waggon Boxes................	1	10
1 hole Augur & large gouge.............		10
4 Sickles 15/ sundries of old Iron 60/....	3	16
Plow & Jacklings 90/ 3 pr Iron king Hams 5/..........................	4	15
1 sprouting Hoe & Iron Rod............		5
1 White saw £ 4 1 X cut Do £ 3........	7	
3 hilling hoes 8/ 3 Mattocks Brode ax & spade 25/........................	1	13
[Page 65]		
Amount Brought forward: [none]		
3 Bells, & 2 Collars 10/................		10
small stone hammer, & nailing hammer..		3
Sundree bridle bits....................		5
A grine Stone 5/. 1 Rifle gun 90/.......	4	15
Do 1 Rifle gun.......................	3	

[total not given]
Wm   Cummins,)
Geo Pomeroy   )
James Galloway)

Whereas Certain Malicious persons have propagated a report, of my having said that Robert Floyd, and the rest of the family, were of the Mustic Bread, or mixed with Mulatto blood,

I do hereby Solemnly Swear, that I never reported any such thing, respecting the said family, and the report is altogether false, and groundless—Given under my hand this 3d day of June 1783.

Mylassah Mayfield

Sworn to before me one of the Magistrates of Jefferson County, this 4th June 1783.

Wm Oldham

At a Court held for Jefferson County on the 3d June 1783. The above Concession was acknowledged, by Micajah Mayfield, and at the request of Robert Floyd, order'd to be recorded—

Teste Mer'th Price Clk Jeff. Cur

Know all men by these presents that I Pleasant Lockett of the Ileanoze [Illinois] Farmer, for divers considerations & good causes, me hereunto moving, have made, ordained, constituted & appointed and by these presents, make, ordain, Constitute and appoint my truly friend John Reburn of the Country aforesaid Gent'n my true & lawfull attorney, for me, in my name, and to my use to ask demand, recover or receive of and from Royell Lockett, Thomas Mosley Excter, boath in the Colony of Virginia and County of Cumberland, the sum & equal part of all my Father's Estate, that is to say negroes, & all other goods & chattels, giving & by these presents granting to my said attorney my sole & full power & authority to [Page 66] take pursue ad folow such legal courses for the recovery, receiving, and obtaining of the same as I myself might could dow, ware I personally present. and upon the receipt of the Same, acquittances and other suficient discharges for mee, and in my name to make signe, and Sale, and deliver, as allso one more attorney, or attorney's under him to Asbotitute, [sic] or appoint, and again at his pleasure to revoke and further to dow perform, and finish for mee, & in my name all & singular thing, or things which shall, or may be necessary tuching and concerning the premisses, as fully, thoroughly, & entirely as I the said Pleasant Lockett, in my own person might; or could Dow, in & about the same ratifying, allowing & confirming whatsoever my said attorney shall lawfully, or cause to dow in and about the execution of the premisses by virtue of these presents In witness whereof I have hereunto Set my hand,

& Sale the 24th day of February in the Eight year of Independence, and in the year of our Lord God 1783

In the presence of us,   )   Pleasant Lockett (Seal)
John Alison John Chambers)
Henry O'Harrey   )

At a Court held for Jefferson County, on the 3d June 1783. The above power of attorney was proved, & admitted to record—
Mer'th Price Clk J. C

At a Court held for Jefferson County on the 3rd June 1783— On the motion of James Anderson, his mark was admitted to record viz: a Crop and half Crop, in the left swallow fork in the right Ear—
John McManus same order, viz: a Crop & Slit in the right Ear.

THE Last Will & Testament of Tho's McGee—For fear of fraud or ferther trobel, after his deth: I take this method to ceap down anea trobel hearafter—I do intend to make John McGee Maniger of my holl afairs to Setal them wright and just as I will them: I do alow my Brother James five hundred ackers of land, on Boshearses Crick, part of William White peamption. I do [Page 67] alow him one site of my cloas—I do alow Nancy Froman's youngest Dauter Mary one thousand ackers of land, part of too peremtions laying in Elk horn & Licton Crickes—I do leave my Brother John's oldest Son or Thomas McGee five hundred ackers lying on Boshearses Crick, part of White's peremption. I likewise leave the said Mary Fromans young Dauter Marey three hundred ackers of land in Cockses Creek at the Mout of Froman's Roon Likewise leave the said Marey one fether Bed, & all the Bed close thear belonging—I leave hur Six puter plates, three Stone plates one Dish one mog to be hurs as hur one property forever—the said McGee doth leave two hundred ackers of land laying on Cockes Creek, to Wiliam Mcanulty Son of Richard Mcanulty—I likewise leave one Coat & Jacket to Patrick McGee—I leave all the rest to John McGee his hayrs or asigns axsept three cows hee is to give the said Marey when she is marid, or coms to agge, if the said Mary dies before shee com to agge, hur part is to be divided the rest ackealloy according to what is left them—

76

This said will is witnesed, in presents of us this 25th of September 1781 to be his Last will & Testement

Tested Boy	)	Thomas McGee
Joseph Brooks	)	
his	)	
Barend x Ridig	)	
mark	)	
his	)	
Lucke x Vores	)	
mark	)	

At a Court held for Jefferson County on the 5th of August 1783 the above will was proved, & admitted to record—

Test Mer'th Price Clk. Jeff Cur.

In the name of God amen I Joseph Black being in a low state of helth: but in perfect memorey blessed be my Redeemer, do order and make this my Last Will & Testamint in manner as followeth—after paying my just dets I give & bequeathe to my Sons Joseph Black, & John Black a Surtin tract of land on the North side of Green River against the mouth of Little Barrin, to be equal divided between them Both—Mr Joseph Barnet is to divide it and to make them Deeds for it for the Consideration of one [Page 68] Stear paid him by me Joseph Black. I give & bequeath to my Loving wife Sarah Black²⁴ son John Black Six Cows & Calves to take them as they can without picking of them—I giv all my household furniture to my wife forever: likewise to my Son Joseph Black I giv two Cows & Calves Likewise to my Daughter Abigal Black two Cows & Calves. Likewise to my wife & youngest son John Black I give six Drey Cattel. and to my son Joseph Black and Daughter Abigal I giv two Drey Cattle a piess. likewise I giv to my Son Joseph Black one Bay horse three years old last spring. Likewise I giv to my Son John Black one two year old filley—Likewise to my Son Joseph & my Daughter Abigal I giv each of them one Ew lamb, and the remainder of my Stock of Sheep I giv to my wife and to my Son John Black. My son Joseph Black is to find my wife in Bread until my youngest Son is abel to make it for hur without she marreys—In case she marreys the said Cattel that I left to hur & my son John is to be equally divid'd between thim both,

77

at the day of marrage. It is my desire that my Daughter Abigal
will stay with hur Stepmother until she Coms of age or marreys.
then at hur own disposal—I do ordain this my last Wil & Testament. assign'd & witnessed this eleventh day of April 1783

Test   )   his
     his   )   Joseph x Black
James x Cook   )   mark
    mark   )
Joseph Cartwright   )

    August Court 1783. The above will of Joseph Black deceased
was duly proven and admitted to record

Teste Mer'th Price. Clk. Jeff. Cur

    At a Court held for Jefferson County on the 5th day of August
1783— On the motion of William Johnston, who made oath according to Law. Certificate is granted him for obtaining letters
of administration of the estate of Robert Johnston deceased
giving Security Whereupon he together with James Sullivan and
David Standiford his Securities entered into & acknowledged
bond [Page 69] in the penalty of One hundred pounds, Conditioned for his faithful administration of said Decedants Estate

Teste Mer'th Price Clk. Jeff. Cur

    We the appraisers appointed by the Court of Jefferson County
to appraise the goods & effects of the late deceased, Hugh
McCloughin, being duly sworn according to law have appraised
the following articles viz:

	£	S	D
1 Gray Horse £ 6 1 Buck Skin 5/	6	5	
1 striped Cotton Coat £ 1.10 1 p thread stockings 16/	1	16	
1 Linnen hankerchief 10/ 1 p shoes & old stockings 6/		16	
1 p leggins 3/ 1 Jacket & shirt 6/ 1 Bell 2/6		11	6
10 Bushels of Salt at 1¾	12		
Total amount	21 .	8 .	6

    Given under our hands at New Holland Station this 8th day
of Feb'y 1783

John Colman
Fran's Leach
Geo. Leach

At a Court held for Jefferson County on the 5th day of August 1783. The above Inventory of the estate of Hugh McCloughin was returned & ordered to be recorded
                              Teste Mer'th Price Clk. Jeff. Cur

At a Court held for Jefferson County August 5th 1783—Satisfactory proof being made to the Court that Benjamin Biggs is entitled to a pre emption of 1000 acres of land by virtue of an Improvement made in the year 1776. and the said Biggs was in the CONTINENTAL SERVICE at the time, the Commissioners, for adjusting claims, to unpatented lands, Sat to do business in this Country: Ordered therefore that it Certified that the said Benjamin Biggs is entitled to the pre-emption of 1000 acres which he located on a Branch, the waters of Salt River, to include his Improvement & a Tree marked B. B.
                              Teste Mer'th Price. Clk. Jeff. Cur

[Page 70] In the name of God Amen. I Edward Skidmore being of sound memory but in a weak, and low state of Body do make this my last will & Testament in manner & form following—Imprimis—I do recommend my Soul to God from whom it came hopeing for a blessed resurrection in the other world—2d I do leave to my Son Benjamin my rifle gun, powder horn & pouch. 3rdly & Lastly I do leave all my other wordly affairs to my beloved wife Debora for her only use & behofe—as witness my hand Seal this 17th day of Oct'r 1782

Witness   John Cameron)   his
          John Cameron)   Edward   x   Skidmore (Seal)
                                          mark

At a Court held for Jefferson County on the 6th day of August 1783. pr adjournm't. The above will of Edward Skidmore was proved & ordered to be recorded
                              Test Mer'th Price Clk Jeff Cur

KNOW ALL MEN by these presents that I John Williams of Jefferson County a Colony of Virginia, (for divers, considerations & good causes, me hereunto moving) having made ordained constituted and appointed and by these presents do make ordain constitute & appoint my Brother Isaac Williams of Washington County in Pennsylvania my true & lawful attorney for me and in my name and to my use to ask, demand, recover or receive of and from my Several Debtors, all debts due me in said County of Washington & Westmoreland in the state of Pennsylvania giving and by these presents granting to my said attorney, my sole & full power & authority to take pursue & follow, such legal counsel for the recovery receiving & obtaining of the Same, as I myself might, or could do, were I personally present, and upon receipt of the same, acquittances & other sufficient discharges, for me, and in my name to make, sign seal & deliver as also one or more attorney or attorneys under him to substitute or appoint, and again at his pleasure to revoke, and further to do, perform & execute, for me, and in my name all and Singular thing, or things, which shall or may be necessary touching & Concerning the premisses as fully, thoroughly, and entirely as I the [Page 71] said John Williams, in my own person ought or could do in & about the Same ratifying allowing & confirming whatsoever my said attorney shall lawfully do, or cause to be done, in & about the execution of the premisses by virtue of these presents: In Witness whereof I have hereunto Set my hand & Seal the sixth day of August. 1783 Seal'd & delivered

In presence of Mer'th Price)   his
                W. Daniel   )   John x Williams (Seal)
                Ben Pope   )   mark

September Term 1783.

The foregoing power of attorney from John Williams to Isaac Williams was proved, & ordered to be recorded.

Teste Mer'th Price. Clk. Jeff. Cur

Sullivan's New Station August 20th 1783—

We the Subscribers being appointed by the Worshipful Court of Jefferson County, to value, & appraise the estate of Robert Johnston deceased do value & appraise the Same as followeth viz—

	£	S.	D.
1 Virginia Cotton Coat a 17/6 1 striped Vest Ditto 12/..................	1	9	6
1 Pair Breeches Ditto 12/ 1 pr Ditto 1/3 2 pr old Stockings 4/.............		17	3
1 Pr spectacles 1/6 1 pr scissars 1/3 1. Razor & Case 1/3		4	

80

1 pr Heams, 6/ 1 Cocoa chest, shell 2/ 2 Lancets 6 d.		8	6
1 Hook & line 1/3 1 awl 6 d 1. Hand vice 5/ 1 gun Screw 6d.		7	3
1 pr Bullett Moulds 2/ 1 gun wiper Screw 1/3.		3	3
1 Charger 6d. 1 snuff Box 6d. Flint soap & needles 2/.		3	
1 sculping Knive, 3/ 1 cutteau²⁵ 6d. 1 pr garters 6d.		4	
1 old Sheet 2/6 1 Bed tick 20/ 1 pt Bottle 9d.	1	3	3
1 pr saddle Bags 15/ 1 Inkstand 8d. 1 pr spurs 18/.	1	13	8
1 shaving Box 4/6.		4	6
£	6	18	2

The Total amount being six pounds Eighteen shillings & two pence specie Virg'a Curr'y

Given under our hands the date above

Aquilla Whitaker Francis Adams James Qutermous

[Page 72] Sworn to before me one of the Commonwealths Justices of the peace this 2'd Sept'r 1783. Rich'd Chenoweth:

September Court 1783

The above Inventory of the estate of Robert Johnston deceased was returned, & ordered to be recorded.

Teste Mer'th Price Clk Jeff. Cur

At a Court held for Jefferson County Sept. 3d 1783.

Nicholas Brashears, orphan of William Brashears. deceas'd comes into Court and choose Benjamin Pope, as his guardian, who enters into bond of five thousand pounds, with William Pope his Security:

Teste Mer'th Price Clk. Jeff Cur.

At a Court held for Jefferson County Sept'r. 3'd 1783.

Administration of the estate of William Asher deceas'd is granted to Richard Chenoweth he giving Security whereupon he together with William Pope his Security entered into & acknowledged their bond in the penalty of three hundred pounds, Conditioned for his faithful administration of Said Decedant's Estate.

Same Term.

Administration of the estate of Christian Neitler deceas'd is granted to Abraham Raymour who enters into bond with John Handley & Jacob Barrackman his Securities in the penalty of three hundred pounds, Conditioned for his faithful administration of Said Decedants Estate:

Same Term.

Administration of the Estate of William Hynch is granted to Elizabeth Hynch his Relict she giving security Whereupon she together with Philip Phillips, & John Handley his Securities entered into and acknowledged their bond in the penalty of four hundred Conditioned for her faithful perf of said Decedants estate

Teste Mer'th Price Clk. Jeff. Cur.

At a Court held for Jefferson County, September 3'd 1783—

On satisfactory proof made to the Court that John [Page 73] Pearman a Soldier in the CONTINENTAL Service, was entitled to a pre-emption of 1000 acres, and that he was in the Service of the United States at the time that the Commissioners were Setting to do business in the Country Ordered therefore that it be Certified to the Register of the Land Office, that Samuel Pearman heir at law to the said John Pearman is entitled to the pre-Emption of 1000 acres to include his Improvement made in the year 1776. on a West Branch of Froman's River, a branch of Cox's Creek, about ½ a mile, or ¾ below the forks, of the trace leading to Froman's and Rogers stations, and on the right hand of the road, so as to have the Cabin, ⅔ of the length of the survey, nearest the Western End, the survey to be twice as long as wide, and the longest line, at equal distance from the Cabin:

Also as Heir at Law, for Elisha Pearman, deceased to include his improvement about five or Six miles, Westwardly from Rogers station, on the right hand side of Froman's Waggon road. to the Salt works, supposed to be on the head waters of Wilson's Creek, and also to include a Small Buffaloe Lick, in the South East corner of the land, which is on the North side of the Trace, 200 poles from each of the including lines.

Also as Heir at law, for Tho's Pearman, deceased, who was entitled to the pre-emption of 1000 acres, in Consequence of an

Improvement for him by the said Samuel Pearman, in the year 1776. made lying on the South side of Salt river near the mouth running down the Ohio and up Salt river at equal distance for quantity to include the Improvement about ¾ of a mile up the river—The said Thomas Pearman being in the service at the time the Commissioners Sat to do business in this Country

Teste Mer'th Price Clk. Jeff. Cur

To ALL WHOM it may Concern, KNOW Ye that I. Baldwin Cliffton of Jefferson County & State of Virginia, out of the especial confidence, & trust I repose in Burditt Cliffton of the County & State aforesaid, do appoint the said Burdett Cliffton [Page 74] my lawful attorney to claim demand, & receive, and by all lawful means to recover all moneys due to me lawfully— Given under my hand and Seal this first day of September A. D. 1783.

Test John Ray Junr.   Baldwin Cliffton (Seal)

At a Court held for Jefferson County September 3d 1783— The above power of attorney from Baldwin Cliffton to Burditt Cliffton was acknowledged & ordered to be recorded—

Test Mer'th Price Clk. Jeff. Cur.

To all whom it may Concern Know Ye that I John Carr, of Jefferson County & state of Virginia. out of the especial confidence and trust I repose in Baldwin Cliffton of the County & State aforesaid, I do appoint by these presents, and doth lawfully constitute & appoint the aforesaid Bald'n Cliffton my lawful attorney to claim, demand, & receive, and by all means, to receive, obtain & recover of Andrew, Lynk of Westmoreland County & State of Pennsylvania, one negroe man which he received of me, or the value of s'd Negroe, lawfully. Given under my hand, & Seal this 28th day of August 1783

Test Geo. Hartt. John Burke)   John Carr (Seal)

At a Court held for Jefferson County on the 3d September 1783. The above power of attorney from John Carr to Baldwin Cliffton was acknowledged & ordered to be recorded—

Test Mer'th Price. Clk. Jeff. Cur

To all whom it may Concern: Know Ye that I, Burditt Cliffton of the County of Jefferson & state of Virginia, out of the especial trust & confidedence I repose in my trusty friend

Baldwin Cliffton of the County & State aforesaid, do appoint by these presents, & doth lawfully Constitute & appoint by these presents, the said Baldwin Cliffton, my lawful attorney to claim demand, and recv'e and by all lawful means to receiv, obtain & recover of any [per]son²⁶ or persons whatsomever, that now Stand indebted to my [est]ate, either by contracts at my last Sale, in Westmoreland County, Pennsylvania on the first day of October 1782 or for any [Page 75] any other debts to me whatsomever lawfully Given under my hand, and Seal this first day of September A D 1783.

Test Wm Lite, John E King)   Burditt Cliffton (Seal)

At a Court held for Jefferson County Sept 3d 1783—
The above power of attorney from Burdett Cliffton to Baldwin Clifton was acknowledged & ordered to be recorded—
                          Test Mer'th Price. Clk. Jeff. Cur

To all whom it may Concern Know Ye. that I. William Pile of Jefferson County & state of Virginia, out of the especial confidence & trust I repose in my trusty friend Baldwin Cliffton of the County & State aforesaid do appoint by these presents & doth lawfully Constitute and appoint said Bald'n Cliffton my lawfull attorney to claim, demand, & receive and by all lawful means to receive obtain, & recover of Charles Broughton of Westmoreland County & State of Pennsylvania the just Sum which he owes me. for a colt he bought of me, & to receive also the forfeiture or the Sum, the bond he gave me, mention'd lawfully.

Given under my hand & Seal this 3rd day of September A D 1783—

Test Ben Pope Mer'th Price   Wm Pile (Seal)

At a Court held for Jefferson County the 3rd day of September 1783. The above power of attorney from William Pile to Baldwin Cliffton was acknowledged. & ordered to be recorded
                          Teste Mer'th Price Clk. Jeff. Cur

Same Term
On the motion of Jacob Tiveback ordered that his mark be recorded viz. A Swallow fork in each Ear—
                          Teste Mer'th Price Clk Jeff Cur

At a Court held for Jefferson County September 3d 1783—
Samuel W Culbertson, & George Wilson are appo[inte]d
guardians to Ann Lynn Daughter of Colo William Lyn[n]
deceased—who entered into, and acknowledged their bond in
the [lawf]ul sum of five hundred pounds, Conditioned for the
faithfu[l di]scharge [Page 76] of the trust & confidence in them
reposed.

Teste Mer'th Price. Clk Jeff. Cur

At a Court held for Jefferson County at the Town of Louisville
on Tuesday the 3rd day of June 1783. The Last will & Testament of Thomas McGee produced & proved by the oath of
Joseph Brooks a witness thereto—And at a Court held for
Jefferson County on Tuesday the 5th August 1783—The Last
will and Testament of Thomas McGee farther proved by the
oath of Luke Voress and ordered to be recorded: and probate
thereof granted John McGee who takes the oath prescribed by
law, & enters into bond of £ 1000 with Jacob Vanmetre & Henry
Floyd Securities—

In Witness whereof and that the foregoing are truly Copied from
the records of my office I the Clerk of said Court do hereto set
my hand this 28th day of May, 1816.

Worden Pope.[17]

[1]The original bears this notation on the margin: "Original taken out of the office."

[2]The name Garret Pendergrass was also spelled Pendergrest (*Illinois Historical Collections*, VIII:21), and Pendergrast. (*Collins*, II:615.) He was killed and scalped by Indians at Harrodsburg January 28, 1777. (Bodley's *George Rogers Clark*, 39.) Colonel William Fleming in a diary entry of January 19, 1783, mentions one Wilson, "who married Wid'w Pendergrass." (Bodley's *History of Kentucky*, 326.)

[3]It is possible that Spanish milled dollars are referred to, for early Kentucky prices were high, but such items as "To a mare…4000" seem to indicate that they were Continental paper dollars, issued originally with a par value of 4 shillings 6 pence. (Shuckers' *The Revolutionary Finances*, 22.) These depreciated so rapidly that by May, 1781, one Spanish dollar equalled between 500 and 1000 of the Continentals. (*Op. cit. 90.*) This money was used in Kentucky and Illinois, because friction arose in 1780 between the Illinois Regiment and the Vincennes French over the recall of certain issues. (Bodley's *Clark*, 153.) The disputed issues were of 1777 and 1778, and were recalled because of counterfeiting. (*Journal Continental Congress*, XIII:21-2.)

[4]This is properly trammel, the hook for suspending kettles over the fire.

[5]This item was evidently copied twice, because with it included, the sum is 4636, but, omitting it, the appraisers' total, 4606, is correct.

[6]This item is unintelligible, although the writing is legible.

[7]"Lincey," given more frequently as "linsey" or "linsey-woollsey," is a familiar word in pioneer writings, representing the homespun cloth of cotton and wool.

[8]"Valines" is evidently intended for valances, or draperies.

[9]This addition is incorrect, but is given as found in the original. Many similar instances will be encountered.

[10]This word is unintelligible unless it be a corruption of pina, a fine material for handkerchiefs and other articles of this character.

[11]In other places Demara is spelled Demaria, Damarie, and Demaree.

[12]This Simon Butler is probably Simon Kenton, who assumed the name of Butler when he left Virginia in the belief he had killed William Veach, his rival in love. It was not until 1782, eleven years afterward, that he learned otherwise and resumed the name of Kenton. (*Collins*, II:442,449.)

[13]Opost was a common name among the Kentuckians for Vincennes. (*Illinois Historical Collections*, VIII:300.)

[14]The name is as given, although it is Christy in the signature and other parts of the document.

[15]The names are as given, Nicholas and Nicholson, although they evidently refer to the same person.

[16]By "chin" is probably meant "chien," meaning the cock or hammer of a gun. (French-English glossary, Sawyer's *Firearms in American History*, p. 109.) If this surmise is correct, the Kentuckians evidently borrowed the term from the Illinois French.

[17]The appraisers in this inventory and in that of Thomas Davis (p. 77), where the scale of depreciation is 200 to 1, do not seem to have followed the General Assembly's act of November, 1781, where the scale was fixed for December of that year at 1000 paper dollars for one dollar specie. (Hening's *Statutes* X:473.)

[18]This name well illustrates the phonetic basis of pioneer spelling. In this book it appears as James Quoturmous, Quertermous, Quertermas, Qutermous, Catermous, and Catamus. Jillson's *Old Kentucky Entries and Deeds*, p. 275, gives three other forms, Quattarmus, Quartermus, and Quatremus, while the *Early Jefferson County Marriage Records* (Filson Club Archives) has it Quertermus and Quertermousy.

[19]Perhaps a glass ornament.

[20]A four-pint pot.

[21]Leonard Helm was one of Clark's four captains on the Kaskaskia Expedition, and was in command of Vincennes when Hamilton captured it. His intrepid refusal to surrender without terms, although almost all the militia had deserted and he stood nearly alone in the fort, is one of the finest examples of courage in our history.

[22]This is probably Chartier's Creek, now in Allegheny County, Pennsylvania. (Crumrine's *The Boundary Controversy between Pennsylvania and Virginia*, map, p. 518.) Cf. Shurtee's Creek, Bodley's *George Rogers Clark*.

[23]The assumption is justifiable that this was the John Handley who was a trustee of and most active in founding Vienna, now Calhoun, McLean County. See article on the beginning of old Vienna in the April issue of THE HISTORY QUARTERLY.

[24]After "Sarah Black" were the words "six Cows & Calves," which were afterward erased.

[25]French "couteau," knife, undoubtedly another term from the Illinois.

[26]Words appearing partly in brackets indicate that the original is torn at those points.

---

[27]Footnote by the Managing Editor of THE HISTORY QUARTERLY:

The foregoing is the third and last part of Minute Book A, Jefferson County, Kentucky, March 7, 1781, to September 3, 1783, copied by Alvin L. Prichard for publication in THE HISTORY QUARTERLY. As indicated in the last paragraph, and as stated in the introduction by Mr. Prichard, this record was transcribed in 1816. Some years ago Mr. R. C. Ballard Thruston, realizing that Minute Book A, also Minute Books 1, 2, and 3 of Jefferson County, extending from April 6, 1784, to December 6, 1793, were rapidly disintegrating, had them photostated and presented the photostats of the four volumes to The Filson Club. Book A is not the original, but a transcribed copy, and does not begin with the organization of the county in May, 1780. Furthermore, between its last entry and Book 1 there is an interval of some seven months. It looks as though the original was badly disintegrated, that a portion of each end was lost, and that what now exists is the transcribed copy of what was still preserved in 1816. Furthermore, it is evident that the pages of the transcribed copy were numbered independent of the original, also that in the small index accompanying the copy the transcribed pages are referred to.

MINUTE BOOK NO. 1, JEFFERSON COUNTY KENTUCKY
APRIL 6, 1784—DECEMBER 7, 1785

Copied for Publication

By Miss Ludie J. Kinkead

In Four Parts

Part One: April 6—May 17, 1784

Introduction

Minute Book No. 1 of the Jefferson County Court Records—here divided into four parts for convenience in printing—was preceded by Minute Book A, which was published in 1929, in Volume III of this Quarterly. Minute Book A extends from March, 1781, to September, 1783. Minute Book No. 1 begins in April, 1784.*Between the two books there is a period of about six months, the records of which can not now be found. The now existing copy of Book A was transcribed in 1816 by Worden Pope. If he transcribed the entire book, the missing months are probably recorded in a book marked B. On the other hand it is possible that all the original entries were on separate sheets of paper and were gathered together by Mr. Pope and transcribed by him in one volume. In that case it is possible that the records now missing were recorded in a book existing in 1816, or, being on separate sheets, had already been misplaced or destroyed. There is no documentary evidence that they were lost or destroyed and it is therefore possible that some day these missing records will be found in book or sheet form.

A photostat copy of Book No. 1 is in the archives of The Filson Club. The Club also has photostat copies of Book A and Books

---

*Pages 1-87, this volume.

No. 2 and No. 3, extending down to August, 1792, or about to the time when Kentucky was separated from Virginia.

Minute Book No. 1, like its predecessor and its immediate successors, is a storehouse of information bearing on the early history of Jefferson County. It is the original volume and consists of 166 pages, 7 ½ by 12 inches.

Part One covers a variety of subjects. Hundreds of names are recorded and thereby a documentary evidence of the existence of these persons is presented. Among many other records are tavern licenses and the prices set for drinks served in public places. Roads and the surveyors in charge are given. One entry shows that George Rogers Clark was "Principal Surveyor for the Virginia State Line." On page 28 is recorded the recognition of a marriage by judgment of court. On page 37 is an entry to the effect that a certain man was found guilty of a breach of an Act entitled "Divulgers of False News" and was fined "2000 pounds tobacco." *

And so in the other three parts of Minute Book No. 1, much material is made available to students of early Jefferson County history, the interest and importance depending upon the subject that is being pursued.

In preparing these records for printing the original has been followed as closely as possible. No attempt has been made to correct any of the spelling or to add any notes. The original paging is indicated by the numbers in brackets. Money is expressed in pounds, shillings and pence. The following abbreviations, kindly interpreted by Mr. Frank Coyle, are among those that occur frequently:

Al. Ca., Alias Capias	Imp'l., Imparlance
Att., Attachment	N. G., Notice Given
C. W., Commonwealth	O. R., Ordered Recorded
Cons'n., Consent	Plt., Plaintiff
C. O., Continuation Ordered	Rec'd., Recorded
C'j., Corrected judgment	Sp., Special
Deft., Defendant	Subp'd, subpoenaed
Dis'd, Dismissed	Su'y, Surety
G., Granted	W. E., Writ of Extension

*The page references found in this transcription refer to pages in the original Minute Book No. 1.

[Page 1] At a Court held for Jefferson County, on the Sixth Day of April, Anno Domini 1784.

Present: Isaac Cox, Richard Chinewith, George May, & William Oldham, Gentlemen Justices.

Benjamin Pope, Deputy Sheriff, personally appeared in Court, and resigned his said Commission, which was accordingly accepted of.

Appraisement of the Estate of William McCullum dec'd returned and ordered to be recorded.

Also an Appraisement of the Remainder of the Estate of Jonathan Rodgers—returned & O. R.

The last will and Testament of George Grundy, deceased, was proved by the oaths of William Owens and William Allen, two of the subscribing witnesses, and O. R.

On the Motion of Elizabeth Grundy and John Grundy, the Executors therein mentioned, they the said Executors ent'd into Bond with Benjamin Pope and Richard Simmonds their Securities in the penal sum of one thousand pounds conditioned for their true & faithful Discharge of s'd office.

Ordered that William Owens, Benjamin Roberts, Peter Cummis & James Rodgers, or any three of them, being first sworn to appraise the Goods & Chattels & Slaves, if any of said Decedent's Estate and return an Inventory thereof to next Court.

License granted to Richard Simmonds to keep a Tavern at Dowdall's Station on Salt River, who with John Green his Surity entered into Bond, &c according to Law.

License granted to Richard Parker to keep a Tavern at his House on Cartwrights Creek, who with Morgan Wright, entered into Bond etc., according to Law.

[Page 2] Commissions were produced and read, appointing John Campbell, George Wilson, Isaac Morrison, Samuel Culberson, Philip Phillips, Charles Polke, & David Cox, Gentlemen, Justices of the Peace for this County in addition to those now holding that office, whereupon Isaac Morrison, one of the Gentlemen therein mentioned, took the Oath of Allegiance & Fidelity to this Commonwealth and also the oaths of office.

A Commission was also produced & read appointing the said John Campbell, George Wilson, Isaac Morrison, Sam'l Culberson, Philip Phillips, Charles Polke, and David Cox, Gentlemen, Commissioners of Oyer & Terminer for said County in Addition to those now holding said Office, whereupon Isaac Morrison, Gent. one of the Justices therein named, took the Several Oaths of Office, according to Law.

A Deed of Conveyance from George Walls to Mary Joynes for a Lot of Ground in the Towne of Louisville proved by the oaths of John Downe & William Johnston and ordered to be recorded.

James Patten, James A'Sturgus & Robert Floyd are by the Consent of Parties appointed to arbitrate a Matter of Controversy now depending in said Court between Samuel Wills, Adm'r of the Estate of Sam'l Wills dec'd, and John Whittaker, whose Award shall be the Judgment of the Court.

Ordered that Court be adjourned untill Tomorrow Morning 8 o'Clock.

Isaac Cox

[Page 3] At a Court held, as pr adjournment, April, 7th, 1784.

Present: Isaac Cox, Richard Chinewith, William Oldham, & Isaac Morrison, Gen. Justices.

Edmund Rogers produces a Nomination from Geo. May, Gent., Surveyor of this County and also a Certificate of his Fitness & abilities to execute said office, from William Johnston & William Clark, who were formerly appointed by Court for that purpose, whereupon he takes the Oath of Allegiance & Fidelity to the Commonwealth, & also the Oath of Office, & is accordingly app'd to execute the same.

Andrew Hynes, Gent., present.

Gilbert Imlay & Robert Breckenridge produced Nominations from Geo. May, Gent., Surveyor of this County.

Benj. Stevens, Gilbert Imlay, James Elliott & Robert Brackenridge produced nominations from the County Surveyor appointed them Deputies under him, whereupon Alex. Brackenridge, Wm. Clark, Wm. Shannon, & John Hardley or any two of them are appointed to examine into their capacity etc. & report.

Sam. Bell produced a nomination as a Deputy Surveyor from the County Surveyor & a cert'e from the Examiners of his capacity etc. & took the Oaths of Allegiance & of Office according to Law etc.

Rob't Brackenridge produced a nomination etc. of a Dep. Surveyor & Cert'e of his capacity, whereupon he had the Oaths of Office & allegiance administered to him.

George May and Samuel Smyth, Gent, present.

[Page 4] The last Will and Testament of Robert Catlett deceased as verbally by him delivered to Meridith Price, William Pope & William Oldham, & by them committed to Writing was proved by the Oaths of William Pope & William Oldham and ordered to Record.

A Writing purporting the last Will and Testament of Meridith Price deceased, was produced, and the said Writing was proven to be that of said Price, by the Oaths of William Clark and George Wilson, and O. R. [Ordered Recorded.]

License is granted Robert Daniel to keep a Tavern at the Salt Works in this County, he giving Security whereupon he together with William Pope his Security entered into & acknowledged their Bond in the penalty of 50£ according to Law.

A Bond for Conveyance of Land from George Hart to John Donne, proven by the Oath of William Walker & by him the Evidence of Rob't Sper, & O. R.

George Wilson, Samuel Culberson, & Philip Phillips Gent., Justices, named in the Commissions from his Excellency the Governor & Council, took the Oath of Allegiance & Fidelity to this Commonwealth and also the general Oaths of Office.

Present, George Wilson, Samuel Culberson, and Philip Phillips, Gentlemen.

License is granted Edward Tyler to keep a Tavern at the Falls of Ohio, giving Security, whereupon he together with Mark Thomas his Security entered into Bond & according to Law.

Absent, Isaac Cox and Andrew Hynes, Gentlemen.

Isaac Cox Gent, produced a Commission from Benj. Harrison Esquire, & the Council of this State appointing him, the said Isaac Cox, County Lieut. of the Militia of this County, whereupon he took the Oaths of Allegiance & Fidelity and also the Oath of office etc.

[Page 5] William Pope Gent. produced a Commission from Benj. Harrison Esqr Governor & the Council of this State, appointing him the said William Pope ensign in the Militia in said County, whereupon he took the Oath of Allegiance & Fidelity and also the Oath of Office.

Andrew Hynes Gent. produced a Commission, directed as above, appointing him the said Andrew Hynes, Major of the Militia of this County, whereupon he took the Oath of Allegiance & fidelity & also the Oath of Office.

Absent, George Wilson & Isaac Morrison, Gent.

Commissions appointing George Wilson & Isaac Morrison Gentlemen, Coroners for this County, were produced & read, whereupon they the said George Wilson and Isaac Morrison Gent. took the Oaths of Allegiance and fidelity and also the Oaths of Office.

William Pope, High Sheriff, appoints John Grundy as Deputy Sheriff for this County, who takes the Oath of Allegiance & fidelity & also the Oath of Office, accordingly.

The Examiners appointed, report the Fitness & Abilities of Gilbert Imlay, Benjamin Stevens & James Elliot to execute the office of Deputy Surveyors, who severally took the Oath of Allegiance & Fidelity & the Oath of Office.

William Barnett & Jos. Tobin produced a nomination from Geo. May, Gent, Surveyor of this County, and a Certificate of their fitness and Abilities being also produced from the Examiners, they severally took the Oaths prescribed by Law, & are accordingly appointed to s'd office.

Freeman vs Saunders. Continued.

Absent William Oldham, Gent.

Logan & al. vs McMullin & al. Judg'm, 2.12.4 & Costs.

Christo. Greenup Gent. produced a License to practice as an att'o at Law & took the Oaths of office allegiance and Fidelity &c.

Present, William Oldham Gent.

[Page 6] Logan & al. vs McKenny & al. Judg'm, 2.12.4 & Costs.

Same vs Brenton & al. same, 3.3.5—Do.

Absent Richard Chinewith Gent.

Logan & al. vs Chinewith, Judg'm by cons'n, 2.12.4.

Same vs McNeal & al. same for 2.5.9.

Absent, Andrew Hynes, George Wilson & Isaac Morrison Gent.

Pittman, Asse. vs Edgcomb, Judg't according to note.

Absent Geo. May, Gent.

Cristy. Ex'r vs Martin, Dism. & plts. Costs.

Present Geo. Wilson, Gent.

Ballard vs Floyd—Judg't according to note.

Logan & al. vs Troutman, Judg, 2.2.10 &c.

Pittman vs George, Dism'd Plts. Costs.

Shorlock vs Bailey, Judg for 3.5.—. & Costs.

Logan & al. vs Froman Judg, 1.15.2

Same vs Cair—abates Deft. Death.

Present, Andrew Hynes Gent.

King vs Chinewith Judg for 10/ & Costs.

Present, Isaac Morrison Gent.

King vs Donne, Continued.

Squire Boone produces a nomination from Geo. May Gent, Surveyor of this County, and also a Certificate of his fitness & abilities for the office of a Deputy Surveyor, from the Examiners appointed, takes the several Oaths prescribed by Law, and is accordingly appointed to said office.

Thomas McCarty, Common Bail for Edward McDonald at the suit of James Elliot, comes into Court and gives up his Charge, who is committed to the Custody of the Sheriff.

Ordered that the Clerk of this Court do furnish the present Delegates for this County with a petition to the Gen'l Assembly for a Division of said County agreeable to a former Order of this Court.

[Page 7] Administration of the Estate of Adam McClentick deceased is granted unto his Relict, Jane McClentick, who made Oath according to Law, she giving Security whereupon she together with Samuel Martin and James Beaty entered into & acknowledged their Bond in the penalty of five hundred pounds conditioned for the faithful Administration of said Decedants Estate. [Marginal notation:] rec'd.

Ordered that Edward Goodin, John M. Castline, Aist'n Jones and Samuel McClentick, or any three of them being first sworn, do appraise the personal Estate and Slaves, if any, of Adam McClentick deceased, and return an Inventory thereof to Court.

On the Motion of William Pope Gent, one of the Executors named in the last will and Testament of John Floyd Gent. deceased, Certificate of obt'g Probation Form of the said Decedants Estate is granted him in Conjunction with Jane Floyd, Relict and Widow of said John Floyd deceased, he giving Security, whereupon he together with Squire Boone, Isaac Morrison & Philip Phillips entered into & acknowledged their Bond in the penalty of £2000 conditioned for the faithful Discharge of said office. [Marginal notation:] rec'd.

Dodge vs Ballard. Referred to William Shannon and George Walls or their umpire.

The arbitrators appointed to settle a matter in Difference between Samuel Wills adm'r of Samuel Wills deceased & John Whittaker, make their report, whereon Judgment is granted accordingly.

Ordered that Abigal Kimble, aged 12 years, Orphan of Haner Kimble deceased, be bound unto John McManus, according to Law. [Marginal notation:] rec'd.

Ordered that Hannal Kimble, aged 9 years, orphan of said Deceased be bound unto Samuel Culberson according to Law. [Marginal notation:] rec'd.

Ordered that Court be adjourned untill Tomorrow Morning 8 o'Clock.
Isaac Cox

[Page 8] At a Court held, per adjournment, April 8th, 1784.

Present: Isaac Cox, Samuel Smyth, Geo. Wilson, Samuel Culberson, Isaac Morrison, Gent. Justices.

On the Motion of Samuel Smyth, Gent. ordered that his mark be recorded, Viz, an upper Bit and an under Bit and a Crop off each Ear. [Marginal notation:] rec'd.

On the Motion of William Johnston, ordered that his Mark, Viz a slit in one Ear and an half Crop in the other, be recorded. [Marginal notation:] rec'd.

Ordered that Susanna Jones, aged 10 years, and Sarah Jones aged 8 years, orphans of Michael Jones deceased be bound unto Jacob Vanmatre according to Law. [Marginal notation:] rec'd.

Ordered that Eliner Garner, a base born Child of Margret Garner, aged 13 years, be bound unto Evan Williams according to Law. [Marginal notation:] rec'd.

The viewers appointed make Return of the Road from Beards Town to the County Line and established accordingly.

Present, Andrew Hynes Gent.

Cuny vs McAdams. Referred to Isaac Morrison and Joseph Barnett, or their Umpire.

Present, Geo. May & William Oldham Gent.

Edward McDonald and Stephen Harris & Robert Tyler acknowledge themselves bound unto Benja' Harris Esq'r' his Heirs or Successors in the penalty of one hundred pounds, that is to say, the said Edward McDonald in the penal sum of fifty pounds, & Stephen Harris and Rob't Tyler each in the Sum of Twenty five pounds, to be levied off their & each of their Goods, & Chattles, Sands & Tenements & etc. Conditioned, that if the above bounden Edward McDonald, shall not henceforward, molest, maim, wound or otherways disable Sarah Watson, who complains of s'd Edward, or do anything tending to disturb the good peace of this Commonwealth, or any of the Liege Subjects thereof, then this Recognizance to be void or else to remain &c.

[Page 9] Absent, George May & Andrew Hynes Gent.

Administration of the Estate of William Scott deceased is granted James Morrison, he giving Security, whereupon he together with William Oldham and Thomas Cuny entered into & acknowledged their Bond in the penalty of 200£ &c according to Law.

Absent, William Oldham Gent.

Ordered that Andrew Hynes, John Handley, Philip Phillips & John Virtress or any two of them being first sworn do appraise the personal Estate & Slaves if any of said Decedant & return an Inventory to Court.

A Power of Attorney from Robert Elliot to James Elliot proven by the Oaths of William Johnston & Rob't George, and O. R. [Marginal notation:] p'd.

A Bond of Insurance from Dave Brodhead Jr. to James Wilkinson, acknowledged & O. R. [Marginal notation:] p'd.

Also a Bond of Insurance from said Dave Brodhead, Jr. to James Armstrong. acknowledged & O. R. [Marginal notation:] p'd.

A Bond for the Conveyance of 1000 Acres of Land from James Purvis to James Dunlap acknowledged & O. R. [Marginal notation:] p'd.

A Bond from James Patten, Ben Pope, Wm. Roberts & James Purvis to Wilkinson Armstrong Dunn & Co. for the Conveyance of 7500 Acres of Land, acknowledged and ordered to be recorded. [Marginal notation:] p'd.

William Pope Gent. Executor appointed by the last Will of Charles Colston, resigns his said Charge, & on the Motion of

Nimlock Colston, Administration of the Estate of said Charles Colston deceased, is granted him, he giving Security, whereupon he together with Benja' Pope and Robert George entered into & acknowledged their Bond in the penalty of 200£ etc. according to Law.

Ordered that James Kimble, aged 10 years, Orphan of Kimble deceased be bound unto Saml Culbertson according to law. [Marginal notation:] rec'd.

Present, Geo. May, Andrew Hynes, & Philip Phillips.

[Page 10] Ordered that Mary Meridith, aged 10 years, Orphan of Susana Meridith deceased, be bound unto William Oldham Gent, according to Law. [Marginal notation:] rec'd.

License is granted William Kincholoe to keep a Tavern at his House in this County, he giving Security whereupon he entered into Bond with Ben Pope Su'y, according to Law.

Present, William Oldham Gent.

Present, Isaac Cox Gent.

On the Complaint of Cain Withers against William McFarline for a Breach of the peace—on hearing the parties, ordered that the said William McFarline enter into a Recognizance, himself in £100 with two Securities in £25 each for the said William McFarline Appearance at the next grand Jury Court to answer an Indictment, then to be preferred against him. [Marginal notation:] ch'd.

Also it's Ordered that the said William McFarline farther recognize in the Sum of £50 with two Securities in £25 each for the said William McFarline's good Behavior 12 months.

On the Complaint of Cain Withers vs. Ed. Shain for a Breach of the peace, on hearing the parties, ordered that the said Ed. Shain, enter into a Recognizance himself in £100—with two Securities in £25 each for the said Ed. Shain's Appearance at the next grand Jury Court to answer an Indictment, then to be prepared against him. [Marginal notation:] rec'd.

Also it's ordered that the said Ed. Shain farther recognize in the Sum of 50£ with two Securities in £25 each for the said Ed. Shain's good Behavior for 12 months.

John Allan Tharp acknowledges himself bound unto Benja' Harrison Esquire Govr. of this State, in the penal Sum of 100£, to be levied off his Goods, Chattels &c. Condition'd that if the said John Allan Tharp shall appear at the next grand Jury Court to be held for this County, to testify & the truth to say in Behalf of this Commonwealth against Jacob Knight, in Custody who is bound to appear, Then his obligation. [Marginal notation:] ch'd.

[Page 11] Satisfactory proof being made to the Court that John Brand, a Soldier in the Illinois Regiment and discharged within 12 Months past, is entitled to a Settlement & preemption in the District of Kentucky, which he locates (viz. his Sett'm) on the Waters of Dunning, Lick Creek, adj'n 1000 Acre Survey of Ben Neal's on the S.W.S. to be bound in by the Lines of a 400 Acre Survey, made by W. Shanon for s'd Brand, which includes his Imp'r & the Mo. [?] of the Cany fork of Dunning's, L. cr., & his Preemption adj'n His Sett't. Neals' 1000 Acre Survey and 12,335 acre Survey of Squire Boones, to be bounded by the Lines of 1000 Acre Survey made by W. Shanon for s'd Brand & that he was in the Service when the Com's sat to do Business in this Country, & Ordered to be certified accordingly.

Ordered that the Sheriff do Summon Twenty four able free-holders of this County to appear at the Court House of said County on the first Tuesday in May next to be sworn a grand Jury of Inquest for the Body of this County.

C. Wealth [Commonwealth] vs. Jacob Knight, in Custody.

Ordered that the said Jacob Knight enter into a Recognizance with two Securities, himself in £50 [and two] Securities each in £25 for the Appearance of the said Jacob Knight at the next grand Jury Court to answer an Indictment then to be preferr'd against by the atto' for the County for petit Larceny. Whereupon Philip Barbour and Josa Archer his Securities Recognized each in the sum of £25 for the s'd Knights appearance as afores'd & waive any advantage from the s'd Jacob's not being in Court. [Marginal notation:] ch'd.

Present, George Slaughter Gent.

Cain Withers acknowledges himself bound &c unto the Gov'r of this State, in the Sum of £[blank] to be levied off his Goods, &c etc. Conditioned for the Appearance of the s'd Cain Withers at the next grand Jury Court to be held for this County, to testify & the Truth to say in Behalf of this Comonw' against William McFarline and Edward Shain in Custody for a Breach of the peace & Then etc.

[Page 12] Ordered that William May, Gent. be recommended & nominated as a proper person to act as County Surveyor of this County in the Room of Geo. May, Gent. who is about to resign, etc.

Ordered that William Clark, Philip Phillips and James Morrison Gent or any two of them are appointed to examine into the State and Situation of the Surveyors office in this County, if the Records are properly kept according to Law and make Report thereof to Court.

The last Will and Testament of Zephaniah Blackford deac'd produced in Court & proven by the Oath of Wil'm Pritchet, one of the subscribing Witnesses, and also proven by the Oath of George Walls, to be the Hand Writing of said Zephaniah Blackford decd. & O. R. Reubin Blackford, Executor therein named, made Oath thereto according to Law; & on s'd Ex'r motion who entered into Bond etc. accordingly with William Shanon and Ths. Cunningham his Sec'y in the penal Sum of £500 condition'd &c, Certificate is granted himself of obtaining Letters of Administration or a probat in due form.

Ordered that James Harrod, John Hinch, Michael Humble, & Sam'l Hinch be appointed to appraise the personal Estate & Slaves if any of s'd dec'd in Lincoln County & return an Inventory to Court.

License is granted Patrick McGee to keep a Tavern on the South Side of Salt River, giving Security whereupon he gave Security etc. according to Law.

Logan & all vs Wells Judg't, 2.2.1 & Cost.

Same vs Dunbar, same for Costs.

Same vs Wright & all, same for 3.2.6. & Cost.

Same vs same, same, 3.7.6. same.

Same vs Martin, same, 1.11.6. same.

McKay vs Cox & al, Cont'd.

Freeman vs Nelson, Judg't for 1.10 & Costs.

Same vs same, same, 1.11 same.

Absent, An. Hynes & Geo Wilson, Gent.

[Page 13] Applegate vs Knight, Judg't for 3£ & Costs.

Saunders vs Nelson, same, 4.5, same

Calhoun vs Hoglans Adm'n now Subp'd for 3.4.8 [Date ?]

Pillars vs Stapleton, Continued.

William Pope Gent, one of the Executors named in the last Will & Testament of Mer. Price dec'd, enters into Bond with George Wilson and Patrick McGee in the penal sum of £100 conditioned etc. and Certif'te is accordingly granted him for obtaining a Probate in due form.

Kilpatrick vs Handley, Cont'd Deft. Costs.

Harris vs French N. G. with leave C'j.

Young vs Chinewith, Dism'd.

Brodhead vs Miles, Dism'd, Deft Costs.

Nelson vs Pyeatt, Cont'd Deft.

Syndray's Adm'n vs Carr, abates deft. Death.

Moss Exr. vs Stephenson, Continued.

Edward Mathews enters himself Special Bail for Edward and W. E. McDonald at the Suit of James Elliot. Judge' by Nihil dicit.

Case vs Johnson, Continued.

Whittaker vs Case, issue joined, Jury to wit, empannelled & sworn according to Law, Viz. Jacob Funk, William Rowan, Jacob Vanmatre, James Morrison, Will Shanon, William Clark, Joseph Phelps, Daniel Brodhead, Saml. Wills, Joseph Brooke, Jacob Banackman, & James McCullock, who bring in their Virdict in these Words. We of the Jury find for the Plaintiff £42.0.0. Jacob Funk.

Sutherland vs McCartline, Continued.

Ex'r. G. Grundy decd. vs Moss Ex'r. Sine facias.

Cox vs Moore, Judg't by non sum informatics.

Isaac Cox Gen. absent.

Same vs Whittaker, discont.

Same vs Folkes, same Deft. Costs.

Same vs Newkirk, C. O.

Same vs prior, C. O.

[Page 14] Judgement Logan & all vs Dunbar is satisfied.

James McCauley enters himself Special Bail for John Allan Tharp at the suit of Jacob Knight

Geo. Slaughter. Gent, present.

Satisfactory proof being made to the Court that James Helms is the true & lawful heir of his Bro'r William Helms decd. and also that William Russel is the Heir of his father Benj. Russel, who each dec. in the Service, ordered that the same be certified.

Present Isaac Morrison & Philip Phillips Gent.

Ordered that Stephen Kimble orphan of Kimble decd. be bound unto Mark Thomas untill he arrives to the Age of 21 Years, the said Thomas to learn him the Art of a Taylor, Indenture to be entered into, which was accordingly done & O. R.

Ordered that Joseph Barnet, Alex Breckinridge, & John Hundley do examine into the fitness & ability of John Veach as a Deputy Surveyor, who produces a nomination for the purpose

The Examiners app'd report that John Veech is duly qualified, who takes the several Oaths accordingly

On the Motion of Mark Thomas who made Oath according to Law, Administration is granted him of the Estate of Hanna Kimble decd. giving Sec'y, whereupon he with Abner Fields & Cain Withers entered into Bond &c. according to Law.

Appearances.

Chinewith vs. Young, dism'd.

Wadkins vs. Pyeatt O. & Sp. Imp'l, Wm. Popes, Bail.

Logan & all vs. Ashley & all.—abates as to Ashly & C. O. against A'Sturgus, Admr. of A.'Sturgus.

Lindsay's Adm'r. vs Chinewith, Oyer & Sp'c Imp'l.

Sherlock vs Nelson. C. O. aj'r, Def't & Bail.

Decker vs Sullivan & all. Oyer & sp. Imp'l.

Matron vs Same, Same.

[Page 15] Logston vs Ashcraft, discont'd.

Brooker vs Moss, C. O.

Logan & all. vs Lynn's Adm'r, Oyer & Spc. Imp'l.

Leach vs Sullivan cont'd for Plf.

Sullivan vs Netherland, Oyer & Sp. Imp'l.

Culbertson vs Ride. Cont'd for Plt.

Brooker vs McCarty & al Dism'd Plt Costs.

Warren vs Davis Discont'd.

Brooker vs Purcell & Uxr. C. O.

Same & Uxr vs same. C. O.

John Sinclear vs John Vaughn Referred to Ben Pope & Bland Ballard as their Umpire.

Walls vs Nelson, N. G. with Leave C'j.

Daulin vs Henry, Cont'd.

Nelson vs Walls, N. G. with Leave C'j.

Pope vs Scott. C. O.

Alvay vs Whitledge, Sp'l Imparlance.

Lynn's Adm'r vs Sullivan, Oyer & Sp. Imp'l.

Boush vs Johnson, Cont'd.

Wm McFarlane & Jno Dorret acknowledge themselves bound &c—viz s'd McFarlane in £50 and John Dorret in £25 etc. Conditioned, that if the above bound Wm McFarlane shall well and truly behave & demean himself as a good quiet & peacible Citizen of this State, as well with Regard to the Security & Safety of Cain Withers, who has complain'd of s'd McFarlane, as to all other the good subject of this State, then etc. [Marginal notation:] ch'd.

Edward Shain & Josiah Phelps acknowledge themselves bound etc. s'd Shain with £50, s'd Phelps in £25—the Conditioned, that if the above bounded Edward Shain shall well & truly etc as above. Then this etc. [Marginal notation:] ch'd.

[Page 16] Robert George & Richard Simmonds, enter themselves special Bail for James O. Tinn at the Suit of Eli Cleveland. Ind.

License to keep a Tavern at the Falls of Ohio in the Town of Louisville, is granted John Dorrett who gave Bond & Security according to Law.

Ordered that George Walls, Cain Withers, Gab'l Johnston & William Clark or any two of them being first sworn do appraise the personal Estate & Slaves if any of Meridith Price dec'd, and return an Inventory to Court.

Present, Andrew Hynes & Geo. Wilson Gent.

Cleveland vs Tinn, Oyer & Sp'l Imp'l Walker. Daniel Ginn is appointed by the Court as Attorney for the Defendant.

Ordered that Court be adjourned until Tomorrow morning 8' o.Clock.   Isaac Cox.

At a Court held, for Jefferson County, p'r adjournment, April 9th, 1784.

Present: Isaac Cox, William Oldham, George Wilson & Philip Phillips, Gent.

Thomas Cunningham produced a Commission appointing him Captain of the Militia of the County, whereupon he takes the Oath of Fidelity & oath of Office according to Law.

Present, Samuel Smyth, & Isaac Morrison, Gent.

Present, Andrew Hynes, Gent.

Philip Phillips Gent. produced a Commission—appointing him a Captain of the Militia of this County, whereupon he takes the several Oaths of office according to Law.

Joseph Kilpatrick Gent, produced a Commission appointing him an Ensign of the Militia of this County who takes the several Oaths of Office, according to Law.

[Page 17] George Slaughter Gent., present.

John McMannus comes into Court, and relinquishes his Charge of Abigail Kimble, Orphan of Hanna Kimble deceased, who was bound unto him by a former Order of this Court, Whereupon at the request of said Orphan its ordered that she be bound unto Mark Thomas according to Law. [Marginal notation:] rec'd.

George Slaughter Gent., absent.

Hinton's Admt. vs Shannon. Jury to try the Issue, viz. Alexander Skinner, Daniel Brodhead, Jr., William Orr, Benjamin Stevens, James Harrod, Samuel McAdams, Cain Withers, Thomas Philips, Josiah Phelps, Graves Wappshot, Niblock Colson, & William Allan, who being sworn according to Law, bring in their verdict in these Words, We of the Jury find for the plaintiff, the Sum of five hundred pounds Damages. A. Skinner, Foreman. Ordered that Verdict be set aside, on acc't of excessive Damages & a new Trial be had on the second day of May C't.

On the motion of William Pope Gent, administration is granted him of the Estate of Robert Catlett deceased, who gave Bond and Security according to Law.

Ordered that George Walls, Cain Withers, Gabriel Johnston and William Clark or any three of them being first sworn do appraise the personal Estate of Robert Catlett dec'd. and return an Inventory to next Court.

It appearing that some of the Rates as formerly settled by Court for Ordinary keepers are too low. Ordered that for 1 Gallon of Corn there be allowed, nine pence, Dinner 1/6, 1 quart of Toddy 1/6, Lodging 6d, whiskey pr ½ pint 9d.

Craig vs Nelson, Benj. Pope, sp. Bail & sp. Imp'l.

Yates admxr vs Cook, Oyer & Sp. Imp'l.

Wm. Pope is appointed Guardian to Wm. Linn, heir at Law to Wm Linn dec'd, also to Asael Linn another Son of William Linn dec'd. Whereupon the s'd Wm. Pope gave Bond in £2000 for the [Page 18] faithful discharge of his Office with James Sullivan & Joseph Barnett his Securities etc. [Marginal notation:] Rec'd.

Brooker vs McGee. Issue, Jury to wit, Joseph Barnett, Richard Terrell, Jacob Vanmeter, Joseph Tobin, Squire Boone, James Welch, William Barnett, Th's. Whitledge, James Sullivan, Robert Tyler, James Carnihan and James Hoglan, who being impannelled & sworn, return verd't for Deft. & Jdgt. etc.

Ordered that George Yount be allowed five Days Attendance as a Witness in the Suit Hinton's Adm'r vs Shannon.

Logston vs Asturgas, Cont'd.

Mathew vs Braden, Cont'd.

Kindergrass's Adm. vs Henry Wm. Pope & Jos. Brooks. Sp Oyer & Sp. Imp.

Asturgas vs Edgcomb, cont'd

Newland vs Purvis, same.

Floyd vs Patten & al Jdg't by confession according to Specialty.

Pope vs McCasline. C. O.

Lee vs Phelps, abates by return.

Lock vs Barrackman, cont'd.

Whitacre vs McGee, dism'd.

M'Cawly & Uxr vs Moore, cont'd.

Logan & al vs Vitteloe, Att.

Dodge vs Ballard, cont'd.

Elliot vs Hutchinson. C. O.

Floyd vs Newkirk. C. O.

Same vs Lock. C. O.

Same vs Hogland. C. O.

[Page 19] Boone vs Elliot, abates by Return.

Nelson vs Walls, Oyer & Sp. Imp.

Sullivan vs Rogers, discont'd at Pv. costs.

Joins vs Shannon, dismd. deft. cost.

Same & Uxr vs same, Dismd. Deft. costs.

Commonwealth vs Nelson, discont'd.

Knight vs Allenthorp. C. O.

Wilkerson vs Owens, cont'd.

M'Carty vs Cox & al, N. Guilty with leave.

Hutchison vs Netherland, cont'd.

Clark vs Archer, Dism'd, Pv costs.

M'Donald vs Elliott, countermanded by return.

Withers vs Shain & al. Dism'd.

Wells vs Floyd, cont'd for return.

104

Asturgas vs Hogland's Adm'r al, capias.

Commonwealth vs Bell. C. O.

Young vs Hume, Oyer & Sp. Imp'l.

Same vs Jean Hume, Plea filed & Time.

Waters vs Stevenson, Oyer & Sp. Imp'l.

Sullivan vs Brodhead discont'd.

Brotsman vs Knight. C. O.

Ronan vs Wall. C. O. vs Def't. & Lee.

Wells vs. Brodhead. cont'd.

C. Wealth [Commonwealth] vs Collins. C. O.

Same vs John Bell. C. O.

Same vs Mc.Gee. C. O.

Brodhead ajd. vs Stevenson, Wm Pope Sp. Bail & Sp. Imp.

Squire Boone produced a Capt'n Commission, Rob't Tyler a Lieut. Com'r of Militia & had the oaths of fidelity and office adm'd etc.

[Page 20] Tyler vs Chinewith, Judg. for 3.6— & Costs.

Geo. Wilson Gent produces a Commission appointing him Captain of the Militia of this County and had the Oaths of Fidelity and of office etc.

Ordered that Cain Withers, John Jackson, John Bailey, & Ralph Matson, or any two of them, being first sworn do appraise the Estate of Hanna Kimble deceased and return an Inventory thereof to Court.

Pres't, Geo. Slaughter & Sam. Culbertson, Gent.

Absent, Geo. Slaughter Gent.

Phelps vs George, Jury to try the Issue to wit, Alexander Skinner, Graves Wepshot, Abner Fields, Jacob Vanmeter, James Welch, Saml. McAdams, William Orr, William Allan, Cain Withers, William Clark, Richard Terrell, & George Walls, who being impannel'd & sworn, bring in their Verdict, for Defendant. A. Skinner, foreman.

Mark Thomas Gent. produces a Commission appointing him Captain of the Militia, where upon the several Oaths are administered to him according to Law.

Ordered that Court be adjourned until Tomorrow Morning 8. O'Clock.

Isaac Cox.

105

[Page 21] At a Court held for Jefferson County, April 10th, 1784, per adjournment.

Present: Isaac Cox, William Oldham, George Wilson, Isaac Morrison, Saml. Culberton, Gent. Justices.

Ralph Matson Gent. produced a Commission appoint'g him a Lieutenant of the Militia of this County, where upon he had the several Oaths of offices administered etc.

Floyd vs Damewood & al, Cont'd.

Cave vs Stevenson, Judge conf'd, & W. E. G.

Burros vs Cochran, Cont'd. def'ts. Costs.

Farrar vs Walls, Adm. Dism'd.

January vs Stephenson, Judge Conf'd, & W. E. G.

Barfield's Admr vs Gregory, J. Conf'd, & W. E. G.

Cave vs Garvey, Referred to Joseph Phelps, Jacob Vanmatre and their umpire.

Withers vs Shain & al, discont'd, Defts. Costs.

Wells vs Clear, Judgt pr Award.

West vs Bolling, Jury to try the issue to wit, Jonathan Clark, Danl. Brodhead, Robert George, Joseph Phelps, William Orr, Michael Hogg, John Jackson, Jas. Elliot, Ralph Matson, James Stuart, James Harrod & Nathan'l Braiden, who being sworn, bring in a Verdict for the Plaintiff, and Judgment etc.

Same vs Same. Cont'd.

Francis Adams is appointed Constable for the Town of Louisville.

James McKeg at Lynn's Station, same Order.

James McCauley on Fern Creek, same Order.

Wm. Beard & Richard Connor, So. Side Salt River, same Order.

[Page 22] Ordered that Richard Chinewith Gent, do take the List of Tithables at the Spring Station, Middle Station, New Holland, Sullivan's old Station & Hoglan's Station, and make Return agreeable to Law.

Ordered that Samuel Culberson Gent, take the List of Tithables at Lynn's Station, A'Sturgus Station, Dan'l Sullivan's, Brashear's and Dunning's Lick Creek, and make return agreeable to Law

O. that William Oldham Gent, take the List of Tithables at the Poplar Level, Sullivan's New Station and Falls of Ohio agreeable to Law.

O. that Geo. Wilson Gent, do tythe Kuykendall's & Kellar's Stations, Fern and Fish pool Creeks, Bullit's Lick and the Stations on the No. Side of Salt River agreeable to Law.

O. that Andrew Hynes Gent, take the List of Tythes at Hynes' Station and on all the Waters of Green River agreeable to Law.

O. that Philip Phillips Gent, tythe the Inhabitants on the So. Side Beech fork, including the Rolling Fork, & make Return according to Law.

O. that Sam'l Smyth Gent, take a List of Tithables in Cap. Samuels and Rogers Companies and report according to Law.

O. that Isaac Morrison, Gent, take the Tithables, all those that are situate between the Beech Fork and Salt River

Younger vs Moss Ex, Cont'd. for Deft.

Gregory vs purcell, Cont'd.

George Slaughter and James F. Moore Gent are recommended to his Exc'y, the Govr. as proper persons to act as Sheriffs, one of whom is to be commissioned for that purpose, for one year.

Gregory vs Purcell, Cont'd.

McMullin vs Brookes, dism'd.

[Page 23] Sullivan vs Henry, Cont'd.

McTall vs Hawkins. Discont'd.

Buchanons Ad'r vs Barbour, Cont'd

Brooks vs Tobin, Judg't. N. Dicit, & W. E. G.

Grundy vs Dorrett, Cont'd.

Lynn's Adm'r vs Derimiah. Same.

Glenn vs Williams, N. G. with Leave.

Burros vs Harrod, Cont'd for Plt.

Same vs Same, same, same.

Same vs Williams, same.

Admt. Grant vs Reid, Cont'd for Deft.

Lynn's Adm'r vs Sullivan, Cont'd for Deft.

McGee vs Hinckston, Cont'd.

Clear vs Wells, Dism'd.

Moss Ex'r vs Williams, Dism'd. agreed.

Pittman vs Clark, Issue wav'd & J. acc'g to specialty.

Wells vs Moss Ex'r Cont'd for Deft.

Lindsay's Adm'r vs Saunders. Jury to try the Issue, to wit, Jonathan Clark, Benj. Stevens, George Walls, John Jackson, Alx. Skinner, William Clark, James Stuart, Ralph Matson,

Joseph Phelps, William Orr, John Rogers & Cain Withers, who being sworn, bring in their Verdict for the plaintiff and Judgt accordingly £22.5.11 & Costs.

Pyeatt vs McCarty. Cont'd at Plt Charge.

Laurence vs McMullin, same Jury to wit, Jonathan Clark etc, etc, who being accordingly sworn, bring in their verdict, for the plaintiff & Judgment accordingly. £15.11.11 & Costs.

[Page 24] Little vs McGee, dis'd. Deft. Costs.

Patton vs McAdams, abates plt. Death.

Lyndsays Adm'r vs Triggs & all, Jury to try the issue to wit, James Sullivan, William Shanon, Jacob Vanmatre, Thomas Phelps, Dav'd Hawkins, Joseph Tobin, Reubin Blackford, Robt George, Danl Brodhead, John Parker, Dennis Burns & Gabriel Johnston, who being sworn, bring in a Verdict for the plaintiff & judgment accordingly.

M. Carty vs Grundy, Cont'd.

Henry vs Doulin, Judg't for £30 & Costs.

Ordered that George Wilson Gent, be desired to furnish Scales and Weights agreable to Law for this County, & that the Sheriff out of any public Money collected pay him for the same & his trouble.

McCra & Co. vs Killars [or Kellare] Adm'r, Jury to wit, Jonathan Clark, Benjamin Stevens, George Walls, Alexander Skinner, William Clark, Jas Stuart, Joseph Phelps, William Orr, John Rogers, Cain Withers, Thos Cunningham & Richard Terrel, who being sworn, bring in a Verdict for pl't and Judgment accordingly.

Glenn vs Dozier [or Doyice?] Judg't Cont'd & W. E. G.

Scott vs Cliffton, Dism'd.

McNew vs Mason, Dism'd.

Cooke vs Phelps, discont'd.

Matron vs Sappington, atty, dism'd Plt. Costs.

Tyler vs Johnson, Judg't 1.10. & Costs.

Present, Geo. Slaughter Gent.

Absent, Geo. Wilson, Gent.

[Page 25] Standiford vs Start, Same Jury as in McCra & Co. vs Killars Adm'r, who were sworn a Juror withdrawn by Consent, Case stands Continued.

Present, Geo. Wilson, Gent. & Sam'l Culberson, Gent.

Ordered that Richard Chinewith, Gent. do appear at May Court, to settle for the County Levys as assessed in the year 1781.

Also ordered that William Pope, Gent. do appear at said Court to settle for the Collection of said Levy. Absent G. Wilson, Gent.

Sullivan Ass'e vs Nelson & al, Jury to Wit, James Patton, Jacob Vanmatre, John Bailey, Rob George, Reubin Blackford, Martin Carney, Jno Parker, James Harrod, Robert Beale, Abner Field, Burditt Cliffton and William Roberts, who being sworn, Plaintiff being called & not appearing, ordered that he be non suit.

Ordered that James A'Sturgess, Surveyor of the road from the South fork of Bear Grass, begin to clear his Road from the place where James Sullivan has cleared to, which is considered as the main South fork of Bear Grass.

Also ordered that those persons who have served under James Sullivan, be exempted from any Attendance on said James A'Sturgess until his said Road is put in a similar situation to s'd Sullivan's.

Ordered that the Clerk of this Court do immediately, as soon as may be, furnish himself with Blanks and such Books as may be necessary and a press to keep them in, which are to be paid for out of the next public Collection, and under an Acc't to Court.

Ordered that James Sullivan, Edward Tyler, Mark Thomas, and James Patten, do view, search out and examine the nearest and most convenient Way from the Court House at the Falls [Page 26] of Ohio, to Lynn's Station and report the Conveniences and Inconveniences attending the same.

Ordered that David Cox, Charles Polk, Andrew Vaughn, Jr., and Thomas Cunningham do view & search out the nearest and most convenient Way from Colo Isaac Cox's to Beard's Town and report accordingly.

Daniel Sullivan is appointed Surveyor of the Road from the South Fork of Beargrass to where James Sullivan has cleared, in the Room of James A'Sturgess, and that the same inhabitants[?] attend him as were laid off for A'Sturgess, in the Execution of his Office.

William Clark produces a Nomination as a Deputy Surveyor and also a Certificate from the Examiners of his fitness & Abilities, whereupon he takes the several Oaths of Office and is accordingly appointed.

Ordered that James Davis, Benja Lynn, Sam'l Pottinger & Sam'l McAdams do view the nearest & most convenient way from Beard's Town to Pottinger's and report accordingly.

Ordered that Squire Boone, Daniel Sullivan, William Shannon and James T. Moon do view the nearest & most convenient way from Boone's Station as far as Kentucky [River] on the Road to Lexington, to some conv't place or opposite Lee's Town Xing [crossing] on Kent'y river.

Also ordered that the same Viewers do view from Boon's Station to Lynn's Station on Beargrass & report, etc.

Ordered that Court be adjourned untill Court in Course.

Isaac Cox.

[Page 27] At a Court held for Jefferson County on the 4th day of May, 1784.

Present, Isaac Cox, Andrew Hynes, George Slaughter, William Oldham, Gent. Justices.

James Buchanon produces a nomination as a Deputy Surveyor from Geo. May Gent., Whereupon William Clark and Alex Breckenridge are appointed to examine into the Fitness & Abilities of said Buchanon & report accordingly.

The viewers appointed make Report of the Road from the Neighbourhood of Beard's Town to the Salt Works, and the same is established accordingly.

On the Motion of Cain Withers ordered that his Mark, Viz a Slit in each Ear, be recorded. [Marginal notation:] Rec'd.

A Bond from John Eastwood to Benja Netherland being proven by the Oath of Robert Floyd and the Testimony of John Sanders the other subscribing Witness being also proven by the Oath of said Floyd, the same is O. R. [Marginal notation:] Rec'd.

On the Motion of Samuel Wills, Ordered that his Mark Viz. a half Cross out of the left Ear, be recorded. [Marginal notation:] Rec'd.

Administration of the Estate of William Stevens dec'd is granted his Relict Mary Stevens, who made Oath & entered into Bond etc. with John Chambers, & Bland Ballard her Securities, in the penalty of £250 & C. [Marginal notation:] Rec'd.

Ordered that Isaac Morrison, Zachariah Hold, Chas Duma & Thos Cunningham, or any two of them being first sworn do appraise the Estate of said Decedant & make Report at next Court.

Present Isaac Morrison, George Wilson & Sam'l Culbertson, Gent.

The Examiners app'd report the fitness & Abilities of James Buchanon, who takes the several Oaths of office as D'y Sur'y accordingly.

[Page 28] Ordered that Thomas Curry be exempted from personal Attendance on the Road, in assisting the Surveyor thereof to clear the same, on Acc't of Inability.

Philemon Waters produces a Com. appointing him Cap't of the Militia, whereupon he takes the Sev'l oaths etc.

William Clark Foreman & John Martin, William Cummins, John Shaw, Samuel Hubbs, Rob't Main, Christd Jones, Samuel Martin, Abram Whittaker, Josiah Phelps, Reubin Case, Samuel Wells, James Qutermous, James A'Sturgess, & Robert Floyd were sworn a Grand Jury of Inquest for the Body of this County, & having rec'd their Charge, Withdraw and after some Time returned and presented.

M'Clure vs M'Linbick, Dism'd, Deft Costs.

License to keep an Ordinary at the Falls of Ohio is granted Andrew Hath, who gave Bond and Security according to Law.

Rowan vs Edgcomb, Al. Ca.

Satisfactory proof was made to the Court that Daniel McCoy & Elsa Ryley were joined together in the Estate of holy Matrimony and it not appearing to the Court that he had any other wife or Heirs, ordered the same Recorded.

Moses Spear and John Allan Tharp enter themselves Special Bail for James Stephenson, at the Suit of Daniel Brodhead, Jr. & Philemon Waters.

James Francis Moore, Gent. produces a Com'n appointing him a Liu't Colonel of the Militia, whereupon he takes the several Oaths of office accordingly.

License to keep a Tavern at the Falls of Ohio is granted John Joynes who gave Bond and Security agreable to Law.

Ordered that Court be adjourned untill tomorrow Morning 8 o'Clock.   Isaac Cox.

[Page 29] At a Court held for Jefferson County, May 5th, 1784. Pr. Adjournment.

111

Present, Isaac Cox, Geo. Slaughter, William Oldham, George Wilson, & Isaac Morrison, Gent. Justices.

An Appointment of the Estate of Merideth Price deceased returned and O. R. (absent, Isaac Morrison, Gent.) [Marginal notation:] Rec'd.

Administration of the Estate of John Carr deceased is granted Isaac Morrison Gent, who gave Bond & Security according to Law. [Marginal notation:] Rec'd.

Ordered that James Samuels, John Esra, Robert Mosely & Alex'r Keith or any three of them being first sworn do appraise the said Decedant's Estate & make Report thereof to Court.

Ordered that Josiah Phelps be fined 500 lbs Tobacco, for a Contempt, to this Court offered, in not attending as a Grand Juryman after having been duly Sworn. [Marginal notation:] Dism'd.

Hawkins vs Trueman, Judg't by Confession £3.3. & Costs.

Cherry vs Willson, Dism'd plaintiff & Costs.

Hughes vs Brachey, Discont'd.

Rowan vs McCune, Judg't for £5 & Costs.

Damewood vs Sherlock, at Sp'o.

Stephen Harris vs Shields, O Sp Imp.

Sullivan vs Rogers.

Geo. Slaughter & Bland Ballard Sp Bail O. & Sp'l Imp'l.

Freeman vs Sanders set for Trial next Court.

Pillars vs Stapleton, dism'd no app.

Calhoon vs Hoglane, Adm'n, Cont'd for plt.

McKey vs Cox & Moon, Dism'd plt Costs.

King vs Donne, C. O.

Archer vs Pope, O. Sp. Imp.

A'Sturgus vs Hoglane, Adm'r Cont'd.

[Page 30] Cliffton vs Parker, Cont'd for return.

Tobin vs Nelson, C. O.

Rowan vs Edgecomb, Do.

Harrod vs A Sturgus, Do.

Tyler vs Culbertson, O. Sp. Imp.

Kirkham vs McCarty & al, Wm. Oldham Sp B'l O. Sp. Imp.

McGee vs Moss Ex'rs & Ben Pope Wm Oldham Sp. B'l for B. Pope, O. Sp. Imp. for all.

Case vs Whittaker, O. Sp. Imp.

Aldridge vs Carr & Al, Abates to Carr J. O. Sp. Imp. for Morrison

McClure vs Martin, O. Sp. Imp.

Donne vs Archer, Sp. Imp.

Seekwright vs Badtitle, Co. Order.

Masterson vs Walls, O. Sp. Imp.

Owens vs Same, Same.

Woods vs. Boone, Al's Cap's.

Same vs Same, Al's Cap's.

Overtons Ex'r vs Moore, Sp'l Imp'l.

Boyd vs Waters, Sp'l Imp'l.

Blaine vs Hartford &c, abates & return, as to Hartford, Isaac Morrison Sp. B'l, for Baird O. Sp. Imp.

Vanmater vs Chenewith, Wm Pope Sp. B'l Jr, Sp. Imp.

Case vs. A'Sturgus Adm'r, C. O.

Colson Ad'r. vs Shannon, O. Sp. Imp.

Rankin vs Gaughney, Dism'd, no app'al.

Wilson vs Rogers (Geo. Slaughter & Bl'd Ballard Sp'l Bail.) & Sp'l Imp'l.

Doherty vs Walls, O. Sp. Imp.

Walls vs Nelson, O. Sp. Imp.

Deifenbach vs Floyd, Will Pope Sp. B'l. O. Sp. Imp.

[Page 31] Harrod & al vs Villetoe, Judg. & Writ of Enqr.

Grundy vs Moss Ex'rs, Sp'l Imp'l.

Shaw vs Swank, Discont'd.

Present, Richard Chinewith, Gent.

Harris vs French, cont'd at pltf. Expense.

Grants Adm'r vs Reid, Jury to try the Issue to wit, Robert Tyler, James Welch, John Bailey, John Ball, Patrick McGee, Dan'l McClure, William Barrett, Joseph Brooks, John McManus, Nillock Colson, Robert George and Edward Trueman, who being sworn, bring in a verdict for pl't., which on acc't of excessive Damages a New Trial's Ordered by Court.

Ordered that Rum, Wine, or good Peach Brandy be rated at 2/3 pr. half pint, for 1 Gallon Corn 1/., for Ordinary keepers or Merchants.

Ordered that a former Order of Court directing James Fr's Moore, Aquilla Whittaker, Wm. Shanon, Dan'l Sullivan, & Squire Boone, to view the nearest & most convenient way, from the Falls of Ohio to Boon's Station & Lee's Town on Kentucky, be set aside & instead thereof that J. F. Moore, Aq. Whittaker, Sq. Boone, Rob. Tyler & Alex. Breckenridge, or any three of them do search out & mark that nearest & most convenient way from the Falls afores'd to the best crossing place on Kentucky, near Lee's Town & report accordingly,

Sam'l Burks Gent, produces a Com'n appointing him a Lieutenant of Militia for Jefferson County, whereupon he takes the several Oaths as prescribed by Law &c.

[Page 32] Presentments of the Grand Jury were made and an Indictm't, C. Wealth vs Jacob Knight, found a true Bill. W. P. Clark, Foreman, And having nothing forther to present were discharged.

Present, Sam'l Culbertson Gent. & Andrew Hynes Gent.

C. Wealth [Commonwealth] vs Skinner. Formality waved, ordered that the presentment be dismissed.

Absent, Isaac Cox, & Geo. Slaughter Gent.

George Rogers Clark Gent. produces a Commission appointing him, the s'd G. R. Clark, principal Surveyor for the Virginia State Line, under the Act for Surveying the Lands given by Law to the officers &c, with a clause in s'd Com'n that he the s'd G. R. Clark give Bond & two suff't Secur's in the penal sum of three thousand pounds, conditiond &c, whereupon after having fully complied with s'd Clause, he took the sever'l Oaths prescribed in such cases by Law &c.

Hintons Adm'r vs Shannon (present, I. Cox Gent.) Jury to try the Issue, agreable to the Order of last Court, Viz. Peter Muhlenburg, Ric'd Anderson, Presly Neville, James Elliot, John Lewis, Jacob Vanmater, John North, Ed'd Trueman, James Welch, Joseph Brooks, Thomas Cunningham, & Robert Green, Who being sworn, bring in a verdict for plaintiff & Judg't &c.

Orderred that Court be adjourned till tomorrow Morning 8 O'Clock.
                                                            Isaac Cox.

[Page 33] At a Court held for Jefferson County, per Adjournment, May 6, 1784.

Present, Isaac Cox, Andrew Hynes, Geo. Slaughter, I. F. Moore, George Wilson, Isaac Morrison, & Sam'l Culberson Gent. Justices.

Ordered that George Yunt be allowed for attending the Distance of 80 miles two several Court Days, in the Suit Hintons

Adm'r vs Shannon, April Court. also that he be allowed one Days Attendance this term & for riding the distance of 80 miles, &c.

O. that John Stapleton be allowed four days Attend'ce in s'd Suit, same Term & one day the present Court & the distance aforesaid.

O. that Ro. Tyler be allowed 4 days attend'ce in s'd suit same Term & 1 day the present term.

Ordered that John Vertrees be appointed Surveyor of the Road from the Salt works crossing Salt River as far as the Lick on Long Lick Creek.

Paul Froman Surveyor of the Road from the Lick on Long Lick Creek to Bardstown.

Wm. Kincheloe Surveyor of the Road from Bardstown up Cartwright's Creek three miles road measure from the mouth.

Richard Parker Surveyor of the Road from three miles road measure up Cartwright's Creek from the mouth to the main Fork of Pleasant Run.

Thomas Cunningham Surveyor of the Road from Pleasant Run to the County Line.

Andrew Hynes Gent. to give a List of the Hands on Green River Waters to work on [Page 34] the Road of which John Vertrees is Surveyor.

Isaac Cox, Samuel Smith, & Isaac Morrison Gent. to allot the hands to work on the Roads of which Paul Froman, Wm. Kincheloe, Rich'd Parker, & Tho's Cunningham are Surveyors.

Ja's. Fr. Moore is security for Costs in the suit McMullin vs Enoch Springer.

Absent, Geo. Wilson Gent.

Administration of the Estate of Garret Pendergrass deceased, is granted unto Geo. Wilson and Margaret his wife, who gave Bond & Security according to Law, in the penalty of £1500 &c.

Ordered that Squire Boone be fined agreable to Law for not attending as a witness in the Suit Hinton Adm'r vs Shanon when he was duly sum'd.

Present, Geo. Wilson Gent.

Elliot vs McDonald Jury to wit, Jacob Vanmater, James A'Sturgus, Sam'l Hubbs, James Welch, Thos. Spencer, John Jackson, Thomas Phelps, John Hawkins, Robert Chaffin, Martin

Carney, & Jacob Barkman, who being sworn bring in a Verdict for plt. & Judg't &c.

Present, Will Oldham Gent.

Kilpatrick vs Handley Cont'd.

Cox vs Newkirk, Judg. Cont'd & W. Enq.

Same vs Prior, Same Order.

Watkins vs Pyeatt, owe nothing C'j.

Logan & al vs A'Sturgus Ádm'r Judg. Con. & W. E.

Lindsays Ad'r vs Chinewith, owe nothing C'j.

Sherlock vs Nelson, Judg't con. & W. Enq.

[Page 35] Decker vs Sullivan, N. Guilty with Leave C'j.

Matson vs Same, &c Same Order

Brooks vs Moss, J. Con. & W. E.

Logan &c vs Lynn's Adm'n owe nothing C'j.

Leach vs Sullivan, Dism'd at plt. Costs.

Sullivan vs Netherland, further Imp.

Culberson vs Rice, N. Guilty with Leave C'j.

Brooks & Uxr vs Purcell, J. C. & W. E.

Brooks . . . vs. same & Uxr, same Order.

Doulin vs Henry, Cont'd.

Pope vs Scott Judg't, Con. & W. E.

Alvay vs Whiledge, N. G. with Leave C'j.

Lynn's Adr. vs Sullivan, N. G. with Leave C'j.

Boush vs. Johnson, C. O.

Cleveland vs Finn, N. G. with Leave C'j.

Craig vs Nelson, Non Assumpsit C'j.

Yates vs Cooke, N. G. with Leave C'j.

Logston vs A'Sturgus &c, Cont'd.

Matthews vs Braiden, Discont'd no App'l.

Pendergrass Adm'r vs Henry, owe nothing.

Sturgus vs Edgcomb, Dism'd, Deft. Costs.

Newland vs Purvis, C. O.

Pope vs McCastline, Judg. Cont'd & W. E.

Lock vs Barkman, Dism'd, with Costs.

McCauley & Uxr vs J. F. Moore, same order.

Elliot vs Hutchenson, C. O.

Floyd vs Newkirk, J. C. & W. E.

Same vs Lock, Same Order.

Same vs Hogland, Same.

[Page 36] Nelson vs Walls, N. G., with Leave C'j.

Knight vs Allan Tharp, J. C. & W. E.

Wilkinson vs Owens, C. O. vs Deft & Sec'r [?].

Walls vs Nelson, Jury to wit, Geo. Ro. Clark, James Elliot, John Harrison, Presley Neville, George Rice, Will'm Barnett, Sealy Rawlings, Benj. Fields, Dennis Springer, Thos. Whitledge, Patrick McGee & Graves Whipshot, who being sworn, bring in a Verdict for plt. & Judg. &c.

Ordered that John Nelson be fined 5/ for profane swearing in open Court.

Hutchinson vs Netherland, Dism'd with Costs.

Sullivan vs Netherland. James Sullivan came into Court and sweareth &c that William Shannon is a material Evidence in his suit vs Netherland, and the said Shannon being to remove from this County on a Dangerous Tour, Ordered that a Dedimus issue to take the Deposition of s'd Shanon.

Wells vs Floyd, Dism'd no Return.

C. Wealth [Commonwealth] vs Bell, N. Guilty C'j.

Nelson vs Walls, Non Suit plt. not appearing.

C. Wealth vs Knight, not guilty whereupon same prisoner being set to Bar, pleads the same Jury as in Walls vs Nelson, who bring in a Verdict, we of the Jury find the Defendant not Guilty. G. R. Clark, foreman.

Ordered that the prisoner be discharged.

[Page 37] George Pomeroy being brought before the Court charged with having been guilty of a Breach of the Act of Assembly entitled "Divulgers of false News" on Examining sundry Witnesses and the s'd Pomeroy heard in his defence, the Court are of opinion that the s'd George Pomeroy is guilty of a Breach of the s'd Act & it is therefore ordered that he be fined 2000 lbs tob'o for the same.

And it is farther ordered that the s'd George Pomeroy give Sec'y for his good behaviour himself in £1000 with two Sec'ys in £500—and pay Costs.

Whereupon the s'd Pomeroy Recognized in £1000 and Thomas Curry & Wm Cummin his Sec's each in £500 for his good behaviour 12 months.

Ordered that John Grymes be allowed 2 days Attendance in the prosecution C. Wealth vs Knight.

Or. that a former Order of Court appointing or binding Hanna Kimble Orphan of Hanna Kimble dec'd be reversed, & that she be bound unto William Cummins agreable to Law. [Marginal notation:] Rec'd.

Cristy Ex'r vs McCarty, on the Motion of plt. Judg't is granted him for the am't of Replevey Bond given by Def't, notice being proven.

On the Motion & Oath of Bland Ballard, Ordered that a Didimus issue to take the Depo' of Th's. McCarty at the Suit of Dodge.

[Page 38] Ordered that Court be adjourned until tomorrow Morning 6 o'Clock.
Isaac Cox.

May 7th 1784. Court met according to Adjournment.

Present, Isaac Cox, Geo. Slaughter, William Oldham, Geo. Wilson, & Isaac Morrison, Gent. Justices.

Ordered that William Saltsman, Orphan of Phil Saltsman, aged 12 years be bound unto Joseph Burnett &c.

Fr's. Adams being appointed Constable by an Order of last Court, takes the Oaths of office &c.

McManus vs Wm. Lynn, Heir at Law of Wm. Lynn deceased. On hearing the cause upon the Bill & Answer of the Heir at Law by Guardian, & hearing the Testimony adduced, It is decreed, that nine hundred Acres of Land part of two Tracts of Land lying on the waters of Goose Creek & Harrod's Creek containing four thousand Acres, which stands entered in the name of James Merriwether, part of which Tract is said to belong to Wm. Lynn's Heir at Law, be conveyed by the Defend't to the s'd John M'Mannes, agreeable to the Contract of Wm. Linn dec'd. & the s'd John M'Mannes, unless the s'd Heir at Law shall within six months after he arrives at lawful age shew cause to the contrary by petitioning for a new Trial or otherwise & obtain a Decree in his Favor.

Standeford vs Hart, continued.

Glenn vs Dozier. Same.

McCarty vs Grundy, abates Deft Death.

[Page 39] Pyeatt vs McCarty, Cont'd for plt.

Wills vs Moss Exrs., Cont'd for pl.

McGee vs Hinkston, Cont'd.

Burros vs Williams, Dism'd for Want pro.

Same vs Harrod, same.

Same & Uxr vs Same, Same.

Glenn vs Williams & al, Dism'd for Want pro.

Grundy vs Donett, Cont'd.

Brooks vs Tobin, same.

Buchanons Admn vs Barbour, Dism'd for Want pro.

Sullivan vs Henry, Cont'd.

Gregory vs Purcell, Dism'd for Want pro.

Same vs Same. Same.

January vs Stephenson, Discont'd.

West vs Bolling Jury to wit, Peter Muhlenburg, George Rogers Clark, Ric'd Anderson, Chas Dabney, Jas Knox, John Lewis, Geo. Walls, John North, Elias Savyham, Nathl Welch, Jacob Vanmatre & Thos Whitledge, who being Sworn, bring in a Verdict for plt. & Judgt &c.

Burros vs Cochran, Dism'd no pro.

Case vs Stephenson. Jury to wit, Alex. Skinner, Benja Roberts, Benja Fields, Thos Spencer, Thos Cunningham, John Rogers, Ralph Matron, Martin Carney, Graves Wipshot, James Sullivan, Jno Sinclear & Jonah Phelps, who being sworn bring in a Verdict for plt and Judgt &c.

Ordered that Abner Field & Fred Parker be fined agreeable to Law for not attending as a Juror in the suit Case vs Stephenson.

[Page 40] Floyd vs Damewood & Uxr, Discont'd.

Brodhead vs Stephenson, Owe nothing jd.

C. W. [Commonwealth] vs Collins, Judgt for 60£, 50 whereof is to be discharged by paymt of 1.15.8

C. W. vs Bell, not guilty C'j.

C. W. vs McGee, Same.

Wells vs Brodhead, Dism'd.

Rowan vs Walls, Judg't £10 & Costs.

Brotsman vs. Knight, J. conf'd & W. E.

Waters vs Stephenson, further Imp.

Young vs Jean Hume, non suit for ws App'l.

Young vs Hume, N. G. with Leave C'j.

Curry vs McAdams, Judgt pr award for 1.12.—&c.

Order by Cr., Costs not to exceed Damages.

Case vs Garvey, C. for Award.

Sinclear vs Vaughan, Same.

Lynn's Admr vs Sullivan, same Jury as in West vs Bolling, who being sworn, bring in a Verdict & Judg't &c.

Dodge vs Ballard. Ordered that the former Order of Reference be reversed, & N. G. with Leave C'j. be the situation of the suit.

Lynn's Adm'r vs Deremeah   Jury to wit, Benja Roberts, Thos Spencer, Thos Cunningham, Ralph Matron, Martin Carney, Joseph Barnett, Abner Fields, Josiah Phelps, Benja Fields, Wm. Banett, John Fookes, & Graves Wisshot, who being sworn, bring in a Verdict for plt. & Judg. &C.

Ordered that Lynn's Adm'r pay Ths McCarty for 16 days attendance in the Suit vs Sullivan.

Also Tho's Curry 19 days, same Suit

Also Edward Tyler 16 days, same Suit.

[Page 41] Ordered that Peter Young pay Ths McCarty for 12 days att'n as a Witness in the Suit vs Hume.

Also to Ths. Curry, 9 days same Suit.

Also Edward Tyler, 8 days same Suit.

Ordered that James Qutermous, Peter Newkirk, Francis Chain, and Jas McCauley, or any three of them, being first sworn do appraise the personal Estate & Slaves if any of Garret Pendergrass decd and Return an Inventory to Court.

Isaac Cox Gent, absent.

Banfields Adr. vs Gregory, Cont'd.

McCarty vs Cox & al. Not guilty Jd. By consent of parties a Jury to try the Issue, to wit, The same as Lynn's Admr vs Deremiah, who being sworn, find for the Defendant.

Ordered that Jn'o Deremiah pay Ths Curry for 7 Days attend'ce as a witness in the Suit Lynn's Adr. vs Deremiah

O. that a Summons issue requiring Jas F. Moore & Ric'd Chinewith, Gent, to shew Cause, why Report has not been made of the State & Situation of the papers & Records of this Court as deb'd [?] to Will Johnston present Clerk, agreable to a former Order of this Court &c.

Satisfactory proof made to the Court that Alex. McMunn is entitled to a preem'n of 1000 Acs. in Jeff'n County including his Imp't on the Waters of Clear Creek, made in the year 1776, sometime in June, to include a Spring & s'd Imp't in the Center of a Square, nearly a N. of East Co'r. from Boone's Station, on the upper Side s'd Clear Creek & that he was in the Service when the Com'n sat to do Business in this Country.

Ordered that the same be certified. N. B. The Spring is remarkable by gushing out of a round hole out of a large flat Rock, being to the Westw'd of a small rising.

Ordered that Court be adjourned untill Court in Course.

Isaac Cox.

[Page 42] At a Court held for Jefferson County on the 16th Day of May, 1784, for the Examination of Charles Morgan and Mathew Jones committed to the Gaol of this County for feloniously stealing four Geese the property of Jacob Minor.

Present, Rich'd Chinewith, J. F. Moore, William Oldham & George Wilson, Gentlemen Justices.

The Prisoners being set to the Bar and it being demanded of them whether they were guilty of the offence wherewith they stand charged or not guilty, they say they are no wise thereof guilty. Whereupon Jacob Minor a Witness was sworn & examined, upon consideration of whose Testimony, it is the opinion of the Court that they are guilty of the s'd Felony & its therefore ordered that each of them recognize in the Sum of £1000, with two Securities each in the Sum of £500 for their Appearance at the next Grand Jury Court, or be recommitted to Gaol until such Security is given.

Jacob Minor recognizes himself in the penalty of £500 &c &c conditioned for his Appearance at the next grand Jury Court to be held for said County, to give in his Testimony against the said prisoners, & thence not to depart without Leave.

Ordered that Court be adjourned.

Rich'd Chenowith.

[Page 43] At a Court held for Jefferson County on the 17th Day of May 1784, for the Examination of John Ox committed to the Gaol of this County, on Suspicion of feloniously taking Sundry Goods, viz, 1 Rifle Gun, powder horn & po., the property of Samuel Dunbar.

Present: Rich'd Chinewith, Jas F. Moore, William Oldham, & Geo. Wilson, Gent. Justices.

The prisoner being set to the Bar and it being demanded of him whether he was guilty of the offence wherewith he stands charged, or not guilty, he says he is in no wise guilty thereof. Whereupon Sam'l Dunbar a Witness was sworn and examined upon Consideration of whose Testimony, it is the opinion of the Court that he is not guilty thereof & he is therefore discharged.

Ordered that Court be adjourned.

Rich'd Chenoweth.

MINUTE BOOK NO. 1, JEFFERSON COUNTY KENTUCKY
APRIL 6, 1784—DECEMBER 7, 1785

Copied for Publication

By Miss Ludie J. Kinkead

In Four Parts

Part Two: July 6—November 4, 1784[1]
*

[Page 44] At a Court held for Jefferson County on the 6th day of July, 1784.

Present: Isaac Cox, Richard Chinewith, William Oldham, & Isaac Morrison, Gents [Marginal note:] Jack Coim, D. C.

William Buckner produces a nomination from Geo. May, Gent, as a Deputy Surveyor and having also produced a Certificate of his Ability to execute this said office, from Examiners appointed, takes the Several Oaths of office &c. [Marginal note:] P'd.

A list of Surveys made in this County from Nov. 6th, 1782, untill June 10th, 1784, was Returnd by the princip'l Surveyor and O. R.

An Inventory of the Estate of Henry Houghland dec'd was returned & O. R. [Marginal note:] Record'd.

---

[1]As stated in the Introduction, no attempt has been made, in preparing this Minute Book for printing, to correct any of the spelling. The penmanship in the original is such that some of the proper names and other words are subject to more than one reading. The following abbreviations, kindly interpreted by Mr. Frank Coyle, are among those that occur frequently:

Al. Ca., Alias Capias	C'j., Corrected judgment	O., Ordered
Att., Attachment	Co., Costs	O. R., Ordered Recorded
Ca. Sa., Capias ad Satis-faciendum	Deft., Defendant	Plt., Plaintiff
	Dis'd, Dismissed	Rec'd., Recorded
C. W., Commonwealth	G., Granted	Sp., Special
Cons'n., Consent	Imp'l., Imparlance	Subp'd, subpoenaed
C. O., Continuation	N. D., Nihil Dicit	Su'y, Surety
Ordered	N. G., Notice Given	W. E., Writ of Enquiry

*The page references found in this transcription refer to pages in the original Minute Book No. 1.

122

A Deed of Conveyance from James M. Corcle to Alex'r Robertson, was proven by the Oaths of William Robertson & Sam'l Givens, &c. and O. R. [Marginal note:] P'd 12/6.

A List of Tithables taken by Isaac Morrison, Gent. Returned & O. R.

James Boyd & John Cowan produce nominat's. from Geo. May, Gent, as Deputy Surveyors, whereupon Wm. Shannon & Jno Handley are appointed to examine into their abilities &c.

A List of Tythables taken by Rich'd Chinewith, Gent, Returned & O. R.

James Boyd & John Cowan having produced Certificate of their Abilities as Dept'y Surveyors from the Examiners, take the several Oaths &c. [Marginal note:] p'd 6/ each.

Robert Daniel enters himself Special Bail for James Hunt adv Wm. Tho's Taylor—Judg't by N. D. & W. E.

Present George Wilson, Gent.

Ordered that a Dedimus issue to take the Depo. of Van Swearengan, in the Suit Young vs Hance & Uxr.

[Page 45] James Mc Cauley, takes the Oath of Allegiance & Fidelity and also the Oath of a Constable.

William Cooke produced a Nomination as a Deputy Surveyor, and having also produced a Certificate of his Abilities, takes the sev'l. Oaths &c.

Wilson vs Swan, Wm. Shannon, Special Bail Cont'd.

Walls vs Knight, Christ'n Kepley, Sp'c Bail. Judg't. Accord'g to specialty by nihil dicit.

Elliot vs. Hutchenson, Jn'o Abbot sp'c Bail, Judgmt. by Nihil dicit & W. Enq'y.

Ordered that Wm. Rowan, Sam'l Wells, Ja's Stephenson and Henry Bowling or any three of them being first sworn do appraise the Estate of Tho's Talbot dec'd and report &c.

O. That, on the motion of Nicholas Meriwether, Ex'r of Geo. Meriwether dec'd, Colo. Wm. Pope, Wm. Johnston, Capt. Wm. Oldham, and James Winn or any three of them, being first sworn do appraise the Estate of said George Meriwether dec'd, and Report accordingly, and also that the said persons do settle the accts. of the s'd Ex'r against the s'd Decedants Estate. [Marginal note:] rec'd.

Present Philip Philips, Gent, and Andrew Hynes, Gent.

Newland vs Fookes. Reubin Case Sp'c Bail, J. by N. D. & W. E.

The Examiners report the Abilities of Wm. Cooke, who thereupon takes the Oaths of Allegiance &c. [Marginal note:] Ch'd to I. Morrison.

O. That Jacob Ashcraft, Philip Phillips, Isaac Lassee and Joseph Kilpatrick or any three of them do view the nearest & most convenient Way from Nolin to the Mouth of the Beech Fork. & Report &c.

Absent, William Oldham, Gent.

Present, James Fr. Moore, Gent.

[Page 46] O. That a Dedimus issue to take the Deposition of Peter Newton, in Behalf of Jn'o Allan Tharp ad'r Jacob Knight.

Ordered that Court be adjourned untill Tomorrow Morning, 7 o'Clock.

Isaac Cox.

Court met according to adjournment July 7th, 1784.

Present: Isaac Cox, Rich'd Chinewith, S. F. Moore & George Wilson, Gent Just's.

A Bargain & Sale of a Negro Wench from Moses Henry to James Sullivan acknowledged & O. R. [Marginal note:] Rec'd.

Also a Bill of Sale from James Sullivan to William Johnston, Sen'r, Acknowledged & O. Record. [Marginal note:] Recor'd.

Present Philip Phillips & Isaac Morrison, Gent.

It appearing to the Court that John Carr is still alive, Administration of whose Estate was granted to Isaac Morrison, Gent, from Sundry Evidence, Ordered That all farther proceedings thereon be enjoined untill a Certainty can be had whether John Carr is alive or not.

A Bill of Sale from John Deckar to Moses Henry Acknowledged and Ordered to Record. [Marginal note:] Recorded.

Present, Andrew Hynes, Gent.

Inventory of the Estate of Adam McClintick dec'd Returned and O. Record. [Marginal note:] Recorded.

Harris vs McCastline. Jonas Scaggin enters himself Special Bail. Judg't by N. Dicit & W. Eq'y.

McMullin vs Springer. George Owens enters himself Sp'l Bail. Same Order.

Claypoole vs Deckar. Isaac Cox, Jas. F. Moore & George Wilson enter Sp'l Bails Same Order.

124

[Page 47] Grants Adm'r vs Reid. Jury to try the Issue to Wit, Philemon Waters, John Waller, Thomas Spencer, James Patten, Joseph Brooks, James McKegg, John Saunders, James Pillars, Joseph Harris, Tho's McMullin, Jesse Evans, & Joseph Burnett, who being sworn bring in a Verdict for the plaintiff, which on acc't of one of the Jurors being on the former Trial, it's ordered by the Court that the Verdict be set aside & a new Trial had.

Jackson vs McGrew, Judg't for 40/ & Costs

Hoak vs Virtress, Geo. Wilson Sp. Bail, Sp. Imp.

Daniel Lindo produces a Commission appointing him an Ensign of the Militia, Whereupon he takes the Oath Of Allegiance &c, & the Oath of office.

Joseph Kilpatrick and John Alvay are appointed Constables for one year.

Johnston vs Sturgus, Judg't for 3.12. & Costs.

Same vs McCarty, Same for 1.16. & Costs.

Brodhead vs Carney, Same 4.10. & Costs. [Marginal note:] Settl'd.

Fookes Ass'evs Wells. Dism'd Deft's Costs.

Walls vs Bryant, Judg't for 3.12. & Costs.

Robert Burge, Andrew Barnes & John Oliver being brought into Court on Suspision & being Chargd with feloniously taking a Chair and Staples of the value Twenty shillings and consenting to wave the priviledge of an examining Court & to submit to the Determination of the present Sitting Members, and it being demanded of them, Whether they were guilty of the offence wherewith they stand charged, or not guilty, they say they are in no Wise guilty thereof. Whereupon upon the examination of Sundry Witnesses who were sworn, upon consideration of whose Testimony, it is the opinion of the Court that the prisoners be dismissed and that they Recognize each of them in the Sum of twenty pounds each with one Security each in the Sum of £10. Whereupon William Hickman, Jr. [Page 48] and Elias Long have Recognized as Securities for Andrew Barnes & John Oliver each in the Sum of £10, for their good Behavior 12 Months, and also Jos. Arnold & Geo. Owens as Securities for Robert Burge each Recognize in the Sum of £10 for their good Behaviour 12 months.

Ordered that Court be adjourned untill tomorrow Morning 6 [?] O'Clock.

Isaac Cox.

Court met according to Adjournment. July 8th, 1784.

Present: Isaac Cox, George Wilson, Philip Philips & Isaac Morrison Gent. Justices, and Andrew Hynes, Gent.

Absent Isaac Cox, Gent.

Ordered that John Rogers be fined 400 lb Tob'o for not attending as a Juror in the Suit, Cox vs Price.

Cox vs Price, Jury to try the Issue to wit, Joseph Bozer, Cain Withers, James McKey, Jas. Pillars, Andrew Reid, Nottley Dival, John Alvay, Van Swarengan, John Tibbs, Ralph Matson, John Crowe & John Cotlett, who being Sworn, bring in a Verdict for Pl't & Judg't &c. [Marginal note:] Fifa. ch'd.

Ordered that a Dedimus issue to take the Deposition of Joseph Bozier in Behalf of Reid adm'r. Grants Adm'r. [Marginal note:] Pd.

Brodhead vs Patten, Judg't for £3 & Costs.

Walls vs Knight, Cain Withers and Jas Pillars enter Special Bail for s'd Knight J. by N. D. & W. En'y. [Marginal note:] Wrong.

Ordered, that William Allan, Wm Owens, John Grundy and Graves Wepshot or any three of them being first sworn do appraise one Horse, the property of James Holmes decd, & make Report &c.

[Page 49] A list of Tythes taken by Sam'l Smyth, Gent. Ret'd & O. R.

Also a list taken by Andrew Hynes, Gent. Ret'd & O. R.

Ordered that all Costs which are legally due, and proven be allowed for Witnesses Attendance in the Suit, Lynn's Adm'r vs. Sullivan.

Ordered that Court be adjourned untill Court in Course.

Isaac Cox.

At a Court held for Jefferson County on the 3rd Day of August 1784.

Present: James F. Moore, William Oldham, George Wilson & Isaac Morrison, Gent. Jus's.

An Inventory of the Estate of Zephaniah Blackford deceased was Returned & O. R. [Marginal note:] Reco'd.

A Power of Attorney from Michael Dennis to James Morrison acknowledged in open Court & O. R. [Marginal note:] P'd. Reco'd.

A Power of Atto. from Moses Henry to John Campbell proven fully by the Oath of W. Johnston one of the subscribing Witnesses and O. R. [Marginal note:] Reco'd. P'd.

Ordered that Court be adjourned untill Court in Course.

J. F. Moore.

[Page 50] At a Court held for Jefferson County on the 5th Day of October 1784.

Present: Isaac Cox, Rich'd Chinewith, George Wilson & Sam'l Culbertson, Gent.

Administration of the Estate of Jacob French deceased is granted Rebecca French and John Paul who gave Bond & Security agreable to Law. [Marginal note:] Pd. Reco'd.

A Deed of Conveyance from Jacob Pyeatt to Philip Trant, proven and adm'd to Record. [Marginal note:] Pd. Reco'd.

Ordered that Jacob Vanmater, Jn'o Vertreess, John Handley and Stephen Rawlings or any three being first sworn do appraise the Estate of Jacob French dec'd & make Return, &c.

Inventory of Th's Talbots Estate Ret'd & O. R. [Marginal note:] Recorded.

Ordered that Court be adjourned untill Tomorrow Morning 8 O'Clock.

Isaac Cox.

Court met according to Adjournment Oct. 6th.

Present: Isaac Cox, William Oldham, George Wilson & Sam'l Culbertson, Gent.

A Bond from John Montgomery & Martin Carney to Lawrence Protzman & Co. proven by the Oath of James Patten fully & O. R. [Marginal note:] Rec'd. Pd.

[Page 51] O. That a Dedimus issue to take the Deposition of Eliza Hacker in behalf of David Glenn vs. Mayes & all. [Marginal note:] Pd.

An Assignment for Lot No. 23 old No in the Town of Louisville from Levi Theel to W. Johnston fully proven by the Oath of Sam'l Wells, and O. R. [Marginal note:] Recor'd.

Matthews vs Pritchett dismissed. [Marginal note:] Pd.

Barbour vs Colman, Same. [Marginal note:] Pd.

James McGill and John Carr enter themselves Sp. Bail in Behalf of Mathew Mayes adr. Cameron. O. & Sp. Imp.

Sinclear vs Wells, dism'd Defts Costs.

Philemon Waters enters himself Sp. Bail in behalf of John McGee ad'r John Haggin O. & Sp. Imp.

Ordered That John Handley & David Standeford examine into the Abilities of Abraham Nelson, who produces a Nomination as a Deputy Surveyor and report &c.

Barbour vs Moon, dism'd defts Costs. [Marginal note:] Pd. 6/3.

Brodhead vs Estis, Att.

Wilson vs Pollock, Jdg't for 4.5.10 & Costs. [Marginal note:] Ca Sa.

Fitzgerald vs A'Sturgus &c, same for £3, same.

Spencer vs Curry, Cont'd.

McCarty vs McKey, Dism'd.

Cox vs Stevens, Dism'd, agreed.

Hoak vs Hart, Jdg't, 4.19.6. & Costs.

Same vs Teavenger, Dism'd.

And. McCune vs Rowan, Cont'd.

Gudgell vs. Withers, Jdg't for 1.11.6, & Cost.

Wells vs McCarty. Same for 4.15, & Cost. [Marginal note:] Ca Sa.

Sinclear vs Floyd, Cont'd.

Same vs Alvoy, Jdg't 1.10. & Costs.

[Page 52] The Examiners report the Fitness of Abraham Nelson, Who thereupon takes the Several Oaths &c.

Brodhead vs McCarty, Jdg't 2.15. & Costs.

Same vs. Sanders, Same for 3.1.10, & Co.

Same vs Sherlock, Same 1.13.6, & Co.

Same vs Deifenbach, Same 2.8., & Co.

Barbour vs Jones, Cont'd.

Same vs Pritchett, Judg't, 3.5.4, & Co.

Same vs Chinwith, Same, 3.17.9, & Co. [Marginal note:] Ca Sa.

Same vs Oliver, Same 4.19. & Co. [Marginal note:] Ca Sa.

O. That the former Examiners enquire into the abilities of James Nourse & James Breckinridge as Deputy Surveyors and report accordingly. [Marginal note:] Ch'd.

James Nourse and James Breckenridge being returned qualified as Deputy Surveyors take the Several Oaths prescribed by Law &c. [Marginal note:] Ch'd.

Brodhead vs Pritchett, Dism'd, deft. Co. [Marginal note:]Pd.

McFarline vs Luns, Dism'd.

Pillars vs Hughes, Cont'd.

Gregory vs A'Sturgus, Jdg't. 2.5. & Co.

Inks vs Lock, Cont'd.

Abbit vs Knight, Dism'd.

Same vs Sullivan, Same.

Same vs Hagland, Same.

Damewood vs Floyd, Same.

Same vs Theel, Same.

Haggin vs Phelps, Same.

Kuykendall's Exr vs Williams, Jdgt. 2.7. & Co.

Same vs Day, Same, 2.2.6. & Co.

[Page 53] Damewood vs Theel, dism'd.

Colman vs Tuel, Jdg't. 1.4.6. & Co.

Young vs Purcell, Same 1.12. & Co.

A Bond from Bartlett Searcey & G. R. Clark to Lawrence Protzman & Co. fully proven and O. R. (Oath, R'd Brashear.) [Marginal note:] Rec'd. Pd.

Knight vs Kepley, Cont'd.

A Bond from V. T. Dalton and W. Clark to Lawrence Protzman & Co. proven fully by the Oath of John Sanders, & O. R. [Marginal note:] Rec'd. Pd.

A Bond from John Tebbs & others to Lawrence Protzman & Co. fully proven by the Oath of John Dorsett & O. R. [Marginal note:] Rec'd. Pd.

Knight vs Floyd, Cont'd.

Same vs Pittman, Same.

Same vs Chinewith, same.

Blackfords Exr. vs Clark, Jdgt. for £3, & Co.

Same vs Same,—Same, Same.

Seekwright vs Badtitle in Ejectm't Jury to try the Issue to wit, John Vertress, John Handley, Thomas Purcell, David Standeford, Sam'l Wells, Benja Johnson, John Philby, Stephen Rawlings, George Leach, John Bailey, James McE'Hatton, & Philemon Waters, who being sworn bring in a Verdict for Defendant.

Welch vs Theel, jdg't by Cons'n for 3.18. & Co. [Marginal note:] Settled.

On the Motion of Jemima Pelton, Administration of the Estate of Benjamin Pelton deceased is granted her, who thereupon gave Bond and Security, &c. [Marginal note:] Rec'd.

Ordered that Sam'l Pottinger, Sam'l McAdams, Mesheck Carter and James Cook, or any three of them being first sworn, do appraise the Estate of s'd Decedant and make Return, &c.

[Page 54] Applegate vs Ford, Cont'd.

Same vs Shannon, Jdgt. 30/ & Co.

Same vs Same,—Same.

Same vs Same,—Same.

Campbell vs Rowan, Cont'd.

Hoak vs Dodge, dism'd. [Marginal note:] Pd.

Ordered that Court be adjourned untill Tomorrow Morning 8 O'Clock.   Isaac Cox.

October 7th, 1784. Court met according to Adjournment. Present the same Members as Yesterday.

A Deed from John Leverns to Stephen Rawlings acknowledged and O. R. [Marginal note:] Recorded.

Also from said Leverns to Edward Rawlings, Same Order. [Marginal note:] Recorded.

Also from said Leverns to Jacob Vanmatre, Same Order. [Marginal note:] Recorded.

Grants Adm't vs Reid, Referred to Wm Kincheloe, Jesse Davis, James Rogers, Philip Philips and John Vertrees, when award shall be the Judgm't of the Court.

Aldridge vs Carr, dism'd plt. Costs.

Donne vs Archer, Same.

A Bond from Philemon Waters to Gab Johnston, acknowlledged and O. R. [Marginal note:] Pd. Recorded.

A Mortgage from Daniel Sullivan to James T. Moore & others, fully proven by the oaths of Alex'r Skinner and And. Heth, and O. R. [Marginal note:] Recorded.

[Page 55] A Deed of Conveyance from the Trustees of the Town of Louisville to James McCauley for Lot No. 57, acknowledged & O. R. (Same to Mark Thomas, Square No. 7., Same): [Marginal note:] Rec'd.

do. Same to John Conway, No. 13. Same.

do. Same to James Patton, No. 133. Same.

do. Same to Jacob Myers, O. No. 63, New No. 79. Same.

do. Same to Ro. Johnston's Heirs, No. 124. Same.

do. Same to Jane Grant, No. 136. Same.

do. Same to Jacob Myers, No. 2. Same.

do. Same to Jos. Roberts, O. No. 76, New 60. Same.

do. Same to Joseph Brooks, No. 128. Same.

do. Same to Th's McGee's Heir, No. 46, New 34. Same.

do. Same to Jos. Irwin's Heirs, No. 139. Same.

do. Same to Patrick Shone, No. 68. Same.

do. Same to John Rayburn, No. 137. Same.

do. Same to Same Heir &c, No. 138. Same.

George Rice is appointed Guardian to Elizabeth and Jane Boyd, Orphans of John Boyd deceased, Whereupon he gave Bond in the Sum of £1000, conditioned for his faithful Discharge of said office, with James Sullivan and John Philly his Securities. [Marginal note:] Rec'd.

Glenn vs Dozier, dism'd, Def't Costs.

Appraisement of the Estate of George Meriwether deceased, Returned & O. R. [Marginal note:] Rec'd.

Ordered, That Ed Tyler be allowed 4 days attendance in the Suit Lynn's Adm'r vs Dermiah.

Return being made of a Settlement of the Exr's [—] vs the Estate of George Meriwether deceased, agreable to a former Order of Court for that purpose, the same was allowed and O. R., also O. that a Receipt be given the said Ex'r for the same.

[Page 56] Kellar vs Leach, Dism'd. Def't Costs.

The Court are of Opinion, that all the Witnesses attendance which are proven in the Suit Lynns Adm's. vs. Sullivan, are legal, and that the same be taxed.

Ordered that Nic'o Meriwether, John Bailey, John Sinclear and John Dorrett or any three of them being first sworn, do appraise the Estate of Hanna Kimble dec'd & make Return &c. [Marginal note:] Ch'd.

Pittman vs Prior, Jdj't. £3/15 & Costs. [Marginal note:] Ca Sa.

Owens vs Thomas, Same 2.8., same.

Damewood vs Sherlock, Cont'd.

Hardy Hill vs Chinwith, Jdj't. £3.9.9¾. [Marginal note:] Ca Sa.

Pittman vs Burks, Same £4. & Co.

Jordan As'e vs. Floyd, Same 2.1.1.

Welch vs Slaughter, Cont'd.

A'Sturgus vs Owens, abates by Return.

Dixon vs Joynes, dism'd. p'tt, Co.

Springer vs. Bailey, Cont'd.

Hickman vs Dolman, Cont'd for return.

Pope vs Murphey. Jdg't, 4.13.6. [Marginal note:] Settled. Pd.

Wilson Ex'r vs Pyeatt, Same 1.7.6. & Co.

Lewis vs Nelson, Jdgt. 2.14. & Co. [Marginal note:] Ca Sa.

Moses Kuykendall produces a Commission appointg him a Capt. of the Militia, who thereupon takes the several Oaths &c.

Sam'l Prior, also as a Lieut, who takes the sev'l Oaths &c.

Commonwealth vs Fookes &c. Jdg't Confess'd, former Order. [Marginal note:] Ca Sa.

Holts Adm'x vs Boone, Same 4£, [?] & Co. [Marginal note:] Ca Sa.

Grundy vs Dorrett, Dism'd.

Present, Ric'd Chinwith, Gent.

[Page 57] Issues:

Treeman vs Sanders, Dismissed.

Harrod &c vs Vittitoe, Cont'd.

Harris vs French, abates Def'ts. Death.

Kilpatrick vs Handley, Cont'd.

Cox vs Newkirk, Dism'd, Def't Co.

Sutherland vs McCasland, Cont'd.

Case vs Johnson, Same.

Moss Ex'rs vs. Stevenson, Same.

Watkins vs Pyeatt, Same.

Logan &c vs Ashley &c., Cont'd.

Patterson vs Chinwith, Same.

Sherlock vs Nelson, Same.

Deckar vs Sullivan, Same.

Matson vs Same, Same.

Brooks vs Moss, Same.

Logan &c vs Lynn's Adm'r. Same.

Culberson vs Rice, Same.

Brooks vs Purcell, Same.

Same & Uxr vs Same, Same.

Pope vs Scott, Same.

Alvay vs Whitledge, Same.

Lynn's Adm'r vs Sullivan, Same.

Cleveland vs Finn, Same.

Craig vs Nelson, Same.

Yates vs Cooke, Same.

Pendergrass Adm'r vs Henry, Same.

Pope vs McCastline, Same.

Floyd vs Newkirk, Same.

Same vs Lock, Same.

[Page 58] Floyd vs Houghland, Continued.

Nelson vs Walls, Same.

Knight vs Allan Tharp, Same.

C. Wealth vs Bell, Same.

132

Dodge vs Ballard, Same.
McGee vs Hinckston, Same.
Brodhead vs Stevenson, Same.
C. Wealth vs Bell, Same.
Same vs McGee, Same.
Brotzman vs Knight, Same.
Young vs Hume, Same.
Banfields Adm'r vs Gregory, Same.
Wells vs Moss Ex'rs, Same.
Pyeatt vs McCarty, Same.
Standeford vs Hart, Same.
Taylor vs Hunt, Same.

Elliott vs Hutchinson, &c. Jury to try the Issue to wit, Bland Ballard, Ric'd Brashear, Moses Kuykendall, Graves Wipshot, John Philby, Geo. Leach, Lancelot Jenkins, John Sanders, Willm Rowan, Peter Lovell, John Hall & Joshua Archer, who being sworn, bring in a Verdict for Pl't & Jdgt.

Ordered That Thomas Purcell recognize himself in the Sum of 20£ with two securities in 10£ each, for his good Behaviour towards Samuel Culberson, Gent. & family, 12 Months, Whereupon he together with Daniel Sullivan and Alex'r Breckenridge recognized Purcell in £20 and each Su'y in £10 each, for his good Behaviour 12 Months, &c. [Marginal note:] Ch'd.

[Page 59] Newland vs Fookes, Continued.
Harris vs McCastline, Same.
McMullin vs Springer, Same.
Claypoole vs Deckar, Same.
References:
Calhoon vs Hoglan's Adm'r Jdg't 3.4.8. & Costs.
King vs Donne, Jdg't Con. & W. Enq'y.
Harris vs Shields, Cont'd.
Sullivan vs Rogers, Same.
Archer vs Pope, Dism'd.
A'Sturgus vs Hoglan's Adm'r, Same.
Cliffton vs Parker, C. O.
Tobin vs Nelson, abates p't Death.

Rowan vs Edgecomb. Jury to try the Issue to wit, Same as in the Elliot vs Hutchinson, except Josiah Phelps, who being sworn, bring in a Verdict for the pl't, 6.10.6. Judg't Accordingly.

Harrod vs A'Sturgus, Jdg't C. & W. E.

Seekwright vs Badtitle, on the Motion of the plaintiff An Appeal is granted her to the 8th Day of the next Supreme Court for the District of Kentucky, Who thereupon gave Bond and Security according to Law.

Tyler vs Culberson, N. G. with Leave J'd.

Kirkham vs McCarty &c, Same.

McGee vs Moss Ex'rs, Same.

Carr vs Whittaker, Same.

McClure vs Martin, N. G. with Leave J'd.

[Page 60] Masterson vs Walls, N. G. with Leave J'd.

Owens vs Walls, Same.

Overtons Ex'r vs Moon, Cont'd.

Boyd vs Waters, Same.

Blaine vs Hartford &c, Same.

Vanmater vs Chinwith, Same.

Carr vs Sturgus Adm'r, I. C. & W. E.

Colson's Adm'r vs Shannon, Cont'd.

Wilson vs Rogers, Same.

Doherty vs Walls, Same.

Walls vs Nelson, Same.

Diefenbach vs Floyd, Same.

Grundy vs Moss Ex'rs. Same.

Sullivan vs Netherland, Same.

Doling vs Henry, Same.

Boush vs Johnson, I. C. & W. E.

Logston vs A. Sturgus, C. O.

Newland vs Purvis, I. C. & W. E.

Wilkinson vs Owens, Same.

Brooks vs Tobin, Cont'd. (at issue).

Sullivan vs Henry, Same.

Waters vs Stevenson. Same Jury as in Rowan vs Edgecomb, except Jas Nourse insted of Jno Phelby, who being sworn, bring in a Verdict for pl't 16£ Jdg't & Co. [Marginal note:] Ca Sa.

Case vs Ganary, Cont'd for Award.

Sinclear vs Vaughan, Same.

Nelson vs Pyeatt, Cont'd.

Wilson vs Swan, Cont'd.

Tyler vs Conger, Same.

Hook vs Vertress, Same.

[Page 61] An Obligation from William Aldridge to Dan Sullivan acknowledged and O. R. [Marginal note:] Recorded.

On the Motion of Joseph Fliming, Ordered that his Mark, Viz the left Ear cropped & an under Bit out of the right Ear be Recorded. [Marginal note:] Pd. Recorded.

Dan'l Sullivan enters himself Sp. Bail for James Pillars advs Barkman. O. & Sp. Imp'l. [Marginal note:] Recorded.

An Assignment from John Carr to Dan Sullivan & Sullivan's Agreem't thereunder written, acknowledged and O. R.

Appearances: Casebear vs Hayes, Cont'd.

Ordered that Court be adjourned untill Tomorrow Morning 8 o'clock.

Isaac Cox.

Court met according to Adjournment October 8, 1784.

Present: Isaac Cox, Rich'd Chinwith, William Oldham & Geo. Wilson, Gent.

Appear'd:

Woods vs Boone, C. O.

Same vs Same, C. O.

Harris vs Mathews, C. O.

Jones vs Sinclear, John Bailey Sp. Bail O., & Sp. Imp'l.

Fitzgerald vs Edgecomb, C. O.

Same vs Sturgus &c, Same.

Hughes vs Stevens, Same vs Df't & Su'y.

Griffin vs Collett, C. O.

Stevens vs Thomas, C. O.

Lindsay's Adm'r vs Carr's Adm'r C. O.

[Page 62] Junkins vs Sullivan, Cont'd.

Young vs Hume, C. O.

Smith vs Richards, dism'd, deft Costs.

Same vs Bailey, Same.

Yokem vs O'Bannon, same pl't Co.

Freeman vs Floyd, C. O.

Peague vs Walls, W. Johnston sp bail O. & Sp. Imp'l.

Sullivan vs Williams &c, Att'a.

Same vs A'Sturgus, C. O.

Same vs Jas Sturgus, Same.

Walls vs Floyd, Wm Pope Sp. B'l, O. & Sp. Imp'l.

Thomas vs Stevens, Same.   Same.

Walls vs Phelps, Josiah Phelps Sp. b'l, O. & Sp. Im.
Phelps vs Hoak, Judgm't. [Marginal note:] Ca Sa.
Lynn vs Pope, Continued.
Culberson vs Same, Same.
McElwee vs Thomas, Same.
Dawson vs Grymes, Dism'd pl't Costs.
Grymes vs Owens, Same.
Samuels vs Calhoon, C. O. vs Deft & Sp. bail.
Same vs Same, Same.
Dye vs McCarty, C. O.
Winn vs Fin'ey, C. O.
Deckarts vs Whittaker, C. O.
Lindsay's Ex'r vs Sullivan, Same.
Dunlap vs Braiden, Cont'd.
Culberson vs Pees, C. O.
Elliot vs White, Dism'd.
Richards vs Wickesham, C. O.
Campbell vs Richards, Dism'd.
[Page 63] Burk vs Ewing &c, dism'd pl't Costs.
Aldridges vs Stevenson, C. O. vs Deft & Su'y.
Vaughan vs Johnston, dism'd pl't Co.
Johnston vs Vaughan &c, C. O.
Moore vs Pope, Dan'l Sullivan Sp. b'l, O. & Sp. Imp'l.
Dodge vs Damewood, Dism'd pl't C.
McMullin vs Carr, Continued.
Young vs Culberson, Same.
Daniel vs Boin, Same.
Trueman vs Hopkins, dism'd.
Enlows vs Cox, C. O.
Hamilton vs Allan Tharp, C. O.
Wible vs Williams, Att'a.
Same vs Same &c, C. O.
Hammond vs Abbot, Cont'd.
Haggin ap'r vs McGee &c Jno Grundy Sp B. O. & Sp. Imp.
Same vs Phelps, Jno Grundy Sp. b'l. O. & Sp. Imp.
Same vs Same, Same, Same.
Collier vs Chinewith, Bland Ballard Sp. b'l. O. Sp. Imp.
McBride vs Thomas, Dism'd, no Appear'ce.
Shute vs Hunter, Cont'd.
Clear Ap'r vs McCarty, C. O.

Shrayder vs Same, Same.
French vs Hoak, dism'd pl. Costs.
Waller vs Phelps, Same.
Sandurs vs Floyd, dism'd pl. Costs.
Burks vs Grundy's Exrs, dism'd, No App'ce.
Moore vs McElhose, Attu
Curry vs Taylor, W. Pope Sp. b'l, O. & Sp. Imp.
[Page 64] Horton vs Gregory, Cont'd for Return.
Meriwether vs Davis &c, C. O.
Hutchinson vs Mason, C. O.
Mason vs Hutchinson, C. O.
Hubbs vs Knight, C. O. vs Deft & Su'y.
Rohrer vs Same, Dism'd, pl. Costs.
Mahel vs Yoder, C. O. vs Deft & Su'y.
Yoder vs Mahel, Same.
Brodhead vs Froman dism'd.
Harrison Ap'r vs Pope, Continued.
Oliver vs Rice, Dism'd.
Turner vs Brookes, W. Pope Sp. b'l, O. & Sp. Imp.
Rowan vs. Campbell, C. O.
Carnahan &c vs Sullivan, dism'd, no App'r.
Shannon vs Same, dism'd, no app'ce.
Sanders vs Floyd, C. O.
Same vs Chinewith, M. Thomas Sp. b'l, O. Sp. Imp.
Davis vs Starks, C. O.
Standeford vs Imlay, Dism'd, nonsuit, no Delat'r.
Sturgus vs Sherlock, C. O. vs Deft & Su'y.
Brodhead vs Tebbs, C. O.
Same vs Owens, Same & Su'y.
Watson &c vs Lesley, Same.
Same vs Same, Same.
White vs Gills, Dism'd.
Kellar vs McKee, Same.
Jno Tebbs vs Dan'l Brodhead. Dism'd, no App'er.
Pittman vs Knight, C. O.
[Page 65] Brodhead vs Brashears, C. O. vs Deft & Su'y.
Same vs Pittman, Same vs Deft & Wife.
Same vs Goodin, Same vs Deft & Wife.
Same vs Cummins, Jdg't by Cons. acc'o to Specialty.
Same vs Peague, C. O. vs Deft & Su'y.

Heth vs Myers &c, C. O.
Findley vs Coldwater, Dism'd, No App'er.
Brodhead vs Thomas, Jdg't by Cons. acc'o to Specialty.
Madison vs Slaughter, Cont'd.
Brooks vs McEl'Hatton, C. O. vs Deft & wife.
McMullin vs Dogan, dism'd.
Grundy's Exrs. vs Montgomery, Scire facias.
Doherty vs Morris, abates by Return.
Hammond vs Medlin, C. O.
Pomroy vs Tebbs, C. O.
Sterrett Vs. Mayer, A. C.
Protzman &c vs Nelson, Dism'd.
Nicholson vs Hogg, C. O.
Slaughter vs French, Dism'd, pl Costs.
Thomas vs Bradley, Dism'd, Same.
Culberson vs Purcell, Continued.
Walls vs Oliver, Jdg't acc'o to Specialty.
Wilson vs Nichodemus, dism'd, pl Costs.
Sheridan vs Springer, dism'd, no App'er.
Ballard vs Slaughter, A. C.
Freeman vs Johnson, C. O. vs Deft. Su'y.
Goodin vs Triplett, A. C.
Leach vs Sullivan, C. O. vs Deft & W'f.
Thomas vs DuBois, Dism'd.
Cunningham vs Parker, Jno Grundy, Sp. Bail O. & Sp Imp.
[Page 66] Glenn vs Same, Same.
Sutherland vs Severns, Dism'd, P. Cost.
Campbell vs Chinewith, Cont'd.
Kindall vs Robertsons, Cont'd for Return.
Morgan vs Kimble's Adm'r, Dism'd.
Thomas vs Rucker, C. O. vs Deft. & Su'y.
Mathews vs Rowan, Cont'd for Return.
Parks vs Lowden, Same.
Craig vs Baird, A. C.
Woods vs Boone, Cont'd, for Return.
Frier vs Montgomery, W. Pope Sp. b'l O. & Sp Imp.
Higgins As'n. vs McGee, O. & Sp. Imp.
Hunter vs Briggs, Cont'd for Return.
Jordan vs Blackford, A. C.
Smith vs McMullin, A. C.

Ordered that the Sheriff do summon twenty four of the most able freeholders in his bailwick to appear before our Justices &c on the first Tuesday in November next, to be sworn a Grand Jury &c agreable to Law.

Ordered that on Acc't of the Death of the States Att'o the pleas of the Common Wealth be continued.

Ordered that the C erk do transmit a Letter to Christ'o Greenup Esq. requesting his Att'ce at the next Court to assist the Court in the County Business.

Ordered that Court be adjourned untill Court in Course.

Isaac Cox.

[Page 67] At a Court held for Jefferson County the 2d November 1784.

Present: Isaac Cox, Richard Chinewith, Andrew Hynes, William Oldham, George Wilson, Isaac Morrison, & Sam'l Culberson, Gent. Justices.

Tyler vs Culberson, dism'd, pl Costs.

Shannon vs Sullivan, Same.

Mathews vs Rowan, Same def Costs.

Sullivan Asse. vs Norward Francis & Lawrence Rulipson, Sp. bail O. & Sp Imp.

Simbroh vs Divon, Tho's Spencer Sp b'l, O. & Sp. Imp.

Sullivan vs Owing, J. F. Moore. Sp. b'l O. & Sp. Imp.

Inventory of the Estate of James Holmes decd Ret'd & O. R. [Marginal note:] Rec'd.

Brodhead vs Brachears, W. Pope Sp. b'l, O. Cont. & W. Enq.

Present Samuel Smyth, Gent.

Shannon vs Sullivan, J. F. Moore Sp b'l, O. & Sp Imp.

Same vs Same, Same.

Hickman vs Doleman, abates by Return.

Welch vs Slaughter, Al. Ca.

Johnston vs Spears, Dism'd. Deft Costs. [Marginal note:] Pd.

Patterson vs Culberson, Dism'd, pl Costs.

Wells vs Spritzman, Al. Ca.

Dorrett vs Nash, Same.

Price vs Browmfield, Same.

Craig vs Baird, dism'd by Return.

Ballard vs Slaughter, Plus. Cap.

139

[Page 68] License is granted Nickolas Meriwether to keep a Tavern at his House at the Falls of the Ohio Who gave Bond & Security etc.

John Wible vs Williams, dism'd pl. Costs.

Sullivan vs Same, Same.

Goodin vs Triplett, Same.

Wm. Shannon, Foreman, & David Standiford, Charles Polk, Jacob Deckar, Wm. Piles, Henry Floyd, Shadrach Carter, Marsham Brashears, Frs Simbril, Jacob Coleman, John Potts, Jno Fookes, Peter Coleman, Andrew Vaughan, Reubin Carr, and Wm Keith were sworn a Grand Jury of the Body of this County, and having rec'd their Charge withdrew and after some Time Returned and presented.

Ordered that on the Motion of W. Johnston Judgm't be granted him vs Jacob Leman & W. Pope & Su'y for the Am't of their duly Bond & Costs.

vs Edward Tyler, Same £3.2.9. [Marginal note:] Ca Sa.

vs Henry McQuaid & Sq Boone, Same £1.6.8. [Marginal note:] Pd.

vs Isaac Pritchett & Ed Tyler, Same £1.7.2. [Marginal note:] Ca Sa.

✓ vs Isaac Finly & Su'y Jno Dorrett, Same £6.15.4. [Marginal note:] Ca Sa.

vs Jno Stoner & Su'y Jas. Patun [Paten], Same £1.12.3. [Marginal note:] Pd.

Administration of the Estate of Niblock Colson dec'd is granted his Relict Sarah Colson, who gave Bond & Security according to Law etc. [Marginal note:] Recor'd.

Ordered that Court be adjourned untill Tomorrow Morning, 8 o'clock.   Isaac Cox.

[Page 69] Court met according to Adjournment Novr. 3d 1784.

Present: Isaac Cox, Andrew Hynes, William Oldham, George Wilson, Isaac Morrison, Philip Phillips, & Sam'l Culberson, Gent. Justices,

Wm May, Gent, having produced a Commission as principal Surveyor of Jefferson County, enters into Bond with Security agreable to Order of the Governor for that purpose, & takes the several Oaths of Office.

140

Cliffton vs Parker, Jno Grundy Sp b'l I. Cont. & W. Enq.

Johnston vs Brashears, W. Pope Sp b'l O. & Sp Imp.

Kellar vs Simbrel, Ed Trueman Sp b'l O. & Sp Imp.

Hunter vs Briggs, Same, Same.

Absent, Isaac Cox, Andrew Hynes, Wm. Oldham, Gent.

Isaac Cox, Andrew Hynes, Wm. Oldham, & Jno Handley produced nominations from W. May, Gent, Surveyor of Jefferson, take the several Oaths &c.

The last will and Testament of Andrew Vaughan [Jr.] dec'd proven by the Oaths of Isaac Cox & W. May, two of the Subscribing Witnesses, & O. R. [Marginal note:] Rec'd.

Ordered that Rice Meridith, an Infant 6 years old, Orphan of Widow Meridith be bound unto Willm Oldham, &c. [Marginal note:] Rec'd.

The Last Will and Testament of Peter Paul dec'd proved by the Oath of John Paul, one of the Subscribing Witnesses. [Marginal note:] Rec'd.

Administration of the Estate of Peter Paul dec'd granted his Relict Eunice who gave Bond and Security according to Law, etc. [Marginal note:] Rec'd.

Present, Isaac Cox and Hynes, Wm. Oldham & Sam'l Smyth, Gent.

[Page 70] Saml Bell, John Helm, David Standiford, Rich'd Woolfolk, & John Ray, having produced nominations from Wm. May, Gent, Surveyor of Jefferson takes the several oaths, etc. [Marginal note:] Pd.

Moore vs McElhon, Shadrach Carter, Sp. bl O & Sp. Imp.

Peter Catlett produces a nomination as D'y Surveyor from W. May, Gent, & takes the several oaths, etc.

Thomas Whitledge also produces etc. as above. [Marginal note:] Pd.

George Wilson, Gent. Same as above.

Ordered that Isaac Dye, John Davis, Atkinson Hill & James Crookes or any three of them being sworn do appraise the Estate of Peter paul decd. etc. [Marginal note:] Pd.

Sullivan vs Welch, dism'd Deft. Costs.

Lovel vs Phelps, Dism'd p'l. Costs. [Marginal note:] Pd.

Campbell vs Rowan, Refered to Sam'l Oldham, Jacob Vanmater & Richard parker.

Rowan vs Campbell, Same.

James Breckenridge, Alex Brekenridge & W. Pope having produced nominations as D'y Sur'rs take the Several Oaths, etc.

A Deed of Conveyance from the T. T. [Town Trustees] Louisville to Daniel Sullivan, for Lot No. 54 and Sullivan Assignm't thereon to Jacob Regar acknowld, & O. R. [Marginal note:] Rec'd.

Also from Jacob French to Jacob Regar, same Order.

Kirkpatrick vs Handley, referred to Joseph Barnett, Stephen Rawlings, & Isaac Morrison. [Marginal note:] Rec'd.

Merriwether vs Finley, W. Pope, Ignatius Brashear, Marsham Brashears, Jno Helm, Peter Catlett, Peter Cummins, and James Pillars, Sp. bail, Jdg't Cont. & W. Enq.

[Page 71] Absent, Sam'l Smyth, Gent. & Isaac Morrison, Gent., & Philip Phillips.

James F. Moore, Isaac Morrison, Samuel Smyth, Wm Breckenridge & Philip Phillips, having produced nominations from W. May, Gent, take the several Oaths etc.

Present, Sam'l Smyth, Isaac Morrison & P. Philips, Gent.

Meriwether vs Finley, the s'd plt. came into Court & protested against Bail being admitted for the Def'ts in said Suit, because the same is illegal.

Grants Adm'x vs Reid, the arbitrators having Returned their Award, Ordered the same be continued.

Backman vs Pillars, dism'd def Costs. [Marginal note:] Colo' Moore to pay.

Abraham Nelson produces a Nomination as D'y Sur. from W. May, Gent, & takes the several Oaths &c.

Maehl vs Yoder. James Pillars & Geo. Owens, Sp. bail, O. & Sp Imp.

Ordered that the following Arrangements be made in the Survey on of the Road from Long Lick Creek to the County Line, Viz.—Paul Froman Surveyor from Long Lick on Long Lick Creek to the parting of the Roads from the Salt Works, to Fromans and Rodgers. Wm. Kincheloe from thence to the Beech fork. Richard Parker from thence to the first main x-ings of Pleasant Run, and Philemon Waters, who is appointed in the Room of Thomas Cunningham, from thence to the County Line.

Fitzgerald vs Edgcomb, Bland Ballard Sp b'l J. by N. D. & W. E.

The Viewers of the Road from Nolin Station to the Mouth of the Beech Fork, having made Report, the Same is accordingly established.

[Page 72] Ordered that Samuels' Company assist Paul Froman, Surveyor of the Road in discharge of his office.

O. that Cap't Cunningham's Company and such of Rogers' Comp'y as live on the East side of Buff'o Run, assist Wm. Kincheloe Surv'r, etc.

O. that the Residue of Rogers' Co. assist Paul Froman Surveyor, etc.

O. that Cap't Polkes Comp'y and those of Pottingers Co as live on the West Side of Princes Creek assist Richard Parker Surv'r, etc.

O. that Capt Waters' Co. and the Residue of Pottinger's Co. assist Philemon Waters, etc.

On the Motion of Richard Chinewith, Gent, it's considered by the Court that the petition he intends to prefer to the Legislature concerning the Exp's incurred by him in first building the Garrison at the Falls of Ohio [Fort Nelson], is reasonable & that the same be certified [Marginal note:] Pd.

Campbell vs Rowan. Rowan vs Campbell. The Arbitrators having ret'd their Award, Ordered that the same be confirmed. [Marginal note:] Pd.

Sullivan vs ASturgus, Refered to Alex. Skinner & John Veech. Who having accordingly ret'd their award.

Ordered that the same be confirmed.

License is granted William Pope to keep a Tavern at his House in Louisville, Who thereupon gave Bond and Security according to Law. [Marginal note:] Pd.

Jediah Ashcraft produces a Com'n appointing him a Lieut. Whereupon he takes the Several Oaths, etc.

Hamilton vs Allan Tharp, dism'd, pl Costs.

An Indenture between Bishop Forsyth and Jacob Regar, acknowledged by each party, and a Mem'o on the Back thereof from s'd Regar, also ackn'd & O. R. [Marginal note:] Recorded.

[Page 73] Trant vs Tyler, dism'd, pl. Costs.

Wilson vs Swan, Jdg't by N. D. & W. Enq.

Ordered That Isaac Larue be appointed Surveyor of the Road from the Mouth of the Beech Fork to Nolinn & that Cap't

143

Phillips' Co. on the So. Side of the Rolling Fork attend said Surveyor in his s'd office.

Daniel Sullivan produces a Nomination as a D'y Sur. and takes the several Oaths etc. [Marginal note:] Pd.

Grundy's Exrs. vs Montgomery, Jdg't by former Order.

John Veach produces a Nomination as D'y Sur'r and takes the several Oaths etc. [Marginal note:] Pd.

Abst. Isaac Cox, & Geo. Wilson Gent.

O. that certain Matters in difference between Dan'l Sullivan Surveyor of the Road & John Galloway relative the S'd Surveyors Office etc, be refered to the first day next Court, to be then settled by two or more of the then present Magistrates.

O. that a Dedimus issue to take the Deposition of such Witnesses as may be called on by Ben Johnston on Monongolia in his Suit vs Brashears.

Ordered that Court be adjourned untill Tomorrow Morning 8 o'Clock.   Rich'd Chenowith.

Court met according to adjournment November 4th 1784.

Present: Isaac Cox, William Oldham, George Wilson, Isaac Morrison, Saml. Culberson & Philip Phillips, Gent.

Glenn vs Mayes etc. Referred to Wm. Kincheloe, Peter Evans, James Rogers, Jesse Davis & Isaac Davis.

[Page 74] License is granted Reubin Cave to keep a Tavern at his House in Jefferson County, Who gave Bond & Security, etc. [Marginal note:] Pd.

Present Samuel Smyth, Gent. & And. Hynes, Gent.

A Deed from Geo. Wilson to Isaac Cox acknowledged and O. Record. [Marginal note:] Rec'd.

An Indenture from Richard Scott to Alex. Skinner acknowledged and O. R. [Marginal note:] Rec'd.

Ordered That the Levy to be laid on each Tythable person for the ensuing year be Six Shillings, and that the Collection be rated at £345.

Jefferson County, Dr:

To George Wilson, Gent, for Scales Weights & Measures,	£200.
To W. Johnston for Extra Service blank books, etc.,	26.
The Adjutant,	50.
The Sheriff 2000w Tob'o,	17.10
A Depositum for future Demands,	51.10
	£345.

A Bond from James Stevenson and Sarah his wife to Moses Spear, ackn'd & O. R. [Marginal note:] Rec'd.

The grand Jury having returned and made their presentments, are as follows, etc., and having nothing farther to present were discharged.

Present, Richard Chinewith & J. F. Moore, Gent.

Charles Polkes and David Cox, two named in the Commission of Peace for this County, & for the Court of Oyer & Terminer, take the Oath of Allegiance and Fidelity and also the Oath of Office.

Present, Charles Polkes & David Cox, Gent.

Absent, J. F. Moore, Gent.

[Page 75] Common Wealth vs Charles Morgan and Mathew Jones, the prisoners being again set to the Bar, agreable to a former Order, and no person appearing to prosecute them they were discharged.

Ordered that an alteration be made in the prison Bounds, Viz. to Begin on the brow of the second bank opposite a large poplar below Mark Thomas his house, thence running along the bank in a direct Line, to strike the Cross Street by John Sinclear's, up said Street so far, that Lines, at R. Angles, will include 10 Acres.

On the Motion of Andrew Vaughan, Ex'r named in the last Will and Testament of Andrew Vaughan Jr. dec'd, Adm'r of s'd Estate is granted him, Who thereupon gave Bond and Security according to Law, etc. [Marginal note:] Recor'd.

Ordered that Thomas Polke, Charles Polke, Tho's Cunningham and William May or any three of them being first sworn do appraise the Estate of Andrew Vaughan Jr. & make Return etc. [Marginal Note:] Pd.

Ordered That Francis Adams, John Morrison, Jno Dorrett, John Brown, or any three of them being first sworn, do appraise the Estate of Niblock Coleon dec'd & report &c.

William Shannon produces a Nomination as Dep'y Surv'r from W. May, Gent, and takes the several Oaths etc.

A Bond from James Stevenson to Edward Mathews proven fully by the Oaths of Th's McCarty & Th's Spencer & O. R.

Barbour vs Jones, Jdg't by Confession.

On the Motion of Alexander Skinner who was presented by the Grand Jury for profane swearing, Ordered that His protest

145

against the legality of said Jury, on acc't of one of them not being a freeholder, be admitted.

Ordered That Nicholas Meriwether & W. Johnston examine into the Minutes of this Court relative the Suit Lynn's Adm'r vs Sullivan, in the Attendance of the Witnesses therein, and report their opinion thereon to next Court.

[Page 76] Sullivan vs Shannon. Jacob Colman Special Bail, O. & Sp. Imp.

Ordered that the Clerk do transmit to the Governor a List of the Magistrates for this County, distinguishing those that are dead and that are removed out of the county. Also ordered that John Campbell and Anguis Cameron, Gent, be summoned to attend Court and give their Reasons for refusing to act or do it by Letter,—agreable to Order of the Governor and Council.

Absent, W. Oldham, And. Hynes, Philip Phillips, Sam'l Culberson & Isaac Morrison, Gent.

Present Sam'l Culberson, Gent.

Ordered that Ordinary keepers be allowed 2/3 for Good Spirits per ½ pint.

Ordered that Court be adjourned untill Court in Course.

Isaac Cox.

MINUTE BOOK NO. 1, JEFFERSON COUNTY KENTUCKY
APRIL 6, 1784—DECEMBER 7, 1785

Copied for Publication

By Miss Ludie J. Kinkead

In Four Parts

Part Three: December 6, 1784—August 10, 1785[1]

*

[Page 76, continued.]   December 6th, 1784.

William May on a Treasury War't No. 6201 and part of a Treasury W. No. 6200 makes an addition of 2300 acres to his several Entries on Little Mudy Waters of Green River, amounting to 6500 Acres which said addition is to lie on the East Side of said Entries, the whole length thereof.

[77] At a Court held for Jefferson County December 7, 1784.

Present: Richard Chinewith, Sam'l Smyth, William Oldham, George Wilson, & Sam'l Culberson, Gent. Justices.

A Deed from William Christy to Geo. Wilson proven fully by the Oath of Will Johnston, and O. R.

Also a power of Att'y from s'd Christy to s'd Wilson. Same Order.

A Deed from Jacob Myers to John Davis proven fully by the Oath of Will Johnston, Iac. Graybill & Nat. Wilson, and O. R.

---

[1] As stated in the Introduction, no attempt has been made, in preparing this Minute Book for printing, to correct any of the spelling. The penmanship in the original is such that some of the proper names and other words are subject to more than one reading. The following abbreviations, kindly interpreted by Mr. Frank Coyle, are among those that occur frequently:

Al. Ca., Alias Capias	C'j., Corrected judgment	O., Ordered
Att., Attachment	Co., Costs	O. R., Ordered Recorded
Ca. Sa., Capias ad Satis-	Deft., Defendant	Plt., Plaintiff
faciendum	Dis'd, Dismissed	Rec'd., Recorded
C. W., Commonwealth	G., Granted	Sp., Special
Cons'n., Consent	Imp'l., Imparlance	Subp'd, subpoenaed
C. O., Continuation	N. D., Nihil Dicit	Su'y, Surety
Ordered	N. G., Notice Given	W. E., Writ of Enquiry

*The page references found in this transcription refer to pages in the original Minute Book No. 1.

147

Isaac Kellar produces a Commission as Lieut. of the Militia. Whereupon he takes the Oath of Allegiance & Fidelity and also the Oath of office.

William Buckner and Geo. Calhoon produce Nominations from W. May, Gent, Surveyor of this County & being formerly exam'd again take the several Oaths &c. [Marginal note:] Pd.

Ordered, that Isaac Hite, Alex. Breckenridge & Will Shannon, or any two of them, do examine such persons as may be nominated during this Term by W. May, Gent. who have not been formerly examined & report, etc.

Isaac Hite produces a Nomination etc. & takes the Oaths etc. [Marginal note:] Pd.

Abraham Hite & Bernard Gaines, being returned duly qualified as Dep'y Surveyors, take the several Oaths, etc.

George Muter and Th's Perkins, Gent, having produced Licenses to practice as Attornies, take the Oaths of Allegiance & Fidelity and also the Oath of Office.

On the Application of Benja. Sebastian, Gent, who gave satisfactory Information to the Court, he is admitted to practice as Att'o at Law, Whereupon he takes the Sev'l Oaths, etc.

Ordered that Court be adjourned untill tomorrow Morning 8 O'Clock.   Rich Chenowith.

[78] Court met according to Adjournment Dec'r 8, 1784.

Present: Richard Chinewith, Samuel Smyth, William Oldham, George Wilson, & Sam'l Culberson, Gent, Justices.

Young vs Hume, dism'd plt. Costs.

Same vs Same & Uxr. Same.

Culberson vs Rees, dism'd Plt Costs.

Spencer vs Curry, dism'd no App'r.

McCune vs Rowan, Jdgt. pr. An's.

Sinclear vs Floyd, dism'd plt Costs.

Pillars vs Hughes, dism'd plt Costs.

Inks vs Locke, dism'd No App'r.

O. That Geo. Clear be sum'd to appear at next Court to shew cause why the Complaint of Sam'l Wilson, his apprentice should, not be heard. [Marginal note:] Rec'd.

Knight vs Floyd, dismissed.

Same vs Pittman, Continued.

Same vs Chinewith, Cont'd.

Applegate vs Ford, dism'd plt. Costs.

O. That said Ford be allowed for 3 days att'e in said Suit, and Rich'd Breeding 2 days as a Witness.

Damewood vs Sherlock, Cont'd.

Springer vs Bailey, Same.

Rohrer & Co. vs Richards, Same.

Herret vs Mayes. Dan Sullivan Sp' bail O & Sp Imp.

Present J. F. Moore, Gent.

Pomroy vs Wells, Judgt £4 & Costs.

[79] Owens vs Pyeatt, dism'd by Return.

Fookes vs McKey, Al Sp'a [Alias Subpoena].

Johnston vs Pyeatt, Jdg't on stay Ex's to Jan'y 1st, 1785.

Mathews Asso. vs Rowan, Continued.

Keiner vs Lutes, Al Sp'a.

Watson vs Springer, Jdg't 4£ & Costs.

Jones vs Sinclear, Refered to Jos. Hunter, Bland Ballard as umpire.

Smith vs McMullin, C. O. Deft & Su'y.

Jordan vs Blackford, Same Order.

Sullivan vs Winn, W. Pope Sp b'l O, & Sp Imp'l.

Sutherland vs Severns. Continued.

Christo Greenup, Gent, produces a Nomination as D'y Sur'r, & being ret'd, qualified, takes the Several Oaths, etc.

Purcell vs. Culberson. Cont'd.

Administration of the Estate of Rob't McGrew is granted. Dorothy McGrew, his relict, who with Reubin Case, her Sec'y, gave Bond according to Law. [Marginal note:] Rec'd.

Knight vs. Kepley, Ref'd to Joshua Owens & W. Shannon.

Boush vs Hardin, Refered to Stephen Rawling, Isaac Vertress, John Helm, & John Handley, as Umpire.

O. that J. F. Moore, Geo. Wilson, James Gutermous & Joseph McGrew, or any three of them, being first sworn do appraise the Estate of Rob't McGrew, dec'd & make Return, etc.

Ordered that Court be adjourned untill tomorrow Morning, 8 OClock.   Rich'd Chenowith.

[80] Court met according to adjournment Dec. 9th, 1784. Present Richard Chenowith, Sam'l Smyth, George Wilson & Sam'l Culberson, Gents.

Yates vs Cooke, dism'd.

149

McGee vs McMullin. Reubin Case Sp. B'l. Owe Nothing.
Campbell vs Oldham. W. Pope Sp. b'l, O & Sp Imp.
Case Ass'e vs Winn, Dism'd, no app'n.
Brodhead vs Froman. Att'n.
Wilson vs Brown. C. O., on Def'ts Su'y.
Dozier vs Garvey, Att'n Cont'd for Garnishee. [Marginal
note:] Nota.
Price vs Brownfield. Plu's Cap's.
Wells vs Sprotzman. same.
Dorsett vs Nash. Same.
Ballard vs Slaughter. Cont'd.
Welch vs Slaughter. Cont'd.
Sullivan vs Shannon, dism'd, No app'n.
Grundy's Exr. vs Burks, Sp. Imp.
Shannon vs Sullivan, Sp. Imp.
Koschendorfer vs Stevenson, discont'd, Plt'fs Costs.
McGee vs Sullivan, Dism'd with costs (plts.).
Cleaver vs Collins, Al Ca.
Fookes vs Hogland, Same.
Same vs McCasline, Cont'd.
Archer vs Dunlap & Co. Sp. Imp.
[81] Sullivan vs Howell, Al Ca.
Floyd vs Goodin, C. O.
Same vs McClintick, C. O.
Wilson vs Elliott & Co, C. O.
Douglass vs Campbell, O. & Sp. Imp.
Winn vs Lacassange, Same.
Neilson & Co. vs Winn, Imp.
Same vs Sanders, & Same W. Pope, Sp. B'l, O. & Imp.
Joyes vs Mackee. Ric'd Chiniwith B'l, J by N. D. & W. En.
Cleveland vs Imlay & Co., C. O.
Preferences:
Casebear vs Hayes, Contin'd.
Cannon vs Mayes, Jdgt by N. D. & W. Enq.
Harris vs Shields, Cont'd.
Sullivan vs Rogers, further Imp.
Overtons Eer. vs Moore, No Ap'r, j'd.
Boyd vs Waters, Non Dit, j'd.
Blaine vs Hartford, etc. Paym't. j'd.
Vanmater vs Chiniwith, discont'd.

Colion vs Shannon, abatis pl't Death.

Wilson vs Rogers, conditions perform'd, j'd.

Doherty vs Walls, dism'd.

Walls vs Nelson, Owes nothing, j'd.

Dieponbach vs Floyd, J. by N. D. & W. Enq.

Grundy vs Moss Exrs. Continued.

Sullivan vs Netherland, N. G. with Leave, j'd.

Doling vs Henry, dism'd.

Logston vs A'Sturgus, Cont'd.

Sullivan vs. Henry, Jdgt. for Costs.

[82] Case vs Garvey, Cont'd for Award.

Sinclear vs Vaughan, Same.

Nelson vs Pyeatt, C. O.

Tyler vs Conger, C. O. Deft. & Su'y (Js. Patten).

Hoak vs Vertress, dism'd.

Woods vs Boone, J. Con'f.

Same vs Same, Same.

Harris vs Matthews, J. Conf. & W. Enq.

Jones vs Sinclear. Cont'd.

Fitzgerald vs A'Sturgus & Co. Judg't vs Def. & Sur. W. E.

Hughes vs Stevens, dism'd, pl. Costs.

Griffin vs Collet, Jdg't Conf. & W. Enq.

Stevens vs Thomas, N. G. with Leave j'd.

Lindsay's Adm. vs Case's Adm'r. discontin'd.

Jenkins vs Sullivan. W. Pope Sp. b'l, O & Imp.

Freeman vs Floyd, Jdg't conf. & W. Enq. vs Def. & Sheriff.

Peaque vs Walls, dism'd.

Sullivan vs A'Sturgus, Judgment vs Bond.

Walls vs Floyd, Paym't j'd.

Thomas vs Stevens, N. G. with Leav j'd.

Walls vs Phelps, paym't Issue.

Lynn vs Pope, Continued.

Culbertson & Uxr vs Same. Same.

Elwee vs Thomas, N. G. with Leave j'd.

Samuels Ass'n vs Calhoon, Jno. Grundy Sp. b'l paym't. & disch'e j'd.

Same vs Same, Same bail Owe Nothing, j'd.

Dye vs McCarty, J. Conf'd & W. Enq.

Winn vs Finley, same.

Deckarts vs Whitam, Cont'd.

[83] Lindsay's Exrs. vs Jas. Sullivan, Sam'l Culberson, Sp. b'l, Owe Noth'g j'd.

Dunlap vs Braiden, dism'd.

Richards vs Wickesham, dism'd no app'n.

Aldridge vs Stevenson, Cont'd.

Johnston vs Vaughan & Ux'r, J. Con., & W. Enq.

Moore vs Pope, N. G. j'd.

McMullin vs Case, Cont'd.

Young vs Culberson, N. G. with Leave j'd.

Daniel vs Boin, C. O. vs Deft & Sur'y.

Enlows vs Cox, Jdg't Cont, & W. Enq.

Wible vs Williams etc, J. O. & W. Enq.

Hammond vs Abbitt, Same.

Haggin Ass. vs McGee & Co, Continued.

Same vs Phelphs, Continued.

Same vs Same, Same.

Collier vs Chinewith, Same.

Shute vs Hunter, Same.

Clare Ass'e vs McCarty, Same.

Shrayder vs W. McCarty, Same.

Curry vs Taylor, N. G. J'd.

Horton vs Gregory, dism'd.

Hutchinson vs Mason, J. Conf. & W. Enq.

Mason vs Hutchinson, dism'd.

Hubbs vs Knight, J. Conf. & W. Enq.

Yoder vs Maehl, Same.

Harrison, Ass. vs Pope, Cont'd.

Turner vs Brookes, Cont'd.

Sanders vs Floyd, N. G, with Leave J'd.

Same vs Chinewith, N. Ap's. j'd.

[84] Davis vs Starks, J. Conf. & W. Enq.

A'Sturgus vs Shirlock, Same.

Brodhead vs Tabbs. J. Conf. & W. Enq.

Same vs Owens, Same.

Watson &c vs Lesley, N. G. with Leave j'd.

Same vs Same, Same.

Pittman vs Knight, J. Conf. & W. Enq.

Brodhead vs Pittman, Same.

Same vs Goodin, Same.

Same vs Peague, Same.

Heth Ass'e vs Myers, Same, An's to Specialty.
Brooks vs McEl'Hatton, Cont'd.
Hammond vs Medlin, dism'd.
Pomroy vs Tebbs, Jdg't, an's to Spec'y.
Nicholson & Uxr vs Hogg, J. Conf. & W. Enq.
Culberson vs Purcell, do, C. O.
Freeman vs Johnson, J. Conf. & W. Enq.
Leach vs Sullivan, Cont'd.
Cunningham vs Parker, N. G. with Leave j'd.
Campbell vs Chinewith. Cont'd.
Kindall vs Robertson, dism'd, no app'n.
Thomas vs Rucker, Jdgt, an's to Spec'y.
Parks vs Louder, dism'd.
Woods vs Boone, Al Cap.
Frier vs Montgomery, J. Con'f, N. D., & W. Enq.
Higgins Ass'e vs McGee, Owe noth'g, j'd.
Sullivan Ass'e vs Knight, Owe nothing, j'd.
Simbrel vs Divon, dism'd, pl Costs.
[85] Sullivan Ass'e vs Owens, Tinder. j'd.
Shannon vs Sullivan, Owe Nothing, j'd.
Same vs Same, Same.
Johnston vs Brashears, Cont'd.
Kellar vs Simbrel, dism'd.
Hunter vs Briggs, Cont'd.
Moore vs McElHow, farther Imp.
Kilpatrick vs Handley, Cont'd for award.
Maehl vs Yoder, dism'd, no App'n.
Glum vs Mayes, Cont'd for award.
Sullivan vs Shannon, further Imp.
Same vs Same, Same.
O. That John Hinch be appointed Captain of the Militia at
the Salt Works.
Ordered that Court be adjourned untill Court in Course.

Rich'd Chenoweth.

[86] At a Court held for Jefferson County, on the 12th day of
January, 1785, for the Trial of Negro Peter, the property of Capt.
Watts, committed to the Joal [Gaol] of this County, for upon a
suspicion of felaniously taking sundries, the property of Trent
& Co.

153

Present: Richard Chiniwith, Wm. Oldham, Sam'l Culberson & Chas. Polke, Gent. Justices.

This prisoner being set to the Bar and it being demanded of him, whether he was guilty of the offence wherewith the stand charged, or not guilty. He says he is in no wise guilty thereof, whereupon Capt. Abner Dunn one of s'd Co. being called and examined, upon Consideration of whose Testimony, it is the opinion of the Court, that there being no person appearing to prosecute the prisoner, He is therefore discharged. [Marginal note:] Ch'd.

Ordered that Court be adjourned.

Richd. Chenoweth.

January 14th, 1785. William May, ass'e of Stephen May, withdraws his Entry of 6800 Acres on part of a T. War't No. 17446 on a large Creek, Waters of Rough Creek. William May Ass'e etc. enters 2604 Acres with Wm, as above, Beg'ng in the forks of Meriwithers Creek, about ½ a Mile from the Junction, on the E. Side of a small branch which empties into the East Fork of the Creek, at a White Oak, beech & 2 sugar trees, thence run S. W. 756 po., thence northly from each End of s'd line so far that a Cross Line will include the quantity. [Marginal note:] Copied.

Also 2279 Acres, Beg'ng at the South East Corner of the above, thence running East 688 po., thence off North from each End of s'd line, till a Cross Line will include the quantity.

[87] Also 1500 Acres, on the same War't on the Ohio below the third Island below the Mouth of Salt River, Beg'ng on the Ohio at the upper Corner of an Entry of 10,000 Acres in the Name of Edmund Taylor & John Helm, thence running up the Ohio to the Lines of Thomas Marshall's Entries, thence Eastwdly for quantity.

At a Court held for Jefferson County, February 1st, 1785.

Present: William Oldham, Sam'l Culberson, George Wilson & Philip Phillips, Gent. Justices.

Joseph Barnett being nominated by Wm. May, Gent. Survor of this County, & being formerly examined again takes the several oaths of office etc. [Marginal note:] Pd.

The last Will and Testament of Philip Trant dec'd fully proven by the Oaths of William Johnston and Walter Davies and

O. Recorded & adm'r granted Pat Joyes who gave Bond, etc. [Marginal note:] Rec'd.

O. that a Dedimus issue to take the Deposition of James Agnew & Jacob Bee in the Suit, Holliday vs Backman.

O. That a Dedimus issue to take the Deposition of David Rankin in the suit Curry vs Taylor.

Ths. Curry vs Sam'l McAdams. Sine facias.

O. that a Dedimus issue to take the Deposition of Geo. Day, William Purcell, David Millburn in Behalf of Th's Mason, Ads Yoder.

O. That Andrew Heth, Nath Wilson, Sam'l Culberson & James Patten, or any three of them, being first sworn do appraise the Estate of Philip Trant dec'd & return &c.

Ordered that Court be adjourned untill Court in Course.

William Oldham.

[88] At a Court held for Jefferson County on Tuesday the first day of March, 1785.

Present: Richard Chinewith, William Oldham, George Wilson & Sam Culberson, Gent. Justices.

George Slaughter, Gent. having produced a Commission appointing him high Sheriff of the County of Jefferson takes the Oath of Allegiance & Fidelity and also the Oath of Office.

Edward Thomas & William Payne being nominated as Deputy Sheriffs by Geo. Slaughter, Gent. takes the several Oaths prescribed by Law accordingly.

A Deed from W. Johnston to Benj'a Roberts and Sam'l Orr, acknowledged and O. R.

Jones vs Sinclear, the Arbitrators having ret'd their award, Ordered that the same be confirmed.

William Pope and Edmund Taylor, Gent., two named in the Commission of the plan for the County of Jefferson, & of Oyer & Terminer, take the several Oaths prescribed by Law and also the Oath of Office.

Present: William Pope and Edm'd Taylor, Gent.

A Deed from Trustees of Louisville to W. Johnston for Lot No. 8 acknowledged & O. R. [Marginal note:] Rec'd.

A Power of Att'y from James Southall to George Slaughter acknowledged & O. R. [Marginal note:] Rec'd.

A Bond from Dan'l Sullivan to W. Johnston for 821 Acres Land, acknowledged and O. R.

O. That David McClean, Orphan of James McClean, be bound an Apprendice unto Moses Kuykendall to learn the Art of weaving. [Marginal note:] Rec'd.

Walls vs Knight on pl'ffs Motion, Jdgt. is given for amt. of Replevey Bond for Deft. Notice being proven.

[89] A Bond from George Wilson to James Elliott and Elliot's Ass'e thereon acknowledges and Orders to Record. [Marginal note:] Rec'd.

Also Bond from said Wilson to W. Johnston, acknowledged and O. R. [Marginal note:] Rec'd.

Ordered that Court be adjourned untill Court in Course.

Rich'd Chenoweth.

At a Court held for Jefferson County on Tuesday the 5th day of April, 1785. [Marginal note:] Rec'd.

Present: Willia Pope, Edmund Taylor, George Wilson, Richard Chinewith, William Oldham, & Sam'l Culberson, Gent. Justices.

George Slaughter, Gent. complains that the Seal of this County at present is insufficient for the purpous necessary & excepts to the insufficiency thereof.

Ordered that Court be adjourned until Tomorrow Morning 8 o'clock. Will. Pope.

William May, Ass'e of Will Johnston ass'e of Ben Johnston & Sam'l McCraw, enters thirty acres on a T. War't No. 157 [159?] on Salt River, joining Jacob Myers preemption that includes Dowdall's Station, on the End next the River, Beg'ng on the River Bank at a Buck Eye, White Oak, & Elm, upper corner to s'd preemption, thence down the River with a line thereof to the lower Corner, thence off at R. Angles from each End of s'd Line south'dly for quantity. April 6th, 1785.

[90] Court met according to Adjournment April 6th, 1785.

Present: Edmund Taylor, Geo. Wilson, James F. Moore, & Sam'l Culberson, Gent. Justices.

Thomas Winn, being nominated by Geo. Slaughter, Gent. as Deputy Sheriff, takes the several Oaths of Office.

O. That a Dedimus issue to take the Deposition of Boston Frederick in the Suit, Catt vs Pyeatt, on behalf of the plaintiff.

Caleb Worley & Nath'l Owens produce Nomination from Wm. May, Gent., as deputy Surveyors. Whereupon John Handley & William Shannon are appointed to examine them & such others as may be nominated by W. May during this Court. [Marginal note:] Pd.

On the Motion of Geo. Slaughter, Gent. O. That the County road be continued round the field at Sullivan's Old Station, upon his making a Bridge convenient & clearing the same agreeable to Law. [Marginal note:] Ch'd.

Wm. Roberts produced a Nomination from Wm. May, Gent. & being formerly examined, again takes the several Oaths of Office. [Marginal note:] Ch'd.

Also Benjamin Stevens, Same Order. [Marginal note:] Pd.

O. That Alexander Breckenridge, Alex'r Skinner, Rich'd Taylor, Rich'd Terrill, Rob't Breckenridge, James Nourse, & David Merriwether, Gent. be recommended to his Excellency the Governor as proper persons to be in, & added to, the Commission of Magistrates for this County. [Marginal note:] Copy sent.

Present: William Pope Gent.

A Deed from the Trustees of Louisville to Buckner Pittman, proven and O. R. [Marginal note:] Rec'd.

[91] O. That John McClean, Orphan of Jas. McClean, aged 14 yrs. be bound unto Th's McClean, to learn the Art of shoe maker, according to law. [Marginal note:] Rec'd.

A Deed from Jacob Myers to Dunlap & Co. fully proven by the Oaths of W. Johnston & Jno. Davis, & O. R. and afterwards acknowledged. [Marginal note:] Rec'd. Sh'd.

Petitions: Knight vs Kepley Cont'd for awards.

Henderson vs Reid. Wm. Shannon Special bail.

Caleb Worley & Nath'l Owens, being returned duly qualified, take the several Oaths of Office etc. [Marginal note:] Pd. 6/8 Re'd.

Floyd's Exrs. vs Galloway & Others, Dism'd.

Ordered that Abram Banta, Th's Fleming, be allowed each one days attendance in the Suit above, and 80 miles distance riding. [Marginal note: Examination order issued] Ex. o iss'd.

Knight vs Pittman, dism'd def'ts Costs.

Pres: R. Cheneweth. Abs: J. F. Moore & S. Culberson, Gent.

C. [Common] Wealth vs Dodge, dism'd on hearing.
Same vs Rankin, Discontinued.
Same vs John Abbit, same.
Same vs Moore, Same.
Same vs Culberson, Same.
Same vs Gilliland, Same.
Same vs Sullivan, Same.
Same vs Boyd, Same.
Same vs Colvan, Same.
Same vs Same, same.
Same vs Hickman, Same.
Same vs Sullivan, Same.
Same vs Ewing, Same.
Same vs Harrod, Same.
[92] C. Wealth vs Chapman, Discont'd.
Same vs Jeffries, Same.
Same vs Wills, Same.
Same vs Conway, Same.
Same vs King, Same.
Same vs Watts, Same.
Same vs Cliffton, Same.
Same vs McCollum, Same.
Same vs Green, Same.
Same vs Purcell, Same.
Same vs Pllantein, Same.
Same vs Kuykendall, Same.
Same vs Donett, Same.
Same vs Shannon, Same.
Same vs Ryan, Same.
Same vs Buffington, Same.
Same vs Abbitt, Same.
Same vs Spangler, Same.
Same vs Campbell, Same.
Same vs Skinner, Same.
Same vs Moore, Same.
Same vs Sullivan, Same.
Same vs Trant, Same.
Same vs Smiley, Same.
Same vs Pyeatt, Same.
Same vs Asturgus, Same.

Same vs Mathews, Same.

Same vs Talbert, Same.

[93] Damewood vs Sherlock. Judg't, 2.5.6, & Costs. [Marginal note:] Petos.

Springer vs Bailey. dism'd, agreed.

Abs't: W. Pope, Gent, pres't: Sam Culberson.

Rohm & Co. vs Richards Jdg't, 2.0.6, & Costs.

Hubbs vs McCune, dism'd.

Roberts vs Pellons, Adm'r. Same.

Galloway vs Sullivan, dism'd.

Fookes vs Whig, dismissed.

Black vs Louden, Same.

Donett vs Williams, Jdg't, £1.14.6, & Costs.

On the Motion of Ann Gafney, Administration is granted her of the Estate of her Husband, Jas. Gafney dec'd, who thereupon gave Bond with B. Sebastian Surity in penalty of £150. [Marginal note:] Rec'd.

O. That James Patten, R. J. Waters, John Donett & Jno. Brown, or any 3 of them, being sworn do appraise s'd Dec'd estate & report accordingly. [Marginal note:] Iss'd.

C. Wealth vs Mathews. on Hearing dism'd.

Same vs Swan, discontinued.

Same vs Freeman, Same.

Same vs Moss, Same.

Same vs Higgins, Same.

Same vs Holmes, Same.

Same vs Arderton, Same.

Same vs Wells, Same.

Same vs McGrew, Same.

Same vs Jackson, Same.

Same vs Damewood, Same.

Same vs [?]mas, Same.

Same vs Tyler, Same.

Same vs Sullivan, Same.

Same vs Van matre, Same.

[94] A Power of Attorney from James Kirby and James Earickson to Sam'l Kirby proven by the Oath of Benj'a Earickson, & O. R. [Marginal note:] Reco'd.

O. That Benj'a Sebastian, Gent, be recommended as a proper person to act as Deputy Attorney for the Commonwealth in this County.

Richard Easton being appointed by Geo. Slaughter, Gent, as a Deputy Sheriff takes the sev'l Oaths accordingly.

Humble vs Houghland, Cont. [Marginal note:] Pet'os.

Same vs McCaslin, Same.

Tyler vs Conner, dism'd, agreed.

Watts vs Shannon, Judgm't, 1.16.8, & Costs. [Marginal note:] CaSa.

Johnston vs Chinewith, dism'd, def't Costs.

Barkman vs Knight. Jdg't, 2.12, & Costs. [Marginal note:] CaSa.

Richmond vs Barkman, dism'd.

Nash vs Cooke, dism'd, no app'n.

Culberson vs Curry, Dism'd.

McIntire vs Slaughter, Al, Sp'e.

Purcell vs Fulton, Same.

Murphy vs Kindall, Cont'd.

Black vs McClintick, dism'd, each pays equal costs.

Neilson & Co. vs Jones, dism'd.

Same vs Same, Same.

Same vs Same, Same.

McElwee vs Louden, Al Sp'ae.

Barbour vs Jones & Co. jdg't, 2.18.8, & Costs.

Tyler vs Sparks, Al Sp'ae.

Winn Ass'e. vs Clare, Same.

Watts vs Girdler, Same.

Sullivan Apr. vs Tyler, Jdg't, 5£, & Costs.

[95] James Sullivan vs Sparks, Al Sp'ae.

Neilson & Co. vs McClintick. Dism'd with Costs.

Same vs Allan Tharp, Al Sp'a.

Same vs White, Same.

Same vs Spears, Jdg't, 26., & Costs.

Same vs Colman & Co. dism'd, def't. Costs.

Same vs Patterson, dism'd, def. Costs.

Same vs Kerr, Al Sp'a.

Same vs Dunlap. Dism'd, def't, Costs.

Ordered that Court be adjourned 'till Tomorrow Morning 8 o'clock.   Will Pope.

Court met according to adjournment April 7th, 1785.

Present: William Pope, George Wilson, Jas. F. Moore, & Sam'l Culberson, Gent. Justices.

A Deed from Robt. Daniel to Mess. Parker & Howell, fully proven by the Oaths of W. Johnston & And. Heth & O. R. [Marginal note:] Rec'd.

Dickin Ass. vs Boone, Jdgt. £5 & Costs. [Marginal note]: ptos.

Young Ass. vs Claw, Al Spa.

Young vs Young, Al Spa.

Davis vs Williams. Judgm't ans to Specialty & Costs.

Mainsell vs Winn, Dism'd, deft Costs, p'ff paying Att'y.

Purcell vs Tuel, Jdgt. 2£ & Costs.

Mathew Ass'n vs Rowan, Same ans to Specialty.

Knight vs Chinewith, Judgm't 5£ & Costs.

[96] On the Motion of Barsheba Hughes, administration is granted her of her husband's Estate, she giving Security. Whereupon she with Jno. Handley and Jacob Coleman entered into Bond in the penalty of £500, according to Law. [Marginal note:] Recor'd.

Ordered that Squire Boone, John Roberts, Aquilla Whittaker and Abraham Whittaker, or any three, being Sworn do appraise s'd Estate &c. [Marginal note:] P'd.

Ordered that John Brown be appointed Constable for the town of Louisville for one year in the room of Fr's Adams.

Also John McClintick on Beargrass.

Keiner vs Lester, dism't p'ff Costs.

Dozier vs Garvey, dism'd.

Sturgus vs Fulton, Jdgt. & ordered that the watch attach'd of the deft. be sold. Watch in the Hands of Sam'l Culberson, Gent.

Owens vs Matson. Cont.

Brodhead vs Estis. Cont.

Same vs Froman. Same.

A Bond from Chinewith & others to Ths. Hughes, acknowledged and ordered to record. [Marginal note:] Rec'd.

Also from said Rich'd Chinewith & others to Charles & Rich'd Swan, acknowledged & O. Record. [Marginal note:] Rec'd.

Madison vs Slaughter, discont'd.

Welch vs Same. Al S'poe.

Pres't: R. Chinewith, & Abs't, G. Wilson, Gent.

Sam'l Kirby, Benj'a Earickson & John Waters are appointed to examine the Court House of this Cty, if built agreeable to contract & report accordingly.

Ballard vs. Slaughter, dism'd.

Ordered that the Sheriff do repay Jno. Galloway 13/1 which was by mistake collected by the former Sheriff, which is to be allowed in his acc't.

[97] Price Ass'n vs Brownfield, dism'd, No. app'n.

Wells vs. Sprotzman, Oyer.

On the Motion of Mary Brenton, administration of the Estate of James Brenton dec'd is granted her, whereupon she, with Jno. Campbell, & James Sullivan, her Securities, entered into Bond, penalty of £200 acc'd to Law. [Marginal note:] Rec'd.

Ordered that John Roberts, Sam'l Wells, Aquilla Whittaker & Abraham Whittaker, or any 3 of them, being first sworn do appraise said Estate &c.

A Deed from Jacob Myers to Thos. Hynes acknowledged and ordered to Record. [Marginal note:] Rec'd.

Donett vs Nash, C. O.

Cleaves vs Collins, dism'd, pl'f. Costs. Pres: J. F. Moore, Gent.

O. That a dedemus issue to take the deposition of Thomas Hogan and George Barker in the suit, Clark & Skinner vs Sanders for plaintiff.

Fookes vs Houghland, dism'd.

Woods vs Boone, plu's [pluries] cap.

Sullivan Ass'n vs Howell, abates no Inhabitant.

Clark Ass'n vs Sullivan, Al. Cap.

Martin al Murdoch vs Helm, Cont'd for return.

Stevenson vs Sinclear, Oyer & Spe. Imp.

May vs Daniels Admrs., dism'd agreed.

Seekwright by the demise of William Pope, Dan'l Sullivan admitted def't, lease entry & ouster confessed, & Gen. Is. adg'd.

Nelson vs Davis, N. G. with leave j'd.

Marshall ass'n vs McGee, O. & Sp. Imp.

Henderson vs Reid, C. O.

Alvay vs. Clare, C. O.

[98] Boush vs Johnson. Jury to assess the pltff. damage, to wit, Ric'd Brashears, William Lears, Richard Waters, Ezekiel Howell, Bryant Sloane, Jenkins Phillips, Stephen Smith, Burwell

Jackson, Reubin Case, Jno. Fookes, William Roberts & Buckner
Pittman, who being Sworn accordingly bring in a Verdict for P'ff
and Judgm't accordingly.

Kelly vs Martin, N. G. with leave jd.

Walls vs Floyd, dism'd deft. Costs.

Ordered that Court be adjourned until Tomorro Morning 8
o'clock.   Will Pope.

Court met according to adjournment, April 8th, 1785.

Present: William Pope, J. F. Moore, Geo. Wilson & Sam'l
Culberson, Gent.

A Deed from John Sanders to Jenkin Phillips acknowledged &
O. R. [Marginal note:] Rec'd.

Also from W. Johnston to said Phillips same order. [Marginal note:] Rec'd.

Humble vs Oldham, Imp.

Clark vs Richard, abates no Inhab't.

Lovell vs Phelps etc. Oyer & Imp.

Lear vs Cornell, dism'd. Settled. [Marginal note:] 6/8 Rec'd.

Watts vs Shannon. Jno. Handley, Sp. b'l N. G. with leave j'd.

Same vs Same, Same.

Neilson & Co. vs Dalton, dism'd.

Martland vs Coinois, dism'd, settled.

Brodhead vs Goodin, dism'd, def't Costs.

[99] Blaine vs Wibly, C. O. deft & Su'y.

Daniel vs Chinowith, dismis'd p'ff. order.

Patten vs Yoder, dism'd p'ff. costs.

Davis vs Winn, Oyer & Imp.

Clare vs Alvay, Oyer & Imp.

Alvay vs Clare, Same.

Davis vs Marker C. O. vs Def't & Su'y.

C. Wealth vs Davis, N. G. j'd.

Watts vs Shannon for a Breach of peace, the Complaint
lodged against the deft. by Rec'o is dism'd, plaintiff not appearing.

License is granted Rob't Elliott to keep a Tavern in the Town
of Louisville, he giving Security. Whereupon he with William
Shannon entered into bond, etc.

Clark & Co. vs Sanders, C. O.

Lindsay's Exrs. vs Sullivan. Jury to try the Issue to wit,
James Patten, Joseph Phelps, James Stevenson, Joseph Brooks,

Abram Field, William Clark, Isaac Cox, Osborn Sprigg, Jacob Myers, William McElwee, Martin Casny and James Watts, who being Sworn, bring in a verdict & the plaintiff being called and not appearing, Ordered that she be nonsuit'd.

McCarty vs Chinewith, Oyer & Imp.

Asturgus vs Carr, Oyer & Imp.

Brown vs Boone, A. C.

Gribbs vs Owens, C. O. vs deft & Su'y.

Calvan vs Carr, dism'd, with Costs. [Marginal note:] Ca Sa.

Same vs Same & Harrod, dism'd, same.

Williams vs Lynn's adm., O & Sp Imp.

[100] Sullivan vs Williams, Jdgt. by Confession, acco. to Sp.

Divon vs Springer, Ed. Mathew bail, Sp. O. & Imp.

Tyler vs Boone, Al. Cap.

Same vs Estis, Same.

Barkman vs Holliday, dism'd. [Marginal note:] Pd.

Adams vs Johnson, dism'd, agreed.

Hite ass'n vs Boone, Al Cap.

Hite jr. Ass'n vs Same, same.

Kuykendall vs Sullivan, N. D. jd., Jas. Sullivan Sp. Bl.

McGee vs Sullivan, abates, p'ff death.

Sanders vs Skinner & Co. R'd C. Anderson, Spl. Bail O. & Imp.

John Campbell, Gent. one of the Justices named in the Commission of the peace for this County, came into Court and on his motion he had the Oath of Fidelity and also the Oaths of a Justice at Common Law & Ch'y & of Oy'r & Terminer adm'd to him and therefore.

Pres't: John Campbell, Gt.

Absent: George Wilson, Gent.

Wilson vs Carr, C. O.

Springer vs Brown, dism'd, deft. Costs.

Barnett vs Osborn, dism'd, no return.

Holliday vs Barkman, dism'd.

Tyler & Ux'r vs Juynes, dism'd, deft Costs.

Richmond vs Barkman, Dism'd, p'ff. Costs.

McCune vs Asturgus, Same.

Abbit vs Pittman, A. C.

Mayfield vs McKim, dism'd, pff Costs.

Sanburn vs Johnson, dism'd.

Boone vs Elliot, Continued.

[101] Pittman vs Abbit, A. C.
Same vs Same, Same.
Hall vs Cotton, Same.
Thompson vs Asturgus, dism'd, deft. Costs.
Same vs Same, Same.
McCune vs Clore, C. O.
Winn vs Meriwether, O & Imp Sp'y.
Ryley vs Lear, dism'd, no Return.
Lancaster vs Drumgold. Attention.
Skinner vs Neilson. Continued.
Lacassagne & Moore vs Brown, dism'd.
Hinch Ass'n vs Thomas. Nihil debit j'd.
Brodhead vs Chinewith. W. Pope Sp. bl., O. & Sp Imp.
Neilson & Co. vs Same, Same.
Same vs White & Pope. Jos. Brooks Sp. bail. O & Imp.
Same vs Martin, dism'd.
Same vs Wells. O & Imp., Jas. Stevenson Sp. bail.
Same vs Fookes. Reubin Case Sp. bl. O & Imp.
Same vs same, same.
Same vs Tuel & Co. Wm Shannon Sp. b. O & Sp. Imp.
Same vs Applegate, A. C.
Young vs Clore, abates, no habitant.
Ruddle vs Phelps, Same.
Newland vs Sullivan. A. C.
Goodin vs Triplett, Same.
Collins vs McCarty, Same.
Grymes vs Knight, dism'd, no appearance.
Winn vs Pyeatt. Al Cap.
Jackson vs Daniel. N. Guilty with leave j'd.
[102] Johnston vs Pope, Continued.
Meriwether vs Pope. James Sullivan Sp. Bl. Oyer & S. Imp.
Pyeatt vs Dennison, dism'd, no appear'e.
Waters vs Brown, discont'd, no appn.
Same vs Meriwether, O. & Sp. Imp.
Edwards vs Same, Same.
Elliot vs Boone, dism'd.
Same vs Same. Same.
Chiniwith vs McManiss, Al Caps.
Same vs Curry. C. O.
References [Orders of]:

Caselbear vs Hayes, Dism'd no Appn.

Harris vs Shields. Non ditinet j'd.

Ordered that the Sheriff summon Twenty four of the most capable Freeholders of the County to serve as a Grand jury of Inquest for the body of this County in May Court next.

Powell vs Sullivan referred to Ths. Perkins, Danl. Brodhead, Jr. Rich'd C. Anderson, & W. Johnston, or any three of them.

Sullivan Ass'n vs Knight & Co. Jury to try the Issue, Viz. Jos. Brooks, Abraham Fields, Osborn Sprigg, Martin Carney, James Watts, Buckner Pitman, Bryan Sloan, M'cl [Michael] Humble, Robert Gilmore, James Stephenson, James Beatty & Benja Stevens. ret'd Verd't for p'ff and Jdgt. &c.

Watson vs Lesley, dism'd deft paying 30 / & Costs.

Same &c vs Same, dism'd.

[103] Sullivan vs Rogers, Owe Nothing, j'd.

Haggin Ass'e vs McGee etc., dism'd def't paying Costs.

Same vs Phelps, dism'd def't Costs. [Marginal note:] Pd.

Same vs Same, Same, [Marginal note:] Pd.

Freeman vs Floyd, dism'd def't Costs.

Sanders vs Same, dism'd.

Ab't [Absent]: W. Pope, G't.

William Pope, G't, exhibited a Complaint ag't Dan'l Sulivan for misbehaving to him as a Magistrate. Whereupon on hearing of the parties it Ordered that the s'd Dan'l Sulivan give security for his keeping the peace until the next Grand jury Court himself in £10 and two Sec'ts in £5 each and pay costs.

Ordered that Court be adjourned until tomorrow Morning 8 o'clock.   Will Pope.

Court met according to adjournment April 9th, 1785.

Present: William Pope, George Wilson, James F. Moore, & Sam'l Culberson, Gents.

Grundy vs Moss Exrs. paym't, j'd.

Logston vs ASturgus, Continued.

Case vs Garvey, discont'd, agreed.

Sinclear vs Vaughan, Cont'd for award.

Nelson vs Pyeatt, Jdg't, Conf. & W. Enqr.

[104] Tyler vs Conger, Jdg't, Conf. & W. Enqr. vs Def't & Suy.

Jenkins vs Sullivan, Owe nothing, J'd.

Deckarts vs Whittaker. N. Guilty, with Leave j'd.

Aldridge vs Stevenson, Cont'd.

McMullen vs Casi. C. O.

Caniel vs Boin, dism'd.

Collier vs Chinewith. N. G., with leave j'd.

Shute vs Hunter. Non ap's. Same within 5 years. J'd.

Clore Ass'e vs McCarty. Jdgt. conf. & W. Enq.

Shrayder vs Same. Same ans. to Specialty [Marginal note:]
Ca. Sa.

Harrison Ass'e vs Pope. Imp, Nil Deb., j'd.

Turner vs Brookes, Owe Nothing, j'd.

Brooks vs McElhatton, Jdgt. conf. & W. Enq.

Culberson vs Purcell, dism'd.

Leach vs Sullivan, dism'd no app'n.

Campbell vs Cheniwith, Owe nothing, j'd.

Johnson vs Brashears, Not guilty, w'h leave j'd.

Hunter vs Briggs, Same.

Moore vs McJhose, plea filed & time.

Kilpatrick vs Handly, con't per award.

Glenn vs Mays & Ux., Same.

Sullivan vs Shannon, Nil deb. j'd.

Same vs Same. Same.

Merritt vs Mays, nil. deb, j'd.

Smith, Adm'r, vs McMillin. Non est fait, as to part. Nil deb.

Jordan vs Blackford, Confirm'd am't to Sp'ly.

Sullivan vs Winn, Non ap's, j'd.

Sutherland vs Swans., C. O.

Purcell vs Culberson, dism'd.

Prest: Jno. Campbell, gt.

[105] Boush vs Hardin, Referens set aside, & N. G. with Leave
j'd.

Campbell vs Oldham, dism'd, pff. Costs.

Wilson ass'n vs Bronen, Jdg't conf. & W. Enq.

Grundy's Exrs. vs Burks, dism'd, agreed.

An Article of Agreement between Rob't Daniel and R. J.
Waters being proven by the Oaths of Benj'a Earickson and
Stephen Smith was ordered to Record. [Marginal note:] Reco'd.

Also between said Waters and William Johnston. Same Order.
[Marginal note:] Reco'd.

Shannon vs Sullivan, Owe Nothing, j'd.

Fookes Ass'e vs McCaslin, Continued.

Archer vs Dunlap & Co, Cond's, perf'd j'd.

Floyd vs Goodin, dism'd pff's Marriage.

Same vs Same.

Wilson vs Elliot & Co., Jno. Campbell sp. bl. Cond's perf'd. j'd.

Douglass vs Campbell, N. Assump't j'd.

Winn vs Lacassagne, N. Ass. j'd.

Neilson & Co. vs Winn, paym't j'd.

Same vs Sanders, & Same. Non Apt. j'd.

Cleveland vs Imlay, Alex Bengrey, Sp Bl. Usury & Time, alias vs fee [?].

Yoder vs Mason, O & Sp Imp.

Sullivan Ass'e vs Owens, Jury to try the Issue, to wit, Ric'd J. Waters, Benj'a Earickson, Ezekiel Howell, Daniel Standiford, Joseph Brookes, Benj'a Pyeatt, John Davis, James Turner, Th's McMullin, Norward Francois, and Stephen Smith & Wm. Rowan, who being Sworn bring in a verdict for Def't and jdgt. etc.

[106] A Bond from Jacob Reager to Patrick Joyes, acknowledged and O. R. [Marginal notes:] Reco'd, ch'd.

On the motion of John Knight and Norward Francis, an injunction is granted them to stay proceedings at Common Law in a Judg't obtained ag'st them by James Sulivan ass'e of Dunlap Elliot Kughtly & Co. until the same shall be heard in Equity. Bond & Su'y to be given in the Clerk's office.

O. that the Clerk do return the Thanks of this Court, by way of letter, to Dan'l Brodhead for his favor of toDay, in his present of a County Seal. [Marginal note:] Iss'd.

O. That Thos Gardner be allowed 3 days attendance in the Suit, Sullivan Ass'e vs Owens.

License is granted Jos. Brookes to keep Tavern at his House in this County for one year, he giving Security. Whereupon he gave Bond and su'y acc'd to Law. [Marginal note:] 6 ⁄ 3 rec'd.

Wilson & Ux vs Swan. Jury to assess the damages, viz, Abram Chaplin, William Roberts, Joshua Owens, Bryan Sloan, Burwell Jackson, Will'm Chain, Baldwin Cliffton, Benja Stevens, Christ. Williams, Wm. Payne, Reubin Case & John Fookes, who being sworn, bring in a verdict for plft. which on acc't of excessive damages is set aside & a new trial ordered next Court.

Ordered that Court be adjourned until Court in Course.

Will. Pope.

[107] At a Court held for Jefferson County on May the 3d, 1785.

Present: William Pope, John Campbell, James F. Moore, & Sam'l Culberson, Gent. Justices.

On the Motion of Mr. Thomas Hall, he is admitted to practice as an Attorney at Law. Whereupon he takes the Oath of Allegiance & fidelity & also the Oath of Office. [Marginal note:] ch'd.

Ordered that Court be adjourned untill tomorrow Morning 10 o'clock.   Will. Pope.

Court met according to Adjournment May 4th, 1785.

Present: William Pope, William Oldham, Edmund Taylor, Geo. Wilson, Gents.

Appearances:

Goodin vs Sloane, N. Guilty, j'd.

Catt vs Pyeatt, C. O.

Sparks vs Brant, Continued.

Joyes & Hooper vs Yoder, abate of return.

Pope vs Heth, dism'd, no return.

Sullivan vs Springer, Owes Nothing, J'd.

[108] May vs Stevens, dism'd agreed.

Simpson vs Myers & Co, ruled to answer.

Stevens vs May, dism'd agreed.

Dorret vs Mathews & Co. O. & Imp., Jno. A'sturgus, Sp. bl.

Sullivan vs Williams, C. O. vs deft. & Su'y.

Same vs Owens, O. & Imp.

Carr vs Winn, abates of return.

Galloway vs Sullivan, Jas. Sullivan Sp. bl., O & S Imp.

Frye vs Sprigg & Co., A. C.

Same vs. Price's Exr., O. & Sp. Imp.

Heth vs Pope., A. C.

Floyd's Exrs. vs Pomeroy., O. & Sp. Imp.

Same vs Cummins, Same.

Same vs Shaw, Same.

Same vs Vouss, Same.

Martin vs Boone, A. Cap's.

Ballard vs Slaughter, dism'd, agreed.

Moore vs Montgomery, dism'd.

Montgomery vs Burks, A. Cap's.

Same vs Sullivan. Jas. Sullivan sp. bl., O & Imp.

Same vs Naylor. A. Cap's.
Same vs Floyd. O. & S. Imp., Geo. Pomeroy Sp. bail.
Same vs Fosts & same. Same.
Same vs Reager. A. Caps.
Edwards vs Applegate., C. O. vs deft. & Suy.
Eliott vs Hall, dism'd no return.
Hazleriggs vs Brookes & Uxr., Sp. Imp.
Neilson vs Montgomery, dism'd no return.
Coleman vs Applegate., C. O. vs def't & Su'y.
[109] Heth vs Sullivan, dismissed, agreed.
James Dunlap & Co. vs Same, Jas Sullivan Sp. bl., O. & Imp.
William Briggs vs Rob't Floyd. C. O. vs def't & Su'y.
Gordon vs Harris, Same.
Spears vs Sullivan, dism'd, def't Costs. [Marginal note:] 6/8.
Dunlap & Co. vs Pope, Sp. Imp.
Same vs Same. O. & S. Imp.
Same vs. Cunningham & Co., A. Caps.
Same vs Burks & Co., A. Caps.
Same vs Floyd & Co., Geo. Pomeroy Sp. Bl., O & Sp. Imp.
Pope vs Heth, O. & Imp.
Cummins &c vs. Floyd's Exrs., Sp. Imp.
Ross vs Applegate, dism'd. Plu's Capias.
Brown vs Boone, Pl. Caps.
Clark vs Sullivan. Jas. Sullivan Sp. bl., O & Imp.
Goodin vs Triplett. Ben Roberts Sp. bl., O & Imp.
Collins vs McCarty. Co. O. vs deft. & Su'y.
Winn vs Pyeatt. O & Sp. Imp., Wm. Shannon Sp. bail.
Cheniwith vs McManiss. N. Guilty, with leave j'd.
Tyler vs Boone. Plu's Caps.
Same vs Estis, dism'd, p'ff costs.
Hite vs Boone. P. Caps.
Same vs Same. Same.
Abbit vs Pittman, not det'emt, j'd.
Pittman vs Abbit & Uxr., Sp. Imp.
Same vs. Abbit. Same.
Hall vs Cotton, abates of return.
Newland vs Sullivan. Jas. Sullivan Sp. bl., O. & Sp. Imp.
[110] Woods vs Boone. Al [?].
Neilson & Co. vs Applegate, dismissed.

Petitions:

Young vs Young. Al. Spa.

Same vs Clare, abates by return.

Neilson & Co. vs Carr. Als. Spa.

Same vs Allan Tharp, Same.

Sullivan vs Sparks, Same.

Watts vs Girdler, Same.

Winn vs Clare, abates of return.

Tyler vs Sparks. A. Spa.

McElwee vs Louden. Same.

McIntire vs Slaughter. Judgm't 3£, P. C. & Costs. [Marginal note:] Ca. Sa.

Purcell vs Fulton, dism'd.

On Reference:

Knight vs Kepley. Cont. for award.

Humble vs Hogland, Jdgt. 4.3.4. & Costs.

Same vs McCasline. Continued.

Murphey vs Kindall. Judgm't for £1.13 & Costs. [Marginal note:] Ca. Sa.

Rowan vs Naylor, Al. Spa.

Simbull vs Glenn, dism'd no return.

Bolling vs McCasline, Jdgt. 3.12. & Costs. [Marginal note:] Ca. Sa.

Absent: Wm Pope; and Pres't J. Fr. Moore, Gent.

Fleming vs Floyd. Ex'or dismissed.

Banta vs Same. Same.

Lawrence vs Springer, abates by return.

Humble vs Pope, dismissed.

A power of atto. from James Elliot, atto., for Rob. Elliot to Will Johnston proven and admitted to record. [Marginal note:] reco'd.

Ab't: Geo. Wilson, & pres't: W. Pope, Gent.

[111] Williams vs Daniel. Jdgt. for 600' w. Tob'o. & Costs.

Gaffneys Adm'r vs Bailey. Jdgt. 3.15. & Costs—3/6 [Marginal note:] Ca. Sa.

Welch vs Slaughter. Jdgt. 4.12. & Costs. [Marginal note:] Ca. Sa.

Edwards vs Applegate, Al. Spa.

Wm. McElwee vs Sparks, Same.

Same vs Same, Same.

Mathews vs Lock. Same.

Owens vs Matson. dism'd, no Bond ret'd. [Marginal note:] Attach.

Asturgus vs Sullivan, Squashed.

Simon & Campbell vs Knight, dism'd.

Same vs Diefenbach. Same.

Brodhead vs Estis. Cont'd for return.

Same vs Froman. Jdgt. for 200£ to be disch'd by pay't 75£ &c.

Lancaster vs Drumgold, dism'd by return.

Prest: Sam'l Culberson, Gent, & ab't: Geo. Wilson, Gent.

A power of atto. from Henry Banks of Richmond to Philip Barbour & William Johnston, proven by the Oath of John Rogers and O. R. Prest: John Campbell, Gent. [Marginal note:] Reco'd.

Wilson & Uxr vs Swan. Jury to wit. Rich'd J. Waters, Thomas Hynes, Edward Watson, Christ. Jones, Edward Goodin, Sam'l Wells, Sam'l McCarty, Reubin Camp, Wm. Goodin, Francis Chain, Charles Bratton, & George Pomeroy, who being sworn well & truly to assess the Damages of the p'ff. who bring in a verdict for plaintiff & Judgm't accordingly, from which the def't. prayed an appeal to the 8th day of the next district Court for Kentucky, which was granted, giving Bond and Security agreeable to Law, he having assigned Reasons, as on the other Side mentioned. [Marginal note:] Ca. Sa.

[112] Brodhead vs Peague, Jury to Wit. Sam'l Orr, Rob't Floyd, Sam'l Applegate, Bryant Sloane, Sam'l Watkins, James Pillars, John Patterson, Stacey Applegate, Hugh Grymes, Jos Beeler & Philemon Waters and James Sullivan, who being sworn bring in a Verdict for p'ff and Judgm't & C.

William May, Gent, informed the Court that he intends to resign his Com. as Surveyor of Jefferson County. Whereupon Alexander Breckenridge is recommended as a proper person fitly qualified &c to act in his stead.

Absent: Jno. Campbell, Gent.

The reasons assigned by the def't in the appeal granted in the suit Wilson & Uxr vs Swan, are as follows, Viz: For that it appeared in Evidence that tho' a certificate was granted to the said Woodard, he was at the Time of making the Settlem't for which the Certif't was granted a hired Servant of one James Swan, and that the said James has now possession of said settlem't & preemption in consequence of s'd Woodards being in his service and that tho' the Certif'e was granted to Woodard, as afores'd, yet he, the s'd Wm. Swan was prevented by the reasons above assigned from making a purchase of said Certif by an Act of the Law.

Wm. Pope and Sam'l Sullivan, Gent., upon Council in Judgm't relative the lawfulness of Wm. Swan's being permitted to give Bond & Su'y in the above appeal without being personally present or having producing his written power Attorney to do it for him, am of opinion, that unless such is the case, that Bond cannot be granted.

Edm'd Taylor & J. Fr. Moore, Gent, are of opinion that it is not necessary that a written power should be produced by s'd Swan's attorney in Order to give Bond.

Ordered that Court be adjourned till tomorrow Morning, 10 o'clock.   Will Pope.

[113] Court met according to adjournment May 5th, 1785.

Present: William Pope, William Oldham, Edmund Taylor, & George Wilson, Gents.

Wells vs Sprotzman, N. App'n. j'd.

Dorrett vs Nash, dismissed.

Stevenson vs Sinclear. Nil debit j'd.

Marshall vs McGee. Continued.

Henderson vs Reid. J. C. [Judgment confessed] & W. Enq.

Humble vs Oldham. N. Guilty j'd.

Lovell vs Philips. N. Guilty with leave j'd.

Blaine vs Wible, Continued, Deft. Costs.

Davis vs Winn, dism'd deft. Costs.

Clare vs Alvay. N. G. with leave, j'd.

Alvay vs Clare, N. Ass't j'd.

Same vs Same. J. C. & W. Enq. vs deft. & Su'y.

Davis vs Mackee. Jdgt. acco. to Spec. vs deft & Su'y.

Cameron vs Mayes &c. Jury to wit, James Sullivan, John Sinkler, Francis Chair, Charles Bratton, Sam'l McCarty, Reubin Camp, Thos Tobin, Jacob Pyeatt, William Jackson, Jno. Blancott, Bryant Sloane, Sam'l Oldham, who being sworn &c bring in a verdict for the plaintiff, £150 (-) & Jdgt. accordingly.

Jos. Brooks is appointed Constable for the Neighbourhood of the Fish pools in the stead of James McCauley.

Clark &c vs Sanders. Jdgt. Conf'd. & W. Enq.

McCarty vs Chinewith. N. G. with leave, j'd.

[114] Nicholson & Uxr vs Hogg. Jury to wit, Benja. Roberts, James McCauley, William Shannon, R. J. Waters, Robert Cree, John Baily, Philemon Waters, Sam'l Wells, James Asturgus, John Handley, John Cameron & John Galloway, who being sworn, bring in a verdict for p'ff £9.5.0 & jdgt. accordingly.

From the Judgm't of the Court in the Verdict Cameron vs Mayes &c the deft. by Ths. Perkins, his atto. prayed an appeal &c for the reason following. That it did not appear by the evidence that the plaintiff lost her marriage in consequence of the words alledged to be spoken in the plaintiff declarative & also for that the evidence did not support the declaration in this particular, for that the words were alledged to have been spoken in Sept. 1784 and the evidence proved them spoken sometime in the year 1783 or January 1784, which is granted upon the defendant's in person giving Bond & Security agreeable to law, but refused to allow Jno. Carr who was the deft's. Sp. bail to give Bond and Security for him in his absence.

Absent: W. Pope, and pres't: John Campbell, Gent.

On the Motion of William Pope, Gent. O. that the Sheriff do pay him 2800 of tob'o. as laid in the last levy out of the first Moneys collected by him from the County.

Ordered that Philemon Waters be allowed 3 days attend'ce in the suit Cameron vs Mays, be & also 110 miles & ferriage.

Also John Galloway, Anne Harris & Eliza Cleaver, same attend. & 90 miles riding & ferriage in same suit.

Also Benoni Demant, 4 days attend'ce in the suit Nicholson & Uxr vs Hogg. [Marginal note:] Ca. Sa.

O. That Christ'o Greenup, Abram Whittaker and Rob't Floyd & Sam'l Hinch be appointed in addition to those already app'd to view the nearest and most conv't way from the Falls of Ohio to Lees Town on Kentucky &c & report.

[115] John Campbell, Gent, is required to take the List of Tythes at the falls of Ohio & Wm Pope's Station. Colo. Slaughter & Jenkin Phillips.

Jas. Fr. Moore, at his own Station, & in the Neighbourhood of him at the Salt Works & on Salt River on the So. Side, as far as the Mouth of Brashears his Creek.

Geo. Wilson, at his own Station, on Cedar Creek, and all those above the Mouth of s'd Creek & on both sides of Floyd Fk.

William Oldham, Gent. at his own Station, Robers, Sullivan run & old Stations, Kuykendalls, & all those on the So. Side thereof.

Edmund Taylor, Gent, at Oldhams upper line on Bear Grass including all the Inhabitants on Beargrass, Goose & Harrods Creeks.

William Pope, Gent, the residue of the County.

Asturgus vs Carr, N. Guilty with Leave j'd.

Grills vs Owens, jdgt. ans. to Spa.

Williams vs Lynn's Ad'n. N. Guilty j'd.

Divora vs Springer, Owes nothing j'd.

Powell vs Sullivan, Cont'd. for award.

Sanders vs Skinner &c, N. G. with Leave j'd.

Seekright vs Dreadnaught, dismissed.

Boone vs Elliot, O & J. Imp.

McCune vs Claw, Continued.

Winn vs Meriwether, N. Assumps. j'd.

Skinner vs Neilson, dism'd.

Brodhead vs Chiniwith. Nil debit j'd.

Neilson & Co. vs Same. Same j'd.

Same vs White &c., Same j'd.

Same vs Walls, Same j'd.

[116] Neilson & Co. vs Fookes, Owe Nothing j'd.

Same vs Same. N. Ass'e. j'd.

Same vs Tuel &c. Nil debit j'd.

Johnston vs Pope, Oyer & Imp.

Meriwether vs Pope, Owe Nothing j'd.

Waters vs Meriwether, Same J'd.

Edwards vs Same. Same.

Chinewith vs Curry. Cont'd for return of C. O.

Logston vs Asturgus, dismissed.

Sinclear vs Vaughan, Cont'd for Award.

Culberson vs Pope. N. G. with leave j'd.

Lynn by guardian vs Same. Same.

Aldridge vs Stevenson. J. C. & W. Enq.

McMullin vs Case. I. C. & W. Enq.

Kilpatrick vs Handley. Cont'd for award.

Sutherland vs Severns. J. C. & W. Enq.

Allison vs McCasline. C. O.

Yoder vs Mason, Continued.

Glenn vs Mayes & Uxr. Same for award.

Ordered that Court be adjourned until Court in course.

Will Pope.

[117] At a Court held for Jefferson County August 2d, 1785.

Present: William Pope, Edmund Taylor, James Fr. Moore, William Oldham & George Wilson, Gents.

Commissions were produced and read appointing John Campbell, William Pope, Richard Chinewith, Edmund Taylor, Jas. Fr. Moore, William Oldham, Geo. Wilson, Sam'l Culberson, Alex'r Breckenridge, Alex'r Skinner, Rich'd Taylor, Ric'd Terrell, Rob't Breckenridge, James Nourse, & David Meriwether, Gent, Justices of the peace for the said County and also Commissioners of Oyer and Terminer. Whereupon the said John Campbell, Edmund Taylor, Jas. Fr. Moore, William Oldham, George Wilson, Richard Taylor, Richard Terrill and David Meriwether, Gents, personally took the oath of Fidelity to the Commonwealth and also the Oath of office and thereupon a Court was held for said County.

Present the said, John Campbell, William Oldham, Richard Terrill, James Fr. Moore, Richard Taylor, & David Meriwether, Gents.

Absent: John Campbell, Gent.

A writ of Certiorari being produced, a Record of the proceedings in a certain suit of Trespass in Ejectin, wherein Mark Thomas is p'ff and Jno. Campbell, Gent, def't, is ordered to be transmitted to 9th day of the next supreme Court.

Appraisem't of the Estate of Ro. McGrew dec'd returned and ordered to be recorded. [Marginal note:] Rec'd

Absent: William Oldham, Gent.

Present: Geo. Wilson, Gent. Present, Jno. Campbell, Gent.

[118] Dunlap and Co. vs Archie. Jas. Sullivan Sp. bail. Oyer & Imp.

Lacasagne vs Davis. Mark Thomas, Same.

Same vs Same. Same.

Same vs Same. Same.

Croghan vs Same. Same.

176

An Injunction to stay proceedings in the suit Wilson & Uxr vs Swan was prefered by said Swan and being sworn to was allowed, he giving Bond and Security agreeable to Law.

A Power of Attorney from John Robertson to And. Heth, proven by the Oaths of Philip Barbour, and Thomas Spenser and O. Record. [Marginal note:] Reco'd.

A Power of Attorney from Jno. Holker Esq of the County of Philadelphia in Penna. to John Rice Jones, being produced and properly certified by the protho notary of s'd county, was admitted to record. [Marginal note:] Reco'd.

Also a power of Atto. from Levi Hollingsworth of the State of Penna. Same Order. [Marginal note:] Reco'd.

John Campbell, Gent, returned his List of Tythes. [Marginal note:] Reco'd.

William Oldham, Gent. Same. [Marginal note:] Reco'd.

Absent: James Fr. Moore, Gent.

Absent: Ric'd Terrell, Gent.

Kerby & al vs Pope, dismissed.

Brookes vs Moss, Same.

McCline vs Mairtin, Same.

Brookes vs Tobin, Same.

Walls vs Phelph, dism'd, def't Costs.

Wilson vs Rogers, dismissed.

Samuels vs Calhoon, Same.

Enlows vs Cox, Same. p'ff Costs.

Turner vs Brooks, Same.

[119] Scoggin vs Fitzgerald, abates by return.

Semple & Co. vs And. Heth. dismissed.

Richards vs Thompson, Same.

Cook vs Craig, Same, agreed.

Chiniwith vs Young, Same.

Blancett vs Pyeatt, dismissed, df't Costs.

Young vs Young, abates by return.

Rowan vs Naylor, Same.

Rogers vs Sherlock. Judgement is given against the Defendant for the am't of his acco. with lawful Interest to be levied in the Hands of Philip Barbour. [Marginal note:] iss'd.

In Inventory of the estate of Jacob French dec'd returned & O. Record. [Marginal note:] Rec'd.

Absent: John Campbell, Gent.

A Bargain and sale from David Standiford to Will Johnston acknowledged and O. Record. [Marginal note:] Reco'd.

A Deed for a Lot in Louisville from Jno. Davis to R. J. Waters proven by the oaths of Sam'l Kirby and Ben Earickson and O. R. [Marginal note:] Reco'd.

A Deed from W. Johnston to Daniel Henry is acknowledged and O. R. [Marginal note:] Reco'd.

A Deed from Sam'l McMullin to Rob't Neilson proven by the oaths of W. Johnston and Ben Sebastian & O. R. [Marginal note:] Reco'd.

Orr vs Blancett, dismissed, p'ff Costs.

Absent: J. Campbell, Gent.

An assignment on & of a Mortgage to J. Fr. Moore from Danl. Sullivan from s'd Moore to Jas. Sullivan, acknow'd & O. R. also from s'd Jas. Sullivan to s'd Danl. Sullivan, same order. [Marginal note:] Reco'd.

A plat or survey of 1000 acres of land in the Illinois Grant as laid off by the Surveyor of s'd grant produced agreeable to law & O. Record. [Marginal note:] Rec'd.

Present: W. Oldham, Gent.

[120] White vs Buchannon. O. that a Dedimus issue to take the Deposition of John Downing, Oath being made accordingly. [Marginal note:] iss'd 3 /re'd.

An Order from W. May, D. S. J. C., to Dan. Sullivan to run the partition Lines between Jno. Campbell & Jno. Conelly, of certain Land at the falls of Ohio agreeable to Act of Assembly, 1783, and said Sullivan's return thereon being produced by said Campbell, & on his Motion is admitted to record. [Marginal note:] Reco'd.

Richard Eastin is appointed Surveyor of the road from the Court House to the South part of Bear Grass together with the Streets of the Town of Louisville, the Inhabitants of said Town attend'g him in discharge of his office.

Ordered that those on the South Side of the So. fork of Bear Grass be added to the District of James Sullivan.

Ordered that License be granted Nicholas Meriwether to keep a Tavern at the Salt Works, he giving Security agreeable to Law.

Ordered that Court be adjourned untill Court in Course.

John Campbell.

[121] At a called Court held for Jefferson County on the 10th day of August, 1785, for the Examination of Negro Peter, the property of Francis Vigo, committed to the Joal [Gaol] of this County on suspicion of felony.

Present: Jas. Fr. Moore, Richard Taylor, William Oldham, & David Meriwether, Gents.

The prisoner being set to the Bar and it being demanded of him, whether he was guilty of the offense wherewith he stands charged, or not guilty, he says he is no wise guilty thereof, whereupon sundry witnesses were sworn and examined before Consideration of whose Testimony and the Circumstances attending the same, it is the opinion of the Court that he is guilty of Burglary and feloniously stealing sundry merchandize the property of Rob't Watson & Co. Therefore it is ordered that he be remanded back to the Joal of this County and from thence be conveyed to the place of Execution, there to be hung by the neck untill he be dead, &c.

Ordered that the above named negro Peter, the property of Thomas Vigo, be valued at Eighty pounds Cont. Money.

Ordered That the said slave Peter be executed on the 24th of this present month agreeable to the above Sentence.

J. F. Moore.

MINUTE BOOK NO. 1, JEFFERSON COUNTY
KENTUCKY
APRIL 6, 1784—DECEMBER 7, 1785

Copied for Publication

By Miss Ludie J. Kinkead

In Four Parts

Part Four: September 6, 1785—December 7, 1785[1]
*

[Page 122] At a Court held for Jefferson County, September 6th, 1785.

Present: Edmund Taylor, William Oldham, Ric'd Taylor, Richard Terrell, & David Meriwether, Gent. Justices.

Appraisement of the Estate of Jacob French dec'd. Returned & O. R. [Marginal note:] Rec'd.

Additional appraisement of Peter A'Sturgus dec'd same. [Marginal note:] Rec'd.

Swope vs Ben. Pope. Abates & ret.

Miller vs Ruke & dism'd p'ff orders.

Montgomery vs Burks alias Plus.

Fields vs Wise . . . . Same.

Lady vs Clare abates & return.

Lacassagne & Moore vs Morris dism'd. agreed.

---

[1] As stated in the Introduction, no attempt has been made, in preparing this Minute Book for printing, to correct any of the spelling. The penmanship in the original is such that some of the proper names and other words are subject to more than one reading. The following abbreviations, kindly interpreted by Mr. Frank Coyle, are among those that occur frequently:

Al. Ca., Alias Capias	C'j., Corrected judgment	O., Ordered
Att., Attachment	Co., Costs	O. R., Ordered Recorded
Ca. Sa., Capias ad Satis- faciendum	Deft., Defendant	Plt., Plaintiff
C. W., Commonwealth	Dis'd, Dismissed	Rec'd., Recorded
Cons'n., Consent	G., Granted	Sp., Special
C. O., Continuation	Imp'l., Imparlance	Subp'd, subpoenaed
Ordered	N. D., Nihil Dicit	Su'y, Surety
	N. G., Notice Given	W. E., Writ of Enquiry

*The page references found in this transcription refer to pages in the original Minute Book No. 1.

Pittman vs Abbitt. Plus Caps.
Lincoln vs Burk. Plus Caps.
Oldham vs Bonter. Plus Caps.
Floyd vs Gregory. Same.
Ford vs Ash. Same.
Harris vs Williams. Same.
Close [Clore] vs McDoggle. abates & return.
Dennison vs Vanmatre. Plus Same.
Byers vs Pennebaker. Same.
Dodge vs Louden. Same.
Same vs Same. Same.
Jeffries vs Sparks. Same.
Hemphill vs Ford. Alias. Sum's.
Neilson & Co. vs Caughey, Alias Sum's.
Same vs Waylock. abates & return.
[123] Neilson & Co. vs White, Alias Sum's.
Same vs Inks. Same.
Barker [Parker] Jr. vs Coleman. Same.
Jas. Sullivan, Jr. vs Brooker [Brookes] Alias Caps.
Holland & Uxr vs Rook, dism'd deft. Costs.
Sullivan vs Mathews. Al. Caps.
Anderson vs Chiniwith. Same.
Neilson & Co. vs Rupert. Same.
Same vs Curry. Same.
Same vs Phelps. Same.
Harbison Ass. vs Shannon. Same.
Young vs Bolling. dism'd agreed.
Absent, Edmund Taylor, Gent.

Alex'r Breckinridge produced a Com. as Surveyor of Jefferson
County and having given Bond & Security agreeable to Order of
Gov'r & Council takes the Oaths of Office & Fidelity &c. Present
Ed. Taylor, Gent.

A Deed from the Trustees of Louisville to Ric'd Terrell fully
proven & admitted to record by the Oaths of W. Johnston &
Sam'l Kirby. [Marginal note:] rec'd.

Ric'd Woolfolk, William Oldham, William Roberts, Sam'l
Bell, David Standiford, William Breckinridge, John Veech, &
William Pope, having produced Nomina's as Deputy Surv's &
being formerly examin'd again take the sev'l Oaths of office.

181

John O'Bannon produces a Com. as Deputy Surv. & a Cert. of his Ability from Alexr. Breckinridge, which being thought sufficient he takes the Oaths of Office &c.

Ordered that James Morrison, Wm. Croghan, & John O'Bannon be appointed to examine into the abilities of such persons as may be nominated by A. Breckenridge as Deputy Surveyors.

[124] A Deed from Ric'd Terrell to David Morgan for lot No. 176 acknowledged, & O. R. [Marginal note:] rec'd.

O. that it be certified that John Rice Jones, who intends to practice as an att'y in this County, is according to the Opinion of this Court, from an acquaintance of 3 months & upwards, a person of probity Honesty & good Demeanor. [Marginal note:] Issd. Pd.

John Helm produces a Nom. as Depy. Surv'r. & having formerly been exam'd again takes the Oaths of office.

Rohrer & Co. vs Sherlock on Attach. Ordered that the remainder of the property of Jas. Sherlock, attached in the hands of Phil. Barbour be subject to the paym't of sd. attachm't. [Inserted in different ink:] Jdgt. £129.13.6 &

Appraism't of the Estate of Hannah Kimble dec'd being Ret'd was O. Record. [Marginal note:] Rec'd.

A power of Atty. from Phil Barbour to Ric'd Barbour, Ben Sebastian & W. Johnston ackn'd & O. R. [Marginal note:] Rec'd.

Adm. of the Estate of Philip Lutes dec'd is granted Mary Lutes & Sam'l Wells, who gave Bond & Sec'y. [Marginal note:] 5/pd. Rec'd.

Adm. of the Estate of Lewis Oliver is granted Turner Oliver who gave Bond & Su'y. agreeable to Law. [Marginal note:] 5/pd. Rec'd.

William Pope & Alexr. Breckinridge, two named in the Com. of the peace for this County, take the Oath of Allegiance & the several Oaths of office.

A Deed from James Patton to Isaac Anderson acknowledged & O. record. [Marginal note:] Rec'd.

A Deed from Isaac Anderson, Jas. Patton & Mary his wife fully proven by the subscribing witnesses and O. Record. [Marginal note:] Rec'd.

Present, Will Pope, Gent.

[125] O. that a Dedimus issue directed to Ric'd Taylor &
David Meriwether to take the Examination of Mary Patten wife
of Jas. Patten relative to a Deed given by her for consent with
sd. James & Isaac Anderson for a Lot in Louisville & report
accordingly.

O. that James Fr. Moore & Alexr. Breckinridge be appointed
to meet at Danville, on the Second Tuesday in the evening
Session of the Supreme Court, to agree on a price for erecting a
Court house & prison for said Sup. Ct. & to apportion the same
agreeable to a Requisition from Sam'l McDowell & Caleb Wallace, Esqrs. & as directed by Law. [Marginal note:] Iss'd.

Absent, Ric'd Taylor.

Charles Tully produced a Nom. & a Certifi. of his abilities as
Depy. Survr. & takes the Oaths of Office &c. [Marginal note:]
Pd.

Ryon vs Cain. Mathew Cain, Sp. bail O & Imp.

Handly vs Flask. Christo. Jones. Same.

A petn. of N. Meriwether, Exr. of Geo. Meriwether, praying
Division of certain lands on Bear Grass being laid before the
Court, On consideration thereof O. that Edmd. Taylor, Ric'd
Taylor & Geo. Wilson, and Ric'd Terrell, be appointed to attend
with the Surveyors of this County to the said Division & report
acc'od'ly. [Marginal note:] Issd.

Jas. Fr. Moore produces a Nomin. as Depy. Surv'r & having
been formerly exam'd takes the Oath of Office &c. [Marginal
note:] Iss'd.

O. that Ro. Shanklin, Ric'd Shanklin & Jarrad Williams view
the nearest & most convenient way from a mile on the upper side
of Jos. Brooks to the Ferry at Dowdall's Station on Salt River &
report accd. [Marginal note:] Iss'd.

O. that Sixpence be allowed for ferriage of a Man & Horse
across sd. River, & wheel carriages increased in sd. proportion or
3d for a single Horse.

Absent Edmd. Taylor, Gent.

[126] Johnston vs Rook. On Atty judgm't & Ordered that the
attach. effects in the Hands of the Sheriff be sold agreeable to Law.

Absent, Ric'd Terrell, Gent. present Alex. Breckenridge.

A Deed from the Trustees of Louisville to Philip Barbour, for
Lot No. 180, proven by the Oaths of W. Johnston & John Donne,
and O. R. [Marginal note:] rec'd.

Same to Thos. Brumfield No. 204. Same Order. Rec'd.

Same to Ric'd J. Waters. No. 212. Same. Rec'd.

Same to Dan. Brodhead, Jr. 190. Same. Rec'd.

Same to Same. . . . . 191. Same. Rec'd.

Same to Same. . . . . 192. Same Rec'd.

Same to Same. . . . . 189. Same. Rec'd.

Same to Kirby & Earickson. . 84 & 48. Same. Rec'd.

Same to Stephen Ormsby. No. 197. Same. Rec'd.

Same to Will Johnston. No. 25 & 88, acknow'd & O. R. Rec'd.

Same to Kirby & Earickson. No. 61 & 77 proven by the oath of Will Johnston. Same. Rec'd.

Same to John Rice Jones, No. 26, old plan, acknowledged & O. Record. Rec'd.

Absent, Will Pope, Gent., present Ric'd Taylor.

Ordered that Court be adjourned till Tomorrow Morning 8 o'Clock.   Will. Oldham.

[127] Court met according to adjournment, September 7th, 1785.

Present: William Oldham, Richard Taylor, Richard Terrell & David Meriwether, Gent.

Johnston vs Tyler & Winn. Judgm't by Confession. for £3.2 and Cost.

William Shannon produces a Nom. as Deputy Surv'r & having been formerly examined, again takes the several oaths of office.

Galloway vs Stevenson, dism'd Deft. Costs.

Cummins vs Same. Thos. McCarty & Jno. Pope, Sp. bail.

Crow ass'e vs Same. Same Sp. Bail.

O. That Alexr. Bullitt, Abraham Whittaker, Aquilla Whittaker, & Jas. Stevenson, or any three of them being first sworn, do appraise the Estate of Philip Lutes, dec'd & return accordingly. [Marginal note:] Iss'd.

Present Edmund Taylor, Gent.

Brodhead vs Shannon, David Standiford sp. bail, Oyer & Imp.

A Deed from W. Pope, Ex'r, Mer'th Price dec'd, to David Morgan for Lot No. 14 in Louisville, acknowledged & ordered to Record. [Marginal note:] rec'd.

Present, Wm. Pope, Gent.

Bland Ballard, David Standiford, Aquilla Whittaker & Hardi
Hill are appointed Captains in this county of the Militia. [Marginal note:] Iss'd.

Robert Tyler app'd Lieut. to Ballard. Zachariah Boone,
Lieut. to Standiford. Sam'l Wells, Lieut. to Whittaker. Jos.
Arnold Lieut to Hill. [Marginal note:] Iss'd.

Jas. Haughland, Ensign to Ballard. Jesse Buzan, Ens'n. to
Standiford. Robert Lemon, Ens'n. to Whittaker. and Martin
Rose Ensign to Hardi Hill.

[128] Winn vs Clore on Attach. Judgm't for Forty Shillings
& 6d, & ordered that the attached effects be sold agreeable to
Law. [Marginal note:] Iss'd.

Absent, Richard Terrell, Gent.

Donne vs McAulay on Attac. Jdgt. for £6.10.10 & costs &
ordered that the effects in the Hands of Dan. Brodhead, Jr. be
sold to satisfy the same. [Marginal note:] Iss'd.

Donne vs Boush on Attach Jdgt. for 6.6.1 & Costs & ordered
as above. [Marginal note:] Iss'd.

O. that Benja. Sebastian be appointed to examine into the
records relative Witnesses attendance Lynn adm'r vs Sullivan instead of N. Meriwether. [Marginal note:] Iss'd.

O. that the Surveyor of Nelson County deliver to the Surveyor
of Jefferson County all the Books &c belonging to said County of
Jefferson. [Marginal note:] Iss'd.

Ordered that Court be adjourned until Court in Course.

Will. Pope.

[129] At a Court held for Jefferson County on Tuesday the
4th day of October 1785.

Present: William Pope, William Oldham, Ric'd Taylor, Ric'd
Terrell, Gent.

Dennison vs Vanmater. Al's Sum's.

Byers vs Penebaker. Same.

Dodge vs Loudon. Plt. Sum Plevins.

Same vs Same. Same.

Jeffries vs Sparks. Same.

Neilson & Co. vs Caughey. Same.

Same vs White. Same.

Same vs Inks. Same.

Park & Howell vs Coleman. Same.

Henry vs Oliver. Alias Sum.
Sullivan & al vs Brooker Jr. [Brookes] Plu. Cap.
Sullivan vs Mathews. Same.
Neilson & Co. vs Rupert. Same.
Same vs Curry. Same.
Same vs Phelps. Same.
Montgomery vs Burks. Plus.
Fields vs Wise. dism'd agreed.
Pittman vs Abbit. Als. Plus.
Lincoln vs Burk. Same.
Oldham vs Bonter. Same.
Floyd vs Gregory. Same.
Ford vs Ash. abates & return.
[130] Harris vs Williams. Alias plus.
Case vs Chiniwith. Same.
Shiell & Co. vs McGrew. Alias Caps.
Tookes vs Hinch. Same.
West vs Bolling. Same.
Lynn's Adm. vs Floyd Etc. Same.
Kennison, Etc. vs Tookes, [Fookes] Etc. Same.
Same vs Boone. Same.
Same vs McGrew. Same.
Thomas vs Blancett. dism'd agreed.
Daniels Admr. vs Terrell. dism'd, deft. Costs.
Young vs Sturgus. dism'd deff. Costs.

Adam Sheperd produces a Nom. as Deputy Surv'r & being formerly ex'd again takes the Oaths of office.

William McClung produces a Com. to practice as Atty. & takes the several Oaths of office.

William Johnston Clerk of this Court gives Bond & Su'y in the penalty of £1000, agreeable to an Act of Oct. 1784, respecting County Court Clerks, and takes the Oath required by said Law. [Marginal note:] Forw'd by Colo. Campbell, Oct. 15th.

Administration of the Estate of Abram Miller dec'd granted Isaac Kellar, who gave Bond & Jas. Qutermous & Abram Hite Su's penalty £200. [Marginal note:] ch'd. rec'd.

O. That Ro. Tyler be allowed one days attendance in the suit Young vs Hume. [Marginal note:] Ch'd.

Present Edmund Taylor, Gent. Geo. Wilson, Gent. & John Campbell Gent. absent W. Pope, Gent.

Admr. of the Estate of Dan'l Whittaker dec'd granted Jas. Sullivan, who gave Bond with Isaac Kellar Su'y in the penalty of £200. [Marginal note:] Reco.

Absent Jno. Campbell, Gent. & Ric'd Terrell.

Handley vs Roberts dismissed, p'tt Costs.

[131] Patterson vs Chiniwith. Jury to wit, Josua Archer, W. McClean, Jno. Sinkler, Ths. McCarty, Buckner Pittman, Geo. Pomroy, Isaac Kellar, Jno. Jackson, Geo. Vinshioner, Sam'l Hubbs, Ths. Steward & Abram Hite, who being sworn bring in a verdict for p'ff and Judgm't. £15.3.7¾. [Marginal note:] Fifa.

Floyd vs Newkirk, abates plaintiff marriage.

Same vs Lock. Same.

Same vs Houghland. Same.

Wible vs Williams, &c. Jury to wit, Edward Goodin, Jno. McCasline, Bland Ballard, Jas. Blackwell, Robt. George, John Potts, Christ. Jones, Han'h Lincoln, Hez'h Ford, Ths. Curry, John Galloway, & James Denny who being sworn bring in a verdict for p'ff 5.11.3, & Judgm't. [Marginal note:] Ca Sa.

Standiford vs Hart. Jury to wit, same as Patterson vs Chiniwith who being sworn bring in a verdict for P'ff and Judg'mt.

Taylor vs Hurst. Same Jury as above, who being sworn bring in a verdict for P'ff one penny and costs.

Newland vs Tookes [Fookes], Jury to wit, same as above who being sworn bring in a verdict for p'ff, £8.1.3½, & Judg't. [Marginal note:] Fifa.

Ryon vs Cain, dism'd p'ff Costs.

McMullin vs Springer. Jury to wit, same as in Wible vs Williams, who being sworn bring in a verdict for p'ff, £8.6.10, & Judgt. [Marginal note:] New Trial.

Harris vs McCasline. Continued.

Harrod vs A'Sturgus. Jury to wit, Alx. McMunn, John McManiss, Benj. Hoak, James A'Sturgus, Elisha Phillips, Mac'h Mayfield, Ro. Floyd, Ths. Purcell, Ric'd Chiniwith, Nacy Brashears, Geo. Crevinsten, & John Alvay, who being sworn bring in a verdict for p'ff £___, and jdgt.

[132] Hubbs vs Knight, Jury to wit, Same as Harrod vs A'Sturgus, who, being sworn, bring in a verdict for p'ff £6.7.6. and Jdgt. [Marginal note:] Fifa.

A power of att'o. from Dan'l Sullivan to John Campbell & Jas. Sullivan proven by the Oaths of John Maitland and John Bailey and O. record. [Marginal note:] rec'o.

Rohrer & Co. vs Nelson &c, Reu. Case & Jno. Bailey, Sp. bail.

Pittman vs Knight. Jury to wit, Bland Ballard, Jacob Barkman, Jno. Sparks, Hez. Ford, Josiah Belt, Wm. Swann, John Bailey, Jno. Nelson, Wm. McElwee and Heth and David Morgan & Peter Colman, who being sworn bring in a verdict for p'ff 6.10.6 & Judgm't.

Fitzgerald vs Hunter. Christ. Jones Sp. Bail.

Brodhead vs Pittman. Dism'd deft. Costs.

Case vs A'Sturgus, adm. Jury to wit, Alex McMunn, Jno. McManiss, Ben Hoak, Josiah Phelps, Elijah Phillips, Ro. Floyd, Macajah Mayfield, Ths. Purcell, Ric'd Chiniwith, Nacy Brashears, Geo. Crevinstin & John Alvay, who being sworn bring in a verdict for p'ff, £25 & Jdgt. [Marginal note:] Fifa.

Ordered that James A'Sturgus admr. of Peter A'Sturgus, dec'd, be sum'd to attend at next Court in Order to settle his acct. as Adm. of sd. Estate. [Marginal note:] Iss'd.

James Denny appointed Guardian to Margaret 'Sturgus, orphan of Peter 'Sturgus dec'd. Whereupon he gave Bond in penalty of £500 with Edw'd Tyler & Ro. Tyler his Securit's. [Marginal note:] rec'o.

Court adjourned till Tomorrow Morning 9 o'Clock.

Will Pope.

[133] Court met according to Adjournment October 5th, 1785.

Present: William Pope, James Fr. Moore, George Wilson, Richard Taylor, & Rich'd Terrell, Gent.

King vs Donne, Contin'd.

Harrod vs Vittetoe. Same.

Sutherland vs McCasline. Same.

Case vs Johnson. Same.

Moss Exr. vs Stevenson. Same.

Watkins vs Pyeatt. Same.

Logan etc vs 'Sturgus, Admr. Same.

Micajah Mayfield produces sundry rec's for provisions furnished the Troops at Fort Nelson from Jas. Finn purch'g Com'y which are thought reasonable, and O. that the prices thereafter rated agreeable to rates fixed July 3, 1782.

Present, David Meriwether, Gent. & Wm. Oldham.

McElwee vs Thomas. Continued. deft. Costs.

O. that Jas. Gilman be allowed one day attendance & 91 miles riding in the above suit.

Rachel Yates, 2 days & 40 miles back & forward same suit.

David McElwee, 2 days & 100 miles same suit.

Tyler vs Conger. Jury to wit, Isaac Kellar, Jas. Denny, George Pomroy, Moses Tyler, Ths. Curry, Jno. Galloway, Micajah Mayfield, Sam'l Wells, Aquilla Whittaker, Ths. Steward, Jas. Hardin, Sam'l Orr, who being sworn bring in a verdict for p'ff, £225 and Jdgt. [Marginal note:] Fifa.

Simpson vs Myers &c in Chancery. On the Motion of the plaintiff, Leave is granted him to make the Trustees of Louisville a party to the Suit & that a Sp'al issue & that the sd. p'ff have leave to amend his Bill. [Marginal note:] Iss'd.

Prest: Jno Campbell, Gent.

[134] A Deed from Nic's Meriwether, Exr. of Geo. Meriwether dec'd, to John Clark proven by the oaths of David Meriwether, Dan'l Sullivan & James Sullivan witnesses thereto and O. record. [Marginal note:] Rec'o.

Donne vs Walls attachm't. Ordered that the same be quashed. Abst., J. Campbell & W. Pope, Gent.

Kellars adm. vs Blain att. quashed.

Lee vs Crevinstin. Jno. Fookes Sp. bail.

Sheperd vs Fookes. Jno. McCasline, Same.

Present Jno. Campbell & Al. Breckinridge, Gent.

Kellar's adm. vs Chappell. Attachm't quashed.

Same vs Rappa. Same.

Same vs Ware. Same.

Same vs Davis. Same.

Same vs Smith. Same.

Same vs Montroy. Same

Same vs Wood. Same.

Same vs Russell. Same.

Same vs Hayes. Same

Same vs Carnes. Same.

Same vs Eagle. Same

Same vs Crauley. Same.

Same vs Panther. Same.

Same vs Bossare. Same.

Same vs Thompson. Same.

Same vs Fay Rose. Same.

189

Same vs King. Same.
Same vs Long. Same.
Same vs Leusander. Same.
Same vs Devist. Same.
Same vs Horner. Same.
Same vs Anderson. Same.
[135] Orr vs Lynn. Jdgt for 40/ & ordered that the attach's effects be sold agreeable to Law.
Kellars adm'r. vs Cocks. Attachm't quashed.
Same vs Cooper. Same.
Same vs McGloughlin. Same.
Same vs Ruddle. Same.
Same vs Duley. Same.
Same vs Duley. Same.
Same vs Cooper. Same.
George vs Foley. Same.
Same vs. Walker. Same.
Same vs Ryon. Same.
Same vs Wallace. Same.
Same vs McDonald. Same
Same vs Seeder. Same.
Same vs Snellock. Same.
Same vs Suffroy. Same.
Same vs Balinger. Same.
Same vs O'Bryon. Same.
Same vs McDonald. Same.
Same vs Bush. Same.
Same vs Ryly. Same.
Same vs Reaper. Same.
Same vs Roberts. Same.
Same vs Bush. Same.
Same vs Anderson. Same.
Same vs Dove. Same.
Brashear vs Allan. Same.
Same vs McKever. Same.
[136] Brashear vs Boss, on att. quashed.
Same vs Howell. Same.
Same vs Curry. Same
Same vs Rubido. Same.
Same vs Foley. Same.

Same vs Morris. Same.

Same vs Allan. Same.

Same vs Corver. Same.

Same vs Blair. Same.

Knight vs Ripley. Continued.

Absent Jno. Campbell & J. Fr. Moore, Gent.

Daniel vs Shannon. Dism'd deft. Costs.

Young vs Floyd. Jdgt. by Cont. for £3 & Cos. [Marginal note:] FiFa.

Same vs McCarty. Jdgt. for £4.8, & Costs. [Marginal note:] FiFa.

Present Ric'd Terrell & Dav'd Meriwether. Gent.

Tyler vs Williams. Mark Thomas Sp'l Bail.

Wilson & Uxr vs Shannon. See fa. It is the opinion of the Court that any farther proceedings herein be stayed until the petition in Chancery, Swann vs Wilson &c be heard.

Swann vs Wilson & Uxr in Chancery. On motion leave is given the Complainant to amend his Bill.

Peter Coleman is appointed Capt. of the Militia on Goose Creek.

Dennis Cain, Ensign to Capt. Coleman.

Present, J. F. Moore, Gent.

Johnston vs Bellshe &c, on Motion Jdgt. granted for amt. of Duty Bond & Costs. [Marginal note:] Ca Sa.

Same vs Brown &c. Same. [Marginal note:] Ca Sa.

[137] Sherlock vs Nelson, Jury to wit, Jos. Brooker, Christ. Jones, Dennis Cain, Han'. Lincoln, Jacob Barkman, Alex. McMunn, Edw'd Goodin, Peter Coleman, James Morrison, Ths. Steward, John Sanders, Isaac Foster, who being sworn bring in a verdict for p'ff £4.8, and Jdgt.

Humble vs McCasline.

A'Sturgus vs Sherlock. Jury to wit, Same as in Sherlock vs Nelson, who being sworn bring in a verdict for p'ff for £30.19.3, and Jdgt. [Marginal note:] Fifa.

Neilson & Co. vs Kerr. Jdgt. for 25/ & costs. [Marginal note:] Fifa.

Same vs Allan Tharp. Jdg. for 60/ & Costs. [Marginal note:] Fifa.

Alvay vs Clare. Jury to wit, Same as in A'Sturgus vs Sherlock, & who being sworn bring a verdict for p'ff £27.12.6, & Jdgt. [Marginal note:] Fifa.

Same vs Same. Same Jury, who being sworn bring in a verdict for p'ff £19.1.9 and Jdgt. [Marginal note:] Fifa.

Sullivan vs Sparks.

Watts vs Girdle. Jdgt. £3.16.3 & Int. & Costs. [Marginal note:] Fifa.

Mitchell vs Steward, con'td p'ff Costs.

Abst. Ric'd Taylor & Ric'd Terrell, Gent.

O. that Jas. Lowry be all'd 2 days attendance in the suit Mitchell vs Steward.

James Sparks same time. same suit.

Ordered that Court be adjourned till 8 o'Clock, Tomorrow morning.   Will Pope.

[138] Court met according to adjournment Oct. 6th, 1785.

Present: William Pope, William Oldham, Ric'd Taylor & Dav'd Meriwether, Gent.

Tyler vs Sparks. Continued.

McElwee vs Louden. Jdgt. £3.12, & Costs.

Edwards vs Applegate. Jdgt. 40/ & Costs. [Marginal note:] Fifa.

McElwee vs Sparks. Jdgt. 3.12, & Costs.

Same vs Same. Dism'd deft. Costs.

Claypool vs Dukar, dism'd.

Lynn's Admr. vs Purcell. Continued.

Camp vs Merriwether. Continued.

Sutherland vs Swanns. Dismissed.

Neilson & Co. vs Sanders & Winn. Issue waved and Jdgt. acc'o to Specialty confessed. [Marginal note:] Fifa.

Brodhead vs Brashears. Jury to wit, Geo. Pomeroy, Thos. Purcell, Jos. Brooks, Jas. Morrison, Jacob Barkman, Abram Wells [Wills], Buckner Pittman, Ben. Hoak, Alex. McMunn, Isaac Foster, Moses Keykendall, & Dennis Cain, who being sworn bring in a verdict for p'ff & Jdgt. for ____.

Clark vs Richards. Han. Lincoln. Spl. Bail.

Brodhead vs Tibbs, same jury as above, who being sworn bring in a verdict for p'ff & jdgt. [Marginal note:] Ca Sa.

Brodhead vs Owens. Same jury as above who being sworn bring in a verdict for p'ff & jdgt. [Marginal note:] Ca Sa.

Dye vs McCarty. Same Jury as above who being sworn bring in a verdict for p'ff & Jdgt.

Watts vs McKeag. Jdgt. 3.12, & Costs. [Marginal note:] Ca Sa.

Haughland vs Farnsworth. Dismissed.

[139] Fitzgerald vs Asturgus &c. Jury to wit, James Stevenson, Geo. Upshot, Ed. Goodin, Geo McClure, Isaac Kellar, Han. Lincoln, Jno. Alvay, Ro. Floyd, Ths. Steward, Jno Brown, Rubin Case, Jno. Sinkler, who being sworn bring in a verdict for p'ff, 44£ & Jdgt. [Marginal note:] Fifa.

Neilson & Co. vs Chiniwith. Issue waved & Jdgt. confessed ans. to Specialty. [Marginal note:] Fifa.

Same vs Fookes. Same. [Marginal note:] Fifa.

Same vs Same. Same. [Marginal note:] Fifa.

Same vs Wells. Same.

Alvay vs Whitledge. Cont'd deft. Costs.

Neilson & Co. vs White &c. Issue waved & Jdgt. [Marginal note:] Fifa.

Brodhead vs Chiniwith. Same.

Humble vs Oldham. Jury to wit, Same as in Brodhead vs Brashears, except Jas. Morrison, in whose place Lewis Dixon, who being sworn bring in a verdict for P'ff which on acco. of excessive damages set aside & new Trial ordered.

Clore [Clare] asse. vs McCarty. Same Jury as in Fitzgerald vs Asturgus, who being sworn bring in a verdict for p'ff & Jdgt. [Marginal note:] Fifa.

Geo. Wilson produces a Nom. as Dep'y Surveyor, & being formerly exam'd, again takes the Oaths of office.

Harrison Ass'e vs Pope &c, same Jury as in Clare vs McCarty, who being sworn bring in a verdict for p'ff & Jdgt. [Marginal note:] Fifa.

Cunningham vs Parker. discontinued.

Present: Geo. Wilson, Gent.

Alexr. Breckinridge appointed Guardian to George and John Floyd, orphans of Jno. Floyd, dec'd. Whereupon he gave Bond, & sec'y in the penalty of £2000, with David Meriwether & Ric'd Taylor Sec'y. [Marginal note:] Reco.

Jeffries vs Shannon, dism'd no Bond returned.

[140] O. that Graves Upshot be allowed 3 days attendance & 80 miles Riding & ferriage in the suit Alvay vs Whitledge.

Atwater vs Lincoln. Benj. Roberts Sp. Bail.

Dukarts vs Whittaker. dism'd.

Edwards vs Meriwether. Jury to wit, Same as in Humble vs Oldham, who being sworn, bring in a verdict for p'ff and Judgment. [Marginal note:] Ca Sa.

Waters vs Meriwether. Same Jury, who being sworn bring in a verdict for p'ff & Judgment. [Marginal note:] Ca Sa

Meriwether vs Pope. Same Jury, who being sworn bring in a verdict for p'ff and Jdgt. [Marginal note:] Fifa

Hemphill vs Ford. Jdgt. 26/ & Costs. [Marginal note:] Ca Sa.

O. That Ths. Steward be allowed 3 days atten'ce the above suit.

McMunn vs Roberts, dism'd p'ff & Costs.

Dedimus to issue to take the Deposition of Cha. West in the suit Alvay vs Whitledge.

Harbison vs Shannon. Geo. Slaughter Sp. bail.

Ordered that Court be adjourned till 8 o'Clock Tomorrow.

Will. Oldham.

[141] Court met according to adjournment October 7th, 1785.

Present: William Pope, William Oldham, Geo. Wilson & David Meriwether, Gent.

Hoak vs Winn. dism'd with Costs. [Marginal Note:] Ca Sa.

Dodge vs Ballard. Jury to wit, Peter Tardiveau, Barth'w Tardiveau, John Williams, Aquilla Whittaker, Robt. Daniel, Han. Lincoln, Edward Tyler, Wm. Barclay Smith, David Morgan, Isaac Kellar, Robert George & John Joynes, who being sworn bring in a verdict for p'll and Jdgt. £5 & Costs.

Logan vs Lynn's admr. continued.

French vs Hoak. Bland Ballard Sp. bail.

Same vs Same. Same.

On the Complaint of Will Johnston against William Shannon for a Breach of the peace, on hearing the parties Ordered that the said William Shannon enter into a Recognizance himself in five hundred pounds, with 2 securities in Two hundred & fifty pounds each, for the said William Shannon's good Behaviour One year and one day. Whereupon the said Shannon recognized in the Sum of £500, with James Sullivan and Michael Humble each in 250£ Securities for his Behaviour as aforesaid, agreeable to Law.

Dedimus to issue to take the Deposition of Lewis Dixon & Ths. Steward in the Suit, Abbitt vs Pittman.

Abbitt vs Pittman. cont'd p'ff Costs.

194

Johnston vs Boone. dism'd Deft Costs.

Skinner vs Watkins. dism'd.

[142] Sullivan vs Rogers referred to Ric'd Taylor & Daniel Henry as Umpire.

Lockhart vs Pope. Jdgt. Confess'd.

Joyes vs Mackie. Discontinued.

Pomeroy vs Daniel. Continued.

Neilson vs Thompson. Jdgt. £1/13. O. & Costs.

Pittman vs Floyd. Jdgt. for the balance due.

The arbitrators having ret'd their award in the suit Sullivan vs Rogers. Jdgt. acco.

O. that Israel Dodge [Hodge] & Ths. Winn be allowed each one days attendance in the Suit, Hoak vs Winn.

Sam'l Woods vs Squire Boone, Judgm't confessed. acco. to Specialty.

Kuykendall vs Sullivan, dism'd deft. costs.

Swann vs Wilson & Uxr. It is the opinion of the Court that all proceedings were stayed by iss'g the Injunction.

On a bill of Exception being filed by the respondent Swan vs Wilson & Uxr. O. That the proceedings be transmitted to the supreme Court.

Present: Ric'd Taylor, Gent. Abs: David Meriwether. Abs. Geo. Wilson. pres't: Al'r Breckinridge, Gent.

Winn vs Finley. Dism'd deft. Costs. [Marginal note:] Ca Sa.

Articles of Agreem't between John Campbell, Jas. Sullivan & Wm. Pope, acknowledged & O. record.

Pres't, W. Pope, Gent.

Lacassagne &c vs Davis, dism'd deft Costs.

Same vs Same. Same.

Same vs Same. Same.

[143] O. that the Sheriff do summons Twenty-four free holders to appear at next Court to serve as a Grand Inquest of the Body of this County. [Marginal note:] Iss'd.

Dodge vs Ballard, on Motion of deft. new trial granted.

Pres't: Geo. Wilson. ab't: Al. Breckinridge, Gent.

Ordered that Court be adjourned till 8 o'Clock Tomorrow Morning.   Will Pope.

Court met according to adjournment October 8th, 1785.

Present: [No names given. See page 147.]

Brown vs Boone.
Hite vs Same.
Same vs Same.
Tyler vs Boone.
Frye vs Sprigg &c.
Heth vs Pope.
Martin vs Boone, abates p'ff Death.
Montgomery vs Naylor, abates & return
Same vs Reagar.
Dunlap & Co. vs Cunningham &c.
Same vs Burks &c.
[144] Pyeatt vs Dennison.
Young vs Chiniwith.
Same vs Same.
Carr vs Tobins Exr.
Grills vs Owens.
Meriwether vs Case &c.
McGee's Exr. vs Campbell &c.
Brooks vs Brodhead.
Meriwether vs Archer.
Christian vs Brashears, Eject.
Lacassagne & Co. vs Davis.
Same vs Same.
Same vs Same.
Sanders vs Phillips.
Dalton vs Tyler &c.
Nielson & Co. vs Brodhead.
Same vs Same.
Lanceford vs Sullivan.
A'Sturgus vs Biggs.
Stevenson vs Pyeatt.
Atwater vs Lincoln.
Loughead vs Chiniwith.
Sinkler vs Jones.
Gray vs Same.
White vs Buchanon.
[145] Bolling vs Colman.
Tuel vs Whittaker.
Handley vs Flack.
Standiford Asse. vs Colman.

Sullivan vs Carnahan & Co.
A'Sturgus vs Sullivan.
Holkes vs Donne.
Dennison vs Evans, dism'd agreed.
Sloan [Slover] vs Sanders.
Cheniwith vs A'Sturgus.
Joyes & Hoops vs Breckenridge.
Dunlap & Co. vs Archer.
Sanders vs Colman.
Glenn vs A'Sturgus.
Croghan vs Davis [Gavis].
Trant's Exr. vs Boone.
Same vs Same.
Edwards vs Wells.
Griffin vs Nourse.
Neilson & Co. vs Boone.
Hite vs Boone.
Same vs Same &c.
Humble vs Pope, dism'd.
Crow Asse. vs Stevenson.
Shull & Co. vs Boone.
Sullivan vs Robinson.
Brodhead vs Shannon.
[146] Roberts vs Davis.
Cummins vs Stevenson.
Edwards vs Spears.
Galloway vs Stevenson.
Ray vs McCasline.
McGuire vs Combs.
Swope vs Wise.
French vs Hoak.
Same vs Same.
Worthington vs Clark &c.
Brashears vs Daniel.
Dunlap & Co. vs Daniels Admrs.
Ford vs Eastin.
Fitzgerald vs Hunter.
Clark vs Richards.
Link vs Richards.
Galloway vs Pope.

Pope &c vs Pittman &c.

Trustees vs Sinkler.

Neilson & Co. vs Vigo.

Brodhead vs McCarty.

Holland vs Rook &c., dism'd & deft. Costs.

Reager vs Peck.

Peck vs Reager.

McCulloch vs O'Neal.

Jackson vs Venshioner.

Venshioner vs Jackson.

Quigley & Uxr vs Sinkler.

[147] Morrison vs Perault.

Cliffton vs Daniel.

Sheperd vs Case.

Court met according to adjournment, Oct. 8th, 1785.

Present: John Campbell, William Pope, Geo. Wilson & David Meriwether, Gent.

Harbison vs Shannon. Sp. Imp.

Dennison vs Evans. dism'd agreed.

Martin vs Boone. abates p'ff Death.

Montgomery vs Naylor. abates & return.

Dedimus to issue to take the Deposition of Zach. Moore in the suit Fookes vs Hinch. [Marginal note:] Iss'd.

Brookes vs Brodhead. dism'd agreed.

Reager vs Peck. dismissed.

Peck vs Reager. Same.

Absent, W. Pope. pres. Rich'd Terrell, Gent.

A Power of Attorney from Ric'd Brashears to Dan'l Brodhead proven by the oath of Dan'l Henry, & O. Record. [Marginal note:] rec'o.

Also from Jacob Colman to said Brodhead, proven by the oath of John Donne, & O. record. [Marginal note:] rec'o.

A Letter dated 16th Apr. '85, also one other dated 12th Mar. '85 from Willis Green to Dan'l Brodhead, proven by the oath of Ths. Perkins, and O. record, on motion of said Brodhead.

Absent: John Campbell. Pres: Will Pope, Gent.

[148] A Deed from Trustees of Louisville to Stephen Ormsby proven by the Oaths of Will Johnston and John Donne. & O. record. [Marginal note:] rec'o.

198

McMullin vs Springer. New Trial granted.
Brodhead vs Estis. Discont'd.
Ordered that Court be adjourned till Court in Course.

Will Pope.

At a Court held for Jefferson County November 1, 1785.
Present: William Oldham, Richard Taylor, Ric'd Terrell &
David Meriwether, Gent.
Young vs Culberson. Jdgt. for Costs.
A Deed from Ths. Phillip to Jos. Brookes, acknowledged &
ordered to record. [Marginal note:] rec'o.
O. that Ths. Curry be allowed twelve days attendance in the
suit Young vs Hume.
Montgomery vs Reager. Jacob Reagar Sp. Bail.
Dennison vs Vanmater. abates & return.
Byers vs Panebaker. Same.
Neilson & Co. vs Caughey. Same.
Same vs Inks. Same.
Pope vs McGill. dism'd deft Costs.
Sullivan vs Sparks. Same.
Present: William Pope, Gent. Abst: Ric'd Taylor.
A Power of attorney from John Campbell to Ric'd Taylor &
James Sullivan proven by the Oaths of John Maitland & David
Meriwether, and O. record. [Marginal note:] rec'o.
Dodge vs Loudon. P. Plu. Sum.
Same vs Same. Same.
Jeffries vs Sparks. Same.
Milligan vs Hudson. Al's Sum [?].
[149] License is granted Sam'l Welch to keep an Ordinary at
his House near Jas. Sullivans, for one year, who gave Bond &
Sec'y, agreeable to Law.
License granted Lawrence Ross to keep an Ordinary at Sulli-
van Old Station, Same order. [Marginal note:] paid.
A sufficient number of Freeholders not appearing as Grand
Jurors, Ordered that those who have appeared be dismissed.
Trustees vs Brookes. Christ. Jones, Sp'l Bail.
Pope vs Sullivan on Ejectm't. discontinued.
Finley vs Thomas. Continued.
Pres: Ric'd Taylor.
Piers vs Wells. dism'd deft. Costs.

Neilson & Co. vs McClintick & Co. Jdgt. vs McClintick for 31/ & Costs.

Parker & Co. vs Slaughter. Jdgt. confessed for 4.19.6, & Costs.

Skinner vs Sanburn. Jdgt. for 3.10.0, & Costs.

Same vs Joynes. Same 5£ & Costs.

Mathews vs Lock. Jdgt. 46/10, with Int. & Costs.

Present, Geo. Wilson, Gent., absent, Ric'd Terrell.

Sullivan vs Netherland. discontinued.

Neilson & Co. vs White. Jdgt. 3.17.9, & Costs.

Parker & Co. vs Colman. Jdgt. 2.2. & Costs.

Henry vs Oliver. Jdgt. 29/2, with Int. & Costs.

Absent: W. Pope.

Pope vs Abbitt. Jdgt. 3.18.9, & Costs.

Lynn's adm'r vs Purcell. Jdgt. 30/ & Costs.

Mitchell vs Steward. ref'd to Jas. Beaty & Reubin Case.

Isaac Hite produced a Nom. as Dep'y Surveyor, and having been formerly Ex'd, takes the sev'l Oaths of office.

Prest: Rich'd Terrell & W. Pope.

O. That W. Christian & Edm'd Taylor, divide the Land on Bear Grass between the relict of John Floyd & his Children agreeable to the last will of said Jno. Floyd. [Marginal note:] Reco.

Ordered that Court be adjourned till Tomorrow 1 o'Clock.

Will Pope.

[150] Court met according to adjournment Nov. 2d, 1785.

Present: William Pope, George Wilson, Ric'd Taylor, & David Meriwether, Gent.

Brown vs Boone. Attachm't. [Marginal note:] Iss'd.

Hite vs Same. Same. [Marginal note:] Iss'd.

Same vs Same. Same. [Marginal note:] Iss'd.

Tyler vs Boone. Oyer & Sp. Imp.

Frye vs Sprigg & Co. Payment j'd.

Heth vs Pope. Oyer & sp. Imp.

Montgomery vs Reager. C. O.

Dunlap & Co. vs Cunningham. W. Pope Sp. B'l O. & Imp.

Same vs Burkes & al. C. O. vs Defts. & Sur'y.

Pyeatt vs Dennison. Sp. Imp.

Young vs Chiniwith. Oyer & Spec'l Imp.

Same vs Same. Same.

Carr vs Tobin's Exr. C. O. vs Deft. & Sh'ff.
Grills vs Oem. [?] C. O. vs Deft, & Sec'y.
Meriwether vs Case. Spl. Imp.
McGee's Exr. vs Campbell & al. Sp'l Imp.
Meriwether vs Archer. Spl. Imp.
Goodtitle vs Badtitle. Nany Brashear deft. in room of casual ejector. Leave entry & ouster confess'd N. G. Jd.
Sanders vs Phillips. Spl. Imp.
Dalton vs Tyler & Ac Oyer & Sp'l Imp.
Neilson & Co. vs Brodhead. Geo. Wilson Sp. B'l. O. & Sp'l Imp.
Same vs Same. O. & Sp. Imp.
Lunsford vs Sullivan. N. G. with Leave J'd.
A'Sturgus vs Biggs. Continued.
[151] Stevenson vs Pyeatt &c, abates to Morton, C. O. vs Pyeatt & Suc'y.
Atwater vs Lincoln. O. & Sp. Imp. Jas. Fr. Moore & Jas. Gilmore, Sp. Bl.
Loughead vs Chiniwith. C. O.
Sinkler vs Jones. Sp. Imp.
Gray vs Jones. Same.
White vs Buchanon. C. O.
Bolling vs Colman. C. O
Tuel vs Whittaker. Non Ass't. with Leave Jd.
Handley vs Flack. Imp.
Standiford vs Colman. C. O.
Sullivan vs Carnahan & C. O. & Sp. Imp.
A'Sturgus vs Sullivan. Wm. Johnston Sp. B'l. Oyer & Sp. Imp.
Holker vs Donne. Jno. Davis Sp. B'l. O. & Sp. Imp.
Slover vs Sanders. Imp. Sp'l.
Chiniwith vs Asturgus. C. O. vs Deft. & Su'y.
Boyes & Co. vs Breckinridge. Imp.
Sanders Ass. vs Colman. C. O. vs Deft. & Su'y.
Glenn vs A'Sturgus. dism'd, no prosecution.
Croghan vs Davis. C. O.
Trants Exr. vs Boone. C. O.
Same vs Same. C. O.
Edward vs Wells. dism'd deft. Costs.
Griffin vs Nourse. Ed. Taylor Sp'l b'l. O. & Sp. Imp.
Neilson & Co. vs Squire Boone, C. O.
Hite vs Same [?]. C. O.

201

Same, Jr. vs Same [?]. C. O.

Sheill & Co. vs Boone. abates p'ff death.

Sullivan vs Robertson. C. O.

Roberts vs Davis. C. O. vs Deft & Suc'y.

Crow Ass. vs Stevenson. Contin'd.

Humble vs Pope. Same.

[152] Cummins vs Stevenson. Imp.

Edwards vs Spears. dism'd deft. Costs.

Ray vs McCasline. discontinued.

McGuire vs Combs, C. O. vs Deft & Sur'y.

Swope vs Wise. C. O. vs Deft & Sur'y.

French vs Hoak. Sp'l Imp.

Same vs Same. Sp'l Imp.

Worthington vs Clark &c. Sp'l Imp.

Brashears vs Daniel. Ric'd Taylor Sp'l Bl. Sp'l Imp. & oyer.

Dunlap & Co. vs Daniels Admr. Sp'l Imp.

Ford vs Eastin. Continued.

Fitzgerald vs Hunter. O. & Sp'l Imp.

Clark vs Richards. Jdgt. by N. Dicit & W. Enq.

Link vs Richards. C. O.

Galloway vs Pope. N. G. with Leave Jd.

Pope & al. vs Pittman &c. W. Johnston Sp. bl. O. & Sp. Imp.

Trustees Louisville vs Sinkler &c. Oyer & Sp. Imp.

Nielson & Co. vs Vigo. discontinued.

Brodhead vs McCarty. C. O. vs Deft & Sur'y.

McCullock vs O'Neal. Continued.

Jackson vs Venshioner. Imp., Reu. Case Sp, Bl.

Venshioner vs Jackson. C. O.

Quigley & Uxr. vs Sinkler. Dism'd, no appr.

Morrison vs Perault. Imp.

Cliffton vs Daniel. Ric'd Taylor Sp. Bl. Sp. Imp.

Sheperd vs Case. Mark Thomas Sp. Bl. Imp.

Same vs Same Jr. Same. [?].

Same vs Fookes, Oyer & Imp.

Neilson & Co. vs Montgomery &c. C. O.

Same vs Colman. C. O.

Same vs Martin &c. abates to Martin. Jno. McCasline Sp. Bail. Impr. for McClintick.

[153] Skinner vs Davis. C. O.

Same vs Johnson Uxr. [?] &c C. O.

Sebastian vs Slaughter. Mark Thomas Sp. Bl. O. & Sp. Imp.
Miller vs Same. Same. Sp. Bl. Same.
Filson vs Jones. C. O. vs. Deft & Sur'y.
McMunn vs Murdock. Ben Roberts Sp. Bl. Imp.
Brodhead vs Thompson. C. O.
Same vs Same. C. O.
Lee Ass. vs Crevinstin. Imp.
Cliffton vs Thomas. Reubin Case Sp. Bl. Imp.
Anderson vs Chiniwith. O. & Sp. Imp.
Tyler vs Williams. Sp. Imp.
Springle vs Nelson. C. O.
Neilson & Co. vs Thompson. C. O. vs Deft. & Sur'y.
Same vs Same. Same.
Same vs Daniels. Continued.
Skinner vs Same. Same.
Same vs Thomas. W. Pope, Sp. Bl. Imp.
Howell vs Daniel. Imp.
Hudson vs Chiniwith. C. O.
Handley vs Roberts. O. & Sp. Imp.
Monroney vs Same. Same.
Rohrer & Co. vs Neilson & Co. Imp.
Pope vs Heth &c. Continued.
Cox vs Daniel. W. Pope Sp. Bl. O. & Sp. Imp.
Beaty vs Coburn. Contd. for answer.
Sinkler vs Donne. Donne Admr. Deft instead of cas [?] Eject.
Leave. Entry & Ouster confessed, N. G. Jd.
Same vs Bailey. Same.
Quigley vs Bradley. C. O.
Reynolds vs Same. C. O.
[154] Kennison &c vs Tyler &c. O. & Sp. Imp.
Winn vs Hoak. Sp. Imp.
Montgomery vs Burk. Att'e. [Marginal note:] Iss'd.
Pittman vs Abbit. Plev. Plev.
Lincoln vs Burk. Same.
Oldham vs Banta. Same.
Floyd vs Gregory. Same.
Harris vs Williams. Cont'd.
Case vs Chiniwith. Sp. Imp.
Sullivan &c vs Brookes &c. O. & Sp. Imp.
Sullivan vs Mathews. A. C.

Neilson & Co. vs Rupert, abates & return.
Same vs Curry. C. O.
Same vs Phelps. Ths. Phelps. Sp. B'l. Imp.
Shiell & Co. vs McGrew. abates defts Death.
Fookes vs Hinch. C. O.
West vs Bolling. Plev. & Cap.
Lynn's Admr. vs Floyd &c. dism'd agreed.
Kennison &c vs Fookes &c. C. O.
Same vs Boone. Plev.
Same vs McGrew. C. O.
Dixon vs Watkins. Al's Cap's.
Henry vs Peck &c. discont'd.
Merdock vs Nelson. Al Cap's.
Allan vs Briscoe. Sp. Imp.
Simon &c vs Springer. Mark Thomas Sp. Bl. O. & Sp. Imp.
Kennedy &c vs Nelson. C. O. vs Def't & Sur'y.
Slaughter vs Campbell. Sp. Imp.
Askins vs Simpson. Imp.
Milligan vs Hudson. Alias Caps.
[155] Searsy vs Simpson. Imp. Sp.
Hoak vs McCarty. Att. [Marginal note:] Iss'd.
Williams vs Same. Att. [Marginal note:] Iss'd.
Brown vs Finam. C. O.
Harris vs Mathews. Al's Caps.
Johnston &c vs Patten. C. O.
Same vs Williams. C. O.
Wells vs Clare &c. Sp. Imp.
Pope vs Meriwether. Imp. Spl.
Henry vs Fitzpatrick & Uxr. C. O.
Simpson vs Trustees Louisville. Time for Bill.
A Rec't and a Bond from John Filson to Dan'l Henry. acknowledged and O. Record. [Marginal note:] Rec'd.
Pomroy vs Daniel. dismissed.
Ordered that Court be adjourned till Tomorrow 10 o'Clock.
                                                    Will Pope.

Court met according to adjournment Nov. 3d, 1785.
Present: William Pope, George Wilson, Ric'd Terrell, & David Meriwether, Gent.
Johnston vs Pope, paym't Jd.

204

Glenn vs Mays & Uxr. Cont'd for Award.
Yoder vs Mason. N. G. with Leave Jd.
Allison vs McCasline. J. C. & W. Enq.
Kirkpatrick vs Handley. Cont'd.
Sinkler vs Vaughan. Same.
[156] Chiniwith vs Curry. Eject. Lease &c confess'd N. G. Jd
McCune vs Clare. Cont'd.
Boone vs Elliott. N. G. with Leave jd.
Powell vs Sullivan. Cont'd for Award.
Wilson vs Elliott & Co. discontinued.
Blaine vs Wible. paym't Jd.
Marshall Ass. vs McGee. N. G. with Leave Jd.
Newland vs Sullivan. Same jd.
Pittman vs Abbit. N. G. with Leave. Jd.
Same vs Same & Uxr. Same.
Winn vs Pyeatt. Paym't Jd.
Collins vs McCarty. J. C. & W. Enq.
Goodin vs Triplett. N. G. with Leave Jd.
Clark vs Sullivan. Paym't Jd.
Cummins vs Floyd Exrs. N. G. with Leave Jd.
Pope vs Heth. Paym't Jd.
Dunlap & Co. vs Floyd &c. Paym't Jd.
Same vs Pope. N. G. with Leave Jd.
Same vs Same. Paym't Jd.
Gordon vs Harris. J. C. & W. Enq.
Briggs vs Floyd. Ro. Eakin, Sp. Bail. Owe Noth'g. Jd.
Dunlap & Co. vs Sullivan. N. G. with Leave Jd.
Colman vs Applegate. J. C. & W. Enq.
Hazleriggs vs Brookes. N. Ap. Jd.
Edwards vs Applegate. J. C. & W. Enq.
Montgomery vs Forts &c. paym't Jd.
Same vs Floyd &c. Same.
Neilson & Co. vs Montgomery &c. Jas. Patten Spl. Bl. Imp.
Montgomery vs Sullivan. paym't Jd.
[157] Floyd's. Exrs. vs Vouss. N. G. with Leave Jd.
Same vs Shaw. Same.
Same vs Cummins. Same.
Same vs Pomeroy. Same.
Frye vs Prices Exr. Paym't Jd.
Galloway vs Sullivan. Same.

Sullivan vs Owens. former Jdgt. in Bar.

Same Asse. vs Williams. Jos'h Phelps Sp. Bl. Imp.

Dorrett vs Mathews. Paym't Jd.

Sparks vs Brant. Cont'd.

Catt vs Pyeatt. J. C. & W. Enq.

Harbison vs Shannon. Paym't Jd.

Dunlap & Co. vs Archer. N. Ass't Jd.

Brodhead vs Shannon. Paym't Jd.

Case vs Evans. Att. Judgm't. 3.9. & O. That the attach'd effects be sold agreable to Law. ab't Ric'd Terrell. p't Ric'd Taylor.

McElwee vs Thomas. Jury to try the issue to wit, Joseph Thompson, Charles West, Edward Goodin, Thomas Stewart, Christ. Jones, Thomas Curry, Jas. Qutermous, John Martin, Janet Williams, Josiah Phelps, Buckner Pittman, and Robt. Gilmore, who being sworn withdrew & after same, returned & being called & one of the Jurors not appearing, O. That a New Trial be had.

Ro. Breckinridge, one named in the Com. of the Peace for sd. County, takes the several Oaths accordingly.

A Bond & power of Attorney, from Jno. Montgomery to Alexr. Breckinridge, proven and ordered to record. [Marginal note:] rec'o.

Pres't, Al. Breckinridge & Ro. Breckinridge, Gent.

O. that the attachm't of Kellars adm'r., Ro. George & Ric'd Brashears be reinstated.

[158] O. That Richard Terrell, James Morrison & Fred Edwards, or any two of them, do settle the acc's of the adm'r of the Es't of Peter A'Sturgus, dec'd and allot the widow her dower & make return acc'd. [Marginal note:] rec'd. Iss'd.

Adm'r of the Estate of Sam'l Martin dec'd granted Daniel McClure who gave Bond with Jas. Sullivan Su'y in the sum of 100£ &c. [Marginal note:] Reco.

On motion of Geo. Wilson, Gent. the Court House of this County, is received from him, and the additional sum of Forty pounds allowed him as a Difference between the first plan of Building the Same and the Manner in Which it is now built, agreable to Report the Viewers for that purpose formerly appointed.

O. That Ed. Goodin, Ro. Gilmore, Abram Wells & James Sullivan, or any 3 of them, do appraise the Estate of Sam'l Martin dec'd & return an Inventory Acct. [Marginal note:] Issd.

Beall vs Chiniwith, Jdgt. by Confession, on Stay of Ex'o & att'o. [Marginal note:] Ca Sa

A report of the Gent. app'd to value the public Buildings of Jefferson, on the Division of sd County, on Motion is admitted to record.

An Indenture from Ann Gaffney & John Gaffney her son to Dan'l Brodhead Jr. proven and O. Record. [Marginal note:] reco.

Roper & Co. vs Nelson. Reu. Case, Spl. Bail. Imp.

Kenady vs Same. Same.

Springle vs Same. Same.

Present: Ric'd Terrell, Gent. ab't: David Meriwether.

An Injunction to stay any farther proceedings on a Judgm't obtained by Reubin Case vs the Adm'r of Peter A'Sturgus dec'd, granted, the sd adm'r having sworn to the Truth of his Bill.

Abs't, W. Pope Gent.

[159] An Injunction in Chancery, to stay proceedings on a Judgm't obtained by Ro. Tyler vs Jno Congee & Jas. Patten as his Bail, granted said Patten, he having sworn to the Truth of his Bill.

Present: William Pope.

Ordered that Court be adjourned till 10 o'Clock Tomorrow Morning.   Will Pope.

Court met according to Adjournment November 4th, 1785.

Present: William Pope, Geo. Wilson, Alexr. Breckinridge, & Ro. Breckinridge. Gent.

O. Deed from Trustees of Louisville to Mic'l Troutman for No. 72, a Lot in said Town, proven by the Oaths of Ben Pope & Isaac Cox and O. record.

Same to Same. Same Order for Lot No. 71. O. P.

Same to Same. Same Order for Lot No. 33. O. P.

Same to Johnston, Lot of 10 acres. Same order.

Kellars Admr. vs Davis. Jdgt. vs Garnishee & amt. of acc't & Order of Sale.

Same vs Chappell. Same.

Same vs Rappa. Same.

Same vs Ware. Same.

Same vs Smith. Same.
Same vs Montroy. Same.
Same vs Wood. Same.
Same vs Russell. Same.
Same vs Hayes. Same.
Same vs Carnes. Same.
Same vs Eagle. Same.
Same vs Crawley. Same.
Same vs Panther. Same.
Same vs Brofran. Same.
[160] Kellars Admr. vs Thompson. Jdgt. for amt. & O. that
the Property in the Hands of Garnishee, be sold agreable to Law.
Same vs LaRose. Same. Same vs King. Same.
Same vs Long. Same. Same vs Linsander. Same.
Same vs Dinst. Same. Same vs Homes. Same.
Same vs Anderson. Same. Same vs Cocks. Same.
Same vs Cooper. Same. Same vs McGloughlin. Same.
Same vs Ruddle. Same. Same vs Duley. Same.
Same vs Duly. Same. Same vs Cooper. Same.
Same vs Hail. Same.
George vs Foley. Same. Same vs Walker. Same.
Same vs Ryon. Same. Same vs Wallace. Same.
Same vs McDonald. Same. Same vs Suder. Same.
Same vs Snellock. Same. Same vs Jaffroy. Same.
Same vs Balsinger. Same. Same vs O'Bryon. Same.
Same vs McDonald. Same. Same vs Bush. Same.
Same vs Reaper. Same. Same vs Roberts. Same.
Same vs Boush. Same. Same vs Ryley. Same.
Same vs Anderson. Same. Same vs Dove. Same.
Brashears vs Allan. Same. Same vs McKever. Same.
Same vs Boss. Same. Same vs Howell. Same.
Same vs Curry. Same. Same vs Rubido. Same.
Same vs Foley. Same. Same vs Morris. Same.
Same vs Allan. Same. Same vs Cowen Same.
Same vs Blair. Same.
Gordon vs Harris. Sp. Bail Janet Williams.
Sullivan vs Williams. Jos'h Phelps Sp. Bail. [?]
Present: Jas. Fr. Moore, Gent.
Lacassagne & Co. vs Lynn. discontinued.
Jones vs Reid. Continued.

Joyes & Co. vs Netherland. Same.

[161] Hale vs Evans. Att. Continued. Abs't, W. Pope Gent. An Injunction in Chancery to stay proceedings on a Judgm't obtained by Wm. Grills vs Geo. Owens &c. granted sd. Owens, he giving Bond & Su'y & having sworn to the Truth of his Bill.

McElwee vs Thomas, Jury to wit, Robt. George, James Watts, John Davis, John Dorrett, William Clark, James Patten, John Harrison, Benj. Roberts, Robt. Daniel, Ric'd Abbitt, Reubin Case, & Nic's Meriwether, who being sworn bring in a Verdict for p'ff £25.10.0, & Jdgt. acco. [Marginal note:] Fifa.

Cox vs Pryor. Jdgt. & replevey Bond, notice being proven.

Kennison vs Ballard. Jdgt. 4.3.6. & Costs.

Washburn vs Thomas. Jdgt. by Confession, for. [Marginal note:] M. Fifa.

Winn vs Hoak. Jdgt. by Confession. Ca Sa.

Same vs Same. Continued.

McClenan vs Tully. Jdgt. acc'd to Spec'y & Costs. [Marginal note:] M. Ca Sa.

Campbell vs Colman. Continued.

Humble vs McCasline. Continued.

Knight vs Kepley. Same.

Tyler vs Sparks. Jdgt. 1.12, & Costs.

Camp vs Meriwether. Continued.

Barkman vs Taylor. Continued. [____?].

O. that James Gilmore be allowed 13 Days attendance and 455 miles, back and forward & ferriage in the Suit McElwee vs Thomas.

David McElwee. Same Time & 500 miles, same order.

Rachel Yates, 3 days & 40 miles, same Order.

Walls vs McCasline. Cont'd.

Ordered that Court be adjourned till Court in Course.

George Wilson.

[162] At a Court held for Jefferson County December 6th, 1785.

Present: William Oldham, Ric'd Terrell, Ro. Breckinridge & David Meriwether, Gent.

Jno. Rice Jones produced a License to practice as Att'y at Law, whereupon he takes the several Oaths, &c.

Prest: W. Pope, abs't: Ro. Breckinridge.

Ro. Breckinridge produces a Nom. as Dep'y Surv. & being formerly exam'd again takes the sev'l oaths. &c.

On the Motion of Geo. Slaughter, Or. that his Mark, viz. a Crop & a Hole in the right & a Crop & an underbit in the left ear. O. Recorded. [Marginal note:] Reco.

Absent: Wm Pope. Pres't: Ricd. Taylor, Gent.

O. That Bartlett Asher, Orphan, aged 18 years, be bound unto David White, to learn the Art of a Carpenter &c. agreable to Law. [Marginal note:] reco.

Knight vs Kepley. Contin'd

Humble vs McCasline. Same.

Camp vs Meriwether. Same.

Barkman vs Taylor. Same.

Winn vs Hoak. Same.

Campbell vs Coleman. Same.

Searcy vs A'Sturgus. Jdgt. 5£ and Costs. [Marginal note:] dism'd.

Davis vs Taylor. Jas. Reager, Sp'l Bail.

Finley vs Thomas. Jdgt. 3.15. & Costs.

Walls vs McCasline. Cont'd.

Jeffries vs Sparks. Pl. Sums.

Filson vs Murphy. Jdgt. 4.1.0, & Costs. [Marginal note:] Ca Sa.

Read vs Mathews. Dism'd agreed. [Marginal note:] paid.

[163] Dodge vs Loudon. Al [?].

Same vs Same. Same.

Mullikan vs Hudson. Same.

Felty vs Crevinstin. Same.

Murphy vs Dimant. Same.

Ray vs McCasline. Cont'd.

Logan vs McElwee. Jdgt. 3£ & Costs.

Davis & Uxr. vs Boone. Jdgt. 3£ & Costs.

Young vs Boone. Jdgt. 36/ & Costs.

Same vs Sam'l Boone. Jdgt. 28/6 & Costs.

Lincoln vs Burk, abates & return.

Oldham vs Bonter. A's P. Plev.

Floyd vs Gregory. Same.

Sullivan vs Mathews, abates & return.

West vs Bolling. P. Caps.

Mullikan vs Hudson. Same.

Harris vs Mathews. abates & return.
Campbell vs Wattson, dism'd agred.
Searcy vs Ford. Als. Caps.
Engle vs Chiniwith. Same.
Campbell vs Burks. Same.
Cunningham vs Cimtlet. [?] Same.
Lyon vs Himblebeam. Same.
Kellar vs Loudon. Same.
Robison vs Young. Same.
Pres't: Geo. Wilson. Gent.

[164] O. that it be certified, that the acco. of Bland Ballard vs the State of Virg'a for Horse Hire, is reasonable, & that he be allowed for said Hire, at such rates, as have been formerly settled by the Gent. Comms. [Marginal note:] pd.

Beaty vs Coburn, on hearing the Cause upon the Bill and answer by the Respondent, It is decreed, that James Coburn convey to James Beaty all the Land claimed by the said Beaty, in Consequence of a Cert'e for a preem. of 400 Ac's. of Land, situate on the Mulberry Fork of Brashears Creek contained within the Lines of said Coburn's Sett'l & preem. on said Fork,

Absent: Ric'd Terrell.
Ordered that Court be adjourned till Tomorrow 10 o'Clock.

Will'm Pope.

Court met according to adjournment, Dec. 7th 1785.
Present: James Fr. Moore, Ric'd Taylor, Ric'd Terrell & David Meriwether.

On the Motion of Robt. Daniel, sufficient evidence being produced to the Court, Ordered that it be certified that said Robert Daniel is Heir at Law to Walker Daniel dec'd. [Marginal note:] Iss'd.

Abst: David Meriwether. prest: W. Oldham & Geo. Wilson.
Harris vs Williams. dism'd p'ff Orders.
Dorrett vs Mathews. Same.

An Injunction to stay any farther proceedings on a Jdgt. obtained by Nics. Meriwether vs Wm. Pope, untill the Acc'ts between the parties can be settled by Comss. granted sd Pope and O. that Ric'd Taylor, Edmund Taylor, Alex. Bullit and Walter Dixon be app'd Coms. for that purpose, or any 3 of 'em.

Simpson vs Trustees Louisville. dism'd p'ff orders.

211

[165] A Deed from James Coburn to James Beaty proven by the Oath of the two subscribing Witnesses and O. record & also acknowledged by said Couburn. [Marginal note:] rec'd 12/.

Present: William Pope. Absent: W. Oldham.

Dan'l Sullivan being nom. as Depy. Sheriff, by Geo. Slaughter, Gent, takes the several Oaths of office acc'd.

A power of Att. from Ed. McCab to Dan Brodhead Jr. proven and Ordered to record. [Marginal note:] ch'd. reco.

A Deed from Jos. Brookes to Jas. Fr. Moore, proven by the Oath of Will Johnston & Mary Pendergrass and O. record. [Marginal note:] redo.

It appearing to the Court that John Leman late soldier in the Illinois Reg't is rendered entirely unable to procure a Livelyhood, in Consequence of said service, O. That it be Certified accordingly.

Adm'r of the Estate of Wm. Johnson dec'd granted Robt. George, who gave Bond with Bland Ballard Sur'y in the penalty of £100. [Marginal note:] rec'o. [The original index of the Minute Book No. 1 shows: "George, Robert, admon. granted Sundry Soldiers Estates (page) 165." This apparently refers to William Johnson and the six following who, accordingly, were also soldiers. All except Henry Hart are listed in Eckenrode's *List of the Revolutionary Soldiers of Virginia*, under "Illinois Papers."]

Adm'r of Henry Hart. Same Order. [Marginal note:] reco.

Wm. Poston. Same Order. [Marginal note:] reco.

John Marah. Same Order. [Marginal note:] reco.

Peter Waggoner. Same Order. [Marginal note:] reco.

Richard Turpin. Same Order. [Marginal note:] reco.

Jeremiah Horn. Same Order. [Marginal note:] reco.

McGee vs Hinckston. Jdgt. for Costs.

Searcy vs A'Sturgus. former Jdgt. reversed.

A power of att. from Ro. George to Dan'l Brodhead acknowledged and O. record. [Marginal note:] ch'd.

A Deed from Geo. Wilson and his Wife to Dan'l Henry proved by the Oaths of the subscribing witnesses and Ordered to record. [Marginal note:] Reco.

Ordered that Court be adjourned 'till Court in Course.

[166] Trants Ex. vs Boone, Dan'l Brodhead, Brackett Owens & Bland Ballard, sp'l Bail.

Same vs Same. Same.

Neilson & Co. vs Same. Same.
Hite vs Same. Same.
Same vs Same. Same.
Brown vs Same. Same.
Hite vs Same. Same.
Same vs Sam'l & Same. Same.
Kennisson Asse. vs Same. Same.

Ordered that Court be adjourned till Court in Course.

William Pope.

[End of Minute Book No. 1]

CALENDAR OF EARLY JEFFERSON COUNTY, KENTUCKY, WILLS

WILL BOOK No. 1: APRIL, 1784—JUNE, 1813

PREPARED BY MISS KATHARINE G. HEALY

[EDITOR'S NOTE: Recorded wills are among the most valuable of documentary evidences available to genealogists. They likewise offer material to compilers of local and regional history. A member of The Filson Club recognizing the importance of this source material and appreciating what our President has done and is doing toward preserving our records, has contributed the cost of preparing calendars of the first three Will Books of Jefferson County, 1784–1846.*

These calendars are brief abstracts and will serve as guides to the contents of the wills. The original wills and the will-book copies are on file in the Jefferson County Court House where they are available to those who wish to read them in detail or make verbatim copies.

Will Book No. 1—a calendar of which is presented in this issue of the Club's QUARTERLY extends from April, 1784, to June 14, 1813—is the original book, a volume of 258 pages. Will Book No. 2 is a transcribed book of 638 pages extending from June, 1813, to December, 1833. Will Book No. 3, also a transcribed book, contains 434 pages and extends from 1834 to 1846.

Hundreds of names occur in these wills as beneficiaries, executors or witnesses. These, with all other names, will appear in our

*Only Will Books Nos. 1 and 2 were ever published in THE FILSON CLUB HISTORY QUARTERLY.

index, where they will serve, in a sense, as entries in a partial directory of the early citizens of Jefferson County.

Thirteen wills were recorded before Will Book No. 1 was begun. They appear in transcribed Minute Book A, March 7, 1781—September 3, 1783, printed in THE FILSON CLUB HISTORY QUARTERLY in 1929, in the January, April, and July numbers:

NAME	DATED	RECORDED	PAGE, BOOK A
John Copage	Oct. 8, 1780	March 7, 1781	1
Joseph Irwin	Oct. 13, 1780	March 7, 1781	1
Mary Christy	Aug. 12, 1781	April 2, 1782	23
Charles Coulson	June 20, 1781	May 7, 1782	26
Leonard Helm	May 2, 1782	June 4, 1782	43
Hezekiah Moss	May 11, 1782	July 2, 1782	45
John Williams	No date	Jan. 8, 1783	55
John Ash	Oct. 29, 1782	Feb. 4, 1783	56
John Floyd	No date	June 3, 1783	57
William Morton	No date	June 3, 1783	60
Thomas McGee	Sept. 25, 1781	Aug. 5, 1783	66
Joseph Black	April 11, 1783	Aug. 00, 1783	67
Edw. Skidmore	Oct. 17, 1782	Aug. 6, 1783	70

It should be borne in mind that the last pages of Minute Book A, extending from September, 1783, to April, 1784, are missing and may contain the records of a few wills. The will of John Floyd listed above is re-recorded in Will Book No. 1, March, 1794.

A calendar of Will Book No. 1 was compiled by William J. Gammon, of Hawesville, Kentucky, and published in *The National Genealogical Society Quarterly*, Washington, in the October, 1917, and January, 1918, numbers, under the title of "Abstracts of the First 131 Wills of Jefferson County, Kentucky." A few years ago the John Marshall Chapter, D. A. R., Louisville, prepared a brief calendar of Will Books No. 1 and No. 2 and presented a manuscript copy to The Filson Club. Although Mr. Gammon's printed copy and the D. A. R.'s manuscript copy are in the archives of The Filson Club, the Publication Committee agrees that such material should not only be made more readily available to its members but should also be presented in a more detailed form than it appears in either of the two preceding calendars.

---

*Pages 1-87, this volume.

After preparing our calendar of the will-book copies, a careful comparison was made with the original wills on file. The county clerks of Jefferson County during the period covered by Will Book No. 1 were Will Johnston, Stephen Ormsby and Worden Pope. They or some of their deputies transcribed the original wills into the Will Book. The writing varies with the character of the writer's penmanship. Some words are subject to more than one reading. An effort has been made to retain, as closely as possible, the original spelling, although it is often erroneous. Some of it is evidently phonetic. A name is sometimes spelled two or three ways in the course of one will. No attempt has been made to suggest the correct spelling.

In the calendar here published the name of the testator appears in capitals and is followed by the date of the writing and the date of the recording of the will. The nuncupative or oral wills that occur are so designated. No annotations are made except in a few instances. Among them are, in brackets, the Will Book number and the page on which the will is recorded.]

GRUNDY, GEORGE, Sr. . . . . . . Sept. 11, 1783—April, 1784.
To wife Elizabeth, goods, chattels, etc; children not of age, Robert, Guardum, Samuel, Charles, Felix, Polly, John and George, Jr.
Executor: Wife Elizabeth. Should she remarry, sons John and George to act.
Witnesses: Richard Lee, William Owens, Will'm Allen, Charles Kinne, And. Scott, Cathrine Callen, Elizabeth Owens. [*B1, p1.*]

CATLETT, ROBERT, Nuncupative will . . Dec. 8, 1783—April, 1784.
Late of County of Frederick. Catlett, living Dec. 5th, 1783, wished his estate to go to his brother Charles: Certain property at Col. Wm. Pope's in Jefferson, and wearing apparel at John Read's in Lincoln.
Signed: Mer'th Price, Wm. Pope, Will Oldham.   [*B1, p2.*]

PRICE, MEREDITH . . . . Dec. 1, 1783—Apr., 1784.
Wife Elizabeth to use property to educate and support their children.
Executors: Wife Elizabeth, John Fox, William Pope, Benjamin Pope, James Patton, William Oldham.

216

Witnesses: None. At April Court, 1784, Wm. Clark and George Wilson made oath that the writing was that of Meredith Price. July 5, 1796, James Patten took oath of Executor, &c. [*B1, p2.*]

BLACKFORD, ZEPHANIAH . . . . . May 12, 1782—April, 1784.
Conductor of military stores of Interior Department, now resident at Ft. Nelson; father was John. To brother Reuben surveying instruments and clothes; rights to property in East Jersey to brothers and sisters there; to Reuben claim against Virginia, 600 acres up Big Kanawha River and two town lots which he bought of Capt. Geo. R. Clark at the mouth of Big Kanawha, and two lots at Clarksville, Ft. Jefferson; to Baptist Society $200.00 for sending Gospel to Illinois country; to Hannah Ruth, daughter of brother Reuben, "Blackford Manor" on "Varbache" [Wabash] River, 1440 acres two leagues above Ft. Vincennes, which was entered in the names of Levi, William, Oliver, George, Joseph, Reuben, Moses, Isaac and Henry Blackford, also 500 apple trees from "my nursery" at Fish Creek; to Phebe, second daughter of Brother Reuben, when eighteen, 360 "arpents" or acres opposite Vincennes, 40 acres bought of John Cardinne, and 500 apple trees; to Elizabeth, third daughter of Reuben, when eighteen, land bought of Randle White; one lot of my father John Blackford, 500 apple trees; to friend Yates Conwell, as token of friendship, 700 apple trees.
Executor: Brother, Reuben Blackford.
Witnesses: Buckner Pittman, Wm. Pritchett, Geo. Shepard.
[*B1, p3.*]

VAUGHAN, ANDREW, JUN. . . . . Aug. 16, 1784—Nov., 1784.
To father, Andrew Vaughan, all property.
Executors: Father, Andrew Vaughan.
Witnesses: William May, John Bennet, Benjamin Purcel. [*B1, p4.*]

TRANT, PHILIP . . . . Oct. 9, 1784—Feb., 1785.
To John Moylan, of Philadelphia, all property.
Executors: Richard C. Anderson, Patrick Joyes.
Witnesses: Wm. Johnston, Walter Davies, William Orr. [*B1, p5.*]

PAUL, PETER . . . . Aug. 3, 1784—Nov., 1784.
To son John, 250 acres of land on Bullskin "joining land I sold my father." To wife Eunice, other land and stock.
Witnesses: John Paul, Dan Melilinger. [*B1, p5.*]

CHRISTIAN, WILLIAM . . . . . . March 13, 1786—May, 1786.
"Now at Kentucky." Having already given to Alexander
Scott Bullitt and "my daughter Priscilla" her share of estate, he
bequeaths to her a pair of stone shoe-buckles and two gold rings;
to wife Anne, 500 acres on Bear Grass Creek, "including improvement whereon I now live and to be laid off by a line running from
the Oxmoor land to Mr. Bullitt's, parallel with the Dutch Station
and Breckinridge's line which joins me," also slaves; to daughter
Sarah Winston Christian, 600 acres adjoining; to Edmond Taylor, Bullitt, Fleming, and daughter Elizabeth 1000 acres, out of
3000 acres, on Elkhorn which adjoins Bryan's Station and Robt.
Johnston, and in Mercer County 400 acres to be sold by executor;
to daughters Anne and Dorothea 1000 acres at mouth of Kentucky, on Ohio River; to son John, "Saltsburg" and other lands;
for seven years the rents of John's lands to be used to educate the
single children; to "my mother," slaves; a good horse and saddle
to each of married children; to daughters Sarah Winston Christian, Betsey, Annie and Dorthea, slaves. Land in Mercer
County was bought from Daniel Trigg.
Executors: Alexander Scott Bullitt, James M. Cowles, John
Brown.
Witnesses: Will proved by oaths of John May, Isaac Hite and
Frederick Edwards. [*B1, p6.*]

LEATHERMAN, CHRISTIAN . . . . Aug. 16, 1786—Sept. 5, 1786.
To wife Julianna, 70 acres bought by me and my father from
Wm. Pope, on waters of Linn's Pond; to sons John, Daniel, Sam-
uel, Peter, David, 1500 acres on Kentucky River, located by
John Reed; mentions unborn child, and schooling of children.
Executors: Wife, Julianna and father, Christian Leatherman.
Witnesses: William Pope, Wm. Payne, Asabel Linn. [*B1, p9.*]

TULEY, CHARLES . . . . Not dated—Mar. 6, 1787.
Wife mentioned, but name not given; real estate to wife and
children, but kept until children marry.
Executors: Alexander Breckenridge, John Tuley, Jr.
Witnesses: Alex. Breckinridge, William Floyd, Nathaniel Floyd.
[*B1, p10.*]

WOODBERRY, JOHN . . . . Feb. 13, 1787—Aug. 11, 1787.
In 1st American Regiment, under Capt. David Segler. To
Patrick Mackerson, all his pay.
Witnesses: Stephen Richards, Robt. George, Griffin Taylor.
Enlisted Oct. 16, 1785, and died Feb. 20, 1787.   [*B1, p11.*]

TURPIN, RICHARD . . . . . Nov. 5, 1780—March 3 & 6, 1789.
Soldier in Illinois Regiment; sick and weak. To brother
Henry, all real and personal property in North and South
Carolina; to brothers Thomas and Jeremiah the remainder in
Virginia and elsewhere.
Executors: Henry, Thomas, Jeremiah Turpin.
Witnesses: George Shepherd, Peter Shepherd.   [*B1, p11.*]

EARICKSON, ELIZA . . . . Jany. 10, 1789—June 2, 1789.
To daughter Ruth, all of estate, she to pay all bills. Men-
tions daughters Elizabeth, Rebecca, Nancy, Caty, and son
Benjamin.
Executor: Son Benjamin.
Witnesses: Richard J. Waters, Stephen W. Richardson, David
Morgan.   [*B1, p12.*]

BRASHEARS, WILLIAM, SR. . . . Sept. 26, 1789—Nov. 3, 1789.
"Much advanced in age and in bad health." Mentions children
Samuel Mason, Mary Ann and Elizabeth; Samuel to keep other
two children until of age; to Samuel land bought of Nicholas
Brashears; other children already had received sufficient "for
their parts."
Executor: Son, Samuel Mason Bearshears.
Witnesses: Anthony Phelps, Joshua Wheeler, Jos. Bearshears,
Edwin Phelps.   [*B1, p13.*]

HITE, ABRAHAM . . . . Mar. 20, 1787—Feb. 2, 1790.
To wife Rebecca real and personal estate, after division in
accordance with contract dated August, 1782, with sons Isaac,
Abraham and Joseph Hite; at her death land, slaves, etc. to go to
sons; to John and William Hite, sons of brother Joseph, 200 acres
and 400 acres, respectively, in District of Kentucky; to Hannah
Vanmetre, during life, 600 acres on Jessamine Creek, "given me
by military warrant," adjoining Adam Stephens, John Bowman
(administrators of estate of John Preston) and Nathaniel Evans;

219

to Thomas Vanmetre the 600 acres, after death of his mother Hannah, and 100 acres bought from Daniel McNeal and he from Robert Higgins, also 500 pounds when he is twenty-one or marries. He mentions a suit which Joseph Hite, his father, has against Lord Fairfax.

Executors: Sons, Isaac, Abraham and Joseph Hite.

Witnesses: Vincent Williams, Alexander Doran, Isaac Vanmeter, Thomas Neale, Daniel Ashby, John Batman.   [*B1, p15.*]

REAGER, JACOB . . . . Mar. 15, 1790—June 1, 1790.

Sick. To wife Elizabeth, 10 acre lot adjoining Louisville; To Edward Colgahoon, son-in-law, 320 acres on Goose Creek, and he to pay a debt "due from me" to the estate of my father (late); to stepdaughter, Nancy Colgahoon, all land located for me by Zephaniah and Reuben Blackford on Pocatello and Fish Creeks, 700 acres and lots in Louisville; to Sally Colgahoon, sister of Nancy, land as compensation for what he owes her on her father's estate; mentions "my four children Henry, Sally, Maria, Jacob"; son Henry is to have the house and lot in Louisville "where I now live" and 150 acres in Illinois grant; to son Jacob 500 acres in Illinois grant; to "my daughter Sally" [this does not seem to be Sally Colgahoon mentioned above] a lot in Louisville adjoining Evan Williams.

Executors: Colonel Richard Anderson, Major William Croghan.

Witnesses: Ga. I. Johnston, Edw. Ashby, R. J. Waters. [*B1, p18.*]

HAWKINS, DAVID . . . . Aug. 5, 1786—Nov. 7, 1786.

Wife Alice; sons John, David, William, Thomas. To Henry, land and ferry; mentions daughters Catherine, Sarah, Eleanor, Ann, Mary, Rebecca.

Executors: Wife Alice and son John Hawkins.

Witnesses: Peter Lovel, John McMachon, Joseph Inlow.[*B1, p20.*]

HAWKES, JOHN [HAKES] . . . . . Sept. 2, 1790—Dec. 7, 1790.

To wife Cateron, one-third of estate, balance to children, but does not name them.

Executors: Philip Smith, Thomas Minter.

Witnesses: Thomas McClean, Adam Mong, Thomas Minter.   [*B1, p22.*]

220

FULLENWIDER, PETER . . . . . . Oct. 22, 1790—Dec. 7, 1790.
To wife Caty one third of land; to son Henry, 150 acres; to daughter Elizabeth balance of land; child unborn.
Executors: Brother Jacob, and Samuel Orycker.
Witnesses: Martin Daniel, Elenner Coper, Mary Cazman.
[*B1, p23.*]

MERRIWETHER, WILLIAM, SR. . . Oct. 26, 1790—Feb. 1, 1791.
To wife Patty the home plantation, 285 acres; to son William the plantation bought of A. S. Dandridge, after wife's death, also balance of tract of land of which James has 100 acres; to son Valentine 203 acres, part of home plantation; to son-in-law James Merriwether 100 acres where he lives on the south fork of Bear Grass Creek bought from Nicholas Merriwether; to son David Wood Merriwether and son-in-law John Hughes, negroes; mentions grand-child.
Executors: David W., William, Valentine, and James Meriwether, and John Hughes.
Witnesses: John Clark, George R. Clark, A. Churchill, Henry Churchill. [*B1, p24.*]

WATSON, WILLIAM . . . . July 31, 1789—Feb. 1, 1791.
To mother, Ervin Watson, of Newcastle County, Delaware, all his property; to Isaac Newland, infant son of Jacob Newland, of Jefferson County, a horse; mentions brother Thomas and youngest sister Margaret Watson.
Executor: Jacob Newland.
Witnesses: William and Samuel Shannon, Henry McWead [?].
[*B1, p26.*]

GOBAN, JOSEPH . . . . Dec. 22, 1790—Feb. 1, 1791.
Wife Lidy and three sons mentioned.
Executors: Pall Spear, Thomas McClean.
Witnesses: John Goben, Pall Spear, Thomas McClean. [*B1, p27.*]

HOLEMAN, NICHOLAS . . . . . . Mar. 14, 1791—June 1, 1791.
[Original will signed Nicholas, given as Nathaniel in notation of court record.] Mentions mother-in-law's four girls, Nancy, Sarah, Patsey and Jane Holeman; mentions uncle Ed Holeman;

221

Lewis Casselman is indebted to him; Daniel Triben and Joseph Maclain, the Taylor are mentioned.
Executor: Zachariah Fisher.
Witnesses: Jas. Fisher, Geo. Holeman, Zachariah Fisher.[*B1, p28.*]

OLDHAM, WILLIAM . . . . . . Sept. 13, 1791—Dec. 6, 1791.
To wife Penelope tract of land on Chenoweth Run, house, furniture and third of stock for ever, certain negroes and residue of estate during widowhood, this to be divided equally between four children John, Richard, Abigail and William Oldham, except pre-emption of 400 acres near Bullitt's Lick: to Elizabeth Homes the 400 acres preemption near Bullitt's Lick.
Executors: Richard C. Anderson, Richard Taylor, Jacob Funk.
Witnesses: George Pearce.   [*B1, p29.*]

NEALE, THOMAS Oct. 2, 1790—Jan. 4, Feb. 4, 1791, & Jan. 3, 1792.
"Starting on a Campaign against the Indians and God may never permit me to return, yet well." To wife Elizabeth property; to children after her death.   *Executors:* None named.
Witnesses: Richard Abbott, John Huckleberry [a third name not legible].   [*B1, p30.*]

LEMEN, ROBERT . . . . Sept. 9, 1786—Feb. 7, 1792.
To father Robert and to mother Isabella Lemen, 224 acres on Brashears Creek; to brothers and sisters John, Samuel, Lucy Newland, Isabella Cox and niece Jean Stevenson two pounds each.
Executors: Brother Samuel and brother-in-law Jacob Newland.
Witnesses: William Watson, Will Shannon.   [*B1, p31.*]

STUART, JAMES . . . . Sept. 16, 1791—Feb. 7, 1792.
In health, but entering campaign against the Indians. After paying debts, estate to friend Thomas Richey and his heirs.
Executors: None named.
Witnesses: William Prince, David Standiford.   [*B1, p32.*]

GREGG, JOHN . . . . Oct. 25, 1791—Feb. 7, 1792.
To wife Ann, house in which he lives, etc.; to son David, farm, etc.; daughters are Margaret, eldest, Lydia, Mary, single.
Executors: Son David, John Todd.
Witnesses: John Perkins, Jas. Ferguson.   [*B1, p33.*]

JOHNSTON, DOROTHY . . . . . . Apr. 27, 1792—June 5, 1792.
To sons Robert and General, negroes; to daughter Nancy Chew Johnston, negroes; to daughter Polly Harrison, bed; John Harrison to see that Nancy Chew is educated; three youngest children mentioned.
Executors: John Harrison, Michael Lacassagne.
Witnesses: Mary Ann Harrison, Elizabeth Reager, Jacob Lytle, August Kaye.   [*B1, p34.*]

CLARK, WILLIAM . . . . Nov. 11, 1791—Dec. 6, 1791.
Late of Clarksville. Bonds payable to William Croghan and Richard Morris to be discharged. To brother Marston Green Clark land in Jefferson County on Beargrass; to brother Benjamin Wilson Clark and sister Lucy Pool 933 acres in the lands given by Virginia to officers etc. of Virginia State Line, being part of his claim for military services performed in last war; to brothers Jonathan and Everard Clark 1000 acres on Russel's Creek, including noted burning spring; also to brothers and sisters land in Illinois grants Nos. 31, 24, 96, 160; to Marston Green Clark certain lots in Clarksville for the term of three years from "the date of my decease"; and if either of brothers or sisters comes to this country to live within the space of three years "after my decease," then he or she shall have lots and houses, if neither of them comes lots and houses remain the property of Marston Green Clark; also to him negro man for seven years, at expiration of which time said negro shall be liberated. To friend and relative Mrs. Elizabeth Anderson, watch. Remainder of estate, 500 acres land, Illinois grant No. 272, of which 200 acres in said grant is at the forks of Silver Cr., remainder of military warrant 733⅔ acres, surveyors instruments, etc. to be disposed of in settlement of estate. Mentions bond he owes Richard Morris.
Executors: "My trusty friends" Richard Clough Anderson, William Croghan, Richard Terrell.
Witnesses: John Clark, Geo. R. Clark, James O'Fallon. [*B1, p36.*]
[The will of William Clark, the surveyor—son of Benjamin Clark and first cousin of General William Clark, of the Lewis and Clark Expedition, and his brother General George Rogers Clark—is published in *Conquest of the Country Northwest of the River Ohio, 1778-1783, and Life of Gen. George Rogers Clark*, by William Hayden English, Vol. 2, pp. 829-832.]

ELLIOTT, JAMES . . . . Aug. 20, 1791—Mar. 5, 1793.
Settlement and preemption "to which I am entitled," to
nephews John, son of William, and John, son of Daniel, and
friend Robert Campbell now of Pittsburg.
Executors: John Campbell, James Francis Moore, Henry Read.
Witnesses: Mic'l Dillon, Wm. Rhodes, Wm. Beard, Daniel Scott,
Charles Scott.   [*B1, p39.*]
[Original will is not now in Will File Box.]

JOHNSTON, PETER . . . . July 31, 1793—Aug. 6, 1793.
Very sick. To brother James, 75 acres in Frederick County,
Maryland, near Ft. Frederick; brother Jacob, he thinks, may be
dead. *Executors:* None named.
Witnesses: Abraham Decker, John Martin.   [*B1, p40.*]

MORGAN, DAVID . . . . Aug. 18, 1792—May 6, 1794.
To wife Elizabeth property in Louisville, also all stock. *Executor:* None named.
Witnesses: James Patten, Samuel Kirby, Evan Williams. [*B1, p41.*]

FLOYD, JOHN . . . . No date—Mar. 4, 1794.
To wife Jenny home farm on Beargrass Creek; to son William
Preston residue of 2000 acres "I live on," being on south side of
Beargrass including stations of Hoglins and New Holland; to
daughter Mourning Floyd and unbaptized son called George
Floyd land in Fayette County called Woodstock, 4000 acres; to
unborn child 1400 acres on waters of Harrod's Creek bought of
Colonel Trigg; certain lands to be sold; other lands on Floyd's
Fork and Harrod's Creek to wife and all children; to heirs of
Colonel Stephen Trigg 1000 acres of land in Fayette called Royal
Spring Tract; to heirs of John McClealland 1400 acres on north
side of Royal Spring Tract and to take up assignment of his of the
Royal Spring now in the hand of Sarah Wilson; to youngest son
Robert Davis, deceased, 25 acres in Amherst County "where I
formerly lived" being the land "I had of his father"; to father
lands in Amherst; all lands in Bottetourt County to be disposed
of by Col. William Preston; to brother Isham 2000 acres entry on
Floyd's Fork called the Horse Shoe Bottom and certain money
for assistance "in removing me to this country"; brothers Robert
and Charles to complete surveying.
Executors: William Pope, Sr., and wife Jenny.
Witnesses: Charles Floyd, Robert Floyd, Robert Eakin. [*B1, p42.*]

[This same will of John Floyd is also recorded in Minute Book A, Jefferson County, under proceedings of June 3, 1783. The appraisement of his estate is recorded in the same book, June 7, 1783. Both will and appraisement are published in *The Filson Club History Quarterly*, Vol. 3, No. 4, July, 1929, pp. 172-176.]

REED, HENRY . . . . Sept. 11, 1793—Apr., 1794.
    Merchant. To Eleanor Elliott, Martha Patton, Elizabeth Wise, of Louisville, 100 pounds each; to brother James Reed of Denny County, Ireland, one-fourth part, but if he is dead, to his children; to sons James Reed, Henry Reed and Robert Reed, one-fourth part each.
Executors: George Wallace of Pittsburg, Andrew Kennedy of Philadelphia.
Witnesses: Thomas Boyd, Bartholomew M. Shane, James McNutt. [*B1, p46.*]

FUNK, JACOB . . . . Apr. 14, 1793—May 4, 1794.
    To wife Ann, home-farm at Lynn Station; to son John, land bought of William Oldham, deceased, and Peyton Short, on which he lives, formerly owned by deceased son Jacob and Robert Martin; to Frederick Geiger and wife 1200 acres; to Philip Aerhert and wife Mary 1220 acres; to Abraham Bairer and wife Elizabeth 1600 acres; to daughter Rosina, wife of Robert Martin, money.
Executors: John Funk, Frederick Geiger.
Witnesses: Thomas Prather, Richard C. Anderson, Ob'd. Newman.
[*B1, p49.*

HITE, ISAAC . . . . Feb. 8, 1794—Mar. 4, 1794.
    To wife Harriet, home-farm 400 acres, part of 1400 acres patented to Abraham Hite; daughters Rebecca Vanmeter Hite, and Elizabeth Rigby Hite, and son Jacob, under twenty-one, mentioned; also refers to saw mill, grist mill, tanyard. All children under age. Abraham Hite mentioned as deceased; Rebecca Hite as legatee; Rebecca, Abraham, Jr., Joseph and Isaac Hite mentioned as partners.
Executors: Robert Breckinridge, Richard C. Anderson, brother Abraham Hite, William Taylor, a family friend, and Moses Kuykendall.
Witnesses: And's Livingston, Wm. Fitzgerald, Timothy Conditt, Samuel Grier, Joseph Hite. [*B1, p51.*]

HUNTER, JOSEPH . . . . No date—Nov. 4, 1794.
To William and Asabel Linn, heirs, 71 and 20 acres, respectively, of land on which "I now live"; mentions Joshua Archer as heir; son Joseph; note on William Pope to Joseph Applegate; Martha Dunn mentioned.
Executors: William Pope, Joseph Hunter.
Witnesses: John Pope, James Stuart, Thomas Long.   [*B1, p54.*]

KIRBY, SAMUEL . . . . Mar. 27, 1795—May 5, 1795.
Miss Nancy Earickson to be maintained out of estate as long as she remains single and to have a lot in Louisville; daughter Nelly and son James to have other property; James Sneed and Miss Earickson to be children's guardians.
Executors: James Sneed, Nancy Earickson.
Witnesses: Michael Lacassagne, Reuben Eastin, Ga. J. Johnston, Evan Williams.   [*B1, p57.*]

WATTS, JAMES . . . . Apr. 3, 1795—May 5, 1795.
To brother John $300.00 and land bought from John Vaughan on Patten's Creek; to sister's son, James Lowry, Jr., watch.
Executors: Evan Williams, John Porter.
Witnesses: Ga. J. Johnston, Jos. Wade, Robert George, John Irwin, Stephen Blackwell.   [*B1, p59.*]

GATEWOOD, JOHN . . . . Feb. 10, 1795—July 7, 1795.
Sons Fleming, James, John, Fielding, Joseph, Fullington, daughters Catherine, Ann, Alsey, Clary, Sarah, Judith, Penelope, Frances; estate in Virginia mentioned.
Executors: Abraham Hite, Fleming Gatewood, Fullington Gatewood.
Witnesses: Ed. Jones, Samuel Bochin, John Brown.   [*B1, p61.*]

VAUGHAN, JOHN . . . . Mar. 18, 1795—July 7, 1795.
Nuncupative will. James Patten to sell lands etc. for payment of debts and benefit of Vaughan's children. Signed by James Watts, John Nelson, John Porter.
Executor: James Patten.   [*B1, p64.*]

MERIWETHER, DAVID WOOD . . . Dec. 7, 1794—Aug. 4, 1795.
To wife Mary one third of estate, balance to children and at her death her share to children; home to be bought for her by

226

executor; names son Henry Wood Meriwether and other children under age. Robert K. Moore indebted to him 150 pounds.
Executors: Friends William and James Merriwether, John Hughes.
Witnesses: Mary Merriwether, Jasper Anderson, Ed Vaughn, John Hughes, Ann Hughes, Ann Read.   [*B1, p65.*]

CHURCHILL, ARMISTEAD . . . . July 29, 1795—Jan. 5, 1796.
    Mentions grandson John Downing, son of his daughter Elizabeth who in 1780 married John Downing; to son John land between Linn's Pond and Fishing Pond, and half of the land "I now hold" in Mason County; to son Henry 1000 acres in Fayette County on waters of Elkhorn and Cedar Creek; to son Armistead 1000 acres in Fayette County on waters of Elkhorn and Cedar Creek; to daughter Mary Churchill when she marries, certain negroes; to son Samuel, under age, "land I live on," after death of his mother; to son William half of lands held in Mason County opposite the Little Miami; to wife Elizabeth "land whereon I now live," household furniture, etc. Besides land, each son and daughter, as well as wife, were left certain slaves by name.
Executor: Wife Elizabeth, sons John, Henry Churchill.
Witnesses: Samuel Oldham, James and Sally Blackwell, James Blackwell.   [*B1, p67.*]

ABBOTT, RICHARD . . . . April 6, 1795—Aug. 2, 1796.
    Recorded in Knox County [Indiana] June 9, 1795. Names wife Elizabeth; sons John and Gabriel bound out; two daughters to live with mother.
Executors: Wife Elizabeth and Jonathan Nixon.
Witnesses: Ab'm. F. Snapp, James Johnson, John Harbin.[*B1,p68.*]

HARDING, HENRY . . . . Oct. 12, 1796—Nov. 1, 1796.
    To wife Rebecca whole estate, at her death to five children, John, Henry, Wilmoth, Caty and Sarah, excepting slave who is to be freed.
Executors: Wife Rebeckah, Moses Keykendall, Jonathan Nixon.
Witnesses: Jos. Kellar, John and Henry Netherton [Netherlands].
          [*B1, p70.*]

CUMMINS, WILLIAM . . Sept. 7, 1795—Dec. 6, 1796, Feb., 1797.
    Wife's name given as Mary, also as Margery. After fourteen years, plantation and land on Patton's Creek to be sold and pro-

ceeds to sons and wife Mary. To daughter Maryann 20 pounds money; to sons David, William and John his farm; sons Henry and Moses to have six months schooling; to daughter Jeany a horse; to son Ebenezer an education.

Executors: Wife Mary, and son David Cummins.

Witnesses: Robert McIntire, Jos. Shaw and Geo. Pomeroy.
[*B1, p71.*]

LINN, WILLIAM . . July 18, 1780—Apr. 3, 1781, Aug. 2, 1796.

Wife Letitia; to youngest daughter Ann, plantation "where I live"; to oldest son William 1000 acres below mouth of Miami; to son Asael [Asabel] 330 acres and one-third of Blue Lick; to son Benjamin 1000 acres adjoining his brother William; to daughters Theodotia Linn and Luoruania [Lavina Anna?] Linn 1000 acres adjoining their brothers; if the daughters "return from the Indians to have this land, if they do not return, land to be divided among my sons"; to daughter Rachel Linn, 600 acres on Harrod's Creek; to her children, John and Josey Linn, "born since I left home," 5 shillings each. To four friends, James and Ben Earickson, James and Samuel Kirby, 1200 acres below the mouth of the Miami.

Executors: James Kirby, James Earickson.

Witnesses: Charles Polke, Sanford Edwards, Thos. McCarty.
[*B1, p74.*]

[In Jefferson County Minute Book A, page 5, is an entry showing that William Linn's will was proved by Thomas McCarty at Court held April 4, 1781. See *The Filson Club History Quarterly*, Vol. 3, No. 2, January, 1929, pages 62, 78, 79.] *

CLARK, ANDREW . . . Jan. 2, 1797—June 6, 1797, July, 1797.

To Richard Taylor and his family, my estate. *Executor:* None named.

Witnesses: Richard Harris, Henry Coleman. [*B1, p75.*]

LACASSAGNE, MICHAEL, July 9, 1796—Oct. 19, 1797, Nov. 8, 1797.

Of Louisville. Authorizes Eli Williams, of Hagerstown, Maryland, to sell 4000 acres on Bear Creek, branch of Green River, 2000 acres on Bacon Creek, 300 acres in Bourbon County; to Robert K. Moore, in trust, for use of Mrs. Elizabeth McClelland, "for my two mulatto children, to be taught to read and write and to receive their freedom at age of 25," and two lots in

---

*Pages 8, 24 & 25, this volume.

Louisville; also to Robert K. Moore, 600 acres in Illinois grant; to John Walker, Sr., 500 acres in Illinois grant, should he die, the government then to use the land to educate children of poor parents; to James Beauvais, 200 acres in the Illinois grant; to sister Jenny Lacassagne of the Republic of France, 500 acres in the Illinois grant; to James Cox of the Western Territory, 200 acres in the Illinois grant; to Cornelius Beatty, of Lexington, 200 acres in the Illinois grant; to Robert K. Moore, house and lots in Louisville; to Charles Clark (negro), 100 acres in the Illinois grant; to Stephen Ormsby, watch which he gave me, and library; to Mrs. Eliz. McClelland, 50 pounds. After debts paid, all moneys to go to Robert K. Moore, James Beauvais, John Thruston, sister, and Ben Sebastian. Executors to send to John Holkes, picture of him "I now have." Directs that he be buried in Richmond, and a well-built brick house be erected over his grave, if he does not die too far away from Richmond to make the burial request impossible. [Does not state but probably refers to Richmond, Virginia.]

Executors: Stephen Ormsby, Robert K. Moore, Cornelius Beatty, St. James Beauvais, John Thruston, John Thompson, Ben Sebastian, Walter Warfield.

Witnesses: Knox County [Indiana], October 19, 1797. Will proven by oath of Henry Vanderburgh, Esq., Judge of Probate, Henry Hurst, G. W. Johnston and Robert Buntell. Signed by Henry Vanderburgh.

October 30, 1797: H. Vanderburgh: above is a true copy of will. Certified copy recorded in Jefferson County, November 8, 1797. Worden Pope. [*B1, p76.*]

JOHNSTON, WILLIAM . . . . . . Sept. 18, 1794—Mar. 6, 1798.

Of Cave Hill, Kentucky. Property to be kept together until wife marries, then she to have one-third and son, Jas. Chew Johnston, to have two-thirds, he being under age. *Witnesses:* None.

Executors: Ben Sebastian, Thomas McMunn. [*B1, p82.*]

SLAUGHTER, CADWALLADER . . Jan. 22, 1798 [?]—Mar. 6, 1798.

Signed Cad. Slaughter. Estate to three sons, Edward, Presly and Francis M [R?]; sons-in-law Charles Morehead and John Churchill have received their parts. *Executors:* None named.

Witnesses: Benoni Diment, William Sullivan, Daniel Donohue. [*B1, p82.*]

TENNENT, HUGH M. . May 19, 1798—Aug. 7, 1798, Dec. 4, 1798.
Of Caroline County, Virginia, at present weak and sick, and in Kentucky. To brother Washington, all lands in Kentucky; sisters are Lucy and Sally Tennent and Polly Ellis; to mother residue of estate for life, and then to three sisters.
Executor: Brother John Tennent.
Witnesses: Presly Thornton, Rice Parker, Richard Taylor, Senr., Colby H. Taylor, And'n Watkins.   [*B1, p83.*]

OGLESBY, RICHARD . . . . Aug. 17, 1798—Mar. 5, 1799.
To wife Nancy real estate. "To my last" children Jesse, Washington, Susannah Ware Oglesby, Matilday, Richard, Woodford, Rachel, Jacob and Willis Oglesby.
Executors: Wife Nancy and Joseph Oglesby.
Witnesses: Joseph Oglesby, William Powell.   [*B1, p84.*]

CLARK, JOHN . . . . July 24, 1799—Oct. 1, 1799.
Includes Codicil dated July 26, 1799. To son Jonathan all real estate and personal now in his possession; to son William and grandsons John and Benjamin O'Fallon, to be equally divided, 3000 acres "which I claim under an entry on Treasury Warrant" 7926 made in surveyors office of Fayette County, March 29, 1783, surveyed and patented in his name. To son Edmond, 1000 acres on waters of East Fork of the Miami River, claimed under entry of military warrant No. 307, made in office of Surveyor for Continental Line, August 16, 1787, also 1000 acres claimed under said warrant No. 307, made in Surveyors office August 17, 1787, these entries made in the name of son John Clark, deceased and "my son Jonathan Clark the heir at law hath relinguished in my favor his rights thereto" also money and negroes. To son George Rogers Clark certain negroes. To son-in-law Owen Gwathmey, estate both real and personal now in his possession, also 1000 acres on waters of Pady's Creek in Logan County, being land deeded by son Jonathan October 24, 1796. To sons-in-law William Croghan and Richard C. Anderson certain negroes. To son-in-law Charles M. Thruston 400 acres in Shelby County on waters of Clear Creek, being settlement part of tract of 1400 acres, also negroes. To son William the tract of land "whereon I now live," together with appurtenances and certain negroes, also the whole of "my lands in Elionise grant," deeded to me by son

George Rogers Clark; William to pay debts; and to grandsons, John and Benjamin O'Fallon when they become of age, 100 and 50 pounds, respectively, also certain negroes.
Executors: Sons Jonathan, George Rogers and William Clark, sons-in-law Richard C. Anderson, William Croghan and Charles M. Thruston, and friend Benjamin Sebastian.
Witnesses: John Hughes, Robert K. Moore, Marston G. Clark.
Witnesses to Codicil: Sam Gwathmy, Jno. Hughes. [*B1, p86.*]
[The will of John Clark is published in *Conquest of the Country Northwest of the River Ohio, 1778-1783, and Life of Gen. George Rogers Clark,* by William Hayden English, Vol. 1, pp. 46-51.]

HOKE, ANDREW . . . . Sept. 23, 1799—Jan. 7, 1800.
To wife Barbara, furniture; to son Jacob one-half of home farm and new stone house where Jacob lives; to son Peter other half of home place; to son Leonard, "my still," 100 bushels of rye due me by August Frederick and part of money due by Henry Gring; Leonard is to live with his mother; to daughter Elizabeth, wife of John Pottorff, hogs, cattle, etc; other daughters Barbara, wife of Jacob Myers; and Clara, wife of John Miller of Baltimore.
Executors: Sons Adam, Jacob and Peter Hoke.
Witnesses: John Miller, Fred. Geiger, Peter Wise. [*B1, p91.*]

GALLOWAY, GEORGE . . . . May 1, 1785—Mar., 1800.
Mentions oldest son William; son James to have note due from Sam and Joseph Galloway; son John; daughter Martha, wife of Launcelot Jenkins, to have certain property, if she comes to this country; son Joseph; daughter Margaret, wife of George Pomeroy. Launcelot Jenkins and George Pomeroy to aid in business affairs. *Executors:* None named.
Witnesses: George Pomeroy, Marget Pomeroy. [*B1, p98.*]

THOMPSON, BENAJAH . . . . Oct. 20, 1799—Apr., 1800.
To wife Druzilla, furniture, etc.; to children, oldest daughter Elizabeth Ford, next oldest daughter Sarah Shaw, oldest son Robert, 10 shillings each; Nancy Walker ten shillings; two youngest children mentioned, Jane and William; to Thomas Thompson, 10 shillings.
Executors: Wife Druzilla and Jesse Ford.
Witnesses: John Core, John Huckelbury, John Beirsol. [*B1, p100.*]

CORNELIUS, WILLIAM . . . . . . Nov. 21, 1800—Jan. 19, 1801
    Wife Catherine; to son Daniel, but if Daniel dies, property to
go to John, Philip and George Hawks.
Executors: Thomas and William Jonson.
Witnesses: James Carmicheal, Samuel Reaugh, Philip Smith.
[*B1, p101.*]

BLANKENBECKER, JACOB . . Died Jan. 2, 1801—Jan. 19, 1801.
    Nuncupative Will. Mentions son Samuel, infants and wife;
youngest son not of age. Signed by John Samuel Mow [Man]
and William Goose. [Written in German.]
Proved by oaths of William Goose and Rev. John Samuel Mow
[Man?].
[Also recorded in Will Book No. 1, p. 111.]   [*B1, p102.*]

CHRISTIAN, JOHN H. . . . . —1800—1801.
    Gives slaves their freedom. Instructs Alex. Bullitt to have
a handsome monument erected over graves of "my father and
mother"; to each of his sisters, ten guineas with which to buy a
locket in memory of him; Aunt Anne Fleming of Virginia and
cousin Leonard Fleming are in debt to him; to Sam Brown a
horse; brother-in-law is Mr. Dickerson, and sister Mrs. Elizabeth
Dickerson; mentions Mrs. Howard and Mrs. Breckinridge; refers to "other Sisters."
Executors: Alexander Bullitt, Dr. Walter Warfield, John Pope.
Witnesses: Mary Howard, Mary Parker.   [*B1, p103.*]

FLEMING, MARTHA . . . . . . Sept. 9, 1800—June 15, 1801.
    To son Ben Rodman, farm "on which I live"; to daughter
Jenny Rodman $91.00; mentions grandson William Pope Rod-
man, son of Thomas, as underage; to son James Rodman $91.00;
to sons John and Samuel Rodman $91.00 and $45.00, respectively;
names Martha and William, children of John Rodman; also son
Alex; grand-daughter Amey Rodman to have "linnin wheal,"
etc.; to son Hugh Rodman, $1.00; also to grandson William, son
of Hugh Rodman, $1.00. *Executors:* None named.
Witnesses: Joseph Oglesby, Mary N. Rodman.   [*B1, p108.*]

BRECKENRIDGE, ALEXANDER . . . May 16, 1797—June, 1801.
    Wife Jany; to brother Robert one third of 3000 acres of land
for "my services in last War." "On northwest of the Ohio, be-

232

tween the Miami and Scioto rivers, located by brother Robert,"
two-thirds to my sons James, Robert and Henry Brown Brecken-
ridge; to sons, also 1000 acres on the Ohio opposite the mouth of
Saline.
Executors: Wife and brother Robert Breckenridge.
Witnesses: None given. Will proved by oaths of Ga. I. Johnston,
James Meriwether, Saml. Wells and Worden Pope.   [*B1, p110.*]

HALE, WILLIAM . . . . May 23, 1801—June 15, 1801.
    [Given as Hall in Will Book, but signed Hale on the original.]
To John Brown and wife estate after debts paid. *Executor:* None.
Witnesses: Robert Dinon, and Henry Puttorf, Minister.[*B1, p111.*]

BLANKENBEKER, JACOB . . . Died Jan. 2, 1801—June, 1801.
    Nuncupative will. "My part of land on which I live to my
wife, her children and mother," etc. Slaves to his son Samuel;
residue to the children of his first wife, with charge to care for his
present wife and infants. [Written in German.]
Signed by John Samuel Mow [Man] and William Goose.
[Also recorded in Will Book No. 1, p. 102.]   [*B1, p111.*]

BAIRD, MARY . . . . Sept. 28, 1798—Oct. 19, 1801.
    To her son Samuel, money due her by sons John and Thomas;
balance to her children Robert, Joseph and Martha, wife of Daniel
McClure; certain personal gifts to Esther, daughter of her son
Thomas; to son Thomas, money of bond in settlement by
Patrict Hartford. *Executors:* None named.
Witnesses: William and George McClure.   [*B1, p113.*]

MYRTLE, JOHN [MERTLE, MURTLE] . . . . . July 27, 1801—
                                            No date of probate.
    To wife Phebe, estate for herself and the children, they to be
reared and supported.
Executrix: Wife.
Witnesses: A. Smoot and Joseph Field.   [*B1, p115.*]
    [Original will is not now in Will File Box.]

MERIWETHER, PATTY . . . . . . Oct. 14, 1801—Oct. 20, 1801.
    To daughter Ann Hughes, for life, negroes and stock, and at
her death to her children. Mentions sons William, Valentine and
sons-in-law John Hughes and James Meriwether. To six children

233

of son David Wood Meriwether, also children of daughter Polly Meriwether, deceased, children of daughter Elizabeth Meriwether, deceased, and only child of daughter Mildred Mitchell, one shilling each. These "children of my three deceased daughters to have nothing more, agreeable to request of my husband at his death."

Executors: Son William Meriwether, sons-in-law John Hughes, James Meriwether.

Witnesses: Robt. K. Moore, C. Prince.   [*B1, p117.*]

THRUSTON, JOHN . . . . Jan. 15, 1802—Mar. 1, 1802.

To wife Elizabeth T. Thruston, negroes, chariot and horses; to son-in-law Thomas January, money from farm "on which I live"; executors to buy 150 acres near Lexington or in Jefferson County for his wife, as she chooses; children, not of age, to be educated; to daughters Elizabeth Taylor, Catherine and Fannie Badello Thruston 3,500 acre lots in Illinois grant, deeded by John Buckner and Charles Thruston, also 1000 acres on the Ohio and Little Sandy Rivers in name of John Harvin, Charles Mynn Thruston and Edmund Taylor and John Buckner. Names five sons, Thomas Whiting, Charles Mynn, Alfred, Lucius Falkland, and Algernon Sidney Thruston, Thomas and Charles being under age. To daughter Mary B., wife of Thomas January, 500 acres on Green River & Rough Creek out of tract conveyed by his father Charles Mynn Thruston to John Buckner and Charles Thruston; to Charles Cary, who lived with him, 100 acres on Green River.

Executors: Wife Elizabeth T., son-in-law Thomas January, Alexander S. Bullitt, Buckner Thruston, Edmund H. Taylor.

Witnesses: Fort. Cosby, John Collins, John Fipps, Rowland Fipps.
[*B1, p120.*]

JONES, CHRISTOPHER . . . . Died April 3, 1802—June 7, 1802.

Nuncupative will. James and Robert, sons, to have land; daughter Mary to have furniture; other children who have not lived with him recently are referred to. Statement written April 5, 1802.

Signed by James McCaslin, and James Farnsley.

Executors: None named.

Witnesses: Fleming Gatewood, Worden Pope.   [*B1, p125.*]

[The original will in Court House is filed in an envelope under name of James M. Caslin.]

234

MORGAN, ELIZABETH . . . . . . Dec. 22, 1801—June 7, 1802.
    Of Louisville. To "Morgan Morgan and David Morgan, sons
of my late husband's brother Nathaniel," house and lot where I
live; Morgan being then under eighteen years of age; to Nathaniel
Morgan and to Elizabeth, Emmons and Peggy Tyson, sisters of
late Husband, 50 pounds "Pennsylvania money"; also to Nathaniel, clothes of late husband and "his bro. David"; to my
sisters Mary Stinson, widow, and Sidney, wife of Moses Dougherty, bed and furniture; to Ben Tyson and James S. Prather, son of
Thomas, and Worden Pope my right to 700 acres on Rolling
Fork, bought of Jacob Yoder; balance of estate to John, James,
William, Francis, Mary, Betsy, Peggy MacConnell, children of
my brother James MacConnell; also to James, Robert, William,
Patsey, Mary Rankin MacConnell, children of brother William
MacConnell; and to John, James and Peggy Dougherty, children
of my sister Sidney Dougherty; and to Thomas Stinson son of my
sister Mary Stinson.
    Executors: Worden Pope, Thomas Prather, Ben Tyson.
    Witnesses: John Collins, James MacConnel.   [*B1, p127.*]

BEARD, SARAH . . . . Oct. 13, 1796—Oct. 4, 1802.
    Of Somerset County, Maryland. To sons John, Charles and
Thomas and daughters Rachel Moor and Mary Beard, certain
bequests, with residue to three youngest children, Charles, Mary
and Thomas.
    Executors: Two honest men to be appointed to divide estate for
three youngest children.
    Witnesses: James Moore, Levin Goslee, Charles Shirman.
                                                        [*B1, p130.*]

BEARD, CHARLES . . . . May 20, 1802—Oct. 4, 1802.
    Lands to youngest brother Thomas; eldest brother John and
sisters Rachel Moore, Mary Beard; John Moore brother-in-law.
    Executor: Brother-in-law John Moore.
    Witnesses: James Moore, Charles Shirman, Thomas Moore.
                                                        [*B1, p131.*]

HUME, JOHN . . . . May 2, 1798—Oct. 4, 1802.
    To wife Jeane, 400 acres for widowhood or life, and then to
grandsons, John and Hume Sturgeon; to Thomas Sturgeon 300

acres of land where he now lives; to Christian Young plantation where he lives, if his wife dies then land to go to her sons Peter and John; mentions daughter Sarah Sturgeon; to children of Mary Soverains 200 pounds.
Executors: Thomas Sturgeon, Robert Breckenridge.
Witnesses: John Potts, George R. C. Floyd, A. Breckinridge.
[*B1, p132.*]

RHODES, WILLIAM . . . . Jan. 27, 1801—Feb. 8, 1803.
To wife Sarah all of estate.
Executrix: Wife Sarah.
Witnesses: James Patton, Sam Vail, John Blanchard. [*B1, p134.*]

SEATON, HOUSON K. B. . . . . . Feb. 19, 1803—May 2, 1803.
Late of Frederick County, Virginia, now of Louisville. To wife Sarah and children, estate here and elsewhere; refers to lots in Wainsburg, Green County, Pennsylvania.
Executors and Trustees: Wife Sarah, Kennon Seaton, William F. Simrall, Alexander Fleming, John Rose.
Witnesses: Geo. I. Johnston, Kenner Seaton, Peter Priest.
[*B1, p135.*]
[The original will is filed in an envelope marked Leaton in Will File Box.]

SHAKE, CHRISTOPHER . . . . . . Nov. 8, 1802—Oct 3, 1803.
To wife Elizabeth all land; children under age each to receive a horse; mentions son George and daughter Caty.
Executors: Elizabeth Shake, Jacob Shreader.
Witnesses: Adam Shreader, Jonathan Thomas. [*B1, p137.*]

ENDRES, VALENTINE [ANDERS?] . . Aug. 30, 1803—Oct. 3, 1803.
To wife, Mary Catharina, during widowhood, personal estate and plantation; at her marriage, she to have one-third, and his sisters and brother, Mary Elizabeth, Esther and Jacob, two-thirds. At wife's death, property to be sold and given to his brothers and sisters, Frederick, John, Mary, Elizabeth, Esther, George, Nicholas, Sussanna, Jacob and Catharina. Peter Brunner, by his father Joseph Brunner, bound by indenture to remain with Ender's wife.
Executor: John Miller.
Witnesses: Charles Malott, Adam Hoke, Peter Winard. [*B1, p138.*]

BERGEN, PETER . . . . —1803—Nov. 7, 1803.
    Nuncupative will. Ill at the house of Richard Edwards. To
William, son of Richard Edwards, his estate. Sworn to October
7, 1803, by Rachel Hall and October 17, 1803, by Matildah
Joynes.
Executors: None named. *Witnesses:* None.   [*B1, p140.*]

MARDERS, ROWLEY . . . . Apr. 15, 1803—Feb. 6, 1814.
    Advanced in years and somewhat feeble. To wife Elizabeth
all property, real and personal; to daughters Nancy Poulter,
Lucy, and Linny, and sons Nathan, Rowley, Abner and William,
each a negro.
Executors: Wife Elizabeth, son Nathan, and William Chambers.
Witnesses: F. R. Slaughter, Samuel Langston, Jacob Fine, Mary
White, Wm. Poulter.   [*B1, p141.*]

POTTORFF, JOHN . . . . —April 2, 1804.
    Nuncupative will. Son of Martin Pottorff. At the home of
Jacob Shreader on Harrods Creek. Estate to go to brother Jacob.
Statement sworn to January 26, 1804, by Jacob and Elizabeth
Shreader.
Executors: None named. *Witnesses:* None.   [*B1, p143.*]

HODGE, WILLIAM . . . . June 7, 1804—Aug. 9, 1804.
    Wife Peggy; To Mrs. Edmund Basye, house where he lives,
and to his child Nelly, after death of his wife and Mrs. Basye.
Executors: Gabriel J. Johnston, Harry Duncan.
Witnesses: Nancy Dodge, Polly Channonhouse, E. Duncan, A.
Walfort.   [*B1, p145.*]

ROYE, JESSE [ROGE?] . . . . . Sept. 17, 1804—Oct. 1, 1804.
    Weak and sick. Orders debts to be paid and balance of estate
to be equally divided among his sisters.
Executors: Jonathan Nixon, Henry Evinger.
Witnesses: John Miller, John Funk, William Coons. [*B1, p145.*]

A'STURGUS, JAMES [STURGUS, JAMES A.] . . . . . July 14, 1792
                                                 —Nov. 5, 1804.
    Farmer. Wife Margaret; sons John and James; Margaret
Asturgus, daughter of son Peter Asturgus deceased; mentions

children of son Minart, deceased. [In writing will, attorney wrote name as James Assturgus, Senr.]
Executors: Wife Margaret, son James.
Witnesses: Alexander Steele, Benjamin and Thomas Johnson.
[*B1, p149.*]
[Indexed also as James A. Sturgus.]

DORSEY, EDWARD . . . . May 2, 1804—Nov. 5, 1804.
Wife Susanna; to daughters Anne (Polly), and Matilda Dorsey, at the age of sixteen, and to sons Elias, Leaven Lawrence and Benjamin Lawrence, at the age of twenty-one, $1,200.00; daughter Patience Luckett to have $10.00.
Executrix: Wife Susanna Dorsey.
Witnesses: Ben and Leavin Lawrence, Willis Hord.   [*B1, p151.*]

PARSLEY, GEORGE . . . . Oct. 27, 1804—Nov. 6, 1804.
Ill. To son William $30.00; to daughter Susannah, a bed; balance of estate to all his children.
Executors: John Obston, William Farquar.
Witnesses: William Hawthorn, John Wallace, William E. Wells.
[*B1, p152.*]

PARRISH, JOHN . . . . June 5, 1802—Dec. 3, 1804.
To wife Ester all of estate; daughters Nelly Holt, Becky Mason, Leah Costen, Sarah Dickinson, Charlotte Reed, one shilling; to sons Richard and Hezekiah, all land after death of wife; to grandson James Holt, at the age of ten, a cow.
Executrix: Wife.
Witnesses: James Moore, Thomas Moor, Charles Shirman.
[*B1, p153.*]

LUCKETT, JOHN M. . . . . Dec. 13, 1804—Jan. 7, 1805.
To brother William M., a horse and saddle; estate, both real and personal, to be sold to pay debts; to sister Eliza N. Luckett his watch; mentions brothers Philip, Samuel N., William M. and Craven [?] and sister Polly.
Executors: Brothers Samuel N. and William M. Luckett.
Witnesses: Charles Anderson.   [*B1, p156.*]

MCMICHAEL, JAMES . . . . Jan. 30, 1805—Mar. 4, 1805.
Weak and sick. To wife Elenor, live stock and furniture; son John mentioned. *Executor:* None named.
Witnesses: George Pomeroy, Joseph Dunbar, Nicholas Buckner.
[*B1, p157.*]

BRYAN, JOSEPH . . . . Nov. 26, 1804—Mar. 4, 1805.
Names children, Samuel, Joseph, John, the youngest, Martha Boon, Rebecca Boon, Mary Howard, Susannah Hinkle, Aylie Howard, Phebe Forbis, Charity Davis, Elenor Adams; grandchildren Aylie, Noah, Joel, Wilah Adams.
Executors: Sons Joseph and John Bryan.
Witnesses: Edward Cox, Sr., David Enoch, Ephraim Hampton.
[*B1, p158.*]

CRAWFORD, DAVID . Dec. 14, 1801—Sept. 20, 1802, Mar. 4, 1805.
To sons David and Reuben, land on Harrods Creek; to Nathan land in Shelby County where he now lives; to daughter Sally Cocke 80 pounds money; money also to daughters Elizabeth Davis and Nancy Jones; to son Charles land bought of Richard Taliaferro adjoining Elias Wells [or Wills]; to sons Nelson and William land in Amherst County, adjoining Buffalo Ridge, granted testator in 1789; to wife part of land where "I now live," bought of Robert Johnston and Wm. Haynes; special gift to Nathan "for him not receiving assistance in setting out in life in a remote and distant country"; to son John one half of all lands in Kentucky surveyed by him.
Executors: Sons John, William S., Nelson and Charles.
Bondsmen: Charles Taliaferro, Nathaniel Warwick.
Witnesses: Wm. Pryor, John Pryor, Stella Sullivan.
Codical dated March 14, 1802. Land to son William to be sold and "divided among my legatees"; son John to manage estate. Sons David and Reuben to be "given equally as much as my other children."
Witnesses: Wm. Pryor, John Pryor, Stella Sullivan. [*B1, p161.*]

HOLT, JOHN . . . . Aug. 26, 1804—Apr. 1, 1805.
Wife Rachel, plantation where he lives; to son Ben, 100 acres on Floyd's Fork; to eldest daughter Sarah McLahlan, 10 acres; to son Isaac, 100 acres; mentions five youngest children, under

twenty-one, Mary, Nancy, Isaac, Rebecca and John; mentions lot in Middletown.
Executors: Kenner Seaton, Robert Tyler.
*Witnesses:*James Anderson, George Hoke, James Moore.[*B1,p173.*]

McMANNIS, JOHN . . . . July 28, 1805—Oct. 2, 1805.
Farmer. To wife Ann, and sons John, George, James, and daughter Margaret Morgan, 50 pounds each; also 50 pounds to step daughter Ruth Williamson; to step-sons George and Moses Williamson a cow; negro to be freed.
Executors: Son George, and friend William Welch.
Witnesses: Thomas Stafford, George Bishop, Richard Mills.
[*B1, p177.*]

STEWART, JOHN . . . . Sept. 25, 1805—Nov. 4, 1805.
Weak in body. [Will not signed.] Wife Elizabeth to live on plantation where he now lives, and to have certain privileges as long as she remains widow; at her marriage she is to have dower right, and balance to children. Children to be educated; sons Isaac, James, Willis, John, under age, to have a bond for 100 acres in Scioto County, in Ohio, opposite Greenup County, Kentucky.
Executor: Wife.
Witnesses: None. Will proven by oaths of John Miller, John Kelly, and Leah McKeown. [*B1, p180.*]

SEATON, RODHAM . . . . Jan. 4, 1804—[Oct. or] Dec. 2, 1805.
To wife Mary, during widowhood, his estate, for her and his childrens benefit. When they become of age, to eldest son Thomas Curry and to youngest son Kenner, the tract of "land on which I live"; to eldest daughter Sarah Seaton and next daughter Bettie Kenner Seaton, money from sale of personals; children under age mentioned.
Executors: Wife, Reuben Smith, of Elks Creek, and John Asher.
Witnesses: Kenner Seaton, James Mundel, Andrew Mundel.
[*B1, p184.*]

LINN, ASABEL . . . . Nov. 25, 1805—Mar. 4, 1806.
Weak and sick; to wife Nancy, one-third of real estate and slaves; children Polly, Lewis, William, all under age.
Executors: Worden Pope and Nath'l B. Whitlock.
Witnesses: Nancy Dodge, Henry Churchil, Worden Pope. Will proven by oaths of William Christy and Worden Pope.[*B1, p188.*]

JOYES, PATRICK . . . . May 24, 1805—July 8, 1806.
Estate to five children, they to take care of their mother,
Nancy Short Joyes.
Executors: Juhn Dunn, Ga. I. Johnston.
Witnesses: Ludlow Clark, Truman Bostwick.   [*B1, p189.*]

MUNDELL, JOHN . . . . Aug. 7, 1806—Oct. 6, 1806.
To daughter Nally, horse of same value as given to other
children; to youngest son John, horse; balance of estate to be sold,
money first for John's education, then one-third to wife Jane,
balance to children James, Andrew, Magaretha, wife of John
Thomson, Polly, wife of Richard Miller, Sarah, Nally and John.
Executor: John Miller.
Witnesses: Thomas Stafford, Bartlett Asher, Charles Wilson.
[*B1, p191.*]

YENOWINE, LEONARD . . . . . . Dec. 26, 1806—Mar. 2, 1807.
Wife Margaret to have living from farm "where I live"; to
son Peter 209 pounds; to son Jacob plantation "where I live"; to
daughters Betsey and Christina, 50 pounds; to daughters Margaret and Madlena, 5 pounds each; to daughter Kathreena,
money; to son John, farm bought of Mr. Irion on Harrods Creek;
to sons George, Leonard, and Frederick farm where they live.
Codicil, Dec. 26, 1806: Son Jacob, to give his mother flax,
yarn, etc., and to give Elizabeth Miller her freedom and certain
live stock and furniture. His still to sons Jacob, Leonard,
Frederick and John; Jacob to give Elizabeth, Christina, Madlena,
Margaret certain gifts. [In German, translated by John Miller.]
Executors: Sons Leonard and Frederick Yenowine.
Witnesses: George Evinger, John Evinger, Henry Evinger.
[*B1, p194.*]

BATE, SUSANNA . . . . Nov. 6, 1806—Mar. 2, 1807.
To daughter Ann Lock, wife of John D. Lock, for life, 200
acres of 400 acres purchased from her sons John and James S., and
at her death to her grand-daughter Elizabeth D. Lock; balance
of said 400 acres to grand-daughters Mariah and Eliza Llewel-
len; sons John and James S.; daughter Philippi Llwellen; grand-
daughters Mariah, Eliza and Susanna Ann Llwellen; daughter
Catherine Wager; grand-children, Catherine Robinson Bate,

James and Robert Throckmorton Bate, children of son James S. Bate; to two granddaughters, children of son John, certain slaves.

Executors: Son-in-law John D. Locke, son James S. Bate.

Witnesses: Richard Higgins, Charles Plummer, Jno'n Toome, Jer'h Plummer. [B1, p200.]

CECIL, THOMAS . . . . Feb. 7, 1807—Mar. 3, 1807.
    Nuncupative will. To wife Nancy, estate.
Signed: William Dougherty and William Lampton.
Witnesses: George Nelson, J. Gwathmey. [B1, p204.]

HARRYMAN, CHARLES . June 15, 1798—Nov. 3, 1806, June 1, 1807.
    To wife Hannah one-third of all estate; to son Job, under twenty-one, the three tracts of land "on which I live" in Jefferson County, certain movable property and two obligations on Jonathan Boon; mentions bonds of Robert Davis and Caleb Firby and 200 acres in Shelby County, part of a preemption in name of Feby Larue for which he paid George Rust; mentions children Josiah, David, Charles, Mary Eliza, Elizabeth and Rebecha. Two slaves to be freed and provided for.
Witnesses: Robert Ward, Cathrane Lock, Drusela Hodgin.
    Codicil June 16, 1798: Wife Hannah and son Job executors. Slaves to live with them until freed.
Witnesses: Robert Ward, Drusila Hodgin.
    April 6, 1807. Job Harryman ordered to take deposition of Catherine Lock, wife of Thomas Horsley, residing in New Madrid, Upper Louisiana; she deposed that she was a witness to the above will. [B1, p206.]

COWAN, JOHN . . . . Aug. 23, 1807—Sept. 7, 1807.
    To wife Mary, during widowhood, his estate; at her marriage Thomas Reysel and Lemuel Lemon to take charge of estate, giving wife her lawful share and balance to his children Elizabeth, Margate, John, William and James.
Executor: Wife Mary Cowan.
Witnesses: Thomas Conn, Elizabeth Little, William Dowland. [B1, p213.]

ASKEW, JAMES [ASKUE?] . . . . . Feb. 5, 1805—Dec. 7, 1807.
To his friend, with whom he lives, Joseph Collet, his estate.
Executor: Joseph Collet.
Witnesses: John Gerking, James McCrery, Samuel Lynd.
[*B1, p215.*]

HOLLIS, WILLIAM . . . . May 2, 1808—June 13, 1808.
To wife Nancy, his estate.
Executrix: Wife.
Witnesses: Isaac Whayne, Roby Mardis, R. Slaughter. [*B1, p216.*]

TAYLOR, JAMES . . . . Sept. 23, 1807—June 13, 1808.
To son James, slaves and tract of land on which son James
lives; to son John Gibson Taylor, 460 acres of land "on which I
live," and slaves; to son Nathaniel P., under age, to be educated,
slaves, 600 pounds, furniture, books, maps; to daughter Elizabeth
Pendleton, slaves and balance of my land "on which I live"; to
daughter Mary Barbour, slaves; to daughter Ann P. Crutchfield, 50 acres of land "adjoining what I have already given her,"
and certain slaves; sons James or John Gibson to execute a deed
for 104 acres for land sold Adam Shrader; lands held with his
brothers, Edmd. Frs. and William to his children.
Executors: Sons James, John G. and Nathaniel P. Taylor.
Witnesses: Richard Barbour, Richard Taylor.   [*B1, p216.*]

PRINCE, SILVANUS . . . . Apr. 26, 1808—July 11, 1808.
To wife Ann, for life, his estate. At wife's death, $1.00 to
each of the sons John, William, Edward and Alburtis, as they
have received their share; residue of estate to his children,
Thomas, Ann Allison, Mary Ross and Rebecca Wells, son Ed-
ward's children, and "my two nieces," Ann and Catharine
Errickson.
Executors: Wife, Thomas Prince, and William Allison.
Witnesses: Edward Jones, Nicholas Stowers, Ronsey [Rawley?]
Kendall.   [*B1, p218.*]

APPLEGATE, THOMAS . . . . . . Dec. 25, 1806—Aug. 8, 1808.
To sons Samuel, Hezekiah, Benjamin, Tunis and Elijah, certain lands, lots Nos. 110, 50, 65 and 70. Movable property pro-

ceeds to children Benjamin, Tunis, Elizabeth, Baldwin, Joanna, McGrew, and Elisha; to son Elisha the place "on which I live."
Executors: Sons Benjamin and Elisha Applegate.
Witnesses: Peter Miller, Frederick Miller, Hiram Malott.
[*B1, p219.*]

DENNY, JAMES . . . . Apr. 1, 1806—Aug. 8, 1808.
To wife Nancy for life, one-third of estate. At her death, anything left, with balance of estate to children Ed. Polly, James, and Synthia.
Executors: Edward Denny.
Witnesses: William Tyler, Patrick Taggart.
Codicil, April 11, 1806, Edward Denny, Executor to have full power to sell and convey any of my property and divide proceeds as directed in will.
Witnesses: Patrick Taggart, William Tyler.   [*B1, p220.*]

OSBORN, WILLIAM . . . . Aug. 20, 1795—Oct. 10, 1808.
Estate, including legacy due by Ralph Murry and Reubin Henry, executors of James Murry's estate, to his children; daughters Elizabeth, Lydia, Nancy, Polly.
Executors: Alexander S. Bullitt, James Meriwether, Richard Taylor, William Murray.
Witnesses: Edward Ashby, William Tuley, Thos. Trueman, William Murray.   [*B1, p221.*]

QUERTERMOUS, JAMES . . . . . Apr. 28, 1803—Mar. 13, 1809.
To wife Elizabeth, slaves and one third of his property for life. At her death, same to his four children and his grandson Thomas Wilson. To his son Elisha and daughter Nancy and the Doctor, the tracts of land on which they live and which was laid off by John G. Moore; to my son James two-thirds of land "on which I live"; to his daughter Rhody Sanders and his grandson Thomas Wilson lands on Bullskin.
Executors: Sons Elisha and James Quertermous.
Witnesses: J. G. Moore, James Robb, Leavin Cooper. [*B1, p222.*]

HITE, REBECCA . . . . Apr. 21, 1809—June 12, 1809.
In poor health. To Jacob, under age, son of Isaac Hite, certain furniture; to Isaac Hite, son of Harriet Bridgeford $50.00, when eighteen, balance of estate to her sons Abraham and Joseph.
Executors: None named.
Witnesses: Elizabeth Jones, Ann Eastin.   [*B1, p224.*]

BRENDLINGER, CONRAD . . . . . Apr. 5, 1806—Aug. 14, 1809.
To wife, Anna Mary, entire estate.
Executors: John Bates.
Witnesses: John Miller, Hezekiah Coats, John Funk. [*B1, p225.*]

PERRY, NOBLE . . . . Aug. 14, 1809—Aug 14, 1809.
Nuncupative Will. To John Hinkle, "in whose home I live,
my estate for his kindness to me."
Signed: John McBain, Jacob Getz.
Witnesses: Wm. Dougherty, And'w Hite. [*B1, p226.*]

NICHOLAS, DR. JOHN . . . . . Feb. 8, 1809—Sept. 11, 1809.
Of Middletown, Kentucky. His undivided part of his
father's estate to his sisters Mary, Matilda and Sarah Ann Jef-
fris Nicholas. To brother William C. Nicholas, library of medical
and historical books, who although now "shows no disposition to
study."
Executors: Marten Brengman, Francis Taylor.
Witnesses: None. [*B1, p227.*]

MOORE, JAMES F. . . . . July 18, 1807—July 8, 1810.
Of Mount Holly, near Man's Lick. Affirms that he was
married to his wife Elizabeth, to disprove rumoured doubts
about it; to Elizabeth Pendergrass, daughter of his first marriage,
and her husband Jesse, slaves and plantation on which they live.
His daughters Cassandra Miller and Zeruah Jones and son Hector
have already received their share of his estate. The farm at
Mount Holly, of 660 acres and slaves, etc., to his wife Elizabeth
for life and then to his children.
Executors: Wife and two sons Hector and Nimrod, and son-in-law
John Jones.
Witnesses: William Jones, Ann Daviess, James D. Breckinridge,
Worden Pope, Craven P. Luckett, Levi Tyler, James Denny,
Presley Ross, Thomas Joyes, John Evans, Jr., James Ferguson,
J. H. Daviess. [*B1, p228.*]

WHITLOCK, CAPT. NATHANIEL BACON Jan. 6, 1810—Jan. 8, 1810.
Nuncupative Will. Died in Louisville December 12, 1809. To
brother George, all estate "for benefit and education of my son
George."
Signed: David Waide, Levi Tyler. [*B1, p232.*]

BRINDLEY, JACOB . . . . Dec. 17, 1809—Jan. 8, 1810.
To wife Catharine for life one-third of his estate, including that share of land "on which I live"; land on north side of Floyd's Fork, to sons Jacob, John, Reubin and Thomas, as well as their mother's share at her death. The sons to pay to his daughter Eve and to his wife's daughter Elizabeth Rainbow certain monies.
Executors: Haley Buckner, John Potts.
Witnesses: Peter Shrote, Mary Potts, James McMillan, Nancy Holt. [*B1, p233.*]

PLUMMER, JEREMIAH . . . . . Aug. 15, 1809—Mar. 12, 1810.
To wife Ann his estate for life; at her death to his children, John, Charles, Ann Williams, Patty Cook, Darkey Plummer, Elenor Tune, Sepphaneah [Zephaniah], and grandson Jetson Taylor.
Executors: Wife and son Charles Plummer.
Witnesses: Wm. Aylett Booth, Samuel Caloway, J. Hite. [*B1, p234.*]

LITER, HANS . . . . Jan. 8, 1810—Mar. 12, 1810.
Wife Elizabeth; to daughter Barbara a saddle; to daughter Sarah $150.00, to son Jonas $150.00, to son Jonathan $150.00, these under age; to son Henry 50 acres; to daughter Magdalena [Polly], wife of Amasa Burt, large German Bible; mentions grandson David Beatty; to his former son-in-law John Beatty, "four and six pence."
Executors: Wife and son-in-law Amasa Burt.
Witnesses: James S. Bate, Wm. Aylett Booth, John Rogan. [*B1, p236.*]

DICKINSON, RICHARD . . . . . Jan. 24, 1806—Sept. 10, 1810.
The law of the land is my will.
Executors: John Breckinridge, Genl. Robert Breckinridge, Worden Pope, George Floyd.
Witnesses: None. Will proven by Col. A. S. Bullitt, John Gwathmey, James Hunter.
September 8, 1810, Worden Pope renounced power to act.
Witnesses: Charles M. Thruston, Edw. Tyler, Jr. [*B1, p238.*]

COVERTON, PRISCILLA . . . . . Dec. 4, 1811—Dec. 9, 1811.
To son Philip, daughter Priscilla, son Able, and daughter Matilda, money, slaves and furniture; Residue to her son Able and

her daughter Matilda. Granddaughter Priscilla given spoons, if she comes to Kentucky to live.

Executor: Son Able Coverton.

Witnesses: Fredk Edwards, John Whips, Joseph T. Edwards.

[*B1, p238.*]

BOSTWICK, TRUMAN . . . . . . Dec. 22, 1811—Jan. 13, 1812.

His slaves to be freed. To his wife Catharine, for herself and small children, his estate, except half an acre of ground in Louisville purchased from William Dougherty, which he give to his son Solomon when twenty-one.

Executrix: Wife.

Witnesses: Thomas Stewart, Jr., William Dougherty, Edw. Tyler, Jr. [*B1, p240.*]

BRANHAM, DANIEL . . . . Mar. 15, 1810—May 11, 1812

To wife Nancy, for life, land on which she lives with appurtenances and slaves. At her death all of estate to five children, Patsy, Richard, Elijah, Julius, youngest son, and Betsy. Son Elijah to be bound to his uncle Richard Branham until he is of age; Julius to be bound to an honest mechanic until of age, at discretion of executors and his grandfather Richard Bohannon; son Richard to comply with contract made with his uncle George Bohannon. Old negro oman to be provided for.

Executors: Isaac Haws, Thomas Sturgeon, George Bohannon.

Witnesses: Larkin Bohannon, Jr., Polly Branham, Richard Branham, Robertston Vaughan. [*B1, p242.*]

STEWART, STEPHEN . . . . No date—May 11, 1812.

To son James Harvey Stewart plantation on Pleasant Run, adjoining lands of Thomas Downs, James Stewart, William Goodwin and Weathers; residue to his three children, James H., Priscilla and Cincha.

Executors: None named.

Witnesses: James Stewart, William Goodwin. [*B1, p244.*]

WRIGHT, SAMUEL . . . . Dec. 30, 1811—June 8, 1812.

To his wife Peggy, slaves and 100 acres land purchased from John Hardin "on which I live in Jefferson County," and all his movable property, and at her death to their two sons by this union. Wife to give to children, by his first marriage, Sally Hardy,

William, Richard, Zephaniah, Nancy, Robert and Peggy Wright, certain monies.

Executors: Wife.

Witnesses: Jas. W. Herndon, Joshua Young, James Collins.
[*B1, p245.*]

YOUNG, ANDREW . . . . Oct. 7, 1811—June 8, 1812.

To wife Martha, a living from the place and appertunances which he possess; son William has had his share; son Andrew to have place on which he now lives; son Walter the mansion place "on which I live"; his daughter Marget to have same as other daughters have had. Walter Shale and Chuse Hoog [Haag?] mentioned.

Executors: William and Walter Young.

Witnesses: John Smith, Henry Smith, James McKeaig.[*B1, p246.*]

LEATHERMAN, FREDERICK . . . . July 8, 1812—Aug. 10, 1812.

Nuncupative Will. Died at home of Michael Leatherman. To wife Peggy one-third of estate; to unborn child, two-thirds of estate. At death of wife, her share to her people, and balance of estate, if child should not live, to his two youngest brothers Jacob and John.

Signed: John Miller, Peter Shrote, George Frederick. [*B1, p248.*]

GEIGER, GEORGE . . . . Jan. 22, 1812—Aug. 19, 1812.

To his mother Elizabeth for life, his estate, including his share of his father's estate. Mentions notes against Able Covington. At mother's death all to his brother John.

Executors: Daniel Fetter, John Edwards.

Witnesses: Fred'k Geiger, Jeremiah Gilman, Jacob Geiger.
[*B1, p249.*]

MASON, THOMAS . . . . May 20, 1812—Aug. 10, 1812.

To daughter Harriet, who is under eighteen, a negro and $1,000.00; to wife Sarah residue of estate for life, and at her death, this, with proceeds of his share of distillery lands, owned by him and Samuel Watson, to daughter Harriett.

Executors: Wife and Samuel Watson.

Witnesses: David Booker, William Watson. [*B1, p250.*]

TODD, SAMUEL . . . . No date—Oct. 12, 1812.
Late of Clay County, Kentucky; weak; estate to son John, sons-in-law John Craig and Thomas Crawford; they to provide for wife Jean.
Executors: None named.
Witnesses: Enoch Magruder, Wm. Edwards, John Stonestreet.
[*B1, p251.*]

WELLS, WILLIAM . . . . Jan. 17, 1810—Dec. 14, 1812.
Now in Fort Wayne, Indiana Territory. Estate to wife and five children; Ann, Rebecca, William Wayne and Polly by former wife, and Samuel Geiger by present wife.
Executors: Wife and brothers, Samuel and Yelverton P. Wells, who are also to be guardians of children. [*B1, p252.*]

STROUD, JOSEPH . . . . Feb. 27, 1813—Mar. 9, 1813.
Nuncupative will. At home, near mouth of Bear Grass Creek. To his wife Polly entire estate. Mentions a child he had lost; says his father may try to claim some of estate.
Sworn to by Elizabeth Kelly, Lorene Yeomans and Francis C. Moss.
Witnesses: Ga. I. Johnston, Justice of Peace, Frances C. Moss.
[*B1, p253.*]

PENN, CLOE . . . . July 22, 1812—May 10, 1813.
To faithful negro servant, Nell, her freedom, and estate to be put in trust for her support in her old age.
Executor: John L. Moore.
Witnesses: James Blair, James Moore, Rachel Moore. [*B1, p255.*]

SIMCO, SIMEON . . . . Mar. 11, 1813—May 10, 1813.
To his wife Elizabeth, estate including tract of land to be bought for her; if she marries, estate to go to four children, Germain, Richard, Sally and Rosetta; unborn child to have equal share with other children.
Executors: Wife Elizabeth, Isaaz Whayne.
Witnesses: R. Slaughter, William Dubberly, Walker Prewitt.
[*B1, p256.*]

KINNISON, STEPHEN W. . . . . No date—May 11, 1813.
Starting on campaign, may never return. To brother Joseph; to John Rice, son of his sister; to Joseph Plasters, son of his sister,

each a horse; to Sally Ann Rice, a lot in Louisville; to sisters Eliza and Nancy a slave; residue of estate to father and mother for life; debts to be paid.

Executors: Abner Field, James Earickson.

Witnesses: Gabriel Field, James Farnsley, William Earickson.

[*B1, p257.*]

DANBY, WILLIAM [DANLEY?] . . June 11, 1813—June 14, 1813.

Nuncupative Will. Of Jefferson County, Kentucky. Died at Vincennes, Indiana, December 12, 1812. To Elias Dorsey, son of Samuel Lawrence, horse, saddle and bridle; to Edward W. Brown, watch; to George Whips, Jr., money; to Corbin H. [N?] Dorsey and Benj. Lawrence, Jr., clothes which are at home of Samuel Lawrence.

Signed: William F. Querey, George Whips, Jr.   [*B1, p258.*]

CALENDAR OF EARLY JEFFERSON COUNTY, KENTUCKY, WILLS

WILL BOOK NO. 2: JUNE, 1813–DECEMBER, 1833

PREPARED BY MISS KATHARINE G. HEALY

IN TWO PARTS

PART ONE: JUNE 14, 1813—DECEMBER 15, 1824[1]

THOMPSON, JOHN . . . . . Jan. 1, 1804—June 14, 1813.
To wife Elizabeth Thompson, all estate on condition that she educate and maintain children during their minority and give to each of the boys, as he becomes of age, a negro; and to each of the girls, as they marry or become of age, a negro woman worth at least $250., a likely horse, saddle and bridle worth $130., furniture and $100. in cash. At wife's death property to be divided among children. Wife to be sole guardian of children.
Executors: Wife, Elizabeth Thompson.
Will proven by Robert Coleman and Philip Thompson.
Codicil: July 24, 1805. About to depart for southern Louisiana, he added codicil. Should wife remarry, property both real and personal, to be divided among wife and children as if he died

---

[1] Editor's Note: A Calendar of Jefferson County Will Book No. 1 (1784-1813) * appears in the January, 1932, issue of this QUARTERLY.

Will Book No. 2 is a volume of 538 transcribed pages covering a period of twenty-one years, during which time Worden Pope was clerk. For convenience in printing, our presentation of this Calendar is divided into two parts. The following statements made in our Introductory Note to Will Book No. 1, pertaining to the interpretations of the penmanship, also apply to the Calendar of Will Book No. 2. **

An effort has been made to retain, as closely as possible, the original spelling, although it is often erroneous. Some of it is evidently phonetic. A name is sometimes spelled two or three ways in the course of one will—in both original and transcribed copies. No attempt has been made to suggest the correct spelling.

In the calendar here published the name of the testator appears in capitals and is followed by the date of the writing and the date of the recording of the will. The nuncupative or oral wills that occur are so designated. No annotations are made except in a few instances. Among them are, in brackets, the Will Book number, *B2*, and the page on which the will is recorded.

*Pages 214-250, this volume.
**See page 214, this volume.

intestate. Executors and guardian of children in case codicil takes effect: John Thomas Houison [Harrison?], William Lightfoot. [*B2, p1.*]

STAFFORD, THOMAS . . . . Oct. 11, 1809—Oct. 11, 1813.
   To wife Eve her wearing apparel, household furniture, roan mare, her riding saddle, two cows, etc., also her maintenance from plantation and her stock; to son John Stafford, plantation on which "I now live," but, should John die before testator, plantation to be sold and proceeds divided among children, Benjamin Stafford, Elizabeth Bishop, Sarah Ward, Mary Newkirk, Mary Sliger [later in will called Margaret Sliger], Thomas Stafford, Martha Young, and Susanah Cury. Sarah Ward's share to be held until her children James and Elizabeth Ward reach maturity. Halves of wagon and wind mill, one third of stock of hogs and property to be sold. Also refers to notes and book accounts.
Executors: John, Benjamin, Thomas Stafford.
Witnesses: Andrew Wilkins, James Guthrie, William Guthrie.
[*B2, p2.*]

EDWARDS, FREDERICK . . . Mar. 6, 1813—Oct. 11, 1813.
   To wife Mary Edwards, for life, one half of home plantation and brick house, slaves with their increase, household furniture, wagon, etc.; to son Joseph T. Edwards other half of plantation, and at wife's death her half, five slaves, mare and filly, and gray, called Eagle. Mentions grandchildren Polly C. Bartlett and her sister Nancy Bartlett, children of Elizabeth Bartlett. Grandson, Pendleton Strother, to be clothed and schooled for six years from this date, and at age of twenty-one to have certain horse, cow, furniture, etc. To grandson Robert Edwards (son of Robert Edwards, killed, on the 22nd of January last, in battle on River Raisen, leaving a widow and one son now about four months old) a negro whose hire is to maintain child. At wife's death, estate to be equally divided among his sons William, John and James Montgomery Edwards, and Elizabeth Bartlett to have her furniture.
Executors: John and William Edwards, without security.
Witnesses: Richard Fenley, Jun., Leonard Harbold. [*B2, p2.*]

WEEMS, JOHN . . . . . . Aug. 29, 1813—Oct. 11, 1813.
To wife Mary S. Weems, and to children, James, Elizabeth M., Kitty, Alice, George, Martha, Julian and David, all personal property, to be equally divided when youngest child is twenty-one years old; wife to have full possession of property until such division. *Executors:* None named.
Witnesses: Edward Garrett, J. L. Murray, George R. Pearson.
[*B2, p5.*]

COLLINS, JOHN . . . . . Sept. 2, 1813—Dec. 13, 1813.
To wife, Betsey Collins, all estate of every kind which she possessed at the time of our intermarriage, and all property he then had and has since acquired, except as hereinafter stated, including judgements, executions, bonds, etc., she to pay all his just debts. To Dr. James C. Johnston, stock of medicines, shop furniture, library, testators interests in the mills on Pond Creek, Jefferson Co., on condition that he rebuild dam and put in operation, if not, interest to revert to Betsey Collins. To brother Daniel and sister Esther, any estate which his father Lemuel Collins, has left or may leave testator.
Executor: James C. Johnston.
Witnesses: Wm. T. Vernon, Worden Pope. [*B2, p5.*]

MYRTLE, JOHN . . . . . . July 27, 1801—Dec. 13, 1813.
To wife, Phebe Myrtle, the use of estate for life, for raising and supporting children who are and remain with her. At her death, the estate to be equally divided among the children.
Executor: Phebe Myrtle.
Witnesses: A. Smoot, Joseph Field.
The signature of Joseph Field was proven by oaths of Alexander Smoot and Reuben Field. [*B2, p6.*]

MARTIN, JOHN . . . . . Aug. 29, 1813—Jan. 10, 1814.
Probated in Bedford Co., Pa., Nov. 4, 1813.
Of Jefferson County, Ky., now in Bedford County, Penn. Servant woman, Patty Barnett, to be freed. To heirs of John Griffith, late of the town Wheelin, Virginia, house and lot in Newilstown, Ohio. Executors to sell real estate at credits of one, two, three and four years, to be payable in negotiable paper at the Lewisville Branch Bank. To Joseph Martin and Joseph [John?]

253

Fleming, both of Mifflin Co., Penn., in trust for sister Marey Walker, $\frac{5}{15}$ of estate during life of her husband, William Walker, at his death to her, and, if she be dead, to her heirs. Joseph Martin and John Fleming to purchase not less than half section of land in Ohio or Indiana for sister Marey Walker. To Joseph Martin, in trust for cousin Priscilla Green, wife of David Green, of Mifflin Co., Penn, one-fifteenth of real estate, to be disposed of as to [as in the case of] sister Marey Walker. To James Overstreet and Wm. Farker in trust for Nancy Misner, wife of Henry Misner, carriage maker, all of Louisville, Ky., three-fifteenths of real estate, to be placed by them in bank stock, she to receive interest yearly, but at death of husband she to receive entire sum; should she die first, above sum to revert to estate. To cousin Mary McGinnis of Lewistown, Mefflin Co., Penn., one-fifteenth part of real estate forever. To cousin Ephya Gray, of Frankfort, Ky., late of Jefferson Co., one-fifteenth part of real estate forever. To sister Elizabeth Fleming, of Mefflin Co., Penn., a family Bible of the best kind. The remaining four-fifteenths of real estate to be placed in bank stock by executors and used in purchase and redemption of two slaves: One, a female called Easter, purchased from Josiah Trueblood of Indiana Territory and now owned by a gentleman near Pinkeyville, Mississippi Territory; Dr. John D. Fawn of Shippingport can give full information about her. The other slave, a boy called Peter, purchased from Thomas Cannon, formerly owned by Taylor and Hamilton of Lewisville, sold to Capt. Brooks, of the U. S. Army, an agent for Col. Constant, who still owns him, to be purchased and set free; in the event he cannot be found and set free within ten years, above sum to be divided between sister Marey Walker and Elizabeth Fleming, and half-sister Polly Campbell, and half-brother Alexander Thompson, the latter two residing in Huntington Co., Penn.

Executors: Archibald Allen, Gen. Robert Brackenridge, Richard C. Anderson.

Witnesses: James, David, and William Piper.

Codicil Sept. 6, 1813. Hugh Morrison and Worden Pope to be given credit for interest due on bond. To Thomas Thuston the amount of his bond, about $47.00 with interest. All bonds, notes, and accounts paid or unpaid found in desk are to be destroyed and not collected.

Witnesses: William, James, David Piper.

Nov. 4, 1813. Will produced in Court in Bedford Co., Penn., by Archibald Allen, Robert Breckinridge and Richard C. Anderson, the *Executors*, and in Jefferson Co., Ky., Jany. 14, 1814. Allen and Anderson declined to qualify; Robert Breckinridge took the oath and gave bond.   [*B2, p7.*]

JONES, ALICE . . . . . . July 8, 1812—Mar. 14, 1814.

To son John Jones, two negroes and $50.00; to grandsons William Scarborough Jones and David Ward Jones one negro each; to daughters Anne Dasheill Jones and Eleanor Smith Jones, negroes, horse, bridle and saddle each. Residue of estate to be divided.

Executor: John Jones.

Witnesses: Thomas and William Lawes.   [*B2, p11.*]

LAWRENCE, BENJAMIN . . . June 12, 1812—Mar. 14, 1814.

To son Samuel Lawrence 220¾ acres on south side of the Sinking Fork of Beargrass, purchased from Col. Frederick Geiger, also land conveyed to testator by Silas M. Noel, about 98 acres, part of survey sold by Sheriff as property of Charles Quincy; also $1709.19. To son Leavin Lawrence tract of land purchased from Yelverton P. Wells; also 500 acres in Ohio County, Virginia, on drafts of Middle Island Creek, provided he pays to estate $1209.25 within two years. To daughter Susannah Williamson, 500 acres of land in Ohio County, Virginia, on waters of Middle Island Creek, and $1600. To daughter Elizabeth Hynes, 500 acres in same location, and $4000.; also negroes. To daughter Rebecca Winchester, $10.00. To grandchildren Benjamin Winchester, Lavinia Snowden, Olivia, Amanda, Polly D., under sixteen, Louisa, under sixteen, and William Chambers Winchester, under twenty-one, the plantation on which Richard Winchester now lives, 200 acres, part of 300 acres purchased of Col. Frederick and Jacob Geiger on north side of the Sinking Fork of Beargrass, also on north side of a new road cut leading to Isaac Fenley's, to be sold when youngest child becomes twenty-one. To granddaughter Polly Chambers, the other 100 acres of this 300 acre tract. To grandson Benjamin Winchester, 500 acres in Ohio County, Virginia, on waters of Middle Island Creek. Mentions Wm. Winchester, Sr. of Baltimore. To grandchildren Polly Hobbs, Matilda L. Dorsey, Elias Dorsey, Leaven L. Dorsey, Benjamin L. Dorsey,

Urath O. Dorsey, each $400., and negro. Also mentions grand-children Math. Brown, Elias D. Lawrence, Leaven Hynes, Lawrence D. Snowden, and Polly D. Haynes.
Executors: Samuel Lawrence, Levin Lawrence, Wm. R. Hynes.
Witnesses: Ben. Head, Francis Taylor, Jno Evans, Sr., Geo. Rudy. [*B2, p12.*]

REED, ABRAHAM [Signed Abram] . Mar. 3, 1814—May 9, 1814.
To mother Mary Reed; to sister Rebecca and brothers John and Joseph Reed certain monies; to brother James Reed part of grist and saw mills in Harrison County, Indiana Territory, with 260 or 270 acres annexed thereto, plat being in name of testator. All horses, cattle, stock and farming utensils to be sold, unless brother James wishes to retain them at fair price.
Executor: James Reed, brother.
Witnesses: Y. Y. Fitzhugh, G. Gray, James Wanton. [*B2, p14.*]

WHIPS, GEORGE . . . . . June 16, 1810—May 9, 1814.
Late of State of Maryland, now of Jefferson County, Kentucky. To eldest son John, the whole of estate, provided he keep the property and family together during life of wife Susana, and pay at intervals of twelve months, beginning twelve months after debts are paid, certain money to children: Reubin, George, Denton, Susan, Rebecca, Westley, Betsy, Joshua and Samuel. John to afford his mother-in-law ("my present wife Susanna") a comfortable support during her life, and that he raise and educate the two youngest sons Joshua and Samuel.
Executor: John Whips.
Witnesses: Wm. Chambers, D. Washburn, R. Winchester.
[*B2, p14.*]

DUNCAN, HENRY . . . . . June 4, 1814—June 13, 1814.
Hatting business, materials, etc. purchased by Daniel S. Howell shall be sold to take up notes in the Louisville Branch Bank for $1500, and to Robert McConnell for $1000. Should Daniel S. Howell make payments on material bought in time to take up note in bank, he be permitted to buy further raw material now on hand, otherwise everything to be sold to protect endorsers (stock and materials of hatting business now in Shelbyville to be removed to Louisville for sale) and to pay a debt of $1000 to Robt.

256

Wickliff. Children to be supported and educated from the rents and profits of estate. Should wife marry, all real and personal property to be disposed of and distributed according to law.
Executors: Wife Nancy Duncan, brother Coleman Duncan, no security.
Witnesses: Ga. J. Johnston, John Todd, Thomas Shipp.
[*B2, p16.*]

SPRADLING, WILLIAM . . . . . No date—Sept. 12, 1814.
Negroes and mare to be sold and this money, with that due from John Speed, to be applied by executor for the purchase and liberation of a woman, Maria, and her four oldest children, belonging to Isaac Miller. Balance of estate to be equally devided between the woman and said four children, Washington, Elvalina, and Ponetan, the name of fourth he did not know, in a manner most effectual toward their usefulness to society and their individual happiness as free people of color.
Executors: David L. Ward, William Pope, Jr., John Speed.
Witnesses: Samuel Casseday, H. Johnston.
Proven by oaths of Samuel Casseday and James C. Johnston.
[*B2, p17.*)

McCONNELL, JAMES [MACCONNELL], Nov. 5, 1814—Mar. 13, 1815.
To wife Melinda all estate, except, if convenient, presents to sister Elizabeth McConnell. Names slaves. Requests wife to retain Caesar as long as she can for her attendant slave.
Executors: Father-in-law Richard Fenley, William Pope, John Bustard.
Witnesses: Richard Mills, Isaac Mills, Margaret Rush, Thomas Armstrong. [*B2, p18.*]

WILHOIT, JOHN . . . . Dec. 3, 1814—Mar. 13, 1815.
To wife Elizabeth for life, or as long as she remains his widow, as much of estate as she needs, balance to be sold, and $100. to be given each child except Aaron, and any over and above, to be divided equally between all children, including Aaron. At wife's death or intermarriage, her portion to be equally divided among children.
Executor: Elizabeth Wilhoit, wife.
Witnesses: Owen Gwathmey, Hen. Harding, William Harding, Jr.

Mar. 10, 1815. Wife declined to qualify and requests that her son Lewis Wilhoit act instead. *Witnesses:* Simeon Wilhoit, William Harding. [*B2, p19.*]

BOHANNON, RICHARD . . . . Oct. 7, 1814—Mar. 13, 1815.
To wife Deborah for widowhood, 125 acres of land on which they live, also certain slaves, furniture and one third of cattle, sheep and hogs; at her death this to be equally divided among three youngest sons, Pearce, William and Henry (under age), with certain monies, slaves, etc., to be used for maintenance. Executors "must not neglect education of my three little sons"; to each, as they become of age, one-third part. To children Elizabeth, Jane, Ambrose and Richard certain slaves, furniture and monies. Ambrose and Jane mentioned as under age. To son Larkin, all his clothes and all bonds, executions held against him. Residue to sons George and Julius.
Executors: Geo. Bohannon, Julius Bohannon, Wife Deborah.
Witnesses: Will Clayton, John Netherton, James Bartlett.
[*B2, p19.*]

DOUGHERTY, WILLIAM . . . Dec. 8, 1814—Mar. 14, 1815.
To wife Elizabeth, house and lot in Louisville, bought of Abraham Rettenger, to sell and pay debts; also slaves and remainder of property for maintenance of herself and children, to be guided by advice of friends Alexander Pope, Levi Tyler and Worden Pope. To daughter Patsey, gray mare. Son William to be kept in school and given good education. Wife to be guardian of children.
Executor: Elizabeth Dougherty, wife.
Witnesses: Worden Pope, James Stewart, Isaac H. Tyler. [*B2, p22.*]

HEMPHILL, SAMUEL . . . . Feb. 22, 1815—May 8, 1815.
Debts to be paid. To mother entire estate, including what he may be entitled to from his father's estate.
Executor: His mother.
Witnesses: Danl. Fetter, J. L. Murray, William Merriwether, Jr.
[*B2, p23.*]

JOHNSTON, GABRIEL J . . . . Apr. 26, 1815—May 8, 1815.
To wife Enfield for life, five-acre lot in Louisville, all slaves, and personal estate in trust for her support; at her death the lot to

258

go to son Gabriel J. and balance to be equally divided among three sons Gabriel J., Benjamin William and Thomas Johnston; slaves of Gabriel or Thomas not to be delivered to them until they become of age or marry. To Benjamin William ten-acre lot in Louisville, conveyed by Fort's [Fortunatus] Cosby. To Thomas corner lot adjoining Public Square. Residue of estate, and, at wife's death, her share to be sold and equally divided among sons.
Executors: Enfield Johnston, wife, Thomas Prather, son Gabriel J.
Witnesses: Worden Pope, Jos. M. Payne.　　　　　　[*B2, p25.*]

TILLICE, GRIFFIN . . . . . Apr. 26, 1815—June 12, 1815.
To William Rose, son of John Rose, plantation on Cain Road to be vested in the father as guardian until William becomes of age, also saddle. To Henson Hobbs, Sr., horse and money due from Robert Shanks (see Z. Carpenter's judgment book) bedding, ten-gallon kettle, etc. To John Rose, hogs, tools and monies due from John Acan and Cornelius Hoak. To Polly Rose, daughter of John Rose, frying pan, etc. To Elizabeth Rose, wife of John Rose, wearing clothes and new hat. Mentions Elisha Freeman.
Executor: John Rose.
Witnesses: Zachariah Carpenter, Edmund Edwards, John Holman.　　　　　　[*B2, p25.*]

PORTER, WILLIAM . . . . July 19, 1815—Aug. 14, 1815.
All property to be divided equally among children, Jane Shawbridge Porter, Eleanor Whittington Porter, Elizabeth Porter, Henry Porter and Julia Ann Porter. Dr. James Porter given privilege of taking obligation due on land, if Edward Broughton does not redeem same, and having land conveyed to himself by paying $1200. to testator's children. Dr. Porter to hold estate until the daughters marry or son Henry becomes of age.
Executor: Dr. James Porter.
Witnesses: John Evans, William Mills, James Porter.
Dr. James Porter qualified with Peter Funk and Abel Covington as sureties.　　　　　　[*B2, p26.*]

HOLLIS, JOHN . . . . . . Mar. 4, 1815—Aug. 14, 1815.
To wife Ruth, estate for life; at her death, land to go to Calvin Luther Agun, but should he die before maturity or without heirs, land to go to testator's son Joshua W. Hollis. Seruah [or Zeneah]

259

Agun, mother of Calvin L. Agun, to have a home in testator's house during her single life. To son Joshua W. Hollis, certain stock and furniture. *Executors:* None named.
Witnesses: A. Smoot, Sen., Lewis Hollis, Ephriam Hollis.

Ruth Hollis, wife, gave bond as administrator, with Alexander Smoot and Philip Shirely as securities. *[B2, p27.]*

McCulloch, Christopher . . Sept. 5, 1815—Sept. 11, 1815.
To executors all possessions to be sold and divided as follows: to wife one-third part of interest of money for her annual support; to children Daniel, Rachel and Alexander, as they reach maturity, the residue of the money equally, except should land given to Daniel in Hardin County, Kentucky, and Rachel in Pennsylvania, by their grandfather, really come to them, they shall each take $100. less from the estate.
Executors: Patrick Taggard, Alexander Pope, Abner Field.
Witnesses: John Gatewood, Thomas King, George Coons.
[B2, p28.]

Zaring, Henry . . . . . Mar. 15, 1815—Oct. 9, 1815.
The sixty acres of land held on bond dated March 14, 1812, from testator's father and mother, Philip and Catheriner Zaring, to be sold at mother's death, and divided among sister Catheriner, brothers Jacob, John, Philip and Benjamin Zaring; balance of estate to four brothers. *Executors:* None named.
Witnesses: Elijah McDaniel, Reuben Ross. *[B2, p29.]*

Richards, Samuel . . . . Nov. 6, 1815—Jan. 8, 1816.
Of Lancaster County, Penn., and now in the town of Louisville, Ky. To friends William Dunn and Mary his wife, all of estate, containing land in Lancaster County, Penn., nine miles from Lancaster Town, some of which came from testator's father, John Richards, deeds held by Daniel Slaymaker; also land due from United States for services as a private soldier in the last war. William Dunn has in his possession testator's discharge papers.
Executors: None named.
Witnesses: Jeremiah Gilman, Joseph T. Edwards, Jno. Y. Blair.
[B2, p30.]

PATTEN, JAMES . . . . Dec. 28, 1815—Jan. 8, 1816.
Estate to be equally divided between wife Phebe Patten, daughter Polly Gracey, formerly McDougle, formerly Vaughan, and son George. As son-in-law, John Nelson, and his late wife Patsey (Martha), testator's daughter, have had their share of estate—lot No. 16, half-lot No. 9, and warehouse formerly there-on—their children are to have no share of estate. Wife Phebe and William Pope to be guardians of son George.
Executors: Wife, Phebe, and Worden Pope.
Witnesses: Worden Pope, Alexander Posey, Elisha Applegate, Moses Bate.
Phebe Patten took oath as executrix, with John I. Honore and John P. McCasland as securities. [*B2, p32.*]

SHIPP, EDMUND, SR. . . . . Jan. 5, 1816—Mar. 11, 1816.
To daughters Nancy Duncan, Sally G. Howell, Betsy and Lucy Shipp, and sons Thomas, Edmond and Ewell Shipp, grand-children Minerva L., Fanny M. and Edmond L. Lampton, certain slaves, monies, furniture, etc. To Ewell Shipp land which ad-joined James Sneed's, and Stansberry's and testator's property. To wife Tabitha, during widowhood, home place 150 acres with all houses, etc., but at her marriage or death to son Edmond; also to wife remainder of estate in fee.
Executors: Tabitha Shipp, wife, Daniel S. Howell, Edmond Shipp.
Witnesses: Henry Churchill, Thomas Stewart, James Sneed, Wor-den Pope. [*B2, p33.*]

MILLER, EDWARD . . . . . Jan. 26, 1816—Mar. 7, 1816.
To wife Hannah room in west of house in which they were liv-ing and certain furniture, slaves, etc. To oldest son Robert, young-est son Thomas B., and daughter Hannah certain slaves; and to Thomas B. tract of land testator now occupies. After paying debts, balance of estate to be equally divided among children.
Executors: Son Robert, son-in-law Isaac W. Dabney.
Witnesses: John Shaw, Thomas M. Jones, Jacob Kalfus. [*B2, p35.*]

REYNOLDS, RICHARD . . . . Oct. 1, 1808—Mar. 11, 1816.
To wife Mary and son Richard ample maintenance from prof-its of estate, including rent of home plantation. At their death plantation to be sold and balance of estate to be divided among

"all of my children." After ample maintenance given wife and son Richard, other profits to be divided among children except Richard. To granddaughter Anne Smith tract of land adjoining Richard Woolfolk which testator purchased from Henry Lyne.
Executors: Andrew Steele, Worden Pope.
Witnesses: Levi Tyler, Arch'd Allen, Stephen Mitchell, Worden Pope, Fred. W. S. Grayson, Isaac H. Tyler.   [*B2, p35.*]

BULLITT, ALEXANDER SCOTT . . Aug. 26, 1815—May 13, 1816.
   To wife Mary, in lieu of her dower, the home plantation with furniture, farming utensils, stock, etc., necessary use of timber, but she is not to clear land; certain slaves, also to have use of slaves willed to children Mary and Thomas. To son Cuthbert P. Bullitt, 1666⅔ acres on Trade Water, Union County, patented in the name of Nathaniel Pendleton. To son William Christian, 950 acres home plantation, subject to wife's life-interest, surveyed in John Ware's name and patented in name of Terrell and Morris, also slaves and library. To son Thomas James, 1000 acres on Poge's Creek, Hopkins County, patented in name of Nathaniel Pendleton, also Bank of Kentucky stock, slaves, etc. To daughters Annie C. and Polly (or Mary) Bullitt certain slaves; and to daughter Helen Massie, in addition to settlement at her marriage, five guineas for a mourning ring.
Executors: Wife, Mary Bullitt, son-in-law Wm. Henry Massie, sons Cuthbert and William C. Bullitt.
Witnesses: Richard C. Anderson, Joseph Frederick, John Willett.
[*B2, p37.*]

STOWERS, NICHOLAS . . . . Mar. 5, 1816—May 13, 1816.
   To wife Fanny Stowers for widowhood plantation, slaves, etc. and 100 acres of land parallel to lot sold to Nicholas M. Lewis. To son William residue of the home plantation, about 100 acres adjoining Robert N. Miller, Stansbury and Nicholas M. Lewis. To son Patrick 100 acres of land at the cessation of wife's legacy, and slave. At wife's death, daughters Barbara Farnsley, Polly Banks, Elizabeth Norrington, Lucy, Letty and Matilda Stowers, to have slaves, furniture, etc. He confirms gifts to sons John and Samuel, and daughters Frances Stinson and Nancy Kendal as their share of estate.
Executors: Son, Patrick, friends Thomas Prince, Nicholas M. Lewis, Hancock Taylor.
Witnesses: James C. Overton, Nathaniel Taylor, Isaac Miller.
[*B2, p40.*]

NEWMAN, OBADIAH . . . . Jan. 24, 1811—Aug. 12, 1816.
To wife Martha W., entire estate. *Executors:* None named.
Witnesses: Elias Newman.
Will proven by oaths of Elias Newman, John Shepherd and
Isaac Miller. [*B2, p40.*]

CHANNONHOUSE, ABEL . . . July 5, 1816—Aug. 12, 1816.
Nuncupative will. Andrew Valley and Joseph Laton, at
Louisville, stated that they were present at Shippingport, Jefferson County, on the first day of present month, when and where
Abel Channonhouse departed this life, that on Sunday the last
day of last month about 5 o'clock in the afternoon, Mary Channonhouse, wife of said Channonhouse, was exceedingly and much
distressed at his approaching dissolution, and that he, the said
Abel, requested the said Mary not to be so distressed for she
would have enough to live on, for it was his will and desire that
she should have all his property after his death.
Sworn to July 5,1816.
Proven by oaths of Andrew Valley, James Berthoud. [*B2, p40.*]

THEOBALDS, THOMAS . . . July 25, 1816—Aug. 13, 1816.
Nuncupative will. Substance of what was considered to be
last will of Thomas Theobold: first that immediate application be
made at County Court, at his expense, "to obtain bill of divorce-
ment of niece, Nancy Pendergrass, from her absconded husband
John Baxter," she to receive her bed, support, etc., so long as she
remain single. After paying debts, residue to be divided among
children. Slaves to be hired out for support of children until
youngest becomes of age, then slaves divided among them, except
Harry to be freed. Will hitherto made, and in the hands of his
brother, to be void.
Signed by Walter Pearson, Rich. Dowling and James H.
Overstreet. [*B2, p41.*]

BUCKNER, AMBROSE . . . . Feb. 6, 1816—Oct. 14, 1816.
To wife Rebecca, entire estate, except slave Elvy, who had
been lent by father-in-law, Benjamin Bridges, Sr.
Executor: Wife, Rebecca Buckner.
Witnesses: Alexander Pope, Samuel Ferguson, John Githens,
Robert Dennis, Jr. [*B2, p42.*]

BROWN, JOHN . . . . Dec. 22, 1814—Jan. 13, 1817.
To wife Susannah P. Brown estate for life; at her death all of
children, nine in number, except Elizabeth Smith now dead, to
receive equal share of estate. To Elizabeth Smith's three children
one tenth part, minus $400. previously given Elizabeth Smith.
Executors: Susanah P. Brown, wife, son John A., and friend Doctor John Willett.
Witnesses: Jas. Logan, Thomas Mount, Thomas Shanks.
John A. Brown qualified with Thomas Ellcott and John Burress as surities.   [*B2, p44.*]

FORWOOD, WILLIAM . . . . Dec. 26, 1816—Jan. 13, 1817.
To wife Hannah for life, enough land to purchase a negro
woman and half of remaining home-land and all moveable property; at her death land to go to son Samuel, he also to receive
twenty-five acres of land located between William James' and
William Scott's in the State of Maryland. To Polly, Hannah,
William and Elizabeth, children of George Pomeroy and his first
wife, Sarah, testator's deceased daughter, the other half of
home-place.
Executor: Samuel Forwood, son.
Witnesses: Haley Buckner, Robert Tyler.   [*B2, p45.*]

HOLLIS, NANCY . . . . . Dec. 13, 1816—Jan. 13, 14, 1817.
To Franky Stenson and Fanny Williams, her wearing apparel.
Slave Celah to be freed at testator's death, and residue of estate
to be sold for maintenance of said Celah.
Executors: Richard Philips, Frederick Henderlider.
Witnesses: Wm. Pope, Jr., Phebe Hollis, R. Slaughter.
Proven by oaths of Wm. Pope, Francis R. Slaughter. [*B2, p47.*]

ARTEBURN WILLIAM [ARTERBURN] Sept. 19, 1815—Oct. 14, 1816.
To granddaughter Lydia McKee $30., to be paid when she
marry or reach lawful age. To wife Nancy "I lend" rest of estate,
and at her death same to be divided among children, Elijah, Wil-
liam, Samuel and Presley Arteburn, Betsey Cornwell and Lydia
Saffer.
Executors: William and Presley Arteburn, sons.
Witnesses: Robert Tompkins, Enos McKee.   [*B2, p48.*]

VEACH, JOHN [VEECH] . . . Apr. 17, 1817—May 12, 1817.
To daughter Frances Beaty Brooky, half-acre lot No. 106, in town of Louisville, negroes, monies due from J. R. C. Floyd and John Floyd, suit now pending, also property of late son James, forwarded from New York. To son Alexander, the tract of land on which he now lives, formerly owned by Major Noel, with addition of part of land whereon testator lives, beginning in Floyd's line, continueing with the bounds till it reaches Polly Osbourn's line; negroes, silver watch, wheat fan, farming implements, etc. To daughter Elizabeth Veach, remainder of land purchased from Polly Osbourn on which testator lives, watch, negroes, etc. To daughter Sarah Veach, 100 acres of land purchased from the late Capt. Frederick Edwards, on north side of road from Louisville to Middletown, negroes, etc. Mentions bond left in his possession by Mr. Galaway for collection. Requests that $50. be presented to the Rev. Robert N. Bishop, as acknowledgment for his kindness to testator's late son James Veach. A sum of money to be deposited with brother George Veach to purchase five Bibles and five copies of the "Westminster Confession of Faith" for four children and John Edwards. Residue of estate to four children.
Executor: Hancock Taylor.
Witnesses: Richd. Taylor, Mary Edwards, James Logan, William Colliar, William Stewart. [*B2, p50.*]

LUCKETT, ELIZABETH . . . Feb. 20, 1817—May 12, 1817.
To granddaughters Elizabeth Jane Love Luckett and Sarah Luckett, daughters of son Otho W. Luckett, and to son Lawson, certain monies, etc. To Elizabeth, large and small likenesses of testator's late husband. To sister Molly Ann Luckett, wearing apparel. To son Thomas H. Luckett, the residue of estate.
Executors: Thomas H. Luckett.
Witnesses: Thos. W. Thruston, Susan P. Luckett, L. Greenup, Worden Pope. [*B2, p51.*]

MERRIWETHER, JAMES . . . Oct. 10, 1800—Aug. 11, 1817.
Proven Louisa Co., Va., July 13, 1801.
Of Louisa County. To wife Elizabeth Merriwether, "I lend" all real estate and personal property; at her death the land on which testator was then living in Louisa to Lancelott Minor, Howard Goodwin and David Bullock (atto.) in trust for daughter

Ann. Leaves all interest in State of Kentucky, to be divided equally between six sons, to David, James, William, Thomas, John and Robert, after deducting 130 acres which he leaves to son Tom, he having paid for it. "I lend" silver spoons to daughter Ann and her children, but if she has no children, to son Tom's daughter, Sally. Also leaves negroes to children. At wife's death, residue of property to be sold and divided among children.

Executors: Col. Wm. D. Callis, Cap. James Winston, and Capt. John Poindexter.

Witnesses: John Garth, Thomas Jackson, Major Ryan.

Codicil: June 4, 1801. Land purchased from Capt. John Poindexter, on Southanna River, at wife's death to sons Robert and Thomas.

Witnesses: Charles Minor, Wm. Tompkins, Gerard Banks, Lancelot Minor.   [*B2, p52.*]

BULLITT, MARY . . . . . Sept. 11, 1817—Oct. 13, 1817.

To daughter Eliza C. Prather, $400., horse and bed; to brother Samuel Churchill $600. in trust for brother William; balance of estate, slaves, real and personal, after paying debts, in trust to brother Samuel Churchill for two youngest children, Mary and Thomas James Bullitt, until they marry or become of age; should either die that share to survivor; should both die to daughter Eliza C. Prather. Farming implements, stock, etc. to be sold. Samuel Churchill to be guardian of infant children, Mary and Thomas James Bullitt. Certain slaves to be maintained.

Executor: Brother Samuel Churchill.

Witnesses: John Downing, Armistead Churchill, Jr., J. L. Mundy, Henry Churchill.   [*B2, p55.*]

TUNSTALL, JAMES M. . . . . Oct. 13, 1817—Oct. 16, 1817.

Surgeon's Mate, U. S. N. To brothers Edmund and George William certain personal gifts; to sisters, Maria S., Lucinda and Jane W. Tunstall residue of estate, including lot No. 29 in Jeffersonville.

Executors: Brother Thomas Tunstall and friend Brooke Hill.

Witnesses: John P. Tunstall, Henry R. Tunstall, Brooke Hill.

[*B2, p58.*]

FERGUSON, SAMUEL . . . . Jan. 12, 1816—Dec. 8, 1817.

To wife Ann Ferguson for life, house and lot where living, two and one-half acres part of five acre lot No. 13, and two-thirds of estate; at her death to son Benjamin, the house and lot; and the two-thirds of estate to sons Samuel, William and George. To grand-daughter Mary Ferguson, daughter of son John, $150. when she becomes of age or marries. To Benjamin, remaining one-third of estate. Fortunatus Cosby, Thomas Prather, John Gwathmey, Cuthbert and Thomas Bullitt to divide estate.

Executors: Wife and sons, John and Benjamin Ferguson.

Witnesses: Fort. Cosby, Mary A. Cosby. [*B2, p59.*]

COLEMAN, ROBERT . . . . . Mar. 5, 1812—Dec. 8, 1817.

To wife Betty, estate, both real and personal.

Executor: Wife Betty Coleman.

Witnesses: W. L. Thompson, Thomas H. Thompson. [*B2, p61.*]

KELLER, WILLIAM . . . . Aug. 5, 1811—Dec. 9, 1817.

Estate to be kept together for the benefit of children and wife during her life or until intermarriage, except to son Abraham, tract of land purchased from Sam Griffin. At death or inter-marriage of wife, land, mill and distillery to sons Abraham and John, jointly. To son John part of home tract of land. To daughters all of personal estate including negroes, except one given Abraham. Gifts to son Abraham and daughter Elizabeth to be charged to them. Negroes to be sold among children only.

Executors: Wife, son Abraham Kellar, son-in-law Abraham Kellar.

Witnesses: Owen Gwathmey, Jonathan Nixon, Ben Clore.

[*B2, p62.*]

[Note: In Jefferson County Marriage Book 1, page 62, is the marriage record of Abraham Kellar and Betsey Kellar, a daughter of William Kellar, whose consent was certified to; the license was issued in August, 1808, and was returned by (Reverend) William Kellar who performed the marriage ceremony.]

QUICK, JACOB . . . . . . Feb. 14, 1818—Mar. 9, 1818.

To wife Eleanor, one-third of estate, and two-thirds to be held in trust to raise and school children, Dennis Jones, John Gray Moore, James Isaiah and Elizabeth Jane, and if any remain to be divided among said four children.

Executors: Wife Eleanor, brother Samuel Quick.

Witnesses: Wm. Cooper, George Lashbrooks, Daniel Wilson.

[*B2, p65.*]

Tunstall, Jane . . . . . July 3, 1817—June 8, 1818.
Recorded in Albemarle Co., Va. Apr. 6, 1818.
Indenture: Between Joseph F. Tunstall and Jane, his wife, John Bell, John P. Tunstall, Leonard H. Tunstall, Henry R. Tunstall, Thomas M. Tunstall and Brooke Hill and Sarah Y. Hill, his wife, of Jefferson County, and William Campbell of Orange Co., and Charles B. Hunton of Albemarle Co., State of Virginia, of the one part, and Joseph T. Tunstall of the other part—indenture made in reference to land and slaves given by will to Jane Tunstall, must at her death be sold and divided among the children of Jane and Joseph Tunstall. Indenture attested to by Frances Walker, Francis Gray, Cuthbert Tunstall, William Alcock, Thomas Hunton and John Bell, Jr., at a court held at Charlottsville, Va., April 16, 1798. Land secured from Robert Means in Military District for Officers and Soldiers of the Virginia State line, in Virginia, now in County of Barren, State of Kentucky, on Nebob [Knoblick?] Creek, etc., March 11, 1805, conveyed to above trustees. Having improved the land, Joseph Tunstall and Jane his wife, being aged and infirm and removed to Louisville, Ky., sold same to their son Joseph T. Tunstall. John P., Leonard H., Henry R., Thomas M. Tunstall, sons and Brooke Hill, son-in-law, and Sarah Y. Hill, daughter (children of Joseph and Jane Tunstall) agree with Joseph Tunstall as to this property he bought. No further claims will be acknowledged against this property and, for sum received, Jane Tunstall conveys property to her son Joseph.

Jane Tunstall's will devises above tract of land and all appurtenances unto said Joseph T. Tunstall for consideration of $3100. and agrees not to alter or revoke this will by future will or codicile. Joseph Tunstall agrees to this devise as though Jane were his widow.

Signed by Brooke Hill, Sarah Y. Hill, John Bell, Wm. Campbell, Chas. B. Hunton, Jos. Tunstall, Jane Tunstall, John P. Tunstall, Leonard H. Tunstall, Henry R. Tunstall, T. M. Tunstall.
Witnesses: Arch'd Allen, Will M. Hughes, Henry W. Merriwether, Norbourne Crawford, John Davies, Worden Pope, Rich'd Duke, Tunstall Rogers, Th. W. Maury.   [*B2, p65.*]

Miller, Anthony . . . . Mar. 12, 1818—June 8, 1818.
To brothers Robert and Buckner real and personal estate and the privilege of buying, at a fair value, three negroes—the three

268

slaves to be sold together, in any event. Money from above to be equally divided among: Thomas Miller, son of brother Thomas Miller, deceased; William son of brother, John deceased; Lavinia Miller daughter of brother Richard Miller; Doratha Jane Miller daughter of brother Buckner; James Buckner Bright, son of sister Nancy Bright; Anthony Miller, son of brother Robert Miller; Wm. Thomas Winlock, son of sister Mary Winlock; Doratha Ann Pomeroy, daughter of sister Jane Pomeroy. When they marry, or become of age, each to get his or her portion.

Executors: Brothers, Buckner and Robert Miller.

Witnesses: Lee White, W. White, Henry F. Kalfus. [*B2, p75.*]

TRIGG, THOMAS . . . . . Oct. 22, 1811—June 8, 1818.

To wife, during widowhood, entire estate both real and personal, for her use and for raising and educating children; at her death or marriage to be divided among children, and wife to get her lawful dower.

Executors: Wm. Duerson, Wm. Edwards.

Witnesses: Thomas Todd, Jr., Joseph Abbott, Enoch Haldern, William Trigg, Jr. [*B2, p77.*]

[Note: Original will is not in will file box.]

KAYE, FREDERIC AUGUSTUS . . Jan. 9, 1818—June 8, 1818.

To wife Mary Dorothy for life, estate; at her death to sons Frederick Augustus, William and Henry, one-half acre lot No. 179 in Louisville, Ky., with buildings, etc.; to sons John and Francis Jacob, lot No. 292, on Jefferson St., where testator lived. Balance of estate to be equally divided among above named sons and daughters: Catharine, wife of Wm. Reed; Mary, wife of John Schwing; and Elizabeth, wife of Coleman Daniel.

Executors: Sons-in-law Wm. Reed, John Schwing.

Witnesses: Daniel C. Banks, Benj. Cawthorn, Benjamin Wilson, David Raymond. [*B2, p78.*]

NORTON, MATHEW . . . . Dec. 15, 1817—June 9, 1818.

To friend Capt. William Huston fifty acres, a part of 200 acres in Huntington, Adams Co., Ohio, deeded by George Schultz. All debts to be paid. If anything is left, give to brother Robert Norton, living in Warren, Trumbull Co., Ohio.

Executors: William Scott, John Lynn, both of Huntington, Adams Co., Ohio. [*B2, p79.*]

WILLIAMS, JEREMIAH . Not dated—Jan. 12, 1818—June 9, 1818.
To wife Martha for life a five and one-half acre lot, furniture, farming implements, waggon, five horses, etc. for her use and support of children. At her death one and one-half acre to son Moses, half acre to youngest daughter Evelyn, three and one-half acres to sons Joseph and Jeremiah. Certain money to daughters: Evelyn, Patsey, Nancy, Elizabeth, and Amelia Williams to be paid when they become of age or marry, also Phoebe Baxter and Carthernia Judkins, and son John. Son Washington to be maintained out of estate.
Executor: Martha Williams, wife.
Witnesses: James Ferguson, Eli Stillwell.   [*B2, p80.*]

PITTS, ROBERT .   .   .   .   .   June 8, 1818—Aug. 11, 1818.
To wife Charlotte, estate for life including real estate; at her death $100. to his half-sister; balance to Rosamond, Julia Ann, Clavin, Felix, Ellen and Washington Pitts, children of Archbald Pitts of Nelson County, and to Thomas, Polly, Sally, Kitty, Sherlotte, children of Thomas Pitt of Nelson County, after deducting $100. devised to Eleanor Aull, half-sister.
Executor: Charlotte Pitts, wife.
Witnesses: James W. Denny, Thomas Glass.   [*B2, p82.*]

SKIDMORE, PAUL   .   .   .   .   Dec. 4, 1817—Aug. 12, 1818.
Signed at New Orleans; probated there Dec. 11, 1817.
One third of estate each: to wife, Frances Matilda, to son John and to daughters, Eliza Bethea, Sarah Ann and Anne Clarke Johnes. Wife to receive rents etc. until son John becomes of age.
Executors: Wife Frances Matilda, and John Gwathmey.
Signed: P. Gilly, Nich. C. Hall, Thos. S. Kennedy, James Purdon, Geo. Wm. Boyd, Alfred Hennen, Geo. G. Minor, I. Pitol Judge.
                    [*B2, p83.*]

ROSS, LAWRENCE   .   .   .   .   Mar. 2, 1810—Sept. 15, 1818.
To wife Susannah, estate, except tract of land purchased from Beall, Galt and Maupin, to son Presley N. At wife's death tract of land on which he lives to Presley, and residue to be divided among his sons Shapley and Presley, and his daughters: Polly, wife of William Peyton; Betsy, wife of Samuel Phillips; Nancy, wife of Jacob Owens and Henry White; Sooky, wife of Matthew

Love; Sally, wife of Nathaniel Sullivan; Anne, wife of Thomas Prince; Milly, wife of Jesse Carter and Fanny wife of Conway Oldham.

Executors: Wife, Susannah Ross, sons, Shapley and Presley Ross.
Witnesses: John Howard, Sam'l Bray, George Hikes, Jacob Augustus.

Conway Oldham and Fanny, his wife, objected to recording will and filed bill of exception. [*B2, p85.*]

BROOKS, JOSEPH . . . . . Sept. 5, 1818—Oct. 12, 1818.
To wife Nancy, estate, except eight slaves, and debts due. To friend Solomon Neill, in trust for son Squire Brooks, 200 acres of land with stock, nineteen negroes, etc. until he thinks Squire Brooks capable to take care of same, he to receive benefits of estate of testator's deceased son David Brooks. Refers to debts by son Squire due D. L. Ward and John Beckwith, Sr. To son-in-law Elisha Standiford and daughter Nancy, his wife, slaves and title to land deed dated Sept. 4th. Confirms gifts to son Joseph Anderson Brooks, and son-in-law Solomon Neill and daughter Margaret his wife, they to live on land left them in trust. Money due from John W. Sanders and his brother David Brooks to be held in trust for Squire Brooks, and also refers to debt due from Robert Breckinridge and Jacob Yoder. To daughter Mary (Polly) Pendergrast and grand-daughter Margaret America Pendergrast, the tract of land known as Clear Station tract; also certain money.

Executors: Son Joseph Anderson Brooks, Solomon Neill, Elisha Standiford.
Witnesses: Thomas Joyes, Elias Dean, Robt. G. Vance.

Codicil Sept. 6, 1818. Should daughter Polly Pendergrast lose suit to recover negroes and they revert to estate, they are to be divided among his children; also to Polly about 649 acres and certain slaves, and revokes gift of money.
Witnesses: Thomas Joyes, Robert G. Vance, Benj. W. Brooks.

Codicil Sept. 25, 1818. To son-in-law, in trust for Squire Brooks, land located between land to Elisha Standiford and Nancy his wife and land already willed to Solomon Neill in trust for Squire Brooks.
Witnesses: John Jones, Wm. H. Allen. [*B2, p87.*]

COLE, CHARLES . . . . . May 1, 1812—Dec. 14, 1818.
To wife Fanny—purchased from John Thorn Clark, St. Mary's County, Maryland—her freedom immediately after testator's death, and to son William his freedom. To wife stock, plantation, utensils and furniture for life and to son William at her death.
Executors: Wife Fanny.
Witnesses: Jno. G. Moore, Wm. Standiford, Levin Cooper, Sr., Samuel Cooper. [*B2, p96.*]

BECKWITH, UPTON . . . . . Not dated—Jan. 11, 1819.
To wife Betsey, slaves and one-third personal estate forever, and one-third real estate for life. To unborn infant, residue of estate; should it die intestate one half to wife and balance to testator's brothers and sisters.
Executors: Brother John W. Beckwith, nephew John B. Summers.
Witnesses: Fred W. S. Grayson, Littleton Quinton, Samuel Albert, J. W. Beckwith. [*B2, p97.*]

HALL, E. . . . . Sept. 4, 1809—Mar. 8, 1819.
Probated as Elisha L. Hall. To wife Fanny Hall all property, real and personal, with implicit confidence that she will provide for children. Betsey Webster to have certain slaves.
Executors: Wife, Fanny Hall, son R. Hall.
Witnesses: James Hunter, John Evans, Jr., Craven P. Luckett, Ga. J. Johnston. [*B2, p98.*]

STAFFORD, EVE . . . . . July 14, 1815—Mar. 8, 1819.
"Widow woman." Mentions eldest son Benjamin and sons Thomas and John, daughters Elizabeth, Sarah, Polly Newkirk, Peggy, Martha and Susan, and son-in-law David Sliger, to whom she leaves personal effects.
Executors: Friend Job Harryman, son-in-law David Sliger.
Witnesses: Isaac Mills, Tuzdaughter, James Graham, Benjamin Smith. [*B2, p98.*]

KELLER, JOSEPH . . . . . Apr. 6, 1818—Oct. 12, 1818.
To wife Sarah for life a dwelling, slave, and $200 annually. To children: Eliza, Isaac, Abraham, Rebecca and Sarah Keller, each a Bible, and residue of estate.
Executors: George Hikes, Sr., Richard Barbour.
Witnesses: Jonathan Nixon, John Smith, John Little.

Codicil [not dated]: Plantation to be kept for wife and children for life; revokes dwelling to wife; slave to each Rebecca and Sarah.
Witnesses: Joel Yeager, Julius Wilhoite, John Little.   [*B2, p100.*]

RICHARDSON, WILLIAM   .   .   .   Oct. 23, 1818—Mar. 8, 1819.
Blacksmith, left in James City County, Virginia, to be hired out until his brother Stanhope Richardson becomes of age. To mother $50; to friend, Richard A. Green, $100; to "Aunt Nancy Green" black horse; balance to be equally divided between brother Stanhope and sister Mary Richardson; interest in his father's estate to be so divided.
Executors: Thomas Boswell, father-in-law, of James City County, Virginia.
Witnesses: Isham Bridges, Addin Cleveland.   [*B2, p101.*]

BUCKNER, HALEY .   .   .   .   .   Feb. 6, 1819—May 10, 1819.
To my wife Lillian for life, one-third profits of land. To sons: Henry S., Patterson C., Presley B., and to daughter Kezia Buckner $512.62½ each, money in the hands of Bullitts and Jones; sons Samuel P. and Avery M. have received said amount. Profits of perishable property to minors as they reach twenty-one years. Residue to six children.
Executors: Sons, Avery M. and Henry S. Buckner.
Witnesses: Thomas L. Moore, William Read, John L. Moore, Alex. Attkisson.   [*B2, p102.*]

WHITE, GEORGE .   .   .   .   .   Mar. 20, 1819—May 10, 1819.
Money for support and education of youngest daughter Anne and son George Rowley. Estate to all children equally. To Ann one dozen silver table spoons engraved G W W.
Executors: Son, Wm. G. White, and Lee White, William D. White, Lawrence Young.
Witnesses: Nathan Marders, William Young, James Johnson.
[*B2, p103.*]

SKIMMERHORN, ANN .   .   .   .   May 17, 1819—June 14, 1819.
To son James Travis $2. his share of estate; residue to brother Coonrod Rush and to son Jacob Skimmerhorn.
Executor: Brother, Coonrod Rush.
Witnesses: Wm. C. Finley, John Heuthorn.   [*B2, p104.*]

WATSON, WILLIAM . . . . Mar. 11, 1819—June 14, 1819.
To wife Anna, for life, estate. At her death, after deducting amounts of gifts previously given, to nine children: Margaret, Sarah, Thomas, Samuel, William, Anna, Narcissa, Narville, James Ryan. *Executor:* None named.
Witnesses: Jacob Oglesby, John Watson, William Kyle. [*B2, p104.*]

MERCER, JOHN . . . . . Jan. 3, 1815—Aug. 9, 1819.
Recorded Spottsylvania Co., Va., Oct. 21, 1817.
Of Fredericksburg, Va. To sister Mrs. Patton, his picture, balance of estate to brother Hugh Mercer and his heirs.
Executor: Brother Hugh Mercer. *Witnesses:* None given.
Proven by oaths of Charles L. Stephenson and Garrett Minor. Robert Patton was security for Hugh Mercer Executor.
[*B2, p105.*]

MERCER, HUGH . . . . . Mar. 20, 1776—Aug. 9, 1819.
Proven in Spottsylvania County, Va. Mar. 20, 1777.
Of Fredericksburg, Spottsylvania County, Va. Wife Isabella and children to live on plantation in King George County, adjoining James Hunter's land, which testator bought from General George Washington. At wife's death, said land to be sold and divided among children—William, John, George, and Ann Gordon Mercer—including land as follows: to William, 2000 acres on River Kentucky, Fincastle County, purchased from James Ducanson; to George, 2000 acres part of 5000 acres, Warrant from Governor of Virginia in consequence of Royal Proclamation of 1763; to John, 3000 acres on Ohio River about seventeen miles above Falls, purchased from Col. Geo. Weedon; to Ann Gordon, 1000 acres on Ohio River twelve miles above Falls, purchased from James Duncanson, also 1000 acres on River Ohio, six miles above the Miama River, purchased from James Duncanson; to unborn child or children 2000 acres, the other part of 5000 above referred to. To executors to be sold house and lots bought of James Hunter adjoining lot of Charles Dick, where family was living, also lot bought from Dr. John Sutherland's estate joining lot of James Allen in Fredericksburg, 300 acres bought of Allen Wylie in tenure of Reuben Zimmerman, three tracts of land on Yoheogany River near Stuart'd Crossing called Mercersburg, Fredericksburg and Winchester, Va., containing 900 acres, pur-

chased from Proprietor of Pennsylvania, also lease of house in Fredericksburg which he then held from John Dalton.
Executors: Wife Isabella, Col. George Weedon, Dr. John Tennant, of Port Royal, and James Duncanson.
Witnesses: John Francis Mercer, John Bell, Elias Hardy.
  On March 20, 1777, Dr. John Tannant qualified with Thomas Lomax and George Baylie, Esq., as surities; and on April 18, 1777, Isabella Mercer and George Weedon, qualified with George Baylie and William Stanard as surities, giving bond for 10,000 pounds.
[*B2, p106.*]

HOUSTON, ELI . . . . . Mar. 20, 1819—Sept. 13, 1819.
  To wife Lucy N., his estate.
Executors: James Houston of Bourbon County, Larence Clore of Jefferson County.
Witnesses: Abr. H. Kellar, Thomas C. Powell, Elijah Clore.
[*B2, p110.*]
  [Note: Recorded will gives Lucy Ann for wife, but original will shows Lucy N. Jefferson County Marriage Book No. 1, p.110, gives marriage record of Allan Wilhoite and Lucy N. Houston, widow of Eli Houston; license issued Oct. 13, and return made, Oct. 14th, 1819, by B. Allen.]

BERTHOUD, JAMES . . . . Dec. 15, 1812—Sept. 13, 1819.
  To wife Mary Anna Julia, for life, estate. At her death, to son Nicholas Berthoud forever.
Executors: Thomas Prather, Fortunatus Cosby, friends.
Witnesses: W. W. Montgomery, Alex Duncan, Jr., Joshua Headington. [*B2, p110.*]

WHEELER, JOHN HANSON . . June 19, 1819—Oct. 12, 1819.
  To wife Deborah, certain slaves, stock, etc.; to daughters, Polly Rose, Mahala Rose, Ann H. Chapline, and the children of Elizabeth Miller, deceased, all property previously given them; and a slave to each of the following children: John, Josiah H., Elias Harden, Elbert Perry, Thomas White, Ulesses and Sarah, Emily, Matilda Perry, Priscilla, Henryetta; at wife's death estate to above named eleven youngest children.
Executors: Wife Deborah Wheeler, son John Wheeler.
Witnesses: John Bate, Sr., Reubin Ross. [*B2, p110.*]

KELLAR, SARAH . . . . . Oct. 2, 1819—Oct. 12, 1819.
Debts to be paid, including one to her brother Isaac Estill. To Rebecca Kellar and her sisters, Betty Evans and Sarah Kellar, daughters of Joseph Kellar deceased, certain money.
Executor: Richard Barbour.
Witnesses: John Little, Hannah Griffy, Francis Evans. [*B2, p111.*]

FUNK, JACOB . . . . . . Oct. 6, 1819—Dec. 13, 1819.
Debts to be paid with estate left him by his father, John Funk; to wife Mary, during widowhood, estate for support and education of children; should she remarry, she is to have only her lawful share, and balance to be put in trust with his brother-in-law, Nathan Taylor, for children,—be divided as they become of age—Rebecca M. Richey, step-daughter, wife Mary's child, Julia Susan, Eliza Temperance, Terracy Louisa, and sons Thompson Taylor and Joseph Perry.
Executors: Wife, Mary Funk, and brother-in-law, Nathan Taylor, now of Harrison County, Indiana.
Witnesses: William Field, Michael Miller.   [*B2, p112.*]

GARAY, BENNETT . . . . Nov. 16, 1819—Dec. 13, 1819.
To wife Charity for life, estate including land purchased from Alexander Gibson and wife Catherine, in State of Indiana. At wife's death, estate to be divided between Margara Garay and Rebecca Smith.
Executor: Wife Charity Garay.
Witnesses: William Brown, Luther Owings, William Eversull, L. A. Tarascon.   [*B2, p113.*]

BRADSHAW, JOHN . . . . Feb. 21, 1794—June 12, 1820.
Property at McGreggs, Pittsburgh, to be sold to pay debts. To friend, Thomas Doyle, Major in service of the United States, all of estate except enough to purchase two rings for the Ladies of Dr. Allison and of H. H. Breckinridge, including tract of land on Little Miama and at Rapids of Ohio. Wm. Perry mentioned.
Executors: Thomas Doyle, H. H. Breckinridge.
Witnesses: H. Marks, Jno. Whistler.   [*B2, p113.*]

HEADINGTON, JOSHUA . . . . Oct. 6, 1818—June 12, 1820.
To son Elliott and daughter Caroline, certain money and land on which living and that leased to John A. Bright. Should either

die without issue, the survivor to receive deceased's share; should both die before age twenty-one, estate to revert to their mother, Maria Headington. Residue of estate to wife Maria. Dr. James C. Johnston, Guardian of son; wife to be guardian of daughter.
Executor: Wife, Maria Headington.
Witnesses: Worden Pope, Wm. F. Pratt, Jas. Peters, C. Whittingham. [*B2, p115.*]

MAPLE, JOHN . . . . . . July 11, 1820—Aug. 14, 1820.
To wife Sarah, estate except gifts to sons Samuel, Peter, John, Arthur and George, and to daughters Hannah, Polly, Sarah Pegga, Rebekah, Nancy Ann and Elizabeth. Should wife remarry, property to be divided among children.
Executors: Wife Sarah Maple, and son, Samuel Maple.
Witnesses: Coleman Duncan, Charles Duncan. [*B2, p118.*]

GRETSINGER, JOHN . . . . June 20, 1820—Sept. 11, 1820.
To mother, a watch and note on brother George for $420.87½; to brother Joseph, a seal. Residue to brothers George and Joseph Gretsinger. *Executors:* None named.
Witnesses: Jacob Hinkle, Daniel McCalister. [*B2, p119.*]

HARDING, JOSIAH . . . . Mar 25, 1820—Sept. 11, 1820.
To brothers Nathan and John Harding, land willed by father in Montgomery County, Maryland. To sister, Deborah Wheeler, for life, the place on which she lives, and at her death to nephews John H. and Josiah H. Wheeler. To wife residue of estate, and at her death $100. each to nieces Elizabeth Kettury and Caroline Harding, daughters of deceased brother, John Harding.
Executors: Wife, Ann Harding.
Witnesses: Enoch Magruder, Edmund Woolfolk, Benj. W. Jones. [*B2, p120.*]

SHAW, JANE . . . . . . Jan. 17, 1820—Dec. 11, 1820.
To daughter Hannah Hartly, clothes; to grand-daughters Nancy and Jane Shaw, daughters of her son Thomas, money for schooling, in the hands of James Pomeroy; to son John, residue of estate.
Executor: John Shaw.
Witnesses: George K. Pomeroy, I. Thursby, James Pomeroy. [*B2, p121.*]

WHITE, MARY . . . . . July 15, 1820—Dec. 11, 1820.
To son William White, certain slaves, and at his death to grandson Lee White; to children of her son George, namely, William G., Lucindy, Mary, Elizabeth White, Sally Glover, Robey and Anne White certain slaves; to daughters Nancy Balthrop, a slave, furniture, etc., and to Mary Floyd 10 pounds. Balance of estate to granddaughters: Winnie Balthorp, Eliza Floyd, Eliza I. and Mary M. White; and great grandchildren Mary Jane and her brother, Robert William Glass.
Executors: Son William White, grandson Lee White.
Witnesses: I. Glass, Benjamin Alsop. [*B2, p122.*]

WHIPS, GEORGE . . . . . Not dated—Dec. 11, 1820.
Nuncupative Will. He died about October 21, 1820. Estate to be divided between sisters Rebecca and Elizabeth Whips.
Signed Thomas Lawes, Josua Whips, P. Payton.
Witnesses: Worden Pope, Clerk. [*B2, p124.*]

HAWES, PETER [HAUSE, HARSE], July 19, 1819—Feb. 12, 1821.
To wife Hannah, furniture and $200 in possession of Peter Funk & Co. To son Benjamin and Peter Omer, plantation until April 1, 1821, and then to be sold and money go to wife Hannah and children: John and Benjamin Hawes; Peggy, wife of Daniel Eby; Sally, wife of John Maple, at her death to her children; Polly, wife of Hiram Melott; Elizabeth, wife of George Fenley; Sybella, wife of Henry Thorn; Hannah, wife of George Seabold; John Hawes, Benjamin Haws and Rebecca, wife of Peter Omer. Note of $421.97 to George Hikes for judgements against Elisha Applegate, bailor for John Hawes to be paid.
Executors: Son-in-law Hiram Melott, son Benjamin Hawes.
Witnesses: Leonard Hoke, Arthur Maple. [*B2, p124.*]

REYNOLDS, CHARLES . . . . Oct. 30, 1820—Mar. 12, 1821.
To wife Margaret, for life, home plantation with slaves, etc.; at her death to children, as well as his share in estate of Richard Raynolds his father. Mentions granddaughter Sarah Noor [Noon?]; sons Thomas, John and Abraham, and daughters: Elizabeth, wife of Basil Williams; Mary, wife of John Noor [Noon?]; Sarah, wife of Jacob Goodman, and her children; and Esther; and brother Edward Reynolds. Wife to confer with

278

friends William Edwards, Abraham Keller and Jacob Frederick, whose decision shall be final on any disputed question.

Executor: Wife Margaret Reynolds.

Witnesses: Andrew Steele, Mary Kuckendall, Nancy Kuckendall.

[*B2, p127.*]

PRESTON, WILLIAM . . . . Jan. 3, 1821—Apr. 9, 1821.
Proven in Montgomery Co., Va., Feb. 7, 1821—Mar. 6, 1821.

Of Jefferson County, Kentucky, but now in State of Virginia, in critical health. Debts to be paid, and, if necessary, Executors to sell lots in Preston's Enlargement adjoining Louisville, and to reserve $6000.00 to educate sons Hancock and William C. Preston. Mentions lots to be laid off adjoining Preston's Enlargement agreeable to verbal agreement with brother Francis, who is to extend his lots on to Main and Market streets. Balance of real estate to descend to children, Henrietta, Maria, Caroline, Josephine, Hancock, William and Susannah, agreeable to law of Virginia, except following tracts of land: two in Indiana, one near Charleston, the other near Posks [Porks?] Mill; four tracts in State of Virginia one on Pocotallico Creek, Kanawha County; one on Piney River, Giles County; one on Big Savannah in Monroe Co.; and other on Muddy fork of Bluestone, Taynnell County; to be sold. Such part of estate to be given to children as they come of age or marry as wife may deem proper "having the fullest confidence in her discretion and justice." Personal property to wife. Wife may take one-third of estate if she prefer. Her father dying intestate, she inherits from him. Refers to land called "Briars Patch" adjoining Louisville. Should wife's mother, Mrs. Hancock, live with wife, children to be sent away to school.

Executors: Wife Caroline Preston, James A. Pearce, Dennis Fitzhugh of Jefferson County; Joseph Cabel Breckinridge, of Lexington; Garnett Peyton of Wythe County, Va., and James McDowell, Sr. of Rockbridge Co., Va.

Witnesses: James A. Piper, John Floyd, Fran's Preston, Letitia Floyd.

Codicil, January 14, 1821. Direct division of estate be by lottery as soon as children arrive at age or marry, in order to equalize same, but redivision not to be made unless executors think there is a palpable inequality.

Witnesses: Eliza Madison, Letitia Floyd, W. R. Preston.

[*B2, p129.*]

YEWELL, LEVY . . . . . Dec. 27, 1820—May 14, 1821.
Of Nelson County. One half of estate to sister Patsey, wife of Thomas Formon, and her children. The other half equally between Benjamin Pope, Martin Yewell, Joel Yeager, Julious Wilhite and Joshua Christly. *Executors*, None named.
Witnesses: Henry Bell, John B. Hobbs, Samuel Bell, Leonard P. Higdon. [*B2, p132.*]

PENDERGRAST, MARY . . . Mar. 13, 1821—May 14, 1821.
[Signed Polly.] To daughter Margaret A. Pendergrast, any title or interest testator has in tract of land in Bullitt County, called Clear Station, 1350 acres, "for the conveyance of which tract of land to the heirs of G. E. Pendergrast by me his daughter Joseph Brooks in his life time gave and executed bond, and which bond in and by his last will and testament, he directed shall be complied with"; to daughter Louisa Brown tract of land on Ponds Creek, Jefferson County, 600 acres. Slaves to daughter. At expiration of ten years, slave Letty to choose which daughter she desires to live with, who shall pay the other $200. James Brown of Beargrass to be guardian for daughter Louisa.
Executor: John Murphey, Justice.
Witnesses: Ch's M. Thruston, John P. Tunstall, Henry R. Tunstall.
Codicil, April 10, 1821. Slave Charles to be sold; proceeds to daughters.
Witnesses: John P. Tunstall, Henry R. Tunstall. [*B2, p132.*]

DORSEY, JOSHUA . . . . . Dec. 6, 1820—May 14, 1821.
Certain monies etc. to granddaughter Caroline Mary Chiles, daughter of deceased son Vachel Dorsey, and to granddaughter Matilda Dorsey Hite, daughter of deceased child Henrietta Hite, when sixteen; to daughter-in-law Matilda L., wife of son Nimrod, $100 for kindness to testator while sick; infant daughters Sarah Ann and Matilda, each $100. for education, or at sixteen years; to son Columbus one-half of mills and distillery, owned by son Nimrod and testator, a slave and one-eighth of residue; other seven-eighths to children: Nimrod, Corilla wife of Henry C. Dorsey, Reagin Hammond, Ruth Maria, Sarah Ann and Matilda Dorsey, and Eliza Chew Booker wife of Richard Booker. Abraham Hite, husband of deceased daughter Henrietta, and Edmond Talbott,

280

husband of deceased daughter Julian, mentioned. Slave Daniel to be freed.

Executors: Nimrod Dorsey, Columbus Dorsey.

Witnesses: Bazil Hobbs, John H. Tyler, James Forsyth, J. H. Wells.

Executors took oath with Bazil Hobbs and David Forsyth as securities. [*B2, p134.*]

HARRISON, JOHN . . . . . June 19, 1821—Aug. 13, 1821.

To wife Mary Ann, slaves, furniture, etc. Estate to be divided equally among five children: Sophia Jones New, Benjamin, Charles, John and James Harrison. To R. A. New, daughter's husband, all he owes testator. Sophia Jones New's portion left to son John in trust for her.

Executors: Sons, John, Charles, Benjamin and James.

Witnesses: Th's Joyes, Isaac Stewart, J[ohn] A. Honore.

Charles L., Benjamin J., John P., James qualified with James D. Breckinridge, Craven P. Luckett, Alexander Pope & Samuel H. Overstreet as Securities. [*B2, p138.*]

RICE, EDMUND, SEN'R. Dec. 10, 1813—Aug. 13 & Oct. 10, 1821.

Wife Mary "should live and enjoy present place of residence" during life, one-half of estate, with exception of a slave to Ebney Baxter, a little girl raised in his family and at her death this, with balance of estate, to adopted son John Rice, whom he raised from infancy.

Executors: Henry Churchill, John Speed, Jacob Lytle.

Witnesses: James Macconel, Wm. Baxter, Jr., Ann Lytle, Linney Macconel.

Proven by Ann Lytle Aug. 13, and on Oct. 10th, 1821, by Mrs. Linney Hauley [or Hanley], "late Linny Macconnell." [*B2, p138.*]

McCUNE, TERRENCE . . . Sept. 6, 1821—Oct. 11, 1821.

To wife Mary McCune, all estate with exception of $150. to Terrence McLissher, of County Fermonagh, Ireland, to pay passage to America, $30; one cart to Hugh Quinn, and a horse to John McCune.

Inventory had been taken by James Fife and Edm'd Hughes.

Executors: None named.

Witnesses: John McCracken, James Fife, Edward Hughes.

[*B2, p140.*]

[Note: In original will spelled McCune and McCracken, but recorded copy is McKune and McKracken.]

HARDING, ANN . . . . . . Oct. 15, 1821—Nov. 12, 1821.
    To niece Verlinda W. Wren and nephew Hezekiah Magruder, equally, her land. Makes gifts to Sarah Ann Wren, daughter of John B. and Verlinda Wren; to nephew Josiah Harding Magruder money, slaves, etc.; and residue of estate to nephews and niece, Hezekiah and Josiah Harding Magruder and Verlinda W. Wren, wife of John B. Wren, sons and daughter of Daniel Magruder. Negroes must not be sold out of family.
Executors: Hezekiah and Josiah H. Magruder.
Witnesses: Enoch Magruder, Wm. Duerson, Benj. W. Jones.
[*B2, p141.*]

BANKS, JOHN . . . . . . Sept. 16, 1821—Nov. 12, 1821.
    To wife Mary, during life, the negroes and one-eighth of money left by his father, John Banks of Virginia. Negroes not to be sold until after wife's death. One-eighth of estate to each of children: Clement, John and Rachael Banks, Betsy, Runah, Bolly and Elias Butler.
Executors: John and Samuel Stowers of Breckinridge County.
Witnesses: Thomas King, Samuel Norrington.   [*B2, p143.*]

POMEROY, GEORGE H. K. . Oct. 19, 1821—Nov. 12, 1821.
    To wife Jane, for life, slaves and half of estate, one half of farm including mansion house. To daughters Ann, wife of James Duncan; Margaret, wife of Alexander Lynes; and Isabelle, wife of James McCully, certain monies; to son James one-half farm, and at wife's death her share.
Executors: Jane Pomeroy, wife, and son James.
Witnesses: Rob't Tompkins, B. Tompkins, W. Wallace.
    James Pomeroy qualified as executor and gave bond with Robert Tompkins and Jonathan Elston securities.   [*B2, p144.*]

CHAPMAN, SAMUEL . . . . Nov. 6, 1821—Nov. 13, 1821.
    Of Shippingport, Ky. To wife Mary, formerly Mary Cummings, and two children, William and Elizabeth, his estate.
Executor: Wife Mary Chapman.
Witnesses: Peter Casson, Shepherd Whitman, James Conner, John Palfrey.   [*B2, p144.*]

GLASS, SARAH . . . . . May 8, 1821—Dec. 10, 1821.
    [Signed Sally.] To nieces Sarah Ann and Mary Vance Bower, $50. each. Debts to be paid and balance of estate to Sister, Mary Vance, and brother Joseph Glass.

Executors: Brothers, Robert D. Vance of Virginia, Joseph Glass of Kentucky, and Samuel Glass.
Witnesses: John Brengman, Bazil N. Hobbs, James Rudy.

Samuel Glass took oath and gave bond with Basil N. Hobbs and Levi Tyler as surities. [*B2, p145.*]

MORRIS, RICHARD . . . . Apr. 2, 1820—Dec. 10, 1821.

Of Louisa County. To son James Maury, all land in County of Louisa, Henrico, city of Richmond, and in County of Buckingham, called the Slate Works, and in New Orleans, farming implements, etc. To son-in-law, Edward Garland, land in Kentucky bought of Hancock Lee. All lands testator is entitled to in County of Flovanna, as well as that held in partnership with David Bullock, five acre lot adjoining town of Charlottesville called the Tan Yard, land in Kentucky near Falls of Ohio, lands in Dismal Swamps called Jones Turnpike tract (should deal pending with Samuel Pain be confirmed), soap and candle factory near Richmond, and shares in Turnpike Company, to be sold or not, at discretion of son James Maury and Edward Garland, and money divided among daughters Martha, Maria, Elizabeth and Clarissa. Son James Maury Morris to furnish each daughter with one dozen silver table spoons, one dozen silver tea spoons, one dozen hard metal pewter plates and three dishes, sorted, and this not to be at expense of the estate. To Fanny and her six children, their freedom, maintenance and education as son thinks best, and that he purchase about 600 acres in the western country and have houses built if necessary for comfort and accommodation of her children, and otherwise provide for them, giving each a slave. Anderson Jones and Charles HaVille mentioned.
Witnesses: John Vest, James Bibb, Thomas Garland, Joshua Morris.

Codicil July 8, 1821. Land on which he lived in Jefferson County ordered to be divided between Thomas and Richard, two oldest sons of Edmond Garland, and John the eldest son of Horatio Gates Winston, testator's grandsons.
Witnesses: Aaron Fontaine, James Summers, Algernon S. Thruston, Joshua Morris.

Administration of estate granted Horatio G. Winston and Isaac Miller. [*B2, p146.*]

EDWARDS, WILLIAM, Sept. 22, 1821—Dec. 10, 1821, and Jan. 14, 1822.

To wife, should she recover and remain a widow, all of estate for support and education of children. Should she marry, one-third of estate to her and balance to children equally, as they come of age.

Executors: Wife, Lyddy, Henry Rudy, brother John Edwards.
Witnesses: John Bate, Will M. Taylor, Andrew Steele, Robert Todd. [*B2, p149.*]

MAIRS, JOHN . Not dated—Dec. 10, 1821, and Jan. 14, 1822.

[Signed John Marssee.] To wife Agnes, the home plantation, except part willed to son Andrew, with slaves, stock, etc., and at her death to children. To daughters and sons: Mary McCaslan, Elizabeth Ross, Agness Nailor, Rachael Mairs and John, Alexander and Nathan, certain money. To son Allen and daughter Sarah, slaves. To son Andrew land near that of Wm. Edwards and Francis Snowden and Tenant. To son-in-law Reuben Ross, furniture.

Executors: Sons, John and Alexander Mairs.
Witnesses: Robert Woolfolk, Sen., Andrew Steele.

Alexander and John Mairs qualified as executors with Andrew Mairs, John Reed and Thomas Joyes as surities. [*B2, p150.*]

[Note: This name is also spelled Marrse, Marrs, Mars; see calendar of will of widow Agnes Marrs; also Jefferson County marriage records.]

GARDENER, SILAS P. . . . . Oct. 30, 1821—Feb. 11, 1822.

[Signed Silas Gardner.] To wife Phebe, entire estate.
Witnesses: N. Martin, Wm. Dodd, Elzy Elzy. [*B2, p152.*]

LITER, ELIZABETH . . . Oct. 21, 1821—Mar. 11, 1822.

Estate to sons Jonah and Jonathan, providing they furnish homes for daughters Barbara and Sally Liter. To son Henry and daughters Mary and Barbara, $1.00 each. Requests that sons hold land on Transylvania Seminary, where they were living, until lease expires.

Executor: Jonathan Liter, son.
Witnesses: Sam'l Steele, Frederick Rudy. [*B2, p153.*]

DEGAALON, HENRY . . . . Apr. 9, 1819—Jan. 14, 1822.
    [Recorded as Henry Degallon.] To wife Jane Degaalon entire estate in trust; should daughter Louisa Degaalon die before wife, then estate is to belong to wife; should reverse be the case, estate to be put in trust in reliable hands for use and benefit of daughter. *Executor:* Wife, Jane Dagaalon.
Witnesses: F. Cosby, John D. Colmesnil.   [*B2, p153.*]

JAMES, SAMUEL . . . . . Dec. 15, 1821—Jan. 16, 1822.
    To sons Griffith and Samuel, a slave and land in State of South Carolina and District of Pendleton. To Katherine Merit and her sons, farming utensils, cattle, etc. Administrator: Squire Brooks. *Witnesses:* Joshua Stewart, Samuel Caple, Geo. Kesacker.
                                                        [*B2, p154.*]

PHILLIPS, JENKIN . . . . Nov. 29, 1819—Feb. 11, 1822.
    To son Thomas, 1616 acres whereon Thomas formerly lived, one lot No. 178 in Louisville adjoining public square where man named Kelly now lives; land whereon testator lives, but Thomas to pay brothers and sisters $5500. to equalize. To Richard land where he formerly lived on the northwest side of South Fork of Beargrass Creek adjoining land of David L. Ward and General Jonathan Clark's heirs and land whereon William Oldham lived; and 100 acres in Illinois Grant in Indiana No. 12, and one-half of another grant No. 161; and choice of two lots in Louisville: No. 119 on Market Street and deeded to testator by John Sanders, or No. 209 on Jefferson and Second Cross-Streets. To children of deceased son Samuel Phillips, lot, in Louisville, No. 175 adjoining Public Square, and other half of tract in Illinois Grant No. 161. To children of daughter Hannah Duberly, 100 acres in Jefferson County on waters of Shively Creek from his 1000 acre survey. To children of deceased daughter Catherine Hunter, negroes; refers to son-in-law Joseph Hunter. To daughter Ann Hamilton, 1000 acres in Hardin County on waters of Green River entered in name of Rheubin Grisslet and patented in testator's name. To daughter Lydia Clark, 355 acres in Jefferson County known as Dutch Spring Tract, where she resides; mentions her husband Ludlow Clark. To daughter Susan Riley money from sale of 750 acres in Montgomery County on waters of Grassy Lick Creek, a branch of Licking River. Negroes to granddaughters Lucy Ann

Hamilton, daughter of his deceased daughter Eleanor and Charles Hamilton, to Mary and Hannah Hunter, and to grandson Jenkin Phillips, son of Thomas. Negro slave Bell to be freed. Residue including negroes to be divided between children and grand-children of deceased son Samuel Phillips and deceased daughter Catherine Hunter.

Executors: Thomas and Richard Phillips, sons.

Witnesses: Samuel Churchill, John Downing, James R. Williams.

[*B2, p155.*]

LEWIS, GEORGE . . . . . Dec. 26, 1821—Jan. 15, 1822·
     To wife, Diana, his estate.

Executors: Diana Lewis, wife.

Witnesses: W. H. Atkinson, Levi Tyler, Israel Monroe. [*B2, p159.*]

ROGAN, JOHN . . . . . . Feb. 6, 1822—Mar. 11, 1822.
     To friend, Thomas Worrall, estate, including lots in Utica, Indiana, Nos. 64, 65, 67 and 105.

Executor: Thomas Worrall.

Witnesses: John Miller, William Martin.

     Thomas Worrall qualified as executor with William Munday, Archibald G. Foster and James M. Edwards, as surities.

[*B2, p160.*]

OFFAND, JOHN M. . . . . Nov. 23, 1818—Mar. 11, 1822.
     Of Shippingport, Ky. Estate to James Pryor, William Mc-Kever and Fortunatus Cosby in trust for wife Henrietta for life and then to children, including what he shall receive from his father, Thomas Offand, of France, where testator was shortly going.

Executors: Wife, Henrietta, James Pryor, Fortunatus Cosby, Wm. McKever.

Witnesses: Thos. Phillips, David Jewell, J. W. Harrison, Samuel Tyler.   [*B2, p161.*]

HAMPTON, EPHRAIM . . . . Oct. 25, 1821—Mar. 11, 1822.
     Estate to wife during life, and then to children, with exception of son Rolin, who has been given his share. *Executors:* None named.

Witnesses: David Hampton, Butler Stonestreet, Jr.   [*B2, p163.*]

PENDERGRAST, MARGARET AMERICA, Jan. 16, 1822—Apr. 8, 1822.
Of Havana, Cuba, late of Kentucky and now sojourning there. To Vincent Gray of Havana, in trust for father, Garrett Elliott Pandergrast, estate, including lot No. 30 in Louisville; tract of land in Bullitt County known as Clairs Station, 1350 acres, together with damages that may be recovered from executors of Joseph Brooks, dec. for non compliance with bond executed to said father by said Joseph in 1799, suit now in General Court of Kentucky; also undivided interest in land near Shelbyville, patented in name of Margaret Pendergrast, suit likewise in General Court of Kentucky. Her desire to comply with last testament of mother, except negro Letitia instead of being sold to half-sister by mother's side, Louisa Brown, be liberated as reward for fidelity and tenderness in nursing mother and testator while ill. Also to Vincent Gray, remainder of legacy left by mother, Mary Pendergrast, by her father Joseph Brooks, which executors have not paid, and requests suit be brought. Should father obtain release from creditors under new bankrupt law of the United States, leaves it to discretion of father and Mr. Gray whether property be conveyed to father without regard to this will.
Executors: Father, Garrett Elliott Pendergrast, and Vincent Gray of Havana.
Witnesses: Elizabeth Pendergrast, John C. Beeler, Tarlton Murphey. [*B2, p163.*]

FENLEY, RICHARD, the Elder . Feb. 11, 1818—Apr. 8, 1822.
Certain lands, slaves, etc. to sons and daughters: To George C., John H., land on Floyd's fork; to Ann, wife of Jacob Lytle, land on south Fork of Goose Creek, also soup spoon; to Elizabeth, wife of Philip Rogers, Amelia, wife of Joshua Fowler, Melinda (otherwise called Verlinda), wife of Hezekiah Hawley, also land on Muddy Fork of Beargrass. To Jacob Lytle, slaves. Residue of estate to children.
Executors: Jacob Lytle, Hezekiah Hawley.
Witnesses: Wm. Chambers, Worden Pope, Wm. C. Bullitt, Nicholas M. Lewis, James W. Denny.
Hezekiah Hawley qualified as executor with Richard Barnes, and John Edwards as surities. [*B2, p166.*]

DUMARSELLARY, ANDREW LECOQ, Apr. 28, 1819—May 13, 1822.
[Signed A. Lecoq Dumarselay.] To wife Theresa Lecoq Dumarsellay, for life, estate, and then to two children Just and Denise Lecoq Dumarsellay.
Executors: Wife Theresa, son Just.
Witnesses: F. Cosby, Moses David.
Theresa Lecoq Dumarsellay, executrix, renounced execution of will. [*B2, p169.*]

MILLS, SAMUEL . . . . . June 27, 1821—June 10, 1822.
Estate to son Jonathan on condition that he care for his mother, Mary Mills, and that he give to his sisters, Sally and Sidney Lee, amounts equal to what the testator had previously given daughters Susan and Polly, already married.
Executor: Jonathan Mills.
Witnesses: M. L. Miller, Henry Welsh, James Welsh. [*B2, p170.*]

WINCHESTER, REBECCA, Mar. 11, 1822—June 10 and July 8, 1822.
To children: Lavinia, wife of Frances Snowden, land in Jackson County, Ind., adjoining town of Valonia and lot in Preston's Enlargement; to Olivia, wife of Captain Alexander Veech, part of lot 115 in Preston's Enlargement, and her children Frances Ann and Rebecca Veech; to daughter Polly Dorsey, wife of Joshua B. Bowles, part of lot 111 on north side of Main St.; to Louise Winchester, only unmarried daughter, part of lot 111, and to Amanda Hall and her husband Richard Hall, part of lot 111; to William Chambers and Benjamin Winchester, and son-in-law Francis Snowden, certain lands, slaves and money. Leaves property in trust with Francis Snowden for children of daughter Amanda Hall and son-in-law Richard Hall, free of Richard Hall (they having conveyed property to testator). Refers to land at Chickasaw Bluff on Mississippi River and to land in Indiana. Mentions fact that daughters Lavinia, Olivia and Amanda were named as residuary legatees in will of Benjamin Lawrence, grandfather.
Executors: Francis Snowden, Joshua B. Bowles, Alexander Veech.
Witnesses: Sam'l Lawrence, L. Lawrence, John Whips.
Francis Snowden and Joshua B. Bowles qualified with John Whips, Edmund G. Byers and James McCrum as surities.
[*B2, p170.*]

BRISCOE, ROBERT . . . . . July 15, 1822—Aug. 12, 1822.
To daughters Ruth, Elizabeth, and Mary, each a slave; furniture, cow and calf, etc; to wife Mary residue of estate.
Executor: Mary Briscoe, wife.
Witnesses: John C. Beeler, Henry Briscoe.
Mary Briscoe qualified as executor with John C. Beeler, Henry Briscoe and James Briscoe as surities. [*B2, p179.*]

FITZHUGH, DENNIS . . . . Dec. 7, 1821—Aug. 12, 1822.
[Signed D. Fitzhugh.] About to leave home he bequeathed to Fanny his wife, estate on condition she support and educate children. At her death, to son Clark, the house and lot on which testator lived, the balance to be equally divided between son Clark and daughter Lucy Ann. Friends Worden Pope and R. C. Anderson, Jr., to advise wife. Refers to stock in Bank of Kentucky, Insurance Co. of Louisville, and Turnpike Company.
Executors: Wife Fanny Fitzhugh.
Witnesses: None named.
Will proven by oaths of James W. Denny, Isaac H. Tyler, Alfred Thruston and John Bustard. [*B2, p180.*]

TRIGG, WILLIAM, SEN'R . . . Jan. 24, 1818—Aug. 12, 1822.
To wife, Ann Trigg, all property for life; at her death to daughter Nancy, wife of Edmund Noel, the place on which she lives on Ohio River and Whortleberry Run and Francis Snowden's farm; to son William Trigg, the home plantation; at wife's death property to be divided equally among sons Daniel, Thomas and William and daughter Nancy Noel, and grandson James Duerson, in lieu of his mother Mary wife of Thomas Duerson. To Miss Offner Carney, whom he raised from infancy, $100.
Executors: Sons Daniel, Thomas and William Trigg.
Witnesses: And'w Porter, Charles B. Tennant, Thomas Foster, John Fenley, Lucy Serly.
Executors gave bond with security signed by James Densford, Edward Talbott, William Mundy, Archibald Foster and Joseph Lavielle. [*B2, p181.*]

PRYOR, JAMES . . . . . Dec. 25, 1814—Aug. 13, 1822.
"The state of our Country rendering life more precarious then usual, induces me to make this my last and only will." Signed at New Orleans. To James Gilly, son of John B. Gilly, when he is eighteen years or marries, $1000.; balance of estate to brothers

Robert L. and Nathaniel Pryor and Robert McClelland and sisters Jane B. Gilly and Eliza Oldham, each one-fifth.
Executors: Jno. B. Gilly.
Witnesses: None given. Will proven by oaths of William McKever and Fry Dabis. [*B2, p183.*]

FRY, SUSAN . . . . . . Aug. 16, 1822—Sept. 9, 1822.
To sister Rebecca Whips, for life, certain furniture, at her death to testator's children; residue of estate to children Polly and William Fry.
Executor: Brother Denton Whipps.
Witnesses: William Hite, Abraham Hite.
Denton Whipps qualified with Joseph Hite and Wesley Whipps surities. [*B2, p183.*]

DELANY, MICHAEL . . . . Aug. 20, 1822—Sept. 10, 1822.
To the Catholic Church of Louisville, Jefferson County, Kentucky, one half of estate. *Executors:* None named.
Witnesses: Timothy Crow, Kerian Campion, Daniel McGreary.
[*B2, p184.*]
[Note: Nothing said regarding the other half of the estate.]

MARRS, AGNES . . . . . Sept. 13, 1822—Oct. 14, 1822.
To son Andrew one slave. Negro Molly to be freed. Estate to children John, Alexander, Nathan, Mary McCaslen, Elizabeth Ross, Nancy Nailor and Allen Marrs. Daughters Rachel Marrs and Sarah Shurley be allowed $60, before division made, they not having been so well provided for in will of testator's deceased husband John Marrs.
Executor: Son Andrew Marrs.
Witnesses: Jeff Overstreet, Sam'l B. Steele, Sarah Trigg.
Andrew Marrs qualified with Samuel B. Steele and James Crutchfield as surities. [*B2, p185.*]
[For various spellings of the name Marrs see note following calendar of will of John Mairs. *B2, p150.*]

SHUTT, FREDERICK . . . . Aug. 1, 1822—Oct. 18, 1822.
[Signed in German.] Estate to son William Shutt.
Executor: John H. Miller.
Witnesses: J. Haney, Nathan Bradley, Christian Menst.
[*B2, p186.*]
[Note: Original will filed as Frederick Smith; signature is indistinct, but will made out and probated as Shutt.]

290

EASTIN, ANN . . . . . . Nov. 27, 1820—Nov. 11, 1822.
To four nieces, Nancy Sneed, Catherine W. Hite, Harriet
Funk and Rebecca Hite, all of estate after debts are paid.
Executors: None named.
Witnesses: George Hite, Joseph Funk. [*B2, p187.*]

EARECKSON, MARY . . . . Nov. 30, 1811—Nov. 11, 1822.
To two nieces, Elizabeth and Susanna Eareckson; sister Anne
Eastin, and brother James Eareckson, certain slaves, monies, etc.
Negro slave Sarah to be freed.
Executors: James Eareckson.
Witnesses: Patrick Taggert, Samuel Eareckson, William Eareckson.
James Eareckson qualified with Samuel Eareckson, Harrison
Arterburn and Thomas Kelly, surities. [*B2, p188.*]

AUGUSTUS, SPRINGER . . . . Not dated—Nov. 11, 1822.
To wife Nancy for life estate, including tract of land on which
living, stock, etc., out of which she is to maintain and educate,
until he is fourteen years old, William Weams, son of Else Weams.
At wife's death, estate to go to the children of brothers John,
David, Jacob and James. Brother James Augustus is about to
take charge of a boat load of produce with view of descending
river to New Orleans, requests that if she die, his death not stop
his proceeding.
Executors: Brother Jacob Augustus, friends Abraham Keller,
Samuel Bray.
Witnesses: Abra. Hite, David Lyman, Henry White.
Abraham Kellar and Jacob Augustus gave bond with David
Lyman, George Hikes, Jr., Moses Kellar, Frederick Rudy and
Frederick Herr as surities. [*B2, p189.*]

LEWIS, DIANA . . . . . Nov. 14, 1822—Nov. 13, 1822.
Nuncupative will. Testator died 8th of August, last. To
Agnes Pye Usher, daughter of Noble and Harriot Usher, late of
the theatre, whom she intended or did adopt, her estate, provid-
ing child's grandfather, Luke Usher, of Lexington, is kept from
control. Agnes P. Usher, Mrs. Lewis thought, would be of age
March next.
Signed, Nocholas Clarke, Emelia Clarke. [*B2, p190.*]

291

CRANE, JOHN H. . . . . . Mar. 10, 1820—Nov. 11, 1822.
To Chauncey Whittelsey, counsellor at law for fee 10% of money collected on debts; Madam Sarah Smith, widow of Rev. Professor John Smith of Hanover, N. H.; William D. Sohen [Shin?] of Boston; and William Smith, Counsellor at law of Hanover, certain monies for mementoes. Residue of estate to Nathaniel Coffin, of Wiscossett, Maine, and his present wife, late Mary Porter.
Executor: Chauncey Whittetsey.
Above sealed and handed us, D. R. Poignand, S. S. Goodwin.
Will proven by oaths of Charles M. Thruston, David C. Pinkham and Isaac H. Tyler. [*B2, p191.*]

WAGGENER, JAMES . . July 27, 1822—Oct. 15, Nov. 18, 1822.
To brothers, Armstead and Reubin Waggener, estate, in trust, for wife Elizabeth and her three children George, Mary and Elesis Waggener. *Executors:* None named.
Witnesses: Ben W. Johnston, William Lewis. [*B2, p193.*]

REAUGH, JOHN . . Mar. 10, 1822—Sept. 9, Dec. 9, 1822.
To wife Margaret, personal property, lands and money for life, and at her death to daughters: Nelly Jonson, Hannah Black, Sarah Hains, daughter of Elizabeth Hains, and to granddaughters Paulina, Susannah Dyer Reaugh, and Asemeth Catherine Langhorn Reaugh. Lands to sons Charles, John and Samuel Reaugh. Confirms gift of land and material for place of public worship on which house of worship now stands for any orderly worshipping society of Christians. Land touches that of Tobias Butler.
Executors: Friends, Isaac Spraggin and George Smith, and Wife.
Witnesses: Matthew Reaugh, Hibb Rosberry, Z. Carpenter.
[*B2, p193.*]

LEWELLEN, SAMUEL . . . . Jan. 28, 1822—Dec. 9, 1822.
[Signed as Sam'l L. Lewellen.] To wife Patty, personal property and one third of real estate, balance to children: Nancy Walton Spreg [Sprague?], Thomas D. Lewellen, Catherine Riggs, Mary Everett, and Samuel R. Lewellen. Mentions land, 67 acres part of 400 acres, owned in Monongahela Co., Va. Mentions land adjoining Louisville in dispute between him and Wm. Doughterty.
Executors: Wife Patty, Daniel McCallister.
Witnesses: James Harrison, Richard Pilcher. [*B2, p195.*]

COLEMAN, BETTY . . . Aug. 4, 1820—Dec. 10 & 11, 1822.
Estate, including slaves, to grandchildren: Melinda Huie, William L. Thompson, Phillip Rootes Thompson, Robert Coleman Thompson, Mildred Ann Thompson, Francis Thornton Thompson, John Thompson Strother; to great grandsons French Strother and Robert Coleman Strother; and Mrs. Jennet Ebert and at her death to her children Elizabeth Ann and George. Six slaves to be freed. To grandson John Thompson, money instead of slaves, as he lived in Louisiana and she did not want them to go there. Slave Cato to have choice of family in which he wishes to live. Executors to lay off quarter acre or more to include graves to be retained as family graveyard.
Executors: Friend, John Peay, and grandson William Lightfoot Thompson.
Witnesses: Wm. C. Bullitt, James Brown. [*B2, p196.*]

RICE, JOHN . . . . . . May 21, 1822—Dec. 11, 1822.
Adopted son and heir by will of late Edmund Rice. Having no relatives and no one having acted so kindly to him as Richard Stintson, he leaves any thing he may have to said Richard Stintson.
Executor: Richard Stintson.
Witnesses: Giles Stephen, Charles L. Harrison, Amelia Harrison.
[*B2, p199.*]

TOMPKINS, ROBERT . . . . Feb. 13, 1821—Jan. 13, 1823.
Estate to wife Fanny during widowhood, at death or remarriage, to children, equally, after advances to William and Benjamin have been deducted from their share.
Executor: Fanny Tompkins, wife, and sons William and Benjamin.
Will proven by oaths of Benjamin Lawrence, Thomas B. Miller, William Cummins. [*B2, p200.*]

SHIPP, EDMOND . . . . . Dec. 11, 1816—Jan. 13, 1823.
[Signed E. Shipp.] In United States Army. Will and codicil dated at St. Louis, Mo. Estate to brother Ewell Shipp of Kentucky.
Executors: John Gwathmey of Louisville and Daniel Howell of Bardstown, Ky.
Witnesses: A. L. Langham, Willoughby Morgan, D. V. Walker.

Codicil March 5, 1817, at St. Louis, Mo. Certain funds in the hands of Joshua Pilcher, merchant, of St. Louis, to be used as follows: $500. to Doctor Bernard G. Farrar for kindness beyond that required by his profession; $400. to pay testator's debts to Gen. Thomas A. Smith; $500. to John Gwafthmey [Gwathmey?] for a monument, model to be furnished by friend A. L. Langham. After five years, servant to be freed and, with testators personal effects, to return to Kentucky.

Executors, in Missouri: Joshua Pilcher, Angus Louis Langham.
Witnesses: D. V. Walker, P. Quarles, I. V. Garnier.

Proven in St. Louis, Mo. Nov. 26, 1822, Slave proved he had served Ewell Shipp five years, court declared him free. Edmond Shipp is referred to as Capt. E. Shipp.   [*B2, p201.*]

FIELD, REUBIN . . . . .   Apr. 22, 1822—Jan. 14, 1823.

To wife Mary Field, forever, entire estate; should their marriage performed in Indiana in 1808 by one they thought was a minister of the Gospel named Smith, but later learned may not have been, be considered illegal, then he bequeathed to her as Mary Myrtle, her former name, said estate forever. *Executors:* None named.

Witnesses: John Jones, Jn. H. Myrtle, Bryan Johnson. [*B2, p203.*]

WOOLFOLK, WILLIAM . . . .   Aug. 8, 1822—Jan. 14, 1823.

To wife Nancy the farm, being part of survey of Wm. Lyne, assignee of Henry Lyne, with all appurtenances on which they live, except twenty acres, a mill seat on Harrod's Creek; she to take care of his two unfortunate children George and Fanny. At wife's death said children to go to his daughter Mary B. Kendall, to whom he gave eight extra slaves for their support. Residue of estate, including place called "Charity Place," land purchased from Anna B. Smith, now Ann B. Calloway, also land in Ohio, to five children, Sophia, James Madison, William, Francis and Mary B. Kendall. Slave Temple to be treated with kindness.

Executors: William, Francis, James M., sons, and son-in-law Amos Kendall.

Witnesses: Smith Felps, Avington Felps, Henry Lawrence.

Executors qualified with Smith Felps, Horatio Magruder as surities.   [*B2, p204.*]

TYLER, EDWARD . . . . Nov. 23, 1822—Jan. 15, 1823.
Signed Edward Tyler, Jr. To wife Rebecca, one-third of estate for life or widowhood; to child or children of this marriage, two-thirds of estate, and at her death her share to go to such children, if no children, estate to be divided among testators brothers and sisters. To Samuel Dickinson one year's rent free. To Elizabeth Dougherty or children, $100.
Executors: Brothers Levi, Isaac H. Tyler.
Witnesses: Edm. T. Bainbridge, Isaac Stewart.
Executors qualified with James Guthrie, Robert Breckinridge, Worden Pope as surities. [*B2, p207.*]

JEGERLEHNER, NIKLAUS . . . Sept. 4, 1822—Jan. 18, 1823.
[Signed in German.] Late of Walkinger, Canton of Berne in Switzerland, now of Shippingport, Ky. To wife Elizabeth, daughter of John Jent of Switzerland, Canton of Argans, estate, but if child she is bearing lives, it is to have two thirds of estate and wife one third.
Executor: Wife, Elizabeth, to appoint whom she wishes.
Witnesses: Aloyse Bachmann, John Buhlen.
Dec. 9, 1822, wife renounced right to quality and asks that testator's brother Frederick be appointed.
Witnesses: Peter Wolford, Benj. Bridges, Jr.
Proven in Jefferson County, Indiana, Nov. 6, 1822. [*B2, p209.*]

KEEN, THOS. F. V. . . . . Apr. 6, 1822—Jan. 18, 1823.
To wife Julia and two children James Louis and Louisa Keen, estate, equally divided. Nominates uncle James Keen as guardian.
Executor: Julia Keen, wife.
Witnesses: Jas. Franklyn, E. Sheridan, Luther Owings.
Executor, Julia Keen, qualified with Lustin Dering as security.
[*B2, p213.*]

OLDHAM, SAMUEL . . . . . Sept. 4, 1820—Feb. 10, 1823.
To wife Ann, home plantation, furniture, slaves, etc.; to son William, farm "Fair Hope" where he lives on Beargrass, also stills, etc.; to son Conway, house and lot in Shepherdsville where son Henry now lives, negro, etc., in trust for Eliza, wife of son Henry, and her children. The 1200 acres, unsold portion of 2000 acres on Pups [?] Creek, a branch of Ohio River, located by James Adams and patented to testator, to be divided one third each to

295

Conway, William, and Conway Oldham in trust as above. Residue of estate to be divided among children: Sarah (Sally) Merriwether; Nancy, wife of Thomas Taylor; Patsy; Oldham; Winnie Mercer; Elizabeth (Betsey), wife of Levi Tyler; to Conway in trust for Mary (Polly) wife of Walter E. Powers; and Amelia wife of Charles L. Harrison; William, Conway and Harry Oldham; at wife's death her portion sold and divided among seven daughters.

Executors: Conway Oldham, and Levi Tyler.

Witnesses: Samuel Churchill, Jenkins Phillips, Jr., Worden Pope.

Codicil Jan 28, 1823. Four old negroes shall not be required to do any involuntary service; they may elect which children they will live with, and if necessary, to be maintained out of estate; negro woman Phebe shall serve daughter Sally Merriwether for three years, then maintained. Two acres of land to be kept for place of interment for family and the blacks.

Witnesses: Richard C. Ferguson., Thomas Phillips.

Conway Oldham and Levi Tyler qualified and gave bond for $50,000, with surety Isaac H. Tyler, Geo. Hikes, Jr., Robert Breckinridge, and Worden Pope.   [*B2, p214.*]

SMITH, DANIEL . . . . . Feb. 21, 1823—Mar. 11, 1823.

To wife Ann E. T. [T. or F.?] Smith, entire estate.

Executor: Friend, William S. Vernon.

Witnesses: Augusta Foreman, Francis Foreman.   [*B2, p219.*]

[Recorded as Reverend Daniel Smith.]

SPARKS, WILLIAM . . . . Nov. 18, 1822—April 14, 1823.

Signed Spearks. To wife Morning, for life, home plantation and appurtences, and at her death to daughters Fanny and Nancy. To son Hampton, tract of land on which he lives; to son Ephraim, land where Moten Pain lives; to son David, balance of land on which testator lives. To son David Sparks, balance of land where testator lives.

Executors: Son Hampton Sparks, son-in-law Rowland Hampton.

Witnesses: John Brown, Joseph Wilhite, Willis Griggs. [*B2, p220.*]

GARRET, SILAS [GARRETT] . . Apr. 1, 1823—Apr. 14, 1823.

To oldest and second son, Olderson W. and Rezin [Regin] W. Garret, certain money. To wife Judith, for life, land recently purchased from Mrs. Benjamin Stafford on waters of Floyd Fork, with appurtenances, slaves, etc. Residue to wife and three youngest children, Peter B., Susan W., and Betsey Ann, except certain personal property to youngest son Peter B. At Wife's death, estate to three youngest children.

Executors: George Seaton, Wm. Markwell.

Witnesses: Wm. Bryan, John McGlauglin, Richard Seaton.

Executors qualified with Edw. Tyler, Senr., Richard Seaton, and John McGlaughlen as surities.   [*B2, p221.*]

LAMPTON, MARK . . . . . Mar. 1, 1823—Apr. 14, 1823.

To wife Susannah Harrison Lampton, for life, the dwelling in which they live on north side of the South Street in Louisville, and certain lands, slaves, stock, etc. Slaves, land, etc. to daughters Minerva L., wife of Ephraim S. Stone, to Fanny M. Lampton, and to son Edmund S. Lampton. Ephraim S. Stone and William Lampton guardians to son Edmund and daughter Fanny. Refers to land purchased from Charles M. Thruston twenty-acre lot No. 2, adjoining Campbell Street.

Executors: Ephraim S. Stone, William Lampton.

Witnesses: Ewell Shipp, Benjamin Tharp, Harriet Lawes, Worden Pope.   [*B2, p222.*]

FONTAINE, AARON . . . . . Mar. 18, 1823—Apr. 16, 1823.

To daughter Barbary C. Cosby, widow of Charles S. Cosby, slave, etc.; also to Messena Fontaine, in trust for family of son James T. Fontaine, a slave. To children Alexander, Henry, Emeline and Aaron, land including home plantation and that in Indiana purchased of Jesse Oatman, Residue of estate to executors, including balance of land in Indiana, to sell for estate or to four above named children; executors to be guardians of children.

Executors: Worden Pope, Alfred and Charles M. Thruston.

Witnesses: Alex Pope, John I. Jacob, Robert Todd, R. S.
                    [*B2, p226.*]

[Note: Original will is not in will file box.]

CROGHAN, WILLIAM . . . . . Aug. 27, 1822—May 12, 1823.

To wife Lucy, for life certain lands and slaves until children become of age or marry, when slaves are to be divided equally, after deducting what had already been given to Mrs. Emelia Clarke. Residue, including much land, to children: John, William, Ann H., Eliza C., George, Nicholas, and Charles, and nephew Nicholas Clarke. To William, son of Nicholas Clarke, five shares Bank of Kentucky stock.

Executors: Wife, Lucy, and sons John, George, William, Nicholas and Charles.

Will proven by oaths of Worden Pope, Charles M. Thruston and Fortunatus Cosby. [B2, p229.]

[Note: In this will he mentions many tracts of land, giving location, when patented, and how acquired, etc.]

FARNSLEY, JAMES . . . . . . Oct. 17, 1817—May 12, 1823.

Certain negroes, monies, etc. to six sons: to David, the eldest, and Joshua the second son, each one-quarter section of land in Harrison Co., Indiana, etc.; to James, land in Jefferson Co., Ky., on Roberts Pond; to Alexander, home plantation in Jefferson Co., Ky.; to Gabriel land in Gibson Co., Ind.; to Joseph land in Nox Co., Ind. To married daughter Mary Earickson, $100., horse, etc.; to single daughter Sarah, furniture, etc. To Alexander, the remainder of estate, provided he will keep youngest sons Gabriel and Joseph until they become twenty-one years of age and educate Joseph.

Executors: Friends, Joseph B. Gatewood, John and Stephen Jones.

Witnesses: John Jones, Stephen Jones, Joseph B. Gatewood.

John Jones (tanner) qualified as executor with David Farnsley and Alexander Farnsley surities. [B2, p234.]

BURTON, JEREMIAH . . . . . Mar. 15, 1823—May 12, 1823.

To wife Polly, $300. and use of land and appurtenances for her comfort and that of children until youngest child, William, reaches age of fourteen, when two-thirds of estate, including slaves, be equally divided among children; Pelina [Paulina?] Davis, Simeon John, Elliott, Charles, Jeremiah and William. Mentions land in Missouri.

Executor: Wife, Polly Burton.

Witnesses: John Noel, Michael Goodknight, Samuel Forwood.

Polly Burton qualified with John Noel, David Enochs and Michael Goodknight, as surities. [B2, p236.]

LUCKETT, SAMUEL N. . . . Apr. 29, 1823—May 13, 1823.
    Estate to be divided between wife Catherine and children,
with exception of son Noland who has had his share.
Executors: Brothers-in-law, Charles M. and Alfred Thruston, and
brother Craven Luckett.
Witnesses: John Miller, George C. Keas.   [*B2, p238.*]
    [Note: In recorded will name of wife is given as Noland, but
in original will it is "wife Catherine," and in Jefferson County
marriage records, Book 1, p. 62, license issued October 1, and return made October 3, 1808, was to Samuel N. Luckett and
Catherine Thruston.]

BARBOUR, THOMAS . . . . May 8, 1818—July 14, 1823.
    To wife, plantation, on which living, with slaves, etc., for her
use and support and education of children, remembering advan-
tages already given to sons Thomas and William; at her death,
estate to children. Hopes children will be dutiful and obedient
to their aged and infirm parent and affectionate to each other.
Mentions his "mill establishment."
Executors: Sons, James, Thomas and William.
    Will proven by oaths of James Ferguson and Charles M.
Thruston.   [*B2, p239.*]

HARDIN, REBECKA . . . . Aug. 21, 1822—July 15, 1823.
    [Signed Rebecca Harding.] To Sally Hancock and Caty
Shreader, her clothes, and to the latter a bureau. Residue to son
Henry Hardin, and daughters Sally Hancock and Caty Shreader.
Executors: None named.
Witnesses: Harding Hancock, Terrel Rucker, Benjamin Hancock.
    William Hancock qualified as executor with Nathan Pugh as
surity.   [*B2, p241.*]

RUCKSBY, JACOB, SR. . . . June 11, 1821—Aug. 11, 1823.
    [Original will filed, also mentioned in papers, as Rookesberry,
but probated as Rucksby.] To wife Elender, estate for life; at her
death, $1.00 each to daughters Nancy Featherengil and Mary
Mayfield. Residue to other children: Sharlotte, Jacob, Caner,
Samuel, Ruban, Thomas and John Rucksby.
Executors: David Forsyth, Isaac Kellar.
Witnesses: Tarlton Goolsby, John Pope, M. H. Pope. [*B2, p242.*]

HOKE, LEONARD . . . . Aug. 13, 1823—Sept. 8, 1823.
Nuncupative Will. He died Aug. 9, 1823. Estate to wife and children. Should wife remarry, she to have one-third and children two-thirds. [Names of children not given.]
Certified by Nimrod Long, James Gunn, Harris Pryor. [*B2, p243.*]

STANDIFORD, JAMES . . . . Jan. 15, 1821—Sept. 8, 1823.
To eldest son Elisha and eldest daughter Nancy Hinch, $1.00 each; to second daughter Betsey Robb, to second son William, to fourth son David, and to youngest daughter, Matilda, furniture, stock, etc. To son Nathan, plantation, he to pay $100. a year rent until youngest son Stewart is twenty-one, when plantation is to be divided between Nathan and Stewart. Residue to lawful heirs.
Executor: Henry Robb.
Witnesses: John Murphey, James H. West. [*B2, p243.*]

FEATHERINGILL, JOHN, SR. . . Mar. 2, 1823—Sept. 8, 1823.
To wife Mary, estate for life. At her death certain furniture to sons Noah, Meredith and John. To youngest sons Noah and Meredith, the land on which testator was living, in Jefferson County, in town of Floydsburg.
Executors: Sons, Noah and Meredith.
Witnesses: James F. Wilson, Isaac Wilson, Elijah Yager.
[*B2, p245.*]

SISSON, ABNER . . Sept. 16, 1823—Sept. 18, Oct. 13, 1823.
Nuncupative will. A few days before his death, Abner Sisson said he wanted his estate, principally of money in Virginia, to go to his wife and children.
Executors: Wife, and brother Armstead Sisson.
Attested: John Sisson, Henry Cummins. [*B2, p246.*]

WHIPS, DENTON . . . . . Aug. 31, 1823—Oct. 13, 1823.
Nuncupative will. Desired brother Samuel Whips to sell all property, except the place on which he then lived, to pay all debts; balance of money to be used for the education of children and support of family.
Executor: Brother, Samuel Whips.
Witnesses: Rich'd Chew, Jacob Hite. [*B2, p246.*]

McCAWLEY, JAMES M.   .   .   .   Aug. 16, 1823—Oct. 13, 1823.

To sons Joshua, and Arthur, land touching stock yards, Brooks' line and the Knobs; to James, Daniel and John money, and to daughters Ann Beverly, land on Little Spring branch to Haywood's Road, and to Margaret McCawley, certain monies, stock and supplies. Requests Arthur and Joshua to build house, twenty-four feet long by eighteen feet wide, of hewn logs with one stone chimney, for Ann Beverly and Margaret McCawley.

Executors: Joshua, John and Arthur McCawley.

Witnesses: David Blackwell, Thomas Gilmore, Joshua G. McCawley.   [*B2, p247.*]

HARDEN, HENRY, SR.   .   .   .   June 27, 1822—Oct. 13, 1823.

To wife Polly, the place on which living, and enough personal estate for her comfort. Balance of estate, including lands, slaves, stock, monies, etc., to be divided equally among nine children: Nancy, Polly, William, Allien, Eliza, Rebecca Jane and Amanda, $300., to make their part equal to the eldest sons, Henry and John, to whom he willed land on which they were living.

Executors: None named.

Witnesses: Ballard Buckner, Martin P. Clark.

Codicil, July 18, 1822. After giving Polly mare and saddle, deduct certain money from hers and Nancy's share of estate. No interest to be paid by children.

Witnesses: B. Buckner, Martin P. Clark.   [*B2, p248.*]

SMITH, JOHN   .   .   .   .   .   .   Nov. 29, 1813—Oct. 13, 1823.

Slaves left by his wife's mother, Ann Green, to two of his children, Henry and Ann Smith, to be valued and deducted from their share of estate. To wife, Ellenor D. Smith, certain lands, home plantation, stock, slaves, etc., for life, and then to children: Henry, Ann, Willis and Elizabeth. Refers to land bought of John Ganowine [Yenawine?].

Executors: Neighbors, Thomas Ramsay, Samuel Chew, Joseph Kellar.

Witnesses: Harriet Bridgeford, Richard Chew, Benjamin Allan.

[*B2, p250.*]

ALDRIDGE, JOHN P. . . . . . Aug. 23, 1823—Oct. 13, 1823.
To wife, her legal third, balance of estate to son William Christian Aldridge, forever.
Executor: Wife.
Witnesses: Wm. C. Bullitt, Merril S. Phelcher, B. Tompkins.
[*B2, p251.*]

NECCO, FRANCIS . . . . . July 20, 1823—Oct. 14, 1823.
To Joseph Massot, partner in trading, $250. To brother Julius Necco, personal estate. To friend Nicholas Barthoud, and brother Julius, the balance of estate, including houses and lots in Shippingport, in trust for his mother Catherine, wife Madelaine Maden Necco and daughter Maria Madelaine Necco, all of Marseilles, France, for their use until daughter reaches age of twenty, then all to go to her for life.
Executor: Brother, Julius.
Witnesses: Geo. Armstrong, Wm. Merriwether, Adam Conradt.
[*B2, p252.*]

QUERTERMOUS, ELIZABETH [QUERLERMOUS], June 13, 1823—Dec. 9, 1823.
Negro Calet to be hired out for four years and then set free, proceeds of hire and all estate to children: Nancy Brown, Elisha Quertermous, James C. Sanders, Polly Quertermous, widow of James Quertermous, and grandson Thomas Q. Wilson.
Executors: Elisha Quertermous.
Witnesses: Wm. Cooper, W. H. Randall, James H. West.
Probation contested by Thomas Q. Wilson; Elisha Quertermous renounced his right to execute above, and Thomas Q. Wilson qualified with John C. Beeler as surity. [*B2, p254.*]

HIGMAN, ABRAHAM . . . . . Jan. 3, 1824—Jan. 12, 1824.
Native of Stock Clims land, Cornwall County, England. Estate in America to dear wife Elizabeth and dear son John, who, when he last heard, were living in Plymouth Dock, Devonshire, England.
Executors: Joseph Middleton, Edward Hughes, both of Louisville.
Witnesses: John Kingwell, Albert Dupont, Isaac Watman.
Edward Hughes declined to qualify; Joseph Middleton qualified with George Keats and David Prentice as surities. [*B2, p254.*]

HENDERSON, JAMES, Jan. 27, 1822—Sept. 8, 1823, Feb. 9, 1824.
Resides with Silas Garrett. To his heir at law, $5.00. To friend Silas Garrett the balance of estate forever.
Executors: Silas Garrett, Arthur Chenoweth, Sr., friends.
Witnesses: Arthur Chenoweth, A. Chenoweth.

On October 17, 1823, Worden Pope, clerk, sent order to Presiding Judge or other court officer of County of Crawford, Illinois, to have Absolem Chenoweth make oath whether or not the "enclosed instrument of writing" was last will of James Henderson. On November 5, 1823, Absolem Chenoweth, in Crawford County, testified that it was. *[B2, p255.]*

WILCKS, SAMUEL . . . . . Aug. 6, 1822—Feb. 9, 1824.
Sons William and Samuel and daughter Mary Caslin, having received part of their share of estate, are willed $50. each. Balance of estate to be equally divided between son Daniel and daughter Patsy Wilcks, including land and mansion.
Executors: Daniel Wilcks, son.
Witnesses: Z. Carpenter, Samuel Bird, Elisha Dehart. *[B2, p257.]*

GAMBLE, WILLIAM . . . . Jan. 14, 1824—Apr. 12, 1824.
Wife Jane to receive entire estate.
Executor: Wife, Jane.
Witnesses: Daniel C. Banks, William Sale, Thomas Stewart, Jr.
[B2, p258.]

PRESTON, WILLIAM . . . . Mar. 29, 1777—Apr. 13, 1824.
Of Montgomery County, [Virginia]. Recommends that his executors employ Mr. James Buchanan and Capt. Francis Smith to examine his books and regulate his accounts, for which they should receive a handsome allowance. To wife, Susannah, as long as she remains single, the use of estate for her support and the education of children. At the end of five years she shall choose tract of land on which she desires to live. Should she marry, she to receive her lawful share only. At her death, estate to be divided among children. Requests that no expense be spared in the education of the children, especially the sons. As sons become of age or marry and daughters marry, wife to give such part of slaves or money as she and executors think just, giving sparingly at first until convinced of their frugality. To daughter Eliza, two tracts

303

of land on Potts Creek adjoining lands of Henry Smith, the Walnut Bottom 350 acres. To son John tract of 2175 acres called "Greenfield," provided wife does not choose either, should she choose that, son to receive "Smithfield," a tract of 1860 acres, to take possession at age of twenty-one, or sooner if he marries. To son Francis, tract of 1230 acres in Columbia where James Nowall dwells, also tract called Marshall's Old Place on the Lick Run, 350 acres, and a tract of 345 acres in the hills south of the place on which James Nowall lives, and Dayley's old place of 85 acres. To daughter Sarah, land on which William Commack dwells, 660 acres on John's Creek, and 250 acres adjoining. To daughter Ann, 390 acres at Forks of Potts Creek. To son William, the Robinson tract on Teek [or Peek?] Creek, branch of New River, except 700 acres to daughter Susannah, papers to title in the hands of Mr. James Hubbard, Atty. in Williamsburg. To son James Patten Preston, land called "Greenfield," 2175 acres, in case wife chooses to live there or "Smithfield." To daughter Mary, 1000 acres of land in the County of Kentucky, "Cane Spring" on waters of Elkhorn. Sons to pay mother certain sums yearly and sister Ann fifty pounds, as they reach twenty-one years.

Executors: Col. Geo. Shelton, Capt. Francis Smith, Capt. John Floyd, Robert Preston, and sons John when twenty-one and Francis when nineteen.

Witnesses: James Byrn, James McGavick, Joseph Cloyd, Jane Buchanan, and Alexander Breckinridge.

Codicil, Feb. 11, 1781. Executors, with exception of sons named in will, for various reasons could not serve, and, in their stead, he appoints son-in-law, William Madison, his nephew John Breckinridge, John Brown and Colo. John Floyd. For child "my wife is now carrying," tract in Kentucky called Horse Shoe Bend. Slave for niece, Susannah Smith, daughter of Francis Smith of Botetourt. To daughter Letitia tract called "Thorn Spring." To Elizabeth Madison 1000 acres in Potts Creek called "Point Bank." Nephew John Breckinridge to be paid for teaching in the family.

Witnesses: James Byrn, James McGavick, Joseph Cloyd, John T. Sayers.

Will proven in Montgomery County, [Va.] August 5, 1783.

[*B2, p259.*]

[Note: Certified copy of original not in will file box.]

STEWART, MATHEW . . . . Sept. 18, 1823—Apr. 12, 1824.
Lands, slaves, farming utensils, furniture, etc., to children
Sally Woods, William, and Hugh Stewart. To sons-in-law William Woods and Joseph Green, $5.00 each. *Executors:* None
named.
Witnesses: Robert N. Miller, Wm. Harrison.
Validity of will contested by Wm. Woods, by Denny and
Nicholas his attorneys, on February 9, 1824. On April 10 Court
upheld will; Woods appealed, with John Jones (tanner) as security, and on April 12 sons William and Hugh Woods, by attorney Pope Tyler, presented will and it was ordered recorded.

[*B2, p270.*]

McKEOWN, MORGAN . . . Apr. 14, 1824—May 10, 1824.
To Polly McKeown, widow of Robert McKeown, present
estate and portion due him from estate of his mother, Leah
McKeown, deceased.
Executor: Polly McKeown.
Witnesses: John C. Bryan, M. Miller, Wm. Bryan. [*B2, p272.*]

SEEBOLT, GEORGE . . . . Apr. 17, 1824—June 15, 1824.
[Signed John George Seebolt.] To wife all furniture; to son
Amos home plantation 160 acres of land on south side of Chenoweth Run, for which he holds the bond of M. L. Miller. Amos to
support and care for his mother in every way. Daughter Margaret, wife of David Evinger, has received her share. Certain
lands, slaves, stock, furniture and money to children Amos, John
and George, Mary, wife of James Welsh, and Betsey, wife of A.
Prewitt.
Executors: George and Amos Seebolt, sons.
Witnesses: Tho. Joyes, James Pomeroy. [*B2, p273.*]

SCOTT, WILLIAM, SEN'R . . . Dec. 30, 1823—Apr. 12, 1824.
[Signed William Scott] To wife Margaret, estate for life and
one-eighth of it forever. Balance to be divided among children
and grandchildren: to Jane, wife of Henry Morris; to children of
daughter Sally, who married David Graig; to Nelly (Nally), wife
of David Stuart, and her daughter Rebecca and sons Lewis and
James; to Peggy, wife of James K. Seaton; to Betsey, wife of
Samuel Ferwood; to sons William and Hugh Scott.
Executor: Son-in-law James K. Seaton.
Witnesses: Richard Seaton, John Miller. [*B2, p276.*]

HOLLOWAY, CHARLES . . . Feb. 23, 1824—May 10, 1824.
To wife Mary Holloway for life, estate, with the exception of
a slave to each of unmarried children: Mary W., Hugh W., Susan
and Clary Ann Holloway. At wife's death, equal division of
estate to be made among children: Mary W. Holloway, Kitty W.
Gray, Emily M. and Charles Anderson, infant heirs of deceased
daughter Emily (one share), Juliet T. Miller, Charles Holloway,
Jr., Hugh W., Susan and Clary Ann Holloway. An equal share
to be lent to daughter Eliza Brown, formerly Eliza Short, for life
and at her death to her children; debt of the late Thomas Short,
her former husband, to be taken out. *Executors:* None named.
Witnesses: James Welsh, Peter Ammer, M. Gow [Gorr].

[*B2, p277.*]

SMITH, PLEASANT . . . . . Oct. 4, 1824—Nov. 9, 1824.
To niece Amandy Artaburn [Arterburn], and nephew Pleasant
Watkins, entire estate. *Executors:* None named.
Witnesses: Jacob Hite, John Arabun, Jr., Nathan T. Ingle.

[*B2, p278.*]

BELL, JOSIAH . . . . No date—Dec. 14, 1824.
To son Horace, his tools of a cabinet maker and mechanic; to
daughter Sarah Hennison, money; to daughter Elizabeth D.,
furniture, etc.; to little daughter Frances, $40. for her education.
Residue of estate to Elizabeth D. and Frances Bell.
Executor: Lawrence Young.
Witnesses: Ben Head, Nathan Marders. [*B2, p279.*]

BROWN, EVERINGTON . . . . . Not dated—Dec. 15, 1824.
Nuncupative will. The above named, in "our presence," a
few days before his death, stated that in gratitude to Eliza Morrison, who had lived with him long and attended himself and his
wife, in their sicknesses, with the care and affection of a child, he
desired her to have whatever estate he had.
Signed: B. N. Sands, Joseph White. [*B2, p280.*]

CALENDAR OF EARLY JEFFERSON COUNTY, KENTUCKY, WILLS

WILL BOOK No. 2: JUNE, 1813–DECEMBER, 1833

PREPARED BY MISS KATHARINE G. HEALY

IN TWO PARTS

PART TWO: JANUARY, 1825—DECEMBER, 1833[1]

HITE, LEWIS . . . . Aug. 28, 1824—Jan. 3, 1825.
Estate to be sold to pay debts and residue to be disposed of according to law.
Executors: William Bryan, Joseph Kellar, Eliza V. Hite.
Witnesses: Abner Field, N. Field, Robert N. Davis. [*B2, p280.*]

TAYLOR, REUBEN . . Jan. 1, 1717 [1818?]—Dec. 16, 1824.
To wife Rebecca land on which living for life, then to sons Francis and Benjamin. Personal estate for use of wife and children unmarried until they marry or become of age, when each shall receive lawful portion. Land: 50 acres bought of John Mercer to son Warner; 400 acres bought of John Daniel, surveyed and patented in testators name on Wolf Pen, to daughters Lucy, Polly

---

[1]Editor's Note: A Calendar of Jefferson County Will Book No. 1 (1784-1813) appears in the January, 1932, issue of this QUARTERLY. *
Will Book No. 2 is a volume of 538 transcribed pages covering a period of twenty-one years, during which time Worden Pope was clerk. For convenience in printing, our presentation of this Calendar is divided into two parts. The following statements made in our Introductory Note to Will Book No. 1, pertaining to the interpretations of the penmanship, also apply to the Calendar of Will Book No. 2. **
An effort has been made to retain, as closely as possible, the original spelling, although it is often erroneous. Some of it is evidently phonetic. A name is sometimes spelled two or three ways in the course of one will—in both original and transcribed copies. No attempt has been made to suggest the correct spelling.
In the calendar here published the name of the testator appears in capitals and is followed by the date of the writing and the date of the recording of the will. The nuncupative or oral wills that occur are so designated. No annotations are made except in a few instances. Among them are, in brackets, the Will Book number, *B2*, and the page on which the will is recorded. In some instances where a name has been found to differ from that given in the Marriage Records, the latter is added with a question mark, in brackets.

*Pages 214-250, this volume.
**See page 214, this volume.

and Elenor Taylor and Polly Leathers and her children Anna, Mariah, John Thompson and Merniva.

Executor: Wife Rebecca Taylor, and sons William, Francis, Warner and Benjamin.

Proven by oath of William Munday.

Jan. 3, 1825. Above Executrix and Executors renounced right to execute and requested Jeremiah Keas be appointed. He took oath and gave bond with Warner Taylor his security.

Jan. 4, 1836. Letters of administration of Jeremiah Keas with Reuben Taylor's will reversed, annulled and set aside by Court and Benjamin Taylor was appointed executor.

[*B2, p281.*]

PATTERSON, JOHN L.   .   .   .   .   Dec. 10, 1824—Feb. 7, 1825.

Negroes and their children to be freed, the latter to remain in service of their parents until twenty-one years of age. Stephen and Washington to be freed but to remain in service of William Hite until they are twenty-one.

Executors: William and Robt. Hite.

Witnesses: P. C. Barbour, Jeremiah Cornwell, William Postlewait.

Jan. 5, 1825. Will ineffectually contested by William H., Elizabeth and the heirs of Sally L. Swope, late Sally L. Patterson, deceased, Thomas L. Patterson, deceased, and Charles Patterson, deceased, all claiming to be rightful heirs and legal representatives of John L. Patterson.   [*B2, p282.*]

STEELE, SAMUEL   .   .   .   .   .   Jan. 20, 1825—Mar. 7, 1825.

To wife Katharine for life estate, and then to children. Mentions son Samuel Andrew Steele, grandchildren John Ward, Eliza Patton and Mary Steele.

Executor: John Edelen, a friend.

Witnesses: Hugh Martin, Nicholas James.

John Edelin made oath and gave bond with William E. Talbot and Zachariah Edelin securities.   [*B2, p284.*]

SHERMAN, CHARLES   .   .   .   .   Mar. 20, 1821—May 2, 1825.

Lands to sons Charles R. and John (under age), including home farm. Any personal property, after debts are paid, to daughter Susannah, wife of Daniel Moore, and to sons named above. At her request no provision is made for "my deserving and beloved wife Priscilla," she having implicit confidence in sons. *Executors:* sons Charles R. and John Sherman. *Witnesses:* Alex. Pope, Worden Pope, Isaac H. Tyler, Patrick H. Pope, and Robert Tyler. [*B2, p285.*]

TARASCON, JOHN ANTHONY . Mar. 25, 1821—Sept. 5, 1825.
Of the Town of Shippingport. Estate to four children Louis, Henry, Marrine [Nanine?], and Josephine. Should children die without issue, estate to brother. Having expended large sums of money in the erection of mills, wharfs and other public and private buildings in the Town of Shippingport, and as it might not be advantageous to children to dispose of property at once, he appoints his brother Louis Anastasius Tarascon to take control with power to manage the business, lease, sell, etc. As children become of age or marry, each to receive proportion of estate.
Executor: Brother, Louis Anastatius Tarascon, without security.
Witnesses: Elijah A. Saltmarsh, John Austin, Luther Owings.
Proven by oaths of Worden Pope, Dabney C. Terrell, and Fortunatus Crosby, Esq. [*B2, p286.*]

MCCLANAHAN, THOMAS . . . July 6, 1825—Oct. 3, 1825.
Estate to parents; brothers, Ezekial H. Field, Willis Field, and William McClanahan; and sisters, Margaret, wife of William Ward; Mary, wife of George Holloway; Anne, wife of William H. Thornton; and Maria, wife of Ansalon Watkins.
Executors: Ezekial H., Willis, Silas Field, Wm. McClanahan of Louisville.
Witnesses. H.[orace] B. Hill, A. H. Wallace, S.[amuel] S. Nicholas. [*B2, p288.*]

BULLITT, CUTHBERT . . . . Jan. 5, 1825—Nov. 11, 1825.
To son Alfred Neville Bullitt 305 acres, half of Richmond Farm on Ohio River in Clark County, Indiana, about two miles above Jeffersonville; land in Knox County, Indiana, adjoining Vincennes, one-fourth part 400 acres "Donation lands", formerly owned by John Gwathmey, conveyed by Wm. Bullitt to Cuthbert and Thomas Bullitt, and by latter to testator; land on Eel River and five lots near Louisville, land laid off by Cuthbert and Thomas

Bullitt; lot in Louisville on which testator lived on northwardly side and adjoining Main St.

To son Neville Bullitt other half Richmond Farm; 156 acres formerly owned by Levi Todd, Illinois Grant; land in Jackson County, Indiana, on Driftwood Fork of White River; lots in Louisville, half acre lot Main Street and 9th Cross Street etc.

To son William Neville Bullitt, land in Vigo County, Indiana, adjoining Terre Haute, lots in Terra Haute; lots near Louisville, part of lot on which testator lived, in Louisville, Main and 5th Cross Street, including small tenement occupied by John and Samuel Thomas.

To son Cuthbert Neville Bullitt outlots adjoining Terre Haute; land in Vigo County near Terre Haute; lots in town of Salem, Indiana; seven lots near Louisville, 52 feet on 9th Cross Street; land on Deer River, Hopkins County, Kentucky, conveyed by Grayson and others to Cuthbert and Thomas Bullitt, and by latter to testator, etc.

To daughter Amanthus Bullitt land in Vigo County, Indiana, northwardly end of testator's part of Square No. 5 in Louisville, 5th Cross Street and Water Street; one-third part of that part of ten-acre lot in Louisville east of Cross Street opened East of Hospital from South Street to Walnut.

To daughter Caroline Bullitt land in Vigo County, Indiana; 560 acres, Lawrence County, Indiana; lots in Louisville, etc.

To daughter Ann Elizabeth Bullitt land in Vigo County, Indiana, 60 acres land near Louisville, part of Boyers Military Survey; part of Walnut Hill tract; land between that of Henry Churchill and heirs of Thomas [Bullitt] deceased, on north end Poplar Street, which is 11th Cross St., of Louisville, continued, on east and Cherry Street on west.

To daughter Amelia land in Jackson County, Indiana, part of 10-acre lot No. 2 in Louisville between grave yard on north, and part of lot testator gave to Hospital on south; part of Walnut Hills, and lot in Louisville, etc.

To sister Sarah Leggett land near Louisville; silver teaspoons, table spoons and salt spoon now in possession Mrs. Peggy Bullitt, widow of Major William Bullitt.

To wife Ann Bullitt about 54 acres of land near Louisville; part of Walnut Hill tract, bounded on west by Salt River Road, on south by land belonging to heirs of Robert McConnel, deceased, and William Reed, on east by Poplar Level Road; a number of slaves, household furniture, plate, carriage, gig, etc.

Rents etc. to be used for seven years for education of minor children. Wife and friend Geo. C. Gwathmey guardians to children: Neville, William, Cuthbert, Amanthus, Caroline, Ann Elizabeth and Amelia.

Executors: Friends, James Guthrie, William C. Bullitt, and James W. Thornberry.

Witnesses: Owen Gwathmey, Ben Lawrence, John Thomas, Alex. C. Bullitt, J[esse] Newton, Worden Pope. [*B2, p289.*]

POPE, JOHN, JR. . . . . . Oct. 19, 1825—Nov. 7, 1825.
Brother William guardian to son.
Executors: William Pope, brother, without security.
Witnesses: Wm. Pope, Minor Pope, James Pope. [*B2, p305.*]

FREDERICK, ANDREW . . . . Sept. 6, 1825—Nov. 7, 1825.
To wife Charity money and a slave. At her death slave to be sold and proceeds with notes held against Henry Isam and Charity Fenly, late Charity Flowson [Floor?], to be equally divided among four daughters, Caty Woblet, Peggy Peek, Susan Shafer and Polly Goben. Son George previously received his share.
Witnesses: Michael Miller, James Pomeroy. [*B2, p305.*]

PEARCE, JAMES A. . . . . Sept. 21, 1825—Dec. 5, 1825.
To wife Ann farm on which living, purchased from Benjamin Temple. Residue of estate to children: Sarah, Edmund, Mary, Eleanor, Ann, Jonathan and Elizabeth, when they marry or become of age. Wife guardian of children.
Executor: Wife Ann Pearce, without security.

Codicil, Sept. 21, 1825. From money due from John C. Richardson and the Millers, the latter for lands sold them in Indiana, pay notes at Bank United States, Louisville.
Witnesses: Wm. Pope, Robert N. Smith, Minor Pope, James Pope, for both will and codicil. [*B2, p307.*]

OLDHAM, CONWAY . . . . . Nov. 5, 1825—Dec. 5, 1825.
To wife Frances for life 553 acres home place, and appurtenances. Six youngest children to be educated. Unmarried children: Samuel, Presley, Mary Ann, John Conway, Feturah, Eliza-

beth, Martha and William Levi to live with mother and be clothed by her until they marry or become of age, and then apportioned, as were Nancy and Susan. To son Samuel, land purchased from Frederick Herr, and to Presley land on Fern Creek purchased from Thomas Armstrong. Sons John Conway and William Levi Oldham to have home place at death of wife Frances; William Levi the part with dwelling house. To daughters: Nancy, wife of Frederick Herr, Susan, wife of John Herr, Jr, Mary Ann, Feturah, Elizabeth and Martha each slaves, and proceeds from sale of land inherited from father, Samuel Oldham, deceased, on Pup Creek, and land bought from Merriweathers, when youngest daughter becomes of age.

Executors: Frederick Herr, John Herr, Jr., and Levi Tyler.

Witnesses: Wm. Bryan, Gowieg Singir [?], John C. Beeler, Geo. Hikes, Jr, John Hikes, Isaac H. Tyler.

Codicil. Nov. 8, 1825. Samuel and Presley, not to be put on their land until they marry or become of age. Wife to have as much of everything as she needs. When son William Levi marries he is to live with his mother and run farm for her.

Witnesses: Gowieg Singer, Wm. Bryant, Isaac H. Tyler.

[*B2, p308.*]

McLAHLAN, JOHN . . . . . July 4, 1825—Dec. 5, 1825.

To sons William, the eldest, John H., and Henson H., and daughter Amanda M., each gifts; to wife Sarah for life the home plantation 141 acres, with balance of estate, and at her death to children. Friend, Daniel Amer, guardian.

Witnesses: Willis Kendall, Joseph Pound. [*B2, p314.*]

SHIVELY, CHRISTIAN . . . . Dec. 28, 1825—Feb. 6, 1826.

To wife Mary for life estate. Mentions: granddaughters, Mariah and Elizabeth Sanders; daughter Sally Jones, Margaret French, Mary Rudy; sons Henry, William, John; grandsons Christen, son of testator's son Henry, and Phillip Crips.

Executors: Warrick Miller, Robert Miller, Sr.

Witnesses: Jos. B. Gatewood, Stephen Jones, Jesse Swindler.

Feb. 4th, 1826, Warrick Miller took oath with Daniel Rudy, Security. [*B2, p316.*]

MURPHY, THOMAS . . . . Jan. 12, 1826—Mar. 7, 1826.
Balance due him on books of Cuddy and Murphy to be
equally divided between brothers and sisters, should he die during
absence from Louisville.
Executors: James McG. Cuddy, John I. Jacob.
Witnesses: Joseph Middleton, Patrick Murphy.　　[*B2, p317.*]

PLASTERS, MARY . . . . . Apr. 19, 1825—Mar. 7, 1826.
Signed Mary H. Plasters. To mother, Amelia Plaster, for life
entire estate. Should she die before youngest sister becomes of
age or marries, estate to go to three youngest sisters, and when
they marry or become of age to go to all brothers and sisters.
Executor: Mother, Amelia Plasters.
Witnesses: Joseph B. Gatewood, Leonard Gatewood, Fleming
Gatewood.　　[*B2, p318.*]

OLDHAM, WILLIAM . . . . Feb. 25, 1826—Apr. 3, 1826.
To wife Elizabeth for life, estate including property with two
three-story brick houses, purchased from Walter E. Powers on
south side of and adjoining Market St., for use of wife and children. When youngest child becomes of age, property, other than
what wife needs, to be divided among all children. Land left him
by his father, Samuel Oldham, to be sold to pay debts.
Executor: Friend, Levi Tyler.
Witnesses: W. Field, D. Halystead, John C. Evans.　　[*B2, p319.*]

SEVEY, SAM, JR. . . . . . Aug. 28, 1822—May 1, 1826.
To brother William, wearing apparel and one fifth of estate,
about $5000. invested in firm of Hinkley and Sevey. After pay-
ing to Uncles Jos., Sam, and Edwin small sums owed them, the
balance to father, S. Sevey.
Executor: William Sevey, brother.
Witnesses: Philip Shively, Jacob Martin ("Written in Dutch"),
Otis Hinkley.　　[*B2, p321.*]

BROOKS, SQUIRE . . . . . Mar. 30, 1826—May 1, 1826.
To sister Nancy, wife of Elisha Standiford, for her and her
children, tract of land left him by father, Jacob Brooks, in codicil
to his will. After paying debts, residue of estate to three children,
George W. Lynn, alias George W. Brooks, America and Joseph
Beeler.
Witnesses: John Jones, Bryan Johnson, Thomas H. Johnson.
　　[*B2, p322.*]

CROGHAN, NICHOLAS . . . . June 30, 1824—June 5, 1826.

To brother Charles all personal property, 300 acres opposite Twelve Mile Island, 1250 acres in Warren County on Rays Fork of Big Barren River. To nephew George Croghan, 1505 acres on Big Barren River near Bowling Green. To niece, Angelica Croghan 830 acres on Clay Lick Ford on Little Barren River and 250 acres on Little Barren River called the Horse Shoe Bend. To sister Ann H. Jessup 900 acres in Warren County, including the Hog Lick Sycamore Spring, a branch of Drake's Creek, and all his land in Indiana. To brother George, all property not mentioned above.

Executors: Charles and George Croghan, brothers, and Genl. Jessup.

Will proven by oaths of William Croghan and Benjamin Tompkins.   [*B2, p323.*]

SEATON, JAMES K. . . . . Aug. 28, 1826—Sept. 4, 1826.

To eldest daughter Cynthiana, wife of William S. Rose, certain furniture, stock, etc. Land, 104 acres on Brush River, to be sold. Wife Peggy for widowhood everything not before mentioned, including slaves. Should she marry, she to have one-third and balance to children: Levi W., Richard, Polly, Sally, Peggy and Rachael Seaton.

Executor: Brother, Richard Seaton.

Witnesses: Allen Rose, James S. Rose.

Richard Seaton gave bond with George Seaton, Allen Rose and James Rose as Securities.   [*B2, p324.*]

RICHARDSON, THOMAS S. . . . July 3, 1826—Sept. 4, 1826.

Wife Margaret to receive entire estate.

Executor: Margaret Richardson, wife.

Witnesses: Daniel F. Strother, Jacob Burkenmire.

Margaret Richardson gave bond with Alfred Richardson and William Richardson as securities.   [*B2, p325.*]

ELSTON, JONATHAN . . . . Mar. 9, 1826—Sept. 4, 1826.

To wife Polly, for life, slaves, plantation, chattels, etc., not otherwise disposed of, for the rearing and schooling of children. Money and extra schooling given son Thomas S. Elston to be his share, he to pay to estate what he owes on note, also the balance

of the Commonwealth money testator loaned him. To son Allen
P. Elston, a horse now in possession of David Blankenbaker. To
daughter Amanda, when she marries or becomes of age, slave and
what her mother thinks proper, and so for each child, except two
first named.
Executors: Robert Teter and James Pomeroy, friends.
Witnesses: James Ward, Reason Williams, Daniel Newkirk,
Presley Tyler.
Codicil March 11, 1826. To son Allen P. Elston $100. and
two suits of clothes.
Witnesses: Presley Tyler, Wm. Watson, Daniel Newkirk.
[B2, p326.]

DORSEY, REZIN HAMMOND . . Aug. 9, 1826—Sept. 4, 1826.
Gifts: to friend Benjamin Lawrence; Mrs. Parmelia Dorsey,
widow of brother Columbus; Mrs. Matilda L. Dorsey, wife of
brother Nimrod; sister, Matilda Dorsey. Balance of estate to
Benjamin Lawrence in trust for testator's sister Mrs. Ruth Maria
Miller and her children. To William C. Hobbs, set of Shakes-
pear works; to Lee White, snuff box.
Executor: Brother, Nimrod Dorsey.
Witnesses: W. C. Hobbs, Lee White, E. O. Hobbs. *[B2, p328.]*

BROWN, PRESTON W. . . . Sept. 22, 1826—Oct. 2, 1826.
Estate to be equally divided among children.
Executors: Wife Elizabeth Brown, brother John Brown.
Witnesses: John Jones, David Jewell, John Speed, Jr., Robert K.
Moore. *[B2, p329.]*

PRENTICE, DAVID . . . . . . Not dated—Oct. 2, 1826.
To wife Margaret, one-third of estate, house in which living,
slaves, furniture and books. To daughter Agness $4000 or one-
fourth of property when she marries or becomes of age. To eldest
son Archibald, old fashioned watch, requesting him not to part
with it. To sons Archibald, George and William the share of the
foundry owned by testator and an equal share of property. Mentions lots at "Albany," at Shippingport, on Main Street, Louisville, and the one between his house and Robert Ransdale's lot.
Executors: George Keats and Joseph Middleton, friends, and
wife Margaret.
Proven by oaths of Worden Pope, Simeon S. Goodwin.
[B2, p330.]

Pope, Alexander . . . . . Nov. 28, 1826—Dec. 4, 1826.
Started writing will in August 1826. To wife Martha Minor Pope, for life, certain slaves, furniture, etc., part of lot No. 273 and all of No. 274, on which living. Part of lots Nos. 275 and 125 on west side of Sixth Cross Street, and No. 121 on Fifth Cross St., other part of lot sold to Hugh Fergerson, to brothers John, William and Nathaniel Pope, appointed guardian of children, in trust for three daughters: Maria G., Penelope and Martha Ann Pope, when they are twenty-five years old. Should they all die before that age, land to go to sons Henry and William Fontaine Pope. Sons to have 1000 acres purchased from Wm. Bryant on Cane Run waters of Floyd Fork in Jefferson County, and that received in contract with Jona Green and Lucas Elmendorf. Five years after testator's death his slaves, Bill and Sophia, to be emancipated and given a lease for life on house and lot where they live. To children, Maria G., Henry and William Fontaine Pope certain slaves. Releases his mother of any claim he may have on his father's estate. Mentions land in Bannons, Jefferson Town, and between Louisville and Mans Lick purchased of William Field. Also mentions brother-in-law Abner Field.
Executors: Brothers John and William Pope.
Witnesses: Worden Pope, James Guthrie, Sam Dickinson, John Pope Trotter. [*B2, p332.*]

Payne, Bennet D. . . . . . Sept. 16, 1826—Jan. 1, 1827.
To wife's mother, her money in testator's hands. To wife Polly Payne for widowhood estate, should she marry she to have her third, and balance, after deducting debts of daughter Margaret Butler and son James from their share, divided equally among children.
Executor: Wife, Polly Payne, son James, and Zachars Peter Carpenter.
Witnesses: George Seaton, Nimrod Hanrick.
Mary D. Payne and James M. Payne qualified as executors with William Rhea and Coleman Wilkes as Securities. [*B2, p338.*]

Pope, William . . . . . Sept. 29, 1819—Jan. 1, 1827.
To son John, all land in Shelby County, a tract on the head waters of Beargrass adjoining Funk Pomeroy, he having paid Joseph H. Findley for land, and a slave who is to be emancipated

316

at the age of forty. To son William 500 acres south of the land on which testator lived in Pond Settlement, and two slaves. Daughters Penelope, Jane, Elizabeth and Hester had already been provided for. To sons Alexander and Nathaniel the residue of estate. To wife Penelope for life three slaves and $200 per year to be paid by son William according to a bond given for that purpose. Debt due by son-in-law Maj. Abner Field to be cancelled,
Executors: Sons John and William Pope.
Witnesses: Minor Pope, James Pope, Wm. Pope, Jr., Cynthia Pope.

Proven by oath of William Pope, Jr., Cynthia Pope being dead, Minor Pope out of United States, and James Pope "being an infant of tender years when he subscribed said instrument as a witness."   [*B2, p340.*]

NEWMAN, MARTHA W.   .   .   .   Feb. 4, 1823—Feb. 5, 1827.
To Charles Newman 400 acres near Big Baren River, deed on record in Warren County, debt due by William Lynn, etc.; to brother-in-law Edmund Newman 475 acres adjoining above; to sons of Elias Newman, Thomas B. and Obediah P., tract of land on which testator was living, slave, etc.; to nephew Obediah Newman a negro; to nephew Thomas Prather, slave and testator's right and title in lands of her father's and mother's estate. Her bonnet, bible, horse, etc. to Mrs. Gibbs; to niece Mary M. Newman slave, books, etc; to Martha Gibbs and Elizabeth Newman furniture; to nephew Elias Newman her right in lot No. 283, Louisville, together with stock, farming utensils, etc.; to sister Williams her clothes. Slave to be freed and furnished with garden, horse, cow and hog, and not to be allowed to suffer want.
Executors: Nephews Elias Newman and Thomas Prather.
Witnesses: Warrick Miller, John H. Gibbs.

Codicil. Nov. 26, 1824. Charles Newman to have 478 acres, to which testator has since made deed of gift, previously willed to her brother-in-law Col. Edmund Newman, who is to take tract willed to Charles Newman.
Witness: Elias Newman.   [*B2, p341.*]

FREDERICK, AUGUSTUS, SEN.   .   Jan. 5, 1826—Feb. 19, 1827.
(Signed in Dutch). To son George his note to testator April 26, 1819, and 150 acres deeded him for his full share; to son Sam-

uel his notes July 11, 1815, and Feb. 4, 1822, and land conveyed
to him as his full share; to children of deceased son John, tract of
land on which they and their mother live, 110 acres on Floyds
Fork; to the children of deceased son Joseph, tract of 130 acres
bought of Benjamin Sebastian, which testator conveyed to their
father. Had given daughters Margaret, when she married
Thomas Moore, and Christina, and her husband Walter Pearce,
their share. To son Jacob slave and note dated March 11, 1818,
and note of $200 due to Locke and Frederick on note of R. C.
Anderson. Makes gifts of money, furniture or slaves to Emily
and Augustus, children of deceased son Andrew; grandchild
Catharine Easom; grandchild, Elizabeth Moore; step-daughter
Dorothea Meddis; sons Waller P. S. and John P. Y.; son Augustus; to wife Polly the rents, stocks, slaves, etc. of plantation on
which she is to live and maintain and educate children Walter
and John P. Y. Should she marry or die, this to be equally divided among sons Walter P. S. and John P. Y., with following
tracts of land 200 acres bought of Alexander Breckinridge; 90
acres bought of Robert Breckinridge; 91 acres bought of heirs of
Thomas Cannon.
Executors: Friend, James Brown, and son Samuel Frederick.
Witnesses: John Miller, Thomas Medis.
    Samuel Frederick qualified as executor and gave bond with
Benjamin Lawrence as security.   [*B2, p343.*]

GILL, THOMAS   .   .   .   .   .Aug. 14, 1822—Apr. 2, 1827.
    To wife Elizabeth for widowhood whole estate. Should she
marry, two-thirds of estate to be given children.
Executors: Wife, Elizabeth Gill and brother George.
Witnesses: Beeda Gill, James L. Gill, Dr. Thornton. [*B2, p345.*]

MATHES, JAMES   .   .   .   .   .   June 13, 1826—July 3, 1826.
    To wife Mirum Mathes for widowhood, the whole place on
which she lives for her and her family's use. William T. Mathes
to be paid what is owed him. Charge all children with what they
have already had and then divide equally the residue among wife
and ten children: Sarah Hutchison, Caty, William T., Rebekah,
Anna O., Poley, Rachel, Keller, James H., and Becky S. Mathes.
Executor: Wife Marium.
Witnesses: Henry Mathes, Thomas Hutchison.   [*B2, p346.*]

FITZHUGH, ELIZABETH S. . . . .Apr. 29, 1825—May 8, 1827.
To daughter Elizabeth one half, to sons Wm. and John each
one-fourth of estate.
Witnesses: I. C. Johnston, Wm. Pickett.   [*B2, p347.*]

SMOOT, ALEXANDER . . . . Sept. 20, 1820—June 8, 1827.
To sons Alexander and Charles equally the home plantation,
Charles to have that part on Big road leading to Salt River includ-
ing house and orchard; Charles to settle debts and raise and
educate testator's son Philip and daughter Abigail. To son
George C. $1. To daughters Saragh Gatewood, wife of James
Gatewood, Elizabeth Shively, and Abigail Hunter Tubbs Smoot,
slaves, furniture, etc. Should Philip die a minor his share to be
divided between Charles and Abigail Smoot. Philip to be bound
to learn a trade as house-joiner, brick layer or plasterer.
Executor: Charles Smoot.
Codicil. Sept. 20, 1820. Son Charles to have use of slaves
willed Phillip B. Smoot until Philip at age of sixteen is bound out
to learn a trade.
Witnesses: Hugh Logan, Vandorem Logan and Sete Logan—for
will and codicil.   [*B2, p347.*]

HOKE, GEORGE, SR. . . . . July 25, 1823—Sept. 3, 1827.
To wife Elizabeth for life one-third of estate, balance to children. The 80 acres given to daughter Elizabeth Stafford to go to
her heirs. The children of son John Hoke, being George Thomas
and Sarah Elizabeth, to receive an equal part with testator's
children.
Executors: Son-in-law Thomas Baird, and son Andrew Hoke.
Witnesses: Alexander Attkisson, Michael Atkisson, Joseph A.
Sweeny.   [*B2, p350.*]

SETTLES, ABRAHAM . . . . July 9, 1827—Sept 3, 1827.
Estate to be divided equally among children: William S.,
Elizabeth, Jesse E., and Mariah Ellis Settles, part being for their
education. Oldest son William to be bound out to learn trade of
house-joiner or blacksmith; oldest daughter to go to her Aunt
Mary Young of Spencer County; youngest daughter to be given
to testator's sister Rebekah Redman; youngest son Jesse E. to

live with John Readman, son of Thomas Readman, Sr. of Spencer County.

Executors: William Coopor and Robert N. Miller.

Witnesses: Robert Miller, Solomon Neill, James Alexander, Andrew Graham. [*B2, p351.*]

BLAKE, JAMES . . . . . . Dec. 7, 1825—Sept. 3, 1827.
   Personal property to wife Jane.

Witnesses: James B. Ward, Charles D. Ward, Elizabeth I. Ward.
[*B2, p353.*]

MILLER, JOHN . . . . . . Apr. 2, 1827—Sept. 3, 1827.
   To infant children, Charles and George Franklin Miller, books, pamphlets, desk and bookcase, except German family Bible to daughter Catharina, who married Peter Smith, and "Doctor Tysots family physician" to son John Miller. To wife Elizabeth furniture, etc., she brought with her at marriage and other furniture, silver, and what testator might have in Tan Yard, crops, etc. for her use, also lot No. 46 in Jefferson Town. Certain property left to Peter Smith in trust for grandson Peter Funk; part to daughters Polly and Fanny. Plantation in Jefferson County to be sold and proceeds to daughter Catharina, Peter Smith in trust as guardian for testator's grandson John Funk, and daughter Fanny. To stepson Samuel Hart $50. for love and attachment, to be paid when he reaches twenty-one. In 1805 purchased tract of land from Bartho'w for son John Miller, 100 acres at $7. per acre, but of said tract about 20 acres were taken by the Trustees of the Transylvania Seminary for which Abraham Hite refunded to testator at rate of $5.00 per acre. In 1806 purchased another tract from John Poully, since conveyed to daughter Polly and her husband Michael Hinterlider, to be considered their part. Wife Elizabeth to be guardian of two infant children, Charles and Geo. Franklin.

Executors: Trusty friend Jacob Hoke, Sr. and Samuel Hinkle.

Witnesses: William D. McHatton, John Yenowine. (Signed in Dutch). [*B2, p354.*]

ARNOLD, ADAM . . . . . Aug. 23, 1827—Oct. 2, 1827.
   Estate to wife Nency Arnold.

Executor: Wife, Nency.

Witnesses: Martin Hashfild, Daniel King, Wm. Johon. [*B2, p359.*]

BLANKENBAKER, SAMUEL, SR. . Feb. 15, 1827—Nov. 5, 1827.
To wife Mary A. [second wife], slaves and plantation with appurtenances during widowhood. Daughters Anna and Polly to live with their mother until they marry. Should wife marry, she to receive one-third of estate, and balance to children: Benjamin, Samuel [under eighteen], Thomas, James, Anna, Mary; daughter Elizabeth provided for, and Harry a saddle; to daughter Rhoda Kamp 80 acres of land in Washington County, Indiana, Highland Creek, and 240 acres adjoining to be rented for wife. Land in Estill County to be sold.
Executors: Wife, Mary A. and sons Felix, Benjamin, Thomas and James.
Witnesses: Minor White, Jacob Newkirk, Abra Ramey, Samuel Newkirk. [*B2, p360.*]

STRINGHAM, JOHN . . . . Sept. 20, 1827—Nov 5, 1827.
"If I should dy in Louisville I request of sweet Nancy Frame to give me a decent burial in the church yard and all over for her sarveses shall remain hers. I mean all the property that I own in I. (Mc)Castles house. This I give her as a dear friend. . . . This to her I leave as my last will and testament."
Witnesses: Mary Ann Vellerais, Sarah Jane Moyers. [*B2, p364.*]

GRAYSON, FREDERICK W. S. . . May 3, 1827—Nov. 5, 1827.
To wife Sally his interest in eight acres of land in Louisville, slaves, etc. To brother Peter W. Grayson, law books and release from debts due testator, provided he pays debts of the late firm Peter W. Grayson & Co. and pays mother $200 annually. Residue of estate to be divided, half to wife for life, and half to James D. Breckinridge in trust for testator's mother Caroline M. Grayson, then to nieces and nephews. To Peter W. Grayson, in trust for sister Eliza M. Breckinridge, one-half of what testator is entitled to from conveyance from Wm Beard and wife for their interest in estate of Arthur L. Campbell, dec.
Executor: James D. Breckinridge.
Will proven by oaths of James Ferguson, James W. Thornbury and James Harrison. [*B2, p365.*]

TYLER, ABSALOM . . . . . Sept. 15, 1827,—Nov. 5, 1827.
Nuncupative Will. Died Sept. 6, 1827. To wife Polly a slave. To nephews Harry and Milton Tyler, living with testator,

each a horse, their schooling and $200. Said in the presence of Thomas B. Miller, John Blankenbaker, on Sept. 6, 1827, and reduced to writing September 15, 1827.   [*B2, p366.*]

WELSH, JOSEPH . . . . . Sept. 27, 1827,—Dec. 6, 1827.
To wife Mary entire estate.
Witnesses: John Jones, Wm. Forrester, Henry Lewis, John Welsh.
[*B2, p366.*]

HAYSE, GEORGE . . . . . Mar. 24, 1813—Jan. 8, 1828.
To oldest son George, plantation on which he lives; to sons George and John certain furnishings and live stock; to son Peter 100 pounds for land on which he lives; to John plantation on which testator lives; to daughters Mary Smith, for use of her three sons, Margaret Sousley and Eave Shively, ten pounds each. To his five children living in Kentucky: George, Peter, John, Mary Smith and Margaret Sousley, testator's loose property.
Executors: Sons George and John Hayse.
Witnesses: James McKeag, Alex. Woodrow and John Slaughter.
[*B2, p368.*]

JONES, SALLY . Apr. 26, 1828—Sept. 4, 1826, Jan. 11, 1828.
To children of nephew William G. Lawes, namely: John Robert, Sally Ann, Andrew Jackson and Eleanor Elizabeth Lawes, the house and lot bought of William Chambers in which Mrs. G. Lawes resides, in Middletown, also certain slaves and furniture.
Witnesses: W. F. Quirey, I. Glass, Thos. Lawes.   [*B2, p369.*]

RUSH, CONRAD . Oct. 10, 1827—Nov. 5, 1827, Feb. 4, 1828.
Estate to be sold and wife Margaret to get half the proceeds. Slave London at age of thirty-one to be freed and given $100. To Richard Bullock, a lame young man, $500.00 for love; to friend John Slaughter Jr., $300. and to Moses Williams, who married Betsey Bishop, $300. Second half of estate to last three in same proportion as above bequests.
Executor: Friend James Pomeroy.
Witnesses: Wm. Bryan, Benjamin Smith.   [*B2, p370.*]

ABERNATHY, JOHN . . . . . Feb. 11, 1828—Mar. 4, 1828.
Nuncupative Will. Dead Feb. 9, 1828. Estate to Mrs. Mar-

garet Monin with whom he boarded and who took care of him in his last illness.
Witnesses: Sworn to by Joseph Applegate and Eveline Tharp.

[*B2, p371.*]

WELSH, MARY . . . . . Feb. 13, 1828—Mar. 4, 1828.
To John Rowan Jones, son of Col. John Jones, one slave; to Jacob Augustus, son of Capt. David Augustus, horse. Residue of estate to be sold; pay Henry Lewis, brother-in-law, $400. Balance to be divided between William, son of deceased brother John Myrtle, and the eldest child of brother Reuben Myrtle, when they reach twenty-one years of age.
Executor: Colonel John Jones.
Witnesses: Bryan Johnson, Thomas Lewis, Thomas N. Johnson, James F. Jones. [*B2, p373.*]

HITE, STEPHEN LEWIS . . . Mar. 16, 1828—May 5, 1828.
To wife Patsey Hite for life estate for her use and the maintenance and education of children until they come of age or marry. To son Joseph one rifle, and the gun given testator by John Cox.
Executor: Patsey Hite, wife.
Witnesses: William Brown, John Miller, James Kelley, George Hite. [*B2, p374.*]

MAUPIN, MATILDA A. . . . June 10, 1828—July 7, 1828.
If money due by uncle Norborne P. Beall exceeds what she owed him, same to his children. To cousin Anne M. McClannaghan $600. Executors to buy and emancipate ten slaves owned by late father Richard A. Maupin. To cousin Norborne A. Galt 550 acres on Ohio River and Muddy Fork of Beargrass in name of Southall and Charlton adjacent to John Edwards's land from estate of her mother Harriet Beall Maupin. To Levi Tyler and Samuel Gwathmey in trust 1180 acres on Ohio River below Louisville in name of Mary S. Beall, inherited from Mattie Beall, to sell and pay to cousin John Floyd $1000, and balance to cousins Harriet M., Louisa, Mary, Samuel and William Beall, children of Norborne B. Beall, to be paid as they marry or become of age. To sisters Maria L., Mildred E.; brother Richard A. Maupin; cousin Harriet M. Beall, Louisa Beall, Mary Beall, certain money not exceeding $20,000; anything over, to cousin Norborne A. Galt. Wearing apparel to friend Rose Anna Hughes.

Executors: Levi Tyler and Samuel Gwathmey.
Witnesses: James Hughes, Rose Anna Hughes, Norborne B. Beall, Eliza Maupin.

Levi Tyler, Samuel Gwathmey took oath and Tyler gave bond with James Guthrie, James D. Breckenridge and John T. Gray his securities; Gwathmey gave bond with Richard Ferguson, George C. Gwathmey his securities. [*B2, p376.*]

McCAWLEY, JOSHUA . . . June 24, 1828—Sept. 1, 1828.

To wife Polly, the farm near home of Samuel Pharis, with stock, etc. for maintenance and education of children: Samuel, James and Arthur. To daughters, Elizabeth Terry, part of farm called Robb Farm; to Margaret McCawley, rest of Robb Farm, and 25 acres on which Thomas McCawley lives; to daughter Sally Terry land near that of Samuel Pharis, Joseph Terry and Arthur McCawley. Residue of estate to three sons Samuel, James and Arthur.
Executors: Brother Arthur McCawley and friend Robert Gailbreath.
Witnesses: Robert Gailbreath, Squire Davis. [*B2, p380.*]

WITHERS, JOHN . . . . Sept. 7, 1828—Oct. 6, 1828.

To wife Sarah Speak Withers slaves and enough of stock to support her, balance to legatees. To daughter Mary, son William, and grandsons William Brooks and Owen Withers, slaves and personal property. Balance to children, except Charley to pay to estate for equal division $100.
Witnesses: William Newkirk, Henry Peyton Field.

An N. B. giving daughter Lucy Withers two slaves is acknowledged and signed by Sarah Speak Withers Oct. 3, 1828, but not signed by John Withers.
Witnesses: John Withers, Waller Withers. [*B2, p382.*]

KING, THOMAS . . . . Aug. 20, 1828—Dec. 1, 1828.

After wife's death, to sons Wesley one slave and 180 acres McQuiddy tract; to John one slave and the home place; to daughters Amy and Mary certain slaves.
Executor: Wife.
Witnesses: John P. Declary, W. R. Davis, Jno. M. Luckett, And. Graham. [*B2, p383.*]

TAYLOR, RICHARD   .   .   .   .   Dec. 22, 1828—Feb. 2, 1829.
  To three sons Hancock, Zachary and Joseph P. Taylor the
home plantation on Muddy Fork of Beargrass to be sold and debts
paid and son Hancock retain $1500 to equalize him with other
children; balance to be divided among children: Hancock; Zachary; Betsey, wife of John G. Taylor; Emily, wife of John Allison;
Sarah, wife of French T. [S.?] Gray; and Geo. Taylor; Sarah's
(commonly called Sally) part to be held in trust by executors
for her use. Mentions slaves.
Executors: Sons, Hancock, Zachary and Joseph P. Taylor.
Witnesses: Charles M. Thruston, Henry Churchill, J. P. Taylor,
Rich'd Ferguson. [Original will not in file box.]   [*B2, p384.*]

KENNEDY, PATRICK W.   .   .   .   Jan. 16, 1829—Mar. 3, 1829.
  To wife Mary during widowhood, estate. Should she marry,
one half of estate to father and mother, John and Elenor Kennedy,
but if dead to brothers Phillip and John.
Executor: James McGlenddy.
Witnesses: John Doherty, James Waters, John Crooks. [*B2, p386.*]

GRAY, GEORGE   .   .   .   .   .   Sept. 13, 1828—Mar. 3, 1829.
  Of Caddone Prairie, Parish of Natchitoches, Louisiana. To
wife Selenah during life, estate, and then to brothers and sisters.
Wife after his death to live with testator's connections in the
State of Kentucky.
Executors: Brothers, John T and Philip R. Gray.
  Will proven by the oaths of Benjamin I. Harrison, Craven P.
Luckett, Geo. D. Gray and Richard Oldham.   [*B2, p387.*]

MARKWELL, GEORGE, SENR.   .   .   Apr. 8, 1828—Apr. 6, 1829.
  To son Elias land on which he lives on waters of Goose River
in Spencer County. At testator's death, Elias to take his son
(testator's grandson) Alfred, and at Elias death Alfred to share
equally with other children. To sons John, George, and grandchildren, heirs of William Markwell, deceased, home place, and
to son George tract purchased from Taylor; to daughter Elizabeth
Smith certain furniture. Residue to all children.
Witnesses: George Marshall, David E. Tyler, Thomas Conn.
                                          [*B2, p388.*]

JOHNSON, JOHN Y.   .   .   .   .   Aug. 12, 1828—July 6, 1829.
To children of his brother Charles Y. Johnson, and his sister
Mildred Y. Pickett, $20. each. Pay debts and balance of estate
to brother William Johnson.
Executor: Brother, William Johnson.
Witnesses: William H. Broaddes, William Pickett, Mich'l I. O.
Callaghan.   [*B2, p390.*]

HART, JACOB   .   .   .   .   .   .   May 3, 1829—July 6, 1829.
Formerly of City of Baltimore, but for seven or eight years a
resident of Louisville. To nephew William Gordon, son of sister
Catharine Gordon of Fredericksburg, Va., estate in trust for testa-
tor's sister Catharine, and at her death to her children.
Executor: William Reed, friend.
Witnesses: Isaac H. Tyler, William D. Payne.   [*B2, p391.*]

VANCE, JAMES [Reverend]   .   .   Feb. 23, 1829—Oct. 5, 1829.
To wife Ruth for life, one-third of estate; to sons Samuel D.
and William R. property in Middletown and on Fern Creek; and
at wife's death her share and residue of estate. Son John has received his share in money.
Executors: Samuel D. and William R. Vance, sons.
Witnesses: James Pomeroy, William M. King, James Tull, Stephen Black.   [*B2, p382.*]

SMYSER, JACOB   .   .   .   .   .   .   Apr. 2, 1829—Oct. 5, 1829.
To wife Nancy for life, estate. At her death to children:
George, John Wesley, Jacob and Catherine his wife, William and
Lewis, Betsy Pottorff and her consort Louis, Nancy, Delila and
Sally Smyser, children of daughter Polly Pottorff. To Frederick
and Nancy Foible, father-in-law and wife, a decent maintenance
and burial.
Executors: John Burkes and Henry Robb.
Witnesses: David Lynam, John P. Williamson, Alex. Woodrow,
Wm. Bryan.
Nov. 2, 1829. Executors named renounced execution and ad-
ministration papers granted to John W. Smyser, son of deceased
Jacob Smyser, who took oath and gave bond with John Burkes,
and George Seabolt his securities.   [*B2, p394.*]

WHEELER, JOHN . . . . . Dec. 16, 1829—Jan. 4, 1830.
Nuncupative will. In the presence of Elisha Applegate and Louisa White, John Wheeler stated that his wife, Christiann Wheeler was to have, at his death, his entire estate.

Christiann Wheeler granted papers of administration.

[*B2, p395.*]

ERICKSON, JAMES . . Dec. 23, 1824—Jan. 5, Feb. 1, 1830.
To sons James and Peregrine and daughters Reabecca Stewart, Elizabeth Banks and Susan Oglisby, and grandsons William, James and Peregrine, sons of deceased son Samuel, certain slaves, also to last three named the home plantation. Residue to his five children and a share to children of deceased son Samuel.
Executor: Samuel Churchill.
Witnesses: William Churchull, Thomas Kelly.
Proven by oath of William Churchill who also made oath that Thomas Kelly did sign as witness, but was then dead. Samuel Churchill renounced the execution, and William Oglesby was named and gave bond with Thomas H. Ayres as security.

[*B2, p396.*]

HOLLIS, RUTH . . . . . . Jan. —, 1830—Feb. 1, 1830.
Nuncupative Will. Sister Rachel Hall with whom she lived to have all personal property. Signed by Jane Shively and Isabella Hollis.
Rachel Hollis granted administration papers and gave bond with John Jones (tanner) as security.   [*B2, p398.*]

MASSIE, HENRY . . . . . Feb. 6, 1830—Mar. 1, 1830.
To wife Helen estate in Kentucky and Ohio. To brother Thomas income from $1400 for life, at his death principal to wife Helen. To each of nieces Constance Massey and Elizabeth Thompson $3000. Remainder to be divided between nephews: Heath Jones Miller of Louisville; Nathaniel Massie of Ohio, son of deceased brother Nathaniel; Henry Bullitt son of Cuthbert Bullitt, and Alexander Scott Bullitt son of William C. Bullitt. Should this residue amount to more than $3000 to each, then the excess is to be divided between them and Constance Massie, Elizabeth Thompson and niece Sally Hawes.
Executor: Wife Helen Massie.
Witnesses: William C. Galt, Neville Bullitt, Edwd. Johnson.

[*B2, p398.*]

ORMSBY, P[ETER] B. . . . . Apr. 3, 1830—May 3, 1830.
To brother Stephen Ormsby estate.
Executor: Brother Stephen Ormsby.
Witnesses: Coleman Rogers, Jno. F. Anderson, Edward Crow.
[*B2, p400.*]

HITE, PATSY . . . . . . May 8, 1830—June 7, 1830.
Personal property to be sold and proceeds to pay her debts
and those of her deceased husband, Stephen Lewis Hite. To son
Joseph Stephen Hite and daughter Mary Ann Hite certain personal belongings; to her father James Pendleton a watch left her
by brother Singleton. Her father to be guardian to two children,
and her relative Geo. Hite to assist him.
Executor: Her father, James Pendleton.
Witnesses: Moses Kellar, James Kelly, Robert Pendleton.
James Pendleton renounced execution, and John L. Hite
named, and gave bond with Joseph Hite as security. [*B2, p401.*]

RUSSELL, LEVI . . . . . Dec. 29, 1824—June 7, 1830.
To wife Nanny during widowhood all lands, certain stock and
furniture. To oldest daughter Sally, wife of Joseph Markwell,
$1.; to daughter Eliza, wife of Blan Smith, certain furniture, etc;
to second son James Russell all land, and should testator's wife
re-marry, James must care for and educate minor children. All
other property to be sold and equally divided between six children
not before mentioned, namely, Hiram, Nancy, Levi, Levisa,
Noah and Mary Russell.
Executor: Richard Seaton.
Witnesses: Rich'd Seaton, George Seaton.
Codicil, May 24, 1830. Disposes of wagon.
Executor: Thomas Waller.
Witnesses: James Reed, James Russell, Thomas Waller.
Richard Seaton and Thomas Waller gave bond with James
Pomeroy and George Seaton as security. [*B2, p403.*]

WITHERS, CHARLES . . . . June 1, 1830—Sept 6, 1830.
To daughter Sadonia Withers a slave and money in hands of
Wm. Hibit of Louisville for her education; to sister Mary Withers
furniture; to Wm. Withers, rifle; to J. Shadburn a shot gun, and
to J. Withers a musket. Slave Philis to be liberated.

Executors: Brother John, and John Shadburn.
Witnesses: Thomas Brown, Nancy Brown, Ann Grant.
    John Withers renounced execution, administration granted
John Shadburn who gave bond with John Doup as security.
                                                    [*B2, p405.*]

McCOLLUM, BARNEY . . . May —, 1830—Sept. 6, 1830.
    [Signed, by his mark, Barney Collum] To wife Elizabeth
McCollum estate.
Executor: Wife Elizabeth.
Witnesses: John Rothwell, Edward Hughes.   [*B2, p406.*]

BYERS, NATHAN . . . . . Aug. 12, 1830—Sept. 6, 1830.
    Estate, including plantation and slave, to be sold and divided
among children. Benjamin Cothan named their guardian.
Executors: Benjamin Cothan, Arthur McCalla.
Witnesses: Thomas H. Vance, James F. Pendergrast.
    Copy of will probated, as identical with lost original, by oath
of Benjamin Cawthorn, Thomas H. Vance, James Pendergrass,
and Samuel Frederick. Benjamin Cawthorn granted administration with Samuel Schwing as security.   [*B2, p406.*]

WILLIAMS, SAMUEL . . . . July 7, 1830—Sept. 6, 1830.
    To wife Nancy during life estate, and at her death to three of
his children, Bensy, Jane and John Williams, the other children
having had their share.
Executor: Son John Williams.
Witnesses: John Womack, Jas. M. Brengman, J. L. Murray.
                                                    [*B2, p408.*]

ROBERTS, THOMAS . . . . Sept 1, 1830—Sept. 7—1830.
    Sell estate, including deed from James Monroe, President of
the United States, for 320 acres in Arkansas; pay debts and divide
balance among the children of his wife Fanny Roberts, when they
reach the age of twenty-one.
Executor: Wife Fanny Roberts.
Witnesses: John Jones, Andrew Graham, Fanny Merritt.
                                                    [*B2, p408.*]

McMULLIN, JOHN . . . . Apr. 17, 1830—Sept. 7, 1830.
To Trustees of the Roman Catholic Church in Louisville, two
horses and one dray.
Will proven by oaths of James Curran and Ann Amiss.
[*B2, p409.*]

QUINN, JOHN . . Jan. 18, 1819—Sept. 6, 1830, June 4, 1832.
To wife Mary, for life, estate. Bequeathed to daughter Jain
Tooms, and John Tooms, to sons Arthur, Fountain and William
Quinn, to Polly, daughter, and Elizabeth Thornbury, small sums
of money and slaves. At wife's death, balance to be divided be-
tween Jain Tooms, William Quinn and Polly Thornbury.
Witnesses: W. W. C. H. Dunbar, Joseph Gailbraith. [*B2, p410.*]

HOLMES, MOSES . . . . . Mar. 16, 1829—Oct. 4, 1830.
Wife Amelia and daughter Margaret to have support from
home farm bequeathed to son Martin G., containing 153 acres,
bought in two parcels from Floid and James Taylor. One dollar
each to: daughter Elizabeth's only heir Theofiles Batman, daugh-
ter Rebeckah Risley [Reily] [Rizley], son Jesse Holmes, son
Matthew Holmes, to whom he had given one-half of farm on
which he lives; to son Timothy the other half of said farm, to son
Benjamin S. a slave. Balance left to wife.
Executor: Son Matthew Holmes.
Witnesses: George G. Barns, Thomas P. Farmer, Isaac Mills.
[*B2, p411.*]

CLARK, GEORGE ROGERS . . . Nov. 5, 1815—Oct. 4, 1830.
Signed G. R. Clark. To friend, William Croghan, Sr., 3600
acres in Bracken County on Locust Creek, a part of 8000 acres
surveyed in name of G. R. Clark and John Crittenden, June 13,
1797, Treasury Warrant No. 15147, also 3920 acres below Mayfield on the Mississippi, an entry made in Lincoln office Nov. 24,
1781. To brother William Clark forever, all lands northwest of
Ohio River. To nephews, John and Benjamin O'Fallon, 1500
acre claim, part of Warrant No. 2292 allowed for military service, entered April 10, 1785, on Clark River, a branch of Tennessee, said to include a silver mine; also 600 acres, part of 1500
acres surveyed on Cumberland River at mouth of Little River.
To brother William Clark, friends Maj. William Croghan, Owen

Gwathmey and Davis [Dennis] Fitzhugh claim to locators fees, part of an entry of 101,000 acres made by testator in Surveyor's office of Lincoln County, which lands are situated between the Tennessee and Mississippi rivers together with all other lands not already disposed of.

Witnesses: Joel Carpenter, John Croghan, Wm. Christy.

George Woolfolk qualified as administrator, with George C. Gwathmey and Samuel Gwathmey as securities.   *[B2, p412.]*

[Note: George Rogers Clark died February 13, 1818, at the home of his sister Lucy, Mrs. William Croghan, near Louisville. This will is published in *Conquest of the Country Northwest of the River Ohio, 1778-1783, and Life of Gen. George Rogers Clark,* by William Hayden English, Volume 2, page 893.]

ADAMS, ISABELLA . . . . .   Apr. 3, 1829—Oct. 4, 1830.

To John Adams, son of Elijah Adams, a slave, he to pay his sister Margaret Ann Adams $100 when she is twenty; Elijah to have use of slaves until John can earn the $100. Money now in the hands of Elijah Adams and proceeds of loose property as follows: to Elizabeth, daughter of Nimrod Hambrick; Sally, wife of John Colbert and her daughter Sarah Elizabeth Colbert; Maria, wife of Nimrod Hambrick; and Elijah Adams.

Executor: Elijah Adams.

Witnesses: Wm S. Rose, Henry I. Payne.

Elijah Adams qualified and gave bond with Samuel P. Buckner as security.   *[B2, p413.]*

DAWSON, JAMES . . . . .   Aug. 22, 1817—Oct. 5, 1830.

To wife Hannah during widowhood, entire estate to "bring up and school" children. If she marries, she is to have one-third, balance to children.

Witnesses: Samuel Phariss, Joshua McCawley, Benjamin Tharp.

                                        [B2, p414.]

HUNDLEY, JOHN W. . . . .   Oct. 16, 1829—Nov. 1, 1830.

All slaves in his service for fifteen years to be set free, others to go to brother Thomas C. Hundley until the expiration of fifteen years service and then be freed; all that have been born his to be freed when they are twenty-five years old, and at brother's death all to be freed. All land in Jefferson County including 60 acre plantation to go to brother Thomas C. Hundley for two years and then be employed "in God's use" forever as follows:

For a Presbyterian Theological Seminary for the training of pious young men for the Gospel Ministry, beneficiaries to be chosen by executors or representatives together with legal officers of the Institution—if blood relations of testator offer themselves and are worthy, they shall be received on the fund. System of theology taught shall be that contained in the standards of the Presbyterian Church and as held by General Assembly of the Presbyterian Church in the U. S. A. If such institution cannot be on his land, property to be sold to create a fund for the education of men for the ministry, both clasical and theological, the sum shall be vested under the charter of Center College, interest only to be used by the "Executive Committee of the Education Society."

To brother Thomas C. Hundley $12,000; to American Tract Society of New York $1000., the interest to be employed by the Branch Society of Louisville, Ky., for the use in Western Country; to an Orphan Assylum $1000, and if the Orphan Assylum now established by law at Middletown in Jefferson County shows signs of stability, it shall receive benefit of interest, on this fund black children, not exceeding five at one time, may be sent. Balance of money on interest to the Education Society of Kentucky if it be established at Danville. To brothers Thomas C. and Joel W. horses and sundry presents.

For the purchase of a slave, then near Woodsville, Miss., $500. if he cannot be purchased then the money is to be given him; $1500 to be put out at interest for use of brother Elisha E. Hundley and his present wife for life, and then to American Bible Society, for distribution of Bibles in Western Country and Texas; mentions Foreign and Home Missionary Societies.

To brother Joel W. Hundley $1000; land in Washington County on which Elisha Hundley now lives to him for life, then to his daughter Mary Jane.

Executors: Rev. Gideon Blackburn, D.D., Thomas C. Hundley, Rev. J. N. Blackburn, Hugh McElroy, Anthony McElroy and James H. Cunningham.

Witnesses: William M. King, Francis Snowden, John T. Hamilton, James Hite.

Appendage: In event Seminary is located on testator's land, brother Thomas C. Hundley to use bed room, pasturage, stables, etc., and gives him rifle gun.

Witnesses: Same as above.

Appendage: Frees certain slaves and changes conditions slightly.

Witness: James Hite.

Second codicil proven by oaths of James Guthrie and Charles M. Thruston.

Executors gave bond with the following as securities: John Frederick, Peter Goately, Mordicai Hardin, James Ewing, Elias Dawson, Henry Pope, John Calhoun, James Bently, Sam Grundy, Andrew Cunningham, John Thomas, Edward Berry, Jesse T. Riney, Wm. B. Harrison, Aba'm McElroy, Alex Hamilton, Pascal D. Craddock, Hugh and Anthony McElroy. The bonds totaled $500,000.   [*B2, p415.*]

Will set aside by Oldham County Circuit Court, and Jack Thomas and Thomas C. Hundley named administrators, June 4, 1832. See Jefferson County Court Order Book No. 16, for 1832, p 106–107.

FIELD, ABNER . . . .   Jan. 16, 1828—Nov. 7, 1831.

To wife Jane (or Jenny) for life 100 acres land on which they were living, on waters of South Fork of Beargrass, etc.; to son John P., a horse. Residue of estate to executors, in trust to pay debts and the following: to daughters Hester E., Betsy, Eleanor G. and Penelope (the latter Lamaster) and sons William, Alexander P., Nathaniel and John P., certain monies. Son Abner has had his share. At wife's death, her share to be divided among children including Abner. Debts to William Thompson, state of Virginia or Pennsylvania, and Robert Wright, late of Henry County, Kentucky, to be paid.

Executors: William Pope and John P. Oldham, also guardian of children.

Witnesses: Worden Pope, Geo. S. Slaughter, Rich'd Oldham.

Codicil, May 21, 1831. Revokes legacy of $100. to William; notes held on Nathaniel and Abner to be settled by assignments; to wife $400, to replace slave which died. Land in Pond Settlement to be sold and divided among heirs. Revokes above executors and appoint Jane Field, Nathaniel Field and William R. Vance.

Witnesses: M. Miller, S. N. Kalfus, Thos. H. Vance.   [*B2, p420.*]

STYER, HENRY M. [STIER] . . Oct. 4, 1830—Dec. 7, 1830.
To Preston Ashby, infant heir of Kitty Ashby, estate including lot purchased from Thomas Joyce.
Witnesses: H[ardin] M. Weatherford, Edward McDade.

[*B2, p424.*]

DENWOOD, MARY . . . . . July 2, 1830—Mar. 7, 1831.
After paying debts, residue to Robert A. Barnes of St. Louis, Missouri, in trust for use of testator's daughter Sally M. Barnes, wife of Richard Barnes, for her life and then to her children.
Executor: Robert A. Barnes.
Witnesses: Wm. H. Booth, Tubman Lawes, John Price.

[*B2, p425.*]

HITE, JOSEPH . . . June 15, 1830—Mar. 7, May 2, 1831.
To be buried in burying ground at brother Abraham Hite's by side of departed companion Sarah Hite. To son John Hite, slaves, etc., and 325 acres, part of land on which testator lived, adjoining lands conveyed to son Lewis Hite, deceased, and son Stephen L. Hite. To Moses Keller, Walker Prewitt and son John Hite, as trustees, for son Abraham balance of farm, 170 acres, negroes, furniture, money, etc. Slaves to grandchildren: Eliza Ann, William Chambers and Lewis Lee White Hite, children of son Lewis Hite, deceased; Mary Ann and Joseph Lewis Hite, under age, children of son Stephen L. Hite, deceased. Refers to land held in copartnership with brother Abraham and heirs of brother Isaac Hite. Appointed John Hite, son, Edmund T. Bainbridge and William E. Graham, friends, trustees to settle all copartnership lands, and divide among children and grandchildren.
Executors: Son John Hite, Mosses Keller and Wm. Bryan.
Witnesses: Abr'm Hite, James Pomeroy, James Hite, James Kelly, Robert Tyler, George Keller, C. L. Duncan.
Codicil, June 21, 1830. Son John to occupy land given son Abraham and pay for its use, also to have slaves to work it.
Witnesses: James Pomeroy, C. L. Duncan, Robert Tyler, George Keller.
June 6, 1831, Codicil rejected, by the court. [*Note:* Codicil not recorded, but filed with original will.] [*B2, p427.*]

WILSON, DANIEL . . . . . Apr. 5, 1831—May 2, 1831.
To wife Henrietta and three children, Mary E, wife W. H. Pope, Thomas E. and Lucinda P. Wilson, estate, subject to the following, to wife two slaves, to be emancipated at her death and provided for, to son Thomas E., medical library; cancel debt due by Rev. D. C. Banks.
Executors: Son, Thomas E. Wilson, and son-in-law W. H. Pope.
Witnesses: Edwd. Johnson, B. Tompkins, R. Johnson. [*B2, p432.*]

ARTEBURN, BRANHAM . . . Apr. 11, 1831—May 2, 1831.
To his mother Rachel Arteburn his portion of his father's estate and 287 acres on which testator was living, purchased from Messrs Peay and Parks. At her death, this to go to his brothers, Burris, Jordon, Tarlton, Norborn, William C., and Covington Arteburn.
Executor: Brother, Jordon Arteburn.
Witnesses: Wm. C. Bullitt, Robert N. Smith.   [*B2, p433.*]

BRENTLINGER, SUSANNAH . . Mar. 22, 1831—May 2, 1831.
To son George a clock and to daughter Rosanna kitchen furniture. Residue to all her children.
Executor: Son Jacob Britlinger
Witnesses: Saml. Burks, M[athew] M. Tower, H[enry] G. Tompkins.
Codicil, March 25, 1831. Having left a clock to George, he is excluded from other bequests. *Witness:* H. G. Tompkins.
[*B2, p434.*]

CAVETT, ANDREW . . . . May 18, 1831—June 6, 1831.
Asks to be buried in Middletown, Ky., beside two children. Interest in cabinet shop on Market Street in Louisville to be sold and all estate, except watch, for the education of daughter Mary Ann Elizabeth at a private boarding school, and estate to be given her when she is fifteen, and large family Bible. Should she die before that age, estate to his sister-in-law Lucinda Morrow. To brother-in-law Ellridge F. Morrow, his Lepine watch.
Executor: William F. Morrow.
Proven by oaths of Peter Acres. William F. Morrow renounced execution and administration granted Thomas Q. Wilson, Esqe., who gave bond with James Guthrie as security.
[*B2, p435.*]

335

Cox, John H. . . . . . . Jan. 4, 1831—June 6, 1831.
To wife Frances Morton Cox, estate.
Witnesses: Richard H. Cox, Vincent Cox, John Hughes, Jr.
[*B2, p437.*]

Masterson, John . . . . Mar. 12, 1831—June 6, 1831.
Of Town of St. Louis, Mo. To brother Aaron Masterson and sister Mary Roberson, $1.00 each. To brother Zachariah, after paying debts, entire estate consisting of a lot in St. Louis, about $60. or $70. in hands of testator's guardian, Michael Goddard; a claim of $27. for wages against Steamboat Cleopatra; and a sum of money from his mother's estate in Pennsylvania.
Executor: Brother, Zachariah Masterson.
Witnesses: Peregrine Craig, Richard Smith, G. Ridgeley.
[*B2, p437.*]

Ballard, Levin I. W. . . . Apr. 29, 1831—June 7, 1831.
To sister Eliza P. Camp estate.
Executor: Ed. S. Camp.
Witnesses: James Tarleton, Gab'l S. Jones. [*B2, p439.*]

Brookhart, Catharine . . June 17, 1828—June 7, 1831.
Sell plantation on which she lived, pay debts and $50. to her daughter Magdaline, balance of money to be equally divided between daughters Magdaline, Lydia, who married Matthew Towers, and son David. Married children have had their share.
Executor: Son David Brookhart.
Witnesses: James Pomeroy, Jacob Hoke.
David Brookhart qualified as executor with Peter Funk and Matthew M. Towers as securities. [Note: In original will son-in-law is Matthew Towers, but recorded as Matthew Dewees, in the will book.] [*B2, p439.*]

Duffy, Michael . . . . . Apr. 24, 1832—June 5, 1832.
Estate to executors in trust for the following uses: to wife one-third estate and furniture; to children Eliza and Nancy each one-third. Should either die before she is twenty-one, after paying Catholic Church of Louisville $200., her share to testator's wife, to sister Honor and Elizabeth Duffay child of Sarah of Cincinnati. To mother, Sarah Beyne for life $50. annually and to said Eliza-

beth $200. for her education. Executors to give Michael Cotter reasonable time to pay his note, or cancel it.

Executors: John O. Beirne and James Rudd.

Witnesses: Garnett Duncan, Joseph Middleton, Jno. O. Beirne, Jeremiah McGrath.   [*B2, p441.*]

STANDIFORD, NATHAN   .   .   .   July 12, 1830—Sept. 3, 1832.

To James Stewart Standiford, eldest son of testator's brother David Standiford, estate except a stand of drawers to his sister Nancy Hench. Executors to have use of property for education of above named until James Stewart Standiford becomes of age, when he is to be given estate.

Executor: David Standiford, also guardian for Nancy Hench.

Witnesses: J. F. Pendergrast, Alfred Thornberry.

David Standiford qualified as administrator and gave bond with Alexander H. Gailbreath and Henry Cummins as securities.

[*B2, p443.*]

CRAWFORD, MARTHA .   .   .   .   July 24, 1831—Sept. 5, 1831.

Of Shelby County. To sisters Mary and Nancy Crawford her estate.

Witnesses: Daniel C. Banks, John G. Simrall, T. W. Cocke.

[*B2, p445.*]

LUCKETT, MOLLY ANN   .   .   .   July 13, 1831—Sept. 5, 1831.

Daughter Eliza N. Moore to have management of slaves left to grand-daughters Sarah L. Thruston; Catharine and Elizabeth Luckett, daughters of Samuel N. Luckett; Mary A. Moore; until they shall marry. Daughter Eliza to have her own certain slaves for life. To grandsons Noland M. Luckett, son of Samuel N. Luckett, a slave; George F. Moore gold watch. Should they move more than twelve miles from Louisville, they are not to take certain slaves, nor are those slaves to be sent out of family. Noland M. Luckett shall pay to executors $30. in specie, with which they shall buy one-half dozen each silver teaspoons, large table spoons, and have engraved on each M. A. L. and send or deliver to grand-daughter Mary Eliza Conway. To grandsons Thomas Nolan Conway and John Middleton Moore, all her interest in land at Noland's Ferry in Loudoun County, Virginia, willed testator by her father. To granddaughter Sarah L. Thruston and grandson

Christopher G. Luckett equally about $600 due on notes of Craven P. Luckett, their father. To grand-daughter Mary Ann Luckett for life two slaves that testator's daughter-in-law, Susan P. Luckett, is to have use of until Mary Ann marries. Notes of James Atkinson and Thomas Woods to daughter Eliza N. Moore. To grandsons James Francis and John F. Moore a slave.
Executor: Daughter Eliza N. Moore, John Jones.
Witnesses: H. W. Holloway, M. H. Miller.   [*B2, p447.*]

WITHERS, MARY . . . . . May 24, 1831—Sept. 5, 1831.
    To sisters Sally and Nancy each a slave, to sister Lucy a horse. Gifts to the following: Delia, sister Sally's child; brothers William and Walter Withers; Gane Brooks. To her mother a set of table spoons; to brother John for Maria Shadburn a slave, and to his daughter Frances set of table spoons to have letter of testator's name engraved thereon; to sister Elizabeth Shadburn, sadle and bridle.
Executor: Brother, John Withers.
Witnesses: Thomas Brown, Sarah S. Ropor.   [*B2, p451.*]

SNELL, CHRISTIAN . . . . Mar. 11, 1830—Oct. 3, 1831.
    To father and mother, John Christian and Frederica Snell, living in Germany, house and lot purchased from Sam'l and Margaret Baxter No. 23 of Preston's Enlargement in Louisville, and at their death to his brothers and sisters also living in Germany. All monies in the office of Discount and Deposit of the Bank of the United States at Louisville also to be so disposed of.
Executors: Friends Christopher Long and Emanual Seybolt.
Witnesses: Samuel Dickinson, William Marshall.   [*B2, p452.*]

RAMSEY, MARGARET . . . . Oct. 1, 1831—Oct. 5, 1831.
    Nuncupative Will. She died at her dwelling on Main Street on "last Thursday a week", and desired her estate to go to Michael Duffay of Louisville in trust for her daughter.
    Will proven by oaths of Mariah Highland and Nancy Cox before Robert H. Grayson, Justice of the Peace.
    Michael Duffay qualified as executor with Edward Hughes as security.   [*B2, p454.*]

SHIRLEY, JOHN . . . . . Sept. 9, 1831—Nov. 8, 1831.
    To wife Jane B. Shirley during widowhood, his estate for the support and education of three children: William Lewis, Andrew

Elias and Arthur Wallace. Should wife marry she is to have only one-third of property.

Executors: Brother Lawrence Shirley and Francis Snowden.

Witnesses: Alfred Luckett, Will M. Taylor.

Codicil. To the widow of Jacob Zearing $2. To wife Jane Shirley for life in case of remarriage, two slaves and their increase over and above her third. Wife to act with above executors.

Jane Shirley and Lawrence Shirley qualified with John Scott and Lewis Shirley as securities. [*B2, p456.*]

BURKS, JOHN . . . . . . Aug. 2, 1831—Jan. 2, 1832.

Renounces any former will that may be in hands of brother James. To brothers James and Samuel Burks, estate with following exceptions: to sisters Polly Williams; Sally Phelps, and then to her children Francis and Emily; Amey Dunn; and Betsy Read, $1000 each. To Perry Burks, if his conduct is good, $30., and to Nancy, an infant, two slaves. Mentions Lydia Shain and Nancy Smyser. Five slaves to be emancipated three months after his death. To nephews James and John Phelps slaves, and impresses upon James to be kind to slave Emanuel as he "was particularly attached to him." Wished to be buried by the side of his father and mother in Bullitt County, and executors to put strong stone wall around graveyard, hoping Mr. Phelps who owned the place would have no objection.

Executors: James and Samuel Burks, his brothers.

Witnesses: John Anderson, George W. Chambers, Tucker Lively.

Codicil. Aug. 4, 1831. To each sister $2000. instead of $1000., but any money due testator by their husbands to be deducted. Witnesses same as above.

James and Samuel Burks qualified as executors with William Pope and Larz Anderson as securities. [*B2, p460.*]

KEARNEY, WILLIAM . . . . Nov. 30, 1831—Feb. 6, 1832.

To wife Sarah and Wm Kearney plantation on which testator lived, slaves, etc, At wife's death property to William. Furniture and stock of every description, etc., to her for life and then to be equally divided between children: James, William, Robert Morris, Susan, Sarah Bivins, and Ann Kearney, also 500 acres in Hopkins County, Kentucky. Lot in Shippingport to be equally divided among children: James, Robert Morris, Susan, Mary

Wells, Sarah Bivins and Ann Kearney. Sons John Kearney and William Kearney trustees to daughter Mary Wells for herself and children.
Executors: Sons John and William Kearney.
Witnesses: John H. Gibbs, David Farnsley.   [*B2, p463.*]

SALE, EDMUND . . . . . . Jan. 30, 1832—Feb. 6, 1832.
To brother William Sale in trust, estate, on following conditions: collect debts, rent out place on Turnpike road, from Louisville to Middletown, about four miles from Louisville, known as Sale's Tavern, hire slaves, sell personal property. Out of proceeds pay debts, and to brothers William, Lewis and Rich'd Sale and their heirs, one-third each. When selling property, before division, reserve a space 400 square feet for burial ground for three brothers and their children, to include grave of deceased wife. To niece, Mary Ann Barker, living with John Harding in Mississippi, a slave. To nephew Thomas Jefferson Sale, horse, etc. and watch.
Executor: Brother, William Sale.
Witnesses: Edw. S. Camp, Thomas Lawes, Levi Tyler. [*B2, p465.*]

TAYLOR, BENJAMIN . . . . July 28, 1831—Feb. 6, 1832.
Any money or property coming to him from Virginia to be divided equally in eight parts for Frank, Edmund, Reubin, Betsy, Jonathan, Jefferson and Sally, colored and formerly owned by testator but freed, except Sally who was born free, he having set her mother free. To nephew Benjamin, son of brother Reubin, the other eighth.
Executor: Benjamin Taylor.
Witnesses: Will D. S. Taylor, Jr., Robert M. Taylor. [*B2, p470.*]

WEIR, ANDREW . . . . . Jan. 10, 1832—Feb. 6, 1832.
Pay debts, residue of estate to wife, Martha R. Weir, for the raising and education of children.
Witnesses: Ch. Quirrey, James Barton Smith.   [*B2, p472.*]

SULLIVAN, JACOB . . . . . Apr. 6, 1832—May 7, 1832.
Desires to be buried by side of brother. His estate, three yoke of oxen and wagon, to Samuel Hopwell providing he pays debts. This in consideration of his care of testator.
Witnesses: Enoch Stout, Wm. G. O. Brien.   [*B2, p472.*]

SHAW, SAMUEL E. . . . . . [Not dated]—June 4, 1832.
Return to wife Catharine all the property, etc. he got by her on and after marriage. Executor to procure from M. D. Averill a gig and harness for wife, for $350. To brother James $500; to Samuel Shaw, son of David Shaw, $250., to be invested in land in some western non-slave holding state. Slave Frank to be sent to Liberia whenever his mother or any of his brothers and sisters, now owned by M. D. Averill, may be sent, or when he is twenty-one, if he is willing to go, expenses paid and $50., and if he will not go, is to be hired out for benefit of American Colonization Society, to which testator left money; to American Home Missionary and Sunday School Societies, certain money. His brother William Shaw of Newburyport being well provided for is not given part of this estate. Residue of estate to be divided among other brothers and sisters, the share of Mary, Sarah and Betsey to be held in trust by James Shaw for them and their children.
Executors: Nathaniel Hardy and Samuel Glass, Jr.
Witnesses: M[arvin] D. Averill, Heath Jones Miller. [*B2, p474.*]

GAILBREATH, JOSEPH . . . . Dec. 15, 1825—July 2, 1832.
To wife Rebecca all personal estate; to sons William, Robert, Alexander, $1. each, having previously given them their share; to son George the farm on which testator lived and at his mother's death, her dower right in it; to daughters Nancy, Rebecca, Mary, Sally and Eleanor, $1. each, they to live with their mother until they marry.
Executor: Son Alexander Gailbreath.
Witnesses: Samuel Gilmore, Joshua McCawley. [*B2, p476.*]

HITE, ABRAHAM . . . . . Oct. 5, 1831—Aug 6, 1832.
Land, 1190 acres, 400 of which was patented to James Sullivan, valued at $29,494. on Bardstown Road, plat made by Alexander Woodrow, Sr., to be divided into five parcels to son James and his wife, Nancy, to sons George, Isaac, Abraham and to daughter Katy Wynkoop. To daughter Harriet Funk 200 acres on Fern Creek known as saw mill tract. To daughter Rebecca 208 acres on south branch of South Fork of Beargrass where old Mr. Briscoe now lives, being undivided one-third conveyed testator by Joseph Hite, Jacob Hite and Robert Breckinridge as executors of Isaac Hite deceased. To sons George and Isaac and daughter Cathar-

ine and Rebecca certain furniture, stock, etc, the other children having been provided with same. All slaves to six of his children: George, Abraham, Isaac, Catharine, Harriet and Rebecca. Sons James, George, Abraham and Isaac and friend Robert Ormsby to be Trustees. Lands held in connection with Isaac and Joseph Hite, both deceased, to be divided by trustees. Requests that a tombstone or tombstones be erected over graves of his father and mother, with inscription of the age and time of decease on each tombstone.

Codicil, Feb. 2, 1832. To son Abraham 50 acres, part of 400 acres conveyed by Thomas Lewis, July 2, 1813; to Catharine W., Isaac, Harriet Funk, other parts of said tract.

Will proven by oaths of William Tompkins and Robert H. Grayson, Justices.   [*B2, p477.*]

HIKES, GEORGE, SR.   .   .   .   .   Oct. 19, 1825—Sept. 3, 1832.

[Signed in German.] To wife Barbara, one third in value of 250 acres on which he lived, money, etc.; to son Andrew other part of land, at $25. per acre; 30 acres in Indiana, in what was called Ilinois Grant on which Brother Jacob Hikes lives, at his death and balance of estate to children equally; eight and one-half acres, adjoining what he has, to son George.

Executors: Son Jacob Hikes and friend William Pope, Jr.

Witnesses: I. W. Thornbury, George Spears, Edmund P. Pope, Abraham Kellar, Worden Pope, Geo. W. Givin.

Codicil, Sept. 19, 1829. Should son Andrew object to taking land at valuation of $25. per acre, same to be sold and divided among children, equalizing his share, after death of wife Barbara.

Witnesses: Robert Tyler, Edmund P. Pope, John Kearney, D. T. Hardin.

Accounts referred to in will and filed with it bear names of Catharine Potorff, Jacob Hikes, George Hikes, Jr., John Hikes, Anna Cannon, Andrew Hikes and Elizabeth Gailbreath, his children.

William Pope and Jacob Hikes qualified as executors with John Hikes, Alex. H. Galbreath, and George Hikes as securities
                                                                        [*B2, p484.*]

LLEWELLYN, RICHARD   .   .   .   Dec. 20, 1829—Sept. 3, 1832.

To sons Jordon, John and Justinian certain slaves, and to Jordon and John and their survivors the residue of estate, to be held

342

in trust for use of daughter Eliza B., wife of Henry C. Dorsey.
Executors: Sons, Jordon and John Llewellyn.
Witnesses: S. S. Nicholas, Carver Mercer, William Pickett.

[*B2, p492.*]

WISE, PETER . . . . . . Apr. 17, 1832—Sept 3, 1832.

Estate, to wife Elizabeth during widowhood, for benefit of herself and children, and their education; to each of children, as they become of age, $65. except Susanna Brown, who has received hers. Wife to retain property in her possession until youngest child becomes of age.
Executor: Joseph A. Sweeney.
Witnesses: Eli Rose, George Rose. [*B2, p493.*]

GEIGER, FREDERICK . . . . Dec. 12, 1831—Sept. 3, 1832.

To wife Margaret, in addition to marriage settlement, a slave and furniture. Balance of estate to be divided in five parts and given one share each: to sons Jacob and Frederick, daughter Julian Hikes, the six children of daughter Nancy wife of John Edwards, (namely, Mary Ann wife of John Reinhard, Frederick, Montgomery, Benjamin, Franklin, John and Alfred Edwards), daughter Polly Turner wife of Robert Turner. Polly's fifth, if any left at her death, to go to her children Samuel and Peyton Wells. Certain old slaves not to be considered in division but to choose with which child they want to live.
Executors: Sons Jacob and Frederick Geiger, sons-in-law John Edwards and Jacob Hikes.
Witnesses: George Doup, Anna Heafer, Daniel Doup, Wm. Pope.

[*B2, p494.*]

BROWN, THOMAS . . . . . Apr. 28, 1832—Oct. 1, 1832.

To Judy, his wife, 100 acres, home place, belonging to Triplett's claim, also slaves, household furniture, etc. To children James, Edward, Thomas and Eliza, slaves, etc.
Executors: Judy and James Brown.
Witnesses: William Withers, Charles W. Field, Lucy Withers.

[*B2, p496.*]

McCONNELL, MARY ANN . . . July 17, 1832—Oct. 3, 1832.

Estate to youngest sister Elizabeth McConnell. Brother-in-law Angerean Gray to be guardian for sisters Elizabeth and Laura.
Executor: Angerean Gray.
Witnesses: Geo. Buchannan, Sam Dickinson. [*B2, p497.*]

READ, JAMES SENR. . . . . Apr. 7, 1829—Dec. 3, 1832.

To sons James and John land purchased from Conrad Wheat; each of above and son William to give their sister Isabella McCormick $100. To six children: William, James, John, Jane, Celia, and Polly, household furniture, slaves, etc., the latter not to be sold out of family, and mothers must not be separated from young children. Money due from Maryland to be equally divided among children. To Isaac Batman $1.00.

Executors: Sons William and James Read.

Witnesses: Zephania Wright, Wm. S. Rose, Elijah Adams.

William and James Read qualified and gave bond with Joseph A. Sweeney and Hezekiah Pounds as securities. [*B2, p498.*]

WATERS, RICHARD JONES . . . _ 30, 1788—Dec. 4, 1832.

To friend Thomas Nicholson fair settlement and accounting for articles, thirty or forty barrels of flour, dried peaches, apples, etc. sold for him in 1787, and great regard to be paid friend and partner David Broadhead for bill of sale testator took on his property. Gives details of business transactions and refers to further details in Diary and Memorandum Book of Richard Jones Waters & Co. To executors 300 pounds Virginia currency to buy slave boy, Tob, and establish him in business where his morals will be preserved, and executors to be guardian and protectors of him, and when he is forty years old to give him absolute deed of manumission. Three years after death, estate to be divided between brother Thomas Jones Waters and four sisters: Mary Waters, Jemima Jones Waters, Rachel James Waters and Ann Jones Waters.

Executors: John Hundley and Thomas Freeman.

Witnesses: R. Daniel, W. Payne, Christian Hondeberg.

By order of Court Jany. 20, 1834 (Chapter 261) Levi Jones withdrew original will of Richard Jones Waters from County Court of Jefferson.

Memo., Sept. 20, 1834, Wm. Pope will deliver to Adam Rankin, formerly of the Redbanks, the will of Richard Jones Waters and oblige Levi Jones, by Wm. Grundy, his agent. [Memo in jacket where original will should be.]

Proven by oaths of Stephen Ormsby and Robert Breckinridge.
[*B2, p499.*]

WHITLOCKE, GEORGE . . . . June 16, 1832—Sept 3, 1832.
Land in the Green River Country to be sold and proceeds to be used to secure a home for his family. All other property to wife during widowhood and the support of family. Should she marry an equal division to be made of estate including Lot No. 180.
Executor: Friend Frederick A. Kaye.
Witnesses: Phillip Myers, Henry Kaye.
Frederick A. Kaye qualified with Henry Kaye, James Harrison, Phillip Myers and Robert Buckner, securities. [*B2, p502.*]

LOVE, MATTHEW . . . . . Jan. 4, 1829—Dec. 3, 1832.
His 500 acres to be equally divided between children George R. Love and Rebecca Owen, except half acre for family burial ground. If not previously built, a stone wall to be built around the plot thirty feet square, and four feet high, with no opening, which would make the wall fall. Farming utensils, etc. and residue of estate to children: Eliza and husband Dr. R. P. Gist; Betsy wife of Dr. Nathl. Ragland, George R. Love and Rebecca Owen, except slaves Sally whom testator received through death of daughter Sally.
Executors: Sons-in-law R. P. Gist and Nathl. Ragland.
Will proven by oaths of Isaac Miller, Worden Pope and Patrick H. Pope. Executors qualified with Robert N. Miller, Abijah Bayless and Allen P. Elston as securities. [*B2, p503.*]

DYE, STEPHEN W. . . . . . Nov. 8, 1832—Dec. 6, 1832.
To wife Eliza H. Dye, all overplus due on accounts, notes, etc., also $800. from estate on Jan. 1, 1833. The residue to be equally divided among children.
Executor: Father-in-law James Plem [Plew?].
Witnesses: Richard M. Bell, Peter Cox. [*B2, p505.*]

RAY, PATRICK . . . . ____, 1832—Jan. 7, 1833.
Nuncupative Will. Pilot of Steamer Tippecanoe, resident of Louisville, but died in New Orleans, Oct. 24, 1832, of Cholera. Pilot on Mississippi and Ohio rivers. Estate to brother David Ray, so stated in the presence of John A. Lake and Mr. Summers, the latter of New Orleans.
Executor: John A. Lake.
Will proven by oaths of John A Lake and Edward M. Smith, who stated Patrick Ray was about twenty-five years of age.

[Note: An unfinished indenture between Thomas R. and his wife Frances B. Parent and Marthara R. Wier, dated November 20, 1831, with no mention of any of above parties in the body of same, but marked on back "Patrick Rays nuncupation will," is filed in the Ray Will envelope.]   [*B2, p505.*]

WELLS, SAMUEL G. . . . . . Nov. 12, 1832—Feb. 4, 1833.
Brother Yelverton Peyton Wells to sell enough of out-of-state land, Kentucky, Indiana and Ohio, to pay debts; to mother Mary Turner, for life, personal estate including slaves. At her death to his said brother.
Executors: Brother Yelverton Peyton Wells and Jacob Geiger.
Witnesses: Wm. Pope, Wm. M. Anderson, Larz Anderson.
[*B2, p507.*]

FARNSLEY, DAVID . . . . Feb. 5, 1833.
Nuncupative Will. Died Jan. 15, 1833. Wife Sarah to control property for maintenance and education of children, until they marry or become of age. Should son-in-law David Phillips, and Mary his wife, want their share, testator's wife to have one-third of personal estate, including slaves and the plantation, until death, then all to be equally divided among children.
Sworn to by John P. Tunstall and Ebenezer Williams.
On February 4, 1833, Sarah Farnsley accepted above as will of David Farnsley. She qualified as executor with David Merriwether, John P. Tunstall and David Phillips as her securities.
[*B2, p508.*]

APPLEGATE, JOSEPH . . . . Feb. 23, 1833—Mar. 4, 1833.
To son Thomas the house and lot on Jefferson St., corner of Tenth, where testator lived. To wife Mary and son Thomas the residue of estate in trust for the use of family. At wife's death same to be equally divided among children, giving Thomas his share in addition to house and lot.
Executors: Thomas Applegate and Mary Applegate.
Witnesses: Garnett Duncan, John M. Talbott, W[illiam] C. Galt.
Executors qualified with Elisha Applegate as security.
[*B2, p510.*]

MERRIWEATHER, VALENTINE W. . Sept. 20, 1832—Mar. 4, 1833.
Executrix to sell land purchased from William Pope, adjoining lands of Sam'l Churchill and Ewell Shipp, and pay purchase money due Pope and all other debts. Balance with residue of estate, including house and lot south side of Walnut St., between Sixth and Seventh, to Lucy Ann, his wife.
Executrix: Wife Lucy Ann Meriweather.
Witnesses: Sam Dickinson, Shapley Owen.   [*B2, p511.*]

SHIPPEN, EDWARD   .   .   .   . Dec. 21, 1832—May 6, 1833.
Died Dec. 23, 1832. In presence of B. R. McIlvaine, the above named, stated he wanted, with a few exceptions, all of his estate to go to his mother for life and at her death to her children equally. To Mrs. Barney, his furniture; to Miss Adelle Barney $100, and a breast-pin; to Mrs. McIlvaine, a watch; to each of her children a suit of clothes; to Daniel Fetter, Junr., horse, saddle and bridle.
Signed and sworn to by B. R. McIlvaine and Geo C. Gwathmey.   [*B2, p512.*]

FINE, JACOB   .   .   .   .   .   . Sept. 2, 1831—June 3, 1833.
To son Wm. R. and daughter Margaret E. Fine, each a negro woman. To grandson John Burks, son of Samuel Burks, one share in Shelbyville and Louisville Turnpike Road Co. To wife Lucy for life, the residue of estate, and at her death, slaves to above mentioned children and to grandson John Burks, under age; balance of estate to children. Children to give a comfortable living to slave Milly, who is to be emancipated at his wife's death.
Executors: Wife and son William R. Fine.
Witnesses: Basil N. Hobbs, L. F. C. Dashiele, W[illiam] S. Thomas, Jos. S. Morris.
[Note: In original will, grandson John Burks is given as "son of Samuel Burks," but this is omitted in the transcribed copy.]
                    [*B2, p513.*]

PURYEAR, HEZEKIAH .   .   .   . Apr. 19, 1833—June 3, 1833.
To son Daniel G. Puryear a slave and twenty shares in Louisville Marine Insurance Company; to Joseph P. Puryear the negro hired to C. Whittingham; to wife Edocia slaves left to her by her grandfather, John Guerrant of Goochland County, Virginia, and

the place on which they lived with everything on it; to two grand-daughters, Mary Jane and Susan Ann Pleasants, daughters of Daniel G. Pleasants of Bowling Green, the balance of negroes and thirty-five shares in the Louisville Marine Insurance Co.
Executor: Joseph P. Puryear.
Witnesses: John K. Clark, Edwin B. Dean.   [*B2, p515.*]

POMEROY, FRANCIS   .   .   .   .   Aug. 4, 1829—Aug. 8, 1833.
    Sell estate, and of proceeds, one-third part to wife Elizabeth, for life, and at her death that to be equally divided among children; to grandson John Francis Elloway, son of daughter Priscilla, $60.; to daughter Sarah, wife of Samuel Peck, $50.; balance of estate to be equally divided among children: Polly, wife of John Clayton; Katharine, wife of John Thompson; Nelly, wife of David McDaniel; Elizabeth, wife of John Acres; and Priscilla, and to the last named all property that is known to be hers.
Executor: James Pomeroy.
Witnesses: Isaac Holt, William C. Seaton, John Rosberry, Kenner S. Whitaker, Bartholomew Elensworth, Allen Rose.
    Codicil. July 1, 1833. Daughter Sarah, wife of Samuel Peck, to have an equal part with the rest of children.
Witnesses: Kenner S. Whitaker, Bartholomew Elensworth, Allen Rose.   [*B2, p516.*]

WHITE, LEE . . . . —Aug. 9, 1833.
    To wife Susan Ann White for life all property and interests he may be entitled to through their marriage, and also his four-story ware-house and lot on Wall Street, Louisville, for life, and at her death to be divided among her children, Mary, Howard and Elias. Slaves to be emancipated provided they will go to Liberia through the American Colonization Society. To Lee Athy 20 acre lot; Transylvania property to William Lee White and all money he owes testator. Property in Natchez to be sold to pay debts. Goose Creek property to Lawrence and Eliza J. Young, on condition they pay his executors $25,000. Sums ranging from $500. to $4000. to the following: Jane M. Gates and her children; Catharine White's three children; Sarah K. Rumsay and children; Nancy Athy and her children; Ruth Vance; Elinora [Elmira?] W. Elston and Geo. W. White; Wm Lee and Elinora White; Charles Lee Beeler; testator's mother; Lewis Lee Hite and

Uncle Daniel Hite, for enclosing graves and erecting tombs, etc. over graves of father and grandmother; Miss Harriet Hobbs; and for graveyard on testator's farm in which he wishes to be buried. *Executors:* Leaven Lawrence, Lawrence Young and Robert W. Glass.
Witnesses: L. M. Mosby, H. G. Smith, R. P. Gist.

Executors qualified with Leaven Lawrence, John Williamson, Edmund T. Bainbridge and Samuel C. Blackburn securities.

[B2, p517.]

MORRIS, PATRICK . . . . . July 11, 1833—Sept. 2, 1833.

To wife Catharine interest in house in which he lived erected on ground leased from Levi Tyler, and stable erected on ground leased from Dr. William Croghan, fronting on Market Street, and personal property.
Executor: Wife Catharine.
Witnesses: Mart. Murphy, James Raverty, Hugh Murphy.

[B2, p519.]

TRUEMAN, WALTER . . . . Apr. 16, 1833,—Sept. 2, 1833.

To wife Mary Ann certain slaves, furniture and farm supplies debt due him by William Sanders, and the City of Louisville, or property owners on Jefferson Street between 10th and 11th Streets for grading. To son Edward, debts due him by Owen Robay of Bullitt County, and from Col. Thompson of Nelson County; to daughters Lucinda, Harriet, Eveline Adams, Elizabeth and Minerva, certain slaves. To above named and children Ann, Ellen, Sarah Ann, Henry, Barilla and Cordelia, equally a debt due him for grading Jefferson Street between 11th and 12th Streets. To son Thomas Trueman, residing with brother John in Hardin County, $100.
Executor: Wife Mary Ann.
Witnesses: Thomas Q. Wilson, Elisha Applegate.   *[B2, p521.]*

PHILLIPS, DAVID . . . . . July 29, 1833—Sept. 2, 1833.

Pay debts and residue of estate, including property he was entitled to out of the late David Farnsley's estate by testator's inter-marriage with Mary; to wife Mary Phillips, also part of the crops now growing on the "late David Farnsley's plantation" to be divided by persons chosen by executor and her mother Sarah Farnsley.

349

Executor: Wife Mary Phillips.
Witnesses: John Hughes, Ebenezer Williams.

Mary Phillips qualified and gave bond with John Tunstall as security. [*B2, p522.*]

BLANKENBAKER, SAMUEL . . July 17, 1833—Sept. 2, 1833.

To wife for life one-half of property on Jefferson and Hand-cock streets, and at her death to son William Frederick; the other half to pay debts; of above named property on Jefferson Street, about twenty-six feet belonged to his brother Thomas. Should son die without issue, his share to testator's sister Mary.
Executors: James and Jeremiah Blankenbaker his brothers.
Witnesses: B. Raverty, John Lang, Gottlieb Kril, John Zeigler, John Hawes.

James Blankenbaker qualified with Jacob Newkirk as security; Jeremiah renounced execution. [*B2, p523.*]

MASSIE, NANCY . . . . . Aug. 8, 1833—Sept 2, 1833.

Signed and recorded as Ann Massie. To niece Ann James of Ohio and her brother Nathaniel James $20. each, for mourning rings. Residue of estate to niece Sharlott James, residing with testator who reared her.
Executors: Brother-in-law Thomas James of Ohio and William L. Thompson of Jefferson County.
Witnesses: William C. Bullitt, Helen Massie, Robert N. Smith.
[*B2, p524.*]

ELLINGSWORTH, THOMAS . . . July 6, 1833—Sept. 2, 1833.

To wife Amelia during widowhood the home plantation and balance of estate. Should she marry, she is to receive only her lawful share; at death or marriage of wife, personal estate to be divided as follows: to children Bartholomey, Elizabeth Thorn, William, Charles, $1.00 each, balance to four children, Ann Stubbens, Charlotte, Katharine and Lucy Ellingsworth. Proceeds of farm to be equally divided between son Littleton and daughter Lucy until she marries or dies, then her share to Littleton and his heirs.
Executor: Friend and neighbor Thomas Waller.
Witnesses: Benoni S. Lackland, Thomas Waller. [*B2, p525.*]

BRECKINRIDGE, ROBERT . . . Sept. 7, 1833—Oct. 7, 1833.
To children of Henry B. Breckinridge one half of estate; the other half to James D. Breckinridge in trust for his daughter Eliza. To Mrs. Henry B. Breckinridge, slaves and the house on Market Street in which she lives; the adjoining house to her daughter Margaret when she marries or comes of age.
Executor: James D. Breckinridge.
Witnesses: W. C. Galt, Richm'd Wautyn, Margaret Kopman.
Codicil. The half estate devised to children of H. B. Breckinridge, now given to Mrs. Maria Breckinridge in trust for their use. Certain slaves to be freed. Signed Robt. Breckinridge, by R. Wautyn.
Witnesses: Richm'd Wautyn, W. C. Galt.
Proven to be will of General Robert Breckinridge. [*B2, p527.*]

HUSTON, WILLIAM I. . . . . Mar. 2, 1833—Nov. 4, 1833.
To daughters, Amelia, eldest, and Henrietta, house and lot adjoining Middletown; to son Joseph and daughter Mary Ann each a watch; residue of estate equally to daughters Mary Ann and Henrietta.
Witnesses: Stephen Black, Hiram Cassell, William Pomeroy.
[*B2, p528.*]

TURNER, ROBERT . . . . . Sept 11, 1833—Nov. 4, 1833.
All wills, particularly one in custody of James Guthrie, Esq., of Louisville, hereby set aside.
Witnesses: Alijah Bayles, and Isaac Gracy, alias Graves.
[*B2, p529.*]

KALFUS, HENRY FREDERICK . Nov. 17, 1831—Nov. 5, 1833.
To daughters Elizabeth Field, of Illinois, and daughter Margaret Ann McHatton and the infant children of his deceased daughter Lucinda Hite, certain slaves and balance of slaves to all heirs equally. To wife for life part of home and maintenance; to son James the tanyard rent free for five years, he to remain on and work plantation; he with his sister Mary Ann to have balance of house until place is sold. At wife's death, plantation to be sold and equally divided among all his heirs, after deducting advances made to sons Simon N., Henry, James, and to each of his daughters.

Executors: James F. and Jacob W. Kalfus.
Witnesses: John R. Moore, Samuel Frederick, Jun.
Executors gave bond with James McHatton, John B. Kalfus, Jeremiah L. Kalfus and Simeon N. Kalfus as securities. [*B2, p530.*]

TULEY, ELIZABETH . . . . Nov. 7, 1833—Dec. 2, 1833.
Nuncupative Will. Negroes to be sold for benefit of heirs, but to remain in county. To daughter-in-law Jane Tuley, daughter Linton and grandson Mils D. Tuley, furniture.
Executor: Thomas Elliott.
Witnesses: Tho. Elliott, Margaret Cooper, Francis P. Elliott.
Codicil, unsigned and without date. Cows to Mrs. Terriel, Jane Tuley and two grand-daughters, Eliz Wicks and Hellen Maria Crook.
Witnesses: Tho. Elliott.
Dec. 2, 1833. This will produced in Court and proved to be the nuncupative will and testament of Elizabeth Tuley, deceased, by oaths of Thomas Elliott; Attest, Worden Pope, Clerk.
[*B2, p532.*]

CROGHAN, CHARLES . . . . Jan. 1, 1832—Dec. 3, 1833.
To sister Mrs. Jessup, property and money due from Mr. Underwood and brother-in-law Mr. Hancock. To children of brother Col. Croghan, real estate including farm six miles above Louisville in which Mrs. Hancock, his sister, is to have life time interest. To brother Dr. Croghan, his servants.
Will proven by oaths of Charles McLoder and William Tompkins. [*B2, p533.*]

McFARLAN, PATRICK . . . Aug. 22, 1822—Dec. 11, 1833.
To wife Rosanna for life or widowhood, estate for the support of herself, testator's step-daughter, Mary Ann McNutt, daughters Elizabeth and Jane McFarlan, and for the education of last named. At wife's death, estate to be equally divided between said daughters and step-daughter, or should wife marry, she to have only one-third and daughters and step-daughter aforesaid two-thirds.
Executor: Wife Rosanna McFarlan.
Witnesses: Isaac H. Tyler, Elisha Applegate, Benjamin Dunn.
[*B2, p534.*]

ORMSBY, ROBERT . . . . __, 1833—Dec. 3, 1833.
Pay debts out of income of estate. Realize on interests in firm of Chambers, Garvin & Co., and pay notes due brother-in-law, William Crawford, Jr., and note given by deceased brother George Ormsby and self to Thomas C. Rockhill [Pockhill?]. To wife, in lieu of dower, all household goods, personal property, slaves, pew in Christ Church, Louisville, liquors and wines, and $2500. annually for life; at her death, the capital of this annuity to be equally divided among the children of deceased brother George Ormsby when the youngest reaches lawful age. To sister-in-law, Elinor Ormsby, widow of brother George, for widowhood, 165 acres known as Cedar Hill estate, with all buildings, etc. Should she marry or die, same to her children, Henrietta, Mary, George, Robert and Collis Ormsby, and their heirs, providing said land is not sold until the youngest child becomes of age. To niece Eliza Ormsby wife of Rev. David C. Page, Rector of Christ Church, Louisville, land purchased from Benjamin Cawthon, June, 1833. Residue of my estate to children, should I have one, if not to my deceased brother George's children equally, when males reach age of twenty-five years.
Executors: Wife, brother-in-law, William Crawford, Jr., of Baltimore, and friend Abraham Hite.
Witnesses: Elisha Athy, Wm. Garvin, Wm. Fellows. [*B2, p536.*]

CALENDAR OF BOND AND POWER OF ATTORNEY BOOK No. 1, JEFFERSON COUNTY, KENTUCKY, 1783–1798

By Ludie J. Kinkead and Katharine G. Healy

In Three Parts

Part One: November, 1783–December, 1788.

Introduction. Among the many documentary sources of interest to historians and genealogists are the various court records. The volumes most frequently searched by investigators are the Will Books and the Minute Books. Some of the other court records are also of importance. Among the lesser known and less frequently investigated volumes are the Bond and Power of Attorney Books. The Filson Club, in its History Quarterly has published Jefferson County Minute Books A and No. 1, also a calendar of Jefferson County Will Books No. 1 and No. 2, and thereby made the contents of these early official records more available to students.

The entries in the early Bond and Power of Attorney Books contain much valuable material. A calendar of Bond and Power of Attorney Book No. 1 is here presented. It extends from 1783 to 1798. Practically every entry, whether pertaining to a bond, power of attorney or other similar transaction, throws some sidelights on genealogy or history. In many instances the record designates from what place the person mentioned came before settling in Kentucky and where he was living in Jefferson County at the time the legal document was drawn. Should the searcher desire more details than given in this calendar he can readily locate the original entry in the original book in the Jefferson County courthouse. The notation at the end of the calendared item shows the number of the book—which in this case is Book 1—followed by the page on which the entry begins.

It must be borne in mind that Kentucky was a part of Virginia until June, 1792, when it became an independent state. It must also be borne in mind that from 1780 to 1784 that part of Virginia known as the District of Kentucky was divided into three counties: Jefferson, Fayette, and Lincoln. Then came Nelson County, formed in 1784, and Bourbon, Mercer, and Madison counties in 1785. Others followed, and by the close of the year 1798 the three original counties were divided into thirty-eight counties. Kentucky now has 120 counties, twenty-eight of which were formed entirely or partly out of what was originally Jefferson County territory. Up to June, 1792, Jefferson County is designated in these records as a county in the state of Virginia or in the District of Kentucky, State of Virginia. This often repeated phrase is omitted in this calendar, except in a few instances where it is retained as a reminder. Most entries are followed by a statement to the effect that the original document was taken out of or withdrawn from the files.

The Minute Books of the Jefferson County Court, beginning with No. 1, contain a brief notation of each bond and power of attorney item, usually followed by a memorandum that it was ordered recorded—that is ordered recorded in the Bond and Power of Attorney Book. Its predecessor, Minute Book A, however, includes in its entries, apparently in full, all items that pertain to the subject of bond and power of attorney. The transcribed copy of Minute Book A (published in THE FILSON CLUB HISTORY QUARTERLY, 1929), extends from March, 1781, to September, 1783.

As stated in the Introduction to the printed presentation of Jefferson County Minute Book No. 1 (published in THE FILSON CLUB HISTORY QUARTERLY, 1932), there is an intermission extending from the end of Minute Book A, September, 1783, to the beginning of Minute Book No. 1, April, 1784, of which no minutes have been found. This lost omission is represented by the first two entries in Bond and Power of Attorney Book No. 1. The third of these entries is noted in Minute Book No. 1, April Court, 1784, and is the first entry of this character in that volume. It appears under the proceedings of April 8, 1784.

All minute book entries, as stated before, are brief. In preparing this calendar of Bond and Power of Attorney Book No. 1 an effort has been made to present the important items and all

---

*See pp. 88-89, this volume.

names occuring in the record, also to follow the spelling of names as they there appear.

"I do assign over all my Right title and claim in all land comeing to me from for serving as a soldier in the Illinois Regiment to Joseph Sanders his heirs or assigns forever for value received. Witness my hand at Fort, 10th February, 1783. Richard Loell. Witnesses present: R. Clark, M. Miles.

"Jefferson County Sct. November Court, 1783. The foregoing assignment from Richard Loell to Joseph Sanders was fully proven by the oaths of the subscribing witnesses and admitted to record.

"*Teste:* Will Johnston, C. Jeff. Ct. [Marginal note:] Original taken out of the office."   [*B. 1, 1st entry.*]

George Hartt, of Lincoln Co., Virginia [now Kentucky], about to explore and locate lands in the western parts of North Carolina, in behalf of himself and company, the lands to be divided between Hartt and his company, binds himself to convey to John Donne 1000 acres of his share of the located land. Mar. 5, 1784. *Witnesses:* Isaac Williams, Robert Sper, William Walker. Recorded, April Court, 1784.   [*B1, p1.*]

Robert Elliott, of Bedford Co., Penn, Jan. 19, 1784, appoints his friend James Elliott, merchant of Philadelphia, to sell in Robert Elliott's name, a settlement and preemption of 1400 acres and 1100 acres on the south side of Clear Creek in Jefferson Co., Virginia [now Kentucky].
Witnesses: Will Johnston, George Walls.
January 24, 1784, James Elliott is also given the power to sell and convey for Robert Elliott one-half part of a settlement of 400 acres at the junction of the Kentucky and the Ohio rivers, also the preemption of 1000 acres adjoining his settlement on the eastwardly and southwardly sides, which land Robert was entitled to by a certificate of a Court for Fayette County, Jan. 13, 1784. *Witnesses:* Robt. George, J. Donne. Recorded April Court, 1784.
                                                          [*B1, p2.*]

Daniel Brodhead, Jr., Falls of Ohio, Jan. 15, 1784, in consideration of forty-two pounds lawful money of Virginia, binds himself to James Wilkinson for the safe arrival at the landing of this

port certain merchandise, valued at 700 pounds Virginia costs, on board a boat in the Ohio River under command of Capt. Abner Dunn, and daily expected to arrive, and if lost this sum to be paid to James Wilkinson, six months from day on which the said loss shall be certainly ascertained. This obligation to James Wilkenson to have the same tone, validity and effect in law as if it were a formal policy of insurance.
Witnesses: B. Tardivean, William Clark. Recorded April Court, 1784.   *[B1, p4.]*

Dan Brodhead, Jr., Falls of Ohio, Jan. 15, 1784, for twenty-five pounds Virginia money, binds himself to James Armstrong for the safe arrival at the landing of this port of 500 pounds Virginia cost of merchandise now on board a boat on the Ohio River under command of Capt. Abner Dunn. This obligation is to be of the same validity in law as a formal policy of insurance.
Witnesses: B. Tardiveau, W. Clark. Recorded April Court, 1784.
[B1, p5.]

James Purvis, Wm. Pope and Wm. Oldham of Jefferson Co. bind themselves in the sum of 1000 pounds specie currency money of Virginia, March 10, 1784, to grant to James Dunlap on or before the 20th of March next, 500 acres first-rate land and 500 acres equal to second-rate land, in Jefferson Co., not to exceed ten miles either from Brashears Creek or Salt River, being part of 5000 acres of a 10,000 acre claim of said Purvis.
Witnesses: Wm. Meriwether, Will Johnston. Recorded April Court, 1784.   *[B1, p6.]*

James Patten, Benjamin Pope, William Roberts and James Purvis, give bond, Feb. 11, 1784, for £4000 Virginia money to convey within one year good title to Wilkinson, Armstrong, Dunn & Co. for 3000 acres of first-class land and 4500 acres of second-rate land as well watered and timbered as lands commonly are in the county within thirty miles of the Ohio Falls and within two miles of Ohio river or else on the waters of Brashears Creek.
Witnesses: Wm. Orr, Josh Blake. Recorded April Court, 1784.
[B1, p7.]

John Eastwood of Jefferson Co., gives bond unto Benja. Netherland of Fayette Co., Virginia [now Kentucky], for £1000, to

make a good deed to a 900 acre tract surveyed March 8, 1781, obtained by a Treasury Warrant No. 3132, issued February 29, 1780, to the said Benja. Netherland, or if the right of Virginia is not valid, Eastwood is not bound to perform this bond. Sept. 29, 1783.
Witnesses: Robt. Floyd, John Sanders. Recorded May Court, 1784. [*B1, p8.*]

John Decker [Deckert?] of Jefferson Co., July 7, 1784, sold to Moses Henry, of St. Vincennes on Wabash River, negro girl, Poll, who was recently purchased from Jeremiah Claypoole of Hampshire Co.
Witnesses: William Johnston, Andrew Heth. Recorded July Court, 1784. [*B1, p9.*]

Moses Henry sells to James Sullivan of Jefferson Co., July 7, 1784, a negro girl, Poll.
Witnesses: Will Johnston, And'w Heth. Recorded July Court, 1784. [*B1, p10.*]

James Sullivan sells to William Johnston, Sr., of Jefferson Co., July 7, 1784, a negro girl, Poll. Acknowledged in open Court. Recorded July Court, 1784. [*B1, p10.*]

Michael Dennis of Jefferson Co. on Aug. 4, 1784, appointed Capt. James Morrison, of Westmoreland Co., Pennsylvania, his lawful attorney with power to take possession of all his landed property in Westmoreland, to sell same, to sue for, levy and recover all debts due Dennis in Pennsylvania or elsewhere. Recorded August Court, 1784. [*B1, p11.*]

Moses Henry, of St. Vincents on the Wabash, owning 300 acres of land on the Monongolia River, obtained in consequence of application to John Lukens, Surveyor General of Pennsylvania, dated at Philadelphia, May 9, 1769,—see order of survey No. 3211 from Robert Dill for said Lukens,—to be surveyed in Cumberland County on east side of said River, including his improvements by consent of Maj. Murray, appoints John Campbell of Jefferson County, his attorney to dispose of all above mentioned land. Dated July 17, 1784.
Witnesses: Will Johnston, Richard C. Anderson, James Reed. Recorded August Court, 1784. [*B1, p12.*]

John Montgomery and Martin Carney of Jefferson Co. give bond unto Lawrence Protzman, Frederic Rover [Rorer?] and Nathaniel Morgan of Washington County, Maryland, to convey to them the first 500 acre lot of the property or claim of Capt. Edward Worthington in the Illinois Grant. Aug. 3, 1784. *Witnesses:* James Patten, John Dorrett, Abra. Wells. Recorded October 6, 1784.   [*B1, p13.*]

Bartlett Searcey of Fayette Co., and George R. Clark of Jefferson Co., give bond to Lawrence Protzman, Frederick Rover and Nathaniel Morgan of Washington Co., Md. to convey to them 400 acres first-rate land in Fayette Co. on the Seven Mile Creek which empties into the Ohio River about ten miles below the mouth of Licking Creek. August 3, 1784. *Witnesses:* Richard Brashear, James Harrod, Sr. Recorded October 6, 1784.   [*B1, p14.*]

Valentine Thomas Dalton of Illinois Grant and William Clark, both of Clarksville, give bond to Lawrence Protzman, Frederick Rorer [Rover] and Nathaniel Morgan of Jefferson Co. The conditions are that Dalton and Clark are to convey to Protzman, Rorer and Morgan 500 acres of land on the Illinois Grant, being said Dalton's first choice of four lots in said Grant as soon as the same shall be surveyed. When this is done the above obligation is void. [Signatures look like F. F. Dalton, W. Clark.] Sept. 8, 1784. *Witnesses:* John Sanders, Elizabeth Reager. Recorded October 6, 1784.   [*B1, p15.*]

John Tebbs, William Pope, James Patten and Mark Thomas of Jefferson Co. give bond to Lawrence Protzman, Frederick Rorer and Nathaniel Morgan of Washington Co., Md. to convey to them, on or before February first next, 500 acres of land on Bank Lick Creek in Fayette Co., being part of a 15,000 acre survey made for Thomas Young and John Tebbs as tenants in common, being part of a 3250 acre tract. Aug. 5, 1784. *Witnesses:* John Dorrett, Jacob Myers, Martin Carney. Recorded October 6, 1784.   [*B1, p17.*]

Philemon Waters gives bond to Gab'l J. Johnston to convey to Johnston one lot, in Louisville, No. 125. *Witnesses:* Will Johnson, George Wilson.   October 7, 1784.   Recorded October 7, 1784.   [*B1, p18.*]

William Aldridge of Lincoln Co. obliges himself to transfer to Daniel Sullivan 400 acres, pre-emption warrant issued in the name of Adam Pain, on Bull Skin about six miles above the Forks, being a branch of Brashears Creek. October 6, 1784.
Witness: John Maitland. Recorded October 7, 1784.
Original taken out of the office by Samuel Lampton, attorney for Daniel Sullivan. [*B1, p20.*]

Contract between Thomas Tuke and John Carr, Nov. 23, 1783. Thomas Tuke makes good his title to a settlement and pre-emption entitled to him by Fayette Court, 1783. The condition is that if Tuke's right and title is not lawful to said tract, Tuke is to make good his right to any other place in Fayette County or either of the other counties in Kentucky. Signed Thos. Tuke. Oct. 6, 1784. John Carr assigns to Daniel Sullivan all his rights in the above obligation for value received.
Teste: John Handley, James Reid. Recorded October 7, 1784.
Original taken out of the office by Col. Campbell, att'y for Daniel Sullivan. [*B1, p20.*]

James Stevenson and Sarah his wife grant to Moses Spear of Jefferson Co. four head of horn cattle and thirteen head of hogs. Nov. 4, 1784.
Witnesses: Thomas McCarty, Nichlas McCarty. Deed of gift recorded November Court, 1784. [*B1, p21.*]

James Stevenson of Jefferson Co. sells to Edward Matthews of the same place one sorrel horse to guarantee him against an execution issuing out of Court of Common Pleas at Jefferson Co.
Witnesses: A. Rowan, Jonas Scoggin, Thos. McCarty, Thos. Spence. Recorded November Court, 1784. [*B1, p21.*]

William Christy of Jefferson Co. appoints his friend George Wilson, Gentleman, of same county, his attorney with full power. Nov. 14, 1784.
Witnesses: Will Johnston, Betsey Johnston. Recorded December Court, 1784. [*B1, p21.*]

James Southall, Williamsburg, letter of attorney to George Sclaster, Esq., Falls of Ohio, dated June 24, 1704, [1784?] sending description of land and copy of three deeds, also an old plot from

Mr. Douglas, pasted together so as to be of advantage in finding the two tracts of land which lie near the Toocemay [?] Springs, with owner's name mentioned on each survey. He states Mr. Douglas also says that John Tood [Todd] and W. Hight are well acquainted with the lands and deeds of his lands at the Falls, etc. March Court, 1785, this letter of attorney, on motion of George Slaughter, was admitted to record. [*B1, p21.*]

James Kirby and James Earickson of Queen Ann Co., Md., appoint Samuel Kirby of same county and state, their lawful attorney to receive all debts due from any persons of any part of the Western country called and known by the name of Kentucky, and to act in their stead in all legal matters and transfers. October 18, 1784.
Witness: Benjamin Earickson. Recorded April Court, 1785.
[*B1, p22.*]

Richard Chenewith and Mark Thomas of Jefferson Co. and Alexander Keith of Nelson Co. give bond unto Thomas Hughes of Washington Co., Pa., to convey to Thomas Hughes 400 acres of land on the North Fork of Licking Creek in Fayette Co., Hughes to have third choice out of 8000 acre survey.
Witnesses: Thomas Johnston, Jonathan Harrod, Absalom Vanmetre. Recorded April Court, 1785. [*B1, p23.*]

Richard Chenewith and Mark Thomas of Jefferson Co. and Alexander Keith of Nelson Co. give bond unto Charles and Richard Swan of Washington Co., Pa., to make good a deed to Charles and Richard Swan for 1000 acres of land on the North Fork of Licking Creek in Fayette Co. part of an 8000 acre survey 2nd rate land. If deed cannot be made good on Licking, then like amount in Fayette or Jefferson Co., same distance from Ohio. April 1, 1785.
Witnesses: Thomas Johnston, Jonathan Harrod, Absalom Vanmetre. Recorded April Court, 1785. [*B1, p24.*]

Agreement between Robert Daniel and Richard Jones Waters, both of Jefferson Co. Daniel is to sell to Waters 1000 acres of land, part of a 5000 or 6000 acre survey which Daniel has right and title to on Ohio River near the Big Bone, at rate of £25 per 100 acres Virginia currency, to be surveyed in two tracts of 500 acres each, not to adjoin each other, and deed to be made out with a clause of warranty against claims "from the beginning of the world up to time of conveyance." For this Waters obligates himself to pay certain money on the following articles: flour at 30 shillings per 100; whiskey at 6 shillings per gallon; shrub at 10 shillings per quart; castings at 1 shilling 3 pence per lb.; bar-iron at 1 shilling 3 pence per lb. The money is to be paid by the fall boating in 1786 and 1787; if not in money, then in aforesaid articles. Feb. 14, 1785.

Witnesses: Benjamin Earickson, Stephen Smith. Recorded April Court, 1785.   [*B1, p26.*]

Agreement between William Johnston and R. J. Waters, both of Jefferson Co. Johnston has sold to Waters 5000 acres of land in Jefferson Co., on Green River, being part of a survey of 37,216 acres made in the name of Johnston as assignee of Henry Banks. The 5000 acres are to be laid off after 12,784 acres mentioned prior are surveyed, and good official deeds with a clause of warranty given up to date of conveyance "from the beginning of the world." For this Waters is to pay at rate of 7 pounds 10 shillings specie Virginia currency per 100 acres, or merchantable articles, as may be agreed upon. Payment to be made within next four years, but if Waters cannot do this, he is to have three more years in which to make settlement. Feb. 11, 1785.

Witnesses: James Winn, Francis Adams. Feb. 12, 1785. Received of Richard J. Waters certain money. Will Johnston. Recorded April Court, 1785.   [*B1, p27.*]

Jacob Reager gives bond to Patrick Joyes, both of Jefferson Co. that he has sold to Patrick Joyes one lot in Louisville, No. 54, which he warrants from all claims "or in case the act relative to the establishment of the Town should be any ways repealed," then Reager binds himself to return the purchase money of this lot. November 4, 1784.

Witnesses: Andrew Heath, Jacob Peyatt. Recorded April Court, 1785.
Original delivered to Thomas Joyes July 17, 1819.   [*B1, p29.*]

Agreeable to bond of James Elliott, Louisville, to George Wilson for the conveyance of 1100 acres of land, the property of

Robert Elliott in Jefferson Co.—see power of attorney from Robert Elliott to James Elliott—James Elliott is to pay all expenses, and, by said Wilson's bond to him, Wilson is to reconvey to James Elliott one-half of said 1100 acres which James Dunlap and James Elliott have been bargaining for at a certain price; and if he does not take it, George Wilson is authorized to dispose of the said one-half. If a patent for the 1100 acres is obtained before James Elliott's arrival in Kentucky, George Wilson is to act as his attorney. May 18, 1784.
Witnesses: John Hundley. Recorded May Court, 1785.[*B1, p30.*]

Henry Banks of Richmond, appoints his friends Philip Barbour and William Johnston of Jefferson Co. his attorney to sue for all debts due him in District of Kentucky or in the country adjacent thereto, and to sell and convey all his lands whether obtained by purchase, by location of a Treasury Warrant, or by a military claim. Feby. 14, 1785.
Witness: Jno. Rogers. Recorded May Court, 1785.   [*B1,p31.*]

John Robinson of Washington Co., Pa., appoints Andrew Heth of Jefferson Co. his attorney to collect debts.
Witnesses: Phil. Barbour, Thos. Spencer. Recorded August Court, 1785.   [*B1, p31.*]

John Holker, of the Township of the Northern Libertins, Philadelphia, Pa., appoints John Rice Jones of Philadelphia as his lawful attorney to settle all accounts with Bartholomew Tardiveau, the elder, of Kentucky District in Virginia, and by all lawful means demand all debts due him, and convey in his name to his heirs all lots, etc. to which he is entitled by location, preemption right, warrant, survey, patent, deed or otherwise, in any place, county, etc., westward of the Alleghaney Mountains in the State of Virginia or as far as the line of the boundary of the United States runs.
Witnesses: Meers Fisher, Charles Vancouver.
Philadelphia, April 26, 1785, said John Holker acknowledged the power of attorney as his act before Sam'l Wharton, Wm. Adcock, Justices of the Peace, and Jonathan Bayard Smith, Prothonotary, certified as the justices of peace.
Recorded in Jefferson Co., August Court, 1785.   [*B1, p32.*]

Levi Hollingsworth, merchant of Philadelphia, Pa., appoints John Rice Jones, at present at Philadelphia, now going to visit in the western parts of the State of Virginia, his lawful attorney, to take possession of lands in District, or County westward of the Alleghaney Mountains in Virginia, and to lease or dispose of his lands. April 26, 1785.

Witnesses: Elliston Proop [?], Meers Fisher. Recorded, August Court, 1785. [*B1, p35.*]

Philip Barbour, late of Orange, now of Jefferson Co., appoints his friends Richard Barbour of Lincoln Co., and Benjamin Sebastian and William Johnston of Jefferson Co., his attorneys. Sept. 3, 1785.

Witnesses: Thomas Minor Winn, Jos. Archer. Recorded September Court, 1785. [*B1, p37.*]

Daniel Sullivan of Jefferson Co. appoints John Campbell and James Sullivan of same county his lawful attornies to lease or farm-let all lands to which he is entitled in the District of Kentucky. Apr. 25, 1785.

Witnesses: John Maitland, Jno. Bailey, Dan. Sullivan, Jr. Recorded October Court, 1785. [*B1, p38.*]

George Wilson of Jefferson Co. makes bond to James Elliott, of same county: whereas James Elliott, as attorney for Robert Elliott, sold to Wilson 1100 acres of land on waters of Clear Creek, being part of a settlement and preemption of 1400 acres of Robert Elliott, and whereas James Elliott became a joint purchaser with Wilson, he, George Wilson, will grant to James Elliott the one-half or moiety of the 1100 acres. May 16, 1784.

Witness: Will Johnston.

May 17, 1784, For value received James Elliott assigned to William Johnston, Sr., his rights to this land.

Test: G. J. Johnston. Recorded March Court, 1785. [*B1, p39.*]

George Wilson and [blank in book], both of Jefferson Co., give bond to William Johnston to defend him against any damages that might arise against Wilson and Johnston as a party in articles of agreement by which George Wilson and William Johnston are jointly bound with James Francis Moore for the location of 250,000 acres of land warrants, as Johnston has this day relinquished all claim he has in the articles. Jan. 2, 1784.

Witnesses: James Elliott, John Hughes. Recorded March Court, 1785. [*B1, p40.*]

Richard Brashear of the Natchez, in the Spanish American Domain, appoints his friend Daniel Brodhead of Louisville, in the Commonwealth of Virginia, his lawful attorney to act for him, and if necessary to appoint one or more attorneys under him to complete his, Brashear's, work. May 23, 1785.
Witnesses: Wm. Leas, Jno. K. Simpson, Daniel Henry. Recorded October Court, 1785. [*B1, p41.*]

Jacob Coleman of Jefferson Co. appoints his friend Daniel Brodhead his lawful attorney to demand and receive from Josiah Tannehill and John Gibson certificates and interest thereon for his, Jacob Coleman's, services as an officer in the late Virginia Line. July 2, 1785.
Witnesses: J. Doone, James Alder. Recorded October Court, 1785. [*B1, p42.*]

John Filson of Jefferson Co. gives bond to Daniel Henry, merchant of same place, in sum of £2000 lawful money of Virginia, to deed to Daniel Henry a tract of 240 acres of land on west branch of Brandywine Creek, about two miles south of the Gap road in East Fallowfield Township, Chester County, Pa., by the first day of April, 1787. Dated Oct. 14, 1785.
Witnesses: Dan'l Buckley, Martin Carney, John Williams, James Morrison. Recorded November Court, 1785. [*B1, p43.*]

John Filson of Jefferson Co. acknowledges receipt from Daniel Henry of full and ample payment for a tract of land on the West branch of Brandywine Creek in Chester Co., Pa., containing 240 acres, viz. £735 lawful money of Pennsylvania, the stipulated sum. October 15, 1785.
Witnesses: Rob. K. Moore, John Dorrett, Dan'l Buckley. Recorded November Court, 1785. [*B1, p44.*]

Robert George, late of the District of Kentucky, now living in Clarksville on North West side of Ohio River, appoints Daniel Brodhead, Jr., his lawful attorney. December 5, 1785.
Witnesses: William Trigg, J. Donne. Recorded December Court, 1785. [*B1, p44.*]

Edward McCabe of District of Kentucky, but lately of Northumberland Co., Pa., appoints Daniel Brodhead, Jr., his lawful attorney to sell a 324 acre tract of land in Northumberland Co., Pa.; see certificate of survey June 19, 1769. Dated December 5, 1785.

Witnesses: Ben Sebastian, J. Donne. Recorded December Court, 1785.   [*B1, p45.*]

John Campbell of Jefferson Co. appoints James Sullivan and Richard Taylor, of same county, his lawful attorneys to sue for debts, to rent, lease-out or farm-let any lands he has or may have in consequence of a title by entry, survey or patent from the authority of the state of Virginia or by purchase, etc; they to have power to appoint other attorneys under them. Oct. 10, 1785.

Witnesses: M'l Lacassagne, Jno. Rogers, D. W. Merriwether, J. Donne, John Maitland, Lewis Field. Recorded November Court, 1785.   [*B1, p45.*]

John Montgomery, of Red River Settlement, Va., appoints Alexander Breckinridge of Jefferson Co. to transact all his business of every kind and to act for him in all claims to land in the Illinois Grant. April 13, 1785.

Witnesses: Ro. Breckinridge, W. Vanleare. Recorded November Court, 1785.   [*B1, p46.*]

Whereas Alexander Breckinridge has been John Montgomery's security in a bond to Major William Veanlere, this is to impower him, in case of Montgomery's death or failure to comply with said bond in the time limit, to keep or sell as much of Montgomery's lands in the Illinois Grant as to give him full compensation for the demands of said bond. April 13, 1785.

Witnesses: Ro. Breckinridge, W. Vanlear. Recorded November Court, 1785.   [*B1, p47.*]

Daniel Brodhead, Jr., merchant of Jefferson Co., appoints Benjamin Sebastian, Bartholomew Tardiveau and John Donne his lawful attornies with full power to buy and sell lands and in general to perform all business transactions, and if necessary to appoint other attornies under them. Dec. 8, 1785.

Witnesses: Amos Ogden, William Trigg, J. Taylor, P. Phillips. Recorded March Court, 1786.   [*B1, p47.*]

Benjamin Sebastian of Jefferson Co. sells to Alexander Scott
Bullitt for £850 Virginia currency, nine negroes with all their
future increase. Feb. 21, 1786.
Witnesses: Alexr. Breckinridge, Js. Breckinridge. Recorded
March Court, 1786. [*B1, p48.*]

Daniel Henry, merchant of Baltimore Town, Md., appoints
his friend John Belle [Bell?] of Louisville, Jefferson Co., District
of Kentucky, State of Virginia, his attorney in fact. Jan. 20,
1786.
Witnesses: Ridh'd Eastin, Reuben Eastin. Recorded March
Court, 1786. [*B1, p49.*]

Mary Kellar, widow of Abraham Kellar, dec'd, appoints her
friend and kinsman John Donne of Jefferson Co. her lawful attorney and in her name to receive of Isaac Kellar, administrator of
the estate of her late husband, Abraham Kellar, all lands, etc.
that belong to her in right of widowhood, or otherwise, and also
lands of the State of Virginia due her or her late husband. Jan.
6, 1786.
Witnesses: Benjamin Reeder, Francis Hughes. Recorded March
Court, 1786. [*B1, p49.*]

Memorandum of agreement between John Helm and Moses
Kuykendall of Jefferson Co. Said Helm agrees to take the following warrants, the property of Kuykendall: No. 9906 Dec. 14,
1781, for 500 acres of land; No. 9907 Dec. 14, 1781, for 500 acres;
No. 10846 Feb. 2, 1782, for 1000 acres; No. 10848 Feb. 2, 1782,
for 1000 acres; No. 8801 Nov. 10, 1781, for 500 acres; a total of
3500 acres. Helm obligates himself to enter and locate in the
District of Kentucky as good land as vacancy will permit, with
the different surveyors of the counties of Jefferson, Lincoln and
Fayette, on agreement that said Kuykendall gives one-half of
said 3500 acres to Helm for his trouble in locating, surveying and
laying off. Helm agrees to lay off 500 acres of above warrants
of the Kuykendall quoto on this side of Salt River. June 4, 1782.
Witnesses: Wm. Johnston, John Ray, Daniel Sparks. Recorded
April Court, 1786. [*B1, p50.*]

Agreement between James Francis Moore of Jefferson Co. and
John Gay Moore of Baltimore Co., Md: James Francis Moore

sold to John Gay Moore 333 acres of land in Jefferson Co., on waters of Floyd's Fork, and as some of this land is in dispute, James Francis Moore agrees that if any of the 333 acres is otherwise claimed, he and his heirs will assign an additional quantity of land to offset any losses to John Gay Moore. April 3, 1786. *Witnesses:* Thomas Stansbury, James Quartermous, Will Shannon. Recorded April Court, 1786. [*B1, p52.*]

David Mitchell impowers Benjamin Sebastian, as attorney, to join with Capt. George Wilson to convey 800 acres of land to Jacob Moonie which Capt. George Wilson sold to the said Moonie, being part of a tract of land of 2000 acres in Jefferson Co. granted to George Wilson and David Mitchell. Feb. 15, 1786. *Witnesses:* George Smith, George Wilson. Recorded May 3, 1786. [*B1, p53.*]

Articles of agreement between John Campbell and James Sullivan of Jefferson Co. and William Pope of same place. For certain consideration John Campbell and James Sullivan, purchasers under Daniel Sullivan, have this day quited claim and released William Pope of an agreement between said Pope and Daniel Sullivan relative to certain lands on the head waters of Beargrass in Jefferson County and give Pope possession of said lands, except reserving to John Campbell and James Sullivan the property of all grain now on said premises; the people living in houses on this land to be permitted to remain until Jan. 1, 1786. In consideration, William Pope in like manner quit-claims and releases Daniel Sullivan to John Campbell and James Sullivan, as purchasers from said Daniel, from the articles aforesaid and gives to Campbell and James Sullivan possession of all lands mentioned in agreement to have been delivered to Pope by Daniel Sullivan. John Clark and Richard Taylor are to be chosen to value all improvements that have been made. Pope also agrees that Campbell shall enjoy 111 acres of land, being part of said land on Beargrass which sold by Daniel Sullivan to Thos. Parsley [Pursell?] and by him to Campbell. Oct. 6, 1785. *Witnesses:* Will Shannon, Mich. Humble, Lewis Field. Recorded October Court, 1785. [Marginal note:] Had been mislaid and not recorded in proper place. [*B1, p53.*]

Williams Roberts of Jefferson Co. gives bond to William Johnston, agent for Henry Banks, Merchant in Richmond, Va. Whereas Roberts and Johnston have made an agreement for the locating, surveying, etc. of certian military land warrants for the Virginia State Line, and Johnston furnishes Roberts with warrants as per list annexed to the amount of 5,733½ acres and one other warrant in the name of George Walls for 7,110 ⅔ acres, (one half already located and not considered here); when William Roberts locates these warrants, surveying the same and delivers to Henry Banks a patent for 2,866 ⅔ acres clear of all and every contingent, also the remainder of warrant of George Walls, then this obligation is void. Mar. 18, 1785.

Witnesses: Dan'l Brodhead, Jr., Fred'k Edwards, Martin Carney.

List of warrants: Granville Smith, No. 2932, acres 2666 ⅔; Robert Boush, No. 3411, Acres 1666 ⅔ and No. 3412, acres 700; Wm. Reynolds, Ass'n James Alexander, No. 3441, acres 100; Saml. Crouch, Ass'n Elisa Jones, No. 3439, acres 100; Adam Armstead, No. 3420, acres 100; Richard Spinner, No. 3435, acres 100; Robert Casey [Carey?] No. 894, acres 100; David Harper, No. 3452, acres 200; total 5733½ acres; George Walls, No. 3315, acres 7110 ⅔; Burgess Longwith, acres 2666 ⅔; making in all 15510½ acres.

May 21, 1785: Received of Wm. Johnston agent one other land warrant No. 2818 for 2666 ⅔, taken in the name of Burgess Longwith, March 25, 1784, to be located and surveyed as the aforesaid.

April 12, 1786: Henry Banks by Will Johnston, his att'y, assigns to Gabriel Johnston all his interest in the aforesaid lands, and patents are to be issued in said Johnston's name; and G. J. Johnston assigns to William Johnston all his rights in aforesaid lands.

June 6, 1786: all above ordered recorded. [*B1, p56.*]

James Sullivan of Jefferson Co. gives bond to William Johnston of said county that, when he receives deed, for the land on which he lives, from Haptonstall and Lee, he will convey by deed, to William Johnston, 115 acres of land, being part of said tract. This to begin at Southall and Charlton's survey of 6000 acres on Beargrass. Sept. 23, 1785.

Witnesses: D. Meriwether, Wm. Peyton, Wm. Sullivan. Recorded June 6, 1786. [*B1, p58.*]

Isaac Hite of Jefferson Co. appoints Capt. Abraham Hite of said county his lawful attorney to make deed of conveyance to a lot in the town of Moorefield, Hardy Co., [now in W. Va.]. Sept. 5, 1786.
Recorded September 5, 1786.   [*B1, p60.*]

Henry Bolling of Jefferson Co. gives bond to William Johnston of said county to convey to Johnston by deed a tract of 240 acres of land on waters of the Ohio River in Ohio Co. [now in W. Va.] on McMechen branch, bounded on the north by land of Thomas West, on south by McMechen, on the east by Wm. Greathouse, and on the west by the land formerly owned by Jacob Walker, which he, Bolling, purchased of William West, and the land whereon Benja. Johnston lives, and shall give to William Johnston immediate possession, and shall, in deeds of conveyance, insert clause of geneal warranty "from the beginning of the world." Sept. 8, 1785.
Witnesses: Thos. McWinn, Benj. Sebastian. Recorded September 5, 1786.   [*B1, p61.*]

Andrew Hare and Hugh McCaughey of Kentucky, merchants, acting partners of Hare, McCaughey & Co., appoint Richard Taylor of Jefferson Co., their lawful attorney for the said company. Sept. 27, 1786.
Teste: Pat Joyes, Jas. Dunlap. Recorded November 7, 1786.
                                                              [*B1, p62.*]

James Withers of Fauquier Co., Va., appoints his friend Abner Field attorney in fact to divide certain lands which he has in parnership with William Pope of Jefferson Co., and to do everything he, Withers, is obligated to do by his bond to Pope.
Teste: Lewis Field, George Slaughter. Recorded November 7, 1786.   [*B1, p63.*]

James Francis Moore of Jefferson Co., by deed conveyed to Samuel Shannon 500 acres of land on Brashear Creek, adjoining on the east of Colo. Daniel Brodhead's survey of 862 acres. Oct. 9, 1786.
Witnesses: David Standiford, Abraham Field, Williams Shannon.
Recorded November 7, 1786.   [*B1, p63.*]

James Patten of Louisville, Jefferson Co., appoints William Roberts of same county his lawful attorney in fact, said Roberts being his security with others for the conveyance of lands in this county to Wilkinson, Armstrong, Dunn & Co. In order that Roberts will be exempt from all damages, Patten authorizes him to satisfy said bond by conveying any of Patten's land to make himself safe, and to void a bargain between Patten and the Morrisons for lands, subjecting the lands to the satisfaction of the bond. Dec. 20, 1786.
Witnesses: And'w Heth, Wm. Payne, Henry Reed. Recorded January 2, 1787. [*B1, p64.*]

John Montgomery of Davidson Co., N. C. appoints Alex'r Breckinridge of Jefferson Co. his attorney and agent to bring suit on all bonds of his in the hands of Breckinridge, notes and open accounts, he to retain all money and any bonds and other instruments of writing of an obligatory nature. In order that said Alex'r Breckinridge may comply more fully with a contract entered into between William Vanlear and John Montgomery, for the compliance of which contract Breckinridge entered security, Montgomery declares all other powers of attorney given in the court of Kentucky null and void, except one give to Breckinridge April 13, 1785. All money after paying expenses of surveying and patenting his lands in the Illinois Grant to be applied to Montgomery's order. March 24, 1787.
Teste: Ballard Smith, Abner Field, Ro. Breckinridge. Recorded June 5, 1787. [*B1, p65.*]

John Rogers of Caroline Co., Va., appoints his friends William Clark and Edmund Rogers of Jefferson Co., District of Ky., his lawful attorneys. April 2, 1787.
Test: Joseph Pollard, W. Croghan. Recorded July 3, 1787. [*B1, p66.*]

James Sullivan of Jefferson Co. gives bond to William Johnston of same county, that, if on or before Jan. 1, 1799, ensuing, Sullivan obtains a deed for the land on which he now lives, from Haptonstall and Lee, he will convey to Johnston a parcel of land on Beargrass Creek, beginning in a line of 115 acres, part of this survey formerly purchased by Johnston from said Sullivan, about

371

ten yards from Preston's line, and touching Taylor's line. July 2, 1787.
Witnesses: Wm. Clark, Edm'd Rice, Geo. Rice. Recorded July 3, 1787.   [*B1, p66.*]

Henry Bolling of Jefferson Co., bargains to sell to William Johnston, for a valuable consideration, a 287 acre tract of land in Ohio Co., Va., [now in W. Va.] on McMechen Run, waters of the Ohio, being the land which Bolling purchased from William West, and on which Benja. Johnston now lives. See bond given by Bolling this day to Wm. Johnston for the conveyance of said land, including all houses, out-houses, orchards, waters, fences, ect., dated September 6, 1785.
Witnesses: Thomas M. Winn, Ben. Sebastian. Recorded July 3, 1787.   [*B1, p67.*]

Henry Shyrock of Washington Co., Md., had sent under the care and management of Luke Foster certain goods, wares and merchandise to Kentucky for disposal. On the return of Foster he left the awards to the determination of Rezin Davis and John Lee both of "this place". Henry Shryock appoints George Wilson and William Oldham, both living in or near Kentucky, his lawful attorneys to make settlement with Luke Foster. Nov. 20, 1786.
Witnesses: Alex'r Clagett, Ad'm Old.
November 20, 1786 Washington Co. said Shryock acknowledged this letter of attorney as his act and deed. Alex. Claggett, Justice. Elie Williams, clerk, certifies that Claggett is a justice. Jefferson Co: Recorded August 11, 1787.   [*B1, p68.*]

Benjamin Roberts of Jefferson Co. sells to William Shannon four slaves, on Roberts' plantation, and dwelling house on Brashears Creek. October 4, 1786.
Witnesses: David Standiford, John Roberts. Recorded September 4, 1787,   [*B1, p69.*]

Robert Daniel, heir at law of Walker Daniel, sells to William Johnston of Jefferson Co. 800 acres of land, part of a 1000 acre survey made in Walker Daniel's name in said county and adjoining Johnston's survey at the confluence of Salt River with the Ohio, at the upper end thereof on Ohio River. Dec. 29, 1787.
Witnesses: Susannah Johnston, Enfield Fowke, Matilda Slaughter. Recorded January 1, 1788.   [*B1, p70.*]

George Slaughter of Jefferson Co. sells to Cadwallader Slaughter two negro slaves. March 4, 1788.
Witnesses: Saml. Oldham, Robt. Floyd, Wm. Peyton. Recorded March 4, 1788. [*B1, p71.*]

William Pope, of Jefferson Co., gave bond to George Wilson: whereas Pope for certain valuable consideration from George Willson, on July 3, last, sold to said Wilson a tract of 1056 acres, surveyed for Pope July 18, 1787, in said county, beginning in east line of Pope's preemption of 400 acres on Fish Pool Creek, thence to Sampson Matthews and to the banks of Fern Creek and corner to said Matthews survey of 300 acres, thence to Flats of Fern Creek, thence to north corner of James Withers' 500 acre survey, thence to a line of said Withers and Pope's military survey of 100 acres. Pope on July 23 also sold to George Wilson another tract of 700 acres surveyed in the name of Osborn Sprigg, sold by Joseph Sprigg his attorney to William Pope. This land begins at north corner to Sprigg's 1100 acre survey that Joins James Withers' 500 acre survey on the Fish Pools, thence to William Pope's 1056 acre survey. Pope stands under bond until Wilson is given good title to these tracts of land. Nov. 8, 1787.
Witnesses: R. J. Waters, Steph'n. Ormsby, Elijah Phillips. Recorded March 5, 1788. [*B1, p71.*]

John Kinnison, of Jefferson Co. appoints his friend Abraham Wells of Nelson Co. his lawful attorney in the following suits: an action of debt against Reuben Case and John Foakes [Fowkes?]; against Edward Tyler and William Pope; against Squire Boone. Mar. 6, 1788.
Witnesses: B. Johnston Recorded April 1, 1788. [*B1, p72.*]

Richard Chenowith bond to Thomas Hughes and others: Whereas Richard Chinewith of Jefferson Co. in 1785 sold Thomas Hughes and Charles and Richard Swann 1400 acres of land on the North Fork of Licking Creek, conveyance of which was to be made sometime past, but was not made within time prescribed and time was extended, for this indulgence and further security, Chenowith binds himself to give Hughes and the Swanns 2000 acres of land in Jefferson Co., on Paddy's Run, waters of Ohio, being half of a 4000 acre entry made in the name of John Edwards

and of whom Chenowith purchased said 2000 acres. May 28, 1788.
Witnesses: Will Johnston, Enfield Fowke, Betsey Johnston. Recorded July 1, 1788.   [*B1, p73.*]

Robert Daniel of Jefferson Co. appoints Daniel Brodhead, Jr., merchant of said county, to collect his debts. December 8, 1785.
Witnesses: J. Donne.

Robert Daniel further grants to Daniel Brodhead his attorney his full authority to sell and convey lands.
Witnesses: J. Donne, W. Croghan, Edmd. Rogers, G. R. Clark. Recorded September 2, 1788.   [*B1, p74.*]

Daniel Bordhead, Jr. of Jefferson Co. sold to Richard Jones Waters of said county his goods, chattels and all his personal property, farm implements, cattle, sheep, a negro woman, also horses, including young stallion purchased from John Severns, his interest in a stud horse late the property of Samuel Boon purchased at Sheriff's sale by Brodhead in partnership with Samuel Wells, 4 wagons, gears for 16 horses, etc., log chains and trace chains, stock of all kinds, timbers belonging to Brodhead, in Louisville or elsewhere, his furniture, rifle-gun, rugs, cherry cupboard, one chocolate pot, pewter ware, etc. August 4, 1788. Recorded September 2, 1788.   [*B1, p75.*]

Letter dated Redstone, April 21, 1783, to "James O'Finn, living at the Falls of Ohio," beginning "Dear Child" and signed John O'Finn. It states that he had received a letter forwarded by John Ward, and that he had received two letters from James O'Finn's sister, and that James' brother-in-law expects to come to the backwoods soon, and that he, John O'Finn, expects to see James at the Falls in a short time. He sends greetings to Mr. and Mrs. Pyatt and all their friends at the Falls. He further instructs James to sell tract of land on Bulls Creek and to take as pay for his trouble John O'Finn's lot at Falls of the Ohio.
Recorded September 2, 1788.   [*B1, p76.*]

John Asturgus gives authority to Daniel Brodhead, Jr., to assign and convey to himself Asturgus' settlement and preemption. June 3, 1785.
Witnesses: Richard J. Waters, Thos. McCarty. Recorded September 2, 1788.   [*B1, p77.*]

Daniel Brodhead of the Burrough of Reading, Berks Co., Pa. appoints his son Daniel Brodhead, Jr. his lawful attorney to collect from James Francis Moore and James Sullivan of Kentucky, his former agents, all money and all such other matters as they had in trust for him. March 1, 1787.
Witnesses: Charles Jno. Biddle, John Christian Hondebier. Recorded September 2, 1788.   [*B1, p77.*]

William Pope of Kentucky gives bond to George Wilson, same place, to make a deed of conveyance, as soon as a patent can be obtained, to George Wilson for 800 acre part of a larger tract known as the Fern Creek tract. June 27, 1780.
Witnesses: Mer'th Price, Joseph Saunders. Recorded October 7, 1788.   [*B1, p78.*]

George Wilson obtained a deed from Wm. Pope for sundry lands on the waters of Fish Pools. It now appears that, sometime since, Pope attempted to make a conditional line. If his action effects Wilson's lands and takes from it, then Wilson will accept that much land on the opposite side of the tract. October 6, 1788. Recorded October 7, 1788.   [*B1, p78.*]

David W. Meriwether, John Hughes and James Meriwether give bond to Edmund Randolph, Governor of Virginia; whereas Daniel Meriwether has been appointed inspector of tobacco at Campbell's Warehouse in Jefferson Co. by commission from the Governor, June 19, past, if said Meriwether shall well and truly perform his duties as inspector and according to an act "to amend and reduce the several acts of Assembly for the inspection of tobacco into one act," then this obligation is void. October 7, 1788.
Teste: Will Johnston. Recorded October 7, 1788. Original sent to the clerk of the Council of Virginia. Signed Wm. Croghan, Esqr., November 4, 1788.   [*B1, p79.*]

John Clark, John Hughes and James Merewether give bond to Edmund Randolph, Governor of Virginia: whereas John Clark has been appointed Inspector of Tobacco of Campbell's warehouse in Jefferson Co., by commission from the Governor, June 19, last, if said Clark truly performs his duties as inspector and, according to act of Assembly "to amend and reduce the several acts of Assembly for inspection of tobacco into one act," then this obligation is void. October 7, 1788.

Teste: Will Johnston. Recorded October 7, 1788.   [*B1, p79.*]

John Holker of Philadelphia appoints his friend Michael Lacassagne, now of Louisville, Va., his lawful attorney to collect debts, etc., from persons in the Western Country, on waters of Ohio and Mississippi Rivers. Oct. 8, 1787.
Witnesses: Charles Wilson, R. E. Tobart.
Philadelphia, Pa., Oct. 12, said John Holker acknowledged letter of attorney before Wm. Pollard. Recorded November 7, 1788.
[*B1, p80.*]

James Patten of Louisville, Jefferson Co., Va., appoints his friends Benjamin Roberts of Nelson Co., and Benjamin Johnston, Sr., of Louisville, to be his lawful attorneys to act in all things, except the sale of lands during his absence, including collecting rents, etc., for merchandise stored in his warehouse. Should he not return, or in the event of his death while away, said attorneys are to search the records for his lands and property in which Patten is in partnership in Virginia. November 4, 1788.
Witnesses: George Wilson, Benja. Johnston. Recorded November 7, 1788.   [*B1, p81.*]

Mark Thomas of Jefferson Co. binds himself to give Lawrence Muse 3000 acres of land on Brashear Creek in consideration of his marrying Mark Thomas' daughter Elizabeth Thomas, to be conveyed to him within the next twelve months. Aug. 9, 1788.
Witnesses: John Vaughan, William Elim. Recorded December 2, 1788.   [*B1, p82.*]

Osborn Sprigg, Washington Co., Maryland, appoints his three friends Col. William Oldham, Benjamin Sebastian and Stephen Ormsby, Esquires, of the District of Kentucky, of the State of Virginia, his attorneys to convey to Ralp Humphreys so much of his land in Kentucky as will satisfy a bond he on Oct. 6, 1787, gave Humphreys. Nov. 10, 1788.
Witnesses: Lewellin Price, James Likens. Recorded December 2, 1788.   [*B1, p82.*]

CALENDAR OF BOND AND POWER OF ATTORNEY BOOK No.1, JEFFERSON COUNTY, KENTUCKY, 1783-1798

By Ludie J. Kinkead and Katharine G. Healy

In Three Parts

Part Two: January, 1789–1796

Thomas Turpin of Jefferson Co. appoints his friend Jacob Owens, same county, as his attorney in any court of law. January 8, 1789.

Power of attorney proven by oath of George Shepherd, and ordered recorded, March 3, 1789. [*B1, p83.*]

Daniel Sullivan, of Post St. Vincent, assigns to William Oldham, Sheriff of Jefferson Co., 2,000 acres of land on Pond Creek, which Sullivan claims by an agreement from Richard Woolfolk, which writing he delivers to Benjamin Johnston his deputy; also 400 acres of land on Brashears Creek adjoining Squire Boone tract of 12,335 acres. The same is delivered up to discharge an ex'o against Daniel Sullivan and William Shannon for 52.16.1, in behalf of Zach'y Johnson; and Sullivan vests Oldham to sell and convey the land in his name, the overplus, if any, to be returned to Sullivan's order. March 26, 1789.
Witnesses: Will Johnston, Rich'd Cheniwith, B. Johnston. Recorded April 7, 1789. [*B1, p83.*]

William Linn of Jefferson Co. binds himself to Donald Kennedy, of Philadelphia, to make a deed to Kennedy with a general warranty for 500 acres of first-rate land at or adjoining what is called the Lower Station, a little below or oposite the mouth of the Big Miami, and not exceeding one-half mile from the Ohio River, within twelve months of this date. March 21, 1789.
Witnesses: Phil Nolan, Dorsttet Sortmass [Sortman?]. Recorded May 5, 1789. [*B1, p84.*]

377

William Linn of Jefferson Co., gives bond to Patrick Simpson, of Philadelphia, to make a deed to him with general warranty for 500 acres of land at or adjoining to what is at present called the Lower Station, a little below or opposite the mouth of the Big Miami, not exceeding one-half mile from the Ohio River. March 17, 1789.

Witnesses: Phil Nolan, Donald Kennedy. Recorded May 5, 1789. [*B1, p85.*]

William Murray, of Philadelphia, appoints William Murray, the younger, of same place, an attorney-at-law, his lawful attorney to sell a 1,000 acre tract of land in Jefferson Co. June 8, 1786. *Witnesses:* Edmd. Milne, Alex'r Stedman. April 5, 1788, Edmd. Milne came before the Hon. Thomas McKean, Doctor of Laws, Chief Justice of the Commonwealth of Pennsylvania, made oath that he saw William Murray and Ale'x Stedman sign the above. Recorded May 5, 1789. [*B1, p87.*]

An agreement between Richard Taylor and Benoni Demant, both of Jefferson County: Richard Taylor has rented and farm-let to Demant 50 acres of land on Beargrass, on upper corner of his survey adjoining the lines of Southall, Charleton and Sullivan, from the 1st of January next for the term of ten years, and further agrees that Demant shall be permitted to make three crops on land Demant has cleared, and where he lives, rent free. September 4, 1786.

Witnesses: Will Johnston, George Demant.
Col. Taylor agreed to give Benoni Demant rent-free on land for one year, making in all eleven years. Recorded May 5, 1789.
[*B1, p87.*]

James McGee acknowledges receipt from John McGee a bond for 500 acres of land which was left to James McGee by Thomas McGee, deceased, which he accepts as full satisfaction for his rights and claims to said Thomas McGee's estate. January 1, 1787.

Witnesses: Jonathan McCarty, Patrick McGee. Recorded September 1, 1789. [*B1, p89.*]

George Slaughter, of Jefferson Co. appoints Abner Field his lawful attorney to sell for him certain lands entered for Slaughter in Ohio Co., Va. [now in W. Va.] also to settle all accounts between him and Carter Braxton of Virginia. September 1, 1789.
Teste: Will Johnston. Recorded September 1, 1789. [*B1, p89.*]

Richard Eastin, of Jefferson Co., sold to John Rhea, merchant of Louisville, one negro boy, Moses, March 7, 1789. If Richard Eastin, within eight months, pays Rhea £50, then this bill of sale is void.
Teste: Tho. M. Winn, Will Johnston. Recorded November 6, 1789.   [*B1, p90.*]

Peter Colman of Jefferson Co. appoints John Veach [Veech], of same county, his lawful attorney to attend to the division of his 1,000 acre preemption on a branch of Long Run which empties into Floyd's Fork on the east side of said Fork wherein John May is concerned. After division is made, agreeable to May's bond, Veach is empowered to deed to Colman's moiety, 250 acres to William Anderson, 250 acres to Francis Huffman. He is also to attend to surveying of the entries that were made by warrants for which Colman and Veach gave their bonds jointly to Cooprider and Marks Easter, part of which warrants Colman transferred to himself in consequence of a power-of-attorney from Veach, which assignment the said Colman relinquished and vested a full power in Veach. April 10, 1789.
Witnesses: Jacob Coleman, Jr., George Veach, Robert Floyd. Recorded February 2, 1790.   [*B1, p91.*]

William Pope of Jefferson Co., sells to William Johnston a 500 acre tract of land on Floyd's Fork which was conveyed to him by Richard Taylor, att'y in fact for John Edwards. March 6, 1789.
Witnesses: Tho. M. Winn, B. Johnston. Recorded February 2, 1790.   [*B1, p92.*]

Charity Owens of Jefferson Co., being about to remove, appoints her friend William Elms of same county her lawful attorney to receive all that is due her in Jefferson County and in town of Clarksville. November 25, 1789.
Witnesses: W. Clark, John Owens. Recorded April 8, 1790.
[*B1, p93.*]

Benjamin Johnston, Jr., of Jefferson Co. and District of Kentucky, gives bond to Benjamin Johnston,Sr. of said District; that whereas Benjamin Johnston, Sr. being the surveyor for Yohogania County, Va., entered and deeded lands amounting to 22,001 acres as per list in the name of Benjamin Johnston, Jr.,—the laws of the state then prohibited county surveyors making entries in their own names—and said Benjamin Sr. having confidence in Benjamin Jr., altho he was then under age, made the entries in the name of Benjamin Johnston, Jr., on condition that when he reached the age of 21, he would fulfill the said Benjamin Johnson Sr's wishes. Now having reached the age of 21, it is just to convey the lands to Benjamin Johnston, Sr., in order that he may dispose of them as he wishes. Benjamin, Jr., acknowledges having received satisfaction and a full recompense, and when said land is transferred to said Benjamin Johnston Sr., this obligation is void. February 15, 1790.

Benja. Johnston, Jr., received a deed for a lot and houses in Louisville as a further satisfaction for the above written conveyance. February 15, 1790.
Teste: Ga. J. Johnston, L. Johnston. [*B1, p94.*]

Benjamin Johnston, Jr., gives bond to Benjamin Johnston, Sr: Whereas Benjamin Johnston, Sr. has this day given his bond to Benjamin Jr. to convey unto Benjamin Jr. 920 acres of land in Woodford Co., in Col. Benjamin Harrison's neighborhood, conditioned that the said Benjamin Johnston, Jr. shall not marry without the consent of Benjamin Johnston Sr. February 15, 1790.
Witness: Ga. J. Johnston, Recorded April 8, 1790. [*B1, p96.*]

An agreement between Robert Daniel and Martin Daniel, whereby Martin will endeavor to settle all debts due from Robert to sundry people, and to have all the lands, or as much as is in his power, surveyed that Robert claims in his own name or name of others, but is only answerable for three-fourths of the expenses for surveying. Robert assigns to Martin all bonds, bills, notes, etc., together with judgments, Martin to pay three-fourths of proceeds of sale to those to whom Robert is indebted a nd retain one-fourth for himself. He is also empowered to sell lands on same terms, except the place on which Robert lives, and Robert in satisfaction

to Martin assigns to him one-fourth of all lands, etc; one-fourth of John Copes contract is assigned to Martin Daniel, but Martin is not to have one-fourth of any land he does not survey, unless he should sell same. September 5, 1789.
Witnesses: Wm. Peyton, Moses Pennell. Recorded April 8, 1790.
[*B1, p98.*]

Parmenus Bullitt of Jefferson Co., appoints his friend Daniel Brodhead, Jr., his lawful attorney and enters into a replevy bond in consequence of an execution served on Bullitt's property at the suit of Andrew Hare by the sheriff of Jefferson Co. March 10, 1790.
Witnesses: Richard Jones Waters, Cuth. Banks. Recorded June 1, 1790. [*B1, p100.*]

Whereas Anthony Thornton on March 16, 1789, executed an obligation to Simon Kenton of Bourbon Co. for conveyance of one-fourth part of a 33,750 acre tract of land, and he has further bound himself to convey to Kenton another fourth part of tract, and whereas the said Kenton on March 24, 1790, did assign the obligation to Phillip Buckner for value received; and by his assignment on the back thereof, be it known that Phillip Buckner, of Jefferson Co. in the District of Kentucky, appoints his friend Richard Taylor of Caroline Co., Va., his lawful attorney to sell his rights in the 33,750 acre tract of land. May 22, 1790.
Witnesses: Ben. Sebastian, Thomas Pearson. Recorded June 2, 1790. [*B1, p101.*]

Richard Eastin of Jefferson Co., sells to George Taylor his rights, titles and interests in five negroes which Eastin got for life by marriage with his present wife Sarah, and his interest in one negro lad till Nov. 1, 1791. Dated Oct. 22, 1789.
Witnesses: Hannah Taylor, Owen Batman. Recorded June 1, 1790. [*B1, p103.*]

Ursula McCarty Benoist, the widow of Richard McCarty, deceased, late Captain in the Illinois Regiment in the service of the United States of America, acting for herself and for her son Richard McCarty, and Joseph Francois Perault, merchant, and Ursula his wife and daughter of the said deceased, all of Montreal in the Province of Quebec, heirs at law of the said Richard Mc-

Carty, appoints John Armstrong, Captain in the First United States Regiment, their lawful attorney with full power to settle all accounts of said Richard McCarty as late Captain and discharge all lawful claims in the heirs names, to sell all lands and convey same. Feb. 10, 1790. Signed "Ursula McCarty Benowist for self and agent for my son J. F. Perrault,—Ursula Perrault McCarty."

Witnesses: J. E. Robertson, P. Robertson.

Province of Quebec, City of Montreal, Feb. 10, 1790, power of attorney acknowledged before John Gorbrand Beck, N. P. Jefferson Co. Recorded August 3, 1790. [*B1, p104.*]

Elijah Logan Hall [Hale?] of Louisville, now intending a journey to Fauquier Co., in the Old Settlement, appoints his friend Benjamin Johnston, his lawful attorney, to represent him in all matters of business. Revokes all other powers of attorney, especially the one to Daniel Brodhead, Jr. to transact business with Colo. Harry Lee of Virginia. Aug. 24, 1790.

Witnesses: Richard Eastin, Pat Joyes. Recorded Oct. 5, 1790.
[*B1, p108.*]

Samuel Oldham assigns to William Oldham all his interest in all lands in the name of Conway Oldham, dec'd, which was located on Potinger's Creek or Eaton Creek or elsewhere in the District of Kentucky. Nov. 10, 1786. Recorded October 5, 1790.
[*B1, p109.*]

Jacob Smith sold to William Marshall, Jr., one horse for £23, Sept. 8, 1790. Recorded October 5, 1790. [*B1, p109.*]

Richard Applegate [signed Apelgate], formerly of Westmoreland, Pennsylvania, now Jefferson Co., Va., appoints his son John Applegate of Jefferson Co., his lawful attorney to act in all lawful questions in reference to certain parcels of wheat due from William Hill and Jonathan Hill of Pennsylvania, and money due him. January 30, 1791.

Recorded February 2, 1791. [*B1, p109.*]

William Hill and Jonathan Hill of Westmoreland Co., Pa., give bond unto Richard Applegate of same place to pay to said Richard Applegate 266 bushels of merchantable wheat to be delivered at Joshua Dickerson's before January 1, 1784. April 25, 1782.

Witnesses: Thos. Beer, Mary Harper. Recorded February 2, 1791. [*B1, p111.*]

William Hill and Jonathan Hill of Westmoreland Co., Pa., give bond to Richard Applegate of same place to pay 266 bushels of wheat to be delivered at Joshua Dickerson's mill on or before January 1, 1785. April 25, 1782.

Witnesses: Thos. Beer, Mary Harper. Recorded February 2, 1791. [*B1, p112.*]

William Hill and Jonathan Hill, of Westmoreland Co., Pa., give bond to Richard Applegate of the same place to pay to him 266 bushels of wheat to be delivered at Joshua Dickerson's mill on or before January 1, 1786. April 25, 1782.

Witnesses: Thos. Beer, Mary Harper. Recorded February 2, 1791. [*B1, p113.*]

James Sullivan of Jefferson Co., District of Kentucky, sold to William Sullivan of same county two negro slaves. January 3, 1791. Bill of Sale recorded January 4, 1791.

[*B1, p114.*]

Charles Tuley's will required his estate to be kept together for the support of his widow and children until the children became of age or married. John Tuley, son of Charles, deceased, has married since the death of his father and wants his share of estate. Therefore John and Charles Tuley, sons of Charles, deceased, and Elizabeth Tuley mother and guardian of William, Sarah, Wyatt, Mary, Robert, and Jane Tuley, under the age of 21 years, do set apart for John Tuley as his share: three slaves and certain money. February 25, 1796.

Witnesses: Ben Sebastian, George G. Taylor. Recorded March 2, 1791. [*B1, p115.*]

John Tuley, sold to Thomas Smith of Jefferson Co., three slaves. March 3, 1791.

Witness: B. Thruston. Recorded March 3, 1791. Original delivered to Michael Lacassagne.

[*B1, p116.*]

John Campbell of Jefferson Co., District of Kentucky and State of Virginia, makes void every power of attorney or agency before made, granted or executed. October 18, 1783.
Witnesses: John Purveance, David Ferguson. Recorded March 4, 1791.   [*B1, p117.*]

Jacob Colman, Sr., sold to Rosannah Colman of Jefferson Co., all goods, household furniture, implements, etc. in his possession: 6 head of cattle, 1 mare, 20 head of hogs, plow & tackling, 2 beds, 2 chests, 20wt. of pewter, 2 small pots, 1 dutch oven, 18 gallon kettle, 1 ax and 3 hoes, March 18, 1791.
Witnesses: Thos. Buitt [Bullitt?] Adam Mong. Recorded April 6, 1791.   [*B1, p117.*]

Thomas Smith, sold Michael Lacassagne three slaves. March 5, 1791.
Witnesses: Robt. K. Moore, Ben Sebastian. Recorded May 3, 1791.   [*B1, p118.*]

William Clark, blacksmith, of Jefferson Co., District of Kentucky, quit claimed unto Thomas Garner of same county all quarrels, controversies, suits and demands which he had against him by reason of any matter or thing "from the beginning of the world to the day of date hereof." April 5, 1791.
Witnesses: Moses Cook, Craven Lane. Recorded May 3, 1791.
[*B1, p119.*]

Benj. Johnston, sold to William Johnston and Ga. J. Johnston, one negro woman. April 9, 1791.
Witnesses: Elisha L. Hall, Benj. Johnston. Recorded May 5, 1791.   [*B1, p120.*]

Ga. J. Johnston relinguishes to William Johnston all rights to a negro woman slave, which he and William Johnston purchased in a joint partnership of Ben Johnston, Jr. June 25, 1791.
Recorded July 5, 1791.   [*B1, p120.*]

Kitty Eareckson sold to Elizabeth Eareckson one negro girl. December 16, 1790.
Witnesses: Edw'd Ashby, Fielding Ashby. Recorded July 5, 1791.   [*B1, p121.*]

Rebecca Hite, Abraham Hite and Joseph Hite of Jefferson Co. appoint Isaac Hite of same county their lawful attorney to sign and deliver a deed to James Dinwiddie for 300 acres of land, part of 600 acres on Hickman Creek in Fayette Co., which was granted to Abraham Hite, deceased, July 14, 1789; also 300 acres, the balance of said 600 acre survey, to William Stafford; also 220 acres to Alexander Scott. This land in Fayette Co., on the west side of Hickman Creek, is part of 2,000 acres granted Abraham Hite deceased. June 8, 1791.
Witnesses: Winston Smith, Rich'd Edwards, William McCoy, William Lux [Lare?]. Recorded July 5, 1791.   [*B1, p121.*]

William Johnston and Ga. J. Johnston sold to Benjamin Johnston, Jr., one billiard table with appurtenances. July 30, 1791.
Witness: John Churchill. Recorded August 3, 1791. [*B1, p122.*]

Daniel Henry, due to the absence of Ga. J. Johnston from home, has been prevented from giving him the power to dispose of his two houses and lots. Mr. Davis has delivered some part of the stone. Daniel Henry now gives to Johnston the full power to rent or sell these houses and lots. The lowest price he will accept for the upper house is £130 and for the lower £140 Virginia Currency, or he would take £300 Maryland Currency. In the event of the sale, the money to be remitted by some safe hand to Baltimore Town. Johnston has Richard Elliott's obligation to deliver 2,000 feet of plank and 30 w. nails, and is to inform Mr. Sales when the plank is ready and to dispose of the houses if possible.

Also empowers Johnston to act for him in all his affairs in Kentucky. August 14, 1791.
Witness: Rich'd Elliott. Recorded September 7, 1791.
[*B1, p123.*]

James Bevard appointed Gabriel Jones Johnston his lawful attorney to act in all his business affairs. January 21, 1790.
Witness: William Payne. Recorded September 7, 1791.
[*B1, p123.*]

James Elliott, appoints friend John Campbell his lawful attorney to act in all lawful ways and to procure for him a grant from the State of Virginia for a settlement and preemption in Jefferson

County, Va., to which Elliott is entitled, and sale of which he desires Campbell to make. August 20, 1791.

Witnesses: Mich. Dillon, Wm. Rhodes, William Beard. Recorded September 7, 1791. [*B1, p124.*]

Richard Jones Waters appoints friend Stephen Ormsby, Esq., his lawful attorney to act for him in all legal matters. June 22, 1791.

Witnesses: Jno. Harrison, Jacob Ambrose. Recorded September 7, 1791. [*B1, p125.*]

Isaac Hornback is discharged from Samuel Mason's claim against him as special bail for Pancake and others on his satisfying James Watts to whom the claim is assigned, or Stephen Ormsby, attorney in fact for Watts. Signed Ben Sebastian att'y at law for Samuel Mason. September 7, 1791.

Witness: Stephen Ormsby. Stephen Ormsby acknowledged receipt for balance due on within mentioned judgment. Recorded October 4, 1791. [*B1, p127.*]

Isaac Hornback, of Jefferson Co., Va. appoints friend John Heuston of Nelson Co., Va., his lawful attorney to procure from Michael Harness, John Pancake and Charles Reed of Hardy Co. all costs etc. sustained for being bail for the said Harness and Pancake. November 4, 1791.

Recorded November 4, 1791. [*B1, p128.*]

John Setzer, of Shenandoah Co., Va., son and heir at law to Martin Setzer, of said county, and heir of Michael Setzer deceased eldest son of Martin, appoints Frederick Setzer his brother of same county his lawful attorney to act for him in all legal ways, especially to get a grant or grants from the Commissioners appointed for the grant to the Illinois Regiment, of which he, John Setzer, has a right to claim a portion; also for his brother Michael Setzer, deceased, as heir at law of Michael, who died single about three years before in Kentucky, leaving no will. October 9, 1787.

Witnesses: Martin Setzer, Michael Sommer.

Shenandoah Co., Va., October 9, 1787. Power of attorney was signed by John Setzer, in the presence of Martin Setzer his father and Michael Sommer.

Martin Setzer made oath that Michael his son, deceased, was at the time of his death above the age of twenty-one years and oldest son, and further that John Setzer and Frederick, his third son, are also above the age of twenty-one years. Alexander Hite, J. P., John Williams, C. S. C., certify copy on October 10, 1787.

Jefferson Co., January 3, 1792, above power of attorney recorded. Original delivered to Michael Lacassagne. [*B1, p129.*]

Frederick Setzer, now of Fayette Co., Ky., by virture of power of attorney from his brother John Setzer of Oct. 9, 1787, assigns to Michael Lacassagne, for £35, all claims and interest of Michael Setzer to 100 acres of land in the Illinois Grant, in Lot No. 2B, granted to Michael for services performed by him as a soldier in the Illinois Regiment, and also 100 acres in Illinois Grant No. 2E granted to John Setzer for services in the Illinois Regiment. November 21, 1791.

Witnesses: George Power, Robt. K. Moore, Eliz. Linley. Recorded January 5, 1792. [*B1, p133.*]

Adam Thompson of Jefferson County sold to Wm. Smith of same county one set of blacksmith's tools now on Brash. Creek, for which he received full pay. December 10, 1791.

Witnesses: Wm. Rhodes, George Dement. Recorded January 3, 1792. [*B1, p135.*]

Hezekiah Applegate of Wythe Co., Va., appoints friend Thomas Applegate of Jefferson Co., his lawful attorney to deed to Thomas Spencer of Nelson Co. 200 acres of his, Hezekiah Applegate's settlement on Plumb Creek within four miles of Salt River, also 200 acres to James Evans of Wythe Co. by deed; all his other lands to his said attorney with power to dispose of them as he thinks proper. October 27, 1791.

Witnesses: Benjamin Applegate, Peter Kuykendall. Recorded January 4, 1792. [*B1, p136.*]

An inventory of Patrick Burks' property at different places to be collected by Dan'l McClelan, should accident happen to him on the campaign he "is now going on July 12th," which property he desires David McClelan to sell for the benefit of his brother William Burks, viz: at Dan'l McClelans salt, 11½ lbs;

at W. Jones' one cow and calf and three yards coating; at Robert Holmes, hogs; at W. Harris' his cloathing and crop of corn; likewise four bushels of salt in Dan'l McClelan's hands for Thos. Richey, the salt at 10 shillings per bushel and to be paid in linnen at six pence per hundred of which he has received one shirt at 14 shillings. Debts: to Mrs. Harris one shirt cloth and the making, one pair overalls; to Thomas Minter four bushels of salt. He appoints Daniel McClelan of Jefferson Co. his lawful attorney in all matters to collect and sell and to convey to his brother William Burks by the hand of Wm. Ferguson in Pennsylvania whom he has appointed his trustee in behalf of said brother. July 12, 1791. *Witnesses:* Thomas Ritchey [Ritchie], Mary Holmes. Recorded February 7, 1792. [*B1, p138.*]

John Harrison of Jefferson Co. appoints friend Benhamin Harrison of Bourbon Co. his lawful attorney toward the alienation of a certain tract, 911 acres in Bourbon Co. formerly owned by Benjamin Johnston, deceased. Jan. 30, 1792.
Recorded March 6, 1792. [*B1, p141.*]

Nicholas Meriwether authorizes Capt. Ben Roberts to sell a tract of land on Salt River, location in the name of William Farmer adjoining Col. Christian's survey on Bullitt's Lick. May 17, 1791.
Witness: William Shannon. Recorded April 3, 1792. [*B1, p141.*]

Richard Elliott, power of attorney to Ga. J. Johnston of Louisville. April 7, 1792.
Witness: John Harrison. Recorded May 1, 1792. [*B1, p142.*]

Joseph Calvit of the District of Natchez gives power of attorney to Capt. James Patten to transact all business with Daniel Brodhead, Jr. September 30, 1791.
Witnesses: W. Croghan, W. Payne.
N. B. Also empowers James Patten to sell his interests in two tracts of land in the Illinois Grant, No. 41 on the Ohio, the other No. 50 on Pleasant Run, to anyone for £200 Va. currency or young likely male negroes. Oct. 1, 1791.
Witnesses: W. Payne, Wm. Beard, Reu [Rice?] Bullock. Recorded May 1, 1792. [*B1, p143.*]

Merideth Helm, of Frederick Co., Va. appoints friend Robert Tyler of Jefferson Co., Va. his lawful attorney to make over to Henry Hunter 352 acres of land on the waters of Tick Creek in Jefferson Co., Va., by lease and re-lease. Sept. 2, 1790.
Witnesses: Thos. Throckmorton, John Sherman Woodcock, Justices of Frederick Co.
N. B. As soon as the land is acknowledged this power of attorney is to be void.
Frederick Co., Va., Sept. 6, 1790, Certificate, that above mentioned are justices of the peace, by J. A. Keith, C. F. C.
Jefferson Co., Recorded May 1, 1792. [*B1, p144.*]

Richard Harrison of the Natchez Settlement, late a Captain Lieutenant in the Illinois Regiment, now at Louisville, Ky., gives power of attorney to John Harrison of Louisville, to sell all that part of land that was allotted to him in the land granted to the Illinois Regiment; also all lands coming to or belonging to him in the Continental State Line as heir to his brother James Harrison deceased; also all his other lands in the State Line and all his lands in the state of Kentucky. July 3, 1792.
Witnesses: Will Johnston, Nicholas Harrison. Recorded July 3, 1792. [*B1, p147.*]

Benjamin Pope and Mark Thomas appoint friend James Patten to act for them in all matters concerning the division of a certain tract of 20,000 acres of land in Jefferson Co., entered in the name of Ben Roberts. January 5, 1791.
Witness: Ga. J. Johnston. Recorded March 4, 1794. [*B1, p148.*]

Elisha Lingen Hall of Louisville sold to Gabriel Jones Johnston one negro slave. February 7, 1794.
Witnesses: Thomas Powers, Richard J. Waters.
Proven February 10, 1794, certified March, 1794. [*B1, p148.*]

Elisha Lingan Hall of Louisville sold to Gabriel Jones Johnston, for thirty-four pounds fifteen shillings and one-half-penny current money of Kentucky, one negro boy about 10 years of age. February 7, 1794.
Witnesses: Thomas Powers, Richard J. Waters. Proven February 10; recorded March, 1794. |*B1, p148.*]

Charles Swan and Richard Swan of Washington Co., Pa., appoint Robert Tyler their lawful attorney to act for them in the suit against Richard Chenoweth, Mark Thomas and Alexander Keith. Jan. 30, 1794.
Witnesses: Edward Tyler, Edward Tyler, Jr. Recorded March 4, 1794.   [*B1, p150.*]

Isaac Hite of Long Meadow, Frederick Co., Va., appoints his friends and kinsmen Isaac and Abraham Hite of Kentucky his lawful attornies with power to sell or lease his lands in Kentucky and recover debts due him. June 1, 1793.
Acknowledged and ordered certified Dec. 4, 1793, James Keith, Clerk of Frederick County Court.
Jefferson Co. Recorded June 3, 1794.   [*B,1 p151.*]

Articles of Covenant between Samuel Kirby of Louisville and Henry Fait of Jefferson Co., whereby Samuel Kirby farm lets to Henry Fait one-fourth part of lot No. 4 in Louisville, southeast and next to Andrew Hare's lot No. 5 on the Main Street, for 15 years from date, Fait to erect a stone or brick house thereon, at least 30 by 18 feet, one-story high, 10 feet between floors. July 5, 1793.
Witnesses: B. Thruston, Stephen Ormsby, John Thruston, Ro. Breckinridge, Moses Kuykendall. Recorded June 6, 1794.
                                                                    [*B1, p153.*]

Dorsey Pentecost of Jefferson Co., Ky. appoints Joseph Pentecost, attorney at law of Washington Co., Pa., to sell the several tracts of land, in Kentucky, of 1,000 acres each which were granted by the State of Virginia by patents to him and Levi Hollingsworth, merchant of Philadelphia, on Guyandott, Sandy and Twelve Pole rivers. All former powers of attorney revoked. Aug 12, 1794.
Witnesses: John Thruston, Josiah Belt. Recorded August 19, 1794.   [*B1, p155.*]

Martin Bottorf, of Jefferson Co., sells to Patrick Joyes of Louisville, two bay mares and colts and five cows. Aug. 9, 1794·
Witnesses: Ga. J. Johnston Recorded August 13, 1794. [*B1, p157.*]

Thomas Curry, of Jefferson Co., for natural love for his son, Daniel Curry, sells to him for five shillings the plantation on which he, Thomas, lives, his slaves and all his live stock, furniture, rents and all of the balance of his estate, provided Daniel shall pay certain money to Thomas' daughters Anne, Sary and Catharine, whenever they arrive at lawful age or marry. This deed to act as his last will as far as respects his property. August 18, 1794. *Witnesses*: Will Johnston, Rich. Eastin, Jas. Meriwether. Recorded October 4, 1794.   [*B1, p158.*]

Rev. Alexander Balmain of Frederick Co., Va., appoints his friend Abraham Hite of Jefferson Co., Ky., his lawful attorney to convey to Col. James Knox of Kentucky one-third part of a 1,000 acre tract for which Balmain obtained a patent May 25, 1786, and which land is on waters of Clear Creek, Jefferson Co. for sale of which he made bond, and on April, 1789, empowered attorney to make a good and lawful deed for same. The remaining two-thirds of said tract is to be leased to best advantage, and as a great proportion of the land allotted to him by the State of Virginia as a Chaplain in the late army remains unsecured, he authorizes his attorney to take necessary measures to properly locate, survey, and otherwise secure said land on west side of the Ohio. Nov. 5, 1792.
Frederick Co., Va., Nov. 5, 1792, said letter of attorney acknowledged before Edward McGuire and Robt. Mackey, and on Nov. 6, James Keith C. F. C., Va., certified above.
Jefferson Co. Recorded January 6, 1795.
                                                                [*B1, p160.*]

Francis S. Taylor, of Norfolk Borough, Va., appoints his brother George G. Taylor of Clarke Co., Ky., his lawful attorney to rent his property in said country. July 1, 1794.
Witnesses: Richard Taylor, Sr., Benjamin Taylor, Richard Taylor, Jr., Thompson Taylor, Wm. Taylor. Recorded April 7, 1795.
                                                                [*B1, p163.*]

James Bosley of Davison Co., Territory south of the Ohio River, appoints Charles Bosley of said County and Territory his attorney to act in all matters, particularly in judgments which he has or may obtain against Capt. Thomas Smith of Kentucky at

or near Mans Lick in Jefferson Co., and also to act in reference to bonds and accounts left by James Bosley in the hands of Gabriel Johnston at Louisville. May 25, 1795.
Witnesses: W. Payne, Jesse Harrison. Recorded June 3, 1795.
[*B1, p164.*]

Thomas Daniel sells to Robert Breckinridge two slaves. April 4, 1795.
Witnesses: John Drake, Worden Pope, James Buchanan. Recorded July 7, 1795. [*B1, p166.*]

Margaret Farnsley appoints son James Farnsley her lawful attorney to demand payment due her from William Smith and James Thompson of Lancaster Co., Pa., executors of the estate of Alexander Martin, deceased of said county, a certain legacy or yearly income left her, by said Alexander Martin in his last will. July 29, 1795.
Witnesses: Geo. Leech, Francis Draine. Recorded August 4, 1795. [*B1, p167.*]

William Miller, an heir of Robert Miller deceased of Huntenton Township, Westmoreland Co., Pa. sells to Joseph Galbraith of Jefferson Co. Ky., his part of a tract of land which his father, the late Robert Miller, owned in North Huntenton Township, bounded by lands of Gasper Markel, John Milikin and Robert Hamilton.
Recorded August 4, 1795. [*B1, p168.*]

Letter to Benjamin Sebastian, dated Beargrass, Oct. 26, 1785, from Gilbert Imlay: "Expecting the complicated state of my business in this country will not only require the attention of a person acquainted in landed cases but will require much care and Judgment, I have to request that you will so far undertake it as to be my acting attorney." Imlay requests Sebastian to aid Richard Woolfolk with advise and instructions, and from him get the present state of his, Imlay's affairs. Sebastian is to communicate with General James Wilkinson and James Marshall of Fayette relative to the business of their county and to the state of land comprehended in the sale last made to Imlay by John May in Jefferson and Nelson counties. He is also to consult Isaac Hite

and particularly urge Hite to examine into the state of an entry for 50,000 acres on Green River made in the name of John Lewis, on which there are several others depending, and have it located if possible. Desires Sebastian to constantly urge Hite to forward to the Register's office all such surveys as may be near running out of date, and secure from Woolfolk a complete list of this land abridged with observations upon every entry whether or not surveyed and when recorded. "In order to facilitate the business I shall endeavor to procure a credit on the Treasurer's books of Jefferson and Nelson and provide a fund for the Register's office, but in case I should be disappointed in this business I will inform you from Danville," and further instruct him as to drawing on him for money. There was to be £50 in Colonel Isaac Shelby's hands, which Imlay would order paid him, Sebastian, and, to establish more remote funds, Imlay would leave 2,500 acres of land purchased of Joseph Lewis at the mouth of Cave Creek, a branch of Rough Creek, to be disposed of. Mr. Freeman of the Dutch Station had proposed to view it and if he found it a good place on which to settle, would pay £300 for 2,000 acres, that is a negro woman and two children, one 3 years and one 10 months old, and £20 in hand and his bond for £150 payable in May, 1790, with lawful interest. If Mr. Freeman, after seeing the land, takes it, negroes are to be sold to Mr. Bullitt or Col. Christian. Empowers Sebastian, in case John Lewis came to this country, to sell Imlay's part of the survey made in his name on Floyd's Fork for 22,000 acres.
Letter of attorney, recorded August 21, 1795.   [*B1, p169.*]

George Augustus Sugg, of the Leeded [Lieded or Luded?] Territory South of the Ohio, Davidson Co., appoints Thomas Brashears of Nelson Co., Va. [Ky.], his lawful attorney to collect from Thomas Smith, John Megomery [Montgomery], Lawrance Thompson and others in the State of Virginia, all money due him, and to bring suit against them. September 25, 1792.
Witnesses: Robert Brashears, Levi Brashear. Recorded August 18, 1795.   [*B1, p171.*]

Philip Slaughter of Culpeper Co., Va., gives power of attorney to friend Robert Coleman, now going to Kentucky, to transact his business in Kentucky and in the territory northwest of the

River Ohio, to sell land, make deeds, etc. for his lands in the state and territory aforesaid, to enter into contracts for the purpose of settling or securing any of aforesaid lands, and particularly to sell and convey a tract of land which was granted Slaughter by the State of Virginia by patent bearing date February 10, 1789, for 1,000 acres lying on then orthwest side of the Ohio River opposite Limestone. October 23, 1793.
Witnesses: French Strother, Berkell [Burkett?] Davenport.
Culpeper Co., Va., power of attorney acknowledged February 16, 1795; on March 28, 1795, John Jameson certifies same.
Jefferson Co., Ky. Recorded August 4, 1795.   [*B1, p172.*]

James F. Moore, James Sullivan, William Agun and William Sullivan of Jefferson Co., give bond to Isaac Shelby, Governor of Kentucky. The conditions are that whereas by Act of Assembly and act to establish a town on the lands of James F. Moore in Jefferson Co., and another act to amend the act concerning the Town of Washington in Mason Co. and for other purposes, it is necessary that James F. Moore shall enter into bond for the faithful payment of all sums which he may receive from the sales of lots in said Town. If Moore pay all sums which he receives from said sales, rents, profits and damages, then this obligation shall be void. July 8, 1795.
Witness: Stephn Ormsby. Recorded July 8, 1795. [*B1, p174.*]

[Note. *Statute Law of Kentucky,* by William Littell, Vol. 1, page 233: An Act to establish a Town on the lands of James Francis Moore, in Jefferson County, approved Dec. 13, 1794.

"Whereas it is represented to the general assembly, that one hundred and fifty acres of land near Mann's Lick, the property of James Francis Moore, adjoining the land of James Speed, and lands claimed by Joseph Brooks, has been already laid off into a town, with convenient streets, out-lots, &c., therefore,
Section 1. Be it enacted by the general assembly, That the said town be established by the name of New Town, and the property thereof be vested in Abner Field, Basil Prather, Isaac Hornbeck, Lewis Field, and James Standiford, gentlemen, trustees," etc.]

Agness Miller of Jefferson Co., conveys to son William Miller her goods and chattels on the condition that he furnish her with meat, drink, lodging and clothing during her life and at her death

bury her. February 8, 1792.
Witnesses: John Martin, Thomas Hooper. Recorded September
29, 1795.   [*B1, p175.*]

William Anderson and John McCready both of Westmoreland
Co., Pa., appoint William Wilson of Louisville, Ky., their lawful
attorney to recover all money due them and particularly from
their attorney [blank] Johnston of said county, on a bond duly
executed to the said John McCready and by him assigned to
William Anderson. Aug. 4, 1795.
Witnesses: James Stewart, Robt. Taylor, J. P.
Westmoreland Co., Thomas Hamilton, Prothy, certifies above,
August 4, 1795.
Jefferson Co. Recorded September 30, 1795.   [*B1, p176.*]

Mark Thomas of Jefferson Co., Va., gives power of attorney to
James Patten to sell and convey enough of his lands in said county
and state to satisfy and pay off a judgment recovered in the
Supreme Court of the District of Kentucky in the name of Daniel
Broadhead, Jr., against Mark Thomas and Benjamin Pope as his
security on a bond for the conveyance of land, all costs, interest
and fees, so that said Pope will be fully cleared, released and
acquitted. January 31, 1791.
Witnesses: Enos [?] Moore, Martha Patten, Mary Patten.
Proven October 6, 1795 by oaths of Martha and Mary Patten,
alias Martha Nelson and Mary Vaughan, and Recorded.
                                                           [*B1, p178.*]

Jeremiah Orme, of Montgomery Co., Md., gives power of attorney to Nicholas Brashears of Nelson Co., Ky., to recover a
negro woman slave and her child. Aug. 29, 1795.
Witnesses: R. Anderson. Certified to by Thomas Munroe, Montgomery Co. Md., Clerk.
Jefferson Co. Recorded December 1, 1795.   [*B1, p179.*]

George Rogers Clark of Jefferson Co. appoints his brother
William Clark his attorney to convey to Humphrey Marshall all
his land on the Tennessee, Ohio and Mississippi rivers agreeable
to articles of agreement existing between him and Marshall, also
to sell and convey his moiety of three tracts of land held in

partnership with Major John Crittenden on the Ohio and Kentucky rivers and on Locust Creek, also to receive money due him. August 15, 1796.
Recorded [sic:] October 5, 1796.   [*B1, p181.*]

James McDonald and William Johnston gave bond to Samuel Oldham in sum of £20,000 current money State of Kentucky. Whereas, Samuel Oldham had obtained from the land office of Virginia patents for lands then in the State of Virginia to the amount of 17,367 acres as follows: 593 acres in the Knobs on the Ohio in Jefferson Co; 250 acres, same; 3,500 acres on Adams Creek, a north branch of Rough Creek in Hardin Co; 2,000 acres, same; 1,389 acres on Little Otter Creek in Hardin Co; 1,210 acres, same; 1,210 acres, same; 942 acres, same; 273 acres in Jefferson Co., on the waters of Ohio in the Knobs; 6,000 acres on Little Kentucky River and Drenning Lick Creek. Said patents have been delivered to McDonald and Johnston by Oldham and he is to made deed, but Oldham, his heirs, etc., are relieved from all obligations, and, if any of the said lands be lost by prior entry, McDonald and Johnston shall stand the loss. August 22, 1795. *Witnesses*: Abr. Hite, B. Thruston, Benj. Frye. Recorded January 5, 1796.   [*B1, p182.*]

Benjamin Johnston, one of the representatives of Benjamin Johnston, deceased, of Jefferson Co., assigned unto William Johnston all the rights he, Benjamin, has to the one-seventh part of all lands in Kentucky which were located by Benjamin Johnston, now dead and which were divided among his heirs. March 1, 1796.
Witnesses: Jos. Lewis, James Winn, Davis Floyd. Recorded March 1, 1796.   [*B1, p185.*]

William Johnston gives bond to Benjamin, whereas Benjamin this day conveyed to William lands in Yohogania, now Ohio Co., Virginia, and in Monongalia and other counties in Virginia, as one of the representatives of Benjamin Johnston (now deceased) and sundry claims to land in Kentucky, never to look to Benjamin for any loss of land by prior claim, etc.
Witnesses: Davis Floyd, Jos. Lewis, James Winn. Recorded March 1, 1796.   [*B1, p186.*]

David Humphreys and Charles Scott of Fayette and Wood-
ford counties and Joshua Humphreys and John Postlethwaite of
Fayette Co., Ky., are bound unto Samuel Terrell of Louisa Co.,
Va., £2,000 money of Kentucky. Conditions, whereas Samuel
Terrell has bought from David Humphreys and Charles Scott
332 acres of land in Jefferson Co. on south Fork of Harrod's Creek,
should Samuel lose the land by a better claim D. Humphreys,
J. Humphreys, Scott, Postlethwaite must refund to Terrell the
amount of the loss. October 10, 1795.
Witnesses: Richard Terrell, Richard Harris. Recorded April 5,
1796.   [*B1, p188.*]

Edmund Taylor exchanges with Major William Taylor a location of 500 acres on the Ohio between a survey of Hugh Mercer
and an entry of James Taylor and Edmund Taylor, about thirteen
miles above the Falls of the Ohio, for an equal quantity out of a
tract of land surveyed for Major William Taylor on Floyd's Fork,
also he is entitled to one-third of half the entry of 1,500 acres
joining the same for his part of locating in company with Benj.
Taylor and Edmund, and he is entitled to one-fourth of the other
half of said 1,500 acres as joint proprietor with James, Francis,
and Edmund Taylor. March 23, 1784.
Witnesses: John Thruston, Anthony Sale, Willis Hord. Recorded
July 5, 1796.   [*B1, p189.*]

Whereas Michael Dillon and Lucretia his wife of Louisville, by
indenture January 22, 1794, sold unto Richard H. Goe, late of
Kentucky, now of Connellsville, Fayette Co., Pennsylvania, one
lot in Louisville No. 128, Goe constitutes Archibald Armstrong of
Louisville his lawful attorney to sell said lot and in Goe's name
give clear title subject to an incumbrance mentioned in indenture
from Michael Dillon, etc., Dec. 16, 1794.
Witnesses: William Harbough, Jonathan Harbough.
Fayette Co., Pa., Dec. 16, 1795, acknowledged before Jonathan
Rowland, J. P. and Ephraim Douglas, Prothy, certified same.
Jefferson Co. Recorded January 5, 1796.   [*B1, p189.*]

Joseph Brooks of Jefferson Co., gives bond to Hugh Grimes of
same county. Whereas Hugh Grimes and his wife have this day
conveyed to Joseph Brooks by deed 100 acres in Jefferson Co., on
the waters of Pond Creek, which land was conveyed to Grimes by

Richard McMahan by deed April 1, 1788, it is the intent of Brooks to take the risk of the title. October 4, 1796.
Recorded October 4, 1796. [*B1, p191.*]
[Note: This bond is recorded twice, and the two pages on which it is recorded are numbered 191 in original book.]

Robert Karney Moore releases and quit claims unto Tardiveau Brothers from all manner of actions, bills, bonds, obligations, mortgages, especially one of sundry tracts of land dated Sept. 15, 1791, debts due judgments, executions, quarrels, etc. both at law and in equity against Tardiveau Brothers. June 4, 1796.
Witnesses: Walter E. Strong, Joshua Barbee, Robt. Rochester, Benj. Field, Jacob Yuie [Yuse?]. Recorded November 1, 1796.
[*B1, p192.*]

Peter Carr of Goochland Co., Va., appoints his friend Richard Terrell of Kentucky his lawful attorney to execute a deed to Dr. Walter Warfield for certain lands granted Carr by Virginia of the land set apart for the officers and soldiers of the Virginia State Line. March 17, 1794.
Witnesses: Eliza B. Christian, Annie H. Christian, P. Harrington. Letter of attorney was proven by the oaths of Eliza B. Dickinson, formerly Eliza B. Christian, and Anne H. Christian. Recorded November 1, 1796. [*B1, p193.*]

Indenture between Elizabeth Bowyer Christian, spinster, and Walter Warfield dated August 29, 1795, whereby fourteen slaves were to be transferred in trust to said Walter Warfield for the sole use of Elizabeth Christian. Since then she has married Richard Dickinson, attorney at law, and desires to revoke the said deed of trust; and it is hereby revoked. March 16, 1796.
Witnesses: Rich'd Terrell, H. Churchill, Thos. Prather, Chas. Nabb. Recorded November 1, 1796. [*B1, p194.*]

Nicholas Coonse of Jefferson Co., gives bond to William Pope of same county: whereas John Todd in his life time, as assignee of John Faith, assigned to William Pope a pre-emption warrant for 400 acres of land, which had been located on the head waters of the South Fork of Beargrass, including the plantation whereon Nicholas Coonse lived, and which was patented in the name of William Pope, and whereas John Todd, at the time of making the assignment, passed his obligation to Pope to warrant the title, and Pope on this day conveyed to Nicholas Coonse 105 acres of land, part of the before mentioned tract, Coons will not hold Pope or his heirs for loss by virtue of prior or better claim. Nov. 1, 1796. *Witnesses*: E. Hall, M. Love, John Pope, Henry Churchill. Recorded November 1, 1796. [*B1, p195.*]

John Gerault, residing in the District of Natchez, appoints W. Phillip Nolan of the same place as his lawful attorney to settle all manner of business for him, sell lands, etc. April 16, 1796. *Witnesses*: James Johnson, Wm. Johnson. On April 16, 1796, John Gerault acknowledged power of attorney before Dr. Carlos de Grand Pre Colonel in the Royal Armies charged with the military and civil government of that place. In testimony whereof he set his hand and "seal of my arms at the seat of government of Natchez," signed "Carlos de Grand Pre." Jefferson Co. Recorded December 6, 1796. [*B1, p196.*]

Joseph Brooks gives bond to John Kinnison [Kennison]. Kinnison has conveyed to Joseph Brooks 150 acres of land which was conveyed to Kinnison by Rich'd McMahon April 1, 1788, being part of a 1,000 acre tract in Jefferson Co. on waters of Pond Creek granted to said Richard McMahan by a patent June 7, 1786. Should Brooks be ejected of whole or any part of the 150 acres by another and better claim, he shall not call on John Kinnison or heirs for any part of money paid by Brooks. November 8, 1796. *Witnesses*: John Pope, Henry Ditto, William Pope, Jr., Ga. J. Johnston. Recorded December 6, 1796. [*B1, p197.*]

John Kinnison conveys to Joseph Brooks 150 acres in Jefferson County on Pond Creek, by deed with special warranty. This is land conveyed to Kinnison by Richard McMahan on April 1, 1788. As it is the intent of the agreement that Brooks shall take the risk of the title without any claim against Kinnison, he empowers Brooks to institute any suits, etc. in his name against McMahan in case of breach of the covenants or warranty. November 8, 1796. *Witnesses*: John Pope, Henry Ditto, Wn. Pope, Jr., Ga. J. Johnston. Recorded December 6, 1796. [*B1, p199.*]

CALENDAR OF BOND AND POWER OF ATTORNEY
BOOK No. 1, JEFFERSON COUNTY, KENTUCKY, 1783–1798

By Ludie J. Kinkead and Katherine G. Healy

In Three Parts

Part Three: February, 1797—March, 1799

John Irwin appoints friend Ga. J. Johnston his lawful attorney to collect all his debts and to take the necessary steps to enforce payments. October 5, 1796.
Witness: Worden Pope. Recorded February 8, 1797.

[*B1, p200.*]

William Fleming of Chesterfield Co., Va., appoints General Robert Breckinridge of Jefferson Co., Ky., his lawful attorney to sell 1,200 acres of land, part of a 10,200 acre tract in said county, granted to Fleming by patent Dec. 6, 1788. Breckinridge is to make all settlements and conveyances and to farm and let-out or lease any unoccupied part of this land. He is also empowered to purchase from John Lewis, or whoever claims under him, about 200 acres southeast of Cummins on the road to Mann's Lick and adjoining the aforesaid grant, near the southeast and towards James Madison's corner. September 23, 1796.
Witnesses: Stephen Ormsby, Worden Pope, John Drake, Alex. Breckinridge. Recorded March 8, 1797.   [*B1, p201.*]

William Austin, of Richmond, Va., appoints Fortunatus Cosby his attorney to act for him in all legal matters, and revokes a former power of attorney given to Richard Terrell of Kentucky Sept. 23, 1796.
Richmond, Va., Sept. 23, 1796, power of attorney acknowledged before Robt. Mitchell, Mayor of Richmond.
Jefferson Co., Ky.   Recorded June 6, 1797.   [*B1, p202.*]

John Winston of Hanover Co., Va., appoints Fortunatus Cosby his lawful attorney to enter, locate, survey and secure any claim for lands which he does or ought to possess in the State of Kentucky and in the Territory Northwest of the Ohio River. October 5, 1796.

Hanover Co., Va., October 5, 1796, power of attorney acknowledged before Jno. Browne, William Fontaine.

Jefferson Co., Ky., Recorded June 6, 1797.   [*B1, p205.*]

William Glassell, merchant, Fredericksburg, Va., appoints Fortunatus Cosby, attorney at law, his lawful attorney to recover money due him in Kentucky on his own account or as attorney in fact for John Glassell, formerly merchant in Fredericksburg, either in his name or as surviving partner of Hunter and Glassell, and Andrew Johnston and Co.   October 10, 1796.

Fredericksburg, Va., Power of attorney acknowledged before William Harvey, N. P.

Jefferson Co., Ky., Recorded June 6, 1797.   [*B1, p206.*]

John Mortimer, of Fredericksburg, Va., appoints Fortunatus Cosby, attorney at law, his lawful attorney to make entry and pay taxes for a 4,125 acre tract of land in Shelby Co., on Pattens Creek, and to make a lease for a term of not over three years, and to defend the land against all other claims.   October 3, 1796.

Fredericksburg, Va., power of attorney acknowledged October 4, 1796, before William Harvey, N. P.

Jefferson Co., Ky., Recorded June 6, 1797.   [*B1, p207.*]

Charles Yates, Fredericksburg, Spottsylvania Co., Va., for himself, for the late House of Payne, Moore & Co., of Falmouth in Stafford Co., Va., as managing partner thereof, and for the estate of Daniel Payne, deceased, of Falmouth, appoints Fortunatus Cosby, attorney at law, his lawful attorney to collect debts amounting to £500, 14 shillings, 3¾ pence due the above mentioned.   September 29, 1796.

Witness: William Payne.

Fredericksburg, Spottsylvania Co., Va., certified before William Lovell, J. P., and on October 1, 1796, John Chew, Clk., testifies that Will Lovell is duly qualified.

Jefferson Co., Ky., Recorded June 6, 1797.   [*B1, p208.*]

John Ryburn of Fredericksburg, Spottsylvania Co., Va., as attorney in fact for James Ritchie & Co. merchants, in Glasgow, appoints Fortunatus Cosby lawful attorney for said James Ritchie & Co., to collect money due them, £346, 16 shillings and 8 pence farthing Virginia Currency, and to give acquittances to those making payments.   October 3, 1796.
Fredericksburg, Va., acknowledged before William Harvey, N. P., October 3, 1796.
Jefferson Co., Ky., Recorded June 6, 1797.   [*B1, p209.*]

John Miller, of Botetourt Co., Va., appoints William Preston Anderson, of Fayette Co., Ky., his lawful attorney to transact all his business in Kentucky and Tennessee in reference to selling and conveying lands.   March 7, 1797.
Botetourt Co., Va., March 7, 1797, above acknowledged before Pat. Lockhart, Joell Bott, and Henry Bowger certifies that these men are acting magistrates.
Jefferson County, Ky., Recorded July 4, 1797.   [*B1, p210.*]

John Peyton Harrison, of Fauquier Co., Va., by power of attorney September 13, 1790, recorded in Loudoun Co., authorized Burr Powell of said County to pay off and convey to Isaac Hite, Andrew Hynes and John Handley, one-fourth part of the lands located by them for Harrison under a contract between them and Leven Powell, May 1, 1790.   Burr Powell in the execution of said power assigned to Isaac Hite, to whom the others had relinquished their right, 162 acres, part of a 1,000 acre tract on the waters of or near Simpsons Creek, which tract was afterwards conveyed by Hite to Leven Powell.   It appears that Harrison, previous to giving the power of attorney, had sold the said 1,000 acres to one Chinn, but neglected to make reserve of it in said power of attorney, therefore there are two claimants under unimproved lot of 162 acres, and in order to clear claim, Harrison empowers Burr Powell to lay off and convey to either of the parties interested 184 acres out of a tract located and surveyed for him by Isaac Hite on Floyd's Fork, which originally contained 1,000 acres, but one-fourth of it has already been conveyed to Isaac Hite and by him to Leven Powell.   February 27, 1797.
Fauquier Co., Va., February 27, 1797, acknowledged and recorded by F. Brook.
Jefferson Co., Ky., Recorded July 4, 1797.   [*B1, p211.*]

402

Leven Powell, of Loudoun Co., Va., appoints his son Burr Powell of same county his lawful attorney to regulate and direct his affairs in the District of Kentucky. September 13, 1790.

Loudoun Co., Va. September 13, 1790, acknowledged before Chas. Bemis; recorded April 10, 1797.

Jefferson Co., Ky., Recorded July 4, 1797. [*B1, p213.*]

Christopher Bryon, now of Jefferson Co., Ky., appoints John C. Owings of Clark Co., his lawful attorney to effect a division of 1,000 acres of land between Bryon and Edward Worthington, according to agreement given by Bryon to Worthington April 17, 1789. The land is in Bourbon County on Rose Run, a branch of State, running on the east side, which land was granted to Thomas Clark by patent May 28, 1787, and conveyed by deed March 25, 1789 to Bryon. February 18, 1797.

Witness: Worden Pope, Proven August 2, 1797. [*B1, p214.*]

Garrett Pendergrass releases Jesse Pendergrass from any expense connected with suit to recover any part of estate of Garrett Pendergrass, deceased, Jesse Pendergrass having made a general sale to Garrett of all his rights in the estate of Garrett Pendergrass, deceased, with certain exceptions. July 5, 1797.

Witnesses: Jno. Harrison, Ths. M. Winn. Recorded July 5, 1797. [*B1, p215.*]

Josiah Bell in consideration of $120 sold to William White certain property, including a horse purchased from Joseph Gaul [Gaut or Gant?] and tools of various kinds including "a holdfast"; Joseph Gaul purchased of William White a gray horse, for which Gaul and Bell gave bond to pay by April 1st next. December 17, 1796.

Witnesses: Elisha Jeter, John Daniel, Benjn. Bridged. Recorded August 1, 1797. [*B1, p215.*]

Peyton Short appoints his friend Col. Alexander Scott Bullitt his lawful attorney for the purpose of selling the following lands: 3,900 acres on the Ohio, about five miles below the Falls on the south side, and called Flemings Military Survey, resurveyed by Thomas Hopkins July 27, 1793; 600 acres being part of Harrison Military Survey, adjoining survey of Fleming; 314 acres being

part of Roberts Pre-emption below the Falls of Ohio, which tract was conveyed by Benjamin Roberts to Lacassagne and from Lacassagne to Short. July 7, 1797.
Witnesses: Richard Eastin, Edmund Basye, Henry Churchill, John Pope. Proven and Recorded August 2, 1797. [*B1, p217.*]

John Shannon, Jr., of Shelby Co., Ky., appoints Ga. J. Johnston, of Louisville, his attorney in fact for the purpose of selling a tract of 800 acres in Jefferson County on the waters of Floyd's Fork, adjoining a survey of Simeon Tripletts by patent assigned by the Commonwealth of Virginia and signed January 18, 1786 by Patrick Henry. September 20, 1797.
Witnesses: WELAM, John Allen. Recorded September 26, 1797. [*B1, p218.*]

George Rogers Clark, of Jefferson Co., Ky., appoints his brother William Clark his lawful attorney in fact to act and transact all manner of business in Kentucky, the Territory North West of the Ohio River, or any other place within the United States or elsewhere. November 3, 1797.
Witness: Elisha Embree. Recorded December 5, 1797.
[*B1, p219.*]

John Abbott, for natural love, gives to his son William Abbott certain cattle, horses and colts; to son Johnson Abbott, one bay mare and colt; to daughter Rebecca Abbott, one sorrel mare and colt; to daughter Mildred, one slave and a mare; to daughter Nancy, two colts. December 6, 1797.
Witness: Richard Harris. Recorded January 2, 1798.
[The above is recorded as five separate deeds of gift]
[*B1, pp220-223.*]

James McKim, of Rappeace district, Province of Louisiana, appoints John Handley of Hardin Co., Ky., his lawful attorney to claim all property in Pennsylvania willed him by his brother John McKim, deceased, and to sell, lease or otherwise dispose of same, and revokes all previous powers-of-attorney. January 4, 1798.
Recorded January 6, 1798. [*B1, p223.*]

Jacob Larue, of Frederick Co., Va., appoints Alexander and Robert Breckinridge of Jefferson Co., Ky., his lawful attorneys to ascertain all the interfering claims within the bounds of two surveys of 18,000 acres, between Floyd's Fork and the trace leading from the Falls of the Ohio to Bullitt's Lick, and to adjust and settle all disputes to the interest of said Larue. March 9, 1795. *Witnesses:* Worden Pope, John Drake and James Buchanan. Recorded March 6, 1798. [*B1, p224.*]

Henry Lyne, of Henry Co., Va., appoints Stephen Ormsby, of Jefferson Co., Ky., his lawful attorney to convey, by deed, unto Richard Reynolds two-third part of 500 acres of land granted to Henry Lyne by patent May 27, 1785, in Jefferson Co., on the Ohio and adjoining lands of William Fleming and George Lyne, agreeable to a division made of the said tract between Richard Reynolds and Isaac Hite of Jefferson Co., and also to convey to Isaac Hite a deed for the other third of the 500 acres. May 25, 1793.
Witnesses: J. Colman, Joseph Kellar. Recorded July 20, 1798.
[*B1, p225.*]

Benjamin Sebastian, of Jefferson Co., releases Michael Horine, of Lincoln Co., Ky., from any actions or causes of actions, debts, bonds, contracts, covenants, etc., which he ever had against him. October 23, 1797.
Witnesses: Jno. Speed, Jas. A. Sturgus [A'Sturgus], Charles Beeler, Lewis Field. Recorded February 6, 1798. [*B1, p226.*]

Cad. Slaughter agrees to a recorded obligation from Col. Richard Taylor to Benoni Demant. June 5, 1790.
Witnesses: Francis R. Slaughter, James Sloane. Recorded March 6, 1798. [*B1, p226.*]

James Smith, of Jefferson Co., being endebted to John Stucky, of same county, for £40 lawful money; and John Stucky having gone James Smith's bond for certain money to William Allison, and also for several others in small debts; James Smith, in order to pay debts, assigns and sells unto the said John Stucky all manner of goods, chattels, debts, money, and one sorrel horse. February 20, 1798.
Witnesses: Jno. Miller, John Ad Bory [Booy?], Martin Pottorff. Bill of Sale recorded March 6, 1798. [*B1, p227.*]

James Meriwether and Thomas Johnson, Jr., administrators of the will of George Meriwether, deceased, appoint W. James Poindexter, of Louisa Co., Va., attorney to complete their administration on the said George Meriwether's estate in Kentucky. *Witnesses:* Geo. Poindexter, David Morris.

Louisa Co., Va., Aug. 30, 1797, James Meriwether and Thomas Johnson Jr., acknowledge this power of attorney as their act and deed, before Henry Garrett and Richard Johnson, acting magistrates of Louisa Co., and on August 31st, John Poindexter, certifies that they are duly qualified to act.

Jefferson Co., Power of attorney ordered recorded June 5, 1798.
[*B1, p228.*]

Thomas Smith of Bullitt Co., appoints John Eastin of Louisville his lawful attorney to dispose of a 5,000 acre tract in Tennessee, supposed to be on waters of Cumberland River and in the Middle District, granted June 8, 1797, by North Carolina to Stokely Donelson, and by him on Aug. 19, 1797, conveyed to Thomas Smith by indenture. April 9, 1798.
Witnesses: Worden Pope, Ro. Floyd. Recorded June 5, 1798.
[*B1, p229.*]

John Obannon, of Woodford Co., gives bond to Abraham Hite, of Jefferson Co., in the sum of £500 current money, to deed to him one-half of a 1,000 acre plot with certificate of survey made in the name of Jonah Thompson, on the waters of Bank Lick Creek, and which had been assigned to John Obannon. October 31, 1794. *Teste:* Will McClung.

On April 3, 1798, Abraham Hite for value received assigned his rights to the within bond and land to William Hite. *Teste:* Isaac Batman.
Witnesses: Saml. Gwathmey, Worden Pope. Recorded June 5, 1798. [*B1, p231.*]

Henry Fait and Margaret Fait his wife, of Jefferson Co., give bond in the sum of £2,000 to John Hugh and Alexander Ralston, of Bullitt Co., to deed to them the 110 acres of land in Jefferson Co., on the waters of Beargrass, whereon the mill, commonly called Falls, now stands, as per James Sullivan's deed to Fait, June 1, 1798.

Witnesses: Worden Pope. Samuel McClintuk and John Gilmore heard Margaret Fait acknowledge the above as her act and deed. Deed proven and ordered recorded June 5, 1798.
Marginal note: Original delivered to J. Heugh.   [*B1, p232.*]

Helana Collier [Colier?] of Somerset Co., Md., executrix of the will of Dowty [Douty] Collier, deceased, late of said county, appoints Charles Shearman of Jefferson Co., her attorney to receive all money due her from Josiah Record and James Tulley by their bond granted to said Dowty Collier and John Leatherbury whom Collier survived.   March 16, 1798.
Witnesses: James Reed, James Reed Jr.   Recorded July 20, 1798.   [*B1, p233.*]

Somerset Co., Md., Esme Bayley, Register of Wills, certified that on ———————28th, 1797, the will of Dowty Colier was approved and on Dec. 4, 1797, letters testamentary were granted to Hellena Colier, the executrix.   March 15, 1798.
Witness: William Jones, Juctice of the Orphans Court.
Jefferson Co., Ky.,   Recorded July 20, 1798.   [*B1, p234.*]

Thomas Smith, of Bullitt Co., bill of sale to Henry Churchill, of Jefferson Co., for certain slaves, including those purchased from Thacker Washington, of King George Co., Va.   April 23, 1798.
Witnesses: Thos. Sanders, Robert Matthews, Daniel Hillary.
Recorded July 11, 1798.   [*B1, p236.*]

Memorandum of articles of agreement entered into by George Wilson with James F. Moore.   It is agreed by George Wilson that William Fleming in his life time was entitled to a portion of two claims, one for 200 acres and the other for 600 acres including and adjoining Mann's Lick, designated by a decree of Supreme Court for the District of Kentucky, when the said Fleming was complainant and the heirs of John Todd and one James Speed were defendants.   George Wilson on January 5, 1790, purchased from William Fleming one-fourth part of the 200 acre entry made in the name of John Todd, to include Mann's Lick, and one-third part of the 600 acre entry made in the name of James Speed, to adjoin the 200 acre entry.   On January 5, 1790, Fleming passed an obligation to George Wilson to convey within the proper time; see bond, now transferred to James F. Moore by assignment. George Wilson releases and transfers to said James F. Moore all the George Wilson rights in the two entries, and obliges himself to dig or cause to be dug a new horse well of the common size near what is called the forward well and to put the same in order for use on or before May 1, 1799. George Wilson reservs for himself and heirs the free and uninterrupted use (to be conveyed by the channel it is at present) of salt water and the use and occupation of the old house. April 20, 1798.

Witnesses: Ga. J. Johnston, Joseph Brook, John Pope, James Sullivan. Recorded August 7, 1798. [*B1, p237.*]

Abram Haptonstalle received of James Sullivan £50 for which he is to give Sullivan credit on his bond for £300 worth of land. July 6, 1798.

Witnesses: John Drake, Geo. R. C. Floyd. Recorded July 9, 1798. [*B1, p241.*]

Abram Hamptonstalle received of James Sullivan a deed from William Sullivan and wife to Hamptonstalle for 250 acres for which he is to give James Sullivan credit for £250 on his bond for £300 worth of land. July 6, 1798.

Witnesses: Geo. R. C. Floyd, John Drake. Recorded July 9, 1798. [*B1, p241.*]

George Wilson received of James F. Moore full satisfaction for all debts, etc. to date and for all actions, suits, quarrels and controversies, the two having reached a compromise and made a final settlement and each has passed to the other an acquittal. April 28, 1798.

Witness: Ga. J. Johnston. Recorded August 7, 1798.[*B1, p241.*]

James F. Moore received of George Wilson full satisfaction for all debts, etc. to date and for all actions, suits, quarrels and controversies, the two having reached a compromise and made a final settlement and each has passed to the other an acquittal. April 28, 1798.

Witness: Ga. J. Johnston. Recorded August 7, 1798.[*B1, p242.*]

Philip Graham of Somerset Co., Md., states that knowing the practice of holding his fellow men in perpetual bondage and slavery is "repugnant to the golden law of God," and the right of mankind as well as to every principal of the "late Glorious revolution which has taken place in America," he emancipates, sets free and discharges all his negroes, by name and age of each, and the date freedom is to be granted each, between date of document and the year 1812.

Witnesses: Isaac Handy, Samuel Curtis.

Somerset Co., Md., May 1, 1787, Philip Graham acknowledged above as his act and deed. John Williams, by Thomas Haywood, Clk. William Done, Clk., Somerset County Court, made certified copy of above on February 27, 1798.

Jefferson Co., Ky. Transcript of manumission was recorded August 7, 1798. [*B1, p243.*]

Indenture between David Malot, an infant orphan of———— Malot, deceased, and Robert Hindman of Jefferson Co.: David Malot with the consent of his mother and the approbation and consent of the justices of Jefferson Co. in consideration of certain covenants, etc. has placed himself an apprentice to Robert Hindman to dwell with him and serve in the capacity of an apprentice until he is twenty-one years of age, to faithfully serve his master in all lawful business, and be honest, orderly and obedient, and the said Hindman is to provide for him sufficient meat, drink, apparel, washing, lodging and instruct the said apprentice in the art and mystery of a weaver and the occupation of a farmer, and shall teach him, or have him taught, to read and write, also common arithmetic, including the rule of three. At the expiration of his service he is to pay David £3 and 10 shillings, a horse, saddle and bridle and two new suits of cloths. August 7, 1798.

Signed by James Denny, presiding justice of said Court on behalf of Infant, and Robert Hindman. Indenture was, with the consent of the court, ordered recorded, August 7, 1798. [*B1, p246.*]

John Shannon, age fourteen, infant orphan of James Shannon, apprenticed to William Kearney, according to law, to learn the trade of carpenter and house joiner. June 8, 1798. Chas. Quirey, presiding justice of the court. Recorded August 7, 1798.
[*B1, p247.*]

PRISON BOUNDS, JEFFERSON COUNTY JAIL, LOUISVILLE, 1798

Reduced facsimile of a Court Record of 1798 presenting the plat and description of Prison Bounds—the bounds within which certain prisoners were permitted at certain times. For a transcription of this page, see our page 164.

In cases of imprisonment for debt, Prison Bounds were extended, in 1820, by the State to the town limits of each county seat. In 1821 imprisonment for debt was abolished, except in cases in which fraud was shown.—*Collins*.

Anthony Foster appoints Fortunatus Cosby his lawful attorney to convey his right to a tract of land in Franklin Co., on the Kentucky River opposite Frankfort, it being an entry and survey of 1,700 acres.   May 2, 1798.
Witnesses: Richd. Harris, John Collins, James Fountaine,   Recorded August 7, 1798.   [*B1, p249.*]

James Shannon, infant orphan, aged about nine years, apprenticed, according to law, to James Anderson of Jefferson Co., to learn the trade of cabinet maker.   Chas. Quirey, presiding justice of the court.   August 7, 1798.   Recorded same day.
[*B1, p250.*]

[PRISON BOUNDS: We present a reduced facsimilie of the page devoted to the recording to the plat and description of the Prison Bounds.   The text, copied in full, is as follows:]
"Surveyed for the Prison Bounds or aisles of Jefferson County Ten acres of Land in the Town of Louisville represented on the above Plat by red lines [double lines] and Bounded as follows Vize Beginning at the N. W. corner of the Jail [on Sixth Street], thence N. 3° E. 52 poles [1 pole is 5½ yards] through Mrs. Morgans & Harrisons Lots into the main Street [Main Street] about one pole from the N. W. Corner of Harrison's Brick House, thence up main Street N. 87° E., 30 po. & 15 Links to a Stone in the edge of One of the South or Cross Streets and about two poles & 17 links from N. E. Corner of Bustards Store, thence So. 3° W. 53 po. up Cross Street on the West edge to a stone near a thorny Bush at the edge of E. William's Lot, thence on a direct course to the Southeast corner of the Jail and including the same.
"Worden Pope Sv.
"At A Court held for Jefferson County Aug't the 7th, 1798
"The foregoing Platt & Cer't of the prison Bounds of said County was returned and Ordered to be Recorded.
"*Teste* Worden Pope."
[The plat indicates that the town lots shown were owned by the following:
North side of Main Street: Johnston, Joyes, Wilson, Prather, Lentz, and Nabb.
South side of Main Street: Harrison, Nelson, Elliott, Howell, Waters &c., and H. Reagar.

411

North Side of Market Street: Harrison, J. Phillips, J. Eastin, Waters, and Johnston.

South side of Market Street: Mrs. Morgans, Ga. J. Johnston, Ths. Phillips, Kaye, and S. Reagar.

North Side of Jefferson Street: Hoops, and Williams: also the Court House and the Jail.]

Plat and description recorded August 7, 1798.

[*B1, p252.*]

Henry Churchill and John Pope, guardians of John, Richard and Abigail Oldham, children and infant heirs, legal representatives of Lieut. Col. William Oldham, authorize and empower their Friend ————— of ————— to act for them and receive money due the above heirs in right of their father as a pension or otherwise from the United States. October 3, 1798. Recorded same day. [*B1, p253.*]

John Holker of Frederick Co., Va., now in the city of Philadelphia, appoints Robert Kearney Moore of Louisville, Jefferson Co., Ky., his lawful attorney to receive from the heirs, executors or administrators of Michael Lacassagne, late of Louisville, all such deeds, conveyances and assurances in the law for vesting in John Holker all the lands, tenements, etc. in Kentucky or in the Northwestern Territory of the United States which Michael Lacassagne sold to John Holker or held in trust for the use of him. April 13, 1798.

Witnesses: Henry K. Helmuth, James Gibson.

Philadelphia: May 1, 1798. Power of attorney acknowledged before Henry [Hilary?] Baker, Mayor.

Jefferson Co., Recorded September 27, 1798. [*B1, p254.*]

John Rice, age five years, with the approbation and consent of the justices of the County Court of Jefferson Co. is apprenticed, according to law, to Edmund Rice to learn the occupation of a farmer. Signed by John Miller and Edm. Rice. October 4, 1798. [*B1, p256.*]

Bill of Sale: Jon'n Nescon sold at public sale at the dwelling house of F. Bareckman, two old slaves for $80.50, belonging to the estate of Richard Abbott, deceased. January 1,1798. Recorded June 5, 1797[sic]. [*B1, p257.*]

Simeon Spring of Louisville appoints Lyman Harding of same place his lawful attorney to sell and covey a 640 acre tract of land in Sumner Co., Tenn., being all that land deeded to Simeon Spring by William Shaw, assignee of the heirs of John Best; to collect all debts due him from any person in Kentucky; to pay any debts owed by him to Robert Craddock of Danville in Mercer County. November 13, 1798.
Witnesses: Robert McConnell, Geo. Cooper. Acknowledged before John Miller, J. P., and Henry Duncan, J. P. Recorded November 30,1798. [*B1, p258.*]

Able Sprigs, age six years, with the consent of the justices of Jefferson Co. Court, is apprenticed, according to law, to William McManamy, to learn the art and mystery of a carpenter. Executed in open court by Will McManamy and Moses Kuykendall. Dated and recorded December 3, 1799. [*B1, p260.*]

Jacob Springer of Allegheny Co., Penn., states he is "entitled for my services during the late war to thirteen hundred and sixty-six and two-thirds acres of land which was surveyed to me by virtue of a Military Warrant from the State of Virginia, situate in Green Co.", Kentucky, and appoints his friend William Harrison of Kentucky his lawful attorney to manage and settle all matters pertaining to and concerning the obtaining of a patent for the said land and to sell it. He revokes all former powers of attorney he may have given. September 13, 1798.
Witnesses: Mich'l Jones, L. Stewart.
Allegheny Co., September 13, 1798: Above acknowledged before Jno. Wilkins, J. P; and James Bryson, Clerk of the Peace of Allegheny Co., certified that John Wilkins was a Justice of the Peace.
Jefferson Co. Recorded December 4, 1798. *Teste.* Sam. Gwathmey, D. C. J. C.
[Note: In original book the page numbers 260 and 261 are duplicated] [*B1, p260.*]

John Callender, of Boston, Suffolk Co., Mass., administrator of Elieazer Callender, late of Virginia, deceased, appoints Richard Taylor, of Kentucky, his lawful attorney to receive all money, goods, wares, merchandize, and other effects due him personally or as administrator; and to sell, convey and execute deeds where necessary for his lands; to receive any plat or plats of land and lodge the same in the register's office in Kentucky or Virginia, and to take necessary steps for obtaining patents of land belonging to the said Elieazer Callender in consequence of warrant 1703. One-third of this warrant for 3133⅓ acres his attorney is authorized to convey to William Croghan. December 19, 1797.

Witnesses: Sheayashal [?] Bourne, Eben'r Gray, Justices of the Peace, and before whom above was acknowledged. Charles Cushing, Clk. of the Court of Common Pleas, for Suffolk Co., certified, before Sam'l Cooper a Notary Public, that they were Justices.

Jefferson Co., Recorded January 1, 1799.   [*B1, p262.*]

Memorandum of agreement between Lieutenant Spencer Morgan, late of Virginia Continental line, but now residing at Granby in the District of Orangeburg, S. C., and Captain Simeon Spring, of the District of Kentucky, State of Virginia. Morgan authorizes his friend Simeon Spring, as his lawful representative and attorney, to obtain for him such military warrants for lands as may become due to him from the United States and the State of Virginia. In consideration of this service, agrees to convey to him one-half of all such lands. March 20, 1790.

Witnesses: James O'Fallon, James Maleng.

Simeon Spring on January 4, 1797, records that he has sold on January 1, 1797, to Jonathan McFadden and Simeon McNeal 666⅔ acres on the south side of Big Baron River, Warren Co., entered, surveyed and patented in the name of Spencer Morgan.

Teste: Worden Pope.   [*B1, p265.*]

Robert Todd appoints Richard Terrell his attorney in fact to transfer his lot of 500 acres, in the Illinois Grant, No. 55, to William Croghan or to Patrick Joyes if he holds the same under said Croghan (as he says he does). October 4, 1798.

Teste: P. Butler, James Hawkins.

P. S. Mr. Terrell, in conveyance, is to recite Robert Todd's sale of same to William Croghan and from William Croghan to Joyes, which will make the matter appear straight. Recorded January 15, 1799.

414

Letter from William Croghan, dated January 4, 1799, states he bought two or three 500 acre surveys from Capt. Robert Todd lying in the Illinois Grant, the whole of which he had sold several years ago, parts to Elie Williams, Benjamin Sebastian, and Alexander S. Bullitt, and the remainder to Joyes & Hoops, and therefore he has no claim to any of Todd's lands.

[*B1, p267.*]

George Nicholas of Clarke Co. gives bond to Jacob Shreader, Jr., of Jefferson Co. The conditions are that whereas George Nicholas owns a 4,000 acre tract of land on Harrod's Creek which was entered in the name of Samuel Beale, and George Nicholas having sold 258 acres to Jacob Shreader, Jr., agreeable to a survey made for him by Abraham Hite, it is agreed that if George Nicholas can obtain a deed for the 4,000 acres from the heirs of Samuel Beale [Beall], deceased, and convey the said 258 acres to Jacob Shreader, Jr., this obligation will be void. January 11, 1797.
Witness: William Logan. Recorded February 17, 1799.

[*B1, p268.*]

George Nicholas of Mercer Co. gives bond to Jacob Shreader of Jefferson Co., that as soon as he can obtain from Samuel Beale [Beall] a deed to 4,000 acres, owned by George Nicholas on Harrods Creek, entered in the name of Samuel Beale, he will give deed for 600 acres of this tract which he sold to Jacob Shreader agreeable to survey made by Abraham Hite. September 3, 1796.
Witnesses: Thos. Deqe Owings, Wm. Shreader. Recorded February 17, 1799. [*B1, p269.*]

George Nicholas of Fayette Co. gives bond to Jacob Shreader, Jr., of Jefferson County that as soon as he can obtain from Samuel Beale [Beall] a deed to 4,000 acres, owned by George Nicholas on Harrods Creek, entered in the name of Samuel Beale, he will give good deed to the 239 acres and 49 poles of same land sold to Jacob Shreader, Jr., agreeable to a survey thereof made for him by Alexander Woodrow. May 25, 1798.
Witness: Abra. Hite. Recorded February 17, 1799.

[*B1, p270.*]

Robert K. Moore of Jefferson Co. appoints his friend John Eastin of same county his lawful attorney. Whereas William Chambers obtained in 1792 from Ebenezer Denton of the Province of Louisiana a bond for $422.00 payable the 1st day of April following, and said bond was assigned to Michael Lacassagne for collection, Robert K. Moore now empowers John Eastin to demand and receive of Ebenezer Denton the amount of the bond. March 6, 1799.
Acknowledged before Henry Churchill and Chas. Quirey, Justices of the Peace. Recorded March 18, 1799. [*B1, p271.*]

Patrick Simpson, of Knox County, Territory of the United States North West of the Ohio, appoints General Washington Johnston his lawful attorney to assign all Simpson's rights to two tracts of land in Kentucky to Mary Kellar, representative of Abraham Kellar, deceased, and assigned to him by said Mary Kellar, who is now Mary Linn, and her husband William Linn: One platt contains 730 acres, and is on the east branch of Marrowbone Creek, which creek the superintendants through mistake in making the entries called Crocus Creek, a branch of Cumberland River. The other tract contains 400 acres and is on the Cumberland River, as will appear by the platts of surveys lodged by Simpson in the hands of William Croghan, of Jefferson Co., surveyor of said lands. May 15, 1797.
Witnesses: Robert Baird, Robert Johnson.
Territory of the United States North West of the Ohio River, Knox County, May 5 [15], 1797: Patrick Simpson acknowledged before James Johnson, Justice of the Court of Common Pleas this power of attorney to be his act and deed.
Jefferson Co. Memorandum dated March 6, 1799. Recorded March, 1799. [*B1, p273.*]

[End of Bond and Power of Attorney Book No. 1.]

CALENDAR OF DIVISION BOOK No. 1 JEFFERSON COUNTY COURT, 1797-1850 *

By Ludie J. Kinkead and Katharine G. Healy

In Four Parts *

Part One: 1797-1819

Introduction: Division Book No. 1 Jefferson County Court extends from 1797 to 1850. It is an official record of the division of estates. Its entries include much material that is of special interest from the standpoint of genealogy. In fact the chief purpose in presenting this calendar is to make more available the names and kinships of persons participating in the division of the estate cited.

The volume is a transcribed copy and evidently was made many years ago. The whereabouts of the original volume is now unknown. The book contains 442 pages, not including the few pages of a very brief index. In some instances the description of land is accompanied by a small sketch map drawn in the book. The entries indicate that Worden Pope was clerk up to 1838, when he was succeeded by Curran Pope, his son. Division Book No. 3 ends in 1916, after which time records of this character were recorded in the Circuit Court.

The spelling of names is here printed as written in the transscription. In some instances a name that is apparently the same is spelled in various ways. In other instances the given name, or its abbreviation, appears, according to the clerk's penmanship, in more than one way, as, for example, the given name of Ed., E., Edw., Edw'n, Edw'd, and Edmond may appear in connection with a certain family name, and in some instances, notwithstanding the variations, all may refer to the same individual. In the detailed index to be published at the end of this History Quarterly—Vol. 8—the names will be spelled as written in the transcribed record and no attempt will be made to group the various spellings of any name under any one of the spellings.

---

*Of the four parts promised, only Parts One and Two (to 1832) were published.

At the instance of Thomas Pickett, Attorney in fact for John Pickett, the commissioners appointed by the Court for the County of Jefferson, in virtue of an act of General Assembly entitled "an act to appoint commissioners for the division of lands," made division of a certain tract of 3000 acres, which, on April 29, 1780, Joseph Jones, guardian, had entered by virtue of a military warrant on Floyd's Fork, about five miles above the trace leading from the Falls to Harrodsburg. Original survey was dated October 29, 1783. Of this tract 250 acres were thrown out, being claimed by others, 550 were given to the locator for his services, leaving 2200, but by resurvey actually was 2230 acres. One half was given to John Lewis, eldest son of Charles Lewis, deceased, and one half to John Pickett. May 15, 1797. Robert Breckinridge, commissioner. Recorded November 8, 1797. [B1, p1.]

Having examined a tract of 1000 acres on Floyd's Fork, patented in the name of Jacob Harmer, and from agreement dated March 28, 1780, the commissioners, James Meriwether and John G. Moore, reported on May 2, 1797, that John R. Gather is entitled to 200 acres. Recorded November 8, 1797. [B1, p2.]

Wm. Garrard, Fred Edwards, and Jas. Drury, commissioners, appointed by April Court, 1803,

Benjamin Johnston estate, divided Lot No. 6 in the town of Louisville among the heirs of Benjamin Johnston, deceased, and ordered equal shares given to the following: Wm. Johnston, Grabiel J. Johnston, Mary A. Harrison, Benjamin Johnston, Susannah Floyd, Robert Johnston, General W. Johnston, Ann C. Johnston. April 13, 1803. Recorded May 2, 1803. [B1, p2.]

Heirs of Edm. Taylor, deceased, being entitled to 85 acres each, from part of 3000 acres of which 1250 was in name of Joseph Jones, parts 1 and 2, of 85 acres each, fell by ballot to [name left blank] and parts 3 and 4 to Wm. Christy, who is entitled to three shares besides his own, and four of the other heirs, Christy's share being 340 acres. Wm. Taylor, Ro. Breckenridge, commissioners. Recorded May 17, 1796. [B1, p3.]

E. Taylor's 1000 acre military warrant, lying on Ohio River, divided by commissioners Wm. Taylor and Ro. Breckenridge between Wm. Taylor, Wm. Christy, Fanny Taylor, Sally Taylor, Thruston Taylor, Edm'd H. Taylor, Geo. Taylor, Reubin Eastin, Francis Taylor, and Polly Taylor. [*B1, p3.*]

At instance of Richard Woolfolk, Jr., agent for representatives of Ed. Taylor, deceased, and John Eastin, one of the legatees, W. White and Fredk. Edwards, commissioners, proceeded to divide four lots in Louisville, two of ten acres each, Nos. 7 and 8, and two of five acres each, Nos. 8 and 9. John Eastin produced papers which showed that he purchased the parts of four of the legatees to wit: Reubin Eastin, husband of Hannah Taylor; Rich. Taylor, Jr., husband of Polly Taylor; Wm. Christy, husband of Patsy Taylor; Geo. Taylor, heir at law, therefore the said John Eastin, husband of Sally Taylor, with his part was entitled to one half of the lots and balance allotted to Fanny Taylor, Francis Taylor, Thruston Taylor, Edward Taylor, heirs at law. Recorded. [*B1, p4.*]

Lot No. 219 on Third Street, Louisville, was equally divided between Nathaniel B. Whitlock, Henry Reager, and Mariah Reager, March 10, 1804, by Fred L. Edwards and Wm. Garrard. Wm. B. Whitlock paid forty-eight shillings, and Geo. Cullner paid four shillings. [*B1, p4.*]

Jacob Reager, deceased. Division of Lot No. 205, Louisville, between Henry B. Reager, his sister Mariah Reager, and Nathaniel B. Whitlock for himself and son George Whitlock, issue of his marriage with Sally Reager, deceased, another of the sisters of Henry and daughter and heir of Jacob Reager, deceased. Jos. Denny and Wm. Garrard, commissioners. August 8, 1804. [*B1, p5.*]

Division of 1500 acres of land, patented in the name of Edm'd Taylor, deceased, on resurvey contained 1654 acres, on Harrods Creek, but part was an interference of claim entered in name of Jacob Myers, which was not divided. Remainder divided between the following: Wm. Taylor; James Taylor; Wm. Christy, representative of Edw. Taylor deceased, and who has other claims of Geo. G., Mary, Hannah, and Martha Taylor; Frances Taylor who intermarried with Dr. ——— Wallace; William Taylor, Jr.; Thruston Taylor; and Edmund H. Taylor. Some of this land touched line of Benjamin Taylor. Fred'k Edwards and Sam'l Wells, commissioners. Recorded November 4, 1805.

[B1, p5.]

Ro. Breckinridge and Rd. Barbour, commissioners, reported on division of land of Jones and Lewis—1250 and 3000 acres on Floyds Fork—surveyed for Joseph Jones and Joseph Jones guardian, between the heirs of Lewis and the heirs of Edmund Taylor, deceased, in obedience to court order of December, 1807. In the division one-fifth or 850 acres were laid off for heirs of Edmund Taylor; four-tenths for William Christy, who claimed same as assignee of Geo. G. Taylor, Hannah Eastin, Edmund H. Taylor and Martha Taylor wife of Christy; two-tenths for William Christy as assignee of John Eastin and Sarah his wife and Francis S. Taylor; one-tenth for each Richard Taylor, in right of his wife Polly, William Taylor, Thruston M. Taylor and Fanny Wallace wife of Dr. John Wallace. Recorded October 17, 1808. *[B1, p7.]*

Edmund Taylor, deceased, in his lifetime tried to locate a military right for 3000 acres in Kentucky for representatives of the late Charles Lewis and a treasury right for 1250 acres for Joseph Jones, for which he was to have a fifth part. Col. Jas. Taylor and Hubart Taylor, in behalf of the representatives of Edmund Taylor, applied to Lewis and Jones for the fifth part allotted, and Col. Jas. Taylor, with consent of Joseph Jones, protracted on the surveys taking 250 acres from said Jones and 650 acres from Lewis. Dated April 27, 1798. Certified to on January 26, 1808, by Hubbard Taylor of Clark Co., Ky., and sworn to before Jno. Renick, J. P. of Franklin Co. James Taylor of Caroline Co., Va., certified before Lan. Bassaile, J. P., Caroline Co., Va., on September 28, 1807, that he laid off said 850 acres as above on Floyds Fork. Recorded October 17, 1808, by Worden Pope, Clerk, Jefferson Co. *[B1, p9.]*

Christopher Shake heirs. April Court, 1809, on motion of Philip Bowyer, husband of Elizabeth Shake, ordered that Thomas Ramsey, Joseph Kellar, Solomon Clure and Samuel Phillips be appointed commissioners to divide 195 acres of land on Harrods Creek, plantation whereon Christopher Shake died, giving to Elizabeth one third part. On April 24, 1809, commissioners qualified before Samuel Hening. Jos. Wood, D. S. J. C., surveyed 195 acres on Harrods Creek; widow's share was 65 acres. Commissioners made division according to survey. Recorded June 12, 1809. [B1, p10.]

Edward Dorsey heirs. At June Court, 1808, Thomas Ramsey, James Taylor, Joseph Kellar, John Edwards, Aaron Fontaine and Frederick Edwards were appointed commissioners to divide lands of Edward Dorsey, deceased, between Susanna Dorsey, widow and relict, and Samuel N. Luckett, Basil N. Hobbs and Polly his wife, Elias Leavin Lawrence, Benj. Lawrence and Matilda with Dorsey heirs and representatives according to respective claims and report.

At September Court, 1808, John Edwards, Thomas Ramsey, Aaron Fontaine, George Rudy, Martin Brengman and Owen Gwathmey were appointed to divide a tract of land on which Edward Dorsey, deceased, lived, between Susanna Dorsey, widow, and his children agreeable to their respective claims.

Plat shows part of interference of Samuel Beall's 4000 acre survey with Jas. Catlett's 1000 acre, and this apparently was agreed upon as conditional lines between lands of Edward Dorsey and Jacob Shreader and run by A. Woodrow in 1802.

Division between Mrs. Susan Dorsey, widow, and his heirs: Basil N. Hobbs and wife Polly, daughter of Edward, deceased; Levin L. Dorsey, and Elias L., infant sons of Edward Dorsey; Eurith O. Dorsey and Matilda L., infant daughters of Edward; Samuel N. Luckett late husband of Patience L. Luckett deceased, daughter of Edward. Surveyed, August 18, 1808, by Alexr. Woodrow, S. J. C. House and lot in Middletown to Benjamin Lawrence Dorsey and he is to pay to the other five children $13.80 to equalize their shares. Recorded June 12, 1809.

[B1, p11.]

Ben Johnston estate. Letter from Gabriel J. Johnston to John Evans, September 15, 1809, advising commissioners would meet next day to divide lots and lands, of which Nancy C. Gray, formerly Nancy [Ann] C. Johnston, died possessed, among heirs of Ben Johnston, deceased. Gabriel claimed three parts out of six of the one half of said lot, and advised Evans to notify Major Harrison, as Evans purchased from him. Attached was the order of August Court, 1809, that on application of Ga. J. Johnston, claiming as heir of Nancy Gray, deceased, an heir of Benjamin Johnston, deceased, and as a purchaser under Davis Floyd, who married Susannah Johnston another heir of Nancy, and claiming under Betsey Johnston, now Betsey Collins, who married William Johnston, another heir of Nancy, it was ordered that Cuthbert Bullitt, Dennis Fitzhugh and Nathaniel B. Whitlock be appointed Commissioners to divide real estate of Nancy Gray that fell to her by descent from Benjamin Johnston. Commissioners made report of division September 16, 1809, into six lots one each to Ga. J. Johnston, Davis Floyd husband of Susannah Johnston, Betsy and James Chas. Johnston, John Harrison husband of Polly Johnston, Benjamin Johnston, General Washington Johnston. Recorded October 10, 1809. [*B1, p14.*]

Charles Beeler estate. At December Court, 1807, on motion of John C. Beeler, administrator of Charles Beeler, deceased, David L. Ward, Jesse Carter, Abner Field and John Howard were appointed commissioners to set apart to Sarah Beeler, widow of Charles, her dower of lands, slaves, etc., and to divide rest of slaves between other heirs. Commissioners made report May 31, 1809, and alloted to Sarah Beeler, widow, 196 acres, as per A. Woodrow's survey, and five slaves. John C. Beeler claimed, by purchase, right to brother Nathaniel's slaves, but refused to receive slaves then as he had entered suit for tract of land on which he resided. Other slaves were divided among Charles, Thomas, George Beeler and Charles Lemaster.

The foregoing allotment of dower to Sarah Beeler was not to preclude her from her right to land on which John C. Beeler resided, on waters of Beargrass, should he lose his suit. The report of A. Woodrow, S. J. C., May 31, 1809, gave the boundary lines of the 198 acres to Sarah Beeler beginning at N. W. corner of Wm. Pope's 400 acre pre-emption, and along Pope's 100 acre survey on military warrant, it also mentions "to a point in the middle of the lane leading to Ward Mann's lick," and a field occupied by Elias Mallott. Recorded October 10, 1809.

[*B1, p15.*]

Edward Dorsey estate. At April Court, 1807, William White, William Chambers, Silas M. Noel, Martin Bringman, George Rudy and Joseph Pomeroy were appointed commissioners to divide lot in Middletown, now occupied by James Fontaine and Leavin Lawrence, between heirs of Edward Dorsey, deceased, Samuel Lawrence and Leavin Lawrence, according to their rights. December Court, 1807, commissioners to report to court by order of Silas M. Noel. April court, 1807, commissioners made report which was quashed and other report ordered. On April 26, 1809, commissioners report on dividing lots 52 and 57 in Middletown between heirs of Edward Dorsey, deceased. It appeared from the bond from Edward Dorsey to Levin Lawrence annexed and by admission of Leavin Lawrence and Susan Dorsey, guardian, that the heirs of Edward Dorsey, deceased, are entitled to one moiety of property, Samuel Lawrence one-sixth and Leavin Lawrence remaining two-sixths. Descriptions of the lots include beginning on the Main Cross Street at a point where the store house joins the tavern, running parallel to the Main St. and precisely through the middle of the logs which form the partition between said store and tavern, thence southwardly to a stone opposite the junction of the dwelling house occupied at this time by Leavin Lawrence and the said store house, etc., to include the house now occupied by John Ballard as a tavern. Allotted to Leavin Lawrence that part of lot including the room then occupied by him with the ground it stands on, and ''so much of the chamber as will extend to the log partition between that chamber and the chamber over the room allotted to Samuel Lawrence,'' Leavin and those claiming from him, to have use of that part of the chamber over the store room of Samuel, only so long as he keep it covered with a good tight roof and no longer than the duration of that building. Leavin also to have his kitchen. Samuel's lot is also further described, and he is to have so much of the cellar and ground as is occupied by store room and only so much of chamber on second floor as was embraced in the small room over the store. This was approved by Susanah Dorsey, L. Lawrence and Samuel Lawrence. Recorded October 9, 1810.   [*B1, p18.*]

Indenture between Edward Dorsey and heirs of Leavin Lawrence, dated January 20, 1803, in which Dorsey gave bond in sum of 1500 Spanish milled dollars to sell to Lawrence one-third of all houses and lots purchased of Charles Quirey in Middletown. Witnesses, Geo. Brinkam, Wm. Jones.

Indenture dated April 23, 1802, whereby Charles Quirey and Catherine his wife sold to Edward Dorsey lots Nos. 51 [57?] and 52 in Middletown. Witnesses, John Miller, W. White, Abijah Swearingen. Recorded October 9, 1810. [*B1, p21.*]

Edmund Taylor estate. At December Court, 1810, Henry Duncan, James Patton, James Hunter, John Nelson, Major William Taylor and John Evans, Jr., were appointed commissioners to divide lots Nos. 171 and 229, of one-half acre each, in Louisville, between John Wallace and Frances his wife, George G. Taylor, Edmund H., Francis S., William, and Thruston M. Taylor, William Christy and Martha his wife, Richard Taylor, Jr., and Polly his wife, William Eastin infant son and heir of Reubin Eastin and Hannah his wife deceased (who was Hannah Taylor) and Myra Eastin infant daughter of John Eastin and Sarah his wife, deceased (who was Sarah Taylor). Commissioners also to appoint Edmund H. Taylor and Major Wm. Taylor guardians to infants William and Myra Eastin to make division for their wards.

Commissioners James Hunter and John Evans, Jr., and Edmund H. Taylor, guardian, found that Edmund H., William, Thruston M., and Francis S. Taylor had sold their rights to John Wallace. One-half of lot No. 171 therefore went to said Wallace and the other half to William Eastin, William Christie and his wife Martha, George G. Taylor, Richard Taylor and wife Polly and Maria Eastin. Recorded December 21, 1810. [*B1, p23.*]

At October Court, 1810, on motion of James C. Johnston, it was ordered that John Nelson, John Martin, Thomas Prather, James Hunter, Cuthbert Bullitt and Ga. J. Johnston be appointed to divide lot No. 5 of five acres in Louisville between heirs of Benjamin Johnston and devisees of William Johnston, deceased. October 24, 1810, division was made between Ann C. Johnston, William Johnston, John Harrison and G. W. Johnston. Recorded December 10, 1810. [*B1, p24.*]

Isaac Hite estate. At December Court, 1810, on motion of Abraham Hite, an executor of Isaac Hite, deceased, ordered that

Jonathan Clark, David L. Ward, Wm. F. Simrall, John Howard, Peter B. Ormsby, Frederick Geiger, Edmund Clark and John Bell divide slaves amongst heirs of Isaac Hite, agreeable to his will. December 11, 1810, division made, six slaves to Rebecca V. wife of Charles Fishback, late Rebecca V. Hite, only daughter, and eight to Jacob Hite, only son of Isaac Hite, deceased. Recorded January 14, 1811.   [*B1, p25.*]

Jacob Augustus estate. At March Court, 1811, on motion of John Speed and David Augustus, administrators of Jacob Augustus, deceased, it was ordered that David L. Ward, Jonathan Clark, John Howard, Samuel Bray and Abraham Hite set apart to Sally Augustus, widow and relict of Jacob Augustus, deceased, her slaves and dower in tract of land whereon Jacob died. Report returned March 29, 1811, allotting to the widow one-third part of personal estate, as per inventory, amounting to $808.96½. Also to widow part of land on Beargrass purchased from Norborne B. Beall, surveyed by order of commissioners, in lieu of Lawrence Ross's land, including spring house, containing 68½ acres. On April 8, 1811, on motion of John Speed and David Augustus, administrators, ordered that commissioners divide slaves among heirs. They reported division, allotting two slaves to each John, David, Springer, Jacob and James Augustus. Recorded April 8, 1811.   [*B1, p26.*]

Robert McKeown estate. At March Court, 1811, it was ordered that Nathan Taylor, John Miller, Hiram Malott and George Oldham allot and lay off to Leah McKeown her widow's dower in lands on which Robert McKeown her husband formerly lived near Bruners Town. The lands adjoined property of Augustus Frederick, Frederick and Philip Zilhart and George Wolf. Recorded June 10, 1811.   [*B1, p30.*]

Jacob Owen estate. At June Court, 1811, on motion of William Munday and his wife Elizabeth, the daughter and heir of Jacob Owen deceased, the Court appointed Samuel Wells, Amos Shadburn, Samuel Bray, John Herr, Col. Richard Taylor and John Howard to divide lands on Beargrass of which Jacob Owen died seized. Division was made equally between Elizabeth Munday and her husband William Munday, Preston, Camilla, Shaply, Ann and John Owen. Recorded July 8, 1811.
[*B1, p31.*]

Charles Beeler estate. At March Court, 1810, on motion of John C. Beeler, it was ordered that Ga. J. Johnston, Samuel Hinch, John Y. Moore, Samuel Bray, and John Howard be appointed to divide land of Charles Beeler among heirs, except John C. Beeler, who claimed land on which he lived, and the widow who received her dower. Beech Spring Tract (according to plat Mill Creek runs through land and Fish Pool Creek through S. E. portion) and land near the licks (Mann's) containing 275 acres, conveyed by executors of Isaac Hite to heirs of Charles Beeler, divided between Nathaniel, Charles, George, and Thomas Beeler and Charles Lamaster, with John Speed guardian. Approved December 5, 1811, by James Vance, guardian, for George and John C. Beeler. Approved December 4, 1811, with slight change asked by John Speed guardian of Charles Lemaster and Thomas Beeler, an infant on April 28, 1810, but now twenty-one years of age. Witness John Speed Smith. Recorded December 9, 1811.   [*B1, p32.*]

James Meriwether estate. At March Court, 1811, on motion of John P. Booker and Edward Booker, it was ordered that Joseph Smith, Thomas Hannah, and David Standiford divide two tracts of land in Shelby County among the heirs of James Meriwether. Land surveyed July 17, 1811, by John Harbison, D. S. S. C., containing 281 acres, including seven acres which had been sold to John Doyel off northeast corner, described as beginning at N. E. corner of John Breckenridge's 1000 acre survey on North Fork of Clear Creek being the same on which Bolings Lick lies, etc., and in line of Allin's military survey. Also another tract in Shelby County on Clear Creek containing 136 acres and touching Benjamin Van Cleave's pre-emption, surveyed by Harbison and divided between Judith, Elizabeth and Sarah Booker, and William, James, Jane, and Richard Meriwether. Report made August 17, 1811. Recorded December 10, 1811.   [*B1, p36.*]

In obedience to order of March Court, 1812, to divide lot No. 10, in Louisville, of five acres between heirs of Nathaniel B. Whitlock and Samuel N. Luckett, and in the presence of James D. Breckinridge, guardian for heirs, Ga. J. Johnston, and Jared Brooks and Thomas Prather met and made division: to Samuel

N. Luckett three acres on which John Gwathmey lives and which adjoins that occupied by R. C. Anderson, and remainder of lot to heir of said Whitlock, deceased. Also on June 8, 1812, divided five-acre lot No. 11, in Louisville, between same. Recorded.
[*B1, p40.*]

At August Court, 1812, on motion of Elliott Headington, by Joshua Headington his guardian, and Robert McConnel, it was ordered that John Gwathmey, Hugh Morrison and James Ferguson divide the five-acre lot No. 12 in Louisville between said Elliott Headington and Robert McConnel. On August 27 above commissioners qualified before James Ferguson, J. P. J. C, and divided the lot which touched that owned by Richard C. Anderson, Sr., between Elliott Headington, infant heir of Joshua Headington guardian, and Robert McConnell. Recorded September 14, 1812. [*B1, p41.*]

Jacob Owen heirs. At December Court, 1814, on motion of Jacob Augustus and Camilla his wife, one of the children and heirs of Jacob Owen, deceased, it was ordered that James Brown, John Howard and Samuel Bray divide and set apart to Jacob Augustus and Camilla their share of the six slaves and their increase. The order of previous day to divide among all heirs was set aside. Commissioners report allotted to Augustus and Camilla two slaves and the sum of $33.33 1/3 from the other two heirs, Shapley and Preston Owen, to equalize their part. Recorded January 9, 1815. [*B1, p43.*]

Richard Terrell estate. December Court, 1814, appointed Matthew Love, Nicholas M. Lewis, John Hughes and John Hughes, Jr., commissions and they, on December 27, 1814, at the home of Isaac Miller, guardian, made division of the estate of Richard Terrell, deceased, among the heirs: Lucy Ann, Martha I., Virginia, Dabney C., and Mary Jane Terrill. Recorded January 9, 1815. [*B1, p44.*]

Jacob Owen heirs. At January Court, 1815, on motion of John Owen, Frederick Rudy and Ann his wife, Jacob Augustus and Camilla his wife, Shapely Owen and Preston Owen by Presley N. Ross their guardian, children and heirs of Jacob Owen who died intestate, Frederick Rudy claiming in right of his wife and under William Munday and Elizabeth his wife, daughter of Jacob Owen, it was ordered that Samuel Bray, Col. Richard Taylor and John Edwards divide between above heirs, a tract of land of 317 acres on waters of Beargrass. James Stewart, D. C. J. C. Commissioners qualified January 12, 1815, before John Miller, J. P. J. C. Division made among above heirs. Recorded March 13, 1815.   [*B1, p46.*]

Joshua Headington estate. At March Court, 1815, on motion of Robert McConnel, husband of Sarah McConnel formerly Sarah Elliott, and Joshua Headington, father and guardian of Elliott Headington, infant and only child of Joshua and Nancy his wife, who was Nancy Elliott, it was ordered that John A. Honore, John Harrison, John Hinkle, Paul Skidmore, Jared Brooks, Samuel C. Dickinson and John I. Jacob divide the half acre lot No. 77 in Louisville between said McConnel and wife and Elliott Headington. Isaac H. Tyler, D. C. J. C. C. On June 9 commissioners made report that they had divided lot between heirs giving to each a front on Main Street. The property touched that of J. Honore and heirs of Henry Duncan, deceased. Recorded June 12, 1815.   [*B1, p48.*]

William Beard estate. At January Court, 1816, on motion of Martha Beard, widow of William Beard, deceased, it was ordered that Robert Breckinridge, John Sutton, Archibald Allen, John Gwathmey and James McCrum set apart said widow's dower, one-third part of half acre lot No. 95 in the new plan of Town of Louisville. They reported that on March 27 the property on South side of Main Street was divided into three parts, one-third to the widow. Recorded May 13, 1816.

[*B1, p49.*]

Jacob Crum estate. At October Court, 1815, on motion of Brite Prewitt, it was ordered that Jonathan Nixon, William Kellar, Benjamin Clore and Lawrence Clore allot to Elizabeth Prewitt, late Crum, widow of Jacob Crum, deceased, her dower, one-third part of lands and divide balance between David, George, Elizabeth, Polly and Jacob Crum. Tract surveyed March 7, 1816, contained about 73 acres, adjoined Ed'd Stevens line and Jonathan Nixon's property, Widow's share 24 acres and mansion-house, and to each of other heirs about 10 acres. Widow allotted her share, but heirs part not divided as it was impracticable at the time. Recorded May 13, 1816.   [*B1, p49.*]

Edmund Taylor estate. John Evans and James Hunter appointed by Court to divide half acre lot in Louisville on Main Street, No. 229, on December 13, 1810, did divide same, but incorrectly described lots on map, and by order of May Term of Court, 1816, directed to rectify same and did examine and found division incorrect. Lot divided into two equal parts of 52½ feet, one part to John Wallace and wife in right of himself, Edmund H., Francis S., William, and Thruston M. Taylor, whose interest Wallace had bought, and other part to Richard Taylor, Jr. and wife, William Eastin, George G. Taylor, Maria Eastin, William Christy and wife, Edmund H. and William Taylor guardians appointed by court to make division for William and Maria Eastin infants. Recorded June 11, 1816.   [*B1, p50.*]

Robert Camp estate. At May Court, 1816, it was ordered that Levi Tyler, Charles Anderson, Archibald Allan and Walker Alsop allot to Mrs. Catherine A. B. Camp her dower in tract of land on which Robert Camp, her deceased husband, lived and died. Commissioners qualified June 11. To Catherine A. B. Camp one slave and blacksmith tools, as per an agreement between the heirs, and which was considered fair.

Articles of agreement entered into June 11, 1816, between Catherine Camp, widow of Robert, and Ambrose and Elizabeth Camp heirs of Robert, gave to widow slave, etc., and money in lieu of dower. She resigned administration to Ambrose Camp. Recorded June 11, 1816.   [*B1, p52.*]

Richard Terrell estate. Richard Taylor, James S. Bate, William Croghan and Nicholas M. Lewis commissioners were appointed by Court to make division of land between heirs of Richard Terrell. Divided property into five portions and drew lots. No. 1, to Dabney C. Terrill, 200 acres, adjoining Finley and Hare's land, part of Abbotts Station; No. 2, to Virginia Terrell, and No. 3, to Martha J. Terrell, 180 acres each, adjoining above; No. 4, to Mary Jane Terrell, including farm where

Mr. Gill lived, 200 acres; No. 5, to Lucy A. Terrell, on bank of Ohio River, Diamond Island, Six Mile Island, the tract in the Ponds [Settlement] and a settlement on Harrods Creek. January 28, 1815. Recorded August 12, 1816.   [*B1, p54.*]

Lucy Ann Terrell estate. Commissioners Richard Taylor, W. Croghan, and Nicholas M. Lewis, dividing lands and slaves of Lucy Ann Terrell, deceased, between heirs of Richard Terrell, deceased, made report. They allotted to each Martha J. Terrell and Virginia Carr one undivided moiety of Diamond Island; to Dabney C. Terrell 180 acres in Pond Settlement and Six Mile Island; to Mary Jane Terrell 60 acres on bank of Ohio, tract on which Richard Terrell lived, also 50 acres on Harrods Creek conveyed by deed from Frederick Barrackman to Richard Terrell; also divided slaves. October 20, 1815. Recorded September 9, 1816.   [*B1, p54.*]

Solomon Clore estate. At March Court, 1815, it was ordered that James Barbee, John Smith, Thomas Ramsey, Abraham H. Kellar and Adam Snider allot to Rosanna Clore her dower of lands in estate of Solomon Clore, deceased. Widow allotted 103 acres and two slaves. August 1, 1815. Recorded August 12, 1816.   [*B1, 55.*]

Edmund Taylor estate. On motion of Edmund H. Taylor and other heirs and devisees of Edmund Taylor, deceased, it was shown that he died seized of 1000 acres of land, in Jefferson County, on Floyds Fork, and devised real estate to children. Commissioner's were appointed to make partition among his children: George G., Francis S., Edmund H., William, Thruston M., Hannah, Martha, Sarah, Polly and Frances Taylor. Martha married William Christy; Hannah married Reubin Eastin, died intestate leaving William an only child; Sarah married John Eastin, both dead leaving Maria their only child; Polly married Richard Taylor; Frances married John Wallace. Commissioners appointed were William Taylor of Floyds Fork, Joseph Oglesby, and Thomas Elliott, who in 1816 submitted division of land into ten lots, giving 100 acres to each child. Property adjoined that of John Evans and Benjamin Temples. Surveyed by William Taylor. Recorded January 14, 1817.   [*B1, p56.*]

In pursuance of order of January Court, 1817, James Prather, James A. Pearce and Joshua Headington appointed commissioners to divide half-acre lot No. 133 in Louisville, on Market and Eighth streets, and on March 10, 1817, made report of division: to Josh. Wilson, in his right by his wife, and in right of Ruth Roach and John Rice, 49 feet front on Market Street; to Griffin Taylor 20 feet; to William Sullivan's heirs 20 feet; and to McCormick's heirs 16 feet. Also ordered to divide a ten acre lot in Louisville, No. 6, and same commissioners reported on February 24, 1817, division between, P. B. Ormsby, Griffin Taylor, McCormick heirs, William Sullivan's heirs, Joshua Wilson in his right by his wife and in right of John Rice. Recorded March 10, 1817.   [B1, p59.]

James Merriwether estate. At December Court, 1817, on motion of William Merriwether, guardian of infant heirs of James Merriwether, deceased, James W. Thornberry, Craven P. Luckett, Hector W. Moore, Robert Pollard and Hancock Taylor were appointed commissioners to divide and allot to the children and heirs of James Merriwether the slaves and personal estate of deceased. They qualified December 26, 1817, before John Bell, J. P. J. C., and same day met at tavern of Nathan Whips in Louisville, and made division, allotting eight slaves to William Merriwether, the only one of age. [Other children are not named.] Recorded January 12, 1818.   [B1, p61.]

Charles Thruston estate. At December Court, 1817, it was ordered that Daniel Fetter, Levi Tyler and Abraham Hite divide and allot to the children and heirs of Charles Thruston, deceased, the slaves of which he died possessed. On December 30 commissioners qualified before D. Fitzhugh, J. P. J. C. and made division to Charles and Ann Thruston, of seventeen slaves. Recorded January 12, 1818.   [B1, p62.]

John Bryan estate. At January Court, 1818, on motion of Elizabeth Bryan widow of John Bryan, deceased, it was ordered that Henry C. Dorsey, William Logan, Elijah Yeager and Thomas Buckner be commissioners to allot to said Elizabeth her dower. On March 6, 1818, they allotted to Elizabeth Bryan 82 acres of land adjoining that of Samuel Hinkle and John Redd, also four slaves. Recorded March 9, 1818.   [B1, p63.]

William Sullivan estate. At August Court, 1817, on motion of Daniel P. Sullivan of full age, and William, Rebecca and Sophia Sullivan, infants, by John C. Sullivan, their guardian, it was ordered that Isaac Miller, Samuel Dickinson and Levi Tyler divide and allot to each of the heirs of William Sullivan, deceased, the real property he owned in Jefferson County. On February 28, 1818, made division of lots—Nos. 140, 145, 146, 157, 158, 159, 241, 242 and 243 in Louisville, located between 10th Cross Street and 11th Cross Street, Jefferson and Market streets—to William, Rebecca, D. P. and Sophia Sullivan. There was a pond on lot No. 145. This division was approved by Daniel P. Sullivan, attorney in fact for Daniel P. Sullivan and guardian for William, Sophia and Rebecca Sullivan. Recorded March 10, 1818.   [*B1, p64.*]

Jacob Myers estate. At May Court, 1817, on motion of James Barbee, it was ordered that James Taylor, Samuel Hening, William F. Quirey, Roger Taylor and John Williamson divide and allot to Barbara Myers, widow of Jacob Myers, deceased, her dower of lands on Harrods Creek and set apart to each of the other heirs their portions. Land surveyed by Paschal E. Smith, D. S. J. C., 290 acres on Harrods Creek adjoining land of John Shreader: To Barbara Myers, widow, 96 2/3 acres, including house; balance to Joshua Barbee and Elizabeth his wife, William Jean and Catherine his wife, Enoch Wilhoit and Polly his wife, John, Sally and Louisa Myers. Leonard Hoke appointed guardian to John, Sally and Louisa Myers. When recorded Sally Myers was Sally Risinger. Recorded June 8, 1818.   [*B1, p66.*]

Samuel Ferguson estate. June Court, 1818, ordered that Fortunatus Cosby, Thomas Prather, John Gwathmey, Cuthbert Bullitt, and Thomas Bullitt divide and allot to the widow of Samuel Ferguson and to Benjamin Ferguson their portions of the slaves and personal property of Samuel Ferguson, deceased. Commissioners met in presence of James Ferguson, agent for the widow and Benjamin, and divided slaves agreeable to the will; to the widow seven and to Benjamin three slaves, total $6,000. Recorded June 9, 1818.   [*B1, p68.*]

James Merriwether heirs. Agreeable to court order, division of thirteen slaves was made by commissioners Isaac Miller,

Robert N. Miller and John P. Tunstall: to James, Richard and Jane Merriwether. Recorded January 11, 1819.   [*B1, p69.*]

Martin Brengman heirs. At June Court, 1818, on motion of John Brengman, administrator, it was ordered that John Williamson, John Miller, John Evans and Samuel Lawrence divide and allot to Margaret Brengman her dower, and to John Brengman, Sarah Geiger, Catherine Brengman, Frederick G. Brengman, Joshua Martin Brengman and Margaret Norah Brengman their shares in the estate. Commissioners qualified December 30, 1818, before Thos. Lawes, J. P. J. C. Eighteen slaves valued at $8,825, were divided, seven to Mrs. Brengman, and balance to Martin, Samuel, and Margaret Noah Brengman, Minor White, John Brengman, Frederick G. Brengman, and Frederick Geiger. Mrs. Brengman relinquished her right to all property in Middletown, and took her dower in the plantation 209½ acres, including the mansion-house, etc. In-lots Nos. 16 and 17 could not be divided to advantage, and therefore advised that they be rented. Refers also to tanyard lot and lot No. 18. Out-lots divided among Frederick G., S. M., John, M. N. and Samuel Brengman and Minor White and Frederick Geiger. Report made February 1, 1819. Also examined account of estate in hands of Mrs. Brengman and John Brengman, administrator. Besides those mentioned, Sarah Geiger and Kitty White are named. Mrs. Brengman is referred to as very advanced in years. Recorded August 9, 1819.   [*B1, p69.*]

Thomas Prince heirs. At October Court, 1818, on motion of James Farnsley, Jr., Major John Hughes, John Hughes, Jr., Henry Churchill and John Jones were appointed commissioners to divide and set apart to Ann Prince her dower and to Frances O. Farnsley, wife of James Farnsley, Jr. and devisee of Thomas Prince, deceased, her share of real estate of which Thomas Prince died possessed. Widow's dower 106 1/3 acres. Six lots divided among Frances O. Farnsley, wife of James Farnsley, Jr., Lawrence Prince, Thomas Ann, Shapley, Susan and Presley Prince. Survey made by Geo. Armstrong, D. S. J. C., September 13, 1819. Commissioners qualified September 13 before M. White, J. P. Recorded October 11, 1819.   [*B1, p74.*]

William Oldham heirs. At August Court, 1819, on motion of Charles L. Harrison, Jesse Clark, John Shake and Ignatus

Wheeler were appointed commissioners to divide, between John P. and Richard Oldham, heirs of William Oldham, deceased, and Joseph Sprigg, two tracts of land of 500 acres each on Floyd's Fork entered, surveyed and patented in the name of Joseph Sprigg. Clark qualified May 6, 1819, before F. Cosby, J. P. J. C., and Shake on September 14, before Ro. Breckinridge, J. P. On May 19, 1819, at request of Charles L. Harrison the commissioners met and divided the upper tract to William Oldham's heirs and other tract on first survey to Joseph Sprigg. Recorded October 12, 1819.   [*B1, p76.*]

John W. Davis estate. At September Court, 1819, on motion of Isaac Balee, Benjamin Head, Samuel Lawrence, Thomas Buckner and Leavin Lawrence were appointed commissioners to divide and allot to Caroline Davis, widow of John W. Davis, deceased, her dower in slaves and 400 acres of land in Jefferson County, on Long Run, conveyed by Isham Bridges and his wife to John W. Davis, and the balance to his children and heirs: John W., Jr., Salem L., Francis, Susan, Matthew, Patsey, Mark and Mary Davis, the last named now the wife of Isaac Balee. Commissioners qualified December 11 before M. White, J. P. J. C. Division made to widow, 112½ acres, adjoining property of William Crutchfield and Graybles original lines, and one slave, November 8th. Balance not then divided. Recorded December 13, 1819.   [*B1, p77.*]

CALENDAR OF DIVISION BOOK No. 1 JEFFERSON COUNTY COURT, 1797-1850

By Ludie J. Kinkead and Katharine G. Healy

In Four Parts

Part Two: 1820-1832*

Adam Snyder estate. At December Court, 1819, James Barber, Henry C. Dorsey and Jacob Shreader named commissioners to allot to Mildred Snyder, widow of Adam Snyder, her dower in slaves and lands. Reported February 10, 1820, that the widow and her two sons had made division of land; the widow received four slaves. Recorded June 13, 1820. [*B1, p79.*]

Jacob Newkirk, Sr. estate. At June Court, 1820, Peter Yenowine, Sr., Samuel Blankenbaker, Sr., Robert Tompkins and Jacob Hoke appointed to settle the accounts of Jacob Newkirk, administrator of Jacob Newkirk, deceased, and to allot to Margaret Newkirk, widow of Jacob Newkirk, her dower in the real estate. On July 3, 1820, the above commissioners qualified before John Miller, J.P. J.C. Commissioners made report, July 22, dividing the 28½ acres of land adjoining Thomas Blankenbaker, calling for one line to cross the springs and one to pass through the entry of the dwelling house, giving to the widow that part of the house built by Jacob Newkirk with "full privilege of free ingress and regress threw the passage doors of the house adjoining, without molestation, disturbance or hinderance of any person or persons whatsoever occupying the other part of the house built in addition thereto." Recorded August 14, 1820. [*B1, p79.*]

---

*As stated in the Introduction to the Four Parts of this Calendar, the spelling of names is here printed as written in the transcribed volume of Division Book No. 1, and no attempt is made to group the various spellings of any name under any one of the spellings. The compilers of this Calendar as well as the proof readers and the editor are aware that in many instances a name in the course of one entry frequently has more than one spelling. Among such names are Shrader, Wilhoite, Meriwether, Allen, Pendergrast and Poulter, also Leaven, Reuben and Diana.—*Editor.*

*Of the four parts promised, only Parts One and Two (to 1832) were published.

Thomas and Ann Prince heirs. At January Court, 1822, on motion of Harrison Arteburn and James Farnsley, Jr., it was ordered that Robert N. Miller, Warwick Miller, John Jones, (Tanner), Major John Hughes, and Henry Churchill, divide into six lots the slaves of Thomas Prince, deceased, held as dower by his widow Ann Prince, then deceased, and the slaves of Lawrence Ross, deceased, which should be allotted to the heirs of Thomas and Ann Prince: to Harrison Arteburn, for his wife Susan, one-sixth part; to him as guardian of Presley and Thomas Ann Prince, two-sixth parts; to James Farnsley, Jr., guardian for Lawrence R. and Shapley R. Prince two-sixth parts; and to James Farnsley, Jr., for his wife Frances O. one-sixth part. On January 21, 1822 [sic], the commissioners reported they met at dwelling place of Mrs. Ann Prince, deceased, and made division of ten slaves valued at $2460.00, as above directed, each child's portion amounting in value to about $410.00. Recorded January 14, 1822 [sic].   [B1, p81.]

William Porter heirs. At December Court, 1820, on motion of John Watson, Jr., "who intermarried with Elleanor W. Porter," and guardian to Julia Ann, Henry, and Elizabeth Porter, who is of full age, heirs of William Porter, deceased, with the consent of James Porter, executor, it was ordered that Henry C. Dorsey, Elijah Yeager, John D. Welch and James Carr divide the slaves among the heirs. Commissioners qualified before John Williamson, J. P. J. C. Commissioners reported on January 5, 1821, that they had allotted the nine slaves, valued at $2950.00 to John Watson, husband of Elleanor Porter, to Elizabeth Porter, Henry Porter, and Juliana Porter. Recorded January 13, 1821.   [B1, p82.]

John Shaw heirs. At January Court, 1821, on motion of Peter Funk, Joseph Funk and John Funk, it was ordered that James Brown, Robert Tompkins and John Miller divide a tract of land on the waters of Floyd Fork among the heirs of John Shaw, the said Peter, Joseph and John having produced the obligation of Robert Shaw for his portion of the land. The commissioners reported February 6, 1821, that the land could not be divided without injury to the estate. Recorded March 12, 1821.
                                                                     [B1, p83.]

Jacob Brindley estate. At the June Court, 1820, on motion of John Potts, guardian to the heirs of Jacob Brindley, deceased, it was ordered that John Miller, Samuel Blankenbaker, Elias Christler and John Moore, divide the estate on Floyds Fork, which Jacob Brindley devised to his sons Jacob, John, Reuben and Thomas Brindley. Commissioners met and John Potts guardian agreed to take 90 acres for Reubin and Thomas, the rest of the 179 acres were allotted to Jacob and John. Recorded March 3, 1821. [*B1, p84.*]

Nancy Owen heirs. At January Court, 1821, on motion of John Owen, ordered that Samuel Bray, John Howard, John Hikes and Jacob Hikes divide the slaves of Nancy Owen (who was the daughter and devisee of Lawrence Ross, and which slaves had been allotted to her by commissioners) among her heirs: John, Shapley, and Preston Owen, and Elizabeth wife of William Munday, Ann wife of Frederick Rudy, Camilla wife of Jacob Augustus, and Paulina White. On March 13, 1821, commissioners appointed to divide negroes of Susanna Ross allotted to the heirs of Nancy Owen by Commissioners of Lawrence Ross, deceased, report that as there were five negroes and seven heirs it is impossible to divide in kind, and ask to be dismissed. Recorded March 13, 1821. [*B1, p88.*]

Henry Duncan estate. At May Court, 1821, on motion of John C. O'Beirne and Nancy his wife, it was ordered that Robert Breckinridge, Alexander Pope, Edward Tyler, Jr., and James W. Thornberry, allot to Nancy O'Beirne, wife of John O'Beirne, formerly Nancy Duncan, her part of the estate of Henry Duncan, her former husband, agreeable to his will, and to divide the balance of the estate between Garnett, Ann E., Mary S., Henry and Coleman Duncan, children of Henry Duncan. The commissioners allotted to Nancy her one-third of slaves, and part of lot No. 73, balance not divided until her dower cease, and to the children lots Nos. 79 and 128, with rents, etc. Recorded June 11, 1821.
[*B1, p89.*]

Abraham Fry heirs. At October Court, 1821, John Edwards, John Herr, George Hikes, Sr., and Leavin Lawrence were appointed commissioners to allot to Susanna Fry, widow of Abraham Fry, her third of his estate and divide the balance among the heirs: daughter Sally, wife of Peter Pottorff, and John, Nancy, Abraham, Elizabeth, Polly and William Fry. Susanna for herself and as guardian for Polly and William Fry, and Peter Pottorff as guardian to John, Nancy, Abraham and Elizabeth, consented to the order. Edwards, Herr and Hikes qualified December 26, 1821, before John Williamson, J. P. J. C., and on December 30, Leavin Lawrence qualified before Ben Lawrence, J. P. J. C. The land consisting of about 234 acres, on North Fork of Goose Creek, and touching the lands of Thomas Prather, Caleb Dorsey, and William Hite, was part of a 500 acre tract in the name of John Cook. In the division one-third was allotted the widow, including the house and orchard consisting of about 260 young bearing apple trees and other fruit, excepting the old house once occupied by Abraham Fry as a dwelling, which they direct Peter Pottorff, as guardian of the five eldest children, shall have right to remove. The children were to receive about 26 acres each. Recorded March 12, 1822. [*B1, p91.*]

Jacob Blankenbaker estate. At January Court, 1822, on motion of Samuel Blankenbaker, it was ordered that James Brown, John Howard, Samuel Lawrence and Robert Tompkins divide nine slaves of the estate of Jacob Blankenbaker, deceased, among: Ambrose Garret and Elizabeth his wife, Samuel Blankenbaker, Henry Jacob and David Blankenbaker, administrators of Henry Blankenbaker, deceased; Nicholas, Thomas, Jeremiah, Phillemon, John Blankenbaker, and Ambrose Tyler and Mary his wife. On February 14, 1822, Howard, Lawrence and Tompkins qualified before James Brown, J. P. J. C. Each received one slave and certain money. Recorded April 8, 1822. [*B1, p95.*]

Levi Yewell estate. On motion of Julius Wilhoyte, Martin Yewell, Joshua Christler, Joel Yeager and Benjamin Pope, at the November, 1821, Court, it was ordered that Richard Barbour, William Fishback, Jacob Shrader, Lewis Wilhoyte, Phillip E. Barbour, James Taylor and Isaac Owens divide land of Levi Yewell, deceased, containing about 170 acres on the waters of Harrods Creek into two parts, one to Patsey, wife of Thomas Foreman, and the other to be equally divided between Julius Wilhoyte, Martin Ewel [Yewell], Joshua Christler, Joel Yager and Benjamin Pope. Commissioners qualified November 19, 1821, before James Barbour, J. P. J. C. Land was surveyed by Richard Barbour, and contained 158½ acres, and touched Taylor's military line. Division was made according to instructions. Simeon Yewell had purchased portion of Martin Yewell, Joshua Christler and Joel Yager. Recorded June 10, 1822. [*B1, p96.*]

William Kellar estate. On motion of Abraham H. Kellar and Joel Heitt at the September Court, 1821, it was ordered that Richard Barbour, James Barbour, Felix Seymour, Solomon Dunagan and Philip C. S. Barbour divide the 237½ acres of land between the North and South Forks of Harrods Creek, late estate of William Kellar, allotting to Abraham H. Kellar and Joel Heitt seven-ninths, and to Pauline and Diana Kellar two-ninths. Abraham Kellar and Joel Heitt claimed one-ninth each, Abraham in his own right and Joel in right of his wife Sarah, late Sarah Kellar, and five-ninths by right of purchase from the five other heirs. Pauline and Dianna claim their one-ninth each as heirs of William. Rebecca Kellar, mother and guardian of Pauline and Diana consented. Richard Barbour, S. Dunagan and Felix Seymour qualified and made division. Recorded August 12, 1822.
[*B1, p98.*]

John Funk estate. At March Court, 1822, on motion of Margaret Funk, widow of John Funk, it was ordered that James Brown, Robert Tompkins, George Hikes, Sr., and John Peay assign to the widow her dower of lands. They assigned to the widow 118 acres, including the house in which she lives, and which adjoins the Henry Harrison old military survey, the Colonel Richard C. Anderson line and the Robert Tompkins line, also 60 acres adjoining above tract, part of which was claimed by Andrew Brentlinger. The tract within the bounds of Harrison's survey, the commissioners were advised, was not subject to dower and was not considered. Recorded August 12, 1822.
[*B1, p100.*]

Joshua Dorsey heirs. At January Court, 1822, on motion of Nimrod Dorsey, Henry C. Dorsey and Corilla his wife, late Corilla Dorsey, Richard Booker and his wife Eliza, late Dorsey, Rezin H. Dorsey and Sarah Ann Dorsey, by Henry C. Dorsey

their guardian, and Ruth M. and Matilda Dorsey infants by Nimrod Dorsey their guardian, all heirs of Joshua Dorsey, deceased, it was ordered that John Williamson, Charles G. Dorsey, Elias Dorsey be appointed to divide 160 acres of land on Floyds Fork, which was devised to applicants by their ancestor unincumbered by dower. On January 23 commissioners Williamson and Dorsey qualified before Charles G. Dorsey, J. P. J. C., and Dorsey qualified before John Williamson, J. P. J. C. Division made, giving to each about 20 acres. Recorded August 12, 1822.
[*B1, p102.*]

Henry Blankenbaker estate. At December Court, 1821, on motion of John Henry Blankenbaker, it was ordered that Elias Christler, Robert Tyler, Samuel Blankenbaker, John Miller, William Field, Robert Tompkins and Peter Yenowine divide real estate and slaves of Henry Blankenbaker, deceased, into eight parts and allot to his heirs. Commissioners qualified on March 8, 1822, before John Miller, J. P. J. C. The land was valued at $5.00 per acre, 200 acres $1000.00 and seven slaves $2105.00. Division made to David Blankenbaker, 100 acres and one slave; to George and Allen Tyler and Jacob, Aaron, Rosane Blankenbaker, one slave each; one slave to Henry and Nicholas Nunemacher; to John H. Blankenbaker 100 acres, part of survey calls for line of a 1322 acre survey made for Thomas Luirk, line of Abr. Brackenridge, corner to survey of 6000 acres made for Nathaniel Sanders. Having on October 16, 1824, arrived at full age, Nicholas Nunemacher acknowledged receipt of property from John H. Blankenbaker, his guardian. Recorded October 7, 1822. [*B1, p104.*]

John Thruston heirs. At July Court, 1822, on motion of Thomas January and Mary B. January his wife, Worden Pope and Eliza T. his wife, Thomas W., Charles M., Alfred, Lucius F., Algernon S. Thruston, also Elias Rector and Frances B. his wife, by Hugh W. Hawes their attorney, it was ordered that Samuel Dickinson, Matthew Love, Isaac Miller, John I. Jacob, James W. Thornsberry, William Pope, Jr., and William Farquar, divide and allot to Worden Pope and wife, Samuel N. Luckett and wife, Thomas W., Charles M., Alfred, Lucius F. and Algernon S. Thruston and Elias Rector and Frances B. his wife, one-ninth each, and the one-ninth interest of Thomas January and wife, to Thomas W., Algernon S. and Charles M. Thruston, they having purchased same. The slaves were devised for life by John Thruston to his wife Elizabeth T. Thruston, late Elizabeth T. Fontaine wife of Aaron Fontaine. On November 19, 1822, Jacob, Pope and Farquar qualified before Robert Todd, J. P. J. C. Commissioners met at the home of Capt. Aaron Fontaine and made division of slaves which had been devised to the widow and then to the children heretofore named: 41 slaves valued at $10,150.00 Charles M. Thruston is referred to as administrator of Elias Rector. Recorded November 20, 1822.

[*B1, p107.*]

Thomas Prince heirs. On motion of Harrison Arteburn and James Farnsley at the January, 1822, Court it was ordered that Robert N. Miller, Warwick Miller, John Jones (tanner), Major John Hays and Henry Churchill divide into six lots the slaves of Thomas Prince, deceased, held as dower by his widow Ann Prince, also deceased, and the slaves of Lawrence Ross, deceased, and allot to the heirs of Thomas and Ann Prince, deceased: one-sixth part to Harrison Arteburn in right of his wife Susan, and two-sixth parts as guardian to Presley and Thomas Ann Prince, also two-sixth parts to James Farnsley, Jr., as guardian for Lawrence R. and Shapley R. Prince, and one-sixth part to Farnsley in right of his wife Frances O. January 21, 1822, commissioners qualified before Matthew Love, J. P. J. C. and met at dwelling place of Ann Prince, deceased, and made division of slaves as ordered. The ten slaves were valued at $2,460.00. Recorded January 14, 1822. [*B1, p109.*]

Thomas Prince heirs. At December Court, 1822, on motion of Harrison Arteburn, guardian of Presley N. and Thomas Ann Prince, and James Farnsley, guardian of Lawrence R. and Shapley R. Prince, it was ordered that James W. Thornsberry, John Jones, Robert Miller and William Meriwether divide and allot slaves of Thomas Prince, deceased, among above mentioned infant heirs. Commissioners met at home of Harrison Arteburn and late residence of Thomas Prince and made division of the seven slaves valued at $2000.00, giving one-fourth part to each of above named heirs. Ordered recorded January 14, 1823.

[*B1, p110.*]

Abraham Fry heirs. At November Court, 1822, on motion of Denton Whips, guardian of Poll and Wm. Fry, it is ordered that Leaven Lawrence, John Williamson, Caleb Dorsey and John Herr divide in seven parts the slaves of Abraham Fry, deceased, allotted as her dower to his widow Susannah Fry, now deceased, and allot one part each to his children: John, Nancy, Abraham, Elizabeth, Polly and William Fry, and Sally, wife of Peter Pottorff who is mentioned as guardian of Nancy, Abraham and Elizabeth Fry. Settlement made December 28, 1822, and recorded February 10, 1823. [*B1, p112.*]

Betty Coleman heirs. At December Court, 1822, William L. Thomson, executor of the last will of Betty Coleman, appointed William C. Bullitt and John G. Taylor to divide slaves among her heirs. John Edwards was appointed to assist them. Slaves valued at $3575.00 were divided among Robert C., Caroline, Mildred Ann, Thomas H., Philip R., Camilla, Francis T., and Elizabeth Thompson, Melinda Huie, and Daniel F. Strother. Recorded February 10, 1823. [*B1, p113.*]

William Meriweather, estate. At October Court, 1822, on motion of William O. Meriwether, Pope & Tyler Attorney, with consent of Levi Tyler guardian of Louisa M., Caroline and Charles W. Meriweather, infants, it was ordered that Frederick Geiger, Samuel Bray, Hancock Taylor, Wm. Pope, Jr., and Conway Oldham divide and allot to Sarah Meriwether, widow of William deceased, her dower in 450 acres of land on Beargrass and slaves, also one-eleventh part to each George W., Samuel, Henry W. Meriwether and Jane his wife, Alex. M. Barker and Lucy his wife, David H., Valentine, Lewis, Louisa Matilda, Caroline, William O., and Charles W. Meriweather, heirs of said William. On November 15, 1822, Geiger, Taylor, and Oldham qualified before Samuel Churchill, J. P. J. C., and division made November 1, 1822.

Henry W. Meriwether from Montgomery County, Tennessee, on August 27, 1822, acknowledged receipt of slaves from William Meriwether during his life for his wife Jane Meriwether, daughter of said William, valued at $1000. Alex M. Baker, from same place, on August 30, 1822, acknowledged receipt of slaves for his wife Lucy from Sarah Meriwether, widow of

William and mother of Lucy. V. W. Meriweather, from Todd County, Kentucky, on August 31, 1822, acknowledged receipt of slaves from father's estate. Recorded February 10, 1823.

[B1, p114.]

William Johnston heirs. At May Court, 1823, Simeon S. Goodwin, B. I. Harrison, and William S. Vernon were appointed commissioners to divide the real estate and slaves of William Johnston, deceased, between James C. Johnston and Elizabeth Collins. Real estate and slaves, as shown commissioners by James C. Johnston, administrator, were divided by allotting to James C. Johnston, part of lots Nos. 25 and 113, also 900 acres first rate land at mouth of Salt River, 600 acres second rate land on Floyd's Fork, and 800 acres on Salt River and Pond Creek, valued at $26,900.00 and 12 slaves valued at $4,600.00. To Elizabeth Collins was allotted part of Lot No. 25, on Sixth Cross Street, and lots Nos. 40, 155, 259, and 260; and slip No. 1, of 5 or 6 acres in upper end of Louisville; 75 feet on Torrace Street, but title disputed and doubtful; lot No. 93 opposite Dr. Galt's, 61 acres on Asturgis Run, 200 acres on Cedar Creek, Jefferson County; 100 acres on Fox Run, Shelby County, 1000 acres on Little Kentucky River, Gallatin County; 550 acres on Russel and Glen Rivers in Adair County; 12,164 acres on Little Sandy River, Greenup County; 200 acres on Drennon's Lick, Henry County; 16,666 on Rolling Fork, Lincoln County; valued at $13,450, and ten slaves. Approved by Elizabeth Collins and J. C. Johnston. Recorded June 9, 1823.
[B1, p116.]

Yelberton P. Wells estate. At January Court, 1823, on motion of Rebecca Wells, widow of Yelberton P. Wells, ordered that Charles G. Dorsey, Nimrod Dorsey, Benjamin Head, John Netherton and John Price allot to Rebecca Wells her dower and divide the remaining part into eight shares for the children and heirs of Yelberton P. Wells. Netherton and Price on February 25 qualified before Charles G. Dorsey, J. P., and Dorsey qualified on April 14 before Ro. Barbour, J. P. The widow was allotted five slaves, and each child to have, in slaves or money, the value of $246.87. The children named were Ann J., William P., Louisiana Wells, Daniel Leach and Elizabeth his wife, late Wells, Mary, Samuel, Caroline and Rebecca Wells. Recorded July 14, 1823.

[B1, p117.]

Abraham Field estate. At May Court, 1823, on motion of William Lewis, it was ordered that John Hughs, Hancock Taylor, John H. Cox, Robert N. Miller and James W. Thornberry allot to Betty Field, widow of Abraham Field, her one-third or dower in his estate. They allotted to her two slaves, the commissioners having qualified before Matthew Love, J. P. J. C. Recorded October 14, 1823. [*B1, p119.*]

Simeon Simcoe heirs. At December Court, 1823, on motion of Lewis I. Simcoe, one of the heirs of Simeon Simcoe, and with the consent of John Herr, guardian for Richard, Sarah and Rosetta Simcoe, the other three and infant heirs, it was ordered that John Edwards, Henry Rudy, John Herr, Jr., and James M. Edwards divide and allot the slaves into four equal parts. The commissioners met at the home of John Herr and made division of the eight slaves valued at $2355.00 to above named heirs. Recorded January 12, 1824. [*B1, p119.*]

Presley N. Ross estate. At September Court, 1823, James Brown, Jacob Hikes, George Hikes, Jr., Abraham Kellar and Thomas Cannon were appointed commissioners to divide and allot to Matilda Burks, wife of James Burks, late Matilda Ross widow of Presley N. Ross, her dower in his estate. Plat of land shows 324¾ acres, part of John Floyd's old military survey of 1000 acres, and 191 acres, part of James Southall and Richard Charlton's 6000 acre military survey on southwest side of Beargrass Creek, same adjoining lands claimed by heirs of John Breckinridge, deceased, touching James Burks' line, near Conway Oldham's fence, to stake on the road between Jeffersontown and Louisville. The widow was allotted as dower 90 acres of cleared land and 85 acres of wood land. Survey made by Alexander Woodrow, Surveyor Jefferson County. Recorded January 12, 1824. [*B1, p120.*]

Edward Lightfoot estate. On motion of William E. Lightfoot, at the December Court, 1823, John Edwards, John G. Taylor and Henry Rudy were appointed to lay off and allot to Martha Lightfoot, widow of Edward Lightfoot, her dower of one third of land and slaves and divide the remainder into four equal parts for the children, William E. Lightfoot, Mary wife of Ab raham Hasbrook, Frances and Goodrich Lightfoot. Slaves valued at $5475.00. To the widow Mrs. Patsey Lightfoot was allotted five slaves, rest divided among children. It was deemed inexpedient to divide the land. Approved by Martha Lightfoot, William E. Lightfoot and Abraham Hasbrook as guardian for Frances and Goodrich Lightfoot. Recorded January 13, 1824.

[*B1, p123.*]

At August Court, 1824, on motion of John Shallcross and Mary Z. his wife, daughter of Jacob Lewis, and with consent of Jacob Lewis, guardian of his children Jane D., Alice Z., and Thomas D. Lewis, it was ordered that John T. Gray, James McCrume, Levi Tyler, John Sutton, James H. Overstreet and Archibald Allen divide and lay off for John Shallcross and Mary his wife one-fourth part of two certain parcels of land in Preston Enlargement to the town of Louisville on the southwest side of and adjacent to Main Street; half acre lot No. 76 and easterly half of half acre lot No. 77, conveyed to Mary Z., Jane D., Alice Z. and Thomas D. by Wm. Zane and wife, deceased, deed dated October 11, 1822, without considering improvements on same made by John Shallcross. Commissioners Gray, Overstreet and Allen qualified before William Field, J. P. J. C. on September 14, 1824. In Division Mary Z. Shallcross, received 62½ feet adjoining Main Street, being lot on which Shallcross' frame dwelling house is erected. Approved by Jacob Lewis, guardian and father of Jane, Alice and Thomas D. Lewis. Recorded September 14, 1824. [*B1, p124.*]

George Evinger estate. At July Court, 1824, on motion of Jacob Evinger, and it appearing to the Court that George Evinger died intestate, the 68 acres on the waters of Beargrass, adjoining Conway Oldham's land, the same whereon Evinger resides, descends to the eleven children: John, George, Henry, Adam, David, Jacob, Frederick, Thomas, Caty, Polly Evinger, and Betty Yenowine, who was Evinger. George, Caty, Adam and Frederick Evinger had sold their parts to David, and Thomas' share sold to John. It was ordered that Alexander Woodrow, Sr., Peter Funk, Abner Field, George Hikes, Sr., Valentine Conrad, and John Peay divide this property which touched that claimed by the heirs of Alexander S. Bullit, also land of Conway

445

Oldham and John Beeler.   John Evinger was guardian of Polly Evinger.   Division made and recorded October 12, 1824.

[*B1, p126.*]

At February Court, 1825, on application of William and Thomas Meriweather and other heirs and devisees of James Meriweather, deceased, Robert and Alexander Woodrow, John Edwards, James Porter and John Burrass were appointed to divide the land of James Meriweather, deceased.   Robert and Alexander Woodrow met at home of Thomas Daniel, April 12, 1825, to divide between the heirs a part of tract of 3000 acres on Floyd's Fork, and waters of Goose Creek.   Lands were in two parts, one of 186 acres in line of James Catlett's 1000 acre survey, made in name of John May, assignee of Nicholas McCarty, where Thomas Daniel lived.   The other part contained 120 acres in line of land devised to Norborne B. Beall, in line of A. Hite. William Meriweather produced a written contract between the late William Littell, attorney at law, and heirs and devisees of James Meriweather by which it appeared William Littell was entitled to one-half of the lands to be divided, and Littell had assigned his half to William Meriweather.   Part of the land, including improvement, was not susceptible to division.   Certain portion was allotted to William Meriweather for himself and that assigned by William Littell, and the balance by lot between Thomas Meriweather, the heirs of James Meriweather, the heirs of David Meriweather and John Meriweather.   Recorded September 5, 1825.   [*B1, p128.*]

Thomas Prather estate.   At June Court, 1825, on motion of John I. Jacob and consent of Matilda Prather, James S. Prather and William Prather, adults, and of Matilda and James S. Prather as guardians of Mary Jane, Matilda, Maria Julia and Catherine Cornelia Prather, infant heirs of Thomas Prather, it was ordered that Robert Breckinridge, Robert Todd (R. S.), Isaac Miller, Samuel Churchill, Levi Tyler and James W. Thornberry were appointed to divide 70 acres of land adjoining Louisville, conveyed by deed May 25, 1812, to John I. Jacob and Thomas Prather by Arthur L. Campbell, acting executor of Arthur Campbell, deceased, and five acres conveyed to Prather and Jacob by James C. Smyrle, known as Campbell's Enlargement of Louisville, No. 18, on west side of Arthur Street. This was divided one-half to John I. Jacob and one-half to James S., William, Mary Jane, Matilda, Maria Julia and Catherine Cornelia Prather, heirs of Thomas Prather, deceased. Breckinridge, Miller and Tyler qualified June 27, 1825, before W. Tompkins, J. P. Recorded September 7, 1825.   [*B1, p131.*]

George R. C. Floyd estate. At October Court, 1824, on motion of Sarah T. Floyd, widow and relict of George R. C. Floyd, deceased, it was ordered that Col. John Jones, Thomas McKnight, Alexander Woodrow, and Solomon Neill be appointed to allot to the widow her dower of one-third part of 480 acres of land, being part of a survey of 1830 acres patented to John Drake. On March 19, 1825, Woodrow, Jones and Neill qualified before Robert Miller, J. P. J. C. Of the 1830 acres patented to John Drake, and divided between Gen. Robert Breckinridge and George R. C. Floyd, 300 acres was conveyed by Floyd to David Meriweather, 200 acres to William Dubberly and 200 to Nathaniel Floyd, leaving 480 acres. Plat on page 134 of Division Book gives details, showing 53 acres at mouth of Mill Creek and other on Pond Creek. The widow was given the 53 acres on Mill Creek and 150 acres on Pond Creek. Recorded October 5, 1825.   [*B1, p133.*]

James Waggoner estate. At September Court, 1825, Samuel Churchill, Harrison Arteburn, James W. Thornberry, William Meriweather and Jesse Swindler were appointed to divide and allot to Elizabeth Waggoner the widow of James Waggoner her dower of one-third of the plantation on which said James lived and died, on Salt River Road, and to divide the remainder between David B. Phillips and George C., Elizabeth and Elseff [Elesis?] Waggoner, children and infant heirs of James. Division of the land, about 232 acres, was made December 7, 1825, allotting to the widow 72 acres, to the children 20 acres and balance to Phillips. Recorded January 4, 1826.   [*B1, p136.*]

Lander Grimes estate. At December Court, 1824, on motion of Rachael Grimes, widow of Lander Grimes, it was ordered that John Williamson, James Brown, Nathan Marders, John Price, Lawrence Young and John Whips divide and allot to

Rachael her dower of lands and slaves. On December 28 Williamson, Price and Young qualified before Charles G. Dorsey, J. P. J. C. They assembled at mansion house of the late Lander Grimes and allotted to the widow 65 acres including mansion house, adjoining land of John Burrass and a lane between Grimes and John and W. Finley, and borders Shelby road. Recorded February 7, 1826.   [*B1, p136.*]

Michael Atkisson estate. At March Court, 1826, on motion of Celia Atkisson, widow of Michael Atkisson, it was ordered that Thomas Waller, James Pomeroy, Richard Seaton, Richard Small and Michael Miller divide and allot to the widow her dower of one-third of slaves and plantation of 100 acres on Floyd's Fork. On April 22, Waller, Small and Seaton qualified before George Seaton, J. P. J. C. Commissioners appraised the nine slaves at $1,650.00 and allotted to the widow two slaves with money to equalize the $550.00. [Division of land not given.] Recorded June 5, 1826.   [*B1, p138.*]

Alexander S. Bullitt heirs. At July Court, 1822, on motion of Cuthbert and William C. Bullitt, Henry Massie and Helen Bullitt his wife, John Howard and Anna Bullitt his wife, and Mary and Thomas Bullitt by Samuel Churchill their guardian, it was ordered that James W. Thornberry, George Hikes, Sr., John Peay and James Brown lay off a tract of land in Jefferson County, on the waters of Beargrass, containing 120 acres. On November 1, 1826, Brown, Peay and Hikes qualified before James Pomeroy, J. P. J. C. The 120 acres was surveyed by Alexander Woodrow, and was part of Hugh Allen's military survey of 1000 acres on waters of South Fork of Beargrass, and was divided into six parts, allotting 20 acres to each of the six heirs. Recorded November 6, 1826.   [*B1, p139.*]

At October 3, 1826, Court, on motion of Nathan Hall and Eliza his wife, it was ordered that Alexander Woodrow, Robert Woodrow, George Seaton, Elias Christler, Richard Seaton and John L. Moon, divide into five parts 1800 acres of land patented in the name of Haden Edwards on the waters of Floyd's Fork, and allot to Eliza one part agreeable to will of Haden Edwards in favor of his daughter Penelope Pope and her deed to Eliza

Hall. When resurveyed tract contained 1946 acres, and adjoins John Pound's meadow, also touches Joseph Sprigs line. Assigned to Eliza Hall 385 acres. Report of commissioners December 2, 1826. (Haden Edward's will is recorded in Bourbon County, August, 1803.) [*B1, p141.*]

Thomas Prather heirs. At December 4, 1826, Court, on motion of Matilda Prather, widow, and James S., William, Mary Jane, Matilda, Maria Julia, and Catherine C. Prather, heirs of Thomas Prather, deceased, it is ordered that Isaac Miller, Simeon S. Goodwin, Nicholas Berthroud, Benjamin Lawrence and James Guthrie divide and allot to widow her dower of slaves and divide the residue equally among the heirs: James, William, Mary, Matilda, Maria and Catherine C. Prather. On December 22, the thirty-one slaves valued at $6650.00 were divided, giving to the widow twelve. Recorded January 1, 1827. [*B1, p144.*]

James Standiford estate. At the December 4, 1826, Court, on motion of Nathan Standiford, it was ordered that Arthur McCawley, John Murphey, Samuel M. Quertermous, John C. Beeler, Joshua McCawley, Alexander L. Woodrow, Robert L. Woodrow divide real estate of James Standiford, deceased, into two equal parts, and allot one-half to Nathan Standiford and divide the other half into seven equal parts, allotting one part to each Elisha Standiford, Mary Hinch wife of Samuel Hinch, Elizabeth Robb wife of Henry Robb, William, Nathan and David Standiford and Matilda McDowell wife of John McDowell, deceased. Alexander Woodrow, John C. Beeler and Samuel M. Quertermous qualified on December 30, 1826, before John Murphey, J. P. J. C., and met at the residence of the late James Standiford, then occupied by Wm. H. Randall. Alexander Woodrow, Jr., surveyed the land and found the tract contained about 153 acres and made division, allotting 49 2/3 acres, including mansion and spring, to Nathaniel Standiford in his own right and in right of Matilda McDowell, and about 21 acres to each of the other heirs, above named. Recorded March 5, 1827. [*B1, p145.*]

At December 4, 1826, Court, on motion of Samuel M. Quertermous and others, heirs of Jesse Pandergrast, deceased, it was ordered that Alexander Woodrow and Alexander Woodrow, Jr.,

Alexander Gailbreath, Joshua McCawley, John C. Beeler, John Burks, and Nathan Byers divide and allot to Quertermous, James F. Pendergrast, Garrett I. Pendergrast and Elizabeth Pendergrast, heirs of Jesse Pendergrast, that portion of real estate of James F. Moore, devised by him to Nimrod H. Moore in Jefferson County and purchased by Quertermous and others. Survey by Robert L. Woodrow, deputy surveyor of land, conveyed by Osborn Sprigg to James F. Moore, showed tract contained 736 acres, adjoining James Withers' 500 acre survey, and line of Levin Powell's 2000 acre survey, and Sprigg's 1100 acre survey. Nimrod H. Moore is only heir mentioned. Further details of bounds of lands refer to George James and Daniel Sullivan's 463 acre survey, Robert Coleman's 12231 acre survey, James Withers' 500 acre survey, George Slaughter's 1000 acre survey, John G. Moore's 1094 acre survey on Lick Run, "otherwise called Chapman's Run," also north bank of Salt Block Run, and Pond Creek. Recorded April 2, 1827.   [*B1, p148.*]

William Preston estate. At the March Court, 1824, William Pope, Jr., John Edwards, Conway Oldham, Levi Tyler, Frederick Geiger and Samuel Churchill were appointed commissioners to divide and allot to Caroline H. Preston, widow of William Preston, her dower in two tracts of land, one near Louisville, the other near the town of Middletown, and all the town lots in Preston Enlargement. Commissioners met at Tavern House of Archibald Allen, Esqr., in Louisville, June 30, 1824, to make division of lots in Preston's Enlargement and allotted to widow parts of lots Nos. 58, 59, 60, 64, 70, 72, 73, 39, 48, 87. Ordered recorded May 7, 1827.

On October 20, 1824, the commissioners met at the home of William Elliott in Louisville and allotted to Caroline H. Preston, one-third of lot No. 62, including four tenements then occupied by John Ruth, George McDaniel and Elizabeth Daugherty and one-third part of a 12 acre lot in Louisville, No. 3. Ordered recorded May 20, 1827.   [*B1, p152.*]

Samuel Hinch estate. At June Court, 1827, Alexander Woodrow, John Murphy, Samuel M. Quertermous, Joshua McCawley and Robert Gailbreath, or any three of them, were appointed commissioners to allot to Nancy Hinch, widow of Samuel Hinch, her dower in lands of Samuel Hinch. On June 15, Woodrow, McCawley and Quertermous qualified before Alex. H. Gailbreath, J. P. J. C., and met at the former dwelling house of Samuel Hinch, having caused a survey made of land formerly executed by James F. Moore to John Hinch for 300 acres, but found to contain 326 acres, ordered Robert L. Woodrow, D. S., to lay off 75 acres as dower to Nancy Hinch. Survey called for line with survey of 2,500 acres in name of Gabriel Jones, and line of lands claimed by Joseph A. Brooks, and a corner to land formerly property of James Quertermous, deceased, then the property of Taylor, and corner to 300 acres conveyed by bond to John Hinch by James Francis Moore, to an old lime kiln in south boundary of 91 acres conveyed in name of Frances F. Moore and patented in name of Samuel Hinch. Ordered recorded July 2, 1827.

[*B1, p154.*]

John Kelly estate. At March Court, 1827, Hiram Malott, Stephen L. Hite, Stephen R. Chenowith and Joseph Funk were appointed commissioners to allot to Sarah, widow of John Kelly, her dower of one-third of lands. Court ordered division of estate to widow and twelve children. Land adjoined that of Hiram Mallott, Samuel Frederick, and to 400 acres originally made in name of Alexander Reed, and to lands of Zilhart, and to road that leads to Bruners Town and to Funk's Mill. To the widow was given about 56 acres and to each of the children one-twelfth of the remaining 116 acres, as follows, Elizabeth wife of Peter Miller, Samuel, David, John, William, James, Daily, Austin Kelly, and Sarah wife of Joseph Beard, Cynthia wife of Michael Miller, Hannah wife of William Johnston, and Jane Frederick. Recorded July 2, 1827.

[*B1, p155.*]

Leonard Gatewood estate. At December Court, 1828, James Farnsley, David Farnsley, James W. Thornberry, Harrison Arteburn and John Jones appointed commissioners to allot to Clara Gatewood, widow of Leonard Gatewood, deceased, her one-third part of his estate and divide the balance in nine parts for William, Littleton, James, Fleming, Upton, Ann Pauline, Mary Ann D., Penelope F. and Leonard I. Gatewood, the last five named being minors. The tract of land by estimation contained 156 acres of which 35 acres, including dwelling house etc., was given to the widow. The survey called for line between lands of the widow and heirs of John Plaster, deceased. The balance of the land was not divided among the children as it could not be done to advantage. Recorded February 4, 1829. [*B1, p159.*]

Samuel Lawrence estate. At May Court, 1829, Lee White, William C. Bullitt, Jacob Frederick, John Whips and John Peay were appointed commissioners to divide in two parts the farm and tract of land on which Samuel Lawrence lived and died, and to set apart to Urath Brown, wife of James Brown, and Benjamin Lawrence two-thirds and to Fry Lawrence, infant heir of Elias D. Lawrence, deceased, the remaining third. On Wednesday May 25, 1829, commissioners met on farm to divide same. Survey of the 479 acres made at instance of Benjamin Lawrence, guardian of Fry Lawrence infant heir of Elias D. Lawrence, deceased, on waters of North Fork of Beargrass. Survey shows this land touches the line of George Rudy, Buckner's corner in Benjamin Head's line, Anderson's corner crossing Turnpike, and James Brown's land. The two-thirds in value was considered about 258 acres and the one-third about 220 acres. Recorded June 1, 1829. [*B1, p161.*]

William Hollis estate. At September Court, 1829, on motion of Thomas, James, Gabriel L., Ann and Jane Hollis, heirs of William Hollis, it was ordered that Robert Woodrow, Alexander Woodrow, John Edwards, John Howard, James Porter and John Burress divide into two equal parts a parcel of land of about 400 acres, part of a tract entered and surveyed in the name of John May in Pond Settlement, east of Smoots Bridge or causeway over a pond on Salt River Road and on Big Run. This land is in line with land conveyed February 6, 1821, to William Lewis and heirs of William Hollis, by John L. Jones and others, by Isaac Tyler commissioner appointed for that purpose by the Judge of the Jefferson Circuit Court. Commissioners allotted 204 acres to William Lewis and 276 acres to the surviving heirs of William Hollis, above named. Recorded November 2, 1829. [*B1, p163.*]

Henry White estate. At November 2, 1829, Court, on motion of Sarah White, widow of Henry White, it was ordered that James Pomeroy, George Hite, John Speed, Abraham Kellar and

James Burks, commissioners, allot to the widow her dower of lands and slave. On Monday January 25, 1830, the commissioners met at the home of Mrs. Sarah White, and by her direction and Andrew Hikes, who married Paulina White only child of Henry White, declined to allot slaves. They directed a survey of the land, exclusive of former dower of Mrs. Augustus, now Mrs. White, which showed 94 acres of cleared land including orchards, etc., and about an acre of wood land, and 44 acres of common land which touched the land of Jacob Hikes. Widow's third allotted January 29, and recorded March 1, 1830.

[*B1, p166.*]

John Sutton estate. At July 6, 1830, Court, George W. Chambers, Philip R. Gray, John Nelson, Nathaniel Hardy, James Rudd, and Archibald Allen were appointed to allot to Emily A. Sutton, widow of John Sutton, her dower of slaves. David Hardin, Deputy Clerk. On January 1, 1830, Rudd, Chambers and Hardy qualified before Robert Miller, J. P. J. C. Same day the eight slaves were valued at $2025.00, of which three were allotted to the widow. Recorded January 3, 1831.   [*B1, p168.*]

Samuel Erickson estate. At December Court, 1830, on motion of Mary Tate, late widow of Samuel Erickson, and her husband James Tate, it was ordered that Henry Churchill, Thomas Phillips, Charles L. Harrison, David B. Phillips and Samuel Phillips allot to Mary Tate her third of this estate. Commissioners on December 17 allotted to Mary Tate one of the three slaves, a girl Louisa, and Mary and James Tate were to support Louisa's child David and such children as she may in future have "until they shall each arrive at the age of fifteen years, after which time she nor her husband is longer to detain any of them in possession." Recorded January 3, 1831.   [*B1, p169.*]

At December Court, 1830, on motion of James W. Thornberry, guardian to Stephen, Susan S., Alex H., Warren, James and Phillip Thornberry, ordered that Thomas Phillips, Hancock Taylor, Henry Churchill, and James Baston be appointed to allot to Stephen Thornberry one equal sixth part of slaves devised to him and above named heirs by his grandfather, John Wiggington, deceased, and which were then in possession of James W. Thornberry. On the 28th, they allotted to Stephen Thornberry a negro boy. Recorded January 3, 1831. [*B1, p170.*]

George Spears estate. At January 4, 1830, Court, on motion of Leah Spears, widow and relict of George Spears, it was ordered that Abraham Hite, George Hikes, Sr., George Hikes, Jr., Samuel Bray, and James Hite allot to widow her dower of one-third in lands and slaves, also to Eliza Brown, late Eliza Spears, wife of Louis Brown, one-sixth part of the estate, and to John K. Spears, son of George, one-sixth part. Survey of land showed 257 acres which touched the line of Walker Prewitt and Joseph Kellar, with Fern Creek running through it. The commissioners allotted to widow three slaves and about 79 acres, the balance divided into six parts, and one part, about 30 acres, given to Eliza Brown and one part to John Kellar Spears. As land could not be divided equally, guardian of John K. Spears ordered to pay to Eliza and Lewis Brown $46.00 and the guardian of other infant heirs to pay them $184.00. Other parts of estate not divided at this time. Recorded February 1, 1830. [*B1, p171.*]

Walton Pearson estate. Port William [now Carrollton], Kentucky, August 16, 1828, to the Justices of Jefferson County Court, the petition of William Winslow and Elizabeth his wife, late Elizabeth Pearson, widow of Walton Pearson, requests her dower in this estate of house and lot in Louisville. At September Court, 1828, on petition of William Winslow and Elizabeth his wife it was ordered that George S. Camden, William Farquar, and Walker Alsop allot to Elizabeth her dower. Commissioners qualified September 1, 1828, before J. Ferguson, J. P., and divided Lot No. 272, fronting 35 feet on Jefferson and Green streets and 210 feet on 7th Cross Street, allotting to the widow 35 feet on Green Street and 105 feet on 7th Cross Street. Recorded September 2, 1828. [*B1, p174.*]

James Paulter heirs. At December 8, 1829, Court, Leaven Lawrence, Samuel Burks, Benjamin Head and John Brengman appointed to allot to John Paulter, Harvey Gregory, William D. Paulter and the infant heirs of James Paulter, deceased, the slaves released to them by Nancy Paulter. On December 28, Head, Burks and Brengman qualified before Sam. D. Vance,

J. P. J. C., and made division of five slaves: to William D. Paulter 2 slaves, and one slave each to John Poulter, Harvey Gregory and infant heirs. Recorded January 4, 1830.

[*B1, p175.*]

Mary Sutton heirs. At July Court, 1830, on motion of Richard A. Woolfolk, ordered that George W. Chambers, Philip R. Gray, John Nelson, Nathaniel Hardy, and James Rudd, divide three negroes between Richard A. Woolfolk and Sarah his wife, Alfred Sutton and Ann Mary Sutton, children and heirs of Mary Sutton, deceased, wife of John Sutton, deceased. November 25, 1830, commissioners valued the three slaves at $875.00 and gave one slave to each heir. Recorded December 6, 1830.

[*B1, p176.*]

David Fay estate. At December Court, 1830, on motion of Michael Pine, it was ordered that Robert McKenzie, Robert Buckner, Edward Hughes and Littleberry Hawkins allot to Nancy Fay, widow of David Fay, her dower in a lot on Portland Turnpike, which was conveyed by Fay to said Pine without release of dower. On January 21, 1831, Hawkins, Buckner and Hughes qualified before Wm. Tompkins, J. P. J. C., and on the 25th made division to Nancy Fay, one-third part of westwardly part of lot next to James W. Fenewick's tract of land, also 18 feet of the west end of dwelling house, being one-half of said house. Recorded February 9, 1831.   [*B1, p177.*]

John Bell estate. At October Court, 1831, on motion of John T. Bell, Ann H. Hunton, Sally I. Camden, Henry R. Tunstall, Liston Bell, Temple E. Bell, Cuthbert Bell, Montgomery Bell, John Meriwether and Jacob A. Horning, guardian for heirs of Patterson Bell, deceased, the heirs and legal representatives of John Bell, deceased, the court appointed George W. Meriwether, John B. Bland, John Price and John P. Bell to divide the lands and slaves. Commissioners divided Lot No. 188 in Louisville fronting on Market Street and on Third Street, and part of half acre lots Nos. 114 and 115 and slaves among the following: John T. Bell, Ann H. Hunton, Sally T. Camden, Polly wife of John Meriwether, Temple E., Cuthbert, Liston T. and Joseph Montgomery Bell, and Lucy R. wife of Henry R. Tunstall, and George

Horning, Lucy wife of Charles Reed, Henderson [Anderson?], Sarah and George Bell who are legal representatives of Patterson Bell, also one of the representatives of John Bell, deceased. Recorded October 5, 1831.   [*B1, p178.*]

July Court, 1831, on motion of Constantine Russell it was ordered that Richard Seaton, George Seaton, Elias Christler and James Pomeroy allot to Russell and Thomas L. Moore, one-fifth part of two tracts of land, one of 1000 acres and one of 800 acres, adjoining, on waters of Floyds Fork, patented December 2, 1783, in name of Headen [Haden] Edwards, and devised by him [will dated Bourbon County, November 10, 1801, probated there August Court, 1803] to George Edwards, Penelope Pope, Nancy Williams, Betsey Chancellor and Penelope Edwards [his granddaughter]. The one-fifth part to be allotted as ordered is George Edwards' part which he conveyed to Alexander Pope, who with his wife Martha M. conveyed same to Russell and Moore by deed dated September 11, 1815. Commissioners on September 8, 1831, made allotment to Constantine Russell and Thomas L. Moore of one-fifth part of said land as shown on plat made by Elias Christler, Richard Seaton and Robert L. Woodrow on December 2, 1826. Recorded November 8, 1831.   [*B1, p181.*]

John Sutton estate. At June 6, 1831, Court, on motion of Richard Woolfolk, husband of Sarah T., one of the children and heirs of John Sutton, it was ordered that Daniel Smith, John T. Gray, Mercer Daniel, and William Sale, allot to Mrs. Emily A. Sutton, widow of John Sutton, her dower of one-third of all the several lands and parcels of land in Louisville and Jefferson County of which John Sutton died seized, and the balance to Sarah, Alfred and Mary Sutton, the only three children and heirs of John Sutton, deceased. On June 23, commissioners made division to the widow, upper part of house on Main Street, lately occupied by John Sutton, together with the passage belonging to the house, also the kitchen under the new addition of house and the east half of lot, with free use of back steps and passage to the alley. To the children the store-room and cellar now occupied by William Miller's iron store and upper part of new building containing four rooms and portico. Recorded July 5, 1831.
                                                                [*B1, p182.*]

Joseph Glass estate. At June 7, 1831, Court, on motion of Samuel D. Vance, guardian of Ruth-Ann and Mary-Jane Glass, infant orphans of Joseph Glass, deceased, ordered that Lawrence Bucks, Benjamin Head, John Bregman and James Pomeroy allot to Jane M. Glass, widow of Joseph Glass, her dower in his estate. On June 22, 1831, the commissioners allotted to the widow two slaves and in-lots in Middletown, Kentucky, Nos. 20 and 21, with improvements. Recorded September 5, 1831.   [*B1, p184.*]

John Wigginton [or Wiggington] estate. December 5, 1831, Court. On motion of James W. Thornberry, guardian of Susan S., Alexander H., Warren, James, and Phillip Thornberry, his infant children, it was ordered that Thomas Phillips, Hugh Stewart, Hancock Taylor and Henry Churchill allot to Susan S. Thornberry, lately married to Jonathan Davis, the one-fifth part of slaves devised to her and her brothers by her grandfather John Wigginton. By consent of Jonathan Davis and Susan S. his wife and James W. Thornberry, guardian for infant heirs, two slaves were allotted to Susan, balance of slaves not allotted. Recorded January 2, 1832.   [*B1, p185.*]

James Lewis estate. At November 8, 1831, Court, on motion of David B. Phillips and Ann Lewis his wife, William Lewis guardian of Eliza Lewis, and Jesse Swindler guardian to Jesse Lewis, and Henry Lewis, it was ordered that Henry Churchill, Robert Miller, Harrison Arteburn and James W. Thornberry divide and allot the slaves of this estate between Ann Phillips, Eliza, Jesse and Henry Lewis, the children and heirs at law of James Lewis, deceased. On December 28, 1831, the commissioners divided among the four heirs the seven slaves as to value. Recorded February 2, 1832.   [*B1, p186.*]

David [Davis?] Wade estate. At December 5, 1831, Court, Warwick Miller, John P. Smith, George W. Meriwether, William A. Cocke and Richard Oldham were ordered to allot to Nancy Wade her dower of one-third part of slaves and real estate of Davis Wade, and to each of the other heirs their share. On December 31, 1831 they allotted to Mary Wade, widow, her third and three slaves, and to Abijah Ruder on account of his wife Sarah Ann heir of David Wade, and to Martha Jane, William M.

and Edwin F. Wade one equal part each of remaining real estate and two slaves each, except Edwin F. received one. Recorded January 2, 1832. [*B1, p187.*]

Elijah Jeter estate. At February 6, 1832, Court, on motion of Barbara Jeter, widow of Elijah Jeter, it was ordered that Jacob Hite, John Whips, Thomas Eaton and Samuel D. Vance set apart to Barbara her dower of 240 acres of land, lying on Goose Creek, being farm on which Elijah died. Infant heirs were John, William, Ragsdale and Elizabeth Jeter. Nathaniel Marders was appointed guardian and administrator. [Plot shows schoolhouse near Goose Creek within this tract.] Widow given her one-third, including buildings, and balance to children. Widow also received four slaves. Recorded May 7, 1832. [*B1, p189.*]

John Sutton estate. At January Court, 1832, on motion of Richard A. Woolfolk, husband of Sarah T., a daughter and devisee of John Sutton, deceased, it was ordered that William Sale, Mercer Daniel, William Pickett and Amos Harris divide slaves, except those theretofore assigned to the widow as her dower, among the children of John Sutton. On January 7, Harris, Daniel and Sale qualified before Sam Dickinson J. P. J. C. With information of Richard Woolfolk and George W. Meriweather, administrator, division was made of four slaves valued at $956.00 among children Sarah, Ann and Alfred. Recorded February 6, 1832. [*B1, p192.*]

Michael Leatherman estate. At November 7, 1831, Court, on motion of Elizabeth Applegate, late widow of Michael Leatherman, deceased, the court ordered that Phillip Bence, Henry Robb, John Burks and Alexander H. Gailbreath allot to Elizabeth her dower of lands and slaves. On December 28th commissioners met at home of Elizabeth Applegate and allotted to her 28 acres and dwelling house and three slaves. The land bordered that of Phillip Bence and that of John Bartlett, Jr. on the north side of the branch. Recorded April 2, 1832. [*B1, p193.*]

INDEX

462

463

Brown (cont.)
  Lewis 454
  Louis 454
  Louisa 287
  Louisa (Mrs.) 280
  Mary 28
  Math. 256
  Nancy 329
  Nancy (Mrs.) 302
  Preston W. 315
  Sam 232
  Samuel 16
  Susanna (Mrs.) 343
  Susannah P. (Mrs.) 264
  Thomas 19, 329, 338,
    343
  Urath (Mrs.) 452
  William 276, 323
Browne, Jno. 401
Brownfield, (?) 150, 162
Brumfield, Thos. 184
Brunner, Joseph 236
  Peter 236
Bruse, Andrew (Col.) 34
  Norman 34
  Norman (Col.) 33
Bryan, Aylie 239
  Charity 239
  Cornelius 19, 41
  Elenor 239
  Elizabeth (Mrs.) 431
  John 239, 431
  John C. 305
  Joseph 239
  Martha 239
  Mary 239
  Phebe 239
  Rebecca 239
  Samuel 239
  Susannah 239
  William 10, 307
  Wm. 297, 305, 312,
    322, 326, 334
Bryant, (?) 125
  Wm. 312, 316
Bryon, Christopher 403
Bryson, James 413
Buchanan, James 303,
    392, 405
  Jane 304
Buchannan, Geo. 343
Buchannon, (?) 178
Buchanon, (?) 196, 201
  James 110, 111
Buchanons, (?) 107, 119
Buchmann, Aloyse 295
Buckley, Dan'l 365
Buckner, (?) 452
  Ambrose 263
  Avery M. 273
  B. 301
  Ballard 301
  Haley 246, 264, 273
  Henry S. 273
  John 234
  Kezia 273
  Lillian (Mrs.) 273
  Nicholas 239
  Patterson C. 273
  Phillip 381
  Presley B. 273
  Rebecca (Mrs.) 263
  Robert 345, 455
  Samuel P. 273, 331
  Thomas 431, 434
  William 122, 148
Bucks, Lawrence 457
Buffington, (?) 158

Buhlen, John 295
Buitt, Thos. 384
Bulger, Edward 9
Bullit, Alex. 211
  Alexander S. 445
Bullitt, (?) 393
  A. S. (Col.) 246
  Alex. 232
  Alex. C. 311
  Alexander 232
  Alexander S. 234, 244,
    415, 448
  Alexander Scott 218,
    262, 327, 367
  Alexander Scott (Col.)
    403
  Alexr. 184
  Alfred Neville 309
  Amanthus 310, 311
  Amelia 310, 311
  Ann (Mrs.) 310
  Ann Elizabeth 310, 311
  Anna 448
  Annie C. 262
  Caroline 310, 311
  Cuthbert 262, 267,
    309, 310, 311, 327,
    422, 424, 432, 448
  Cuthbert Neville 310
  Cuthbert P. 262
  Eliza C. 266
  Helen 262, 448
  Henry 327
  Mary 262, 266
  Mary (Mrs.) 262, 266
  Neville 310, 311, 327
  Peggy (Mrs.) 310
  Permenus 381
  Polly 262
  Sarah 310
  Thomas 262, 267, 309,
    310, 432, 448
  Thomas James 262, 266
  Thos. 384
  William 311
  William (Maj.) 310
  William C. 262, 311,
    327, 350, 442, 448,
    452
  William Christian 262
  William Neville 310
  Wm. 309
  Wm. C. 287, 293, 302,
    335
Bullitts, (?) 273
Bullock, David 265, 283
  Reu 388
  Rice 388
  Richard 322
Buntell, Robert 229
Burbridges, John 8
Burcell, (?) 116
Burge, Robert 125
Burk, (?) 136, 181, 186,
    203, 210
  John 21
  Patrick 387
  Samuel 69
  Thomas 28
Burke, John 83
Burkenmire, Jacob 314
Burkes, (?) 200
  John 326
Burks, (?) 131, 137,
    150, 167, 169, 170,
    180, 186, 196, 211
  Amey 339
  Betsy 339

Burks (cont.)
  James 339, 444, 453
  John 339, 347, 450,
    458
  Matilda (Mrs.) 444
  Nancy 339
  Perry 339
  Polly 339
  Sally 339
  Sam'l 114
  Saml. 335
  Samuel 339, 347, 454
  William 387, 388
Burner, Peter 5
Burnett, John 9
  Joseph 118, 125
Burns, Dennis 108
Burrass, John 446, 448
  William 21
Burress, John 264, 452
Burros, (?) 106, 107,
    118, 119
Burt, Amasa 246
Burton, Charles 298
  Davis 298
  Elliott 298
  Jeremiah 298
  John 298
  Paulina 298
  Pelina 298
  Polly (Mrs.) 298
  Simeon 298
  William 298
Bush, (?) 190, 208
Bustard, John 257, 289
Bustards, (?) 410
Butler, Elias 282
  Margaret (Mrs.) 316
  P. 414
  Sampson 47
  Simon 27, 29, 86
  Tobias 292
Buzan, Jesse 185
Byers, (?) 181, 185, 199
  Daniel 20
  Edmund G. 288
  Jacob 46
  Nathan 329, 450
Byrn, James 304
Byrns, John 54
Caghey, Jno 17
  John 17
Cain, (?) 183, 187
  Dennis 191, 192
  Mathew 183
Cair, (?) 94
Calhoon, (?) 112, 133,
    136, 151, 177
  Geo. 148
Calhoun, (?) 99
  John 333
Callaghan, Mich'l I. O.
    326
Callen, Cathrine 216
Callender, Elieazer 413,
    414
  John 413
Callis, Wm. D. (Col.)
    266
Caloway, Ann B. 294
  Samuel 246
Calvan, (?) 164
Calvit, Jos 45
  Joseph 388
Camden, George S. 454
  Sally I. 455
  Sally T. 455
Cameron, (?) 127, 173,

Cameron (cont.)
174
Anguis 146
John 21, 79, 174
Camp, (?) 192, 209, 210
Ambrose 429
Catherine (Mrs.) 429
Catherine A. B. (Mrs.)
429
Ed. S. 336
Edw. S. 340
Eliza P. (Mrs.) 336
Elizabeth 429
John 17, 54
Reubin 172, 173
Robert 429
Campbell, (?) 130, 136,
137, 138, 141, 143,
150, 153, 158, 167,
168, 172, 196, 201,
204, 209, 210, 211,
375
(?) (Col.) 186, 360
Allen 20
Arthur 446
Arthur L. 321, 446
Daniel 20
J. 178, 189
Jno 189
Jno. 162, 167, 168,
172, 176, 178, 187,
189, 191
John 90, 91, 126, 146,
164, 169, 172, 174,
176, 177, 178, 186,
187, 195, 198, 199,
224, 358, 364, 366,
368, 384, 385, 386
Johnson 42, 43
Polly 254
Robert 224
William 268
Wm. 268
Campion, Kerian 290
Camron, Anguis 10
Caniel, (?) 167
Cannon, Anguis 10
Anna (Mrs.) 342
Thomas 254, 318, 444
Caple, Samuel 285
Caps, (?) 186
Cardinne, John 217
Carey, Robert 369
Carmicheal, James 232
Carnahan, (?) 137, 197,
201
Carnes, (?) 189, 208
Carney, (?) 125
Martin 109, 115, 116,
119, 120, 127, 166,
359, 365, 369
Offner 289
Carnihan, James 104
Carpenter, Joel 331
Z. 259, 292, 303
Zachariah 259
Zachars Peter 316
Carr, (?) 100, 113, 130,
134, 135, 136, 164,
169, 171, 175, 196,
201
James 436
Jno. 174
John 3, 16, 25, 26,
83, 112, 124, 127,
135, 360
Peter 398
Reubin 140

Carr (cont.)
Virginia 430
Carter, Elizabeth 64, 65
Jesse 271, 422
Mesheck 129
Shadrach 140, 141
Shadrack 18
Shedrach 64
Cartwright, Joseph 10,
78
Carty, M. 108
Cary, Charles 234
Case, (?) 100, 112, 113,
119, 132, 134, 150,
151, 152, 166, 175,
186, 188, 196, 198,
201, 202, 203, 206
Jacob 19, 41
Joseph 19
Lydia 19
Reu. 188
Reuben 19, 54, 373
Reubin 111, 149, 150,
163, 165, 168, 200,
203, 207, 209
Rubin 193
Casebear, (?) 150
Caselbear, (?) 166
Casey, Robert 369
Casi, (?) 167
Caslin, James M. 234
Mary (Mrs.) 303
Casny, Martin 164
Casseday, Samuel 257
Cassell, Hiram 351
Casselman, Lewis 222
Casson, Peter 282
Castline, John M. 94
Catamus, James 41, 63,
86
Catermous, James 41, 63,
86
Catlett, Charles 216
James 446
Jas. 421
Peter 141, 142
Robert 92, 103, 216
Catt, (?) 157, 169, 206
Caughey, (?) 181, 185,
199
Cave, (?) 106
Reuben 8, 55
Reubin 144
Cavett, Andrew 335
Mary Ann Elizabeth 335
Cawthon, Benjamin 353
Cawthorn, Benj. 269
Benjamin 329
Cazman, Mary 221
Cecil, Nancy (Mrs.) 242
Thomas 242
Cesabear, (?) 135
Chaffin, Robert 115
Chain, Francis 120, 172
Will'm 168
Chair, Francis 173
Chambers, (?) 353
George W. 339, 453,
455
John 76
Polly 255
William 237, 288, 322,
416, 423
Wm. 256, 287
Chamers, John 110
Chancellor, Betsey 456
Channonhouse, Abel 263
Mary (Mrs.) 263

Channonhouse (cont.)
Polly 237
Chaplain, Abraham 41
Abraham (Cpt.) 52
Abram 51
Chaplin, Abram 168
Chapline, Ann H. (Mrs.)
275
Chapman, (?) 158
Abraham 43
Elizabeth 282
Mary (Mrs.) 282
Samuel 282
William 282
Chappell, (?) 189, 207
Charlton, (?) 369
Richard 444
Cheneweth, R. 157
Chenewith, (?) 113
Richard 361
Cheniwith, (?) 167, 170,
197
Rich'd 377
Chenowith, A. 303
Absolem 303
Arthur (Sr.) 303
Rich'd 42, 61, 72, 81,
121, 153, 156
Richard 17, 22, 25,
81, 390
Richd. 154
William 25
Chenowith, Rich 148
Rich'd 121, 144, 149
Richard 1, 149, 373,
374
Stephen R. 451
Cherry, (?) 112
Moses 16
Chew, John 401
Nancy 223
Rich'd 300
Richard 301
Samuel 301
Chiles, Caroline Mary
(Mrs.) 280
Chinewith, (?) 93, 94,
100, 101, 105, 116,
129, 136, 137, 138,
148, 152, 153, 160,
161, 164, 165, 167,
174, 175
R. 161
Ric'd 120
Rich'd 121, 123, 124,
127, 161
Richard 90, 91, 93,
106, 109, 113, 122,
139, 143, 145, 147,
148, 155, 156, 176
Chiniwith, (?) 150, 165,
175, 177, 181, 186,
187, 193, 196, 200,
201, 203, 205, 207,
211
Ric'd 150, 187, 188
Richard 154
Chinn, (?) 402
Chinoweth, Rich'd 37, 43
Rich'd (Cpt.) 39
Chinowith, (?) 101, 163
Chinwith, (?) 128, 131,
132, 134
Ric'd 132
Rich'd 135
Christian, (?) 196
(?) (Col) 388
(?) (Col.) 393

Colman (cont.)
J. 405
Jacob 146, 198
Jacob (Sr.) 384
John 78
Peter 188, 379
Rosannah 384
Colmesnil, John D. 285
Colson, (?) 113, 134
Niblock 103, 140
Nillock 113
Sarah (Mrs.) 140
Colston, Charles 96, 97
Nimlock 97
Colvan, (?) 158
Colvin, James 21
Combs, (?) 197, 202
Edward 21
Commack, William 304
Conditt, Timothy 225
Conelly, Jno. 178
Congee, Jno 207
Conger, (?) 134, 151,
166, 189
Conn, Thomas 242, 325
Conner, (?) 160
James 282
Connor, Richard 106
Conrad, Valentine 445
Conradt, Adam 302
Constant, (?) (Col.) 254
Conway, (?) 158
John 130, 312
Mary Eliza 337
Thomas Nolan 337
Conwell, Yates 217
Cook, (?) 103, 177
James 28, 78, 129
John 438
Moses 384
Patty (Mrs.) 246
Cooke, (?) 108, 116,
132, 149, 160
William 123
Wm. 124
Coons, George 260
William 237
Coonse, Nicholas 398,
399
Cooper, (?) 190, 208
Geo. 413
Leavin 244
Levin (Sr.) 272
Margaret 352
Sam'l 414
Samuel 272
William 320
Wm. 267, 302
Cooprider, (?) 379
Copage, John 2, 4, 215
Susannah (Mrs.) 4
Coper, Elenner 221
Copes, John 381
Corcle, James M. 123
Core, John 231
Corkran, Hugh 16
Cornelius, Catherine
(Mrs.) 232
Daniel 232
William 232
Cornell, (?) 163
Cornwell, Betsey (Mrs.)
264
Jeremiah 308
Corret, John 102
Corrett, John 102
Corver, (?) 191
Cosby, Barbara C. (Mrs.)

Cosby (cont.)
297
Charles S. 297
F. 285, 288, 434
Fort's 259
Fort. 234, 267
Fortunatus 259, 267,
275, 286, 298, 400,
401, 402, 410, 432
Mary A. 267
Costen, Leah (Mrs.) 238
Cothan, Benjamin 329
Cotlett, John 126
Cotter, Michael 337
Cotton, (?) 165, 170
Coulson, Charles 33, 34,
215
Jean 33
Niblock 33
Willm 33
Countryman, Henry 20
Peter 21
Peter (Jr.) 21
Coverton, Able 246, 247
Matilda 246, 247
Philip 246
Priscilla 246, 247
Priscilla (Mrs.) 246
Covington, Abel 259
Able 248
Cowan, Elizabeth 242
James 242
John 123, 242
Margate 242
Mary (Mrs.) 242
William 242
Cowen, (?) 208
Cowles, James M. 218
Cox, (?) 99, 100, 104,
112, 116, 120, 126,
128, 132, 136, 152,
177, 203, 209
David 9, 40, 90, 91,
109, 145
Edward (Sr.) 239
Frances Morton (Mrs.)
336
I. 114
Isaac 9, 16, 17, 24,
40, 90, 91, 92, 95,
97, 100, 102, 105,
106, 109, 110, 111,
112, 114, 115, 118,
120, 122, 124, 125,
126, 127, 130, 135,
139, 140, 141, 144,
146, 164, 207
Isabella (Mrs.) 222
James 229
John 40, 323
John H. 336, 444
Joseph 11, 25
Nancy 338
Peter 345
Richard H. 336
Vincent 336
Coy, John 19
Coyle, Frank 89, 122,
147, 180
Craddock, Pascal D. 333
Robert 413
Craig, (?) 103, 116,
132, 138, 139, 177
John 249
Peregrine 336
Crane, John H. 292
Crauley, (?) 189
Cravetson, George 21

Crawford, Charles 239
David 239
Elizabeth 239
John 42, 43, 45, 239
Martha 337
Mary 337
Nancy 239, 337
Nathan 239
Nelson 239
Norbourne 268
Reuben 239
Sally 239
Thomas 249
Val. 60
Valentine 59, 60
William 239
William (Jr.) 353
William S. 239
Crawley, (?) 208
Cree, Robert 174
Crevinsten, Geo. 187
Crevinstin, (?) 189,
203, 210
Geo. 188
Crips, Phillip 312
Cristy, (?) 94, 118
Crittenden, John 330
John (Maj.) 396
Crittinden, John 43
Crittindin, John 42
Crogan, William (Maj.)
220
Croghan, (?) 176, 197,
201
(?) (Col.) 352
(?) (Dr.) 352
Angelica 314
Ann H. 298
Charles 298, 314, 352
Eliza C. 298
George 298, 314
John 297, 298, 331
Lucy (Mrs.) 297, 298
Nicholas 298, 314
W. 371, 374, 388, 430
William 223, 230, 231,
297, 298, 314, 414,
415, 416, 429
William (Dr.) 349
William (Maj.) 330
William (Mrs.) 331
William (Sr.) 330
Wm. 182, 375
Crokes, James 141
Crook, Hellen Maria 352
Crooks, James 17
Jas 17
John 325
Crosby, Fortunatus 309
Crouch, Saml. 369
Crow, (?) 197, 202
Edward 328
Timothy 290
William 72
Crowe, John 126
Crum, David 428
Elizabeth 428
Elizabeth (Mrs.) 428
George 428
Jacob 428
Polly 428
Crumrine, (?) 63, 87
Crutchfield, Ann P.
(Mrs.) 243
James 290
William 434
Cuddy, (?) 313
James McG. 313

Culberson, (?) 116, 132,
    134, 136, 138, 139,
    148, 149, 152, 153,
    158, 160, 167, 175,
    199
  S. 157
  Sam 155, 159
  Sam'l 91, 108, 114,
    139, 140, 146, 147,
    148, 149, 152, 154,
    155, 156, 161, 163,
    166, 169, 172, 176
  Saml. 144
  Samuel 90, 92, 95,
    106, 133
Culbertson, (?) 101,
    112, 151
  Sam 105
  Sam'l 111, 114, 127
  Saml 97
  Saml W. 25
  Saml. 106
  Saml. W. 25
  Samuel W. 24, 25, 85
Cullner, Geo. 419
Cummin, Wm 117
Cummings, Mary 282
Cummins, (?) 137, 169,
    170, 184, 197, 202,
    205
  David 228
  Ebenezer 228
  Henry 228, 300, 337
  Jeany 228
  John 228
  Margery (Mrs.) 227
  Mary (Mrs.) 227, 228
  Maryann 228
  Moses 228
  Peter 20, 142
  William 20, 42, 111,
    117, 227, 228, 293
  Wm 74
Cummis, Peter 90
Cunningham, (?) 138,
    153, 170, 193, 196,
    200, 211
  (?) (Cpt.) 143
  Andrew 333
  James H. 332
  Jonathan 17
  Tho's 115, 145
  Thomas 102, 109, 114,
    115, 142
  Thos 108, 110, 119,
    120
  Ths. 99
Cuny, (?) 95
  Thomas 96
Curran, James 330
Curry, (?) 119, 128,
    137, 148, 152, 160,
    165, 175, 181, 186,
    190, 204, 205, 208
  Anne 391
  Catharine 391
  Daniel 391
  Sary 391
  Tho's 120
  Thomas 25, 61, 111,
    117, 206, 391
  Ths 120
  Ths. 155, 187, 189,
    199
Curtis, Samuel 409
Curts, Martin 20
Cury, Susanah (Mrs.) 252
Cushing, Charles 414

Custard, Corrod 20
Dabis, Fry 290
Dabney, Chas 119
  Isaac W. 261
Dade, Francis 60
Dalton, (?) 163, 196,
    201
  F. F. 359
  John 275
  Thomas 359
  V. T. 129
Damarie, Saml (Jr.) 20
Damewood, (?) 106, 112,
    119, 129, 131, 136,
    149, 159
  Boston 19
Danby, William 250
Dandridge, A. S. 221
Daniel, (?) 136, 152,
    163, 165, 171, 191,
    195, 197, 198, 202,
    203, 204
  Coleman 269
  John 307, 403
  Martin 221, 380, 381
  Mercer 456, 458
  R. 344
  Rob't 167
  Robert 92, 123, 361,
    372, 374, 380
  Robt. 161, 194, 209,
    211
  Thomas 392, 446
  W. 80
  Walker 211, 372
Daniels, (?) 162, 186,
    197, 202, 203
Danley, William 250
Darling, Catharine 19
  Lambert 20
Dashiele, L. F. C. 347
Daugherty, Elizabeth 450
Daulin, (?) 101
Davenport, Berkell 394
  Burkett 394
David, Moses 288
Davidson, John 5
Davies, John 268
  Walter 154, 217
Daviess, Ann 245
  J. H. 245
Davis, (?) 101, 137,
    152, 161, 162, 163,
    173, 176, 189, 195,
    196, 197, 201, 202,
    207, 210, 385
  Caroline (Widow) 434
  Charity (Mrs.) 239
  Elizabeth (Mrs.) 239
  Francis 434
  Henry 20
  Isaac 24, 144
  James 110
  Jesse 130, 144
  Jno. 157, 178, 201
  John 141, 147, 168,
    209
  John W. 434
  John W. (Jr.) 434
  Jonathan 457
  Mark 434
  Mary 434
  Matthew 434
  Patsey 434
  Rezin 372
  Robert 67, 224, 242
  Robert N. 307
  Salem L. 434

Davis (cont.)
  Squire 324
  Susan 434
  Thomas 23, 63, 86
  W. R. 324
Dawson, (?) 136
  Elias 333
  Hannah (Mrs.) 331
  James 331
Day, (?) 129
  Geo. 155
  William 28
Dean, Edwin B. 348
  Elias 271
Deckar, (?) 124, 132,
    133
  Jacob 140
  John 124
Deckarts, (?) 136, 151,
    166
Decker, (?) 101, 116
  Abraham 224
  John 358
Deckert, John 358
Declary, John P. 324
Deft, (?) 137, 138, 202,
    203
Degaalon, Henry 285
  Jane (Mrs.) 285
  Louisa 285
De Grand, Carlos (Dr.)
    399
Dehart, Elisha 303
Deifenbach, (?) 113
Delany, Michael 290
Demant, Benoni 174, 378,
    405
Demar, Sebastian 42, 43
Demara, John 20
  Samuel 20, 29, 86
Demaree, Peter 16
  Samuel 29, 86
Demaria, Peter 13
  Samuel 86
Demarie, Samuel 29, 86
Demaris, Samuel 29
Dement, George 387
Denney, James W. 287
Dennis, Michael 126, 358
  Robert (Jr.) 263
Dennison, (?) 165, 181,
    185, 196, 197, 198,
    199, 200
Denny, (?) 305
  Ed 244
  Ed Polly 244
  Edward 244
  James 187, 188, 244,
    245, 409
  James W. 270, 289
  Jas. 189
  Jos. 419
  Nancy (Mrs.) 244
  Synthia 244
Densford, James 289
Denton, Ebenezer 416
Denwood, Mary (Mrs.) 334
Deremeah, (?) 120
Deremiah, (?) 120
  Jn'o 120
Derimiah, (?) 107
Dering, Lustin 295
Dermiah, (?) 131
Deumiah, John 10
Devist, (?) 190
Dewees, Matthew 336
Dick, Charles 274
Dickeans, George 45, 48

470

Dickens, George 27, 46, 47, 48
  Susanna 20
Dickerson, (?) 232
  Elizabeth (Mrs.) 232
  Joshua 383
Dickey, Jno 5
Dickin, (?) 161
Dickins, George 17
Dickinson, Eliza B. 398
  Richard 246, 398
  Sam 316, 343, 347, 458
  Samuel 295, 338, 432, 440
  Samuel C. 428
  Sarah (Mrs.) 238
Diefenbach, (?) 128, 134, 172
Dieponbach, (?) 151
Dill, Robert 358
Dillian, Thomas 19
Dillon, Lucretia (Mrs.) 397
  Mic'l 224
  Mich. 386
  Michael 397
Dimant, (?) 210
Diment, Benoni 229
Dine, Andrew 6
Dinon, Robert 233
Dinst, (?) 208
Dinwiddie, James 385
Ditto, Henry 399
Dival, Nottley 126
Divon, (?) 139, 153, 164
Divora, (?) 175
Dixon, (?) 131, 204
  Lewis 193, 194
  Walter 211
Dodd, Wm. 284
Dodge, (?) 95, 104, 119, 130, 133, 136, 158, 181, 185, 194, 195, 199, 210
  Israel 20, 195
  Nancy 237, 240
Dogan, (?) 138
Doherty, (?) 113, 134, 138, 151
  James 21
  John 325
  Niel 20
Doleman, (?) 139
Doling, (?) 134, 151
Dolman, (?) 131
Done, William 409
Donelson, Stokely 406
Donett, (?) 118, 158, 159, 162
  John 159
Donne, (?) 94, 112, 113, 130, 133, 189, 197, 201, 203
  J. 37, 356, 365, 366, 374
  John 20, 183, 198, 356, 367
Donohue, Daniel 229
Doone, (?) 185
  John 92
Doran, Alexander 220
Dorret, (?) 169
  Jno 102
Dorrett, (?) 107, 132, 139, 173, 206, 211
  Jno 140, 145
  John 131, 209, 359, 365

Dorsett, John 129
Dorsey, (?) 421
  Anne 238
  Benjamin L. 255
  Benjamin Lawrence 421
  Caleb 438, 442
  Caroline Mary 280
  Charles G. 440, 443, 448
  Columbus 280, 281, 315
  Corbin H. 250
  Corbin N. 250
  Corilla 280
  Corilla (Mrs.) 439
  Edward 238, 421, 423
  Elias 238, 250, 255, 440
  Elias L. 421
  Eliza Chew 280
  Eurith O. 421
  Henrietta 280
  Henry C. 280, 343, 431, 435, 436, 439
  Joshua 280, 439, 440
  Julian 281
  Leaven L. 255
  Levin L. 421
  Matilda 238, 280, 315, 440
  Matilda L. 255, 421
  Matilda L. (Mrs.) 280, 315
  Nimrod 280, 281, 315, 439, 440, 443
  Parmelia (Mrs.) 315
  Patience 238
  Patience L. 421
  Polly 238
  Polly (Mrs.) 288
  Reagin Hammond 280
  Rezin H. 439
  Rezin Hammond 315
  Ruth M. 440
  Ruth Maria 280, 315
  Sarah Ann 280, 439
  Susan 423
  Susan (Mrs.) 421
  Susanah 423
  Susanna (Mrs.) 238
  Susanna (Widow) 421
  Urath O. 256
  Vachel 280
Dougherty, Elizabeth 295
  Elizabeth (Mrs.) 258
  James 235
  John 235
  Moses 235
  Patsey 258
  Peggy 235
  Sidney (Mrs.) 235
  William 242, 247, 258
  Wm. 245
Doughterty, Wm. 292
Douglas, (?) 361
  Ephraim 397
Douglass, (?) 150, 168
  David 28, 36, 37, 42, 43
Doulin, (?) 108, 116
Doup, Daniel 343
  George 343
  John 329
Dove, (?) 190, 208
Dowdall, (?) 2
Dowland, William 242
Dowling, Rich. 263
Downe, John 91
Downing, Dennis 18

Downing (cont.)
  John 178, 227, 266, 286
  Margaret 20
  Margarett 18
Downs, Thomas 247
  William 21
Doyel, John 426
Doyice, (?) 108
Doyle, John 17
  Thomas 276
  Thomas (Maj.) 276
Dozier, (?) 108, 118, 131, 150, 161
Draine, Francis 392
Drake, John 392, 400, 405, 408, 447
Dreadnaught, (?) 175
Drumgold, (?) 165, 172
Drury, Jas. 418
Dubberly, William 249, 447
Duberly, Hannah (Mrs.) 285
DuBois, (?) 138
Ducanson, James 274
Duerson, James 289
  Thomas 289
  Wm. 269, 282
Duffay, Elizabeth 336
  Michael 338
Duffy, Eliza 336
  Elizabeth 336
  Honor 336
  Michael 336
  Nancy 336
  Sarah 336
Dukar, (?) 192
Dukarts, (?) 193
Duke, Rich'd 268
Duley, (?) 190, 208
Duly, (?) 208
Duma, Chas 110
Dumarselay, A. Lecoq 288
Dumarsellary, Andrew Lecoq 288
  Just 288
Dumarsellay, Denise Lecoq 288
  Theresa Lecoq (Mrs.) 288
Dunagan, S. 439
  Solomon 439
Dunbar, (?) 99, 100
  James 20, 41
  Joseph 239
  Sam'l 121
  Samuel 121
  W. W. C. H. 330
Duncan, Alex (Jr.) 275
  Ann E. 437
  C. L. 334
  Charles 277
  Coleman 257, 277, 437
  E. 237
  Elizabeth 20
  Garnett 337, 346, 437
  Harry 237
  Henry 256, 413, 428, 437
  James 282
  Mary S. 437
  Nancy 437
  Nancy (Mrs.) 257, 261
  Nimrod 28
  Samuel 28
Duncanson, James 274, 275

Galloway (cont.)
  Francis 41
  George 231
  James 7, 41, 74, 231
  Jno. 162, 189
  John 20, 144, 174, 187
  Joseph 231
  Margaret 231
  Martha 231
  Mary 28
  Sam 231
  William 7, 231
Galt, (?) 270
  (?) (Dr.) 443
  Norborne A. 323
  W. C. 351
  William C. 327, 346
Gamble, Jane (Mrs.) 303
  William 303
Gammon, William J. 215
Ganary, (?) 134
Ganowine, John 301
Gant, Joseph 403
Garay, Bennett 276
  Charity (Mrs.) 276
  Margary 276
Gardener, Phebe (Mrs.)
  284
  Silas P. 284
Gardner, Silas 284
  Thos 168
Garland, Edmond 283
  Edward 283
  Richard 283
  Thomas 283
Garner, Eliner 95
  Margret 95
  Thomas 384
Garnier, I. V. 294
Garrard, Wm. 418, 419
Garret, Ambrose 438
  Betsey Ann 297
  Judith (Mrs.) 296
  Olderson W. 296
  Peter B. 297
  Regin W. 296
  Rezin W. 296
  Silas 296
  Susan W. 297
Garrett, Edward 253
  Elizabeth (Mrs.) 438
  Henry 406
  Silas 296, 303
Garth, John 266
Garvey, (?) 106, 119,
  150, 151, 161, 166
Garvin, (?) 353
  Wm. 353
Gates, Jane M. (Mrs.)
  348
Gatewood, Alsey 226
  Ann 226
  Ann Pauline 451
  Catherine 226
  Clara (Widow) 451
  Clary 226
  Fielding 226
  Fleming 226, 234, 313,
    451
  Frances 226
  Fullington 226
  James 226, 319, 451
  John 226, 260
  Jos. B. 312
  Joseph 226
  Joseph B. 298, 313
  Judith 226
  Leonard 313, 451

Gatewood (cont.)
  Leonard I. 451
  Littleton 451
  Mary Ann D. 451
  Penelope 226
  Penelope F. 451
  Saragh (Mrs.) 319
  Sarah 226
  Upton 451
  William 451
Gather, John R. 418
Gaughney, (?) 113
Gaul, Joseph 403
Gaut, Joseph 403
Gavis, (?) 197
Geiger, Elizabeth (Mrs.)
  248
  Fred'k 248
  Fred. 231
  Frederick 225, 343,
    425, 433, 442, 450
  Frederick (Col.) 255
  George 248
  Jacob 248, 255, 343,
    346
  John 248
  Julian 343
  Margaret (Mrs.) 343
  Nancy 343
  Polly 343
  Samuel 249
  Sarah 433
George, (?) 94, 105,
  190, 208
  John 7
  Ro. 206, 212
  Rob 109
  Rob't 96
  Robert 42, 97, 102,
    106, 113, 194, 212,
    226, 365
  Robt 37, 108
  Robt. 187, 209, 212,
    219, 356
  Thomas 7, 8
  Thos 7, 8
Gerault, John 399
Gerking, John 243
Getz, Jacob 245
Gibbs, (?) (Mrs.) 317
  John H. 317, 340
  Martha 317
Gibson, Alexander 276
  Catherine (Mrs.) 276
  James 412
  John 365
Gill, (?) 430
  Beeda 318
  Elizabeth (Mrs.) 318
  George 318
  James L. 318
  Thomas 318
Gilliland, (?) 158
Gills, (?) 137
Gilly, James 289
  Jane B. 290
  Jno. B. 290
  John B. 289
  P. 270
Gilman, Jas. 189
  Jeremiah 248, 260
Gilmore, James 209
  Jas. 201
  John 21, 407
  Ro. 207
  Robert 19, 42, 56, 166
  Robt. 206
  Samuel 341

Gilmore (cont.)
  Thomas 301
Ginn, Daniel 102
Girault, Jno (Cpt.) 45
  John (Cpt.) 44
Girdle, (?) 192
Girdler, (?) 160, 171
Gist, R. P. 345, 349
  R. P. (Dr.) 345
Githens, John 263
Givens, Sam'l 123
Givin, Geo. W. 342
Glass, I. 278, 322
  Jane M. (Widow) 457
  Joseph 282, 283, 457
  Mary 282
  Mary Jane 278, 457
  Robert W. 349
  Robert William 278
  Ruth Ann 457
  Samuel 283
  Samuel (Jr.) 341
  Sarah 282
  Thomas 270
Glassell, (?) 401
  William 401
Glenn, (?) 107, 108,
  118, 131, 138, 144,
  167, 171, 176, 197,
  201, 205
  David 127
  Joseph 21, 54
Glum, (?) 153
Goately, Peter 333
Goban, Joseph 221
  Lidy (Mrs.) 221
Goben, John 221
  Polly (Mrs.) 311
Goddard, Michael 336
Godin, Edward 94
Goe, Richard H. 397
Goodin, (?) 137, 138,
  150, 152, 165, 168,
  169, 170, 205
  Ed. 193, 207
  Edw'd 191
  Edward 172, 187, 206
  Wm. 172
Goodknight, Michael 298
Goodman, Jacob 278
Goodtitle, (?) 201
Goodwin, (?) 140, 163
  Amoss 28
  Edward 28
  Howard 265
  S. S. 292
  Simeon S. 315, 443,
    449
  William 28, 41, 56,
    247
Goolsby, Tarlton 299
Goose, William 232, 233
Gordon, (?) 170, 205,
  208
  Catharine (Mrs.) 326
  William 326
Gorr, M. 306
Goslee, Levin 235
Gow, M. 306
Gracey, Polly (Mrs.) 261
Gracy, Isaac 351
Graham, And. 324
  Andrew 320, 329
  James 272
  Philip 409
  William E. 334
Graig, David 305
Grant, (?) 107, 142

475

Grant (cont.)
Adam 6, 51
Ann 329
Jane 19, 130
Jane (Widow) 6
Grants, (?) 125, 130
Grass, Henry 19
Gratton, John 12
Graves, Isaac 351
Gray, (?) 196
Angerean 343
Eben'r 414
Ephya 254
Francis 268
French S. 325
French T. 325
G. 256
Geo. D. 325
George 325
John T. 324, 325, 445, 456
Kitty W. (Mrs.) 306
Mary 21
Nancy 422
Nancy C. 421
Philip R. 325, 453, 455
Selenah (Mrs.) 325
Vincent 287
Graybill, Iac. 147
Graybles, (?) 434
Grayson, (?) 310
Caroline M. (Mrs.) 321
Eliza M. 321
Fred W. S. 272
Fred. W. S. 262
Frederick W. S. 321
Peter W. 321
Robert H. 338, 342
Sally (Mrs.) 321
Greathouse, Wm. 370
Green, (?) 158
Ann (Mrs.) 301
David 254
John 90
Jona 316
Joseph 305
Nancy 273
Priscilla (Mrs.) 254
Richard A. 273
Robert 114
Willis 16, 17, 198
Greenup, Christ'o 139, 174
Christo 149
Christo. 93
L. 265
Greenwall, Joseph 16
Greenywalt, John 20
Jos 21
Gregg, Ann (Mrs.) 222
David 222
John 222
Lydia 222
Margaret 222
Mary 222
Gregory, (?) 106, 107, 119, 120, 128, 133, 137, 152, 181, 186, 203, 210
Andrew 21
Harvey 454, 455
Richd 21
Gretsinger, George 277
John 277
Joseph 277
Gribbs, (?) 164
Grier, Samuel 225

Griffin, (?) 135, 151, 197, 201
Sam 267
Griffith, John 253
Griffy, Hannah 276
Griggs, Willis 296
Grills, (?) 175, 196, 201
Wm. 209
Grimes, Hugh 397
Lander 447, 448
Rachael (Widow) 447, 448
Gring, Henry 231
Grisslet, Rheubin 285
Grover, Sally (Mrs.) 278
Grundy, (?) 107, 108, 113, 118, 132, 134, 137, 138, 144, 150, 151, 166, 167
Charles 216
Elizabeth 90
Elizabeth (Mrs.) 216
Felix 216
G. 100
Geo. 39
George 2, 12, 13, 16, 54
George (Jr.) 17, 216
George (Sr.) 12, 216
Guardum 216
Jno 136, 138, 141
Jno. 151
John 90, 93, 126, 216
Polly 216
Robert 216
Sam 333
Samuel 216
Wm. 344
Grymes, (?) 136, 165
Hugh 172
John 117
Guerrant, Edocia 347
John 347
Gum, Jacob 41
Gumm, Jacob 42
Gun, Jacob 20
Gunn, James 300
Gutermous, James 149
Guthrie, James 252, 295, 311, 316, 324, 333, 335, 351, 449
William 252
Gwafthmey, John 294
Gwathmey, Geo C. 347
Geo. C. 311
George C. 324, 331
J. 242
John 246, 267, 270, 293, 294, 309, 427, 428, 432
Owen 230, 257, 267, 311, 330, 331, 421
Sam. 413
Saml. 406
Samuel 323, 324, 331
Gwathmy, Sam 231
Haag, Chuse 248
Hacker, Eliza 127
Haggin, (?) 129, 136, 152, 166
John 127
Hagland, (?) 129
Hail, (?) 208
Hains, Elizabeth (Mrs.) 292
Sarah 292
Hakes, Cateron (Mrs.)

Hakes (cont.)
220
John 220
Haldern, Enoch 269
Hale, (?) 209
Elijah Logan 382
William 233
Hall, (?) 165, 170
Amanda (Mrs.) 288
Daniel 8, 18
E. 272, 399
Elijah Logan 382
Elisha L. 272, 384
Elisha Lingan 389
Elisha Lingen 389
Eliza 448, 449
Eliza (Mrs.) 448, 449
Fanny (Mrs.) 272
Henry 4
John 133
Nathan 448
Nich. C. 270
R. 272
Rachel 237
Rachel (Mrs.) 327
Richard 288
Sarah 8
Thomas 169
William 19
Halystead, D. 313
Hambrick, Elizabeth 331
Nimrod 331
Hamilton, (?) 136, 143, 254
Alex 333
Ann (Mrs.) 285
Charles 286
Eleanor (Mrs.) 286
James 19
John 20, 69
John T. 332
Lucy Ann 285, 286
Robert 392
Thomas 395
Hammond, (?) 136, 138, 152, 153
Reagin 280
Hampton, David 286
Ephraim 239, 286
Rolin 286
Rowland 296
Hamptonstalle, Abram 408
Hance, (?) 123
Hancock, (?) 352
(?) (Mrs.) 279, 352
Benjamin 299
Harding 299
Sally (Mrs.) 299
William 299
Handley, (?) 100, 116, 132, 142, 153, 175, 187, 196, 201, 203, 205
Jno 123, 141
Jno. 161, 163
John 17, 62, 63, 82, 87, 96, 127, 129, 149, 157, 174, 360, 402, 404
Handly, (?) 167, 183
John 42, 43
Handy, Isaac 409
Haney, J. 290
Hanley, Linney (Mrs.) 281
Hanrick, Nimrod 316
Hansberry, Benja 17
Hansbrough, Morias 10,

481

Merdock, (?) 204
Meredeth, Uriania 28
Meredy, Dan C. 54
Merewether, James 375
Meridith, (?) (Widow)
    141
    Mary 97
    Rice 141
    Susana 97
Merit, Katherine 285
Meriweather, David 446,
    447
    George W. 458
    James 446
    John 446
    Thomas 446
    V. W. 443
    William 447
Meriwether, (?) 137,
    142, 165, 175, 194,
    196, 201, 204, 209,
    210, 435
    Caroline 442
    Charles W. 442
    D. 369
    Daniel 375
    Dav'd 191, 192
    David 176, 179, 180,
    183, 184, 188, 189,
    193, 194, 195, 198,
    199, 200, 204, 207,
    209, 211
    David H. 442
    David W. 375
    David Wood 226, 234
    Elizabeth 234
    Geo. 123, 183, 189
    George 123, 131, 406
    George W. 442, 455,
    457
    Henry W. 442
    Henry Wood 227
    Ja's 33
    James 33, 233, 234,
    244, 375, 406, 418,
    426, 446
    Jane 426
    Jane (Mrs.) 442
    Jas. 391
    John 455
    Lewis 442
    Louisa M. 442
    Louisa Matilda 442
    Lucy 443
    Mary (Mrs.) 226
    N. 183, 185
    Nic'o 131
    Nic's 189, 209
    Nicho 5
    Nicholas 9, 123, 146,
    178, 388
    Nicholass 5, 9
    Nickolas 140
    Nics. 211
    Patty 233
    Polly 234
    Richard 426
    Sally (Mrs.) 296
    Samuel 442
    Sarah (Mrs.) 296
    Sarah (Widow) 442
    Thomas 446
    Valentine 442
    William 234, 426, 441,
    442, 443, 446
    William O. 442
    Wm. 357
Merritt, (?) 167

Merritt (cont.)
    Fanny 329
Merriweathers, (?) 312
Merriwether, (?) 142,
    192
    Ann 266
    D. W. 366
    David 157, 266, 346
    David W. 221
    David Wood 221
    Elizabeth (Mrs.) 265
    Henry W. 268
    James 118, 221, 227,
    265, 266, 431, 432,
    433
    Jane 433
    John 266
    Lucy Ann (Mrs.) 347
    Mary 227
    Nicholas 221
    Patty (Mrs.) 221
    Richard 433
    Robert 266
    Sally 266
    Thomas 266
    Valentine 221
    Valentine W. 347
    William 221, 227, 266,
    431
    William (Jr.) 258
    William (Sr.) 221
    Wm. 302
Mertle, John 233
    Phebe (Mrs.) 233
Methews, (?) 204
Meyers, Jacob 12
Middleton, Joseph 302,
    313, 315, 337
Miles, (?) 100
    M. 356
Milikin, John 392
Millburn, David 155
Miller, (?) 180, 203
    Abram 186
    Agness 394
    Anthony 268, 269
    Buckner 268, 269
    Cassandra (Mrs.) 245
    Catharina 320
    Charles 320
    Christopher 21
    Doratha Jane 269
    Earnest 16
    Edward 261
    Elizabeth 241
    Elizabeth (Mrs.) 275,
    320, 451
    Fanny 320
    Frederick 244
    Geo. Franklin 320
    George Franklin 320
    Hannah 261
    Hannah (Mrs.) 261
    Heath Jones 327, 341
    Isaac 257, 262, 263,
    283, 345, 427, 432,
    440, 446, 447, 449
    Jane 269
    Jno. 405
    John 231, 236, 237,
    240, 241, 245, 248,
    269, 286, 299, 305,
    318, 320, 323, 402,
    412, 413, 424, 425,
    428, 433, 435, 436,
    437, 440
    John H. 290
    Juliet T. 306

Miller (cont.)
    Lavinia 269
    M. 305, 333
    M. H. 338
    M. L. 288, 305
    Mary 269
    Michael 276, 311, 448,
    451
    Nancy 269
    Peter 244, 451
    Polly 320
    Richard 241, 269
    Robert 261, 268, 269,
    320, 392, 441, 447,
    453, 457
    Robert (Sr.) 312
    Robert N. 262, 305,
    320, 345, 433, 436,
    441, 444
    Ruth Maria (Mrs.) 315
    Samuel 21
    Thomas 269
    Thomas B. 261, 293,
    322
    Warrick 312, 317
    Warwick 436, 441, 457
    William 269, 392, 394,
    456
Millers, (?) 311
Milligan, (?) 199, 204
Mills, Isaac 257, 272,
    330
    Jonathan 288
    Mary (Mrs.) 288
    Polly 288
    Richard 240, 257
    Sally 288
    Samuel 288
    Sidney 288
    Susan 288
    William 259
Milne, Edmd. 378
Minor, Charles 266
    Garrett 274
    Geo. G. 270
    Jacob 121
    Lancelot 266
    Lancelott 265
Minter, Thomas 220, 388
Misner, Henry 254
    Nancy (Mrs.) 254
Mitchell, (?) 192, 200
    David 9, 11, 368
    Joseph 20
    Mildred 234
    Robt. 400
    Stephen 262
    William 20
Moddrel, Adam 28
    Rebecca 28
Momson, Isaac 5
Mong, Adam 220, 384
Monin, Margaret (Mrs.)
    322, 323
Monroe, Israel 286
    James 329
Monroney, (?) 203
    Sylvester 28
    William 28
Montgomery, (?) 138,
    144, 153, 169, 170,
    180, 186, 196, 198,
    199, 200, 202, 203,
    205
    Jno. 206
    John 7, 127, 359, 366,
    371, 393
    W. W. 275

490

491

504